T0178365

Lecture Notes in Computer Science   12022

More information about this series at http://www.springer.com/series/7410

Hongxia Wang · Xianfeng Zhao ·
Yunqing Shi · Hyoung Joong Kim ·
Alessandro Piva (Eds.)

Digital Forensics and Watermarking

18th International Workshop, IWDW 2019
Chengdu, China, November 2–4, 2019
Revised Selected Papers

 Springer

Editors
Hongxia Wang ⓘ
College of Cybersecurity
Sichuan University
Chengdu, China

Yunqing Shi
Department of ECE
New Jersey Institute of Technology
Newark, NJ, USA

Alessandro Piva ⓘ
Department of Information Engineering
University of Florence
Florence, Italy

Xianfeng Zhao ⓘ
Institute of Information Engineering
Chinese Academy of Sciences
Beijing, China

Hyoung Joong Kim ⓘ
Graduate School of Information Study
Korea University
Seoul, Korea (Republic of)

ISSN 0302-9743   ISSN 1611-3349   (electronic)
Lecture Notes in Computer Science
ISBN 978-3-030-43574-5   ISBN 978-3-030-43575-2   (eBook)
https://doi.org/10.1007/978-3-030-43575-2

LNCS Sublibrary: SL4 – Security and Cryptology

Preface

This book is the proceedings of the 18th International Workshop on Digital Forensics and Watermarking (IWDW 2019) which was held in Chengdu, China, during November 2–4, 2019. The IWDW is a premier forum for researchers and practitioners working on novel research, development, and applications of digital watermarking and forensics techniques for multimedia security.

IWDW 2019 received 70 valid submissions of original research papers covering the following topics: digital watermarking, digital forensics and anti-forensics, deep learning for multimedia security, information hiding, steganography and steganalysis, as well as authentication and security. There were three reviewers for each submitted paper with regards to the double-blind peer review process. The decision of the Program Committee was motivated by a highly competitive basis. Only 22 submissions were accepted as regular papers and 12 as short papers. Two prizes were awarded for the best paper and the best student paper, respectively.

February 2020

Hongxia Wang
Xianfeng Zhao
Yunqing Shi
Hyoung Joong Kim
Alessandro Piva

Organization

General Chairs

Hongxia Wang	Sichuan University, China
Xianfeng Zhao	Chinese Academy of Sciences, China

Program Committee Chairs

Yunqing Shi	New Jersey Institute of Technology, USA
Hyoung Joong Kim	Korea University, South Korea
Alessandro Piva	University of Florence, Italy

Steering Committee

Jiwu Huang	Shenzhen University, China
Anthony T. S. Ho	University of Surrey, UK
Mauro Barni	University of Siena, Italy
Ton Kalker	DTS, USA
Nasir Memon	NYU-Poly, USA

Program Committee

Patrick Bas	École Centrale de Lille, CNRS, France
Chin-Chen Chang	Feng Chia University, Taiwan
Rémi Cogranne	Troyes University of Technology, France
Claude Delpha	Paris-Sud University, France
Jana Dittmann	University Magdeburg, Germany
Isao Echizen	National Institute of Informatics, Japan
Jessica Fridrich	Binghamton University, USA
Yi Hu	Northern Kentucky University, USA
Fangjun Huang	Sun Yat-sen University, China
Xinghao Jiang	Shanghai Jiao Tong University, China
Xiangui Kang	Sun Yat-sen University, China
Mohan Kankanhalli	National University of Singapore, Singapore
Stefan Katzenbeisser	TU Darmstadt, Germany
Andrew Ker	University of Oxford, UK
Anja Keskinarkaus	University of Oulu, Finland
Cheonshik Kim	Sejong University, South Korea
Minoru Kuribayashi	Okayama University, Japan
Xiaolong Li	Beijing Jiaotong University, China
Chang-Tsun Li	Charles Sturt University, Australia
Feng Liu	Chinese Academy of Sciences, China

Xiangyang Luo	Information Engineering University, China
Bin Ma	Qilu University of Technology, China
Wojciech Mazurczyk	Warsaw University of Technology, Poland
Rongrong Ni	Beijing Jiaotong University, China
Jiangqun Ni	Sun Yat-sen University, China
Akira Nishimura	Tokyo University of Information Sciences, Japan
Tomáš Pevný	Czech Technical University in Prague, Czech Republic
Yong-Man Ro	KAIST, South Korea
Athanassios Skodras	University of Patras, Greece
Matthew Stamm	Drexel University, USA
Xingming Sun	Nanjing University of Information Science and Technology, China
Andreas Westfeld	HTW Dresden, Germany
James C. N. Yang	National Dong Hwa University, Taiwan
Xinpeng Zhang	Fudan University, China
Weiming Zhang	University of Science and Technology of China, China
Yao Zhao	Beijing Jiaotong University, China
Linna Zhou	Beijing University of Posts and Telecommunications, China
Guopu Zhu	Chinese Academy of Sciences, China

Sponsors

Sichuan University

CSIG Special Committee of Digital
Media Forensics and Security

CSIG Special Committee of Digital Media Forensics
and Security

Multimedia Security Expert Committee
Chinese Institute of Electronics

Multimedia Security Expert Committee Chinese
Institute of Electronics

Contents

Deep Learning for Multimedia Security

GAN-Based Steganography with the Concatenation of Multiple Feature Maps

Haibin Wu[1], Fengyong Li[1,3]([✉]), Xinpeng Zhang[2], and Kui Wu[3]

[1] College of Computer Science and Technology, Shanghai University of Electric Power, Shanghai, People's Republic of China
fyli@shiep.edu.cn
[2] School of Computer Science, Fudan University, Shanghai, People's Republic of China
[3] Computer Science Department, University of Victoria, Victoria, Canada

Abstract. Steganography has been widely used to conceal secret information in multimedia content. Using generative adversarial networks (GAN) where two subnetworks compete against each other, steganography can learn good distortion measurement. Nevertheless, the convergence speed of GAN is usually slow, and the performance of GAN-based steganography has large room to improve. In this paper, we propose a new GAN-based spatial steganographic scheme. The proposed learning framework consists of two parts: a steganographic generator and a steganalytic discriminator. The former generates stego images, and the latter evaluates their steganography security. Different from existing GAN-based steganography, we reconstruct the generator by combining multiple feature maps, and then expand the maximum number of feature channels to 256. The reconstruction generator can effectively generate a sophisticated probability map, which is used to calculate optimal distortion measurement and further provides a better guidance for adaptive information embedding. Comprehensive experimental results show that, with the same discriminant network, the anti-steganalysis performance of our method is better than that of ASDL-GAN scheme and Yang's scheme.

Keywords: Steganography · Generative adversarial networks · Multiple feature maps · Content-adaptive

1 Introduction

As a hotspot in the field of information hiding, image steganography [2–6,11] is an efficient technology that hides secret information in cover images. With the development of steganalysis [8,14,16], the traditional algorithms, e.g., Least Significant Bit (LSB) methods [1], cannot meet the security requirements. To address the problem, more sophisticated content-adaptive steganographic schemes have been proposed to measure each pixel's degree of modification

© Springer Nature Switzerland AG 2020
H. Wang et al. (Eds.): IWDW 2019, LNCS 12022, pp. 3–17, 2020.
https://doi.org/10.1007/978-3-030-43575-2_1

suitability, so that the overall distortion can be controlled. Generally, content-adaptive steganography, such as HUGO [2], WOW [3], HILL [4], S-UNIWARD [5] and MiPOD [6], performs data embedding operations mainly in complex texture regions of cover images. Recently, generative adversarial networks (GAN), that use two subnetworks to compete against each other to gain overall better performance, have been used in image steganography and steganalysis. Researchers have showed that GAN can achieve considerable performance improvement in both steganalysis and steganography.

Regarding Steganalysis. Qian et al. [20] first introduced CNNs to solve steganalysis problem, and then proposed a network structure that consists of five convolution layers and three full connection layers. This scheme uses a fixed Ker-Bohme (KV) kernel in preprocessing layer to obtain image residuals [19], but the detection results over the BOSSBase image database are slightly lower than that of Spatial Rich Model (SRM) [8]. Xu et al. [7] proposed another CNN architecture by considering the knowledge of steganalysis. Similar to Qian's scheme, this scheme also obtains image residuals by using fixed KV kernel, but, it reduces the scope of feature map by adding an abstract (ABS) layer. Ye et al. [21] proposed a 10-layer CNN, in which 30 high-pass filters referring to SRM model are used to initialize the first layer parameters of this network. This scheme reconstructs the activation function by using truncated linear unit (TLU), which is more suitable for the distribution of steganographic noise. By combining channel selection, the detection performance for adaptive steganography can be significantly improved.

Regarding Steganography. CNN-based GAN is still in its nascency. Tang et al. [9] proposed an automatic steganographic distortion learning framework based on generative adversarial network (ASDL-GAN). The steganographic distortion of each pixel in cover image is learned by alternately training two adversarial subnetworks. Although ASDL-GAN can effectively learn steganographic distortion, its anti-steganalysis performance has not yet exceeded S-UNIWARD. Yang et al. [10] improved ASDL-GAN by using Tanh-simulator function to solve a crucial problem in ASDL-GAN, that is, the ternary embedding simulator (TES) is difficult to propagate backwards in ASDL-GAN. Compared with ASDL-GAN, the training time of Yang's scheme is greatly reduced and the anti-steganalysis capability is significantly improved. The above schemes mainly get steganographic distortion by adversarial learning, and then choose appropriate pixels for data embedding. Another thread of research directly generates adversarial examples by adversarial learning [15,22]. Following the design of deep convolutional GAN (DCGAN) [12], Volkhonskiy et al. [15] proposed steganographic GAN (SGAN), which generates cover images more suitable for steganography than natural images. On the basis of SGAN, Shi et al. [13] replaced DCGAN with Wasserstein GAN (WGAN) [17] and further proposed a secure steganographic scheme called SSGAN. Zhang et al. [22] added specific noise to cover image to obtain an enhanced cover so that the stego images can "mislead" the classification of deep learning. Although adversarial example-based steganographic schemes can effectively resist the deep learning-based steganographic analysis methods, they do not perform well under traditional steganalysis schemes using the high-dimensional feature model. The above research has shown that the steganographic distortions can be learnt effectively and cover images can be directly constructed with the adversarial network framework. Nevertheless, the performance with respect to anti-steganalysis capability and training speed, still has much room for improvement.

We are thus motivated to address the above problems by proposing a new spatial spatial steganographic framework that uses GAN to find out the optimal distortion measurement. Overall, we make the following novel contributions in the context of secure steganography:

- We design a novel steganographic scheme based on a reconstructed generative adversarial network (R-GAN). The proposed scheme can learn steganographic distortion measurement effectively and has a fast training speed for optimal parameters. Moreover, our steganographic scheme is resilient to steganalysis.
- Different from the existing GAN-based research, we reconstruct the generator of GAN by combining multiple feature maps. The generator can effectively generate sophisticated probability map, which is used to calculate optimal distortion measurement and provides a better guidance for achieving adaptive information embedding.
- We perform comprehensive test over two image databases, including one large-scale database of natural images as training set and a classical image database, BOSSBase, as testing set. Testing results show that our solution has a higher anti-steganalysis capability than that of existing ASDL-GAN scheme and Yang's scheme.

The rest of this paper is organized as follows. The related work is reviewed in Sect. 2. Our proposed framework is described in Sect. 3. Experimental results and discussions are presented in Sect. 4. Finally, Sect. 5 concludes the paper.

2   Related Work

2.1   ASDL-GAN Model

In [9], ASDL-GAN model is proposed for steganographic distortion calculation. Its structure is mainly composed of two parts:

1. A steganographic generative subnetwork. It mainly focuses on generating the modification probability map for cover image.
2. A steganalytic discriminative subnetwork. Its role is to discriminate cover images and stego images and provides an effective feedback.

In the ASDL-GAN model, the generator G contains 25 groups of convolution networks, a batch normalization process, and rectified linear units (ReLU). When cover images are input into the generator G, the change probability for each pixel is enforced to fall in the interval $(0, 0.5)$. The ASDL-GAN model uses ternary embedding scheme to construct a TES activation function as the embedding simulator. The modification directions are thus $\phi \in \{+1, 0, -1\}$. Since the TES activation function uses the given change probability $p_{i,j}$ ($p_{i,j} \in (0, 0.5)$) and a random number $n_{i,j}$ ($n_{i,j} \in [0, 1]$) as input, the output can thus be denoted as the corresponding modification $m'_{i,j}$.

$$m'_{i,j} = \begin{cases} -1 & , \text{ if } n_{i,j} < p_{i,j}/2 \\ 1 & , \text{ if } n_{i,j} > 1 - p_{i,j}/2 \\ 0 & , \text{ otherwise} \end{cases} \tag{1}$$

As a result, the capacity of the corresponding stego image can be calculated by accumulating the modification probabilities $p_{i,j}^{+1}$, $p_{i,j}^{-1}$, $p_{i,j}^{0}$ for $\{+1, 0, -1\}$, respectively.

The ASDL-GAN model adopts Xu's model [7] as the discriminator. By alternately training the generation network and the discrimination network, the ASDL-GAN model automatically learns embedding change probabilities for each pixel and coverts them as steganographic distortion. Finally, the embedding process uses a minimal-distortion framework, e.g., Syndrome Trellis Codes (STCs) framework [23]. Nevertheless, the performance of ASDL-GAN is still inferior to the traditional adaptive steganography scheme S-UNIWARD. In addition, since TES needs a long time for pre-training, ASDL-GAN is very time consuming.

2.2 Yang's Model

In [10], Yang et al. proposed another adversarial steganographic scheme, which consists of a generator, an embedding simulator, and a discriminator. This scheme uses a more compact generator based on U-NET [24]. With extensive experiments, the authors verified that this generator improves security performance significantly and reduces training time dramatically.

As the key contribution, Yang's model changes the activation function from TES to the Tanh simulator. This process can solve the problem that the parameters in TES are difficult to back propagate and can save two thirds of training time for each epoch. The definition of Tanh simulator is as follows:

$$m'_{i,j} = -0.5 \times \tanh(\lambda(p_{i,j} - 2 \times n_{i,j})) + 0.5 \times \tanh(\lambda(p_{i,j} - 2 \times (1 - n_{i,j}))) \tag{2}$$

$$\tanh(x) = \frac{e^x - e^{-x}}{e^x + e^{-x}} \tag{3}$$

where $p_{i,j}$ and $n_{i,j}$ have the same meaning as in (1) and λ controls the slope at the junction of stairs.

In addition, the channel selection is considered in the design of the discriminator D, so that the learned distortion measurement can guide the design of a more secure steganographic scheme. Compared with ASDL-GAN, Yang's model has a significant advantages w.r.t. training time, but its anti-steganalysis capability still has much room for improvement. In the following, we thus reconstruct the network structures to further improve the secure performance.

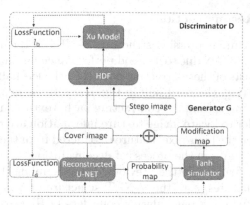

(a) The overall framework

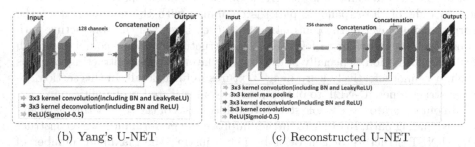

(b) Yang's U-NET   (c) Reconstructed U-NET

Fig. 1. The framework for proposed scheme. (a) The generator and the discriminator. (b) Yang's U-NET structure. (c) Reconstructed U-NET structure. (Color figure online)

3 Proposed Scheme Based on Reconstructed GAN

3.1 The Overall Introduction of Proposed Scheme

Our scheme uses GAN to learn optimal distortion measurement and further guides steganographic embedding. The proposed framework mainly consists of two parts: a steganographic generator G and a steganalytic discriminator D, as shown in Fig. 1(a).

In the steganographic generator G, we reconstruct a new generator by combining multiple feature maps, as shown in Fig. 1(b). For a cover image, the corresponding probability map is obtained by the reconstructed generator. Then, we use the Tanh simulator to construct the embedding modification map, which is used to generate the stego image by referring to the cover image.

For the steganalytic discriminator D, the cover image and the stego image are combined as its input. We use Xu's model to provide feedback so that their anti-steganalysis performance can be evaluated in real time. An optimal probability map can be effectively learnt by the two subnetworks competing against each other. The final probability map is then converted to measure distortion in the design of secure steganography.

3.2   Generator Reconstruction

As a good image texture expression structure, U-NET [24] can be used to construct the generator in GAN due to its good performance for image segmentation. U-NET usually consists of the contracting path (i.e., the left half in Fig. 1(b)) and the expanding path (i.e., the right half in Fig. 1(b)). If the expanding path does not combine feature maps from the contracting path, texture information will be hard to learn. In order to locate image texture information accurately, a common practice is to combine the high-pixel features extracted from the contracting path with the new feature maps in the process of deconvolution. This process can preserve image textural features in the previous down-sampling. Unfortunately, for existing U-NET structures, e.g., the U-NET structure of Yang's model (shown in Fig. 1(b)), the expanding path always considers ONE feature map concatenation, i.e., the feature map at layer i of the expanding path (counting from left to right of the expanding path) is combined with the feature map at the corresponding layer of the contracting path (i.e., layer i of the contracting path counting from the right to left) [10]. This structure does not combine enough feature information, especially in the first few layers on the contracting path. As such, it cannot effectively learn image textures in finer detail. In this section, we reconstruct a new U-NET to obtain a more sophisticated probability map.

In our generator, the whole structure still consists of the contracting path and the expanding path. In order to further improve the performance, we reconstruct the U-NET structure of generator by (1) adjusting the maximum number of feature channels in the contracting path and (2) combining multiple feature maps in the expanding path. The details are as follows.

First, we fix the structure and parameters of each path. Specifically, the contracting path contains a convolution structure (corresponding to kernel size 3×3 and step size 2), batch normalization, Leaky-ReLU, max pooling (corresponding to kernel size 3×3, step size 1). Each expanding path contains deconvolution (corresponding to kernel size 3×3, step size 2), batch normalization, ReLU, concat, convolution (corresponding to kernel size 3×3, step size 1). The total number of layers along a path (i.e., path length) of new generator is $L = 16$ and the maximum number of channels is 256. The specific network structure of the generator is shown in Table 1.

Second, in the contracting path, convolution is used to increase the channel number of feature maps, while max pooling is used to decrease the size of feature maps.

Third, in the expanding path, in order to ensure that the image features learned from the contracting path can be used effectively for image reconstruction, we combine TWO feature maps before and after convolution in the corresponding contracting layer. For example, in Fig. 1(c) and Table 1, the ith ($i \in [9, 16)$) expanding layer combines the $(L - i + 1)^{th}$ feature map after Leaky-ReLU and the $(L - i)^{th}$ feature map after max pooling.

Forth, in the expanding path, since there are many feature channels after concatenation, we further reduce the number of channels by adding the convolution layer (i.e., the red layers at the right side of Fig. 1(c)). This operation can

Table 1. Specific network structure for reconstructed generator.

Layers	Output size	Kernel size	Process
Input	$1 \times 512 \times 512$	/	Convolution-BN-Leaky ReLU-Maxpool
Layer1	$16 \times 256 \times 256$	$16 \times (3 \times 3 \times 1)$	Convolution-BN-Leaky ReLU-Maxpool
Layer2	$32 \times 128 \times 128$	$32 \times (3 \times 3 \times 16)$	Convolution-BN-Leaky ReLU-Maxpool
Layer3	$64 \times 64 \times 64$	$64 \times (3 \times 3 \times 32)$	Convolution-BN-Leaky ReLU-Maxpool
Layer4	$128 \times 32 \times 32$	$128 \times (3 \times 3 \times 64)$	Convolution-BN-Leaky ReLU-Maxpool
Layer5	$256 \times 16 \times 16$	$256 \times (3 \times 3 \times 128)$	Convolution-BN-Leaky ReLU-Maxpool
Layer6	$256 \times 8 \times 8$	$256 \times (3 \times 3 \times 256)$	Convolution-BN-Leaky ReLU-Maxpool
Layer7	$256 \times 4 \times 4$	$256 \times (3 \times 3 \times 256)$	Convolution-BN-Leaky ReLU-Maxpool
Layer8	$256 \times 2 \times 2$	$256 \times (3 \times 3 \times 256)$	Convolution-BN-Leaky ReLU-Maxpool
Layer9	$256 \times 4 \times 4$	$256 \times (3 \times 3 \times 256)$ $256 \times (3 \times 3 \times 768)$	Deconvolution-BN-ReLU-Concat-convolution
Layer10	$256 \times 8 \times 8$	$256 \times (3 \times 3 \times 256)$ $256 \times (3 \times 3 \times 768)$	Deconvolution-BN-ReLU-Concat-convolution
Layer11	$256 \times 16 \times 16$	$256 \times (3 \times 3 \times 256)$ $256 \times (3 \times 3 \times 768)$	Deconvolution-BN-ReLU-Concat-convolution
Layer12	$128 \times 32 \times 32$	$256 \times (3 \times 3 \times 128)$ $128 \times (3 \times 3 \times 512)$	Deconvolution-BN-ReLU-Concat-convolution
Layer13	$64 \times 64 \times 64$	$128 \times (3 \times 3 \times 64)$ $64 \times (3 \times 3 \times 256)$	Deconvolution-BN-ReLU-Concat-convolution
Layer14	$32 \times 128 \times 128$	$64 \times (3 \times 3 \times 32)$ $32 \times (3 \times 3 \times 128)$	Deconvolution-BN-ReLU-Concat-convolution
Layer15	$16 \times 256 \times 256$	$32 \times (3 \times 3 \times 16)$ $16 \times (3 \times 3 \times 64)$	Deconvolution-BN-ReLU-Concat-convolution
Layer16	$1 \times 512 \times 512$	$16 \times (3 \times 3 \times 8)$ $3 \times (3 \times 3 \times 8)$	Deconvolution-BN-ReLU-convolution
Output	$1 \times 512 \times 512$	/	ReLU (Sigmod-0.5)

reduce the number of parameters and the amount of computation while ensuring the symmetry of network structure.

3.3 Discriminator Design

In our framework, discriminator is considered as steganography adversarial tool (also called as steganalytic tool). Since the whole network can be effectively trained by steganography and steganalysis competing against each other, a stronger discriminator can make steganography more secure with a serial of adversarial training.

In order to improve the effectiveness of discriminator so that the trained parameters can better express the distortion measurement, we introduce 10 high pass filters from SRM and consider them as the adversarial basis of discriminator. Since Xu's model [7] has good performance in implementation efficiency and steganalysis, we use it (named as Xu Model in Fig. 1(a)) in our discriminator D. During each round of training, the generator adjusts parameters to resist the analysis of the discriminator, while the discriminator also adjusts the parameters to judge the results of generator. When the process converges (i.e., the parameters in both the generator and the discriminator remain stable or a given maximum number of iterations has been reached), the final parameters are used to calculate the embedding distortion of each pixel.

3.4   Training of Network

Our training framework contains the generator G and the discriminator D. For discriminator D, its function is to determine whether an image is a stego image. The corresponding loss function can be calculated as follows.

$$l_D = - \sum_{i=1}^{2} y'_i \log(y_i) \tag{4}$$

where y_i is the softmax output of the discriminator D and y'_i is the corresponding truth.

For generator G, the main function is to generate optimal probability maps and calculate steganographic distortion measurement for each pixel. Stego images can be produced by combining optimal steganographic distortion measurement and a traditional steganographic method. Thus, its loss function can be defined in two parts: l_D and $GLoss$. l_D makes the produced stego image hard to detect by the discriminator D, while $GLoss$ ensures that the produced stego image can embed payload approximate to a given embedding rate Q.

$$l_G = -\alpha \times l_D + \beta \times GLoss \tag{5}$$

$$GLoss = (C - H \times W \times Q)^2 \tag{6}$$

where H and W are the height and width of cover images, respectively. α and β are used to control the weights of l_D and $GLoss$, respectively.

In this framework, the total capacity of stego image is denote as C.

$$C = \sum_{i=1}^{H} \sum_{j=1}^{W} (-p_{i,j}^{+1}\log_2 p_{i,j}^{+1} - p_{i,j}^{-1}\log_2 p_{i,j}^{-1} - p_{i,j}^{0}\log_2 p_{i,j}^{0}) \tag{7}$$

where $p_{i,j}^{+1}$ and $p_{i,j}^{-1}$ stand for the probabilities of modifying the corresponding pixel by adding 1 and subtracting 1, respectively, while $p_{i,j}^{0}$ represents the probability that the corresponding pixel keeps unchanged. They can be calculated by embedding probability $p_{i,j}$, which is the output of generator G.

$$p_{i,j}^{+1} = p_{i,j}^{-1} = p_{i,j}/2 \tag{8}$$

$$p_{i,j}^{0} = 1 - p_{i,j} \tag{9}$$

By setting a serial of initial parameters (refer to Sect. 4 for the specific values), the generator G and the discriminator D are alternately trained round by round. Each round includes two steps:

Step 1: We divide cover images into batches, e.g., 8 cover images a batch, and put the batch of cover images into the reconstructed U-NET. We then obtain the actual probability maps. Subsequently, Tanh simulator is used to generate the modification maps (i.e., $\{-1, 0, 1\}$) by combining the embedding probability maps and random matrices. Finally, the generator G generates the corresponding stego images by applying the modification maps on the cover images.

Step 2: The batch of cover images and their stego images are input into discriminator D. In discriminator D, we minimize l_D and $GLoss$ by Mini-Batch gradient descent with Adam optimizer, and then the minimal l_G is calculated by Eq. (5).

3.5 Practical Steganographic Scheme

In this section, we present the actual steganographic process by using our reconstructed network. Since our reconstructed network only outputs the embedding probabilities by a serial of adversarial training, the actual embedding distortion (embedding cost) should be calculated with the trained embedding probabilities. Subsequently, with STCs [19,23], the practical steganographic scheme can be achieved easily.

Given a batch of cover images, we use the reconstructed generator G and the discriminator D to alternately train and update the embedding probabilities. When the network model training is completed, an optimal embedding probability map P can be obtained with a serial of adversarial training. With the probability map P, the embedding cost β can be calculated according to Eq. (10). Finally, STCs is used to embed the secret information.

$$\beta_{i,j} = \ln\left(1/p_{i,j} - 2\right), p_{i,j} \in (0, 0.5) \tag{10}$$

4 Experimental Results and Discussion

4.1 Experimental Setup

We test our method over two image sets: Places365-Standard [18] and BOSSBase v1.01 [19]. The Places365-Standard image set is used to train our proposed GAN model, while the BOSSBase image set is used to test the performance. In the training stage, the parameters α and β in Eq. (5) are set to 10^6 and 0.1, respectively. Since the Places365-Standard image set contains a lot of natural images of big size, we select 36500 JPEG color images from this set and use "rgb2gray" function and "imresize" function in matlab to transform JPEG color images into gray images. The images are resized to 512×512. In the testing stage, we use the BOSSBase images to generate 10000 stego images and build 10000 cover-stego image pairs, which are divided randomly into two parts: 5000 pairs for training the classification model, while the rest 5000 pairs for testing.

In addition, we employ ensemble classifier to give an ensemble detection error rate in our experiments. Generally speaking, a higher error rate indicates a stronger anti-steganalysis capability. Adam optimizer with 0.0001 learning rate is chosen to train the model by 160000 iterations and all the experiments were conducted with TensorFlow on DELL W-2102 Workstation with 16 GB RAM and an RTX2080 GPU card.

4.2 Steganographic Results

We first show the experimental results of our proposed scheme. Two embedding payloads, 0.1 bpp and 0.4 bpp, are tested. For illustration purpose, we randomly choose an image ("1013.pgm") from BOSSBase and show the testing results.

The corresponding results are shown in Fig. 2. In this figure, Fig. 2(a) is cover image. Figure 2(b) and (c) are the change probability map and the corresponding modification map of 0.4 bpp, respectively, while Fig. 2(e) and (f) are the change probability map and corresponding modification map of 0.1 bpp, respectively. From this figure, we can see that embedding change probability values of texture regions are larger than the smooth regions. In other words, the embedding modification is concentrated in the texture region (i.e., content adaptive). The experimental results, Fig. 2(c) and (f), also confirm this conclusion.

4.3 Testing for Different Concatenations of Feature Maps

Existing schemes, e.g., Yang's scheme, use one feature map (after the deconvolution layers) to learn texture information. This may not be good enough, because single feature map cannot fully capture image texture information, especially in the first few contracting layers. In contrast, combining multiple feature maps can better utilize the texture information and offers a better guidance for building the probability map. Due to the above consideration, our scheme reconstructs the U-NET structure by combining multiple feature maps in the contracting layers to further improve the learning capability. In this section, we evaluate the effectiveness of different ways of concatenating the feature maps.

Table 2 shows the experimental results. From this table, we can see that concatenating feature maps leads to a significant improvement over the case that no feature map is concatenated. The average gains are 6.3% and 8.5% for 0.1 bpp and 0.4 bpp, respectively. Comparing the case where only one feature map is combined (i.e., Yang's scheme [10]) and the case where two feature maps are combined (i.e., our scheme), the average gains are 2.23% for 0.1 bpp and 1.3% for 0.4 bpp. In the steganography field, such an improvement is nontrivial. In fact, if more feature maps (e.g., three) are combined, we believe the performance may be further improved, but, such an improvement may not be good enough to justify the higher complexity and longer running time.

Since our proposed scheme expands the number of maximum channels to 256 while Yang's scheme is only 128 channels, we are interested in checking whether or not increasing the maximum number of channels also contributes to the performance gain of our method. For this purpose, we modified and tested

Fig. 2. The steganographic results of proposed scheme. (a) Cover image "1013.pgm" in BOSSBase with size 512 × 512. (b) Change probability map with 0.4 bpp. (c) Modification map with 0.4 bpp. (d) Stego image with 0.4 bpp. (e) Change probability map with 0.1 bpp. (f) Modification map with 0.1 bpp. (g) Stego image with 0.1 bpp.

Yang's method with 256 maximum channels. The results are listed as "One (256)" in Table 2. From the results, we can see that increasing the number of maximum channels does not necessarily lead to a better performance, e.g., when the payload is 0.4 bpp, "One (128)" actually outperforms "One (256)". We can thus conclude that the performance gains of our scheme are mainly due to the concatenation of multiple feature maps.

4.4   Comparison with State-of-the-Arts

We compare our scheme with existing state-of-the-art schemes, ASDL-GAN model (Tang's scheme), Yang's scheme and S-UNIWARD scheme. The same image sets as the above experiments are used in this section. To gain more insights, we combine ensemble classifier v2.0 (EC for short) and two classical steganalysis methods, SRM+EC and maxSRMd2+EC. The corresponding experimental results are shown in Tables 3 and 4, respectively. From these tables, we can observe that our scheme outperforms the above three schemes by a large margin. In particular, when SRM+EC method is used, compared with Yang's scheme, the proposed scheme has the error rate gains 2.1% for 0.1 bpp, 1.8% for 0.2 bpp and 1.3% for 0.4 bpp; compared with Tang's scheme, the proposed scheme has the error gains 8.57% for 0.1 bpp, 7.39% for 0.2 bpp and 6.36% for 0.4 bpp. Similarly, when maxSRMd2+EC method is used, the superior performance

Table 2. Error rates for different generators that are constructed by combining zero, one, two feature maps, respectively. Note that "Zero" corresponds to the original U-NET [24], "One (128)" corresponds to Yang's scheme with maximum number of channels equal to 128 [10], "One (256)" corresponds to Yang's scheme with maximum number of channels equal to 256, and "Two" corresponds to our proposed scheme using two feature maps concatenation. **maxSRMd2+EC** is used over BOSSBase.

Payload	Number of combined feature maps			
	Zero	One (128)	One (256)	Two
0.10 bpp	35.02%	39.10%	40.10%	41.33%
0.40 bpp	12.50%	19.72%	19.42%	21.02%

Table 3. Error rates of different steganographic schemes by using **SRM+EC** over BOSSBase.

Payload	Different steganographic schemes			
	S-UNIWARD	Tang's scheme [9]	Yang's scheme [10]	Proposed
0.10 bpp	40.11%	32.84%	39.33%	41.41%
0.20 bpp	32.30%	27.41%	32.99%	34.80%
0.40 bpp	20.18%	15.31%	20.29%	21.66%

Table 4. Error rates of different steganographic schemes by **maxSRMd2+EC** over BOSSBase.

Payload	Different steganographic schemes			
	S-UNIWARD	Tang's scheme [9]	Yang's scheme [10]	Proposed
0.10 bpp	40.24%	32.31%	39.10%	41.33%
0.20 bpp	32.21%	26.75%	32.53%	34.17%
0.40 bpp	19.18%	15.08%	19.72%	21.02%

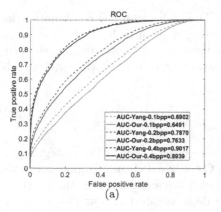
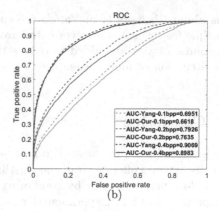

Fig. 3. The ROC curves and the corresponding AUC information for our proposed scheme and Yang's scheme when resisting two steganalysis methods: (a) SRM+EC and (b) maxSRMd2+EC.

Table 5. Training time (DELL W-2102 Workstation with 16 GB RAM and an RTX2080 GPU card.) for different steganographic schemes based on GAN. In this test, 160000 iterations are performed.

Steganographic scheme	Training time
Tang's scheme [9]	52 h 41 m
Yang's scheme [10]	17 h 26 m
Proposed scheme	23 h 44 m

is still obvious. This demonstrates that our scheme has a significant stronger anti-steganalysis capability.

To test the performance thoroughly, we also compare the proposed scheme with Yang's scheme by showing receiver operating characteristic (ROC) curves and the corresponding area under curve (AUC) values, which are calculated by ensemble classifier. The results are shown in Fig. 3. In this figure, the lower ROC curve and the lower AUC value imply that the error rate is higher, or in other words, the steganographic scheme is more secure. We can see that the proposed scheme has a better performance than Yang's scheme [10], whatever the payload is.

In addition, we compared the training time of the three schemes. All the three schemes iterate 160000 times, and 8 cover-stego pairs[1] are used as input in each iteration. All experiments are implemented with TensorFlow platform over DELL W-2102 Workstation with 16 GB RAM and an RTX2080 GPU card. Table 5 shows the comparison of training time. Compared with Tang's scheme, the training time of our proposed scheme is reduced by more than half, but

---

[1] Since RTX2080 GPU card has only 8 GB memory, 8 cover-stego pairs are the maximum number of images that the processor can process at one time.

it is about 6 h more than Yang's scheme. This is because the combination for multiple feature maps involves extra processing steps in each iteration, e.g., the convolution layers are added to reduce the number of feature channels after the concatenation of multiple feature maps (i.e., the red layer at the right side of Fig. 1(c)).

5 Conclusion

We proposed a secure steganographic scheme using GAN to learn steganography distortion. Different from the existing GAN-based steganographic methods, we build a new generator by combining multiple feature maps in the contracting path of U-NET. Experimental results demonstrate that our method effectively generates a change probability map for better distortion measurement, and achieves a more secure steganographic scheme.

In the future, we plan to extend the work in two directions. First, we plan to further simplify the network structure by reducing the training parameters, while maintaining high anti-steganalysis capability. Second, we plan to consider some better-structured neural networks to design discriminator, e.g., Recurrent Neural Network (RNN).

Acknowledgments. This work was supported by Natural Science Foundation of China under Grants (61602295, U1736120), the Foreign Visiting Scholar Program of Shanghai Municipal Education Commission and Postgraduate Innovation and Entrepreneurship Project of Shanghai University of Electric Power (A-0201-19-183Y-20).

References

1. Mielikainen, J.: LSB matching revisited. IEEE Signal Process. Lett. **13**(5), 285–287 (2006)
2. Pevný, T., Filler, T., Bas, P.: Using high-dimensional image models to perform highly undetectable steganography. In: Böhme, R., Fong, P.W.L., Safavi-Naini, R. (eds.) IH 2010. LNCS, vol. 6387, pp. 161–177. Springer, Heidelberg (2010). https://doi.org/10.1007/978-3-642-16435-4_13
3. Fridrich, J., Holub, V.: Designing steganographic distortion using directional filters. In: IEEE International Workshop on Information Forensics and Security, WIFS 2012, pp. 234–239. IEEE (2012). https://doi.org/10.1109/WIFS.2012.6412655
4. Li, B., Tan, S., Wang, M., Huang, J.: Investigation on cost assignment in spatial image steganography. IEEE Trans. Inf. Forensics Secur. **9**(8), 1264–1277 (2014)
5. Holub, V., Fridrich, J., Denemark, T.: Universal distortion function for steganography in an arbitrary domain. EURASIP J. Inf. Secur. **2014**(1), 1–13 (2014). https://doi.org/10.1186/1687-417X-2014-1
6. Sedighi, V., Cogranne, R., Fridrich, J.: Content-adaptive steganography by minimizing statistical detectability. IEEE Trans. Inf. Forensics Secur. **11**(2), 221–234 (2016)
7. Xu, G., Wu, H., Shi, Y.: Structural design of convolutional neural networks for steganalysis. IEEE Signal Process. Lett. **23**(5), 708–712 (2016)

8. Fridrich, J., Kodovsky, J.: Rich models for steganalysis of digital images. IEEE Trans. Inf. Forensics Secur. **7**(3), 868–882 (2012)
9. Tang, W., Tan, S., Li, B., Huang, J.: Automatic steganographic distortion learning using a generative adversarial network. IEEE Signal Process. Lett. **24**(10), 1547–1551 (2017)
10. Yang, J., Liu, K., Kang, X., Wong, E.K.: Spatial image steganography based on generative adversarial network. arXiv:1804.07939 (2018)
11. Li, F., Wu, K., Zhang, X., Yu, J., Lei, J., Wen, M.: Robust batch steganography in social networks with non-uniform payload and data decomposition. IEEE Access **6**, 29912–29925 (2018)
12. Radford, A., Metz, L., Chintala, S.: Unsupervised representation learning with deep convolutional generative adversarial networks. arXiv:1511.06434 (2016)
13. Shi, H., Dong, J., Wang, W., Qian, Y., Zhang, X.: SSGAN: secure steganography based on generative adversarial networks. In: Zeng, B., Huang, Q., El Saddik, A., Li, H., Jiang, S., Fan, X. (eds.) PCM 2017. LNCS, vol. 10735, pp. 534–544. Springer, Cham (2018). https://doi.org/10.1007/978-3-319-77380-3_51
14. Li, F., Zhang, X., Cheng, H., Jiang, Y.: Digital image steganalysis based on local textural features and double dimensionality reduction. Secur. Commun. Netw. **9**(8), 729–736 (2016)
15. Volkhonskiy, D., Nazarov, I., Borisenko, B., Burnaev, E.: Steganographic generative adversarial networks. arXiv:1703.05502 (2017)
16. Li, F., Wu, K., Lei, J., Wen, M., Bi, Z., Gu, C.: Steganalysis over large-scale social networks with high-order joint features and clustering ensembles. IEEE Trans. Inf. Forensics Secur. **11**(2), 344–357 (2016)
17. Arjovsky, M., Chintala, S., Bottou, L.: Wasserstein GAN. arXiv:1701.07875 (2017)
18. Places365-Standard (2019). http://places2.csail.mit.edu/download.html. Accessed Mar 2019
19. DDE Download (2019). http://dde.binghamton.edu/download/. Accessed Mar 2019
20. Qian, Y., Dong, J., Wang W., Tan, T.: Deep learning for steganalysis via convolutional neural networks. In: Media Watermarking, Security, and Forensics 2015, Proceedings of SPIE, vol. 9409 (2015). https://doi.org/10.1117/12.2083479
21. Ye, J., Ni, J., Yi, Y.: Deep learning hierarchical representations for image steganalysis. IEEE Trans. Inf. Forensics Secur. **12**(11), 2545–2557 (2017)
22. Zhang Y., Zhang W., Chen K., et al.: Adversarial examples against deep neural network based steganalysis. In: Proceedings of the 6th ACM Workshop on Information Hiding and Multimedia Security, pp. 67–72. ACM (2018)
23. Filler, T., Judas, J., Fridrich, J.: Minimizing additive distortion in steganography using syndrome-trellis codes. IEEE Trans. Inf. Forensics Secur. **6**(3), 920–935 (2011)
24. Ronneberger, O., Fischer, P., Brox, T.: U-Net: convolutional networks for biomedical image segmentation. In: Navab, N., Hornegger, J., Wells, W.M., Frangi, A.F. (eds.) MICCAI 2015. LNCS, vol. 9351, pp. 234–241. Springer, Cham (2015). https://doi.org/10.1007/978-3-319-24574-4_28

GAN-TStega: Text Steganography Based on Generative Adversarial Networks

Zhongliang Yang[1(✉)], Nan Wei[2], Qinghe Liu[3], Yongfeng Huang[1], and Yujin Zhang[1]

[1] Beijing National Research Center for Information Science and Technology, Tsinghua University, Beijing 100084, China
yangzl15@mails.tsinghua.edu.cn, yfhuang@tsinghua.edu.cn
[2] National Key Laboratory for Novel Software Technology, Nanjing University, Nanjing 210023, China
[3] Department of Geological Engineering, Qinghai University, Xining 810016, China

Abstract. Steganography based on text auto-generation technology is a current topic with great promise and challenges. It has the advantages of large information hiding capacity compared with the modification-based text steganographic methods. The biggest challenge faced by previous methods is that they can hardly generate fluent steganographic texts, and only pay attention to the statistical distribution of individual sentences without considering the overall statistical distribution of all generated texts. This paper proposes a text steganography called GAN-TStega which based on generative adversarial networks (GANs). Firstly, we use strategy update algorithm to solve the problem that traditional GANs are difficult to generate discrete data. Through antagonistic training on different types of text datasets, GAN-TStega can generate high quality texts. Then, by encoding the conditional probability distribution of generator's output at each iteration, GAN-TStega can achieve secret information hiding. Through this method, we achieve the statistical distribution fitting at the sentence level, thus enhancing the security of steganography system. Experiments show that our method has good performance.

Keywords: Text steganography · Generative Adversarial Networks · Text generation

1 Introduction

For information security systems in cyberspace, Shannon has divided them into three categories: encryption systems, privacy systems, and concealment systems [1]. While protecting information security, encryption systems and privacy systems also expose the existence and importance of information itself, which may expose the target to potential attackers and thus is vulnerable to targeted attacks [2,3]. However, the concealment system is different from them. It embeds secret

H. Wang et al. (Eds.): IWDW 2019, LNCS 12022, pp. 18–31, 2020.
https://doi.org/10.1007/978-3-030-43575-2_2

information into a particular carrier, hiding the existence of it to ensure information security. As a very unique information security system, concealment communication system plays an important role in ensuring cyberspace security [4].

In cyberspace, there are different carriers that can be used for information hiding, including image [5,6], audio [7,8], text [9,10] and so on. As one of the most commonly used information medium in daily life, the study of text information hiding technology has great academic and practical value [11]. However, due to the low amount of redundant information in texts, hiding information in text has a great challenge. At present, text information hiding methods can be divided into two types, modification-based [12] and generation-based [9,10,13]. Modification-based text information hiding methods are mainly through a small amount of text modification, such as synonym substitution [12] to achieve secret information embedding. It is characterized by less text changes, so it can achieve a high concealment. However, due to the small redundancy of text information, modification-based text steganography can hardly have a high hiding capacity. Generation-based information hiding methods can automatically generate steganographic texts according to the secret information, thus to have a higher information hiding capacity. However, the main challenge they face is how to generate high-quality natural texts.

Recently, Yang *et al.* [9] proposed an automatic steganographic text generation model based on recurrent neural networks. It first learns the statistical language distribution model from a large amount of normal text, and then generates texts that conform to such statistical patterns. In the process of sentence generating, the conditional probability distribution of each word is encoded by binary tree to realize secret information hiding. But their model only considers the statistical properties of a single sentence, ignoring the overall distribution of batch-generated texts, which is incomplete to the whole security.

In this paper, we propose an automatic steganographic text generation model called GAN-TStega which based on Generative Adversarial Networks (GANs). By introducing antagonistic learning strategies, our model can further optimize the statistical distribution characteristics of the overall distribution of batch-generated sentences, thus further enhance the concealment of generated steganographic texts.

In the remainder of this paper, Sect. 2 introduces some related works, including text generation-based steganography and Generative Adversarial Networks. A detailed explanation of the GAN-TStega and algorithm details of information hiding and extracting are elaborated in Sect. 3. The following part, Sect. 6, presents the experimental evaluation results and gives a comprehensive discussion. Finally, conclusions are drawn in Sect. 7.

2   Related Works

In this section, we will introduce existing steganography methods and compare their advantages and disadvantages. At the same time, we will give a brief introduction of Generative Adversarial Networks.

2.1   Text Generation-Based Steganography

Different from text modification-based steganography, text generation-based steganography does not need to be given a carrier advance, but directly generate steganographic texts according to the secret information needs to be transmitted. However, the generator should keep the statistical distribution of generated steganographic texts as little different from the normal texts as possible.

With the development of natural language processing in recent years, more and more automatic text generation models have emerged [14]. Based on the statistical language model [15], natural language generation can be reduced to a sequence generation problem. For a sequence $S = (w_1, w_2..., w_n)$, whose probability can be expressed as:

$$\begin{aligned} P(S) &= P(w_1, w_2, ..., w_n) \\ &= P(w_1)P(w_2|w_1)P(w_3|w_2, w_1) \cdots P(w_n|w_{n-1}, ..., w_2, w_1). \end{aligned} \tag{1}$$

The generator predicts the probability distribution of the next value of the sequence by the known part of the sequence, and the prediction result can be expressed as $P(w_i|w_{i-1}..., w_2, w_1)$.

Within this framework, the use of Markov chains to generate steganographic text has emerged [10,16–18]. But the markov chain also has the limitation of not catching the long-range dependence. The long short term memory (LSTM) network proposed by Hochreiter and Schmidhuber can well capture long-range dependence [19]. Therefore, the application of LSTM in steganography achieves a better effect than markov chain [9,13].

The performance of text generation-based steganography method depends largely on the text generation method itself. It is a prerequisite to ensure the security of steganography to produce natural, smooth and unbiased text. Currently, most methods use maximum likelihood estimation to train the network [9,13]. However, training with this method will encounter the problem of *exposure bias* [20], that is, if there is a pattern that does not appear in the training data set during the generation process, it will lead to the accumulation of subsequent generation errors, which will produce the generation samples completely deviating from the real distribution.

2.2   GANs for Text Generation

Generative Adversarial Networks was first proposed by Goodfellow in 2014 [21]. The core idea of GANs is antagonistic learning and the main body is the generator G and the discriminator D. The generator generates the sample $G(z)$ by inputting the random variable $z \sim p_z$ to make it obey the real distribution as much as possible p_{data}. The discriminator trains with the generated sample $G(z)$ and the real sample $x \sim p_{\text{data}}$ to determine whether the sample is from the generator or the real data. The training process can be expressed as follows:

$$\min_G \max_D V(D, G) = \mathbb{E}_{x \sim p_{\text{data}}(x)}[\log D(x)] + \mathbb{E}_{z \sim p_z(z)}[\log(1 - D(G(z)))]. \tag{2}$$

However, due to the error back propagation requires that the function is continuous, the basic GANs can not be directly applied to the problem of sequence generation such as text generation. Yu *et al.* [22] proposed to use Policy Gradient in reinforcement learning to train the model, then the GAN can be applied to the task of text generation. Based on this training method, Guo *et al.* [23] proposed LeakGAN to leak the features extracted by the discriminator to the generator in the process of confrontation learning, thus helping the generator obtain more useful information to improve the quality of the generated text. MaskGAN [24] separately designs Critic to provide reward function, and uses the training method of filling in blanks instead of generating whole sentences from left to right to improve the quality of generation and generate text diversity.

Because of its excellent generating effect, GAN has been rapidly applied to image steganography research in these two years [25, 26]. However, due to the discrete nature of texts, GANs has never been applied to generative steganographic texts. In this paper, we use strategy updating method to train text generation network and then generate high-quality steganographic texts, so as to solve the shortcomings of previous text information steganography methods. According to our best knowledge, we are the first to use GANs for text steganography.

3   GAN-TStega Model

This section will introduce the structure and principle of GAN-TStega in detail. Generally speaking, GAN-TStega can be divided into two relatively independent parts: the generating part and information hiding part. Its operation mode is as follows: firstly, a large number of real text samples are trained by generative adversarial networks and optimize the generators; secondly, the trained generators are used to generate text automatically, and in the process of generating, the hidden information is embedded by encoding the conditional probability distribution of each word. This section will first introduce the generation part, then elaborate on steganography and extraction algorithm.

3.1   Generator

Based on the statistical language model, the generation of natural text S can be modeled as a sequential form of $S = (w_1, w_2, ..., w_n)$. The generator reads each word in the sequence in turn, converts each word into a fixed-length word vector, and feeds it into the GRU layer. For GRU, the input is the current word vector $\mathbf{x_t}$ and the last hidden state $\mathbf{h_{t-1}}$. Its forward propagation process is as follows:

$$\mathbf{r}_t = \sigma(W_r \cdot [\mathbf{h}_{t-1}, \mathbf{x}_t] + \mathbf{b}_r),$$
$$\mathbf{z}_t = \sigma(W_z \cdot [\mathbf{h}_{t-1}, \mathbf{x}_t] + \mathbf{b}_z),$$
$$\mathbf{n}_t = \tanh(W_n \cdot [\mathbf{r}_t * \mathbf{h}_{t-1}, \mathbf{x}_t]), \qquad (3)$$
$$\mathbf{h}_t = (1 - \mathbf{z}_t) * \mathbf{h}_{t-1} + \mathbf{z}_t * \mathbf{n}_t,$$
$$\mathbf{y}_t = \sigma(W_o \cdot \mathbf{h}_t),$$

where $[\mathbf{h}_{t-1}, \mathbf{x}_t]$ denotes matrix connection, $*$ denotes element-by-element multiplication between vectors, and σ denotes sigmoid function:

$$\sigma(x) = \frac{1}{1 + \exp(-x)}. \tag{4}$$

The output of its t-th time step is $\mathbf{h}_t$ and $\mathbf{y}_t$, $\mathbf{h}_t$ continues to participate in the next operation as the hidden state of the $t + 1$ time, and $\mathbf{y}_t$ is sent as the output to the next full connection layer of the generator. The purpose of the full connection layer is to project $\mathbf{y}_t$ to the probability by using Softmax to get $\mathbf{p}_t = (P_{t1}, P_{t2}, P_{t3}, ..., P_{tv})$. Among them, P_{ti} represents the conditional probability that the word w_i appears at the position of t in the sequence, that is:

$$P_{ti} \sim P(w_i | w_1, w_2, ..., w_{t-1}). \tag{5}$$

Then, the probability sampling or the value with the highest probability is directly selected as the next element of the sequence, and the iteration can complete the generation of the whole sequence.

3.2 Discriminator

The main purpose of discriminator is to judge whether the input text is a real sentence or machine-generated text. It plays the role of Eve in covert communication system. In GAN-TStega, we use the latest text steganalysis model [27] as a discriminator which uses bidirectional GRU to enhance the discriminant ability. For the discriminator, its input is a complete sequence of $S = (w_1, w_2, ..., w_n)$ consisting of n words, which can get from real data or samples generated by the generator. Similarly, the first layer of discriminator is also the embedding layer, which converts every word in the sequence into a word vector to form a word vector matrix:

$$X = Embed(S) = [\mathbf{x}_1, \mathbf{x}_2, ..., \mathbf{x}_n]. \tag{6}$$

Then the word vector matrix X is input to Bi-GRU layer, and the output is generated through the full connection layer and the activation function of σ to form the final binary classification probability. At the same time, we add Dropout mechanism to the discriminator network to prevent over-fitting.

4   Update Strategy

From the perspective of adversarial learning, for a generator G_θ with θ parameter set, its task is to generate a natural language sequence $S = (w_1, w_2, w_3, ..., w_n)$, to make it as close to the real data as possible, so that the discriminator D_Φ can not distinguish whether the generated sample comes from the real data. Based on the statistical language model, G_θ needs to generate each word in the sequence until the whole sequence is completed. As mentioned before, GAN was originally designed to handle continuous data. However, sequence generation is a typical discrete process, and it is impossible to update generator parameters directly using error return algorithm. For this reason, we use the method of reinforcement learning and use the reward function as the generator loss function to update the generator network.

We first define the concepts of current state, behavior, strategy, etc. For the current time node t, its state is the generated sequence, $s_{t-1} = (w_1, w_2, ..., w_{t-1}) = \mathbf{w}_{1:t-1}$, and the behavior a is the next word added to the sequence, $w_t \in V$, where V is the vocabulary. G_θ is used as a strategy model to guide the choice of next action. At the same time, the discriminator D_ϕ acts as a guide to the generator G_θ to update network parameters. D_ϕ receives samples from real data and generates samples of G_θ in an attempt to distinguish the two. Its discriminant results will guide G_θ to update the weight as an action-value function. D_ϕ is a binary classifier in function. We choose cross-entropy loss as its loss function:

$$L_D = -[y \log \hat{y} + (1 - y) \log(1 - \hat{y})], \tag{7}$$

where, $y, \hat{y} \in \{0, 1\}$, y represents the true result of the sample, $\hat{y}$ represents the predicted result of D_ϕ. The parameter updating process is as follows:

$$\phi \leftarrow \phi - \alpha_D \nabla_\phi L_D, \tag{8}$$

Among them, α_D is the learning rate. For a complete generating sequence, the expected reward can be expressed as:

$$J(\theta) = \mathbb{E}[R_n | s_0, \theta] = \sum_{w_1 \in V} G_\theta(w_1 | s_0) \cdot Q_{D_\phi}^{G_\theta}(s_0, w_1), \tag{9}$$

where R_n is the reward function value of the complete generated sequence, s_0 is the initial state, $Q_{D_p hi}^{G_\theta}(s, a)$ is the expected cumulative reward of choosing the behavior a under the current state of s and following the policy of G_θ. So the goal of G_θ is to maximize the expected reward of $J(\theta)$.

In order to calculate $J(\theta)$, we need to define a behavioral value function of $Q_{D_\phi}^{G_\theta}(s, a)$. Here we use the judgment result of D_ϕ as the behavioral value function, that is:

$$Q_{D_\phi}^{G_\theta}(s = \mathbf{w}_{1:n-1}, a = w_n) = D_\phi(\mathbf{w}_n). \tag{10}$$

But this formula only describes the last step of generation, because the input of the discriminator must be a complete sequence. We are concerned with the quality of the whole sequence, so the Q function needs to predict the long-term quality to some extent while expressing some of the generated quality. So we use Monte Carlo tree search to complete the sequence to get the Q function. Specifically, for an incomplete generating sequence $\mathbf{w}_{1:t}$, the following part of the sample completion sequence $\bar{\mathbf{w}}_{t+1:n}$ is sampled with the strategy M to form a complete sequence, which is then sent to the discriminator D_ϕ to obtain the discriminant result. Here we choose $M = G_\theta$, even if the current generator is used to complete the sequence. Thus the complete Q function can be expressed as:

$$Q_{D_\phi}^{G_\theta}(s = \mathbf{w}_{1:t-1}, a = w_t) = \begin{cases} D_\phi([\mathbf{w}_{1:t}, \bar{\mathbf{w}}_{t+1:n}]) & t < n \\ D_\phi(\mathbf{w}_n) & t = n \end{cases} \tag{11}$$

So for generator G_θ, the weight updating process is as follows:

$$\theta \leftarrow \theta + \alpha_G \nabla_\theta J(\theta), \tag{12}$$

where α_G is the learning rate and the gradient of $J(\theta)$ to θ can be expressed as:

$$\nabla_\theta J(\theta) = \Sigma_{t=1}^n \mathbb{E}_{\mathbf{w}_{1:t-1} \sim G_\theta} [\Sigma_{w_t \in V} \nabla_\theta G_\theta(w_t|\mathbf{w}_{1:t-1}) \cdot Q_{D_\phi}^{G_\theta}(\mathbf{w}_{1:t-1}, w_t)]. \tag{13}$$

The derivation process is as follows. From the definition of behavioral function, we have:

$$Q(s = \mathbf{w}_{1:t-1}, a = w_t) = \sum_{w_{t+1} \in V} G_\theta(w_{t+1}|\mathbf{w}_t) \cdot Q(s = \mathbf{w}_{1:t}, a = w_{t+1}). \tag{14}$$

so the gradient of Q is found when $t < n$ is:

$$\begin{aligned}
&\nabla_\theta Q(\mathbf{w}_{1:t-1}, w_t) \\
&= \nabla_\theta \sum_{w_{t+1} \in V} G_\theta(w_{t+1}|\mathbf{w}_t) \cdot Q(\mathbf{w}_{1:t}, w_{t+1}) \\
&= \sum_{w_{t+1} \in V} [\nabla_\theta G_\theta(w_{t+1}|\mathbf{w}_t) Q(\mathbf{w}_{1:t}, w_{t+1}) + G_\theta(w_{t+1}|\mathbf{w}_t) \nabla_\theta Q(\mathbf{w}_{1:t}, w_{t+1})] \\
&= \sum_{w_{t+1} \in V} \nabla_\theta G_\theta(w_{t+1}|\mathbf{w}_t) Q(\mathbf{w}_{1:t}, w_{t+1}) + \sum_{w_{t+1} \in V} P(w_{t+1}|\mathbf{w}_t; G_\theta) \nabla_\theta Q(\mathbf{w}_{1:t}, w_{t+1}).
\end{aligned} \tag{15}$$

When $t = n$, the formula (11) shows that the value of Q at this time is independent of the parameter θ and therefore we has:

$$\nabla_\theta Q(\mathbf{w}_{1:n-1}, w_n) = 0. \tag{16}$$

Thus the process of finding the gradient of the Eq. (9) can be expressed as:

$$\begin{aligned}
\nabla_\theta J(\theta) &= \nabla_\theta \sum_{w_1 \in V} G_\theta(w_1|s_0) \cdot Q(s_0, w_1) \\
&= \sum_{w_1 \in V} \nabla_\theta G_\theta(w_1|s_0) Q(s_0, w_1) + \sum_{w_1 \in V} P(w_1|s_0; G_\theta) \nabla_\theta Q(s_0, w_1) \\
&= \sum_{t=1}^n \sum_{\mathbf{w}_{1:t-1}} P(\mathbf{w}_{1:t-1}|s_0; G_\theta) \sum_{w_t \in V} \nabla_\theta G_\theta(w_t|\mathbf{w}_{1:t-1}) Q(\mathbf{w}_{1:t-1}, w_t) \\
&= \sum_{t=1}^n \mathbb{E}_{\mathbf{w}_{1:t-1} \sim G_\theta} \left[\sum_{w_t \in V} \nabla_\theta G_\theta(w_t|\mathbf{w}_{1:t-1}) Q(\mathbf{w}_{1:t-1}, w_t) \right].
\end{aligned} \tag{17}$$

The whole training process of confrontation learning is divided into the following steps: first, the generator G_θ is pre-trained through MLE in $\mathcal{S}$, then a pre-training discriminator D_ϕ is combined with real samples and generated samples. Then the two networks alternately confront each other until convergence. In the actual training process, we can make the value Q more stable by averaging multiple Monte Carlo sampling. At the same time, we can also train generators or discriminators according to actual needs each time to prevent one side from being too strong to converge.

5   Information Hiding and Extraction

GAN-TStega mainly implements covert information hiding by encoding the conditional probability distribution of each word in the process of generation. Here we refer to previous work [9] and adopt a fixed-length encoding method, that is, a word is embedded in a fixed-length bits. In the previous paper, we elaborated on the generator training method based on statistical language model. The output of G in each iteration is based on the conditional probability distribution of the generated sequence $w1 : t$ and $\mathbf{p}_t$. In common sentence generation tasks, the words corresponding to the most probabilistic value are often chosen as the next value of the sequence. For a well-trained generator, the most probabilistic words in its probability distribution are often synonyms or can be replaced with each other without obvious damage to sentence quality. This property can be used to hide bit streams. During each generation of the next word, the output of G is arranged in descending order, $\mathbf{p}_t$, and the block of bits to be embedded is converted to decimal as the basis for choosing the next generation word. The specific steganography process is as described in the Algorithm 1.

Algorithm 1. Information Hiding Algorithm

Input:
Secret bitstream: $B = \{0, 0, 1, 0, 1, ..., 0, 1, 0\}$
Embedding rate: k
Trained generator: G
Output:
Generated sentence collection $\mathcal{S}$

1: **while** $B \neq \emptyset$ **do**
2:      **if** The currently generated word w_i is not the end of the sentence **then**
3:          Calculate the probability distribution of the next word $\mathbf{p}_i$ on the dictionary
       V by G
4:          Arrange $\mathbf{p}_i$ in descending order to get $\tilde{\mathbf{p}}_i$
5:          Convert $B[0 : k]$ to decimal b
6:          Select $\tilde{\mathbf{p}}_i[b]$ to be the next output word w_{i+1}
7:          $B \leftarrow B[k :]$
8:      **else**
9:          Randomly initialize the hidden vector z and send into G to generate the
       first word w_1
10: **if** The currently generated word w_i is not the end of the sentence **then**
11:      Generate the complete sentences with G, select the most probabilistic words
       each time

The process of information extraction is similar to that of information hiding. The principle is to decode sentences using the probability distribution of the next word generated by the generator as a tool. The receiver needs to use the same generator as the sender, that is, $G_R = G_S$, which requires that both be synchronized at all times in the actual application process. When the receiver receives the set of sentences $\mathcal{S} = (S_1, S_2, ..., S_m)$, for each of the sentences $S_i = (w_1, w_2, ..., w_n)$, the receiver sends the words in turn to the generator G, and gets the probability distribution of the next word. That is, for $w_i, i \in \{1, 2, ..., n-1\}$, the generator generates the next word probability distribution $\mathbf{p}_i$. After descending the order of $\mathbf{p}_i$, we get $\tilde{\mathbf{p}}_i$, and then find the index l of w_{i+1} in it, and convert the l into binary to get the secret information contained in w_{i+1}.

6   Experiments and Results

This chapter will verify GAN-TStega's effectiveness and concealment in GAN-TStega steganographic task through multiple experiments.

Firstly, we tested the contribution of adversarial learning to improving the quality of generated text. The essence of text generation is sequence generation, so we can define a randomly initialized LSTM network as Oracle, as a sample sequence generator G_O, whose generated sequence sample space satisfies the probability distribution P_O. The object of anti-learning is to train the sample generated by generator G_θ to be as close as possible to the distribution P_O. Note that the output of G_O is a single hotspot vector of dictionary length v, representing the next word in the Oracle sequence, while the output of G_θ is still a probability distribution $\mathbf{p}_i$. We adopted the negative logarithm likelihood loss as the index to measure their similarity:

$$L_O = -\sum_{i=1}^{n} G_O(w_i | \mathbf{w}_{1:i-1}) \cdot G_\theta(w_i | \mathbf{w}_{1:i-1}), \tag{18}$$

In the experimental setting, we used the randomly initialized LSTM network to generate 10,000 sequences with a length of 20 as the real data samples, and then used the maximum likelihood estimation training generator G_ξ and GAN-TStega anti-learning training generator G_θ respectively. Among them, G_ξ training 150 cycles, the first 100 cycles of G_θ are pre-training, and the last 50 cycles are confrontation training. For comparison purposes, the network structure of G_ξ and G_θ are exactly the same. The final learning curves of the two are shown in Fig. 1.

It can be seen that in the first 100 cycles, since both of them use the training generator of maximum likelihood estimation, the loss value is very close, tends to converge after 50 cycles, and the loss value is stable at about 11. Starting from the 101st cycle, GAN-TStega has conducted 50 confrontation training. It can be seen that the loss of GAN-TStega is significantly reduced compared with MLE, and finally stabilized at around 10.2, which proves that GAN-TStega can better generate sequences that conform to Oracle sample probability space P_O.

Next we test GAN-TStega's performance on real data samples and compare it with MLE trained RNN generator [9]. We use Image COCO [28] and EMNLP WMT17 source dataset as the real sample. Among them, Image COCO is the dataset for image captioning. We remove the samples whose sentence length is

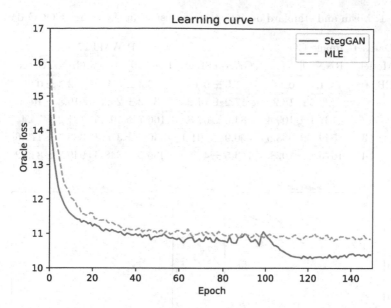

Fig. 1. LSTM maximum likelihood estimation vs. GAN-TStega training process loss

less than 10, and then randomly select 10,000 as the training data. EMNLP WMT17 is a dataset for machine translation. We selected English news data in it to remove sentences with length less than 20 and low-frequency words, and also randomly selected 10,000 as the training data.

In order to ensure the concealment of steganographic text, the statistical difference between steganographic distribution and real distribution should be as small as possible. Here, we use Perplexity to measure the difference between two statistical distributions. In the information theory, ρ is used to represent the fit between the predicted results of the probability model and samples. The lower ρ is, the better the predicted results of the model will be. Its mathematical expression is:

$$\log_b \rho = -\frac{1}{n} \sum_{i=1}^{n} \log_b p(S_i). \tag{19}$$

Where S_i is the i-th sample sequence. In the formula, the base of b is often chosen as 2 in informatics. Here, we use $b = e$ for calculation convenience.

After training the generator separately based on each data set, we generated 1000 sentences on each generator, and then generated steganographic text with different embedding rates under the guidance of randomly generated 01 bit stream. The confusion mean and variance obtained are shown in Table 1. In order to compare the differences between the two models, we made the logarithmic broken line graph of the confusion mean as shown in the Fig. 2.

Table 1. Mean and standard deviation of confusion on the Image COCO dataset

Dataset		Image COCO		EMNLP WMT17	
Model		RNN [9]	GAN-TStega	RNN [9]	GAN-TStega
ER	0	1.4 ± 0.1	1.3 ± 0.1	3.3 ± 1.4	2.3 ± 0.9
	1	22.5 ± 18.2	17.2 ± 14.2	33.2 ± 29.4	19.8 ± 10.5
	2	137.1 ± 109.4	84.6 ± 67.8	166.7 ± 101.5	121.2 ± 74.4
	3	549.1 ± 368.5	300.9 ± 201.1	546.8 ± 376.4	388.7 ± 173.6
	4	1675.5 ± 1028.1	753.5 ± 427.0	1456.5 ± 848.6	949.8 ± 849.2

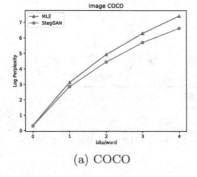 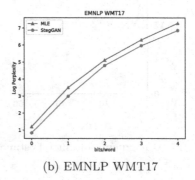

(a) COCO   (b) EMNLP WMT17

Fig. 2. Logarithmic confusion at different embedding rates (ER).

It can be seen from the results that GAN-TStega's confusion is lower than that of RNN under different embedding rates, which is also consistent with previous experimental results – the anti-learning generator can further reduce losses and improve the quality of generated sequences.

In order to more intuitively show the distribution of generated samples and real samples, t-distribution random neighborhood embedding (t-sne) [29] maps the training samples and generated steganographic samples of Image COCO data sets to low-dimensional space. For sequence S, we first transform it into a word vector matrix by word vector embedding, and then map it to two-dimensional space by t-sne algorithm. The result is shown in Fig. 3. It can be seen that training text and steganographic text are inseparable in the two-dimensional space of mapping under different embedding rates.

Finally, we present the steganographic sentences generated by our model on COCO datasets in Table 2. It can be seen that when the embedding rate is 0, that is, no secret information bitstream is embedded, sentences with correct grammar and fluent semantics can be generated. When the embedding rate is 1, the quality of the generated sentences is still high because the steganographic selection space is 2. When the embedding rate is increased to 2, the quality of sentences decreases slightly. We also noticed the pattern collapse of sentences generated at low embedding rates, that is, the structure of sentences and the combination of words tend to be singular.

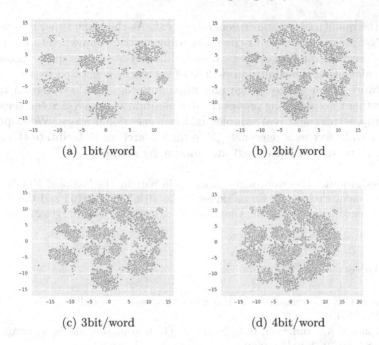

(a) 1bit/word   (b) 2bit/word

(c) 3bit/word   (d) 4bit/word

Fig. 3. Image COCO training text and steganographic text distribution, blue dots for training text, orange dots for steganographic text. (Color figure online)

Table 2. Steganographic sentences generated by our model on COCO datasets

Embedding rate (bpw)	Generated steganographic sentences
0	A person riding a motorbike with people A person wearing red shirt standing next to a shop Man is riding a motorcycle down a beach
1	A cat sitting on top of a wooden bathroom tub A motorcycle parked in front of a temple A pine apple in a corner
2	A safety conscious rock outside of formation in the night direction A blurry mirror cuts a sink and medicine pen A narrow bathroom with a mirror looking toilet behind some ruins

7   Conclusion

In this paper, we propose an automatic steganographic text generation model called GAN-TStega which based on Generative Adversarial Networks (GANs). In the experiment part, we can find that the adversarial learning can further reduce the loss of generator which has been converged under the training of maximum likelihood estimation, which proves that adversarial training is helpful to improve the quality of generator generated text. At the same time, it is verified that GAN-TStega can better fit the real sample distribution when GAN-TStega generates steganographic text sets under different steganographic embedding rates by calculating the confusion degree of sentences generated by the trained RNN network under GAN-TStega and maximum likelihood estimation respectively. Further t-sne mapping proves the inseparability of GAN-TStega generated steganographic text and real samples in low dimensional space. We hope that this paper will serve as a reference guide for researchers to facilitate the design and implementation of better text steganography method.

Acknowledgment. This work was supported in part by the National Key Research and Development Program of China under Grant 2018YFB0804103 and the National Natural Science Foundation of China (No. U1536207, No. U1705261 and No. U1636113).

References

1. Shannon, C.E.: Communication theory of secrecy systems. Bell Labs Tech. J. **28**(4), 656–715 (1949)
2. Petitcolas, F.A., Anderson, R.J., Kuhn, M.G.: Information hiding-a survey. Proc. IEEE **87**(7), 1062–1078 (1999)
3. Bernaille, L., Teixeira, R.: Early recognition of encrypted applications. In: Uhlig, S., Papagiannaki, K., Bonaventure, O. (eds.) PAM 2007. LNCS, vol. 4427, pp. 165–175. Springer, Heidelberg (2007). https://doi.org/10.1007/978-3-540-71617-4_17
4. Fridrich, J.: Steganography in Digital Media: Principles, Algorithms, and Applications. Cambridge University Press, New York (2009)
5. Marvel, L.M., Boncelet, C.G., Retter, C.T.: Spread spectrum image steganography. IEEE Trans. Image Process. **8**(8), 1075–1083 (1999)
6. Luo, W., Huang, F., Huang, J.: Edge adaptive image steganography based on LSB matching revisited. IEEE Trans. Inf. Forensics Secur. **5**(2), 201–214 (2010)
7. Yang, Z., Peng, X., Huang, Y.: A sudoku matrix-based method of pitch period steganography in low-rate speech coding. In: Lin, X., Ghorbani, A., Ren, K., Zhu, S., Zhang, A. (eds.) SecureComm 2017. LNICST, vol. 238, pp. 752–762. Springer, Cham (2018). https://doi.org/10.1007/978-3-319-78813-5_40
8. Yang, Z., Du, X., Tan, Y., Huang, Y., Zhang, Y.-J.: AAG-stega: automatic audio generation-based steganography. arXiv preprint arXiv:1809.03463 (2018)
9. Yang, Z.-L., Guo, X.-Q., Chen, Z.-M., Huang, Y.-F., Zhang, Y.-J.: RNN-stega: linguistic steganography based on recurrent neural networks. IEEE Trans. Inf. Forensics Secur. **14**(5), 1280–1295 (2019)
10. Yang, Z., Jin, S., Huang, Y., Zhang, Y., Li, H.: Automatically generate steganographic text based on Markov model and Huffman coding. arXiv preprint arXiv:1811.04720 (2018)
11. Bennett, K.: Linguistic steganography: survey, analysis, and robustness concerns for hiding information in text (2004)
12. Xiang, L., Sun, X., Luo, G., Xia, B.: Linguistic steganalysis using the features derived from synonym frequency. Multimed. Tools Appl. **71**(3), 1893–1911 (2014). https://doi.org/10.1007/s11042-012-1313-8

13. Yang, Z., Zhang, P., Jiang, M., Huang, Y., Zhang, Y.-J.: RITS: real-time interactive text steganography based on automatic dialogue model. In: Sun, X., Pan, Z., Bertino, E. (eds.) ICCCS 2018. LNCS, vol. 11065, pp. 253–264. Springer, Cham (2018). https://doi.org/10.1007/978-3-030-00012-7_24

14. Yang, Z., Zhang, Y.-J., Rehman, S., Huang, Y.: Image captioning with object detection and localization. In: Zhao, Y., Kong, X., Taubman, D. (eds.) ICIG 2017. LNCS, vol. 10667, pp. 109–118. Springer, Cham (2017). https://doi.org/10.1007/978-3-319-71589-6_10

15. Bengio, Y., Ducharme, R., Vincent, P., Jauvin, C.: A neural probabilistic language model. J. Mach. Learn. Res. 3, 1137–1155 (2003)

16. Dai, W., Yu, Y., Dai, Y., Deng, B.: Text steganography system using Markov chain source model and DES algorithm. JSW 5(7), 785–792 (2010)

17. Moraldo, H.H.: An approach for text steganography based on Markov chains. arXiv preprint arXiv:1409.0915 (2014)

18. Dai, W., Yu, Y., Deng, B.: BinText steganography based on Markov state transferring probability. In: Proceedings of the 2nd International Conference on Interaction Sciences: Information Technology, Culture and Human, pp. 1306–1311. ACM (2009)

19. Hochreiter, S., Schmidhuber, J.: Long short-term memory. Neural Comput. 9(8), 1735–1780 (1997)

20. Bengio, S., Vinyals, O., Jaitly, N., Shazeer, N.: Scheduled sampling for sequence prediction with recurrent neural networks. In: Advances in Neural Information Processing Systems, pp. 1171–1179 (2015)

21. Goodfellow, I., et al.: Generative adversarial nets. In: Advances in Neural Information Processing Systems, pp. 2672–2680 (2014)

22. Yu, L., Zhang, W., Wang, J., Yu, Y.: SeqGAN: sequence generative adversarial nets with policy gradient. In: Thirty-First AAAI Conference on Artificial Intelligence (2017)

23. Guo, J., Lu, S., Cai, H., Zhang, W., Yu, Y., Wang, J.: Long text generation via adversarial training with leaked information. In: Thirty-Second AAAI Conference on Artificial Intelligence (2018)

24. Fedus, W., Goodfellow, I., Dai, A.M.: MaskGAN: better text generation via filling in the_," arXiv preprint arXiv:1801.07736 (2018)

25. Volkhonskiy, D., Nazarov, I., Borisenko, B., Burnaev, E.: Steganographic generative adversarial networks. arXiv preprint arXiv:1703.05502 (2017)

26. Hayes, J., Danezis, G.: Generating steganographic images via adversarial training. In: Advances in Neural Information Processing Systems, pp. 1954–1963 (2017)

27. Yang, Z., Wang, K., Li, J., Huang, Y., Zhang, Y.: TS-RNN: text steganalysis based on recurrent neural networks. IEEE Signal Process. Lett. 99, 1 (2019)

28. Chen, X., et al.: Microsoft COCO captions: data collection and evaluation server. arXiv preprint arXiv:1504.00325 (2015)

29. van der Maaten, L., Hinton, G.: Visualizing data using t-SNE. J. Mach. Learn. Res. 9(Nov), 2579–2605 (2008)

Optimized CNN with Point-Wise Parametric Rectified Linear Unit for Spatial Image Steganalysis

Yi-ming Xue[1]([✉]), Wan-li Peng[1], Yuzhu Wang[1], Juan Wen[1], and Ping Zhong[2]

[1] College of Information and Electrical Engineering,
China Agricultural University, Beijing 100083, China
{xueym,hunanpwl}@cau.edu.cn
[2] College of Science, China Agricultural University, Beijing 100083, China
zping@cau.edu.cn

Abstract. The convolutional neural network (CNN) based image steganalyzers have evolved remarkably over the past few years, and designing suitable CNN structures has been currently the fundamental method to improve the detection accuracy. However, CNN-based steganalyzer with the universal activation functions of the computer vision (CV) field barely achieves significant performance improvement. Therefore, a dedicated activation function is required to improve the detection performance for image steganalysis. In this paper, we propose a point-wise parametric rectified unit (PW-PReLU) which has different adaptively learnable parameters for each pixel of the negative inputs to facilitate the representation capacity of the activated feature maps. Then, in order to further boost the detection accuracy, the feature fusion is realized by the concatenation operation in the first layer. Based on the above components, an optimized CNN-based steganalyzer is proposed for spatial image steganalysis. The results of comparative experiments demonstrate that the proposed network can detect the state-of-the-art spatial steganographic algorithms with better performance than the previous steganalyzers on the 512×512 BOSSbase_1.01 dataset and the resized 256×256 union dataset of BOSSbase_1.01 and BOWS2.

Keywords: Convolutional neural network · Spatial image steganalysis · Point-wise PReLU · Feature fusion

1 Introduction

Image steganography aims to conceal messages into noise residuals of the natural images through making perturbation as slightly as possible. Nowadays, many of the content-adaptive spatial image steganographic algorithms have been proposed [1–6]. As the opposite of image steganography, image steganalysis has also

This work was supported by the National Natural Science Foundation of China under Grant 61872368 and Grant 61802410.

© Springer Nature Switzerland AG 2020
H. Wang et al. (Eds.): IWDW 2019, LNCS 12022, pp. 32–42, 2020.
https://doi.org/10.1007/978-3-030-43575-2_3

made tremendous progress, especially the convolutional neural network (CNN) based image steganalysis.

Recently, CNN-based image steganalysis has achieved remarkable performance and outperformed the feature-based image steganalysis. Tan et al. [9] first attempt to use the stacked convolutional auto-encoders for image steganalysis. Qian et al. [10] employ the Gaussian activation function and KV kernel to extract the effective features. Xu et al. [11,15] put forward a CNN structure (called Xu-Net in this paper) equipped with absolute activation layer, hybrid activation functions, and 1×1 convolutional layer, which first exceeds the spatial rich models (SRM) features [7] with ensemble classifier. Imitating three key steps of the selection-channel-aware SRM algorithm [8], Ye et al. [12] present a CNN structure called YeNet to further improve the detection performance by employing 30 SRM kernels, TLU, and the knowledge of selection channel. It first implements the end-to-end learning for image steganalysis. Inspired by the inception structure of GoogleNet [16] and SRM [7], Li et al. propose a wider network named as ReST-Net which consists of three parallel convolutional subnets equipped with diverse activation modules (DAMs) [13]. Mehdi et al. design a deeper CNN structure called SRNet based on the shortcut operation of the ResNet [17]. The SRNet achieves the significant improvement for image steganalysis [14]. It is pointed in [14] that using the universal activation functions can not bring any performance gain.

The breakthrough is closely related to the rapid development of CNNs in computer vision (CV) field. While, except for truncated linear unit (TLU) proposed in [12], the CNN-based steganalyzers with other universal activation functions, including rectified linear unit (ReLU) [23], leaky-ReLU [25], the parametric ReLU (PReLU) [24], and Exponential Linear Unit (ELU) [26], can not achieve any performance gain [14]. Why is the abnormal phenomenon happening? Can the performance be improved by specially designing an activation function for image steganalysis?

The main reason for the abnormal phenomenon is that since the secret information is embedded by the spatial image steganographic algorithms through adaptively modifying the values of the target pixels, and the cover images are statistically similar to the corresponding stego images, which leads to the difference between cover images and their stego images in the pixel-level. While, the universal activation functions activate the inputs in layer-level rather than pixel-level. In other word, the functions have only one fixed or adaptively learnable parameter for all feature maps generated from previous convolutional layer, which causes the CNN-based steganalyzers with the universal activation functions can not extract more effective feature maps.

From the above investigation and analysis, we believe that a suitable pixel-level activation function will further boost the performance of CNN-based steganalyzers for spatial image steganalysis. In this paper, we first propose a dedicated activation function called point-wise parametric rectified linear unit (PW-PReLU). Different from the commonly used PReLU [24], the PW-PReLU is a point-wise activation function rather than the channel-wise or channel-shared activation function, which can activate the negative inputs in pixel-level. Then in order to further improve the detection accuracy, the feature fusion is realized by the first parallel convolutional layer initialized by 30 random kernels and 30 SRM kernels pointed in [12], respectively. Based on these components, an optimized CNN structure named as PWNet is designed for the spatial image steganalysis.

The rest of this paper is organized as follows. Section 2 introduces the structure of the proposed CNN in detail. The experimental results and analysis are described in Sect. 3. Finally, we conclude the paper in Sect. 4.

2 The Proposed Architecture

In this section, we first introduce the overall framework of the PWNet. Then, the PW-PReLU activation function is described in detail. Finally, we state the design of the feature fusion.

2.1 Architecture Overview

As shown in Fig. 1, the framework of the PWNet with nine convolutional layers is composed of feature fusion module, convolution module, and classification module. For the feature fusion module, the concatenation operation is adopted to fuse the features extracted by two parallel convolutional layers. For the convolution module, a stacked architecture consisting of eight convolutional layers is designed to generate the discriminative features automatically. Each layer utilizes 3×3 random kernels, and except for the 8th convolutional layer with the proposed PW-PReLU activation function, other layers make use of ReLU activation function. Besides, the maximum pooling operation is utilized to increase the receptive field of the deep layers. For the classification module, the global average pooling layer is utilized rather than the fully connect layer [27].

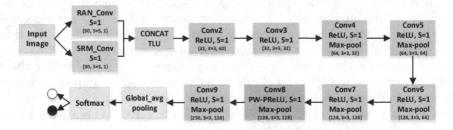

Fig. 1. The framework of the PWNet consists of feature fusion module, convolution module and classification module. They are represented by pink boxes, blue boxes and yellow boxes, respectively. The Conv$N$ is represents the Nth convolutional layer. The RAN_Conv denotes the convolutional layer initialized by the random scheme. The convolutional layer with 30 SRM kernels is presented by the SRM_Conv. The stride of convolutional layer equals 1 (S = 1). The numbers in boxes represent the number of kernels, the size of each kernel and the number of inputs. (Color figure online)

2.2 Point-Wise PReLU Activation Function

It has been demonstrated that activation function is one of keys to the CNNs, and a suitable activation function not only improves the detection performance, but also expedites the convergence of training procedure [23–26]. Nevertheless, a similar study in image steganalysis indicates that the adoption of different existing activation functions does not bring any significant performance improvement [14]. In this paper, we propose a dedicated activation function PW-PReLU which can adaptively activate the negative inputs in pixel-level to further improve the detection performance. The PW-PReLU is defined as follows:

$$f(x_{m,n}^i) = \begin{cases} x_{m,n}^i, & x_{m,n}^i \geqslant 0 \\ \alpha_{m,n}^i x_{m,n}^i, & x_{m,n}^i < 0 \end{cases} \tag{1}$$

where $x_{m,n}^i$ represents one point of the ith input for the PW-PReLU activation function f. $\alpha_{m,n}^i$ is a trainable coefficient controlling the slope for the negative $x_{m,n}^i$. The (m, n) denotes the location coordinate.

The dimension of the adaptively learnable coefficients α is consistent with that of the previous convolutional layer outputs, where α is the tensor composed of $\alpha_{m,n}^i$. Namely, the different point of each feature maps has different coefficient $\alpha_{m,n}^i$. The update formulations of $\alpha_{m,n}^i$ are simply derived from the chain rule and back-propagation algorithm [20]. The gradient of $\alpha_{m,n}^i$ for one layer is:

$$\frac{\partial l}{\partial \alpha_{m,n}^i} = \frac{\partial l}{\partial f(x_{m,n}^i)} \frac{\partial f(x_{m,n}^i)}{\partial \alpha_{m,n}^i} \tag{2}$$

where l is the objective function. The term $\frac{\partial l}{\partial f(x_{m,n}^i)}$ is the gradient propagated from the deeper layer. The gradient of the activation function is given by:

$$\frac{\partial f(x_{m,n}^i)}{\partial \alpha_{m,n}^i} = \begin{cases} 0, & x_{m,n}^i \geqslant 0 \\ x_{m,n}^i, & x_{m,n}^i < 0 \end{cases} \tag{3}$$

For the negative inputs, the PW-PReLU not only has a pixel-level activation values in the forward propagation, but also adaptively learns the most suitable activation coefficients $\alpha_{m,n}^i$ in the backward propagation.

As shown in Fig. 1, it is a specific design that the PW-PReLU is merely adopted in the 8th convolutional layer of the PWNet. There are two reasons for the design: One is that if the PW-PReLU was used in shallow layers, it would reinforce the difference of the cover and corresponding stego images while enhancing the local correlation of image content, which will weaken the representation capacity of the activated feature maps. On the contrary, the PW-PReLU can activate the high-level features which contain more effective residual information than the low-level features extracted by the shallow layers. The other is that as the number of learnable parameters of the PW-PReLU is consistent with the size of the previous convolutional layer outputs, the adaption of PW-PReLU in the deeper layer requires the less learnable parameters than those in the shallow layers. All in a word, the specific design can not only boost the detection accuracy by facilitating the effectiveness of the activated feature maps, but also prevent the overfitting in the training phase.

2.3   Feature Fusion

We implement feature through concatenating the different feature maps generated from two parallel convolutional layers, including the convolutional layer initialized by 30 SRM kernels and the convolutional layer initialized by 30 random kernels respectively. The main goal of random kernels is to obtain the optimal parameters and comprehensive residual information. The SRM kernels serve as the good priori knowledge to accelerate the convergence of the proposed network [12]. Furthermore, the maximum pooling operation is utilized in the layers of the convolution module to keep the texture information and enlarge the receptive field.

3   Experiment

3.1   Setup

We perform the experiments using the proposed network on two datasets, including the 512×512 dataset of BOSSbase_1.01 [18] and the resized 256×256 union dataset of the BOSSbase_1.01 and BOWS2 [19]. For the 512×512 dataset, we randomly select 4000 pairs of cover and stego images to train the compared steganalyzers and 1000 pairs for validation. The remaining 5000 pairs are used for testing. For the resized 256×256 union dataset, it is consistent with the "resample" images of YeNet [12]. The random 14000 pairs are used for training, 1000 pairs for validation, and 5000 pairs for testing. Three steganographic algorithms including S-UNIWARD, HILL, and CMD-HILL are employed to generate the stego images at 0.1 bpp (bit of per pixel) to 0.4 bpp. In the training phase, the input images are randomly mirrored and rotated to make data augmentation.

The experiments are implemented on the Tensorflow1.8.0 and an NVIDIA 1080Ti graphics card. We utilize the Adadelta optimization algorithm [21] to update parameters and the training is run for 350,000 iterations. The learning rate is initialized to 0.4 and decreases to 0.008 at iterations 200,000. The mini-batch size is 32, including 16 cover images and 16 corresponding stego images. "truncated_normal" initialization method with zero mean and standard deviation 0.01 is chosen to initialize the random kernels in the feature fusion module, and the weights from the 2rd to 9th convolutional layers are initialized with the He-initializer [24]. The biases are initialized to 0.2 and the initial value of the coefficients $\alpha_{m,n}^i$ of PW-PReLU are 0.75. Furthermore, in training phase, we make use of the common curriculum learning strategy to accelerate the convergence of CNNs [12,14,29]. For instance, the proposed network for 0.3 bpp payload is fine-tuned on the well-trained network at 0.4 bpp payload. Then, for 0.2 bpp payload, the proposed network is obtained based on the well-trained network at 0.3 bpp payload, and so on.

3.2 Results

Comparison with Prior Arts. To assess the performance of the PWNet for spatial image steganalysis, we conduct several experiments in two datasets with different sizes, including 512 × 512 BOSSbase_1.01 and resized 256 × 256 union dataset of BOSSbase_1.01 and BOWS2, against three spatial image steganographic algorithms.

(1) 512 × 512 dataset: In the Table 1, we compare the PWNet with three CNN-based steganalyzers, including Xu-Net [11], TLU-CNN [12] (YeNet without the selection channel information), and ReST-Net [13], in terms of detection accuracy. From Table 1, it is observed that the PWNet increases the detection accuracies significantly against the three steganographic algorithms at all payloads. When detecting S-UNIWARD, HILL, and CMD-HILL steganographic algorithms, the detection accuracies of PWNet are up to 7.72%, 8.95%, and 6.85% higher than that of Xu-Net, and the improvement is up to 5.08%, 6.39% and 4.67% higher than that of TLU-CNN. Compared with the ReST-Net, the PWNet detection accuracies are improved by 0.25% at least.

Table 1. Comparison of the detection accuracies against three steganographic algorithms: S-UNIWARD, HILL, and CMD-HILL on the 512 × 512 BOSSbase_1.01 dataset.

Steganography	Steganalyzer	0.4 bpp	0.3 bpp	0.2 bpp	0.1 bpp
S-UNIWARD	Xu-Net	0.7985	0.7185	0.6553	0.5882
	TLU-CNN	0.8139	0.7552	0.6906	0.6146
	ReST-Net	0.8544	0.7878	0.7135	0.6567
	PWNet	**0.8569**	**0.7932**	**0.7211**	**0.6654**
HILL	Xu-Net	0.7712	0.7194	0.6248	0.5619
	TLU-CNN	0.7981	0.7285	0.6504	0.5794
	ReST-Net	0.8166	0.7674	0.7064	0.6238
	PWNet	**0.8219**	**0.7725**	**0.7143**	**0.6342**
CMD-HILL	Xu-Net	0.7122	0.6654	0.5859	0.5484
	TLU-CNN	0.7301	0.6882	0.6077	0.5522
	ReST-Net	0.7614	0.7028	0.6514	0.5892
	PWNet	**0.7638**	**0.7135**	**0.6544**	**0.5987**

(2) Resized 256 × 256 union dataset: In order to further test the effectiveness of the PWNet, we conduct the extra experiments compared with TLU-CNN [12] in the resized 256 × 256 union dataset. Table 2 shows the performance in terms of detection accuracy. The experimental results show that the PWNet consistently outperforms the TLU-CNN for the involved steganographic algorithms and the tested payloads. For example, the PWNet increases the detection accuracy of S-UNIWARD at 0.4 bpp by 1.58%.

Table 2. Comparison of the detection accuracies against three steganographic algorithms: S-UNIWARD, HILL, and CMD-HILL on the resized 256×256 union dataset.

Steganography	Steganalyzer	0.4 bpp	0.3 bpp	0.2 bpp	0.1 bpp
S-UNIWARD	TLU-CNN	0.8660	0.8236	0.7483	0.6621
	PWNet	**0.8818**	**0.8357**	**0.7585**	**0.6757**
HILL	TLU-CNN	0.8235	0.7864	0.7241	0.6475
	PWNet	**0.8365**	**0.7943**	**0.7328**	**0.6594**
CMD-HILL	TLU-CNN	0.7625	0.7134	0.6753	0.6042
	PWNet	**0.7735**	**0.7279**	**0.6840**	**0.6179**

The Network Structure Design Choices. To the best of our knowledge, the final accuracy is sensitive to architecture design of the CNN model. In this subsection, We first investigate the impact of the PW-PReLU activation function in the different layers, and then evaluate the other three different structure design choices including the pooling operations, the feature fusion module and the activation functions.

(1) PW-PReLU in different layers: We first investigate the influence of the PW-PReLU activation function in the different convolutional layers. We train several CNN structures using the design illustrated by Fig. 1 with PW-PReLU in different convolutional layers. The experiment results summarized in the Table 3 indicate that the CNN model can obtain the best performance (88.18%) using PW-PReLU activation function in 8th convolutional layer. From Fig. 2, it is observed that the overfitting of the CNN models with PW-PReLU in shallow layers is more serious than that of the other CNN models equipped with PW-PReLU in deep layers.

(2) Other design choices: In the remaining experiments, we evaluate the other three choices. The PWNet is compared with four competitive CNN models, and the detection accuracies are reported in Table 4. The results of a, b and e show that the average detection accuracies of PWNet are 0.98% and 1.46% better than that of the SRM based network and ReLU based network, respectively. The experiments c, d and e demonstrate that the average pool operation and stride convolution lead to the decrease of the detection accuracy. Additionally, Fig. 3 depicts the validation accuracies versus the training iterations for the three design choices, and the results show that the PWNet converges slightly quicker to a higher accuracy.

Table 3. The detection accuracies of PWNet with PW-PReLU on different layers against S-UNIWARD at 0.4 bpp and 0.1 bpp payloads on the resized 256 × 256 union dataset. ("conv-layer" indicates convolutional layer)

ID	The detail description of the PW-PReLU on different layers	0.4 bpp	0.1 bpp
a	Use the PW-PReLU in 2nd and 3th conv-layers	0.8175	0.6089
b	Utilize the PW-PReLU in 4th to 6th conv-layers	0.8344	0.6302
c	Employ the PW-PReLU in 6th to 9th conv-layers	0.8606	0.6534
d	Employ the PW-PReLU in 7th to 9th conv-layers	0.8689	0.6543
e	Use the PW-PReLU in 7th and 8th conv-layers	0.8680	0.6575
f	Utilize the PW-PReLU in 7th and 9th conv-layers	0.8677	0.6537
g	Utilize the PW-PReLU in 8th and 9th conv-layers	0.8606	0.6545
h	Make use of the PW-PReLU in 7th conv-layer	0.8711	0.6672
i	Make use of the PW-PReLU in 9th conv-layer	0.8643	0.6512
j	**The PWNet** **(use the PW-PReLU in 8th conv-layer)**	**0.8818**	**0.6757**

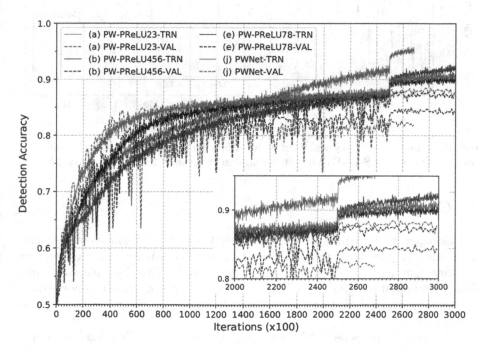

Fig. 2. Detection accuracy v.s. training iterations for PWNet equipped with PW-PReLU activation function in the different convolutional layers against S-UNIWARD at 0.4 bpp on the resized 256 × 256 union dataset.

Table 4. The detection accuracies of PWNet with different components against S-UNIWARD at 0.4 bpp and 0.1 bpp payloads on the resized 256 × 256 union dataset. ("conv-layer" indicates convolutional layer)

ID	The detail description of the different components	0.4 bpp	0.1 bpp
a	Only use a conv-layer with 30 SRM kernels in the first layer	0.8721	0.6658
b	Use PReLU activation function from 2rd to 9th conv-layers	0.8665	0.6617
c	Use the average pool from the 4th to 9th conv-layers	0.8729	0.6623
d	The stride is set to be 2 from the 4th to 9th conv-layers	0.8735	0.6684
e	**The PWNet** **(use the max pool from the 4th to 9th conv-layers)**	**0.8818**	**0.6757**

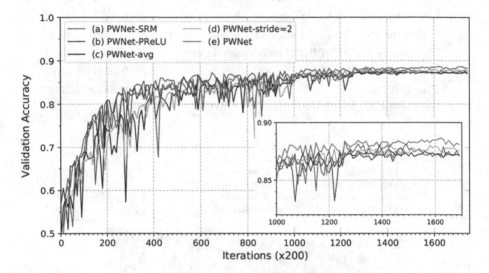

Fig. 3. Validation accuracy v.s. training iterations for PWNet equipped with different components against S-UNIWARD at 0.4 bpp on the resized 256 × 256 union dataset.

4 Conclusion

In this paper, we have proposed an optimized CNN-based steganalyzer by introducing a new pixel-level activation function and the feature fusion to improve the detection accuracy for spatial image steganalysis. The experimental results demonstrate that the proposed CNN structure outperforms three top-performing CNN-based steganalyzers on the 512 × 512 dataset and the resized 256 × 256 union dataset.

However, the proposed CNN-based steganalyzer is specially designed for spatial image steganalysis. In future work, we will focus on exploring the specific structure designs of CNNs for JPEG image steganalysis.

References

1. Fridrich, J., Filler, T.: Practical method for minimizing the embedding impact in steganography. In: SPIE, vol. 6505, pp. 650520-1–650520-15 (2007)
2. Pevný, T.F., Bas, P.: Using high-dimensional image models to perform highly undetectable steganography. In: Proceedings of 12th Information Hiding Workshop, pp. 161–177 (2010)
3. Holub, V., Fridrich, J.: Designing steganographic distortion using directional filters. In: Proceedings of the International Workshop on Information Forensics and Security, pp. 234–239 (2012)
4. Holub, V., Fridrich, J., Denemark, T.: Universal distortion function for steganography in an arbitrary domain. IEEE Trans. Image Process. **2014**(1), 1–13 (2017)
5. Li, B., Wang, M., Huang, J., Li, X.: A new cost function for spatial image steganography. In: Proceedings of the International Conference on Image Processing, pp. 3320–3328 (2014)
6. Li, B., Wang, M., Li, X., Tan, S., Huang, J.: A strategy of clustering modification directions in spatial image steganography. IEEE Trans. Inf. Forensic Secur. **10**(9), 1905–1917 (2015)
7. Fridrich, J., Kodovský, J.: Rich model for steganalysis of digital images. IEEE Trans. Inf. Forensic Secur. **7**(3), 868–882 (2012)
8. Fridrich, J., Holub, V.: Selection-channel-aware rich model for steganalysis of digital images. In: Proceedings of the IEEE International Workshop on Information Forensics and Security, pp. 48–53 (2014)
9. Tan, S., Li, B.: Stacked convolutional auto-encoders for steganalysis of digital images. In: Proceedings of Signal and Information Processing Association Annual Summit and Conference, pp. 1–4 (2014)
10. Qian, Y., Dong, J., Wang, W.: Deep learning for steganalysis via convolutional neural network. In: SPIE Media Watermarking, Security, and Forensics, vol. 9409 (2015)
11. Xu, G., Wu, H., Shi, Y.: Structural design of convolutional neural networks for steganalysis. IEEE Signal Process. Lett. **23**(5), 708–712 (2016)
12. Ye, J., Ni, Q., Yi, Y.: Deep learning hierarchical representations for image steganalysis. IEEE Trans. Inf. Forensic Secur. **12**(11), 2545–2557 (2017)
13. Li, B., Wei, W., Tan, S.: ReST-Net: diverse activation models and parallel subnets-based CNN for spatial image steganalysis. IEEE Signal Process. Lett. **25**(5), 650–654 (2018)
14. Boroumand, M., Chen, M., Fridrich, J.: Deep residual network for steganalysis of digital images. IEEE Trans. Inf. Forensic Secur. https://ieeexplore.ieee.org/document/8470101
15. Xu, G., Wu, H., Shi, Y.: Ensemble of CNNs for steganalysis: an empirical study. In: Proceedings of the 4th ACM Workshop on Information Hiding and Multimedia Security, pp. 103–107 (2016)
16. Szegedy, C., Liu, W., Jia, Y.: Going deeper with convolutions. In: Proceedings of the IEEE Computer Society Conference on Computer Vision and Pattern Recognition, pp. 1–9 (2014)
17. He, K., Zhang, X., Sun, J.: Deep residual learning learning for image recognition. In: Proceedings of the IEEE Computer Society Conference on Computer Vision and Pattern Recognition, pp. 770–778 (2016)
18. Bas, P., Filler, T., Pevný, T.: Break our steganographic system: the ins and outs of organizing boss. In: Proceedings of the Information Hiding Workshop, pp. 225–230 (2011)

19. Bas, P., Furon, T.: BOWS-2 (2007). http://bows2.ec-lille.fr
20. LeCun, Y., Boser, B., Jackel, L.: Backpropagation applied to handwritten zip code recognition. Neural Comput. **1**(4), 541–551 (1989)
21. Zeiler, M.D.: ADADELTA: an adaptive learning rate method. arXiv preprint arXiv:1212.5701 (2012)
22. Glorot, X., Bengio, Y.: Understanding the difficulty of training deep feedforward neural networks. In: Proceedings of the 13th International Conference on Artificial Intelligence and Statistics, vol. 9, pp. 249–256 (2010)
23. Glorot, X., Bordes, A., Bengio, Y.: Deep spares rectifier neural networks. In: Proceedings of the IEEE International Conference on Artificial Intelligence and Statistics, pp. 315–323 (2011)
24. He, K., Zhang, X., Ren, S., Sun, J.: Delving deep into rectifiers: surpassing human-level performance on imagenet classification. In: Proceedings of the IEEE International Conference on Computer Vision, pp. 1026–1034 (2015)
25. Maas, A.L., Hannun, A.Y., Ng, A.Y.: Rectifier nonlinearities improve neural network acoustic models. In: Proceedings of the 30th International Conference on Machine Learning, vol. 28 (2013)
26. Clevert, D., Unterthiner, T., Hochreiter, S.: Fast and accurate deep neural network learning by exponential linear units (ELUs). In: Proceedings of the International Conference for Learning Representations (2016)
27. Lin, M., Chen, Q., Yan, S.: Network in network. In: Proceedings of the International Conference for Learning Representations (2014). arXiv:1312.4400
28. Ioffe, S., Szegedy, C.: Batch Normalization: accelerating deep network training by reducing internal covariate shift. In: Proceedings of the International Conference on Machine Learning (2015). arXiv:1312.4400
29. Bengio, Y., Louradour, J., Collobert, R., Weston, J.: Curriculum learning. In: Proceedings of the 26th International Conference on Machine Learning, pp. 41–48 (2009)

Light Multiscale Conventional Neural Network for MP3 Steganalysis

Jinghong Zhang[1,2], Xiaowei Yi[1,2], Xianfeng Zhao[1,2]([✉]), and Yun Cao[1,2]

[1] State Key Laboratory of Information Security, Institute of Information Engineering, Chinese Academy of Sciences, Beijing 100093, China
{zhangjinghong,yixiaowei,zhaoxianfeng,caoyun}@iie.ac.cn
[2] School of Cyber Security, University of Chinese Academy of Sciences, Beijing 100049, China

Abstract. In this paper, we propose a light multiscale convolution neural network to detect adaptive MP3 steganography, which can be used in attacking both the MP3 steganography based on Huffman codes substitution and the method through modifying sign bit in MP3 encoding. Especially, we decrease the model size and the occupation of graphics memory based on convolution factorization. At the same time, the convolution kernels with different size are applied in one layer, which is conducive to the retaining of the detection performance. And refer to the residual structure, a shortcut connection is used in the proposed network to enhance the performance of the network. The experimental result shows the accuracy can reach more than 90% when the payload rate is high. And the model size is reduced by 70% than the previous networks.

Keywords: CNN · MP3 steganalysis · Multiscale convolution · Residual structure · Adaptive MP3 steganography

1 Introduction

As we all know, audio is one of the most commonly used digital media. Due to the high compression rate and high quality, MP3 is widely used for audio file compression. Steganography is the method of hiding secret information in digital files. Because of the popularity of MP3 format, steganographic algorithms based on MP3 have got much attention. In recent years, many MP3 steganographic algorithms have been proposed. Petitcolas et al. [9] proposed MP3Stego, which is a well know MP3 steganographic method. The basic idea of the algorithm is according to the parity of block length, modify in the inner loop MP3 encoder. Furthermore, Gao et al. [2] and Yan et al. [15] respectively presented steganographic algorithms which embedding secret messages through Huffman coding substitution. The algorithms establish a mapping between the secret bit and the Huffman code. Yang et al. [16] proposed an adaptive algorithm also known as EECS based on equal length entropy codes substitution, which improves the

© Springer Nature Switzerland AG 2020
H. Wang et al. (Eds.): IWDW 2019, LNCS 12022, pp. 43–56, 2020.
https://doi.org/10.1007/978-3-030-43575-2_4

embedding capacity and security. Furthermore, in [17], Yang *et al.* proposed another adaptive MP3 algorithm also known as SBF-JED. They proposed a new distortion function in sign bit domain and embed the secret message by flipping sign bit.

On the contrary, steganalysis is the method to attack the steganographic algorithms. Up to now, many CNN-methods have been proposed to attack the steganographic algorithms of spatial and JEPG images, while in the field of audio steganalysis, people mostly use manually extracted feature to design the steganalysis algorithms. Jin *et al.* [7] proposed a steganalysis algorithm by using one-step transition probability to describe the QMDCT differences along with the row and column directions (Jin-Makrov). In [10], Ren *et al.* find the effect of modifying QMDCT coefficients on the statistical characteristics of inter and intra frame in different domain. They use the multi-order differential coefficients of intra-frame and inter-frame (MDI2) as the handcrafted feature to detect the AAC and MP3 steganography. Besides, Ghasemzadeh *et al.* [3] proposed a new set of feature which is extracted through the reversed Mel-frequency cepstral coefficients (R-MFCC) to against the steganography. In the CNN-method research, Chen *et al.* [1] proposed a convolution neural network (Chen-Net) to detect ± 1 LSB audio steganography in the time domain. After that, an MP3 steganalysis method based on the convolution neural network (WASDN) is proposed by Wang in [13], which takes QMDCT coefficients as input. Furthermore, Wang *et al.* [14] proposed a new network architecture with rich high-pass filtering whose role is to increase the steganographic noise, which shows good performance in steganography detection.

However, the above-mentioned methods have the following disadvantages. For the features of manual extraction, although their detection efficiency is very high, they often have poor performance in detection accuracy. For CNN-based algorithms, good detection results can be obtained, but their network structure is generally complicated. It takes up a lot of computing resources, and the network model also takes up a lot of storage space. Therefore, a light MP3 audio steganalysis network with multiscale convolution (LMCNN) is proposed in this paper to solve these problems. In our design, we are inspired by the design of GoogLeNet [12], applying multiple convolution kernels and residual structures in each convolution sub-nets. In order to reduce the number of parameters of the network, we perform convolution kernel factorization on large-scale convolution kernels. The network is evaluated on various adaptive MP3 steganographic algorithms and payload rates. And our network acquires good results in different algorithms and payload rates.

The rest of this paper is organized as follows. In Sect. 2, we introduce the related work. Section 3 introduces the design of our proposed network in detail. Experiment results and discussion are shown in Sect. 4. Finally, the conclusion is drawn in Sect. 5.

2   Related Work

In recent years, lots of studies focus on adjusting deep neural structures to strike an optimal balance between accuracy and performance. Among these works, three of the most classical structures receive widespread attention, namely multi-scale convolution, convolution kernel factorization, and residual structure. Below we will explain the composition and role of these three network structures in detail.

2.1   Multiscale Convolution Structure

The convolution layer is the most important component of the convolution neural network, and the convolution operation can be seen as the extraction of the feature. In convolution network, a convolution kernel is used to capture the feature within a certain area. Typically, input signals are processed using the same size convolution kernel in one convolution layer. In [11], the author proposes the structure of inception. In the design of inception, different sizes of convolution kernels are adopted in one convolution layer. In principle, large-scale convolution kernels can provide a wider range of receptive field, but small-scale convolution kernels have a finer granularity of detection and can capture more detail. The structure of multi-scale convolution is shown in Fig. 1. In the same convolution layer, various scale convolution kernels are used, such as $1 \times 1, 3 \times 3, 5 \times 5$ and others.

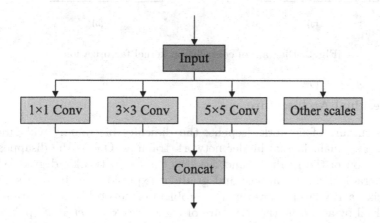

Fig. 1. Diagram of multiscale convolution structure.

2.2   Convolution Kernel Factorization

The purpose of convolution kernel factorization is to reduce the number of network parameters. Generally, large-scale convolution kernels can provide a larger receptive field, but introduce more parameters and reduce the efficiency of the network at the same time. It is proposed in the paper [12] that large-scale convolution kernels can be factorized into multiple small-scale convolution kernel. The form of the two convolution kernel factorization is shown in Fig. 2. A large-scale convolution kernel can be symmetrically factorized into two convolution kernels of the same small size. For example, a 5×5 kernel can be instead of two cascaded convolution kernels which size is 3×3. If two 3×3 convolution kernels are used instead of a 5×5 convolution kernel, the number of parameters will increase $(5 \times 5 + 1)/(3 \times 3 + 1) = 2.6$ times. Besides, the asymmetric factorization can be applied to the small-scale convolution kernel. For example, the 3×3 convolution kernel is factorized into the convolution kernel concatenation of 3×1 and 1×3, and the number of parameters is further reduced by 48%.

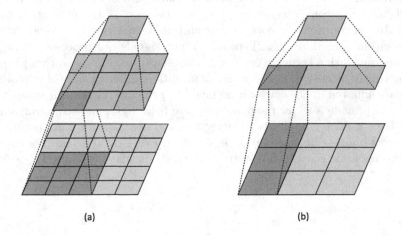

(a)   (b)

Fig. 2. Diagram of convolution kernel factorization.

2.3   Residual Architecture

As the structure of network deepens, the difficulty of training will gradually increase. Two main factors hinder network training. One is the disappearance and explosion of the gradient, and the other is the network's degradation. At present, gradient disappearance and gradient explosion can be well solved by introducing a BN layer. However, the problem of network's degradation needs to be solved by adjusting the structure of the network. He *et al.* [5] pointed out that the simple stacking of convolution layers does not improve the detection accuracy of the network, but may lead to a decrease in detection accuracy. Suppose that two identity mapping layers, i.e. $H(x) = x$, are added to a shallow network, as shown in Fig. 3(a). The experimental results show that the deep network with constant mapping layer is not as good as the previous shallow network in detection accuracy. The cause of this problem is that the training difficulty increases with the deepening of the network, resulting in the mapping relationship $F(x) = H(x)$ being difficult to fit, in other words, the network has degraded. In order to solve this problem, He proposed a structure as shown in Fig. 3(b). Through a shortcut connection, the network training task is changed from $F(x) = H(x)$ to $F(x) = H(x) - x$, which is easier to fit. Small changes in the output signal can also be learned by the network, thereby alleviating the problem of network degradation. For example, we suppose the network needs to learn the map from 1 to 1.5. For the structure without shortcut connection, the mapping is $H_1(x) = F_1(x) = 1.5$, so the training task is $F_1(x) = 1.5$. When the target changes from 1.5 to 1.55, the relative change rate is 3.3%. However, if we use the residual, the mapping changes to $H_2(x) = F_2(x) + x = 1.5$. And the training task is $F_2(x) = 1.5 - x$. Similarly, if the target increases 0.5, the relative change rate is 10%, which is 3 times than before. As can be seen from the above example, the residual network structure can make the network more sensitive to changes in output, thereby improving the efficiency of training.

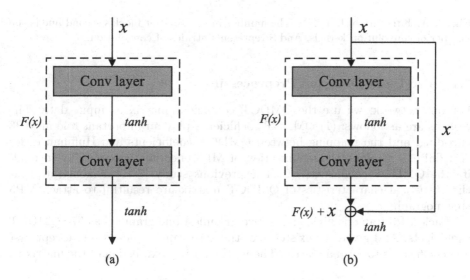

Fig. 3. Diagram of residual structure. (a) is the directly connected structure and (b) is residual structure.

3 The Architecture of Proposed Network

In this section, we describe the architecture of proposed network in detail. The architecture of our network is shown in Fig. 4, which is mainly divided into three parts. The first part plays the role of preprocessor, which contains a high-pass filter and a concat function. The second part contains six sub-net blocks, each block orderly contains three convolution kernels with different scales, a tanh activation function, a BN layer, and an average pooling layer. The last part is the feature classification part, which contains two fully connected layers and followed by the softmax classifier.

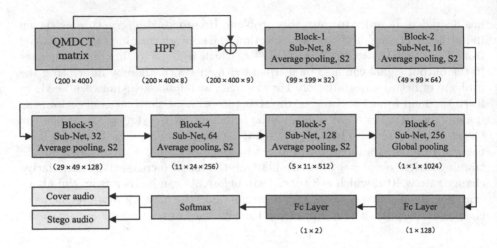

Fig. 4. Architecture of LMCNN. The number in the sub-net block's second line is the number of convolution kernels. And S represents strides of convolution.

3.1   The Input Data and Preprocessing

For our network, we use the QMDCT coefficient matrix as input data. The reasons are as follows: (1) QMDCT coefficients play an important role in MP3 encoding, and the mapping between QMDCT coefficients and Huffman codes is definite. Therefore, the modification of MP3 encoding is essentially to modify the QMDCT coefficients. (2) The previous study [7,10] demonstrate that the statistical characteristics of QMDCT matrix are resultful to attack MP3 steganography.

Each MP3 frame is divided into two granules, one granule has 576 QMDCT coefficients. And given the existence of the zero value region, we intercept first 400 coefficients to form a matrix. The mathematical expression of the matrix is,

$$\mathcal{Q} = \begin{pmatrix} q_{1,1} & \cdots & q_{1,j} & \cdots & q_{1,400} \\ \vdots & \ddots & \vdots & \ddots & \vdots \\ q_{i,1} & \cdots & q_{i,j} & \cdots & q_{i,400} \\ \vdots & \ddots & \vdots & \ddots & \vdots \\ q_{200,1} & \cdots & q_{200,j} & \cdots & q_{200,400} \end{pmatrix} \tag{1}$$

where $q_{i,j}$ represent the QMDCT coefficient, $i \in \{1,2,3,\cdots,200\}$ is the index of granule and $j \in \{1,2,3,\cdots,400\}$ is the index of QMDCT coefficients in one granule.

As shown in Fig. 4, the QMDCT matrix is preprocessed by a high pass filter at the begin of the network to amplify the perturbation introduced by the embedding. And the processed matrix is added to the original before input to the next part, which is proved in [14] that can improve detection accuracy.

3.2   The Sub-net Block

The architecture of the sub-net block is shown in Fig. 5. Each sub-net block has three convolution kernels of different sizes. And in order to reduce the network parameters, we adopted the strategy of convolution kernel factorization. Besides, the residual structure is applied to speed up the convergence of the network and improve the performance.

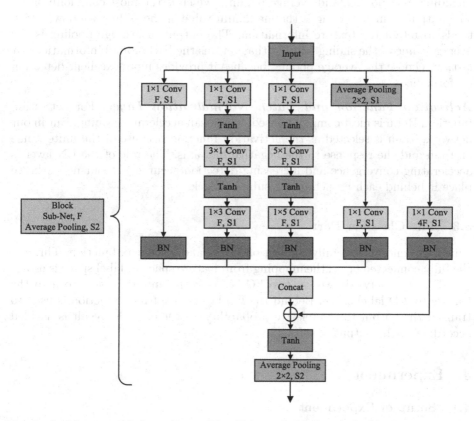

Fig. 5. Architecture of the sub-net. The F in each block stands for the number of convolution kernels.

Multi-scale Convolution. QMDCT coefficients of MP3 are divided into three regions, which are large value region, small value region, and zero value region. Two coefficients in the large region are encoded to a Huffman code, while four them in the small region are encoded to a Huffman code. Considering the rule of coding, we set the size of convolution kernels as 1×1, 3×3 and 5×5 respectively. 3×1 and 1×3 kernels are used instead of a 3×3 kernel. And the 5×5 kernel is factorized to the scale of 5×1 and 1×5 to further decrease the number of parameters. A branch with pooling layer is used to enhance the perception of the network.

Residual Structure. According to the described in Sect. 2, we use the residual architecture in each sub-net block. In order to match with the output data of multi-scale convolution, the data from the previous layer need through one 1×1 convolution layer and BN layer to raise dimension.

Pooling Layer. Pooling layer is used for the reduction of feature dimensions to decrease the quantity of parameters. We experiment with different pooling layer, including max pooling and average pooling, which is the most commonly used. The output of max pooling is the maximum value of the sliding window, which tends to retain the texture information. The output of average pooling is the average value of the sliding window that retains the background information. At last, we choose the average pooling because it provides more excellent detection performance.

Activation Function and Batch Normalization Layer. For activation function, ReLu is most commonly used, which can accelerate training. But in our network, Tanh is selected as the activation function because of the finite range of Tanh and the response to the negative half axis. The role of the BN layer is accelerating convergence and increasing detection accuracy. In our network, we place it behind each branch in the sub-net block.

3.3 The Classifier Part

This part contains two fully connection layers and a softmax function. Through the fully connected layer, the mapping from feature space to label space is established. In our network, we use two FC layers with tanh activation to map the feature to 2-D label space. Behind the FC layers, a softmax function is used to transfer the output to the relative probability. In the end, the result is decided according to the output of softmax.

4   Experiment

4.1   Setup of Experiment

To evaluate the performance of our proposed network, a dataset which consist of 10,000 stereo WAV clips with sampling rate of 44.1 kHz and the duration of 10 s is constructed. Cover files are made by encoding WAV audio files to 128 kbps and 320 kbps MP3 audio files via LAME [6]. Then, two steganography algorithm, SBF-JED [17] and EECS [16], are implemented to generate the stego MP3 audio files. And the bitrate is set to be the same as cover. The EECS algorithm is encoded by Syndrome-Trellis Codes (STC), so the embedding capacity is related to relative payload α. In practice, we can change the width W of the parity-check matrix to control α. The relationship between them is $\alpha = \frac{1}{W}$. In our experiment, we choose the first 50 frames of MP3 file to embed secret message. The width of the parity-check matrix is set from 2 to 6, and the height is fixed at 7. For the SBF-JED algorithm, the settings of parameters are the same as EECS except that the threshold is set to 2. Table 1 shows the specific parameter settings and the corresponding payload rate.

Table 1. The specific parameter settings and the corresponding payload rate

	W		2	3	4	5	6
Payload (kbps)	EECS	128 kbps	5.0	3.0	1.8	1.5	1.0
		320 kbps	11.9	8.0	5.8	4.3	3.9
	SBF-JED	128 kbps	7.1	5.2	3.5	2.9	2.4
		320 kbps	13.0	10.2	7.0	5.6	4.7

We train all networks on NVIDIA TITAN XP GPU with 12 GB graphics memory. Networks are trained with an initial learning rate of 10^{-3}. For decay function, we use exponential decay function with a decay rate of 0.9 and decay step of 5000. Besides, for the optimizer, we use the Adam algorithm [8] with $\beta_1 = 0.9, \beta_2 = 0.999$ and $\epsilon = 10^{-8}$. The fully connection is initialized by Glorot [4]. The batch size of each iteration is 16 (8 cover-stego pairs). Furthermore, an L2 regulation with the gain of 10^{-3} is used to prevent overfitting. And BN layers are dropped when we test our network. False Positive Rate (FPR), False Negative Rate (FNR), and Accuracy Rate (ACC) are used to measure the performance for steganalysis. The three metrics are defined as below:

$$FPR = \frac{FP}{FP + TN} \times 100\% \tag{2}$$

$$FNR = \frac{FN}{FN + TP} \times 100\% \tag{3}$$

$$ACC = 1 - \frac{FPR + FNR}{2} \times 100\% \tag{4}$$

where TP, FP, TN and FN are the number of true positive samples, false positive samples, true negative samples and false negative samples respectively.

4.2 The Selection of Sub-net Structure

To verify the impact of multi-scale, convolution kernel factorization and residual structure on the performance of LMCNN, we designed three different sub-net with dropping part of structures to compare with the sub-net used in LMCNN. In Sub-Net1, we drop the multi-scale structure, and only use a 3×3 convention kernel instead of it. And for Sub-Net2 and Sub-Net3, the convolution kernel factorization and residual structure are dropped independently. We compare the detection accuracy and the number of parameters of the network with different sub-nets under the same condition (EECS, 128 kbps, payload = 1.5 kbps). The experiment results are shown in Table 2.

Table 2. Performance of each sub-net (EECS, 128 kbps, payload = 1.8 kbps)

Sub-net structure	Sub-Net1	Sub-Net2	Sub-Net3	Sub-Net of LMCNN
ACC (%)	79.20	81.50	82.30	**83.20**
Number of parameters (k)	**0.65k**	4.5k	2.2k	2.9k

As the result shown in Table 2, the number of parameters decreases by 35% via the factorization of the convolution kernel. On the other hand, the introduction of multi-scale and residual structure can improve the performance of detection accuracy. Considering of the detection performance and model size comprehensively, the structure we use is optimal.

4.3   The Result of Detecting MP3 Steganography in Different Domains

Table 3. Steganalysis performance of proposed network

Algorithm	Bitrate (kbps)	Payload (kbps)	FPR (%)	FNR (%)	ACC (%)
EECS	128	5.0	3.25	3.70	96.52
		3.0	8.95	9.10	90.98
		1.8	17.20	16.40	83.20
		1.5	23.80	24.10	76.02
		1.0	33.65	36.65	70.03
	320	11.9	0.05	0.00	99.97
		8.0	0.90	0.50	99.30
		5.8	2.35	2.50	97.58
		4.3	5.00	5.95	94.53
		3.9	7.20	8.10	92.35
SBF-JED	128	7.0	0.55	0.55	99.45
		5.2	2.20	4.10	96.85
		3.5	4.95	5.10	94.98
		2.9	7.20	7.60	92.60
		2.4	9.50	8.80	90.85
	320	13.0	0.10	0.00	99.95
		10.2	0.11	0.23	99.83
		7.0	0.60	0.80	99.30
		5.6	1.58	1.04	98.69
		4.7	3.20	2.56	97.12

To verify the performance of our network, we use our network to attack EECS and SBF-JBD in the different payload. The result is shown in Table 3. The result demonstrates that the proposed network can be suitable for detecting MP3 steganography which acts on different domains. From the table, we can see that the ACC is bigger than 95% under the high payload. When the payload drops to about 2.4 kbps, the ACC can still above 90%.

4.4 Comparison with Handcraft Features

To assess the performance of our network, we compare it with two existing state-of-the-art steganalysis algorithm based on handcraft feature, MDI2 [10] and Jin-Markov [7]. We use these methods to attack EECS and SBF-JED in the different payload. The results of detection accuracy are shown in Tables 4 and 5. From the results, we can find that the proposed network outperforms the conventional method based on handcraft feature, which is improved above 25% in average.

Table 4. Detection ACC (%) of EECS algorithm

Bitrate (kbps)	Payload (kbps)	Jin-Markov	MDI2	LMCNN
128	5.0	70.99	71.34	**96.52**
	1.8	57.89	57.48	**83.20**
	1.0	48.52	43.75	**70.03**
320	11.0	73.41	79.95	**99.97**
	5.8	59.25	61.84	**97.58**
	3.9	54.47	56.34	**92.35**

Table 5. Detection ACC (%) of SBF-JED algorithm

Bitrate (kbps)	Payload (kbps)	Jin-Markov	MDI2	LMCNN
128	7.0	51.30	75.64	**99.45**
	3.5	51.31	64.91	**94.98**
	2.4	51.31	59.03	**90.85**
320	13.0	51.25	75.37	**99.95**
	7.0	51.25	69.71	**99.30**
	4.7	51.25	61.71	**97.12**

4.5 Comparison with CNN-Based Methods

In this section, we compare our network with previous CNN-based steganalysis method, WASDN [13] and RHFCN [14], in memory occupation, model size and the number of parameters. From Tables 6 and 7, we can see that the proposed network has significant advantages in model size. Comparing with RHFCN, the model size of our network is reduced from 1.7 GB to 47 MB and the memory occupation is reduced by 40%. In terms of detection performance, the accuracy of our network is better than WASDN. And compared with RHFCN, the detection accuracy stay on same level, even slightly increases in some conditions.

Table 6. Evaluation of MP3 steganalytic networks (EECS, 128 kbps, batchsize = 16)

	WASDN	RHFCN	LMCNN
ACC (%, payload = 5 kbps)	92.39	95.40	**96.52**
ACC (%, payload = 3 kbps)	82.07	89.85	**90.98**
Model size (MB)	932.29	1764.23	**47.20**
Number of parameter (K)	8k	15k	**2.9k**
Memory occupation (MB)	4551	7391	**4439**

Table 7. Evaluation of MP3 steganalytic networks (SBF-JED, 128 kbps, batchsize = 16)

	WASDN	RHFCN	LMCNN
ACC (%, payload = 7 kbps)	99.15	**99.75**	99.45
ACC (%, payload = 5 kbps)	96.07	**97.32**	96.85
Model size (MB)	932.29	1764.23	**47.20**
Number of parameter (K)	8k	15k	**2.9k**
Memory occupation (MB)	4551	7391	**4439**

5   Conclusion

In this paper, we propose a light-weight network with convolution factorization, multi-scale convolution and residual structure to detect MP3 steganography. The experimental results show that our network can be used to detect steganographic algorithm under different bitrates, payload rates, and embedding domains. The detection accuracy of the proposed network is above 90% when the payload is more than 3.0 kbps whether EECS or SBF-JBD. And the proposed network obviously outperforms the conventional schemes under the same experiment condition. Additionally, comparing with other CNN-based methods, our network requires fewer parameters, memory and storage space without dropping out the detection accuracy, which means it has the potential to use in widely scenarios, such as mobile terminal. Furthermore, we will continue to simplify the network structure, and improve the performance in low payload rate.

Acknowledgments. This work was supported by NSFC under 61902391, 61972390 and U1736214, and National Key Technology R&D Program under 2016QY15Z2500 and 2019QY0700.

References

1. Chen, B., Luo, W., Li, H.: Audio steganalysis with convolutional neural network. In: Proceedings of the 5th ACM Workshop on Information Hiding and Multimedia Security (IH&MMSec 2017), pp. 85–90. ACM (2017)
2. Gao, H.: The MP3 steganography algorithm based on Huffman coding. Acta Scientiarum Naturalium Universitatis Sunyatseni **46**(4), 32–35 (2007)
3. Ghasemzadeh, H., Khass, M.T., Arjmandi, M.K.: Audio steganalysis based on reversed psychoacoustic model of human hearing. Digit. Signal Process. **51**, 133–141 (2016)
4. Glorot, X., Bengio, Y.: Understanding the difficulty of training deep feedforward neural networks. In: Proceedings of the 13th International Conference on Artificial Intelligence and Statistics (IJCAI 2010), pp. 249–256 (2010)
5. He, K., Zhang, X., Ren, S., Sun, J.: Deep residual learning for image recognition. In: Proceedings of the 2016 IEEE Conference on Computer Vision and Pattern Recognition (CVPR 2016), pp. 770–778. IEEE (2016)
6. Hegemann, R., Leidinger, A., Brito, R.: LAME (1998). https://sourceforge.net/projects/lame/files/lame/
7. Jin, C., Wang, R., Yan, D.: Steganalysis of MP3Stego with low embedding-rate using Markov feature. Multimed. Tools Appl. **76**(5), 6143–6158 (2017)
8. Kingma, D.P., Ba, J.: Adam: a method for stochastic optimization. arXiv preprint arXiv:1412.6980 (2014)
9. Petitcolas, F.: MP3Stego (1998). http://www.petitcolas.net/steganography/mp3stego/
10. Ren, Y., Xiong, Q., Wang, L.: A steganalysis scheme for AAC audio based on MDCT difference between intra and inter frame. In: Kraetzer, C., Shi, Y.-Q., Dittmann, J., Kim, H.J. (eds.) IWDW 2017. LNCS, vol. 10431, pp. 217–231. Springer, Cham (2017). https://doi.org/10.1007/978-3-319-64185-0_17
11. Szegedy, C., et al.: Going deeper with convolutions. In: Proceedings of the 2015 IEEE Conference on Computer Vision and Pattern Recognition (CVPR 2015), pp. 1–9. IEEE (2015)
12. Szegedy, C., Vanhoucke, V., Ioffe, S., Shlens, J., Wojna, Z.: Rethinking the inception architecture for computer vision. In: Proceedings of the 2016 IEEE Conference on Computer Vision and Pattern Recognition (CVPR 2016), pp. 2818–2826. IEEE (2016)
13. Wang, Y., Yang, K., Yi, X., Zhao, X., Xu, Z.: CNN-based steganalysis of MP3 steganography in the entropy code domain. In: Proceedings of the 6th ACM Workshop on Information Hiding and Multimedia Security (IH&MMSec 2018), pp. 55–65. ACM (2018)
14. Wang, Y., Yi, X., Zhao, X., Su, A.: RHFCN: fully CNN-based steganalysis of MP3 with rich high-pass filtering. In: ICASSP 2019-2019 IEEE International Conference on Acoustics, Speech and Signal Processing, pp. 2627–2631. IEEE (2019)
15. Yan, D., Wang, R., Zhang, L.: A high capacity MP3 steganography based on Huffman coding. J. Sichuan Univ. (Nat. Sci. Ed.) **6**, 1281–1286 (2011)

16. Yang, K., Yi, X., Zhao, X., Zhou, L.: Adaptive MP3 steganography using equal length entropy codes substitution. In: Kraetzer, C., Shi, Y.-Q., Dittmann, J., Kim, H.J. (eds.) IWDW 2017. LNCS, vol. 10431, pp. 202–216. Springer, Cham (2017). https://doi.org/10.1007/978-3-319-64185-0_16
17. Yang, Y., Wang, Y., Yi, X., Zhao, X., Ma, Y.: Defining joint embedding distortion for adaptive MP3 steganography. In: Proceedings of the 7th ACM Workshop on Information Hiding and Multimedia Security (IH&MMSec 2019), pp. 14–24. ACM (2019)

Improving Audio Steganalysis Using Deep Residual Networks

Zhenyu Zhang[1,2], Xiaowei Yi[1,2], and Xianfeng Zhao[1,2(✉)]

[1] State Key Laboratory of Information Security, Institute of Information Engineering, Chinese Academy of Sciences, Beijing 100093, China
zhaoxianfeng@iie.ac.cn
[2] School of Cyber Security, University of Chinese Academy of Sciences, Beijing 100093, China

Abstract. In this paper, we propose an effective audio steganalysis scheme based on deep residual convolutional networks in the temporal domain. Firstly, considering the weak difference between cover and stego, a high pass filter is adopted in the proposed network which is used to calculate the residual map of the audio signal. Then, comparing with convolutional neural networks (CNNs) based audio steganalysis in recent studies, the deeper network structure and complicated convolutional modules are considered to capture the complex statistical characteristic of steganography. Finally, batch normalization layers and shortcut connections are applied to decrease the dangers of over-fitting and accelerate the convergence of back-propagation. In the experiments, we compared the proposed scheme with CNNs based and hand-crafted features based audio steganalysis methods to detect the various steganographic algorithms on speech and music audio clips respectively. The experimental results demonstrate that the proposed scheme is able to detect multiple state-of-the-art audio steganographic schemes with different payloads effectively and outperforms several recently proposed audio steganalysis methods.

Keywords: Audio steganalysis · Deep residual network · Adaptive steganography · Temporal domain

1 Introduction

Modern steganography is a science and art of covert communication that slightly changes the original digital media in order to hide secret messages without drawing suspicions from the steganalyzers [4,10]. Corresponding to the development of steganographic techniques, the steganalysis with the aim of revealing the presence of hidden messages in digital media has also been made considerable progress. Recently, many researches about steganalysis have been reported. However, most existing steganalytic methods are mainly dependent on the high-dimensional steganalysis features and supervised classifiers, which can not adapt itself to the various steganographic algorithms. In this paper, we introduce a deep

H. Wang et al. (Eds.): IWDW 2019, LNCS 12022, pp. 57–70, 2020.
https://doi.org/10.1007/978-3-030-43575-2_5

learning method over audio steganalysis, which achieve better detection accuracy than several recent works.

In the past decade, many statistical steganalysis features have been investigated for detecting audio steganographic algorithms. For instance, the Mel-frequency based features were introduced for audio steganalysis in [12]. Liu et al. proposed an approach based on Fourier spectrum statistics and Mel-cepstrum coefficients to detect the audio steganography [14]. In [15], the authors employed the Mel-cepstrum coefficients and Markov transition features from the second derivative of the audio signal to make steganalysis. In [6], the authors tried to build a linear basis to capture certain statistical properties of audio signal. In addition, there are some effective features to detect audio steganography in the frequency domain, such as MPEG-1 audio layer III (MP3) based steganalysis [9], and advanced audio coding (AAC) based steganalysis [17]. The above researches are based on hand-crafted high-dimensional features, and the performances of these works for the steganalysis of audio in the temporal domain are still far from satisfactory.

Recently, various deep learning architectures are proposed successively, which have achieved state-of-the-art results in many areas, especially in speech recognition and computer vision. However, very few deep learning based methods have been applied for audio steganalysis. Chen et al. [2] first proposed a sample convolutional neural network (CNN) to detect ±1 least significant bit (LSB) matching steganography in the temporal domain and achieved better results than the hand-crafted features. Lin et al. [13] proposed an improved CNN-based method for boosting the detection performance for the low embedding-rate steganography by adopting parameter transfer strategy. Wang et al. [22] presented an effective steganalytic scheme based on CNN for detecting MP3 steganography in the entropy code domain by using the quantified modified DCT (QMDCT) coefficients.

In this paper, we propose a modified deep residual convolutional network model for steganalysis of audio in the temporal domain. The deep residual network introduced in [7] has achieved promising performance on computer vision tasks, and also has been used for steganalysis of digital images [1,23,24]. Compared with the traditional convolutional neural network, the residual network introduces shortcut connections that directly pass the data flow to later layers, thus effectively avoids the vanishing gradient problem caused by multiple stacked non-linear transformations. As a consequence, deeper network constructed with residual block generally gets better performance in comparison with networks that consist of simply stack layers. The proposed network model is empirically designed with shortcut connections and a series of proven propositions, such as tanh activation function and high pass filter. The main contributions of this work are summarized as follows: (1) According to [2,18,25], employing the residual filters before inputting the original signal to neural networks usually results in better performance for steganalytic scheme. Inspired by this, a high pass filter module is implemented in the proposed scheme. (2) From previous researches [19] and [20], it is observed that the network model with larger depth can extract complex optimal functions more efficiently. Following the notions of residual network [7], we repeat the convolutional module twice in each residual block and design the network model with shortcut components. Our experimental results demonstrate that the proposed scheme obtains considerable improvement in terms of detection performance compared with several existing steganalytic methods.

The remaining parts of the paper is organized as follows. In Sect. 2, we describe the structure of the proposed steganalytic network and discuss the details for each component of the architecture. Next, the experimental setup and the overall performance of the proposed scheme for different scenarios are described in Sect. 3 and Sect. 4 respectively. Finally, we conclude the paper and state some directions for future works in Sect. 5.

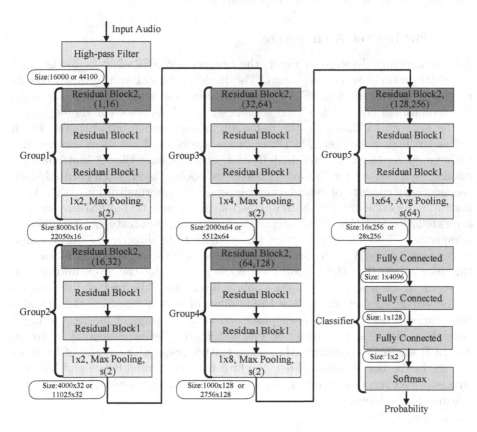

Fig. 1. The architecture of WavSResNet. The parameters in Residual Block2 are the input and output channels respectively. For example, "(m, n)" denotes input with m channels and n output channels. In Max and Avg Pooling layers, "1×2" denotes that pool size 1×2 and s(2) denotes that the stride of slide window is 2. The "Size 8000×16" represents the output dimension of the block, which is the shape of feature maps.

2   Proposed Method

The proposed network architecture is called "WavSResNet", which represents residual network for waveform audio steganalysis. The word "residual" refers to the residual blocks with shortcut connections from deep learning. The shortcut connections help propagate gradients to upper layers and encourage feature reuse in the training process. In addition, residual blocks improve the performance of network because the vanishing gradient phenomenon that often negatively affects the convergence of deep network architectures [5,8]. The remainder of this section is divided into several subsections. Firstly, we describe the architecture of WavSResNet, and then analyze each part of the network in details. Most of the explorations focused on components in each residual block, the activation function, pooling layers and shortcut components.

2.1   WavSResNet Architecture

As schematically depicted in Fig. 1, the proposed WavSResNet is divided into a concatenation of several segments. The Residual Block1 and Residual Block2 represent identity shortcut (Fig. 2) and projection shortcut (Fig. 3) respectively. A convolutional layer with a fixed kernel $(-1, 2, -1)$ is placed at the beginning of the network to transform the input audio data into residual signal, which act as the high pass filter. Then five groups are stacked one after another and each group contains one Residual Block2, two Residual Block1 and one max pooling layer, expect for Group5 with average pooling layer. Each residual block consecutively consists of convolutional layers, batch normalization (BN), Tanh activation function and the shortcut component. Among them, the convolutional layers followed by BN and tanh activation function extract features from different perspectives. The "shortcut" allows the gradient to be directly back-propagated to the earlier layer [8]. Tanh activation function help the network decide whether the information that the neuron received is relevant for the given information or should it be ignored. The max pooling layers keep the texture information of the sliding window and reduce the number of parameters from the previous convolutional layer. Having been processed by five groups of blocks, the input clips data with size 1×16000 or 1×44100 (see the experimental setups in Sect. 3.1) are finally transformed to a 256 feature maps with the size of 1×16 or 1×28. In the last segment, three standard fully connected layers and followed by a soft-max function, which act as a role of "the linear classifier" and map the features to the label space.

2.2   Convolutional Layers

The convolutional layers are the main components in CNN, which use one or several filters to convolve the input data and generate different feature maps for subsequent processing. In the proposed network, there are two kinds of convolutional layers which are the fixed convolutional layer and the common convolutional layer. Fixed convolutional layer is used to capture the minor modification introduced by the data hiding methods through reducing the impact of content information which can be seen as a high pass filter (HPF). The common convolutional layers with parameters are used to generate feature maps. In each convolutional layer, the convolutional kernel with the shape of 1×3 is used with the stride of (1, 1) and the padding is "SAME", which is followed by BN step to speed up training.

2.3 Activation Function

In the proposed network, we choose the nonlinear activation function to introduce nonlinear factors. The Rectified Linear Unit (ReLu) is the most commonly activation function, which seems maybe faster than Tanh for many of the given examples [3]. However, considering the property of audio steganalysis task, the saturation region of the tanh activation function limit the range of data value which can improve the performance of our model (refer to Sect. 4.2, compared with network #3). So we choose Tanh as the activation function instead of the Relu.

2.4 Pooling Layers

In order to extract robust invariant features and reduce the number of parameters from previous convolutional layer, it is very often to insert a pooling layer right after the convolutional layer in neural network. The pooling layer can be regarded as a kind of fixed convolutional layer and realized by average pooling or max pooling. The difference between average pooling and max pooling is the output of pooling. The max pooling keeps the texture information of the sliding window and outputs the maximum value of the sliding window, while the average pooling outputs the average value of the sliding window.

Considering characteristics of audio steganalysis, the max pooling layer and the average pooling layer are used in our proposed network. The size of max pooling layer is 1×2, 1×4, 1×8 with stride (1, 2). The average pooling layer has the size of 1×64 with the stride of (1, 64). In order to keep enough parameters, we just use five pooling layers and each one follows the second Residual Block1 in each group.

2.5 Shortcut Components

The proposed WavSResNet contains two types of shortcut connections because convolutional layers require different shortcut connections. Two main types of shortcuts are the projection shortcut and the identity shortcut, depending mainly on whether the input and output dimensions are same or different. The shortcut connection allows the gradient to be directly back-propagated to earlier layers by skipping over layers and helps deep residual networks from vanishing gradients.

We insert shortcut connections which turn the network into its counterpart residual version. The identity shortcuts can be directly used when the input and

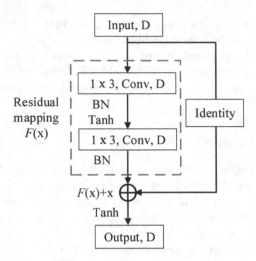

Fig. 2. Identity shortcut with skipping over 2 convolutional layers. The parameters inside the boxes represent kernel size, layer type, and the number of channels respectively. For example, "1 × 3, Conv, D" means a convolutional layer with 1 × 3 kernel size and D channels. "BN" and "Tanh" represent batch normalization layer and activation function respectively.

output are of the same dimensions as described in Fig. 2. When the dimension increases, to make the shortcut still performs identity mapping, the projection shortcut is used to match dimensions as sketched in Fig. 3 (done by 1 × 3 convolution). The difference between projection shortcut with the identity shortcut is that there is a convolutional layer without any non-linear activation function in the shortcut path, which is used to resize the input feature map to a different dimension. In this paper, the shortcut connections skip over 2 layers.

3   Experimental Setup

This section describes the common elements of all experiments that appear in Sect. 4, including the dataset, evaluation metric, training and testing of WavS-ResNet.

3.1   Dataset

The experiments will be carried out on three datasets which are SpeechData1, SpeechData2 and MusicData. SpeechData1 is the dataset used in [2], which includes the 40,000 cover-stego speech pairs. SpeechData2 and MusicData consist of 40,000 speech clips and 40,000 music clips respectively which were downloaded from the public data set [21]. Each clip was recorded with resolution of 16 bits per sample, duration of 1 s and stored in the uncompressed wave audio files (WAV). The SpeechData1 and SpeechData2 include mono speech corpus with

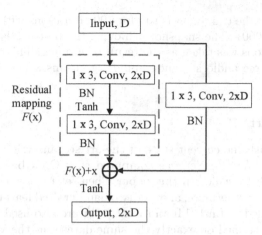

Fig. 3. Projection shortcut with skipping over 2 convolutional layers. The parameters inside the boxes represent the same meaning in Fig. 2.

a sampling rate of 16 kHz, and MusicData is mono audio clips with a sampling rate of 44.1 kHz. Three steganographic algorithms for WAV audio, which are ±1 LSB matching method (LSBM), modification of the amplitude value of sampling (Amplitude Modification) [26] and the adaptive steganographic algorithms (Luo Adaptive) [16], are implemented on original audio clips to generate the corresponding stego audio dataset. The stego clips in SpeechData1 were made by LSBM algorithm with 0.50 bit per sample (bps). The stego clips in SpeechData2 and MusicData were made by another two steganographic algorithms, which are Amplitude Modification with payloads 0.5 bps and Luo Adaptive with payloads 0.3 bps. Totally, each dataset contains 40,000 cover-stego pairs. Half of the pairs are used for training, and the rest are used for testing. In the training stage, the 16,000 pairs are used to train the network, and the rest 4,000 pairs are set aside for validation to chose the best trained model. In Sect. 4.1, we will introduce the experimental results on three datasets respectively.

3.2 Training Part

The WavSResNet has been experimented on speech clips dataset and music clips dataset with the same hyperparameters. The stochastic gradient descend (SGD) optimizer Adamax [11] was used with mini-batches of 32 cover-stego pairs and the training database was shuffled after each epoch. The batch normalization parameters were learned via an exponential moving average with decay rate 0.99. At the beginning of the training, the filter weights were initialized with random numbers generated from zero mean truncated Gaussian distribution with standard deviation of 0.1, and L^2 regularization. The filter biases were initialized to zero and no regularization. For the fully connected classifier layer, we initialized the weights with a zero mean Gaussian and standard deviation 0.01 and no bias.

On our dataset, the training was run for 100k iterations with an initial learning rate of $r_1 = 0.0001$. The snapshot achieving the best validation accuracy in the last 40k iterations was taken as the result of training. This training strategy was applied for three audio steganographic algorithms at three kinds of WAV audio datasets.

3.3   Testing Part

For comparison with the current state-of-the-art steganalytic methods of WAV format audio, the WavSResNet was compared with CNN based method introduced in [2], which we called in this paper ChenNet to distinguish it from the proposed network. Furthermore, another two hand-crafted features based steganalytic methods called as Liu1 [14] and Liu2 [15] were also used to be compared. The ChenNet was trained on exactly the same dataset as the WavSResNet and implemented in TensorFlow.

After choosing the bast trained model, we made the test with mini-batches of 64 audio clips which were randomly sampling from the test dataset without replacement until all data were recycled, and calculated the average detection accuracy. For another two hand-crafted features based steganalytic methods, after training support vector machine classifiers on the training dataset, the classifier was carried on the test dataset to calculate the detection accuracy.

3.4   Evaluation Metric

To evaluate the performance of the proposed scheme and state-of-the-art steganographic algorithms on WAV format audio dataset, the performance is measured by the detection accuracy of audio clips in the testing dataset. The detection accuracy is calculated as the number of correctly detection examples over the total number of the selected audio clips. Mathematically, the detection accuracy can be stated as:

$$\text{Accuracy} = \frac{TP + TN}{TP + TN + FP + FN} \tag{1}$$

where TP, TN, FP and FN represent the number of true positives, true negatives, false positives and false negatives respectively. To obtain convincing results, all the experiments are repeated 10 times by randomly splitting the training and testing datasets.

4   Experiments

4.1   Experiments on Three Datasets

To show the efficiency of the proposed scheme in improving the performance of audio steganalysis in the temporal domain, we use WavSResNet and Chen-Net [2] to make the detection on SpeechData1. Then we make experiments on

Table 1. The average detection accuracy (%) for LSBM algorithm in SpeechData1.

Steganalysis method	Accuracy
ChenNet	88.81
WavSResNet	89.70

Table 2. The average detection accuracy (%) of WavSResNet for different steganographic schemes.

Steganographic scheme	Dataset	
	SpeechData2	MusicData
Amplitude Modification	99.80	99.39
Luo Adaptive	54.69	52.25

SpeechData2 and MusicData to discuss the influence of sampling frequency to the WavSResNet. The stego examples are made as described in Sect. 3.1. We train the WavSResNet for 100,000 iterations with the parameters description in Sect. 3.2, and choose the best trained model to calculate the average detection accuracy on the test dataset. The average detection accuracy of WavSResNet and ChenNet [2] for LSBM on SpeechData1 are shown in Table 1, and the detection on SpeechData2 and MusicData for another two steganographic algorithms are shown in Table 2.

From Table 1, the WavSResNet's detection accuracy has achieved 89.70% on SpeechData1. It can be seen that the WavSResNet has better performance than ChenNet, which demonstrate improvement of WavSResNet for making audio steganalysis. From Table 2, we can see the overall performance on speech is better than that on the music, which may be interpreted as the samples' values of music are more complex than that of the speech clips and the network could not learn the rules efficiently. In addition, we can see that the steganographic algorithms have a heavily efficiency for the detection accuracy. The best detection accuracy is achieved when detects Amplitude Modification in SpeechData2, which reaches 99.80%. However, for the Luo Adaptive algorithm, the WavSResNet can not get the well results. This loss of performance is due to the fact that adaptive steganographic algorithms modify less samples and choose the complex area to embed messages, which makes the WavSResNet difficult to capture the discipline of this modification.

4.2 Comparison with the Variants

In this experiment, we try to show the effective of the WavSResNet by comparing it with its several variants. As listed in Table 3, three variant networks are used in this experiment, indexing from #2 to #4. The components of these variant networks are slightly different from the WavSResNet #1. All the networks have the same hyper-parameters described in Sect. 2 and are analysised on SpeechData1. In order to compare the fluctuation of 50 times experiments' detection accuracy for different networks, we record each experiment's detection accuracy and show the box plot for each network in Fig. 4.

Table 3. Network indices and descriptions.

#1 The proposed WavSResNet
#2 Remove the high pass filter layer
#3 Replace the activation function "Tanh" with "Relu"
#4 Remove all of shortcut connections from Residual Block1 and Residual Block2

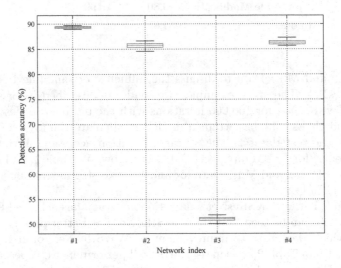

Fig. 4. Box plots of the detection accuracy obtained by different networks for detection LSBM with 0.5 bps.

From Fig. 4, it is observed that network #1 achieves the highest average accuracy of 89.70% and has a very stable performance over different times of testing. Most of detection accuracies of network #2 and #4 are between 84.01% and 87.72%, which are slight lower than that of network #1. The average detection accuracy of the network #3 is 51.02% because of the vanishing gradient problem, which are much lower than that of the proposed network. Moreover, we can observe from Fig. 4 that the accuracies of network #2 and #4 spread out in wide ranges, which indicates that these networks are not stable enough. In addition, we have additionally tested some other variants of the WavSResNet, which always obtain lower classify accuracy compared with the network #1, and we do not report them in the paper because of the limitation of space. As a result, the proposed WavSResNet (#1) converges relatively fast and achieves the best detection accuracy, so it is the most effective network compared to other variants.

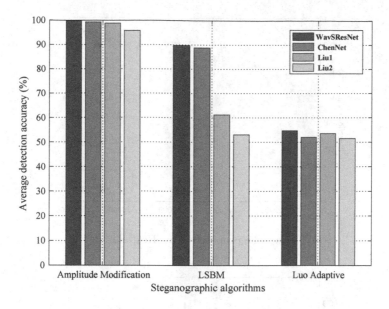

Fig. 5. The average detection accuracy of tree steganalytic algorithms for different steganographic methods.

4.3 Comparison with Previous Methods

In this experiment, we try to show the effectiveness of the WavSResNet by comparing it with three state-of-the-art steganalytic methods, which are ChenNet [2], Liu1 [14] and Liu2 [15]. The average detection accuracy of these steganalytic methods for three steganographic algorithms are shown in Fig. 5. The LSBM algorithm is tested on the SpeechData1 and another two steganographic algorithms are tested on SpeechData2.

As we can see in Fig. 5, the proposed WavSResNet has better detection performance for different steganographic algorithms than ChenNet. The average detection accuracy of WavSResNet improves upon ChenNet by up to 2.32%. The biggest improvement is typically observed for Luo Adaptive steganography. In addiction, we show that both network based detectors clearly outperform the traditional hand-crafted features based steganalytic paradigms. As a rule, the overall detection accuracy of Luo Adaptive algorithms is not very high. The reason is that the adaptive steganographic algorithms modify less samples, which makes the steganalytic algorithms hard to detect audio steganography in temporal domain effectively.

To further evaluate the WavSResNet and ChenNet with relatively good performance, we draw the curves of their training and validation accuracy during the training stage in Fig. 6. It is observed that the training accuracy of both networks steadily increased with more iterations before the convergence of networks. The validation accuracy of the ChenNet almost doesn't increase after about 30,000 iterations, which means that network converges in this case and more iterations

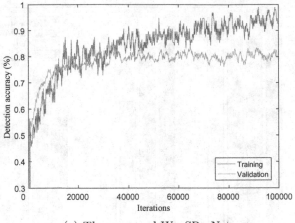

(a) The proposed WavSResNet.

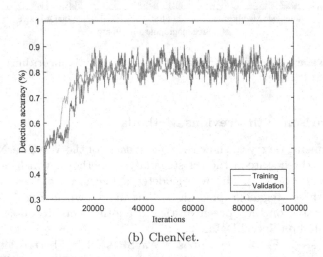

(b) ChenNet.

Fig. 6. The detection accuracy curves of two networks. (a) Our proposed method WavSResNet. (b) Chen's method ChenNet [2].

could not improve its validation accuracy. The WavSResNet, which doesn't converge even after 60,000 iterations, can eventually converge after more 80,000 iterations and its final detection accuracy is higher than that of ChenNet. On the whole, the residual blocks and more layers make WavSResNet need more iterations to be converged, but also make it achieve the better results than the other CNNs based audio steganalysis.

5   Conclusion

In this paper, a novel audio steganalytic method based on residual convolutional neural network is proposed as WavSResNet. Compared with existing CNNs based audio steganalytic methods, the deeper network structure and the short-cut connections are utilized to the WavSResNet. Experimental results demonstrate that the WavSResNet obtains considerable improvement in terms of detection performance compared with several existing steganalytic methods. However, although the proposed method can achieve the state-of-the-art performance, it still has a long way to improve the accuracy of audio steganalysis in the temporal domain to a high level. All of our source codes and datasets will be available via GitHub: https://github.com/Amforever/WavSteganalysis.

Further works will be focus on two directions. On the one hand, the higher quality features of the audio signal can be developed before inputting the original audio data to the convolutional networks. On the other hand, some more powerful neural networks can be adopted to improve the accuracy of audio steganalysis.

Acknowledgments. This work was supported by NSFC under U1736214, 61902391 and 61972390, and National Key Technology R&D Program under 2019QY0700 and 2016QY15Z2500.

References

1. Boroumand, M., Chen, M., Fridrich, J.: Deep residual network for steganalysis of digital images. IEEE Trans. Inf. Forensics Secur. **14**(5), 1181–1193 (2018)
2. Chen, B., Luo, W., Li, H.: Audio steganalysis with convolutional neural network. In: Proceedings of the 5th ACM Workshop on Information Hiding and Multimedia Security, pp. 85–90. ACM (2017)
3. Eger, S., Youssef, P., Gurevych, I.: Is it time to swish, comparing deep learning activation functions across NLP tasks. arXiv preprint arXiv:1901.02671 (2019)
4. Fridrich, J.: Steganography in Digital Media: Principles, Algorithms, and Applications. Cambridge University Press, Cambridge (2009)
5. Glorot, X., Bengio, Y.: Understanding the difficulty of training deep feedforward neural networks. In: Proceedings of the Thirteenth International Conference on Artificial Intelligence and Statistics, pp. 249–256 (2010)
6. Han, C., Xue, R., Zhang, R., Wang, X.: A new audio steganalysis method based on linear prediction. Multimedia Tools Appl. **77**(12), 15431–15455 (2017). https://doi.org/10.1007/s11042-017-5123-x
7. He, K., Zhang, X., Ren, S., Sun, J.: Deep residual learning for image recognition. In: Proceedings of the IEEE Conference on Computer Vision and Pattern Recognition, pp. 770–778. IEEE (2016)
8. He, K., Zhang, X., Ren, S., Sun, J.: Identity mappings in deep residual networks. In: Leibe, B., Matas, J., Sebe, N., Welling, M. (eds.) ECCV 2016, Part IV. LNCS, vol. 9908, pp. 630–645. Springer, Cham (2016). https://doi.org/10.1007/978-3-319-46493-0_38

9. Jin, C., Wang, R., Yan, D.: Steganalysis of MP3Stego with low embedding-rate using Markov feature. Multimed. Tools Appl. **76**(5), 6143–6158 (2016). https://doi.org/10.1007/s11042-016-3264-y
10. Ker, A.D.: The square root law of steganography: Bringing theory closer to practice. In: Proceedings of the 5th ACM Workshop on Information Hiding and Multimedia Security, pp. 33–44. ACM (2017)
11. Kingma, D.P., Ba, J.: Adam: A method for stochastic optimization. arXiv preprint arXiv:1412.6980 (2014)
12. Kraetzer, C., Dittmann, J.: Mel-cepstrum-based steganalysis for VoIP steganography. In: Proceedings of SPIE conference on the Security, Steganography and Watermarking of Multimedia. pp. 5–12. SPIE (2007)
13. Lin, Y., Wang, R., Yan, D., Dong, L., Zhang, X.: Audio steganalysis with improved convolutional neural network. In: Proceedings of the ACM Workshop on Information Hiding and Multimedia Security, pp. 210–215. ACM (2019)
14. Liu, Q., Sung, A.H., Qiao, M.: Temporal derivative-based spectrum and Mel-cepstrum audio steganalysis. IEEE Trans. Inf. Forensics Secur. **4**(3), 359–368 (2009)
15. Liu, Q., Sung, A.H., Qiao, M.: Derivative-based audio steganalysis. ACM Trans. Multimed. Comput. Commun. Appl. **7**(3), 1–19 (2011)
16. Luo, W., Zhang, Y., Li, H.: Adaptive audio steganography based on advanced audio coding and syndrome-trellis coding. In: Kraetzer, C., Shi, Y.-Q., Dittmann, J., Kim, H.J. (eds.) IWDW 2017. LNCS, vol. 10431, pp. 177–186. Springer, Cham (2017). https://doi.org/10.1007/978-3-319-64185-0_14
17. Ren, Y., Xiong, Q., Wang, L.: A steganalysis scheme for AAC audio based on MDCT difference between intra and inter frame. In: Kraetzer, C., Shi, Y.-Q., Dittmann, J., Kim, H.J. (eds.) IWDW 2017. LNCS, vol. 10431, pp. 217–231. Springer, Cham (2017). https://doi.org/10.1007/978-3-319-64185-0_17
18. Shi, X., Li, B., Tan, S.: Preprocessing layer in spatial steganalysis based on deep learning. J. Appl. Sci. **36**(2), 309–320 (2018)
19. Simonyan, K., Zisserman, A.: Very deep convolutional networks for large-scale image recognition. arXiv preprint arXiv:1409.1556 (2014)
20. Sun, S., Chen, W., Wang, L., Liu, X., Liu, T.Y.: On the depth of deep neural networks: a theoretical view. In: Thirtieth AAAI Conference on Artificial Intelligence, pp. 2066–2072 (2016)
21. Wang, Y., Yang, K., Yang, Y., Zhang, Z., Yi, X., Zhao, X.: Audio steganalysis dataset (2019). https://ieee-dataport.org/documents/audio-steganalysis-dataset
22. Wang, Y., Yang, K., Yi, X., Zhao, X., Xu, Z.: CNN-based steganalysis of MP3 Steganography in the entropy code domain. In: Proceedings of the 6th ACM Workshop on Information Hiding and Multimedia Security, pp. 55–65. ACM (2018)
23. Wu, S., Zhong, S.H., Liu, Y.: Steganalysis via deep residual network. In: 2016 IEEE 22nd International Conference on Parallel and Distributed Systems, pp. 1233–1236. IEEE (2016)
24. Wu, S., Zhong, S., Liu, Y.: Deep residual learning for image steganalysis. Multimed. Tools Appl. **77**(9), 10437–10453 (2017). https://doi.org/10.1007/s11042-017-4440-4
25. Ye, J., Ni, J., Yi, Y.: Deep learning hierarchical representations for image steganalysis. IEEE Trans. Inf. Forensics Secur. **12**(11), 2545–2557 (2017)
26. Zou, M., Li, Z.: A wav-audio steganography algorithm based on amplitude modifying. In: Tenth International Conference on Computational Intelligence and Security, pp. 489–493. IEEE (2014)

Cover-Source Mismatch in Deep Spatial Steganalysis

Xunpeng Zhang[1], Xiangwei Kong[2]([✉]), Pengda Wang[1], and Bo Wang[1]

[1] Dalian University of Technology, Dalian 116081, LN, China
zhangxunpeng@mail.dlut.edu.cn
[2] Zhejiang University, Hangzhou 310058, ZJ, China
kongxiangwei@zju.edu.cn

Abstract. In conventional image steganalysis, cover-source mismatch is a serious problem restricting its utility. In our work, we validate that in deep steganalysis, cover-source mismatch still exists. But unlike in conventional scenarios, sharp accuracy reduction just exists in a part of cover-source mismatch scenarios in deep steganalysis. To explain this phenomenon, we use A-distance to measure the texture complexity between databases. Furthermore, to ease the accuracy reduction caused by the mismatch, we adapt JMMD into deep steganalysis and design a new network (J-Net). Extensive experiments prove A-distance and J-Net works well.

Keywords: Steganalysis · Deep learning · Cover-source mismatch

1 Introduction

Steganography is the technique which embeds information into cover image imperceptibly to carry out secret and safe communication. Steganalysis is the technique to detect the existence of steganography, i.e., to judge whether the image is embedded with secret information. When taking steganalysis into real world, the images you want to detect and the images used to train the steganalysis model always come from different distributions. This phenomenon is called cover-source mismatch, which is a serious problem restricting the utility of steganalysis. In conventional steganalysis, cover-source mismatch always causes sharp accuracy reduction, and there are many researchers focusing on solving it [10,13,15]. In recent years, with the development of deep learning,researchers started to solving steganalysis problem using deep neural networks. But in steganalysis based on deep learning, cover-source mismatch problem has not attracted much attention [4], and there are rare works discussing that. Hence, in this paper we study the cover-source mismatch scenario in deep steganalysis.

At first, we do analysis on cover-source mismatch scenario in deep steganalysis and validate that cover-source mismatch still exists. But not like the scenario in conventional steganalysis, sharp accuracy reduction just exists in a part of situations in deep steganalysis. According to that texture complexity is positively

H. Wang et al. (Eds.): IWDW 2019, LNCS 12022, pp. 71–83, 2020.
https://doi.org/10.1007/978-3-030-43575-2_6

related to the steganalysis difficulty, we think it's caused by the discrepancy of texture complexity among databases. To explain this phenomenon, we adapt A-distance [1] to measure the texture complexity among the databases we use.

Now that there is still cover-source mismatch problem in deep steganalysis, we want to address it. But unlike in conventional steganalysis, deep steganalysis models unify preprocessing, feature extraction and classifying into one framework. So methods for conventional cover-source mismatch can't be used to solve the problem in deep steganalysis. Then inspired by researches in domain adaptation which has similar scenarios as cover-source mismatch, we adapt JMMD [12] into deep steganalysis and design a deep adaptive network (J-Net) to address the cover-source mismatch problem. To our best knowledge, there is no research working for solving this problem in deep steganalysis. And experiments prove that J-Net can relieve the accuracy reduction caused by cover-source mismatch.

The contributions of this paper are concluded as follows :

1. We validate that cover-source mismatch still exists in deep steganalysis, and use A-distance to explain it quantitatively, which is instructive for future works.
2. To ease the accuracy reduction caused by cover-source mismatch, We adapt JMMD into deep steganalysis and design a deep adaptive architecture (J-Net).
3. Extensive experiments prove that J-Net can ease the accuracy reduction caused by cover-source mismatch effectively.

2 Related Works

2.1 Deep Steganalysis

With the impressive performance of deep learning in other fields, scholars started to utilize deep neural networks into steganalysis. In 2015, Qian et al. [18] first adapted CNN (convolutional neural network) to abstract the features used for steganalysis. Based on it, according to the speciality of steganalysis, Xu et al. [21] adjusted the details in CNN layers to promote its performance. Inspired by the idea in conventional steganalysis, Ye-Net [22] adapted selection channel knowledge into deep steganalysis and achieved much better performance than conventional methods. Utilizing the residuals, Fridrich et al. [3] designed a network which can be used both in spacial domain and JPEG domain. Adapting spatial pyramid pooling, Zhu-Net [25] could take images in random sizes as input.

In conventional steganalysis, cover-source mismatch attracted much attention [10,13,15]. But in deep steganalysis, there are rare works discussing it. [4] said mismatch in deep steganalysis is not yet really well treated and understood. And [16] proposed that there is no mismatch phenomenon when using CNNs in steganalysis, but we have found sufficient experimental evidence to prove their conclusion might be ill-considered to some degree.

2.2 Deep Domain Adaptation

Domain adaptation focuses on the problem that how to transfer the model trained on labeled source database to the unlabeled target database without sharp accuracy reduction, where the source and target database have different distributions, which is very similar to the cover-source mismatch scenario in steganalysis. To measure the distance between the source database and the target database, Ben-David et al. [1] proposed A-distance to measure the domain discrepancy. With the development of deep learning, researchers did lots of works about the generality of deep neural networks [2,5,7,24]. Glorot et al. [7] proposed that while deep neural networks are more general than conventional networks, they still can't remove the discrepancy across domain. Furthermore, [24] proposed that the features in deep CNNs will transform from general to specific along the network, i.e, the deeper are the layers, the less transferable are the features.

Based on these theories, scholars further studied how to improve the domain adaptation performance of deep neural networks. VRNN [17] learned temporal dependencies to create domain invariant representations; Madasu et al. [14] designed GCN to filter out domain dependant knowledge; Deng et al. [6] proposed an active transfer learning network to get competitive performance using minimally labeled training data.

Among deep domain adaptation researches, MMD (maximum mean discrepancy) is a very popular tool to restrict the discrepancy between source and target domain. MMD is proposed by [19] to measure the distance between two statistic distributions. In 2012, Chen et al. [20] started to adapt MMD into deep domain adaptation. And Long et al. [11] proposed a variant of MMD called multi-kernel maximum mean discrepancy (M-MMD). Then based on M-MMD, Long et al. [12] proposed JMMD which takes the joint distribution of the input images and the predicted labels into account. Inspired by researches above, we adapt JMMD into deep steganalysis to address cover-source mismatch problem.

3 Methodology

3.1 Analysis of Cover-Source Mismatch in Deep Steganalysis

Steganographies with high concealment always embed information into the high frequency part of the image, which has less probability of being detected by steganalysis [9]. It means that, the texture complexity of database is positively correlated to the steganalysis difficulty [16]. Based on it, we believe that there will be cover-source mismatch when the training set and testing set come from different database with different texture complexity. In experiment part, we prove that in spatial domain, there is sharp accuracy reduction when the steganalysis model is trained on less textured set and tested on more textured set.

To measure the texture complexity among databases, we adapt A-distance [1] to be the measurement tool. Next we give a simple introduction of A-distance.

A-distance is proposed to measure the discrepancy between two databases, which is calculated using the following formula:

$$\hat{d}_A = 2(1 - 2 \times error) \tag{1}$$

where *error* stands for the generalization error of a binary classifier (fully connected layers with 2 outputs here) trained on the binary problem to distinguish input samples between the training and testing database. More implementation details will be given in the experiments part.

Although A-distance is just a linear form of binary classifier, it can be used to measure the discrepancy between 2 databases in the latent space depending on the features used for the classifier. When the features for the classifier in A-distance are features used for steganalysis, the latent space where the discrepancy is measured in A-distance is steganalysis-relevant. Therefore, we think that A-distance can measure the attributes which is relevant to steganalysis between 2 databases, including texture complexity. And the experimental results prove its effectiveness.

3.2 J-Net for Cover-Source Mismatch in Deep Steganalysis

Since there is cover-source mismatch problem in deep steganalysis, we try to ease the accuracy reduction caused by cover-source mismatch. Note that cover-source mismatch in steganalysis is really similar to the scenario in domain adaptation: the model is trained on the labeled source database and tested on the unlabeled target database which is in different distribution with the source. Hence, inspired by the impress performance of JMMD (joint maximum mean discrepancy). [12] in domain adaptation, we adapt it into deep steganalysis and design J-Net (Fig. 1). The structure of J-Net can be divided into four part: preprocessing, feature extraction, classifier and JMMD.

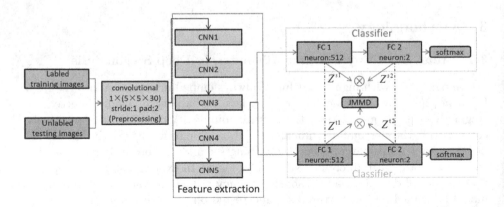

Fig. 1. The structure of J-Net. The dotted line stands for sharing parameters.

As is known to us, the stego signal is always embedded in the high frequency part of image. Hence, to improve the signal to noise ratio (the ratio of stego signal to image signal), we use 30 5×5 high pass filters to preprocess the input images just as Yedroudj-Net [23].

Then the feature extraction part consists of 5 CNN (convolutional neural network) layers. The implementation details of the CNN layers are shown in Table 1. Note that, because the average pooling operation acts as a low pass filter [3] while the stego signal acts as high frequency noise, we get rid of the pooling operation in CNN1. In addition, since in the bottom CNN layers, relatively to image signal, stego signal is very small, ReLU (Rectified Linear Unit) is not suitable for the weak stego signal. Hence, we use TLU (truncate linear unit) [22] as the activation in CNN1 and CNN2. TLU function is defined as:

$$f(x) = \begin{cases} -T, x < -T \\ x, -T \leq x \leq T \\ T, x > T \end{cases} \tag{2}$$

The classifier in J-Net concludes 2 fully connected layers followed with a softmax function which is always used for classifier:

$$y_i = \frac{e^{x_i}}{\sum_{j=1}^{2} e^{x_j}} \tag{3}$$

Note that, the FC layers here have no difference from the fully connected layers in other model. What is special is that, after pre-trained procedure, the FC layers in J-Net will be fine-tuned under the constraint of JMMD.

At last, we use JMMD (joint maximum mean discrepancy) [12] to measure and restrict the discrepancy of features in 2 fully connected layers, separately extracted from the training and testing database which come from different distribution. JMMD measures the distance of P and Q in reproducing kernel Hilbert space (RKHS), which is defined as:

$$D_L(P, Q) \triangleq ||L_{Z^s,1:|L|}(P) - L_{Z^t,1:|L|}(Q)||^2_{\otimes_{l=1}^{|L|} H^l} \tag{4}$$

where P and Q stand for the distribution of the training and testing database respectively, which are called source and target domain respectively here. $L_{Z^s,1:|L|}(P)$ are the features in layer L extracted from P, which are in distribution P, and H represent the reproducing kernel Hilbert space. Assuming that the source domain D_s has labeled n_s points drawn i.i.d from P, while the target domain D_t has n_t unlabeled points drawn i.i.d from Q. The CNN will get features in layer 1 to L as $\{(z_i^{s1}, ..., z_i^{sL})\}_{i=1}^{n_s}$ and $\{(z_i^{t1}, ..., z_i^{tL})\}_{i=1}^{n_t}$. In empirical calculation, we use the estimate of $D_L(P, Q)$, which is defined as :

$$\hat{D}_L(P, Q) = \frac{2}{n} \sum_{i=1}^{n/2} (\prod_{l \in L} k^l(z_{2i-1}^{sl}, z_{2i-1}^{sl}) + \prod_{l \in L} k^l(z_{2i-1}^{tl}, z_{2i-1}^{tl}))$$
$$- \frac{2}{n} \sum_{i=n/2}^{n} (\prod_{l \in L} k^l(z_{2i-1}^{sl}, z_{2i-1}^{sl}) + \prod_{l \in L} k^l(z_{2i-1}^{tl}, z_{2i-1}^{tl})) \tag{5}$$

Table 1. Implementation details of CNNs in J-Net.

CNN1	Convolutional $30 \times (5 \times 5 \times 30)$ stride:1 pad:2
	ABS
	BN
	TLU
CNN2	Convolutional $30 \times (5 \times 5 \times 30)$ stride:1 pad:2
	BN
	TLU
	average_pooling (5×5) stride:2
CNN3	Convolutional $30 \times (3 \times 3 \times 32)$ stride:1 pad:2
	BN
	ReLU
	average_pooling (5×5) stride:2
CNN4	Convolutional $32 \times (3 \times 3 \times 64)$ stride:2 pad:2
	BN
	ReLU
	average_pooling (5×5) stride:2
CNN5	Convolutional $64 \times (3 \times 3 \times 128)$ stride:1 pad:2
	BN
	ReLU
	global_average_pooling (32×32) stride:2

The entire loss function of J-Net is composed of two parts:

$$\min_{f} \frac{2}{n_s} \sum_{i=1}^{n_s} \left(J(f(x_i^s), y_i^s) \right) + \lambda \hat{D}_L(P, Q) \tag{6}$$

where $J(\bullet)$ is classifier loss, $f(x_i)$ represents the predicted output of the input image, $\hat{D}_L(P, Q)$ stands for the JMMD distance between P and Q, in layer L. Note that, in J-Net the features in fc layers are special and less transferable, so L = FC1,FC2 . By minimizing $\hat{D}_L(P, Q)$, the features in FC1 and FC2 can be as similar as possible in the reproducing kernel Hilbert space.

4   Experiment

4.1   Experimental Settings

Database. According to the analysis in Subsect. 3.1, we need textured and less textured database together to conduct experiments. We choose BOSSBase to be the textured database, which contains 10000 512×512 images in pgm format. As mentioned above, cover-source mismatch in steganalysis is a serious problem in

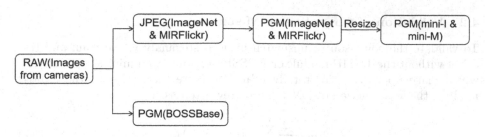

Fig. 2. Database processing programme.

real world, while ImageNet and MIRFlickr are good samples of the real world. Hence, to match the image format and amount of BOSSBase, we randomly select 10000 images from ImageNet and 10000 from MIRFlickr respectively and transform them into pgm format. Then, to maintain the consistency of image size, we resize the images to 512×512. The database composed of 10000 512×512 images in pgm format from ImageNet (MIRFlickr) is called mini-I (mini-M).

Next, based on Fig. 2, we'll utilize a simple inference to illustrate that images in mini-I and mini-M are less textured than images in BOSSBase. As we all known that, the compression from raw format to pgm format is less lossy than the compression from raw format to jpeg format; and the format conversion from jpeg to pgm will bring additional information loss; then the resizing process will further hurt the texture of image. Hence, mini-I and mini-M are less textured than BOSSBase. Note that it's not a serious inference because the images in BOSSBase, ImageNet and MIRFlickr are from different cameras, but we can still think that most images in mini-I and mini-M are less textured than images in BOSSBase (Fig. 3).

Note that, most images in ImageNet and MIRFlickr are smaller than 512×512, so due to the texture hurting, the mini-I and mini-M will be detected with high accuracy. This scenario can not be used in normal steganalysis research, but in our experiments, no matter how we process it, what we need is less textured database. In real world scenario, there will be also many images which are processed in unknown way.

Implementation Details. All the experiments are implemented on pytorch with NVIDIA 1080Ti. And we adopt stochastic gradient descent (SGD) algorithm to update the parameters of J-Net, the learning rate is initialized as 0.001, and multiply 0.9 every 90 epochs. In addition, in all experiments shown in this paper, we use S-UNIWARD [9] and WOW [8] at 0.4 bpp (bits per pixel) as the stegaography methods.

4.2 Validation of Cover-Source Mismatch

To validate the cover-source mismatch in deep steganalysis, we train and test J-Net without the JMMD module on BOSSBase, mini-I and mini-M respectively, which make up 9 scenarios totally (Table 2). Note that, without the JMMD module, the loss function of J-Net can be rewritten as:

$$\min_{f} \frac{2}{n_s} \sum_{i=1}^{n_s} \left(J(f(x_i), y_i) \right) \tag{7}$$

BOSSBase   mini-I   mini-M

Fig. 3. Image samples.

From Table 2, we can see that there is sharp accuracy reduction, when the model is trained on the less textured database (mini-I or mini-M) and tested on the more textured database BOSSBase; while there is little or even no accuracy reduction when using the model trained on BOSSBase to detect mini-I or mini-M. In addition, when using the model trained on mini-I (or mini-M) to test images from mini-M (or mini-I), although there is a little accuracy reduction, the accuracy on test database still reaches upper than 90%.

Unlike the scenario in conventional steganalysis, sharp accuracy reduction just exists in a part of situations in deep steganalysis. This phenomenon may be caused by the strong learning ability of deep neural networks: Since the texture complexity is positively related to the steganlysis difficulty, when trained on textured database, the deep model can learn more intrinsical features for classifier, which can also perform well on less textured database. But how to judge a database is textured or not? In the next part, We use A-distance [1] to measure the texture complexity between databases.

4.3 Texture Complexity Measurement by A-distance

Figure 4 shows that A-distance matches the texture complexity analysis in Subsect. 4.1 and the experimental results above very well, which will be described in detail next:

A-distance between 2 of the 3 databases we use is shown in Fig. 4. Note that in Fig. 4, negative B→I stands for that mini-I is less textured than BOSSBase, and the larger is the absolute value of B→I, the less is the texture similarity of BOSSBase and mini-I. And in the process to get B→I, features used for the classifier are extracted from BOSSBase and mini-I by CNN trained on BOSSBase for steganalysis.

Table 2. Validation of cover-source mismatch (%)

train:BOSSBase			
	BOSSBase	mini-M	mini-I
suni-0.4	81.3	79.9	87.25
wow-0.4	83.323	78.15	85.475
train:mini-M			
	BOSSBase	mini-M	mini-I
suni-0.4	54.425	97.975	94.2
wow-0.4	53.825	97.875	95.675
train:mini-I			
	BOSSBase	mini-M	mini-I
suni-0.4	61.85	93.275	97.325
wow-0.4	63.175	92.45	96.475

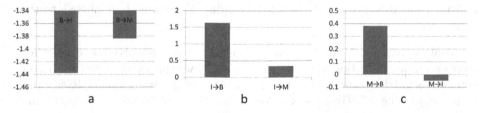

Fig. 4. A-distance among BOSSBase (B), mini-I (I) and mini-M (M).

A-distance in Fig. 4 shows that after the processing programme, mini-I and mini-M are less textured than BOSSBase, which demonstrate the inference in

Subsect. 4.1. It matches the experimental results in Subsect. 4.2 well: there is sharp accuracy reduction when steganalysis model is trained on less textured mini-I (mini-M) and tested on BOSSBase, while there is just little accuracy reduction between mini-I and mini-M which have similar texture complexity. Note that to our best knowledge, there is no research measuring the texture complexity of databases numerically before, we believe that it's instructive for future works.

From experimental results above, we can concluded that not relying on the image content, the cover-source mismatch problem in deep steganalysis is mainly related to the texture complexity of the database, which is very different from mismatch problem in other computer vision fields.

4.4   J-Net for Cover-Source Mismatch in Deep Steganalysis

Table 3. The accuracy promotion of J-Net (%).

train:mini-I test:BOSSBase			
	pre-train	J-Net	promotion
suni-0.4	61.85	68.95	7.1
wow-0.4	63.175	71.2	8.025
train:mini-M test:BOSSBase			
	pre-train	J-Net	promotion
suni-0.4	54.425	63.875	9.45
wow-0.4	53.825	63.725	9.9

At first, it's necessary to introduce the training process of J-Net:

1. Pre-train J-Net on training database without JMMD module, which has been done in Subsect. 4.2;
2. Except full connected layers, fix parameters of J-Net;
3. Fine-tune J-Net with the labeled training images and unlabeled testing images.

Table 3 gives the J-Net experimental results in cover-source scenarios where sharp accuracy reduction happens. From Table 3 we can see that, in these cover-source mismatch scenarios, J-Net can promote the accuracy by 7%–10%, which demonstrate the effectiveness of J-Net. Note that, up to now, this is the first attempt to solve the cover-source mismatch problem in deep steganalysis.

Note that, domain adaptation strategy can only be used in the scenario where the images tested are a set of images. How to address the cover-source mismatch problem when the image tested is a single image will be the future work.

4.5   Parameter Analysis

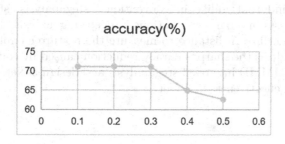

Fig. 5. Analysis of λ in the loss function of J-Net.

In this section, we do analysis on the tradeoff parameter λ in the loss function of J-Net (Fig. 5). The experiment is implemented in the scenario where training and testing set is mini-I and BOSSBase respectively, and the steganography is wow (0.4bpp).

Fig. 5 shows that, along the increasing of λ, the performance of J-Net rise first and then fall, which demonstrates that the adaptation of JMMD makes sense. According to Fig. 5, we fixed all the λ in experiments as 0.2.

Table 4. Experiments in steganography mismatch scenario (%).

train:suni-0.4			
	BOSSBase	mini-I	mini-M
suni-0.4	81.875	97.325	97.975
wow-0.4	78.575	96.275	97.05

train:wow-0.4			
	BOSSBase	mini-I	mini-M
suni-0.4	77.433	97.775	95.375
wow-0.4	83.025	97.925	96.525

4.6   Bonus Experiments

In addition to cover-source mismatch scenario, we do bonus experiments on steganography mismatch scenario (Table 4). Table 4 shows that there is just little accuracy reduction when the training and testing database are embedded with different steganographies. It means that whether the steganography is WOW or S-UNIWARD, J-Net (without JMMD) can learn similar features, which demonstrates the strong learning ability and generality of deep neural network in steganalysis.

5   Conclusion

In this paper, we do analysis on cover-source mismatch scenarios in deep steganalysis, and find that unlike in conventional steganalysis, sharp accuracy reduction just exists in a part of situations in deep steganalysis. To explain this phenomenon, we utilize A-distance to measure the texture complexity between databases. To address the sharp accuracy reduction caused by cover-source mismatch, we adapt JMMD into deep steganalysis and design J-Net. Experimental results prove the effectiveness of J-Net.

References

1. Ben-David, S., Blitzer, J., Crammer, K., Kulesza, A., Pereira, F., Vaughan, J.W.: A theory of learning from different domains. Mach. Learn. **79**(1), 151–175 (2009). https://doi.org/10.1007/s10994-009-5152-4
2. Bengio, Y., Courville, A., Vincent, P.: Representation learning: a review and new perspectives. IEEE Trans. Pattern Anal. Mach. intell. **35**(8), 1798–1828 (2013)
3. Boroumand, M., Chen, M., Fridrich, J.: Deep residual network for steganalysis of digital images. IEEE Trans. Inf. Forensics Secur. **14**(5), 1181–1193 (2018)
4. Chaumont, M.: Deep learning in steganography and steganalysis from 2015 to 2018. arXiv preprint arXiv:1904.01444 (2019)
5. Chen, M., Xu, Z., Weinberger, K., Sha, F.: Marginalized denoising autoencoders for domain adaptation. arXiv preprint arXiv:1206.4683 (2012)
6. Deng, C., Xue, Y., Liu, X., Li, C., Tao, D.: Active transfer learning network: a unified deep joint spectral-spatial feature learning model for hyperspectral image classification. IEEE Trans. Geosci. Remote Sens. **57**(3), 1741–1754 (2018)
7. Glorot, X., Bordes, A., Bengio, Y.: Domain adaptation for large-scale sentiment classification: a deep learning approach. In: Proceedings of the 28th International Conference on Machine Learning (ICML-11), pp. 513–520 (2011)
8. Holub, V., Fridrich, J.: Designing steganographic distortion using directional filters. In: 2012 IEEE International Workshop on Information Forensics and Security (WIFS), pp. 234–239. IEEE (2012)
9. Holub, V., Fridrich, J., Denemark, T.: Universal distortion function for steganography in an arbitrary domain. EURASIP J. Inf. Secur. **2014**(1), 1–13 (2014). https://doi.org/10.1186/1687-417X-2014-1
10. Kodovský, J., Sedighi, V., Fridrich, J.: Study of cover source mismatch in steganalysis and ways to mitigate its impact. In: Media Watermarking, Security, and Forensics 2014, vol. 9028, p. 90280J. International Society for Optics and Photonics (2014)
11. Long, M., Cao, Y., Wang, J., Jordan, M.I.: Learning transferable features with deep adaptation networks. arXiv preprint arXiv:1502.02791 (2015)
12. Long, M., Zhu, H., Wang, J., Jordan, M,I.: Deep transfer learning with joint adaptation networks. In: Proceedings of the 34th International Conference on Machine Learning, vol. 70, pp. 2208–2217. JMLR. org (2017)
13. Lubenko, I., Ker, A.D.: Steganalysis with mismatched covers: Do simple classifiers help? In: Proceedings of the on Multimedia and Security, pp. 11–18. ACM (2012)
14. Madasu, A., Rao, V.A.: Gated convolutional neural networks for domain adaptation. In: Métais, E., Meziane, F., Vadera, S., Sugumaran, V., Saraee, M. (eds.) NLDB 2019. LNCS, vol. 11608, pp. 118–130. Springer, Cham (2019). https://doi.org/10.1007/978-3-030-23281-8_10

15. Pasquet, J., Bringay, S., Chaumont, M.: Steganalysis with cover-source mismatch and a small learning database. In: 2014 22nd European Signal Processing Conference (EUSIPCO), pp. 2425–2429. IEEE (2014)
16. Pibre, L., Pasquet, J., Ienco, D., Chaumont, M.: Deep learning is a good steganalysis tool when embedding key is reused for different images, even if there is a cover sourcemismatch. Electron. Imaging **2016**(8), 1–11 (2016)
17. Purushotham, S., Carvalho, W., Nilanon, T., Liu, Y.: Variational recurrent adversarial deep domain adaptation (2016)
18. Qian, Y., Dong, J., Wang, W., Tan, T.: Deep learning for steganalysis via convolutional neural networks. In: Media Watermarking, Security, and Forensics 2015, vol. 9409, pp. 94090J. International Society for Optics and Photonics (2015)
19. Sejdinovic, D., Sriperumbudur, B., Gretton, A., Fukumizu, K., et al.: Equivalence of distance-based and rkhs-based statistics in hypothesis testing. Ann. Stat. **41**(5), 2263–2291 (2013)
20. Tzeng, E., Hoffman, J., Zhang, N., Saenko, K., Darrell, T.: Deep domain confusion: Maximizing for domain invariance. arXiv preprint arXiv:1412.3474 (2014)
21. Guanshuo, X., Han-Zhou, W., Shi, Y.-Q.: Structural design of convolutional neural networks for steganalysis. IEEE Signal Process. Lett. **23**(5), 708–712 (2016)
22. Ye, J., Ni, J., Yi, Y.: Deep learning hierarchical representations for image steganalysis. IEEE Trans. Inf. Forensics Secur. **12**(11), 2545–2557 (2017)
23. Yedroudj, M., Comby, F., Chaumont, M.: Yedroudj-net: an efficient cnn for spatial steganalysis. In: 2018 IEEE International Conference on Acoustics, Speech and Signal Processing (ICASSP), pp. 2092–2096. IEEE (2018)
24. Yosinski, J., Clune, J., Bengio, Y., Lipson, H.: How transferable are features in deep neural networks? In: Advances in Neural Information Processing Systems, pp. 3320–3328 (2014)
25. Zhang, R., Zhu, F., Liu, J., Liu, G.: Depth-wise separable convolutions and multi-level pooling for an efficient spatial CNN-based steganalysis. IEEE Trans. Inf. Forensics Secur. **15**, 1138–1150 (2019)

Ensemble Steganalysis Based on Deep Residual Network

Qiangjie Li, Guorui Feng$^{(\boxtimes)}$, Hanzhou Wu, and Xinpeng Zhang

School of Communication and Information Engineering,
Shanghai University, Shanghai 200444, China
fgr2082@aliyun.com

Abstract. The performance of the steganography detector built on deep learning has been superior to the traditional feature-based methods, and more adaptive methods for steganalysis are beginning to emerge. However a single model may encounter a bottleneck in classification accuracy due to the absent diversity of training data and parameter configuration, it maybe fails to exert a strong fitting performance of the deep learning network. To make full use of the classification performance of the combination of multiple models, we first obtained multiple base learners from different snapshot and different training sets. Then two strategies to combine multiple base learners: one achieves the optimal ensemble effect by majority voting and product combination, another, in view of the insufficient performance of Softmax classifier, propose a scheme of feature extraction based on convolutional neural network. Experiments show that the ensemble scheme proposed can well fuse the output of multiple convolutional neural networks, thus effectively reduce the detection error rate of a single model.

Keywords: Steganalysis · Ensemble · Feature fusion · Convolutional neural networks

1 Introduction

Steganography is an effective mean to protect the communication security. It embeds information in the communication carrier and then sends it out through public channel without attracting attention of the third party. It pays attention to concealment and security of communication process. Steganalysis, as the confrontation against steganography, aims to determine whether a given object contains secret information, which has important research significance.

The traditional steganalysis adopts machine learning method to extract generalized steganalysis features and combines SVM (support vector machine), neural network and other classifiers to train the general detection model to achieve the detection target of various steganographic algorithms. In the feature construction phase, residual image is often calculated using a high-pass filter, and statistical models are used to extract steganalysis features. Common steganalysis

© Springer Nature Switzerland AG 2020
H. Wang et al. (Eds.): IWDW 2019, LNCS 12022, pp. 84–95, 2020.
https://doi.org/10.1007/978-3-030-43575-2_7

methods of the spatial image include SPAM [16], SRM [4], etc. Early steganalysis of JPEG images followed the principle of constructing features in the embedded domain, usually were based on DCT coefficient to calculate residual and extracting features, such as PEV [17]. Later, JPEG steganalysis constructed residual features by combining phase information in the decompression domain according to characteristics of decompressed signal amplification and block phase, including GFR [19] and MD-CFR [3]. However, with introduction of a series of high-dimensional features represented by rich models, traditional classifiers are no longer applicable due to high training complexity [4]. To address classification problem caused by high-dimensional features, Fridrich et al. proposed an ensemble classifier in 2012, which had become the preferred classifier for processing high-dimensional features since it improved prediction accuracy and reduced training complexity [12].

Recently, scholars have begun to combine steganalysis with deep learning, and use ability of deep learning model to simulate complex representation to achieve the purpose of automatic learning effective feature. The early spatial steganalysis based on CNN model with certain influence was proposed by Qian [18]. The network includes a preprocessing layer, five convolutional layers and three full connection layers in preprocessing layer. The fixed KV kernel (Eq. (9) in [11]) is used to obtain the residual image for subsequent learning and reduce interference of the image content. XuNet [22] was the first architecture with competitive performance, where in the front part of network, the absolute value layer and TanH activation were used, and batch normalization [10] and 1×1 convolution were used to compress feature map as well. In addition, YeNet proposed in [15] used 30 SRM convolution kernels to initialize parameters and used TLU and ReLU activation functions in network. The newly proposed SRNet [1] has achieved better results in both spatial and JPEG domains. SRNet is an end-to-end CNN steganalysis model. The network does not perform pre-processing (learning filters) and only subsamples feature map from the first seven convolutional blocks. To avoid problem of disappearing gradients, layers 2–11 use shortcut mechanism [7].

In order to enable deep learning to play a good role in JPEG domain, scholars have made many adaptive modifications to CNN model. Chen et al. [2] and Xu et al. [20] introduced deep learning into steganalysis of JPEG images in 2017. Chen et al. [2] used traditional JPEG steganalysis idea for reference, and trained different convolutional neural network models based on different phases of JPEG images. Xu et al. [20] proposed a 20-layer deep convolutional neural network to detect J-UNIWARD steganography method [9], and used residual structure to solve vanishing gradient problem. The latest end-to-end network-SRNet [1] can also be used for steganalysis of JPEG domain images with leading results.

In following work [21], they proposed several different collection methods, which use two CNN structures with different widths, called "size 128" and "size 256". Experiments show the best one in S-UNIWARD 0.4 bpp with a detection error of 18.44%. Inspired by Xu et al. [21] and Ni et al. [14], classification performance of ensemble method is often better than that of a single model.

Therefore, we utilize ensemble learning for better performance. In this paper, we build multiple classifiers based on current best end-to-end model SRNet [1], and use the following methods to maximize classification accuracy. Experimental results show that our method achieves better classification accuracy than SRNet model in both spatial domain and JPEG domain.

First of all, we obtain multiple base learners from different training snapshots and different training data. On this basis, we adopt two methods to optimize the classification accuracy: 1. Collected decision output of all models and ensemble multiple models based on majority voting and product combination. 2. As a powerful feature extractor, convolutional neural network is better than most hand-designed traditional feature classifiers. Traditional steganalysis is usually classified by ensemble FLD classifier [12], which can automatically select feature and has good detection performance. The paper proposes to take output of the last convolution module of convolutional neural network as feature, then fuse all feature of base learner into a new complex feature, finally, let the ensemble classifier complete the classification task as the second-level classifier.

The rest of this paper is organized as follows. In Sect. 2, we review the benchmark CNN for ensemble. How to extract base models and two combination strategies are shown in Sect. 3. In Sect. 4, we present the experimental settings and results. Finally, a conclusion is given in Sect. 5.

2   The Framework of SRNet

The proposed ensemble methods require the base learner to be built by SRNet [1], which has been the state-of-the-art model in steganalysis filed. Therefore, we will briefly review architecture and novel tricks of SRNet.

The overall structure of SRNet proposed by [1] is similar to CNN framework for universal image recognition: the first part extracts the features of residual noise; the second part reduces dimensionality of feature maps to extract more advanced semantic features; the third part classifies dimensionality reduction features extracted. Different from previous CNN steganalysis framework, SRNet is a complete end-to-end network, which does not contain any heuristic and prior information like fixed preprocessing high pass filter or SRM [4] kernel used to initialize convolution kernel. SRNet randomly initializes and learns its own filter kernel.

The overall structure of SRNet is shown in Fig. 1, which has 12 layers of convolutional blocks. Generally, it can be classified into four types, 256×256 gray scale images are directly input into network, Types 1-2 (Layers 1-7) completes extraction of low-level features of steganographic signals, Type 3 and Type 4 reduce dimension of feature maps. Finally, the combination of a fully connected layer and Softmax layer achieves linear classification. It should be noted that in order to extract sufficient residual noise features, network disallows average pooling in feature extraction stage (Type 1-2), because average pooling will filter implicit residual signal as a low-pass filter. SRNet introduces shortcut connections [7] for Type 2 and Type 3 to ease disappearance of gradients and encourage feature reuse. In addition, the nonlinear activation function adopted is ReLU, and the size of convolution kernel of all convolution modules is 3×3.

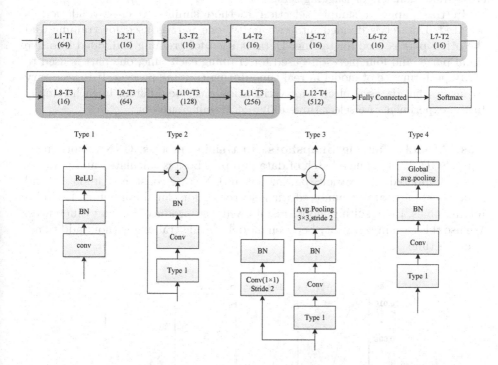

Fig. 1. Framework of SRNet. L1-T1 represents Layer 1-Type 1. BN represents batch normalization. The number in the brackets is the number of 3×3 kernels in convolutional layers.

3　Ensemble Learning

In machine learning, we usually want to train a model with the stable and good performance in all aspects. However, the performance of a single model is often not perfect, and we can only obtain multiple models with advantages and disadvantages. Through ensemble learning, multiple models are combined to improve classification accuracy.

3.1　Extract Base Models

Base Models Varying Training Data. One way to realize the difference between models is to train each model on a different subset of available training data. By using re-sampling methods (such as cross-validation and Bagging), different subsets of training data are naturally trained into model to obtain the models with different weights. This method aims to estimate average performance of model for data not seen in general. The models used in this estimation process can be combined in so-called resampling-based sets, such as cross-validation sets or Bagging sets.

In this paper, a sample selection method similar to cross-validation is adopted. Dataset is divided into two parts, one part is used for training and the other part is used for testing. Dataset used for training is divided into five equal parts, and four pieces are used for training each time, one part is used to verify performance of model in real time during training process. It is necessary to ensure that dataset selected for verification must be different in each sample. In the experiment, we select three different training subsets.

Base Models Varying Snapshots. In training process, CNN adopts mini-batch SGD. Every time a batch of data is input, Loss is calculated and parameters are updated. The various parameters in CNN are constantly updated, and many local parts are encountered when searching for global minimum. The minimum values, the resulting model results will also produce different differences. We use this to gain versatility between models during training without additional training time.

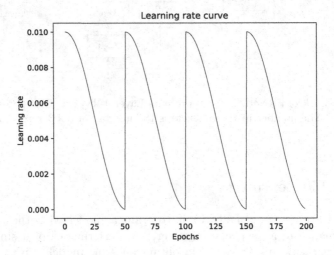

Fig. 2. Learning rate cycling procedure

In fact, the idea was implemented by Huang et al. [5] in 2017, which obtains multiple neural network models by manipulating learning rate without additional training costs. Generally speaking, learning rate represents optimization step of SGD. Adjusting learning rate can make model converge to different local minimum. It saves weight of each local minimum for subsequent ensemble. Specifically, it adopts cyclic attenuation strategy proposed by Loshchilov [13], in which learning rate is cyclically attenuated in the form of cosine function (see Fig. 2), and the sudden increase of learning rate can make model escape from the current local minimum.

Cyclic cosine annealing can be expressed as

$$\alpha(t) = \frac{\alpha_0}{2}\left(\cos\left(\frac{\pi \bmod (t-1, \lceil T/M \rceil)}{\lceil T/M \rceil}\right) + 1\right)$$ (1)

where t is the current number of training iterations, T is the total number of training iterations and $\alpha(t)$ is the current learning rate. In the experiment, we set $M=8$ and $T=400$, that is, complete a cosine attenuation every $400/8 = 50$ epochs. In order to converge sufficiently, this parameter($\lceil T/M \rceil$) increases with the size of training set. At the end of the loop we select the last $m=5$ base models for the subsequent ensemble.

3.2   Combination Strategy

How to make full use of $N = 3 \times 5$ base model obtained in previous section, we propose two methods to fully fuse the obtained 15 models. The first method is to combine the decision output of each CNN model. Another method is to fuse the output of the last layer of the convolutional layer of each model, and finally input the ensemble classifier [12] for the feature classification. Thanks to the excellent classification performance of ensemble classifier [12], the final ensemble result is competitive.

Decision Combination. For classification tasks, ensemble learning will predict a new result in combination with the category labels of all sub-classifiers. In this paper, two schemes are used to combine the decision results of neural network, namely majority voting and product combination.

Majority Voting. The most common combination strategy is the voting. Due to the steganalysis is a binary classification task, we have N base learners mentioned above, and the classification labels have two categories, h_i is the i-th learner. The predictor output of h_i on sample x is represented as a two-dimensional vector $[h_i^0(x), h_i^1(x)]$, plurality voting can be expressed as:

$$H(x) = c_{\arg\max} \sum_{i=1}^{N} h_i^j(x)$$ (2)

where $h_i^j(x)$ is the decision output of h_i on sample x, $j \in \{0,1\}$, $h_i^j(x) \in \{0,1\}$.

Product Combination. Except for majority voting, there is another decision combination strategy: product combination rule. Suppose a data sample $x \in \mathcal{R}^n$, label class is $\omega_j, j = 1, 2..., C$. For steganalysis task, $C = 2$. The Softmax output of the $N = 15$ models introduced in the previous section can be described as:

$$P(y = \omega_j | X = x) = \frac{e^{f_k^j(x)}}{\sum_{c=1}^{C} e^{f_k^c(x)}}$$ (3)

where $f_k(x)$ is the output from the last layer of the neural network for k-th model, $f_k^j(x)$ is the score corresponding to j-th label, and $P(y = \omega_j | X = x)$ is the predicted probability for data x in class ω_j.

In this experiment, the product combination rule for steganalysis can be described as:

$$H(x) = \begin{cases} 0, \prod_{k=1}^{15} P(\omega_0|x) > \prod_{k=1}^{15} P(\omega_1|x) \\ 1, \text{ otherwise} \end{cases} \tag{4}$$

where ω_0 and ω_1 represent cover and stego respectively.

Algorithm 1. Selective decision combination

Input: N base learners
Output: detection error rates on the testing set
1: **for** $i = 1$ to N **do**
2:     **for** $l = 1$ to C_N^i **do**
3:         Calculate error rates of every combinations of classifier on training set
4:     **end for**
5: **end for**
6: Select the combination whose error rate is the lowest, then test on the testing set

---

It has been proved that not all base classifiers participate in ensemble learning is best, therefore we compare detection error rates of all the combinations using two decision combination on training set to obtain the best combination. For we choose i models from N models ($i = 1, 2, 3, ..., N$), there are total $C_N^1 + C_N^2 + ... + C_N^N = 2^N - 1$ combinations, then the best combination whose ensemble detection error rates is lowest on training set will be selected to be tested on the testing set. The method above can be expressed as Algorithm 1.

Feature Fusion. The deep learning model has the nonlinear function approximation ability unmatched by the support vector machine, and can extract and express the characteristics of the data well. The essence of the deep learning model is the feature learner. However, the combined classifier with full connection and Softmax in CNN is often difficult to achieve the desired effect in terms of independent processing classification and regression.

In order to make full use of the features of multiple base learners extracted in the previous section, we use ensemble classifier proposed in [12] to replace the combined classifier with full connection and Softmax. Zhong proposed a similar method [23]: CNN is used to extract features and ensemble classifier in [12] is considered as the second-level classifier. In this paper, the output of the last convolutional layer of every CNN models is fused into a new multi-dimensional feature, and then the high-dimensional feature is classified by the ensemble classifier [12] commonly used in steganalysis. For feature fusion strategy, this paper adopts two fusion strategies: serial fusion and parallel fusion.

Suppose a data sample $x \in \mathcal{R}^n$, the 15 models introduced in the previous section are $D_1, D_2, ...D_{15}$, the 512-dims feature of each model can be described as: $\boldsymbol{v}_x^k = \left[v_{x,1}^k, v_{x,2}^k, \cdots, v_{x,512}^k \right]^{\mathrm{T}}, k = 1, 2, ...15$, and two fusion strategies can be described as follows:

Serial fusion

$$v_x = \begin{pmatrix} \alpha v_x^{1\,\mathrm{T}} \\ \beta v_x^{2\,\mathrm{T}} \\ \cdots \\ \gamma v_x^{15\,\mathrm{T}} \end{pmatrix}^{\mathrm{T}} \tag{5}$$

Parallel fusion

$$\boldsymbol{v} = \left(\alpha \boldsymbol{v}_x^1 + \beta \boldsymbol{v}_x^2 + ... + \gamma \boldsymbol{v}_x^{15} \right)^{\mathrm{T}} \tag{6}$$

In addition, due to the different ways of feature extraction, the values of the features are not balanced. In this case, the features need to be normalized. The normalization of the features of this subsection is normalized by the L2 norm defined by

$$\mathrm{norm}\ \left(v_x^k \right) = \sqrt{ \left(v_{x,1}^k \right)^2 + \left(v_{x,2}^k \right)^2 + \cdots + \left(v_{x,n}^k \right)^2 }$$

$$\boldsymbol{v}_x^{\prime k} = \frac{\boldsymbol{v}_x^k}{\mathrm{norm}\ \left(\boldsymbol{v}_x^k \right)}, k = 1, 2, ..., 15 \tag{7}$$

Feature fusion can derive and obtain the most effective and minimal dimension feature vector set, which is conducive to final decision-making. Besides ensemble FLD classifier can further utilize the fused high-dimensional features.

4   Experiments

4.1   Dataset and Settings

In this experiment, the base model SRNet is implemented by TensorFlow, which is tested on spatial domain steganography algorithm WOW [8] and JPEG domain steganography algorithm J-UNIWARD [9] respectively. The embedding rate used is 0.2 bpp and 0.4 bpp (bpnzac for J-UNIWARD). In terms of data set, we used BOSSBase v1.01 image set commonly used in this field which consists of 10,000 512×512 grayscale images. Limited to Nvidia GTX 1080Ti memory capacity of this experimental hardware platform, we adjust the 512×512 size grayscale image to 256×256 using "imresize" with default setting in Matlab. For the spatial domain image, we directly use WOW steganography algorithm to embed secret information to obtain stego image. For the transform domain image, first use JPEG toolbox to compress 10,000 grayscale images into JPEG images with a quality factor of 75, then use J-UNIWARD (Abbr. JUNI) [9] algorithm to embed secret information, and finally decompress 10,000 pairs of cover-stego pairs into the spatial domain. Note that the integer is not rounded when decompressing.

We compose the original and stego images into image pairs, a total of 10,000 pairs, and guaranteed that the pairs were input into CNN. 5,000 pairs are randomly divided into training sets, and the remaining 5,000 pairs are testing sets, which do not participate in training during the training process. In order to obtain multiple different training sets, the training set is further divided into five subsets, four for training and one for testing.

For hyper parameters, we set epoch $= 400$, and the learning rate adopted the cyclic cosine attenuation mentioned in Eq. 1, $\alpha_0 = 0.002$, $M = 8$ and every $400/8 = 50$ epochs to complete a complete cosine attenuation, and we took the last five models to complete the ensemble experiment. The kernel weights were initialized with the He initializer [6] and 2×10^4 L2 regularization. Eight pairs of images are used as a batch, and the model is saved every 10 epochs, but after each epoch, the training set will be shuffled for training.

4.2   Result and Discussion

We obtain $N = 3 \times 5 = 15$ base models through snapshot ensemble and Bagging, for the $N = 15$ base models, we implement the two combination strategies mentioned in Sect. 3.2. First, according to Algorithm 1, the output probabilities of each base model are extracted and combined, and finally the optimal classification results are selected. According to feature fusion strategy, the 512-dimensional features of the last convolutional block output of each base model are fused into a more complex feature as the input of ensemble classifier. The ensemble classifier will select the different combination of feature to obtain better performance of classification like selective ensemble. Finally, we compare results of different ensemble scenarios. We use the average error rate P_E to evaluate the performance.

$$P_E = \min_{P_{FA}} \frac{1}{2} \left(P_{FA} + P_{MD} \right) \tag{8}$$

where P_{FA} and P_{MD} are the false-alarm and missed-detection probabilities.

Figure 3 shows the comparison of two selective decision combination schemes: majority voting and product combination. Considering different schemes and payload, selective decision combination has low error rates when product combination is used. Table 1 shows results of steganalysis for spatial steganography algorithm WOW and JPEG steganography algorithm J-UNIWARD, respectively. SRNet represents steganalysis error rates of SRNet run by ourselves. Product-Sel indicates the results of selective product combination, SF-EC represents serial feature fusion with ensemble FLD classifier, namely the classification of 512×15-dimensional serial feature classified by traditional ensemble FLD classifier, PF-EC represents parallel feature fusion with ensemble FLD classifier. From results of the table we can conclude that the results of two combination strategies are always better than the best results of a single model. Overview the table, feature fusion performs best in classification. More specifically, SF-EC

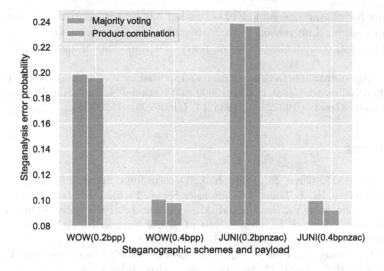

Fig. 3. Steganalysis error rates comparison of different ensemble scenarios

and PF-EC perform best in WOW and J-UNIWARD algorithms, respectively. This means that serial feature fusion and parallel feature fusion have their own applicable scenarios. In addition, feature fusion is more effective than decision combination, compared to results of SRNet, and an improvement of up to 1.35% is observed.

Table 1. Detection errors of different ensemble scenarios

Steganalysis method	WOW		JUNI	
	0.2 bpp	0.4 bpp	0.2 bpnzac	0.4 bpnzac
SRNet	0.2007	0.1074	0.2431	0.0995
Product-Sel	0.1960	0.0984	0.2380	0.0924
SF-EC	**0.1872**	**0.0945**	0.2367	0.0948
PF-EC	0.1878	0.0951	**0.2308**	**0.0887**

5 Conclusion

In this paper, we study several ensemble strategies based on SRNet, which is the state-of-the-art for steganalysis. We first use two methods to obtain multiple base learners. Cyclic cosine decay strategy can manipulate learning rate to obtain multiple models in iterative process, and then use Bagging to obtain multiple models trained by different data. Multiple base models are combined by decision combination and feature fusion. Experiments show that two combination strategies can often perform better than any single classifier, alternatively the feature fusion and ensemble FLD classifier has better performance than decision combination. The reason is that ensemble classifier is more effective than Softmax in dealing with classification, regression and other issues independently.

Acknowledgement. This work was partly supported by the Natural Science Foundation of Shanghai under Grant 19ZR1419000 and National Natural Science Foundation of China under Grants 61902235, U1936214, U1636206, 61525203.

References

1. Boroumand, M., Chen, M., Fridrich, J.: Deep residual network for steganalysis of digital images. IEEE Trans. Inf. Forensics Secur. **14**(5), 1181–1193 (2019)
2. Chen, M., Sedighi, V., Boroumand, M., Fridrich, J.: JPEG-phase-aware convolutional neural network for steganalysis of JPEG images. In: ACM Workshop on Information Hiding & Multimedia Security (2017)
3. Feng, G., Zhang, X., Ren, Y., Qian, Z., Li, S.: Diversity-based cascade filters for jpeg steganalysis. IEEE Trans. Circ. Syst. Video Technol. (2019)
4. Fridrich, J., Kodovsky, J.: Rich models for steganalysis of digital images. IEEE Trans. Inf. Forensics Secur. **7**(3), 868–882 (2012)
5. Gao, H., Li, Y., Pleiss, G., Zhuang, L., Hopcroft, J.E., Weinberger, K.Q.: Snapshot ensembles: Train 1, get m for free (2017)
6. He, K., Zhang, X., Ren, S., Sun, J.: Delving deep into rectifiers: surpassing human-level performance on imagenet classification. In: Proceedings of the IEEE International Conference on Computer Vision, pp. 1026–1034 (2015)
7. He, K., Zhang, X., Ren, S., Sun, J.: Deep residual learning for image recognition. In: 2016 IEEE Conference on Computer Vision and Pattern Recognition (CVPR), pp. 770–778. IEEE, Las Vegas, June 2016
8. Holub, V., Fridrich, J.: Designing steganographic distortion using directional filters. In: IEEE International Workshop on Information Forensics & Security (2012)
9. Holub, V., Fridrich, J.: Digital image steganography using universal distortion. In: Proceedings of the First ACM Workshop on Information Hiding and Multimedia Security - IH&MMSec 2013, p. 59. ACM Press, Montpellier (2013)
10. Ioffe, S., Szegedy, C.: Batch normalization: accelerating deep network training by reducing internal covariate shift. In: International Conference on International Conference on Machine Learning (2015)
11. Kodovsky, J., Fridrich, J., Holub, V.: On dangers of overtraining steganography to incomplete cover model. In: Proceedings of the Thirteenth ACM Multimedia Workshop on Multimedia and Security, pp. 69–76. ACM (2011)
12. Kodovsky, J., Fridrich, J., Holub, V.: Ensemble classifiers for steganalysis of digital media. IEEE Trans. Inf. Forensics Secur. **7**(2), 432–444 (2012)
13. Loshchilov, I., Hutter, F.: SGDR: Stochastic gradient descent with restarts (2017)
14. Ni, D., Feng, G., Shen, L., Zhang, X.: Selective ensemble classification of image steganalysis via deep Q network. IEEE Signal Process. Lett. **26**(7), 1065–1069 (2019)
15. Ni, J., Jian, Y., Yang, Y.I.: Deep learning hierarchical representations for image steganalysis. IEEE Trans. Inf. Forensics Secur. **12**(11), 1 (2017)
16. Pevny, T., Bas, P., Fridrich, J.: Steganalysis by subtractive pixel adjacency matrix. IEEE Trans. Inf. Forensics Secur. **5**(2), 215–224 (2010)

17. Pevny, T., Fridrich, J.: Merging Markov and DCT features for multi-class JPEG steganalysis. In: Security, Steganography, and Watermarking of Multimedia Contents IX (2007)
18. Qian, Y., Dong, J., Wang, W., Tan, T.: Deep learning for steganalysis via convolutional neural networks. In: Media Watermarking, Security, and Forensics 2015, vol. 9409, p. 94090J. International Society for Optics and Photonics (2015)
19. Song, X., Liu, F., Yang, C., Luo, X., Yi, Z.: Steganalysis of adaptive JPEG steganography using 2D Gabor filters. In: ACM Workshop on Information Hiding & Multimedia Security (2015)
20. Xu, G.: Deep convolutional neural network to detect J-UNIWARD. In: ACM Workshop on Information Hiding & Multimedia Security (2017)
21. Xu, G., Wu, H.Z., Shi, Y.Q.: Ensemble of CNNS for steganalysis: an empirical study. In: ACM Workshop on Information Hiding & Multimedia Security (2016)
22. Xu, G., Wu, H.Z., Shi, Y.Q.: Structural design of convolutional neural networks for steganalysis. IEEE Signal Process. Lett. **23**(5), 708–712 (2016)
23. Zhong, K., Feng, G., Shen, L., Luo, J.: Deep learning for steganalysis based on filter diversity selection. Sci. China Inf. Sci. **61**(12), 129105 (2018)

Digital Forensics and Anti-forensics

Weakly Supervised Adaptation to Re-sizing for Image Manipulation Detection on Small Patches

Ludovic Darmet[✉] ⓘ, Kai Wang ⓘ, and François Cayre ⓘ

Univ. Grenoble Alpes, CNRS, Grenoble INP, GIPSA-lab, Grenoble, France
{ludovic.darmet,kai.wang,francois.cayre}@gipsa-lab.grenoble-inp.fr

Abstract. Basic image processing operations like median filtering and Gaussian blurring in general do not change the semantic content of an image, although they are commonly used to cover fingerprints of falsification that does alter image content such as copy-move and splicing. Therefore image forensics researchers are interested in detecting these basic operations. Some existing detectors track local inconsistencies in statistics of the image. However these statistics are very sensitive to image development process. Thus pre-processing operations can be damaging for performances of such detectors. In this paper, we focus on a very common pre-processing operation, *i.e.*, re-sizing, and study how it affects performance when trying to detect several image processing operations on small patches, with Gaussian Mixture Model (GMM) as feature extractor and a Dense Neural Network (DNN) as classifier. We first show performance drops. We then introduce an adaptation method which relies on better fit to testing data for the feature extraction and fine-tuning for the neural network classifier. Experimental results show that our method is able to improve results with very few labeled testing samples. We also present comparisons with an improved version of a recent CNN(Convolutional Neural Network)-based method.

Keywords: Image forensics · Gaussian Mixture Model · Neural network · Feature adaptation · Weakly supervised · Fine-tuning

1 Introduction

Digital images now play a more and more important role in our decision-making processes of daily life, either personal or professional. However, people can be misled by falsified images which can now be created very easily even by non-experts. Under this context, it is necessary to build reliable tools to assess integrity of an image and to tell whether it is falsified or not. This is indeed the goal of image forensics research. In this work, we focus on a specific forensic problem, *i.e.*, the detection of basic image processing operations on very small patches of 8×8 pixels. Basic operations, *e.g.*, Gaussian blurring, median filtering and noise addition, are often used during the creation of a fake image to cover

H. Wang et al. (Eds.): IWDW 2019, LNCS 12022, pp. 99–114, 2020.
https://doi.org/10.1007/978-3-030-43575-2_8

the traces of falsifications that do change the semantic meaning of the image. Detection of such operations on very small patches of 8×8 pixels is challenging due to lack of information, but can make it possible to reliably detect operations applied within a small spatial extent.

In an image development process it is quite common to re-size an image to fit some layout or displaying constraints or else to reduce storage. So this operation is not suspicious in general, as it is a realistic scenario to assume that an image could have been re-sized before being manipulated. This pre-processing operation should not harm performances of forensic detectors. It is not practical to assume that a sufficiently large number of labeled samples are available to re-train models from scratch. From a computing time and power perspective it would be exhaustive and very demanding to perform many times of re-training. A similar issue has been raised in [11] in the field of computer vision, which underlines the importance and benefit of being able to train a model when incomplete or only few labeled samples are available. Training with few labeled samples is also called "few-shot learning" in the machine learning literature [15,16]. In digital image forensics, recently authors of [4] have proposed an interesting method to tackle a related yet different problem of weakly supervised learning. Both considered problem and adopted approach are different from ours. Classifier in [4] is able to distinguish synthetic images from natural ones, and the "target" domain means a new class of samples (*e.g.*, tested on synthetic images created by a new algorithm). The good performance under weakly supervised scenario is mainly due to the design of disentangled latent variables in an auto-encoder-based detector. In this paper, we propose a new and different weakly supervised approach for a classifier based on image statistical models, for the forensics of manipulations on images which have undergone re-sizing pre-processing. In the related field of steganalysis, researchers have expressed some concerns about similar issues of performance drop under the so-called cover-source mismatch [7–9]. In general, popular solutions in steganalysis are to train a classifier with more samples of big diversity, or to train multiple classifiers and later use the most suitable one during specific testing. By contrast, in this paper, we propose a light-weight *adaptation* method to image pre-processing for the detection of basic manipulation operations. Our contributions are summarized as follows:

- We raise the problem of forensic performance drop under re-sizing pre-processing, which until now seems ignored and underestimated;
- For image statistical models that have been trained on samples of original size, we develop a simple *weakly supervised* (making use of around 2000 labeled patches) adaptation method to re-sized testing samples;
- Our method takes into account both feature and classifier adaptation and is very quick and straightforward so as to provide a real shortcut.

We will first introduce in Sect. 2 the research problem. Our approach of weakly supervised adaptation is described in Sect. 3. Experimental results are presented in Sect. 4. Finally, we draw the conclusion in Sect. 5.

2   Background and Research Problem

Image Forensics. Various problems have been considered by image foren-sics researchers [12], such as camera identification [2], identification of synthetic images [4,14], detection of falsification such as splicing and copy-move [3,17], and detection of image manipulation [1,5,10,13]. We are interested in the last topic of detecting image manipulations. Here we distinguish between falsifications, *i.e.*, modifications that alter the semantic content of the image, and *manipulations*, *i.e.*, modifications with basic image processing operations which in general do not change the image's semantic meaning. Regarding manipulation detection, in the literature researchers first focused on building specific and targeted detec-tor for one particular manipulation, *e.g.*, median filtering, JPEG compression, *etc.* Then after achieving successful results with these methods, the community tried to build so-called "universal" detectors. They are detectors not focusing on one particular operation but capable of detecting several ones with same anal-ysis pipeline. Our work follows this trend. Existing universal detectors can be classified into three categories:

1. Explicit statistical modeling of the image (using the Gaussian Mixture Model, GMM) to spot statistical discrepancy [5];
2. Extraction of steganalytic features, *e.g.*, based on SPAM (Subtractive Pixel Adjacency Matrix) or SRM (Spatial Rich Model), combined with classifier training [10,13];
3. "End-to-end" deep-learning-based method [1].

As mentioned earlier, we consider that it is crucial to be able to forensically analyze very small patches, so as to be spatially more accurate and capable of detecting manipulation of a very small region. This has driven us to focus on the first GMM-based approach mentioned above [5], as it appears to be the most promising method for very small patches. The explicit statistical model-ing can be effectively conducted on patches of 8×8 pixels [5], while the other two approaches, as described in their original papers [1,10,13], work on larger patches. These two approaches seem not specifically designed to cope very well with small patches. In particular, the second approach involves an occurrence accumulation step which is more reliable with more contributing pixels, and tends to have decreasing accuracy as the size of patch decreases [10,13]; and CNNs in the third approach [1] normally contain pooling layers, which would cause loss of information and thus is not necessarily very suitable for small patches.

Performance Drop Under Re-sizing. Considered manipulations are bor-rowed from [5] and listed in Table 1. Most of these manipulations are also used in [1], but here we consider a slightly more challenging setting (*i.e.*, distortion introduced by manipulation is smaller) than that in [1]. We decide to focus on these basic operations as they are among the most common in image processing. Moreover, they can be used to cover more complex tampering. For instance,

Table 1. List of considered manipulations.

ORI	No image modification
GF	Gaussian filtering with 3×3 kernel and $\sigma = 0.5$
MF	Median filtering with window size of 3×3
USM	Unsharp masking with Laplacian filter of window size 3×3 and strength factor of 0.5
WGN	White Gaussian noise addition with $\sigma = 2$
JPEG	JPEG compression with quality factor $Q = 90$

Table 2. Testing accuracy (in %) without any adaptation for GMM-based method using log-likelihood ratio (details in Sect. 3.1). The first column gives the re-sizing factors. The performance drop compared to the case without re-sizing (*i.e.*, the row of ×1) is given in parentheses. We do not use ratios like 0.5 to avoid the potential special side effect of such ratios. The last column of "AVG" gives the average accuracy and performance drop of the 5 classification problems.

	GF	MF	USM	WGN	JPEG	AVG
×1	91	86	97	98	89	92
×0.51	64 (−27)	75 (−11)	73 (−24)	69 (−29)	79 (−10)	72 (−20)
×0.76	78 (−13)	81 (−5)	81 (−16)	73 (−25)	84 (−5)	79 (−13)
×1.15	55 (−36)	80 (−6)	87 (−10)	85 (−13)	79 (−10)	77 (−15)
×1.25	51 (−40)	75 (−11)	74 (−23)	81 (−17)	67 (−22)	70 (−22)

one can use Gaussian blurring to smooth boundary between a spliced part and the rest of an image. In the following, "source" indicates training samples that have not undergone re-sizing. "Target" means the testing samples which have undergone re-sizing before applying a possible manipulation that we want to detect. This study is interested in the impact of image re-sizing as *pre-processing* operations on detection of image manipulations. Bi-cubic interpolation is used to re-size testing images as, in general, it is the hardest case for carrying out successful adaptation. Drops of detection accuracy of the GMM-based method, when there is no adaptation, can be observed in Table 2. From this table, we can also see that the method works quite well on 8×8 patches of images of original size, with an average accuracy of about 92%. However, the performance drop, when there is re-sizing pre-processing, is sometimes quite significant.[1] This has motivated our work of detector adaptation presented in the next section.

---

[1] As shown in Sect. 4, performance decrease also exists for CNN-based method [1].

3 Proposed Approach

3.1 Classification Pipeline

Our pipeline is largely inspired by the method of Fan *et al.* [5] as it is one of the state-of-the-art methods for detecting manipulations on small patches. Firstly Gaussian Mixture Models (GMMs) are trained, one for each set of patches (original, Gaussian filtered, median filtered, *etc.*), six models in total (see Table 1). Models are trained to maximize likelihood on patches with the Expectation-Maximization (EM) algorithm. Log-likelihood for sample x_l under a mixture of N Gaussian components, parameterized by $\theta = \{\pi_k, \mu_k, \Sigma_k\}, k=1,2,...,N$, is:

$$\mathcal{L}(x_l|\theta) = \log \left(\sum_{k=1}^{N} \pi_k \mathcal{N}(x_l|\mu_k, \Sigma_k) \right), \qquad (1)$$

with π_k, μ_k and Σ_k respectively the weight, mean and multivariate (full) covariance matrix for k^{th} component in the mixture. Here DC component of each patch is removed so patch mean is 0 thus μ_k are all zeros. After the GMMs are trained, a very quick and efficient technique to produce a decision for a testing sample is to compute log-likelihood for each GMM and compare these values. In the case of binary classification, it means calculating the log-likelihood ratio between the GMM of manipulated patches and that of original patches [5], as:

$$r(x_l) = \frac{\mathcal{L}_{GMM_{manip}}(x_l)}{\mathcal{L}_{GMM_{ori}}(x_l)}. \qquad (2)$$

If the ratio $r(x_l) > 1$ then the decision should be that sample patch x_l is a manipulated one, otherwise it is original.

In the first step of EM (E step), we need to compute component scores which are likelihood values with regard to each Gaussian component in the GMM:

$$r_k^{(l)} = \pi_k \mathcal{N}(x_l|\mu_k, \Sigma_k). \qquad (3)$$

We notice that these component scores form a more detailed descriptor than the log-likelihood value for patch x_l. Therefore in this paper we propose to use them as features to feed a classifier. For binary classification, the $2N$-dimensional feature vector $(r_{1,ori}^{(l)}, r_{2,ori}^{(l)}, \ldots, r_{N,ori}^{(l)}, r_{1,manip}^{(l)}, r_{2,manip}^{(l)}, \ldots, r_{N,manip}^{(l)})$ of patch sample x_l is a concatenation of component scores of the two trained GMMs under comparison, each having N components. We use a small Dense Neural Network (DNN) as classifier whose architecture is described in Sect. 4. As expected, experiments show that performances of baseline scenario (*i.e.*, when testing samples are not re-sized) are almost identical to the detector based on log-likelihood ratio. In the following we propose a weakly supervised adaptation method of our classification pipeline composed of GMMs and DNN.

3.2   Weakly Supervised Adaptation

The proposed adaptation method comprises two sub-steps. First, GMMs are adapted so that they fit better to the testing samples which have undergone re-sizing. Then the DNN classifier is adapted by fine-tuning the network. Both steps are accomplished in a weakly supervised manner, *i.e.*, by using a very limited number of labeled testing samples of 8×8 patches.

In the following, we first show that if DC components of patches are removed (*i.e.*, Gaussian component's means $\boldsymbol{\mu}_k = \mathbf{0}, \forall k = 1, 2, \ldots, N$), the weighted sum of covariance matrices of a GMM is equal to the covariance matrix of the data. We have $\boldsymbol{X} = (X_1, X_2, \ldots, X_p)$ a multi-dimensional random variable. Here $p = 64$ as patches are 8×8. Let f be the Probability Density Function (PDF) of random variable $\boldsymbol{X}$ with DC component removed and f_k the PDFs of each component of the related Gaussian mixture, then we have:

$$f(\boldsymbol{x}_l) = \sum_{k=1}^{N} \pi_k \, f_k(\boldsymbol{x}_l) = \sum_{i=1}^{N} \pi_k \, \mathcal{N}(\boldsymbol{x}_l | \mathbf{0}, \boldsymbol{\Sigma}_k), \tag{4}$$

with $\boldsymbol{x}_l$ a p-dimensional sample of the random variable $\boldsymbol{X}$, $\boldsymbol{\Sigma}_k$ and π_k respectively the covariance and the weight for the kth component in the mixture. Now let us compute elements of the covariance matrix of $\boldsymbol{X}$:

$$\mathrm{cov}(X_i, X_j) = \mathbb{E}_f[X_i X_j] - \mathbb{E}_f[X_i]\mathbb{E}_f[X_j] = \mathbb{E}_f[X_i X_j]$$
$$= \sum_{k=1}^{N} \pi_k \mathbb{E}_{f_k}[X_i X_j] = \sum_{k=1}^{N} \pi_k (\boldsymbol{\Sigma}_k^{(i,j)} + \boldsymbol{\mu}_k^{(i)} \boldsymbol{\mu}_k^{(j)}) = \sum_{k=1}^{N} \pi_k \boldsymbol{\Sigma}_k^{(i,j)}, \tag{5}$$

where superscripts $(i), (j)$ and (i, j) are element index within the corresponding vector and matrix. Considering that variance is a special case of covariance, from Eq. (5) we can see that covariance matrix of the data is equal to the weighted sum of covariance matrices of the Gaussian mixture.

We assume that we have only a few labeled samples on target domain, not enough to train a model from scratch (this needs around 200000 samples of each class) but enough to compute empirical covariance matrix per class on target (around 1000 samples for each class). GMMs' parameters should be slightly adjusted so as to enhance the descriptive capability of the model on target data. GMMs can be adjusted in two ways: the weights or the covariance matrices (the means are zeros). Beside that, our aim is to have a quick adaptation solution. Therefore, we choose to adapt the GMM weights. The weights contain less parameters (only a vector and not matrices). Adaptation of GMMs' weights can be formulated as an optimization problem:

$$\underset{w_k}{\mathrm{minimize}} \left\| \left(\sum_{k=1}^{N} w_k \times \boldsymbol{\Sigma}_k \right) - \boldsymbol{\Sigma}_{data} \right\|_F$$
$$\text{subject to } \sum_{k=1}^{N} w_k = 1, \text{ and } 0 < w_k < 1, \forall k = 1, 2, \ldots, N. \tag{6}$$

In Eq. (6), w_k are adapted GMM weights to be deduced, Σ_{data} is the empirical covariance matrix on target domain, and F stands for Frobenius norm. We do acknowledge that semi-definite positive matrices lie on a Riemannian manifold, thus with a curvature. So a geodesic distance would be more adapted; however we do not notice any differences in classification performances or results of optimization using Euclidean distance instead of geodesic distance, although geodesic distance is way more expensive and slower to compute. Therefore in practice Frobenius norm is used.

These adjustments of weights for each GMM can be seen as a fine-tuning for feature extraction. It is a means of reducing discrepancy between features of source and target domains. In the second step of our method, *classifier adaptation* by fine-tuning the DNN is carried out to cope with drifts in features and therefore enhance discriminative capability of the classifier.

4   Experiments

In this section, we present some experimental results to show the feasibility of the proposed weakly supervised adaptation method.

Dataset and Implementation.   For experiments, we looked for a large database (around 1000 images), in high-resolution (more realistic), in RAW format to be able to control the image development process and with as many image sources as possible. Dresden database [6] is the best match with these expectations with 1200 images, in RAW format from various source cameras, different scenes and exposures and of around 2000×4000 resolution. We select randomly 30% of images as testing images. Re-sizing is performed on the full-sized images (not patches) and before applying the potential manipulations. This is indeed a pre-processing operation which does not alter fingerprints of manipulations but only statistics of images. The remaining 70% are used to train the GMMs and the DNN classifier. This training set is never re-sized. For training, we use 200000 patches of 8×8 pixels for each class. These patches are extracted randomly from images in the training set, with same number of patches coming from each image. This makes 400000 patches for each binary classification problem.

GMMs have $N = 75$ components each. This number has been chosen via cross-validation to reach a good trade-off between classification accuracy and model complexity (as well as training time). For GMM training, we used Scikit-Learn implementation with 5 initializations for π_k and Σ_k with k-means. μ_k are initialized to be zeros. Initialization that obtains best likelihood on data is selected. For the classification part, we perform binary classification of original patches *vs.* manipulated patches. We used Keras (with Tensorflow backend) for the DNN implementation and training. It is a very simple network with two hidden layers of respectively 256 and 128 neurons, ReLU activation, dropout of 0.5 and Adam optimizer with default parameters for minimizing *cross-entropy* loss. This architecture has not been optimized as it is not a crucial part given that classification is quite easy. For fine-tuning, learning rate is reduced to 10^{-4}.

Table 3. Testing accuracy (in %) of DNN fine-tuning, combined without or with weights adaptation of GMMs. The improved accuracy of weakly supervised adaptations, compared to the case of "without adaptation", is given in parentheses. Testing accuracy without re-sizing is also given in the second row for reference. The last column of "AVG" presents the average accuracy (and average accuracy improvement in parentheses, if any) of the 5 classification problems.

	GF	MF	USM	WGN	JPEG	AVG
Without re-sizing	91	86	97	98	89	92
Re-sizing ×0.51 (without adaptation)	64	75	73	69	79	72
Re-sizing ×0.51 (DNN fine-tuning only)	72 (+8)	75 (+0)	91 (+18)	71 (+2)	82 (+3)	78 (+6)
Re-sizing ×0.51 (GMM adaptation + DNN fine-tuning)	78 (+14)	76 (+1)	92 (+19)	70 (+1)	86 (+7)	80 (+8)
Re-sizing ×0.76 (without adaptation)	78	81	81	73	84	79
Re-sizing ×0.76 (DNN fine-tuning only)	78 (+0)	77 (−4)	92 (+11)	81 (+8)	84 (+0)	82 (+3)
Re-sizing ×0.76 (GMM adaptation + DNN fine-tuning)	83 (+5)	82 (+1)	94 (+13)	85 (+12)	84 (+0)	86 (+7)
Re-sizing ×1.15 (without adaptation)	55	80	87	85	79	77
Re-sizing ×1.15 (DNN fine-tuning only)	66 (+11)	82 (+2)	95 (+8)	96 (+11)	79 (+0)	84 (+7)
Re-sizing ×1.15 (GMM adaptation + DNN fine-tuning)	70 (+15)	85 (+5)	95 (+8)	96 (+11)	82 (+3)	86 (+9)
Re-sizing ×1.25 (without adaptation)	51	75	74	81	67	70
Re-sizing ×1.25 (DNN fine-tuning only)	63 (+12)	78 (+3)	95 (+21)	90 (+9)	70 (+3)	79 (+9)
Re-sizing ×1.25 (GMM adaptation + DNN fine-tuning)	66 (+15)	80 (+5)	95 (+21)	95 (+14)	78 (+11)	83 (+13)

Batch size is 128. 1000 samples of each class are used to compute empirical covariance matrices in order to be able to adapt GMM weights and fine-tune the DNN. Code will be soon available on-line.

With DNN Fine-Tuning Only. DNN fine-tuning helps to improve the detection accuracy, but sometimes the improvement is rather limited (Table 3, rows of "DNN fine-tuning only"). By fine-tuning, the classifier's decision boundary is slightly adjusted, somehow similar to the case of selecting a new threshold for the comparison of likelihood (instead of 1 initially). In order to further enhance the discriminative power of the whole forensic pipeline, it is necessary to also adapt GMMs, the underlying feature extractor, which are until now trained solely on the source data while being "blind" to the target domain. Therefore, GMMs should be tweaked, more precisely their weights, in order to better fit the target data (as described in Sect. 3.2).

Table 4. Testing accuracy (in %) of DNN fine-tuning, combined without or with weights adaptation of GMMs, for the case of mixed re-sizing factors. Re-sizing factor is drawn following uniform law within the specified interval.

	GF	MF	USM	WGN	JPEG	AVG
Re-sizing ×[0.48, 0.72] (without adaptation)	71	81	76	72	87	77
Re-sizing ×[0.48, 0.72] (DNN fine-tuning only)	78 (+7)	81 (+0)	91 (+15)	76 (+4)	87 (+0)	83 (+6)
Re-sizing ×[0.48, 0.72] (GMM adaptation + DNN fine-tuning)	83 (+12)	80 (−1)	92 (+16)	80 (+8)	88 (+1)	85 (+8)
Re-sizing ×[1.12, 1.27] (without adaptation)	53	78	81	83	74	74
Re-sizing ×[1.12, 1.27] (DNN fine-tuning only)	63 (+10)	78 (+0)	95 (+14)	91 (+8)	75 (+1)	80 (+6)
Re-sizing ×[1.12, 1.27] (GMM adaptation + DNN fine-tuning)	64 (+11)	83 (+5)	98 (+17)	95 (+12)	78 (+4)	84 (+10)

With GMM Weights Adaptation. We observe in Table 3 some clear improvements (*e.g.*, for WGN and JPEG under upsampling of ×1.25) when fine-tuning of DNN is conducted jointly with GMM weights adaptation. In addition, there is consistent average accuracy improvement under all the considered re-sizing factors (last column of Table 3) for adaptation of both GMMs and DNN, when compared to DNN fine-tuning only. The standard deviation of results is under 10^{-1}. Accuracy increase offered by adaptation of GMMs and DNN depends on manipulations. For example our method is able to recover up to +19% for sharpening (USM) and re-sizing of ×0.51, but there are not such improvements for median filtering (MF). Median filtering is the manipulation with the smallest score (86% in Table 2, row of ×1) on baseline (without re-sizing of testing set) and is also across re-sizing factor one of the hardest to deal with. Beside that, our method works better with upsampling (for example +13% for average accuracy improvement with a factor of ×1.25 and less for factors ×0.51 and ×0.76). Our conjecture is that with downsampling, some striking local dependencies in patches are partially removed so it needs more complex transformation than a simple weights adjustment to allow GMM to well describe them. With upsampling, the dependencies are somehow mildly smoothed so it is easier to adapt.

Mixed Re-sizing Factors. Our method also performs well with a mix of re-sizing factors. As shown in Table 4, our method still obtains good results when factors are randomly (following uniform distribution) drawn within an interval. This is not a surprise as our method only intends to adapt the GMM-based feature extractor to the new covariance of the data and the DNN classifier to these new features, without taking into account the specific factor value and algorithm of the re-sizing pre-processing.

Table 5. Testing accuracy (in %) of an improved version of Bayar and Stamm's CNN-based method [1], for cases of with and without fine-tuning. The improved accuracy of weakly supervised fine-tuning, compared to the case of "without fine-tuning", is given in parentheses. The baseline testing accuracy without any re-sizing pre-processing is given in the second row. Results in this table are to be compared with those given in Table 3.

	GF	MF	USM	WGN	JPEG	AVG
Without re-sizing	79	85	91	86	79	84
Re-sizing ×0.51 (without fine-tuning)	68	82	80	66	76	74
Re-sizing ×0.51 (fine-tuning)	73 (+5)	82 (+0)	85 (+5)	69 (+3)	77 (+1)	77 (+3)
Re-sizing ×0.76 (without fine-tuning)	73	83	89	80	79	81
Re-sizing ×0.76 (fine-tuning)	74 (+1)	83 (+0)	89 (+0)	80 (+0)	79 (+0)	81 (+0)
Re-sizing ×1.15 (without fine-tuning)	59	76	79	86	61	72
Re-sizing ×1.15 (fine-tuning)	67 (+8)	80 (+4)	90 (+11)	86 (+0)	66 (+5)	78 (+6)
Re-sizing ×1.25 (without fine-tuning)	55	72	74	82	55	68
Re-sizing ×1.25 (fine-tuning)	65 (+10)	77 (+5)	91 (+15)	86 (+4)	60 (+5)	76 (+8)

Comparisons with Bayar and Stamm's CNN-Based Method. We compare with the state-of-the-art deep-learning-based method in [1]. The approach is different from ours as feature extraction and classification are carried out in an end-to-end way in the CNN. As shown in the following, the CNN-based method also experiences some performance drops due to re-sizing pre-processing. In order to make the CNN work with 8×8 patches, one or some of the four *pooling* layers of the network in [1] have to be removed. Otherwise outputs of these layers drop to 1×1 and following 2D convolution is not possible anymore. We have tried different configurations and numbers of retained pooling layers (0, 1 or 2 retained layers are technically possible) and found that we obtain better performance without any pooling. This is understandable as pooling layers would cause loss of information. Performances are also better with a learning rate of 10^{-4} instead of 10^{-3} (value suggested in the original paper [1]). Results reported in Table 5 have been obtained with these improved settings, best that we can get after many experiments. We can notice that the baseline scores (without re-sizing) of CNN-based method are lower than our GMM-based method, with an average accuracy of 84% for CNN *vs.* 92% for GMM (see Tables 3 and 5, row of without re-sizing). There is also performance drop for CNN-based method under re-sizing pre-processing, especially for upsampling. The performance decrease can be as big as -24% for detection of JPEG compression with re-sizing of $\times 1.25$ (see Table 5, with a decrease from 79% to 55%). We observe comparable performance drop under re-sizing pre-processing for different settings of CNN that we tried during our experiments. In general, although CNN has smaller amount of accuracy decrease (this point deserves further studies), but the final decreased accuracy without adaptation is comparable for CNN-based and GMM-based methods (*cf.* the corresponding rows in Tables 3 and 5), with a same trend of more accuracy decrease under upsampling for both methods.

For CNN-based method, we used Caffe implementation from authors available at https://gitlab.com/MISLgit/constrained-conv-TIFS2018. Images selected for training and testing, patches generated and number of patches generated are exactly the same as with the GMM-based method. The weakly supervised adaptation is realized by the conventional way of fine-tuning the CNN. Again, we made efforts to try different strategies, *i.e.*, fine-tuning the first few, the last few, and all layers of the network. We find that only fine-tuning the dense layers at the end of CNN gives slightly better performance than other strategies. Learning rate has been reduced to 10^{-5}. This learning rate and fine-tuning setting gave us the best performances of adaptation in our experiments. Fine-tuning of CNN is performed on the same number of re-sized samples (2000 patches per class). Adaptation of CNN helps to improve the accuracy under re-sizing pre-processing, especially for upsampling, as shown in Table 5. In general, our adaptation of GMM-based method gives more improvement and higher improved accuracy than CNN-based method. The final accuracy of GMM-based method is 80%, 86%, 86% and 83% for the four re-sizing factors (Table 3), against respectively 77%, 81%, 78% and 76% for the CNN-based method (Table 5).

In all, it is interesting to see that GMM-based method (using explicit image statistical models) has better performance than CNN for this forensic problem on small patches, in terms of both baseline accuracy without re-sizing and improved accuracy after adaptation to re-sizing pre-processing. It is clear that more theoretical and experimental investigations are needed to better

110   L. Darmet et al.

understand these results. Nevertheless, the results are encouraging for us to continue on this image-model-based approach when nowadays CNN becomes dominating in many image forensic research problems.

Example of Image Forgery Localization. Evaluating and analyzing the use of the proposed image manipulation detection method, probably jointly with other forensic methods, for the localization of image forgery is out of the scope of this paper and constitutes one part of our future work. In the following, we only present an example of forgery localization to show the feasibility of our method for this task. As highlighted in red circle in Fig. 1(a), a small part (89 × 187

(a) Image forgery with spliced part highlighted

(b) Output of GMM-based method on image of original size (F1 score = 0.85)

(c) Output of GMM-based method on pre-re-sized image (F1 score = 0.04)

(d) Output of adapted GMM-based method on pre-re-sized image (F1 score = 0.64)

(e) Output of adapted CNN-based method on pre-re-sized image (F1 score = 0.14)

Fig. 1. Example of image forgery localization (Color figure online).

pixels) has been taken from a *source* image of the testing dataset and inserted into a *host* image also in the testing set. This inserted part (thus the source image) has previously been JPEG compressed with quality factor $Q = 90$, while the host image is an original one. We try to detect this JPEG compression and therefore localize the splicing forgery indirectly.

Output map of our GMM-based detector on image of original size is shown in Fig. 1(b). Just next to it, in (c) we show the output of the same detector but for the situation where source image and host image have been pre-re-sized with factor of ×0.51 before JPEG compression and spliced part insertion, respectively. The map in (d) is the result of our detector after adaptation to pre-re-sizing. In (e) it is the output map with re-sizing pre-processing for the adapted CNN-based detector of Bayar and Stamm [1] (see previous part of this section for details of CNN improvement and adaptation). As we deal with small patches, output map could be noisy, so for better visualization each output map in (b)–(e) has undergone a 3×3 median filtering to smooth the output. The F1 scores given in Fig. 1 are computed on maps before smoothing. As can be expected from the performances on 8×8 patches, manipulation is quite well localized on image of original size in (b) but not well on the pre-re-sized image in (c). In particular, here we show an example where our detector without adaptation has dramatic performance drop on JPEG compressed patches, *i.e.*, in the spliced part which has rich texture, and where there is noticeable improvement after adaptation. This performance drop is however understandable because with downsampling pre-processing (here of factor ×0.51), in general both original and compressed patches can have more mid- and high-frequency components. JPEG compression introduces JPEG grid and also removes mainly high-frequency components within each block. The grid artifact is quite similar with or without re-sizing because it is a pre-processing operation. Therefore, a downsampled JPEG compressed patch with rich texture can be very "similar", in a forensic sens, to an uncompressed patch without re-sizing. This may explain the low accuracy in the JPEG compressed spliced part as illustrated in Fig. 1(c), which is below the accuracy on whole re-sized testing data reported in Table 3.

Our adaptation method improves the localization accuracy, as reflected by the map and F1 score in Fig. 1(d). It is worth mentioning that the localization on pre-re-sized image is harder because spliced part becomes smaller after downsampling pre-processing. The adapted CNN-based method works not as well as our method on this example, in particular with a number of false alarms in the pristine part of the spliced image as shown in (e). As mentioned above, a thorough evaluation and analysis is scheduled as future work.

Computational Cost. Our adaptation method is very quick. Solving the optimization problem in Eq. (6) takes around 1 min, and DNN fine-tuning 2 min. Training six GMMs from scratch each with 200000 samples takes around 12 h in total on CPU, and DNN training about 20 min. Training CNN-based method of Bayar and Stamm lasts around 2 h on GPU for every binary classification problem with 200000 samples for each class. This is quite fast because of small size of patches. Fine-tuning CNN takes about 10 min. We use a standalone computer with Intel Xeon CPU E5-2630, 64 GB RAM and Nvidia 1080 Ti GPU. In all, the adaptation of our method is slightly faster then CNN-base method (about 4 min *vs.* 10 min). The GMM training would be faster than CNN training if we could use a GPU implementation.

5   Conclusion

This work outlined how re-sizing as pre-processing could alter performances of a manipulation detector based on local image statistics and a state-of-the-art CNN-based detector. We propose a method to adapt both GMM-based feature extractor, by adjusting weights, and DNN classifier, by fine-tuning. Experimental results show the feasibility of the proposed weakly supervised adaptation method which tries to better fit covariance of target domain data for the GMM feature extractor. In some cases with our method using 2000 labeled target samples (1000 per class), we obtain almost same results as re-training from scratch with 400000 labeled samples, *e.g.*, detection of Gaussian noise addition with re-sizing of ×1.25. Our adaptation takes a few minutes instead of several hours for re-training from scratch. This provides a shortcut in terms of flexibility and computing power. Our image-statistics-based detector outperforms an improved version of the state-of-the-art CNN-based detector [1], in terms of both baseline and adapted accuracy for the situations without and with re-sizing pre-processing, respectively. However, we are aware that this CNN-based method has been originally designed for bigger patches but not for small ones; in the meanwhile, to the best of our knowledge, there are until now no published results of manipulation detection on 8 × 8 patches for CNN-based and other methods. Therefore, in the future more appropriate CNNs have to be designed for this specific case and compared with image-statistics-based method.

The performance of the proposed adaptation under downsampling needs to be improved, probably with a stronger GMM adaptation which also adjusts the components' covariance structure. We would like to mention that in the literature post-processing is commonly studied when testing a forensic detector, however effects of pre-processing on performances have been much less investigated. In this paper we introduce new concerns related to the pre-processing and a new methodology to carry out light-weight adaptation. We plan to extend this framework to cope with other pre-processing operations, the case of unsupervised adaptation, as well as other forensics domain adaptation scenarios which have been receiving more and more attention among the research community [4]. We also intend to conduct studies on methods based on other type of features such as [10,13]. At last, we think that it is possible to improve adaptation of CNN for specific problems of digital image forensics by using approaches other than fine-tuning and we plan to work on it.

Acknowledgement. This work is supported by French National Research Agency (DEFALS ANR-16-DEFA-0003, ANR-15-IDEX-02).

References

1. Bayar, B., Stamm, M.C.: Constrained convolutional neural networks: a new approach towards general purpose image manipulation detection. IEEE Trans. Inf. Forensics Secur. **13**(11), 2691–2706 (2018)
2. Bondi, L., Baroffio, L., Güera, D., Bestagini, P., Delp, E.J., Tubaro, S.: First steps toward camera model identification with convolutional neural networks. IEEE Signal Process. Lett. **24**(3), 259–263 (2017)
3. Cozzolino, D., Poggi, G., Verdoliva, L.: Splicebuster: a new blind image splicing detector. In: Proceedings of the IEEE International Workshop on Information Forensics and Security, pp. 1–6 (2015)
4. Cozzolino, D., Thies, J., Rössler, A., Riess, C., Nießner, M., Verdoliva, L.: Forensictransfer: Weakly-supervised domain adaptation for forgery detection. arXiv CoRR, pp. 1–12 (2018). https://arxiv.org/abs/1812.02510
5. Fan, W., Wang, K., Cayre, F.: General-purpose image forensics using patch likelihood under image statistical models. In: Proceedings of the IEEE International Workshop on Information Forensics and Security, pp. 1–6 (2015)
6. Gloe, T., Böhme, R.: The Dresden image database for benchmarking digital image forensics. In: Proceedings of the ACM Symposium on Applied Computing, pp. 1585–1591 (2010)
7. Ker, A., Pevný, T.: A mishmash of methods for mitigating the model mismatch mess. In: Proceedings of the SPIE Media Watermarking, Security, and Forensics, vol. 9028, pp. 90280I:1–90280I:15 (2014)
8. Kodovský, J., Fridrich, J.: Effect of image downsampling on steganographic security. IEEE Trans. Inf. Forensics Secur. **9**(5), 752–762 (2014)
9. Kodovský, J., Sedighi, V., Fridrich, J.: Study of cover source mismatch in steganalysis and ways to mitigate its impact. In: Proceedings of the SPIE Media Watermarking, Security, and Forensics, vol. 9028, pp. 90280J:1–90280J:12 (2014)
10. Li, H., Luo, W., Qiu, X., Huang, J.: Identification of various image operations using residual-based features. IEEE Trans. Circ. Syst. Video Technol. **28**(1), 31–45 (2018)
11. Oquab, M., Bottou, L., Laptev, I., Sivic, J.: Is object localization for free? - Weakly-supervised learning with convolutional neural networks. In: Proceedings of the IEEE Conference on Computer Vision and Pattern Recognition, pp. 685–694 (2015)
12. Piva, A.: An overview on image forensics. ISRN Signal Process. **496701**, 1–22 (2013)
13. Qiu, X., Li, H., Luo, W., Huang, J.: A universal image forensic strategy based on steganalytic model. In: Proceedings of the ACM Workshop on Information Hiding and Multimedia Security, pp. 165–170 (2014)
14. Quan, W., Wang, K., Yan, D.M., Zhang, X.: Distinguishing between natural and computer-generated images using convolutional neural networks. IEEE Trans. Inf. Forensics Secur. **13**(11), 2772–2787 (2018)
15. Snell, J., Swersky, K., Zemel, R.S.: Prototypical networks for few-shot learning. In: Proceedings of the Advances in Neural Information Processing Systems, pp. 4077–4087 (2017)

16. Vinyals, O., Blundell, C., Lillicrap, T., Kavukcuoglu, K., Wierstra, D.: Matching networks for one shot learning. In: Proceedings of the Advances in Neural Information Processing Systems, pp. 3630–3638 (2016)
17. Wu, Y., Abd-Almageed, W., Natarajan, P.: BusterNet: detecting copy-move image forgery with source/target localization. In: Ferrari, V., Hebert, M., Sminchisescu, C., Weiss, Y. (eds.) ECCV 2018, Part VI. LNCS, vol. 11210, pp. 170–186. Springer, Cham (2018). https://doi.org/10.1007/978-3-030-01231-1_11

GRU-SVM Model for Synthetic Speech Detection

Ting Huang[1], Hongxia Wang[2(✉)], Yi Chen[1], and Peisong He[2]

[1] School of Information Science and Technology,
Southwest Jiaotong University, Chengdu 611756, People's Republic of China
[2] College of Cybersecurity, Sichuan University,
Chengdu 610065, People's Republic of China
`hxwang@scu.edu.cn`

Abstract. Voice conversion and speech synthesis techniques present a threat to current automatic speaker verification systems. Therefore, to prevent such spoofing attack, choosing an appropriate classifier for learning relevant information from speech feature is an important issue. In this paper, a GRU-SVM model for synthetic speech detection is proposed. The Gate Recurrent Unit (GRU) neural network is considered to learn the feature. The GRU can overcome the problems of gradients vanishing and explosion in traditional Recurrent Neural Networks (RNN) when learning the temporal dependencies. The Support Vector Machines (SVM) plays a role in regression before softmax layer for classification. An excellent performance after the SVM regression has shown in the case of classification ability and data gradient descent. We also obtain the optimal speech feature extraction method and apply it to the classifier for training by a large amount of verification and analysis. Experimental results show that the proposed GRU-SVM models gain higher prediction accuracy on data sets, and an average detection rate of 99.63% has been achieved in our development database. In addition, the proposed method can improve the learning ability of the model effectively.

Keywords: Synthetic speech detection · Gate Recurrent Unit · Support Vector Machines

1 Introduction

Voice has become one of the most important biometric authentication for identifying individuals. Speech signal can be easily collected, transported and stored, which makes the voiceprint recognition widely be used in identity authentication. This speech technique is called Speaker Verification (SV) [1,2]. Nowadays, the speech synthetic technique can transform text to speech with the voice characteristics of source speaker [3–5]. There are very few differences between source speech and target speech, it is easy to fake a person's voice to fool a speaker verification system. Many verification techniques cannot recognize neither kinds

© Springer Nature Switzerland AG 2020
H. Wang et al. (Eds.): IWDW 2019, LNCS 12022, pp. 115–125, 2020.
https://doi.org/10.1007/978-3-030-43575-2_9

of speeches. If the criminals apply the technique to the telephone fraud, it will cause serious social problems and loss. In order to solve this problem, an automatic speaker recognition system has been proposed to identify an individual's identity by using inherent physiological or behavioral characteristics of a computer. Analyzing the signal and extracting its feature will be automatically verified who the speaker is [6]. The typical automatic speaker recognition system mainly includes four parts, preprocessing, feature extraction, training model and pattern recognition [7] and it is shown in Fig. 1.

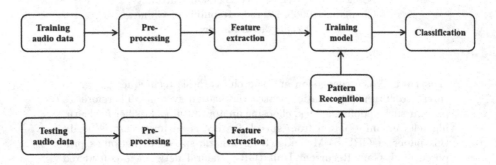

Fig. 1. Automatic speaker recognition system

Existing audio preprocessing includes endpoint detection, pre-emphasis, framing, windowing. Preprocessing is an indispensable part of speech signal processing, which has a significant influence on quality of feature extraction. Feature extraction means extracting feature parameters that can indicate the identity of the speaker. There are a number of studies [7–9] that compare various implementations of the feature on the speech recognition task. Mel Frequency Cepstrum Coefficient (MFCC), Gammatone Frequency Cepstrum Coefficient (GFCC) and Linear Prediction Cepstrum Coefficient (LPCC) are the most common speech features. MFCC is based on the auditory characteristics of human ear. There are many reported works on MFCC, Ahmad et al. [10] motivated the use of combination of MFCC and its delta derivatives (DMFCC and DDMFCC) calculated using mel spaced Gaussian filter banks for text independent speaker recognition. Research studies on classifiers indicate there are many different classification algorithms which are applied to the speech recognition task. Jagtap et al. presented a mainstream machine learning classifier that using Gaussian mixture model (GMM) for classification [11]. Recently, with the rise of artificial intelligence, various neural networks have been proposed by scholars. The classification algorithm based on artificial neural network (ANN) has been successfully applied in speech recognition by Shahamiri et al. [12]. Convolutional neural network (CNN) is a typical deep neural network proposed by Professor Yann LeCun of the University of Toronto in Canada and his colleagues [13], which also has been introduced into speech recognition in recent years. The input needs to be organized as a feature map that can feed into the CNN. RNN is a powerful model for sequential data [14]. Mou et al. [15] proposed that the RNN was inherently deep in time, and the hidden state was a function of all previous hidden states. However, performance of the RNN in speech recognition has so far been disappointing. The Long-Short-Term Memory network (LSTM) and the GRU are special types of the RNN network that can overcome the problems of vanishing and explosion of gradients in traditional RNN. Therefore, we try to choose the application of the RNN and its variants in our own scheme. On the basic of the GRU, we explore a way with adding the SVM to change the GRU network structure, which can improve the detection rate.

The rest of this paper is organized as follows. The proposed GRU-SVM is described in Sect. 2. Then experimental results and discussions are shown in Sect. 3. Finally, a conclusion is given in Sect. 4.

2   Proposed Scheme

2.1   Data Preprocessing

In this paper, MFCC is used as feature for training and taking 20-dimension is the best in our experiments. The standard MFCC extracts the static features of the speech, the dynamic features can effectively improve the recognition performance of the system. Therefore, the first-order derivative of the extracted MFCC is usually performed to obtain ΔMFCC, the 40-dimensional feature parameters of the MFCC $+$ ΔMFCC in this paper is given as:

$$M = \{(C_1, C_2, \cdots, C_m), (\Delta C_1, \Delta C_2, \cdots, \Delta C_m)\} \tag{1}$$

where m is the dimension of the feature parameter of the MFCC.

Now we depict how to feed the speech features to the GRU network further. We form the feature of each speech sample into an L $\times$ 40-dimensional matrix (L is the max frame length of the audio sample), if the frame length of sample is shorter than L, we supply it with zero. Making sure that each feature is a matrix of $L \times 40$ dimensions. All training samples are constructed into a matrix of $L \times 40 \times n$ dimensions, n is the number of training speech samples, the MFCC feature matrix is shown in Fig. 2.

2.2   The Proposed GRU-SVM Model

GRU and LSTM are both variants of the RNN to overcome the vanishing gradient and explosion problem. Compared with the LSTM, the GRU has better performance which is easier to train and improve the training efficiency [16]. Suppose we are given a sequence of input $(x_1, x_2, \cdots, x_{t-1}, x_t)$, the GRU calculates the corresponding hidden layers $(h_1, h_2, \cdots, h_{t-1}, h_t)$ and outputs a vector sequence $(y_1, y_2, \cdots, y_{t-1}, y_t)$. Then the feature parameters are learned through the gating mechanism of the GRU which is implemented by the following composite function.

$$z_t = \sigma(W_z \cdot [h_{h-1}, x_t]) \tag{2}$$

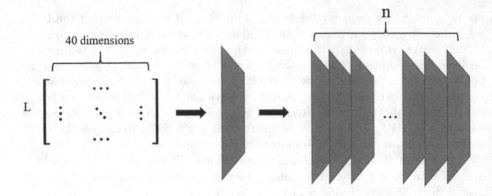

Fig. 2. MFCC feature matrix.

$$u_t = \sigma(W_r \cdot [h_{h-1}, x_t]) \tag{3}$$

$$\begin{cases} \widetilde{h}_t = tanh(W \cdot [u_t * h_{t-1}, x_t]) \\ h_t = (1 - z_t) * h_{t-1} + z_t * \widetilde{h}_t. \end{cases} \tag{4}$$

The reset gate, the update gate and the hidden state are described as Eq. (2), Eq. (3) and Eq. (4) respectively. Where $\sigma(\cdot)$ is element-wise sigmoid function. W_z is the matrix weights of the reset gate and W_r is the matrix weight of the update gate. x_t is the input at time t. The GRU has one less gate function than the LSTM, so the number of parameters is less than the LSTM. On the whole, training speed of the GRU is faster than the LSTM. The adjustment method of hyperparameters is similar to other neural networks. During training, the loss function of the training data sets is minimized. Cross-entropy is chosen to be the function due to the classification task.

SVM is a powerful and efficient machine learning algorithm and it hardly outperform [17,18]. Unfortunately, it is really hard for these algorithms to capture features in synthetic speech detection sometimes. Due to the good robustness and generalization performance of the SVM, it is used for regression of the features captured by the GRU networks in this paper. So we propose a new method for synthetic speech detection based on the GRU network and the SVM. With the introduction of SVM as its second last layer, the parameters are also learned by regression function of the SVM. After regression, the loss network is using cross entropy function Eqs. (5–6).

$$\widehat{y}^{(i)} = min\frac{1}{2}||w||^2 + C\sum_{i=1}^{n} max(0, 1 - y^{(i)}(w^T x_i + b_i)) \tag{5}$$

$$L = \sum_{i=1}^{N} y^{(i)} log\widehat{y}^{(i)} + (1 - y^{(i)})log(1 - \widehat{y}^{(i)}) \tag{6}$$

where w and b_i determine a straight line for classification, $\widehat{y}^{(i)}$ is the forecast value after the SVM regression, $y^{(i)}$ is the real value. C is a constant ($C > 0$).

According to the GRU network, we adopt the 3-layers GRU network and treat the GRU as a simplified LSTM, there is no more cell state, only hidden layer state, so final state of the hidden layer could be obtained. We directly put the final state into the SVM for regression before last layer. We optimize the classification of the results by the SVM regression, evaluation, finally using softmax function to output the classification result. The schematic diagram is shown in Fig. 3.

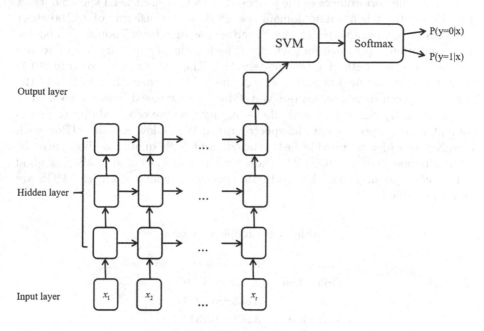

Fig. 3. GRU-SVM neural network

The proposed GRU-SVM model can be summarized as follows:

(1) Feed the speech features $(x_1, x_2, \cdots, x_{t-1}, x_t)$ to the GRU neural network.
(2) Initialize the network parameters such as weights and biases.
(3) The hidden states of the GRU are computed based on the input and its learning parameters.
(4) At the final time step, the output of the model is fed into the SVM using Eq. (5).
(5) The loss of the network is cross entropy function using Eq. (6).
(6) For this task, the Adam optimizer is used as an optimization for minimize loss. Optimization adjusts the weights and biases based on the computed loss.
(7) This process is repeated until the model reaches the highest accuracy.
(8) After all these processes, the trained model can be used for classification.

3 Experimental Results and Analysis

In this section, we firstly introduce the data generation and the environment, then analyze the experimental results.

3.1 Data Generation and Environment Construction

To validate the performance of the proposed model, we use the LJ speech dataset [19]. This dataset is a public domain speech dataset consisting of 13,100 short audio clips from a single speaker, with reading passages from 7 non-fiction books. A transcription is provided for each clip. The lengths of clips vary from 1 to 10 s and have a total length of approximately 24 h. The audio was recorded in 2016–17 by the LibriVox project and is also in the public domain. In addition to the synthetic speech database, we use WaveGlow, a flow-based network vocoder is computationally challenging and affects quality because of the ability to generate high quality speech from Mel-spectrograms. WaveGlow combines Glow with WaveNet in order to provide fast, efficient and high quality audio synthesis. Mean Opinion Scores (MOS) [20] show that it delivers audio quality as good as the other publicly available synthetic speech implementation, the MOS are shown in Table 1.

Table 1. Mean opinion scores

Model	Mean opinion scores
Griffin-Lim	3.823 ± 0.1349
WaveNet	3.885 ± 0.1238
WaveGlow	3.961 ± 0.1343
Ground truth	4.274 ± 0.1340

The MOS are shown in Table 1, the MOS of WaveGlow is 90% higher than other methods, though the MOS of synthetic samples are very close, no methods can reach the MOS of natural audio. The most obvious advantages of WaveGlow are training simplicity and fast speed in training processing. We decide to use WaveGlow to synthesize the speech samples.

In the experiment, both of the natural speech samples and synthetic speech samples have a sampling frequency of 22.05 kHz and are standard mono. We used python and tensorflow to supply with all models and adjust the hyperparameters. The detailed construction of the experiment environments are shown in Table 2.

After defining the hyperparameters, we select 16000 speech samples from each two databases as training samples and put them into the proposed method for training, then we save the generated models. Finally, 8000 speech samples are selected as the testing samples for detection from the remaining speech in the database.

Table 2. Hyperparameters construction

Hyperparameters	GRU + SVM	GRU
Batch	10	10
Hidden-cell-size	128	128
Epoch	100	100
Dropout	0.5	0.5
Learning rate	1e−3	1e−3
SVM-C	0.5	N/A

3.2 Results and Discussions

Generally, performance metrics [21] in synthetic speech detection include Detection Accuracy, False Alarm (FPR) and Missing Alarm (FNR) which are denoted as

$$Accuracy = \frac{(TP + TN)}{(TP + FN + FP + TN)} \tag{7}$$

$$FPR = \frac{FP}{TN + FP} \tag{8}$$

$$FNR = \frac{FN}{FN + TP} \tag{9}$$

where TP indicates positive samples with the correct classification. TN indicates negative samples with the correct classification. FP indicates positive samples with wrong classification, FN indicates negative samples with wrong classification. Commonly, the higher the accuracy and the lower the FPR and FNR, the better the classifier.

Table 3. Accuracy (%) of the different models

Models	Natural speech	Synthetic speech	Hybird speech
Linear SVM	95.70	99.10	97.40
RNN	99.75	47.50	50.11
LSTM	98.55	100	99.28
GRU	99.25	99.85	99.55
GRU + linear SVM	**99.30**	**99.95**	**99.63**

We report the accuracy of different training models as shown in Table 3. In the database of our development, the performance of the GRU network and the GRU-SVM network are always more outstanding than the rest networks. This shows our GRU-based models are more suitable for synthetic speech detection.

Table 4. FPR and FNR (%) of the different models

Models	FPR	FNR
Linear SVM	4.16	0.93
RNN	0.52	34.48
LSTM	1.43	0
GRU	0.74	0.15
GRU + linear SVM	**0.69**	**0.10**

The GRU-SVM model performs better comparing with other methods. Especially, the hybird speech means the average detection accuracy of the natural speech and the synthetic speech, the GRU-SVM is 99.63%, while 99.55% for the GRU, 99.28% for the LSTM, 50.11% for the RNN, 97.40% for the linear SVM. The SVM also has a good performance in classification, which is due to the fact that there are more kernel functions in the SVM and strong classification ability for linearly inseparable data. In particular, as the time step increasing, the RNN can no longer connect the feature information, there is a problem of gradient explosion. The RNN misclassify almost all the test samples into natural speech that is why the RNN is the best in natural speech. The synthetic speech is synthesized using the Mel-spectrograms feature which making synthetic speech feature is more regular than natural speech. Although the LSTM is the best in detecting synthetic speech, it is less effective in detecting natural speech than the GRU and the GRU-SVM. The same problem is also seen in Table 4, the GRU-SVM is the lowest in the false alarm expect the RNN. The GRU-SVM is the lowest in the missing alarm except the LSTM.

With respect to accuracy and loss in training performance illustrated by Fig. 4(a) and (b), we compare with the GRU and the GRU-SVM further. The accuracy rate is a ratio of forecast value and real value in prediction of training processing, which represents the convergence and the classification ability of the whole model. If the accuracy is 1, which means the forecast value is equal to the real value, the model can predict the results with 100% correctly. And loss rate measures the degree of deviation between the forecast value and the real value. If the loss is 0, which means there is no deviation between them. We select the first 4000 iterations and make a statistic. In Fig. 4(a), the accuracy rate of the GRU-SVM is earlier up to peak than the GRU, and the GRU-SVM is more stable in the processing up to peak. In Fig. 4(b), the loss rate of the GRU-SVM is also earlier down to lowest point than the GRU, and the range of the GRU loss varies greatly, especially between 2000 and 2500 iterations. This proves that the GRU-SVM model converges faster than the GRU.

The above experimental results show that the proposed method is feasible and effective in the synthetic speech detection. After the hidden layer of the GRU output, the SVM performs regression to control the entire feature data in a specific feature space, which enhances the feature and facilitates subsequent classification. This is the main reason why the GRU-SVM model success.

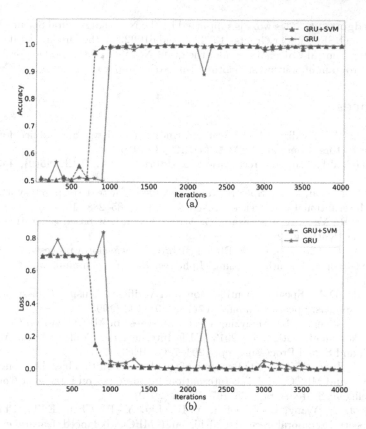

Fig. 4. The accuracy and loss in prediction of training processing. (a) The accuracy of prediction through 4000 iterations of training processingPro1 (b) The loss in prediction through 4000 iterations of training processing.

4   Conclusion

In this paper, we propose a GRU-SVM neural network for synthetic speech detection. The state of the art synthetic speech technique is used to build a synthetic database. MFCC is extracted as the feature parameters. Our method is proved to be effective by the experimental results. The approach of using the GRU-based models to extract useful information from a vast array of speech feature has shown to be excellent. After the hidden layer of the GRU, the SVM performs regression before the softmax layer. In summary, the improvement of the proposed method compared to current classifier is noteworthy. Further research is required to explore other features and multiclass classifiers to enhance the effect of the GRU model.

Acknowledgement. This work is supported by the National Natural Science Foundation of China (NSFC) under Grants 61972269 and 61902263, the Fundamental Research Funds for the Central Universities under the grant No. YJ201881, and Doctoral Innovation Fund Program of Southwest Jiaotong University under the grant No. DCX201824.

References

1. Langford, J., Guzdial, M.: The arbitrariness of reviews, and advice for school administrators. Commun. ACM **58**(4), 12–13 (2016)
2. Campbell, J.P.: Speaker recognition: a tutorial. Proc. IEEE **85**(9), 1437–1462 (1997)
3. Kain, A., Macon, M.W.: Spectral voice conversion for text-to-speech synthesis. In: IEEE International Conference on Acoustics, pp. 285–288 (1998)
4. Prenger, R., Valle, R., Catanzaro, B.: WaveGlow: a flow-based generative network for speech synthesis (2018)
5. Moulines, E., Charpentier, F.: Pitch-synchronous waveform processing techniques for text-to-speech synthesis using diphones. Speech Commun. **9**(5–6), 453–467 (1990)
6. Reynolds, D.A.: Speaker identification and verification using Gaussian mixture speaker models. Speech Commun. **17**(1–2), 91–108 (1995)
7. Zhao, X., Wang, D.L.: Analyzing noise robustness of MFCC and GFCC features in speaker identification. In: 2013 IEEE International Conference on Acoustics, Speech and Signal Processing, pp. 7204–7208. IEEE (2013)
8. Yuan, Y., Zhao, P., Zhou, Q.: Research of speaker recognition based on combination of LPCC and MFCC. In: IEEE International Conference on Intelligent Computing & Intelligent Systems, pp. 765–767. IEEE (2010)
9. Wang, J.-C., Wang, C.-Y., Chin, Y.-H., Liu, Y.-T., Chen, E.-T., Chang, P.-C.: Spectral-temporal receptive fields and MFCC balanced feature extraction for robust speaker recognition. Multimed. Tools Appl. **76**(3), 4055–4068 (2016). https://doi.org/10.1007/s11042-016-3335-0
10. Ahmad, K.S., Thosar, A.S., Nirmal, J.H.: A unique approach in text independent speaker recognition using MFCC feature sets and probabilistic neural network. In: Eighth International Conference on Advances in Pattern Recognition, pp. 1–6 (2015)
11. Jagtap, S.S., Bhalke, D.G.: Speaker verification using Gaussian mixture model. In: International Conference on Pervasive Computing, pp. 1–5 (2015)
12. Shahamiri, S.R., Salim, S.S.B.: Artificial neural networks as speech recognisers for dysarthric speech: identifying the best-performing set of MFCC parameters and studying a speaker-independent approach. Adv. Eng. Inform. **28**(1), 102–110 (2014)
13. LeCun, Y.: Generalization and network design strategies. Ph.D. thesis, University of Toronto (1989)
14. Lipton, Z.C.: A critical review of recurrent neural networks for sequence learning. arXiv:1506.00019 (2015)
15. Mou, L., Ghamisi, P., Zhu, X.X.: Deep recurrent neural networks for hyperspectral image classification. IEEE Trans. Geosci. Remote Sens. **55**(7), 3639–3655 (2017)
16. Kawakami, K.: Supervised sequence labelling with recurrent neural networks. Ph.D. thesis, Technical University of Munich (2008)
17. Tang, Y.: Deep learning using linear support vector machines. arXiv preprint arXiv:1306.0239 (2013)

18. Hu, H., Xu, M.X., Wu, W.: GMM supervector based SVM with spectral features for speech emotion recognition. In: IEEE International Conference on Acoustics, Speech and Signal Processing, pp. 413–416 (2007)

19. The LJ Speech Dataset. https://keithito.com/LJ-Speech-Dataset

20. Hanhart, P., Ebrahimi, T.: Calculation of average coding efficiency based on subjective quality scores. J. Vis. Commun. Image Represent. **25**(3), 555–564 (2014)

21. Mesaros, A., Heittola, T., Virtanen, T.: TUT database for acoustic scene classification and sound event detection. In: 2016 24th European Signal Processing Conference (EUSIPCO), pp. 1128–1132. IEEE (2016)

Median Filtering Detection of Small-Size Image Using AlexCaps-Network

Guiduo Duan[1,2], Jiayu Miao[1], and Tianxi Huang[3(✉)]

[1] School of Computer Science and Engineering, University of Electronic Science and
Technology of China, Chengdu 611731, China
Guiduo.Duan@uestc.edu.cn
[2] Institute of Electronic and Information Engineering of UESTC in
Guangdong, Guangdong 511700, China
[3] Department of Fundamental Courses, Chengdu Textile College, Chengdu 611731, China
huang_tianxi@163.com

Abstract. Digital image forgers often use various image processing software to maliciously tamper with image contents, and then use some anti-forensics techniques such as median filtering to hide the obvious traces of these tampered images. Therefore, median filtering detection is one of the key technologies in the field of image forensics. Recently, with the rapid development of the deep learning, more and more researchers have proposed many image median filtering detection algorithms based on deep learning. Deep learning method can automatically extract the image median filtering features and unify them with classification steps in a deep learning model, which has better detection performance than traditional algorithms. However, existing methods based on deep learning still have the promotion space when facing small size or highly compressed images. To solve this problem, a median filtering detection method of small-size image using AlexCaps-network is proposed in this paper. AlexCaps-network is a joint network combining the classical network Alexnet and Capsule network. Firstly, in order to cope with the difficulty of extracting median filtering features caused by the low-resolution of small size and highly compressed image blocks, we add image preprocessing layer to the first layer of the network to enhance the trace of median filtering. Secondly, the general feature of median filtering in learning images is extracted by shallow ordinary convolutional neural network. The capsule network layer extracts the more complex spatial information in the median filtering image by dynamic routing algorithm and predicts the results. Finally, the experimental results show that the effective detection performance of our proposed method for small size and highly compressed images, even though the size is 16×16 image blocks and QF of compression is 70, is still good.

Keywords: Digital image forensics · Median filtering detection · Alex network · Capsule network

1 Introduction

With the rapid development of digital image technology, digital image forgery cases emerge in endlessly, which has a serious negative impact on many important social

H. Wang et al. (Eds.): IWDW 2019, LNCS 12022, pp. 126–140, 2020.
https://doi.org/10.1007/978-3-030-43575-2_10

fields, such as politics, justice, media and military. In order to judge the authenticity of digital images and detect the methods of image processing, researchers have proposed a variety of digital image forensics algorithms. Exposing the processing history of a digital image is an important part of image forensics, such as the detection of copy-move [1, 2], image re-sampling [3, 4], contrast enhancement [5, 6], JPEG compression [7, 8], median filtering [9–11].

As an anti-forensics technology, median filtering is a common nonlinear operation in image processing. It is generally used to smooth the image, remove noise from the image and maintain edge information. The forger can hide the operation methods of forged images by median filtering. For example, median filtering can reduce the discontinuity of forged parts and other parts in copy-paste or spliced images, and make forged images more real. Therefore, the median filtering detection has been paid more and more attention in the field of digital image forensics in recent years.

Median filtering detection methods are generally divided into two categories. One is the traditional method which based on image features that relies on manually selected features. In reference [9], Kirchner and Fridrich proposed a first-order difference method based on the strip effect and subtractive pixel critical matrix (SPAM) when the image quality factor is less than 70 as the detection feature. In reference [10], Cao et al. proposed a method to calculate the probability of first-order pixel difference of texture region being zero. However, these two methods have a bad performance on JPEG compressed image detection. Therefore, Kang et al. proposed to use the coefficient of the fitted autoregressive model as the feature of median filtering detection in reference [11]. Gao et al. proposed a median filtering detection method based on joint features of differential images in reference [12], which is better than the previous methods in detecting low-resolution images and JPEG compressed images. In reference [13], an untrained one dimensional feature MF detector based on frequency residual-difference is proposed for median filtering detection of JPEG processed images.

Another kind of median filtering detection method is based on deep learning. Deep learning can automatically learn image features and complete classification, which has been applied into the field of image forensics. In reference [14], Chen et al. first proposed the application of deep learning to median filtering detection, which was also the first application of deep learning in the field of forensics, opening a new idea for the subsequent application of deep learning in the field of digital image forensics. Based on the work of Chen et al., Bayar presented a new convolutional neural network structure in reference [15], which can automatically learn the predictive error filter by constrains the new convolutional layer, so as to detect the traces left by image operation. In reference [16], Liu et al. putted the discernible frequency-domain features obtained into the conventional CNN model by adding a transformation layer, and could identify the template parameters of various spatial smoothing filtering operations. In reference [17], Tang et al. added the famous Mlpconv structure layer to the proposed network to enhance the nonlinear classification ability of the network structure in the paper, which greatly improved the ability of detecting the nonlinear characteristics of the automatic learning median filtering of the model.

About the uncompressed image and the high-resolution image median filtering has achieved very high detection precision. Currently, the greatest challenge is median filtering detection of compressed JPEG and small size images. When the low-resolution image is compressed, the trace of median filtering in the image will be weakened, and the detection performance of existing methods will drop significantly. Moreover, most of the existing median filtering detection methods are about whether the median filtering exists which is an image dichotomy problem. In the field of image forensics, it is necessary not only to judge the operation type, but also to detect the specific parameters of its operation. From the above, to overcome these shortcomings, the contributions of this paper are as follows. Firstly, a new network AlexCaps-network combining the classical convolutional neural network Alexnet and the dynamic routing ideas of capsule network is proposed in this paper. In AlexCaps-network, the general feature of median filtering in learning images is extracted from shallow network by convolutional neural network and more complex spatial information is extracted from deep network by capsule network. Secondly, in view of the weakness of median filter trace in small image blocks, image preprocessing layer is added to the first layer of the network to put large image blocks and strengthen the trace of median filter operation. Moreover, our method could also distinguish images with different filtering window sizes. The last, experimental results demonstrated the methods we proposed is effective and have good detection performance, even though all the test images have been compressed significantly (QF = 70) and the sizes as low as 16×16. The detection accuracy of the network proposed in this paper can reach 97.01% for the median filtered images with size of 64 and a jpeg90. As for the same size images, the detection accuracy of median filter window size $3 \times 3, 5 \times 5$ and 9×9 can reach 86.92%.

The outline of the paper is organized as follows: Sect. 2 describes the proposed detection method, including a brief review of the related network, the framework and parameters setting of AlexCaps-network. Simulation results and performance analysis of detection accuracy rate along with the feasibility and advantages of our proposed method are presented in Sect. 3. Finally, the conclusions and future work are presented in Sect. 4.

2 Methods

This paper proposes a network structure that can be used for median filtering detection. By combining the classical convolutional neural network Alexnet and Capsule network, the median filtering features are automatically extracted from small size and highly compressed median filtering images. To distinguish it from other existing networks we name it AlexCaps-network.

2.1 Related Network

In computer vision, Alexnet network proposed by Alex in reference [18] won the champion of image recognition contest in 2012, which aroused widespread attention for convolutional neural network (CNN). In reference [19], Hinton proposed a new network structure in October 2017, called Capsule Network (Capsnet). Capsnet achieving the most advanced results with 0.25% test error in digital recognition of highly overlapped MNIST data sets, initially showing the potential of this network.

Alexnet deepens the network structure on the basis of LeNet, and uses the layered convolutional layer and pooling layer to enhance the richness of image features. The first five layers of Alexnet are convolutional layers, among which the first, the second and fifth layers contain a maximum pooling layer. And the last three layers are full connection layers. The first five convolutional layers can extract effective features through a small number of parameters, which is much more important than the fully connected layer. The Alexnet network structure is shown in Fig. 1.

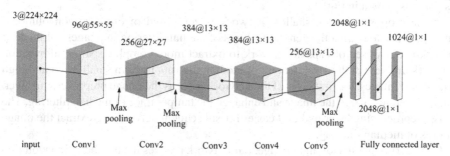

Fig. 1. The Alexnet network structure

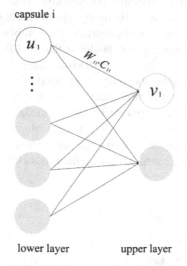

Fig. 2. The capsule structure

The biggest difference between the Capsnet and Alexnet is that the output of neurons changes from a scalar to a set of vectors. The image spatial information is encoded and the probability of the existence of image features is calculated by vector length. In Capsnet, the lower capsule layer is called the primary capsule layer, while the higher capsule layer is generally called the classified capsule. The capsule structure is shown in Fig. 2.

2.2 The Framework of Proposed Network

Inspired by Hinton, in order to explore more possibilities of capsule networks in the field of computer vision, we try to combine the classical convolutional neural network Alexnet and Capsnet, and propose AlexCaps-network that can be used for median filtering detection.

The proposed network in this paper consists of 8 layers. The first layer is image magnification layer, 2 to 6 layers are composed of overlapping convolution layer and pool layer which referring to Alexnet network. The 7th and 8th layers are capsules layer. Taking size of 32 × 32 image input as an example, the network structure proposed in this paper is shown in Fig. 3.

In the proposed model, shallow network is composed of ordinary convolutional neural network to extract the general features of median filtering in images, while deep network is composed of capsule network to extract more complex spatial information in images. In view of the weak feature of median filtering trace in small-sized and high compressed images, the first layer of the network is set as the image preprocessing layer, which is used to enlarge the image and enhance the tamper trace of median filtering. The image preprocessing layer makes it easier for subsequent networks to extract the image features of median filtering.

Considering the size of input image, our network reduces the number of convolution layers in Alexnet, but still uses the overlay convolution layer and the maximum pooling layer to extract the feature information in the image. The proposed network consists of four convolution layers and the maximum pooling layer is set after the third layer.

The main capsule layer contains 10 main capsules, receives the general features detected by the convolution layer, and generates the combination of features into the classified capsule layer. The number of capsules in the classification capsule layer is the number of image categories. In this paper, classified capsules are called median filter capsules. The detection of whether the image has passed through the median filter can be regarded as an image classification problem, and the number of median filter capsules is 2. The module length of the output vector of the median filter capsule layer is the probability of the existence of corresponding image category features, and the vector direction is the spatial information of image features. The final model prediction result is determined by selecting the capsule with the maximum length.

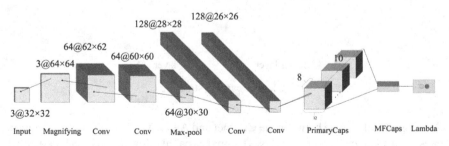

Fig. 3. The framework of proposed AlexCaps-network

2.3 Image Magnification Method

The first layer in the network is the image preprocessing layer, which is used to expose the median filtering trace better in small image blocks after magnifying the image. In this way, network can more easily extract the median filtering feature from the image. The nearest neighbor interpolation, bilinear interpolation and bicubic interpolation are three methods commonly used for image magnification.

Nearest Neighbor Interpolation algorithm is a simple algorithm that does not need extra computation. In the four adjacent pixels to be solved, the nearest adjacent pixel gray scale is assigned to the pixel to be solved, and its formula is as follows:

$$X_{src} = X_{dst} \times (Width_{src}/Width_{dst})$$
$$Y_{src} = Y_{dst} \times (Height_{src}/Height_{dst}) \tag{1}$$

X_{src} and Y_{src} represent the coordinates of the source image, X_{dst} and Y_{dst} represent the coordinates of the target image. Then calculate the coordinates of the original image and fill the coordinate pixel value of the original image into the coordinate position of the target image.

The core idea of Bilinear Interpolation algorithm is to carry out linear interpolation in two directions. The pixel value of the target point is obtained by fitting the pixel value of Q_{ij}, the four nearest points of the target point in the original image. The calculation formula is as follows:

$$f(x, y) \approx \frac{y_2 - y}{y_2 - y_1} \left(\frac{x_2 - x}{x_2 - x_1} f(Q_{11}) + \frac{x - x_1}{x_2 - x_1} f(Q_{21}) \right)$$
$$+ \frac{y - y_1}{y_2 - y_1} \left(\frac{x_2 - x}{x_2 - x_1} f(Q_{12}) + \frac{x - x_1}{x_2 - x_1} f(Q_{22}) \right) \tag{2}$$

$f(x, y)$ represents the grayscale value of the target point, and $f(Q_{ij})$ represents the grayscale value of the four adjacent points.

The BiCubic interpolation algorithm needs to calculate the pixel value at the target point $B(x, y)$ according to the nearest 16 pixel points of the pixel point $A(x, y)$. The pixel value of the target point $B(x, y)$ is equal to the weight $W(x)$ weighted superposition of 16 pixel points. Assumption that point P is the target point $B(X, Y)$ corresponding to the position in the source image. The calculation formula of $W(x)$ is as follows. Parameter **a** takes a value of -0.5, and the parameter **x** represents the distance from the pixel point to point P.

$$W(x) = \begin{cases} (a+2)|x|^3 - (a+3)|x|^2 + 1 & for \ |x| \leq 1 \\ a|x|^3 - 5a|x|^2 + 8a|x| - 4a & for \ 1 < |x| < 2 \\ 0 & otherwise \end{cases} \tag{3}$$

The pixel value of the target point $B(X, Y)$ is calculated as follows:

$$B(X, Y) = \sum_{i=0}^{3} \sum_{j=0}^{3} a_{ij} \times W(i) \times W(j) \tag{4}$$

For the interpolation pixel A(x, y), take the nearby 4×4 neighborhood point (x_i, y_j), i, $j = 0, 1, 2, 3$. Interpolation is calculated according to the formula as follows.

$$f(x, y) = \sum_{i=0}^{3} \sum_{j=0}^{3} f(x_i, y_j) W(x - x_i) W(y - y_j) \tag{5}$$

In order to find the most effective magnification method for median filtering, it is necessary to compare the effects of several magnification methods by analyzing the statistical eigenvalues of several images. Firstly, 800 images were randomly selected from the UCID data set for the central image block clipping of 32×32. The original image block and the median filter image block are respectively magnified twice in three different ways.

By comparing statistical characteristic difference of the three image frequency coefficients of skewness, variation coefficient and kurtosis, the difference in frequency domain between the median filter image block and the original image block can be intuitively obtained. The statistical feature difference between the enlarged image block and the original size image block with different magnification methods is shown in Fig. 4.

In Fig. 4, the horizontal direction is the statistical characteristic difference in the frequency domain of the image block with size 32×32, while the vertical direction is the statistical feature difference in the frequency domain of the image block with size 64×64 after twice magnification. From left to right are skewness, coefficient of variation, and kurtosis. The specific calculation formula is as formula (6) follows.

$$Dif = F(abs(FFT(med(x)))) - F(abs(FFT(x))) \tag{6}$$

Med ($\cdot$) represents the median filtering operation, FFT ($\cdot$) represents the fast Fourier transform of the image block to obtain its amplitude information in the frequency domain, and F($\cdot$) represents the calculation of three different statistical features, namely skewness, kurtosis and variation coefficient.

It can be seen from Table 1 that the slope K of the fitting line is almost all greater than 1. The differences between the median filtered image and original image block are increased to different degrees by these three magnification methods. By comparing the slope K, it can be seen that nearest neighbor interpolation magnification effect is relatively better. Compared with other methods, this method did not introduce new grey value when magnified image and did not destroy the image of the original pixels when enhance the median filtering trace information. The pixel interpolation completely from the original image pixels.

AlexCaps-network is respectively trained on the data set magnified by three different magnification methods. As can be seen from Table 2, the detection accuracy comparison results of different magnification methods show that the nearest neighbor interpolation performs best. Therefore, the nearest neighbor interpolation method is adopted in the image preprocessing layer of this paper to magnify the image.

2.4 Parameters of Proposed Network

In the network proposed in this paper, the input image is firstly extracted the general median filtering features through the basic convolutional neural network and then output

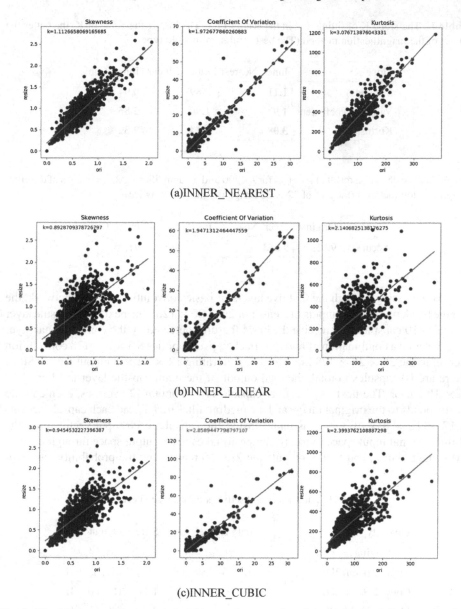

Fig. 4. The difference of three statistical features between the original image and the corresponding median filtered image after different magnification modes. The horizontal direction represents the difference of the statistical features of the original size image, while the vertical direction is the difference of the statistical features after the image is magnified twice

to the capsule layer. The capsule layer is divided into the main capsule layer and the median filter capsule layer. The following table is an example of a 32 * 32 median filtered image dichotomy for the parameters of proposed network.

Table 1. The slope K of fitting line in the scatter plot. The higher the value of K, the better the effect of the magnification method (The best results are in bold type)

Slope K	Inner_Nearest	Inner_Linear	Inner_Cubic
Skewness	**1.11**	0.89	0.94
Variation coefficient	1.97	1.94	**2.85**
Kurtosis	**3.08**	2.14	2.39

Table 2. The detection result of Acc (%) for Jpeg90 and median filtering 3×3 images of different magnification methods (the size of 32×32 image magnification twice).

Method	Original	Inner_Nearest	Inner_Linear	Inner_Cubic
Accuracy	90.23	**92.53**	90.82	91.05

After passing through the first five layers of basic convolutional neural network, the image block of 32×32 outputs the tensor of $26 \times 26 \times 128$. The next main capsule layer contains 10 capsules that receive the basic features detected by the convolutional layer and generate a combination of features. Each capsule applies 8 $3 \times 3 \times 128$ convolution kernel to the $26 \times 26 \times 128$ input tensor, generating $12 \times 12 \times 8$ output tensor. Since there are 10 capsules in total, the total output of the main capsule layer is $12 \times 12 \times 8 \times 10$ tensor. The next median filter capsule layer contains 2 capsules, each capsule corresponds to the original image and the median filter image, and each capsule accepts a $12 \times 12 \times 8 \times 10$ tensor as input. Inside the capsule, each input vector maps the 8-dimensional input space to the 10-dimensional capsule output space through the 8×10 weight matrix, and finally outputs the 2×10 matrix and the probability values of

Table 3. Parameters and settings of proposed network

Layer (type)	Kernel	Kernel_num	Stride	Output shape
Magnifying				(64, 64, 3)
Conv_1 (Conv2D)	(3, 3)	64	1	(62, 62, 64)
Conv_2 (Conv2D)	(3, 3)	64	1	(60, 60, 64)
Max_pool (MaxPooling2D)	(2, 2)		2	(30, 30, 64)
Conv_3 (Conv2D)	(3, 3)	128	1	(28, 28, 128)
Conv_4(Conv2D)	(3, 3)	128	1	(26, 26, 128)
PriCap_Conv (Conv2D)	(3, 3)	8×10	2	(12, 12, 128)
PriCap_reshape (Reshape)				(1440, 8)
capsule_1 (Capsule)				(2, 10)
lambda_1 (Lambda)				(1, 2)

different categories through the Lambda layer to confirm the model prediction results. The detailed network structure parameters are shown in the following Table 3.

3 Experimental Results

3.1 Datasets

In order to evaluate the performance of the network structure proposed in this paper and compare it with other methods, the mixed data set containing 11338 images was tested in the network. The mixed data set composed of the BOSSBase1.01 [20] and the UCID database [21], in which the BOSSbase1.01 provides 10,000 PGM images and UCID database provides 1338 uncompressed tif color images, including images of natural landscapes and man-made objects.

When preparing the data set, the images are first uniformly converted into grayscale images, and the images are processed by median filtering. Then, the images processed by median filtering are centrally clipped to small image blocks of the size required by the experiment. Finally, the small image block is saved as JPEG compression forma. The data set without median filtering in the processed data set is taken as negative sample, and the data set after median filtering is taken as positive sample. The data sets are randomly divided into training set, test set and verification set according to the proportion of 8:1:1 respectively.

3.2 Experimental Results

Performance Comparison of Different Magnification Times. 1000 images were randomly selected from the original mixed data set, and small image blocks with the size of 32 × 32 were cut out from the center of the image blocks for experiment. Then, jpeg compression processing with different quality factors (QF) and median filtering processing with different window sizes were performed on small image blocks respectively. The nearest neighbor interpolation in Sect. 2.3 is used to magnify image blocks by different multiples and train them on the network proposed in this paper. The comparison results of different magnification times are shown in the following Table 4.

Table 4. The detection result of Acc (%) of different magnification times (Jpeg90 + Mf3 represents images processed with compression QF of 90 and processed by median filter with window of 3 × 3).

Original size	Magnification	Jpeg90 + Mf5	Jpeg70 + Mf5
32 × 32	1	94.80	90.28
	2	96.42	92.19
	3	97.05	92.81
	4	97.51	92.38

It can be seen from Table 4 that the detection accuracy of median filtering is positively correlated with the image magnification times. But the detection accuracy is improved slightly and the computational complexity is high when magnification is 3 or 4 times. The detection performance is improved significantly when magnification is 2 times. Therefore, the magnification times of the image magnification layer in the proposed network is twice.

In order to more comprehensively verify the performance of the proposed network on small size and compressed image blocks, image with different compression quality factor, different size and different filtering window size are tested on the proposed network. The size of the image used in the experiment are 16×16 and 32×32, the filtering window sizes are 3×3 and 5×5, and the jpeg QF are 70 and 90. The comparison results of experimental detection accuracy are shown in the following Table 5.

The comparison results show that the detection performance of median filtering decreases when jpeg QF is low and image size blocks are small, but the detection accuracy of 16×16 image blocks on the network proposed in this paper can still reach 86.68% when the QF is as low as 70. It can also be seen from the experimental results that the image magnification layer can significantly improve the detection accuracy and make it easier to distinguish the median filtered images. Among them, the detection accuracy of 32×32 image blocks with QF = 90 is up to 96.42%, on the network proposed in this paper, with superior performance.

Table 5. The detection result of Acc (%) of different parameters. The contrast parameters include image size, quality factor and filter window size. ($16 \times 16 \rightarrow 32 \times 32$ represents the image of size 16×16 enlarged to size 32×32 by the nearest neighbor interpolation)

Image size	Jpeg90 + Mf3	Jpeg90 + Mf5	Jpeg70 + Mf3	Jpeg70 + Mf5
16×16	82.32	88.86	77.47	83.29
$16 \times 16 \rightarrow 32 \times 32$	85.31	91.23	80.84	86.49
32×32	90.23	94.80	85.57	90.28
$32 \times 32 \rightarrow 64 \times 64$	92.53	96.42	86.68	92.19

Performance Comparison of Median Filtering Multiclassification. In the previous experiments, median filtering detection is mainly conducted based on whether the image has median filtering or not which is a image dichotomy problem. In the field of image forensics, it is not only necessary to determine the type of image processing operation, but also to detect its specific operating parameters in many scenarios. The size of median filtering window is directly related to the filtering effect. Different window sizes have different degrees of image blurring and image edge information loss. Therefore, the network proposed in this paper is used for image multi-classification to detect and judge different filtering window sizes which is a median filtering multiclassification problem. The filter window sizes designed in the experiment are 3×3, 5×5 and 9×9. The experimental results of median filtering multiclassification are shown in the following Table 6.

Table 6. The detection result of Acc (%) of Median Filtering multiclassification.

Heading level	Jpeg90	Jpeg70
32 × 32	83.24	71.68
64 × 64	86.92	76.36

Performance Comparison of Different Algorithms. In order to verify the good performance of the network structure in this paper, it is compared with other three median filtering detection methods. Chen [14] added a preprocessing layer to the improved Alexnet network structure, calculated the median filtering residue (MFR) of the image, and took MFR as the input of Alexnet network. Two Mlpconv layers are added to the MFNet structure of Tang [17], which improves the nonlinear expression ability of the network structure. The above two methods are deep learning detection methods based on convolutional neural network. The accuracy comparison results of the three detection methods are shown in the following Table 7.

Table 7. The detection result of Acc (%) of different algorithms (The best results are in bold type).

Input image size	Method	Jpeg90 + Mf3	Jpeg90 + Mf5	Jpeg70 + Mf3	Jpeg70 + Mf5
16 × 16	Proposed	85.31	**91.23**	**80.84**	**86.49**
	MFNet [17]	**86.42**	90.67	77.04	84.86
	AlexNet [14]	NA	NA	NA	NA
32 × 32	Proposed	92.53	**96.42**	**86.68**	**92.19**
	MFNet	**93.06**	95.71	85.23	91.67
	AlexNet	88.39	90.24	79.01	84.50
64 × 64	Proposed	**96.32**	**97.01**	**92.37**	**96.90**
	MFNet	95.97	96.62	91.07	96.86
	AlexNet	95.30	95.62	89.49	93.81

The network proposed in this paper cannot give full play to its advantages when the image size is small and the compression ratio is low. Therefore, under the JPEG 90, when the image size is 16 × 16 and 32 × 32, the accuracy of some detection results of this network is slightly lower than that of mfnet only about 0.5%. However, it can be seen from other comparison results in the table that under other parameter settings, the network detection performance proposed in this paper all performs well and the accuracy rate is slightly better than that of other networks. The above experiments verify that AlexCaps-network proposed in this paper can fully extract and identify median filter features in small-size compressed images, and carry out effective image classification.

Performance of Median Filter Positioning. When a part of the median filtering image is cut and pasted into the non-median filtering image, it is very important to detect the specific location of the median filtering for image forensics. The proposed network can detect the median filtering on small image blocks, which can be used for locating the median filtering on large images.

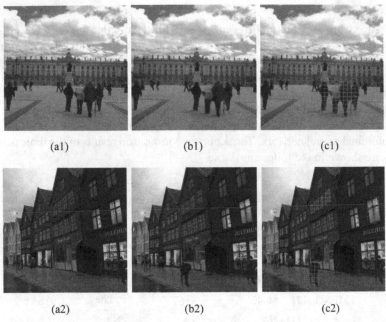

Fig. 5. Cut a part of the median filter image and paste it into the non-median filtering image, and call the trained model to detect the position of the median filter in the image. (a1 and a2) Original image (b1 and b2) forged image (c1 and c2) detection result

Figure 5(a1 and a2) is original image. In Fig. 5(b1 and b2), median filtering image block was pasted to the corresponding position of the original image. For the images to be detected of different sizes, they are divided into small image blocks of input size of the training model. Each small image block calls the trained model to detect successively, and generates the corresponding detection matrix of the image. The non-zero position in the matrix refers to the corresponding position of median filtering in the image. Finally, the non-zero position in the matrix is marked with a color box, and the detection results are shown in Fig. 5(c1 and c2). In the experiment, the detection model was trained on the data set with an image size of 16×16 and median filtering window size of 9×9. It can be seen from the Fig. 5(c1 and c2) that the network proposed in this paper can mark the specific location of median filtering more accurately, and individual errors appear within the acceptable range.

4 Conclusion

Combined with the popular deep learning technology, this paper studies the median filtering operation detection in the field of digital image anti-forensics. This paper propose a network called AlexCaps-network, which combines the basic convolutional neural network with the dynamic routing idea of capsule network. The basic convolutional neural network can extract the basic feature in the median filtering image, while the deep capsule network can mine the highly abstract spatial information in the median filtering image through dynamic routing algorithm. For small size and compressed image blocks, image preprocessing layer is added in the first layer of the network to magnify the image, which makes it easier to extract and identify the median filtering feature from the image. In this paper, median filter detection is considered as an image classification problem, which can satisfy the median filter detection of different parameters by increasing or decreasing the number of capsules in the capsule network.

Several experimental results show that the proposed network can be effectively applied to median filtering detection. And compared with other existing algorithms, the network presented in this paper performs better.

Acknowledgement. This work is supported by the Ministry of Science and Technology Department Foundation of Sichuan Province (No. 2018JY0067, No. 2017GFW0128) and by the Natural Science Foundation of Guangdong Province, China (No. 2017A030313380).

References

1. Wenchang, S., Fei, Z., Bo, Q., et al.: Improving image copy-move forgery detection with particle swarm optimization techniques. China Commun. **13**(1), 139–149 (2016)
2. Rao, Y., Ni, J.: A deep learning approach to detection of splicing and copy-move forgeries in images. In: 2016 IEEE International Workshop on Information Forensics and Security (WIFS), pp. 1–6. IEEE (2016)
3. Popescu, A.C., Farid, H.: Exposing digital forgeries by detecting traces of resampling. IEEE Trans. Signal Process. **53**(2), 758–767 (2005)
4. Hou, X., Zhang, T., Xiong, G., Zhang, Y., Ping, X.: Image resampling detection based on texture classification. Multimed. Tools Appl. **72**(2), 1681–1708 (2013). https://doi.org/10.1007/s11042-013-1466-0
5. Stamm, M., Liu, K.J.R.: Blind forensics of contrast enhancement in digital images. In: 2008 15th IEEE International Conference on Image Processing, pp. 3112–3115. IEEE (2008)
6. Dong, W., Wang, J.J.: Contrast enhancement forensics based on modified convolutional neural network. J. Appl. Sci. **35**(6), 745–753 (2017)
7. Barni, M., Bondi, L., Bonettini, N., et al.: Aligned and non-aligned double JPEG detection using convolutional neural networks. J. Vis. Commun. Image Represent. **49**, 153–163 (2017)
8. Zeng, X., Feng, G., Zhang, X.: Detection of double JPEG compression using modified DenseNet model. Multimed. Tools Appl. **78**(7), 8183–8196 (2018). https://doi.org/10.1007/s11042-018-6737-3
9. Kirchner, M., Fridrich, J.: On detection of median filtering in digital images. In: Media Forensics and Security II, vol. 7541, p. 754110. International Society for Optics and Photonics (2010)

10. Cao, G., Zhao, Y., Ni, R., et al.: Forensic detection of median filtering in digital images. In: 2010 IEEE International Conference on Multimedia and Expo, pp. 89–94. IEEE (2010)
11. Kang, X., Stamm, M.C., Peng, A., et al.: Robust median filtering forensics using an autoregressive model. IEEE Trans. Inf. Forensics Secur. **8**(9), 1456–1468 (2013)
12. Gao, H., Hu, M., Gao, T., et al.: Robust detection of median filtering based on combined features of difference image. Sig. Process. Image Commun. **72**, 126–133 (2019)
13. Li, W., Ni, R., Li, X., Zhao, Y.: Robust median filtering detection based on the difference of frequency residuals. Multimed. Tools Appl. **78**(7), 8363–8381 (2018). https://doi.org/10.1007/s11042-018-6831-6
14. Chen, J., Kang, X., Liu, Y., et al.: Median filtering forensics based on convolutional neural networks. IEEE Signal Process. Lett. **22**(11), 1849–1853 (2015)
15. Bayar, B., Stamm, M.C.: A deep learning approach to universal image manipulation detection using a new convolutional layer. In: Proceedings of the 4th ACM Workshop on Information Hiding and Multimedia Security, pp. 5–10. ACM (2016)
16. Liu, A., Zhao, Z., Zhang, C., Su, Y.: Smooth filtering identification based on convolutional neural networks. Multimed. Tools Appl. **78**(19), 26851–26865 (2016). https://doi.org/10.1007/s11042-016-4251-z
17. Tang, H., Ni, R., Zhao, Y., et al.: Median filtering detection of small-size image based on CNN. J. Vis. Commun. Image Represent. **51**, 162–168 (2018)
18. Krizhevsky, A., Sutskever, I., Hinton, G.E.: ImageNet classification with deep convolutional neural networks. In: Advances in Neural Information Processing Systems, pp. 1097–1105 (2012)
19. Sabour, S., Frosst, N., Hinton, G.E.: Dynamic routing between capsules. In: Advances in Neural Information Processing Systems, pp. 3856–3866 (2017)
20. Bas, P., Filler, T., Pevný, T.: "Break our steganographic system": the ins and outs of organizing BOSS. In: Filler, T., Pevný, T., Craver, S., Ker, A. (eds.) IH 2011. LNCS, vol. 6958, pp. 59–70. Springer, Heidelberg (2011). https://doi.org/10.1007/978-3-642-24178-9_5
21. Schaefer, G., Stich, M.: UCID: an uncompressed color image database. In: Storage and Retrieval Methods and Applications for Multimedia 2004, vol. 5307, pp. 472–480. International Society for Optics and Photonics (2003)

Double JPEG Compression Detection Based on Markov Model

Jinwei Wang[1,2,3,4,5], Wei Huang[2], Xiangyang Luo[4(✉)], and Yung-Qing Shi[6]

[1] Jiangsu Collaborative Innovation Center of Atmospheric Environment
and Equipment Technology (CICAEET), Nanjing University of Information Science
and Technology, Nanjing 210044, China
wjwei_2004@163.com
[2] Department of Computer and Software, Nanjing University of Information Science
and Technology, Nanjing 210044, Jiangsu, China
[3] Shanxi Key Laboratory of Network and System Security, Xidian University,
Xi'an 710071, China
[4] State Key Laboratory of Mathematical Engineering and Advanced Computing,
Zhengzhou 450001, China
xiangyangluo@126.com
[5] State Key Laboratory of Information Security, Institute Information Engineering,
Chinese Academy of Sciences, Beijing 100093, China
[6] Department of Electrical Computer Engineering,
New Jersey Institute of Technology, Newark, NJ 07102, USA

Abstract. In this paper, a feature based on the Markov model in quaternion discrete cosine transform (QDCT) domain is proposed for double JPEG compression detection. Firstly, a given JPEG image is extracted from blocked images to obtain amplitude and three angles (ψ, ϕ, and θ). Secondly, when extracting the Markov features, we process the transition probability matrix with the corresponding refinement. Our proposed refinement method not only reduces redundant features, but also makes the acquired features more efficient for detection. Finally, a support vector machine (SVM) is employed for NA-DJPEG compression detection. It is well known that detecting NA-DJPEG compressed images with QF1 $\geq$ QF2 is a challenging task, and when the images with small size (i.e., 64×64), the detection will be more difficult. The experimental result indicates that our method can still achieve a high classification accuracy in this case.

Keywords: Color image forensics · Double JPEG compression detection · Quaternion discrete cosine transform · Markov model

1 Introduction

With the rapid development of multimedia technology, a variety of powerful and easy-to-use image processing software is widely used to edit and process images, such as Photoshop and ACDsee, etc. While these softwares bring convenience,

H. Wang et al. (Eds.): IWDW 2019, LNCS 12022, pp. 141–149, 2020.
https://doi.org/10.1007/978-3-030-43575-2_11

they also pose potential threats. Indeed, some tampered color images were illegally used in the fields of formal media, scientific discovery and forensic evidence. There is no doubt that these tampered color images have a negative effect on social stability. Therefore, many techniques [1–5] have been proposed to detect whether a digital image has tampered or not. JPEG compression is a popular image compression standard [6] in recent years, which has the advantages of saving image storage space and ensuring the quality of highly compressed images, so a large number of color images are stored in JPEG format. Due to the widespread use of JPEG compression, double JPEG compression detection becomes increasingly concerned.

It is well known that peculiar artifacts caused by double JPEG compression leave in the DCT domain. Accordingly, many proposed detection methods [7–9] focus on the analysis of first order statistics of DCT coefficients. The methods in [7,8] based on the distribution of first (and sometimes second) significant digits (FSDs) in block DCT coefficients, and the one in [9] relies on Benford-Fourier analysis. However, a major drawback of these methods is that they are designed to work on the entire image, ie, to detect whether the image is completely subjected to single or double JPEG compression, and it is difficult to estimate statistics under small blocks or image blocks. Therefore, when only part of the image is manipulated, these methods are not suitable for this detection scenario.

In the NA-DJPEG scenario, several other methods for detecting double compression have been proposed, and these features are extracted from both pixel domain and DCT domain. Specifically, a method in [10] is proposed to detect both aligned and non-aligned double JPEG compression. The scheme works by combining periodic artifacts in spatial and frequency domains. A set of features is computed to measure periodicity of blocking artifacts, which is altered when a NA-DJPEG compression occurs, and another set of features is used to measure periodicity of DCT coefficients, which is perturbed in presence of A-DJPEG. This approach for non-aligned recompression detection is outperformed by [11]. Furthermore, in [12] Bianchi and Piva proposed a forensic algorithm for tampering localization when DJPEG compression occurs, either aligned or not. The proposed scheme is as an extension of their analysis carried out in the paper, where a unified statistical model characterizing JPEG artifacts in the DCT domain is considered. In [13], a calibrated RID (C-RID) feature vector generated by a reference feature is proposed for final binary classification. However, in order to achieve accurate detection, spatial resolutions lower than 256×256 pixel are not considered. A method based on CNN is proposed in [14]. A detector is builded by using the CNN-based method and works in the noise domain. The CNN-based detector in the noise domain (Cnoise) is able to correctly classify images compressed by NA-DJPEG. Although the low resolution is considered, this scheme works well as long as $QF2 > QF1$. Motivated by this recent trend, the goal of this paper is to design approaches based on Markov in the QDCT domain for the classification of single and double JPEG compressed images. Specifically, we are interested in working with small size images.

The paper is organized as it follows: in Sect. 2 we give some basics on quaternion discrete cosine transform and discuss their usage for color image. Then, in Sect. 3 we present the Markov-based methods proposed to solve the problem of NA-DJPEG compression detection addressed in the paper. Finally, Sect. 4 is devoted to the experimental results. Section 5 concludes the paper.

2 Theoretical Introduction of Quaternion Discrete Cosine Transform for Color Image

2.1 Representation of Polar Coordinates of Quaternion

Quaternion includes a real part component and several imaginary part components, which is usually regarded as the generalization of complex number. The definition of quaternion is introduced as follows:

$$q = w + xi + yj + zk \tag{1}$$

where w, x, y, z are real number, i, j and k are operators of complex number and vector. They all satisfy Hamilton rule as

$$ij = k, jk = i, ki = j, ji = -k, kj = -i, ik = -j \tag{2}$$

And they also satisfy $i^2 = j^2 = k^2 = ijk = -1$, but they do not satisfy the commutative property of multiplication.

When the quaternion model is used to represent a color image, where the coefficients of three imaginary numbers (i,e,. i, j and k) represent the RGB three channels, respectively.

Since the amplitude and angles are used in the paper, the introduction of polar coordinates of quaternion is introduced The polar coordinates of the quaternion consist of amplitude ($|q|$) and three angles (ϕ, θ and ψ), which can be expressed as

$$q = |q|e^{i\phi}e^{j\theta}e^{k\psi} \tag{3}$$

where the $|q|$ is the modulo of the quaternion, $\phi \in [-\pi, \pi]$, $\theta \in [-\pi/2, \pi/2]$, $\psi \in [-\pi/4, \pi/4]$, and these three angles are given by

$$\phi = a\tan(2(cd + ab), a^2 - b^2 + c^2 - d^2)/2 + k\pi, k \in \mathbf{Z}$$
$$\theta = a\tan(2(bd + ac), a^2 + b^2 - c^2 - d^2)/2 \tag{4}$$
$$\psi = \arcsin(2(ad - bc))$$

2.2 Quaternion Discrete Cosine Transform

Due to the successful application of QDCT in the field of real and complex Numbers, relevant researches have been carried out. The basic principle of QDCT was proposed by Feng and Hu [15], and the definition of L-QDCT and R-QDCT are as follows:

L-QDCT:

$$J_q^L(p,s) = \alpha(p)\alpha(s) \sum_{m=0}^{M-1} \sum_{n=0}^{N-1} u_q \cdot h_q(m,n) \cdot T(p,s,m,n) \qquad (5)$$

R-QDCT:

$$J_q^R(p,s) = \alpha(p)\alpha(s) \sum_{m=0}^{M-1} \sum_{n=0}^{N-1} h_q(m,n) \cdot T(p,s,m,n) \cdot u_q \qquad (6)$$

where $h_q(m,n)$ is a $M \times N$ quaternion matrix, m and n is row and column of the matrix respectively, here, $m \in [0, M-1]$, $n \in [0, N-1]$, u_q is a unit pure quaternion, which can represent the direction of axis of transformation and satisfies $u_q^2 = -1$. p and s is row and column of the transform matrix, respectively. The definition of $\alpha(p)$, $\alpha(s)$ and $T(p,s,m,n)$ are given by

$$\alpha(p) = \begin{cases} \sqrt{1/M} \ p = 0 \\ \sqrt{2/M} \ p \neq 0 \end{cases} \quad \alpha(s) = \begin{cases} \sqrt{1/N} \ s = 0 \\ \sqrt{2/N} \ s \neq 0 \end{cases} \qquad (7)$$

$$T(p,s,m,n) = cos[\frac{\pi(2m+1)p}{2M}]cos[\frac{\pi(2n+1)s}{2N}] \qquad (8)$$

The spectral coefficient of $J(p,s)$ through transformation is still a $M \times N$ quaternion matrix, which can be expressed as

$$J(p,s) = J_0(p,s) + J_1(p,s)i + J_2(p,s)j + J_3(p,s)k \qquad (9)$$

In our algorithm, L-QDCT are chosen for block QDCT. Since the computational complexity of QDCT transform can be seen from its definition, to avoid wasting of resources resulted from complicated calculation, the approach of QDCT is designed on the basis of DCT that is widely used in the field of real number and complex number.

3   Proposed Method

In this subsection, the extraction procedure of Markov features in QDCT domain are described. At first, apply 8×8 block QDCT on the reconstructed color image pixel array, and the corresponding QDCT coefficient array is obtained to calculate the amplitude and three angles. The amplitude and three angles are then rounded to integer and take absolute value to form four arrays. Secondly, difference 2-D arrays are formed from the four arrays. These difference 2-D arrays are modeled by Markov process and then the transition probability matrix is calculated with corresponding refinement process. In addition, a threshold technique is developed to greatly reduce the dimensionality of the transition probability matrices.

3.1 Difference 2-D Arrays

The horizontal, vertical, main diagonal and minor diagonal intra-block difference 2-D arrays F_h, F_v, F_d and F_m are calculated by applying Eq. (10).

$$
\begin{aligned}
F_h(u, v) &= F(u, v) - F(u + 1, v) \\
F_v(u, v) &= F(u, v) - F(u, v + 1) \\
F_d(u, v) &= F(u, v) - F(u + 1, v + 1) \\
F_m(u, v) &= F(u + 1, v) - F(u, v + 1)
\end{aligned}
\tag{10}
$$

where u, v denote coordinates in a QDCT coefficient 2-D array, and $u \in [0, D_u - 2], v \in [0, D_v - 2]$, D_u, D_v denote the 2-D array's dimensions in the horizontal direction and vertical direction, respectively. Thus, $F(u, v)$ denotes a QDCT coefficient 2-D array formed by each coordinate.

In order to reduce computational cost further, we set the threshold $T = 4$ in this implementation. That is, if the value of an element in the difference array is either larger than 4 or smaller than -4, it will be represented by 4 or -4, respectively.

3.2 Transition Probability Matrix Derived from Difference 2-D Arrays

Since JPEG compressed operation changes the correlation between image pixels, according to random process theory, Markov random process is a tool to characterize the correlation. Instead of applying Markov process directly to coefficient 2-D array, Markov process are applied to the difference array introduced above. The horizontal, vertical, main diagonal and minor diagonal transition probability matrices of F_h, F_v, F_d, F_m are calculated by applying Eq. (11).

$$
\begin{aligned}
P_{hh} &= \frac{\sum_{v=0}^{D_v-2} \sum_{u=0}^{D_u-2} \delta(F_h(u, v) = a, F_h(u + 1, v) = b)}{\sum_{v=0}^{D_v-2} \sum_{u=0}^{D_u-2} \delta(F_h(u, v) = a)} \\
P_{vv} &= \frac{\sum_{v=0}^{D_v-2} \sum_{u=0}^{D_u-2} \delta(F_v(u, v) = a, F_v(u, v + 1) = b)}{\sum_{v=0}^{D_v-2} \sum_{u=0}^{D_u-2} \delta(F_v(u, v) = a)} \\
P_d &= \frac{\sum_{v=0}^{D_v-2} \sum_{u=0}^{D_u-2} \delta(F_d(u, v) = a, F_d(u + 1, v + 1) = b)}{\sum_{v=0}^{D_v-2} \sum_{u=0}^{D_u-2} \delta(F_d(u, v) = a)} \\
P_m &= \frac{\sum_{v=0}^{D_v-2} \sum_{u=0}^{D_u-2} \delta(F_m(u, v) = a, F_m(u + 1, v + 1) = b)}{\sum_{v=0}^{D_v-2} \sum_{u=0}^{D_u-2} \delta(F_m(u, v) = a)}
\end{aligned}
\tag{11}
$$

where, $a, b \in (-T, -T + 1, \cdots, 0, \cdots, T)$, and

$$
\delta(A = a, B = b) = \begin{cases} 1, if\ A = a\ \&\ B = b \\ 0, Otherwise \end{cases}
\tag{12}
$$

Proverbially, since there exists correlation between coefficients in a coefficient 2-D array, the distribution of the elements in the difference array is somehow surrounding zero. The extent to which the distribution of the elements is concentrated on zero reflects the strength of the correlation among coefficients. According to the theory of random process, a Markov process can be characterized by a transition probability matrix. Motivated by this observation, we further think about the transition probability matrix.

3.3 Refinement Process in Amplitude and Three Angles

It is well known that the DC and AC coefficients differ greatly in amplitude, and the result obtained after the difference and threshold processing will only be the maximum or minimum value, so that the transition probability matrix formed will have a lower sensitivity in reflecting the change of the coefficient. Therefore, before forming the transition probability matrix, the points obtained by DC-AC (named as DA points) in the difference matrix are eliminated first.

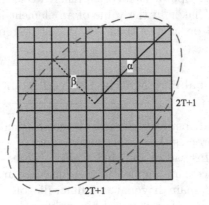

Fig. 1. Illustration of the proposed feature selection method.

The illustration of the proposed feature selection method in three angles is shown in Fig. 1. An elliptical box is used to select features on the transition probability matrix and then those selected features are retained. It is known that the size of the transition probability matrix is $(2T+1) \times (2T+1)$. Since the concentration along the minor diagonal of transition probability matrix spreads from the minor diagonal towards the rest of the matrix, we set the center of the elliptical box to $(0, 0)$ and the size of the long axis is fixed to the minor diagonal length, while the short axis moves along the main diagonal. If α and β represent the semi-major axis and the semi-minor axis, respectively, the range of the semi-short axis can be expressed as

$$0 < \beta < \frac{2N-1}{\alpha}(N = 1, 2, \cdots, T+1) \tag{13}$$

It can be deduced from Eq. (13) that there is a ratio relationship R between β and α . Therefore, choosing an appropriate R will help to further improve the detection accuracy.

4   Experimental Results

The color images selected from the UCID database [16] are cropped to size 64×64 for experimental investigation, and the database includes 1338 uncompressed images of size 384×512 and 512×384. All of these images are divided into positive and negative samples with equal quantity, half of which are used for training, and the other half for testing. Positive samples have NA-DJPEG compressed color images with random cropping vector shift $((x, y) \neq (0,0))$ and quality factors QF1 and QF2. On the other hand, the negative samples are singly JPEG compressed with quality factor QF2. Next, in order to better classify these tampered images, the soft-margin SVM [17] is used. The Gaussian kernel is used and the parameters c and γ are determined by a grid-search over a multiplicative grid $(c, \gamma) \in \{(2^i, 2^j) \mid i \in \{-7, -6, ..., 7\}, j \in \{-7, -6, ..., 7\}\}$ in the SVMs. A 5-fold cross validation is used for training and the average classification accuracy rate is reported.

Table 1. Experimental results of the Markov features

QF1	QF2				
	50	60	70	80	90
50	93.87	95.17	96.48	96.94	98.25
60	94.11	95.64	96.01	97.06	97.65
70	93.66	95.38	96.28	97.00	97.98
80	93.69	95.41	96.07	96.66	98.10
90	93.88	94.72	96.31	97.17	97.95

To evaluate the proposed method, the experimental results for detecting NA-DJPEG compression are listed in Table 1. It is worth noting that NA-DJPEG compression detection with QF1 $\geq$ QF2 is a challenging task. When QF1 $\geq$ QF2, the primary JPEG compression trace is not only weaker than the secondary one, but is easy to be covered by the secondary one in double JPEG compressed images, so the primary JPEG compression trace is difficult to catch for detection. For instance, in the cases of (QF1, QF2) = (70, 50) and (QF1, QF2) = (90, 90), the Markov features still achieve the accuracy of 92.25% and 97.31%, respectively.

For the cases of QF1 < QF2, the proposed method still has certain advantages in detection. The detection accuracy of the proposed method is greater than 95% in all cases.

5   Conclusion

In this paper, a novel method has been proposed to detect Non-aligned double JPEG (NA-DJPEG) compression for color images. We first analyze the quaternion discrete cosine transform for color image. Based on the analysis, the Markov features are obtained by mapping the reconstructed color image into QDCT domain. Finally, with the extracted Markov feature, the support vector machine classifier is employed for NA-DJPEG compression detection. Experimental results show that the proposed method has certain advantages.

Acknowledgement. This work was supported in part by the Natural Science Foundation of China under (Grant No. 61772281, U1636219, 61502241, 61702235, U1636117, U1804263 and 61572258), in part by the National Key R&D Program of China(Grant No. 2016YFB0801303 and 2016QY01W0105), in part by the plan for Scientific Talent of Henan Province (Grant No. 2018JR0018), the PAPD fund and the CICAEET fund.

References

1. Li, C., Li, Y.: Color-decoupled photo response non-uniformity for digital image forensics. IEEE Trans. Circ. Syst. Video Technol. **22**(2), 260–271 (2012)
2. Wang, J., Li, T., Shi, Y.-Q., Lian, S., Ye, J.: Forensics feature analysis in quaternion wavelet domain for distinguishing photographic images and computer graphics. Multimed. Tools Appl. **76**(22), 23721–23737 (2016). https://doi.org/10.1007/s11042-016-4153-0
3. Ma, Y., Luo, X., Li, X., Bao, Z., Zhang, Y.: Selection of rich model steganalysis features based on decision rough set positive region reduction. IEEE Trans. Circ. Syst. Video Technol. **11**(2), 99–102 (2018)
4. Zhang, Y., Qin, C., Zhang, W., Liu, V., Luo, X.: On the fault-tolerant performances for a class of roubust image steganography. IEEE Trans. Signal Process. **146**, 99–111 (2018)
5. Wang, J., Li, T., Luo, X., Shi, Y.Q., Jha, S.K.: Identifying computer generated images based on quaternion central moments in color quaternion wavelet domain. IEEE Trans. Circ. Syst. Video Technol. **29**(9), 2775–2785 (2018)
6. Wallace, G.K.: The JPEG still picture compression standard. Commun. ACM **34**(4), 30–44 (1991)
7. Korus, P., Huang, J.: Multi-scale fusion for improved localization of malicious tampering in digital images. IEEE Trans. Image Process. **25**, 1312–1326 (2016)
8. Taimori, A., Razzazi, F., Behrad, A., Ahmadi, A., Babaie-Zadeh, M.: Quantization-Unaware double JPEG compression detection. J. Math. Imaging Vision **54**(3), 269–286 (2015). https://doi.org/10.1007/s10851-015-0602-z
9. Pasquini, C., Schöttle, P., Böhme, R., Boato, G., Pèrez-Gonzàlez, F.: Forensics of high quality and nearly identical jpeg image recompression. In: Proceedings of the 4th ACM Workshop on Information Hiding and Multimedia Security, pp. 11–21. ACM (2016)
10. Chen, Y.-L., Hsu, C.-T.: Detecting recompression of JPEG images via periodicity analysis of compression artifacts for tampering detection. IEEE Trans. Inf. Forensics Secur. (TIFS) **6**, 396–406 (2011)
11. Bianchi, T., Piva, A.: Detection of nonaligned double JPEG compression based on integer periodicity maps. IEEE Trans. Inf. Forensics Secur. (TIFS) **7**, 842–848 (2012)
12. Bianchi, T., Piva, A.: Image forgery localization via block-grained analysis of JPEG artifacts. IEEE Trans. Inf. Forensics Secur. (TIFS) **7**, 1003–1017 (2012)

13. Yang, J., Zhu, G., Wang, J., Shi, Y.Q.: Detecting non-aligned double JPEG compression based on refined intensity difference and calibration. In: Shi, Y.Q., Kim, H.-J., Pérez-González, F. (eds.) IWDW 2013. LNCS, vol. 8389, pp. 169–179. Springer, Heidelberg (2014). https://doi.org/10.1007/978-3-662-43886-2_12

14. Barni, M., et al.: Aligned and non-aligned double JPEG detection using convolutional neural networks. J. Vis. Commun. Image Represent. **49**, 153–163 (2017)

15. Feng, W., Hu, B.: Quaternion discrete cosine transform and its application in color template matching. IEEE Congr. Image Signal Process. **5**(2), 252–256 (2008)

16. Schaefer, G., Stich, M.: UCID - An uncompressed color image database. In: Proceedings of SPIE. Speech, Signal Process, pp. 472–480 (2004)

17. Chang, C.C., Lin, C.J.: LIBSVM: a library for support vector machines. ACM Trans. Intell. Syst. Technol. (TIST) **2**(3), 1–27 (2011)

Anti-forensics of Image Sharpening Using Generative Adversarial Network

Zhangyi Shen[1], Feng Ding[2(✉)], and Yunqing Shi[1]

[1] New Jersey Institute of Technology, Newark, NJ 07102, USA
{zs226,shi}@njit.edu
[2] State University of New York Albany, Albany, NY 12203, USA
fding@albany.edu

Abstract. Image sharpening is an image enhancement method which has been widely used to improve the quality of images. Therefore, in image forensics, it is required to be identified as all possible manipulations applied in images need to be detected. In recent years, sharpening detection get evolved with new detectors proposed every year to gradually boost the detection performance. This situation continues for several years till the introduction of convolutional neural networks (CNNs). With the assistance of CNNs, the detection of sharpening seems to be completely solved that the detection performance for sharpening achieves perfect, even when the images are weakly sharpened. Is it true that we should no longer pay attention to sharpening forensics any more? To answer this question, in this paper, an anti-forensics method based on generative adversarial network (GAN) is proposed to investigate the philosophy. The images generated via our method possess the feature of sharpening, however, they cannot be simply considered as sharpened images because no traditional sharpening manipulation is applied during the procedure. Observed from the experimental results, even the state-of-art sharpening detector based on CNN can be deceived with the GAN generated images.

Keywords: Image anti-forensics · Deep learning · Generative Adversarial Network · Image sharpening

1 Introduction

The explosive development of internet makes the propagation and distribution of information easier than ever. Under this circumstance, it also enables the dissemination of false information which brings immense harm to the community. Therefore, it is necessary to justify the authenticity and integrity of information from all possible channels. Generally speaking, people prefer visualized information such as images and videos over information in other forms. Thus, the research of image forensics [1–3] is the guardian to protect people from all kinds of image attacks.

© Springer Nature Switzerland AG 2020
H. Wang et al. (Eds.): IWDW 2019, LNCS 12022, pp. 150–157, 2020.
https://doi.org/10.1007/978-3-030-43575-2_12

The research about detecting USM sharpened images beginning in 2009. In 2009, Cao *et al.* found that there were aberrations in the histograms of sharpened images and proposed an algorithm to detect such aberration [4]. However, regarding to their report, this algorithm is not very effective when detecting the images without wide histogram. Then, Cao *et al.* revised their algorithm in order to improve the performance on images with narrow histogram and proposed a new detecting algorithm [5] in 2011. The algorithm employs a set of side-planar crosswise pixel sequences to locate on the basis of edge pixels of the detected image. Then, a set of overshoot strengths is calculated for each side-planar pixel sequence. The average of the overshoot strengths measures the overshoot metric of the whole image. Finally, the detected image will be identified refer to which interval this average overshoot strength belongs to.

After solving the problem about detecting images with narrow histogram, another weakness of their algorithm has been found, that is, the performance is limited when detecting images with JPEG compression. This drawback limits its generality use in practical applications. However, Ding *et al.* [6] proposed an novel algorithm based on local binary pattern (LBP) [7,8] in 2013. The authors thought that the appearance of overshoot artifacts can be regarded as a special kind of texture modification. Meanwhile, LBP is a widely used texture classification technique. As a result, the performance of the LBP-based algorithm exceeds all the sharpening detection algorithm before. However, after that, Lu *et al.* [9] proposed a method to remove overshoot artifacts for anti-forensics of USM sharpening.

Then, Inspired by the LBP-based method, Ding *et al.* [10] proposed a much more effective algorithm to detect USM sharpening. The algorithm is called Edge Perpendicular Binary Coding (EPBC). Since that the texture modification generated by USM sharpening is mainly along the perpendicular direction of image edges, EPBC employs a long rectangular window, which is perpendicular to the edges of images, to extract features of image textures and uses a binary coding strategy to reduce the size of feature sets. Furthermore, an improved algorithm, which is Edge Perpendicular Ternary Coding (EPTC), is proposed in [11]. EPTC replaced the binary coding with ternary coding in EPBC, which outperformed the EPBC.

The sharpening forensics was further improved later since CNN was introduced. The detection scheme based on CNN came out in 2018. Ye *et al.* [12] proposed an advanced CNN architecture that contains four convolutional modules with 4 layers each. By using max pooling as the pooling function and 'Relu' as the activation function, the results of this paper showed that the detection accuracy on all the cases were over 98% on the CNN model they trained. And this work represents the state-of-art on image sharpening detection at present.

Since the forensics on sharpening detection has achieved tremendous success, an anti-forensics sharpening algorithm via GAN is proposed in this paper to deeply challenge the current state-of-art. The rest of this paper is organize as follows. Section 2 shows the architecture of pix2pix. The experiment results with analysis are shown in Sect. 3. Finally, Sect. 4 made a conclusion for this paper.

2 Pix2pix

Pix2pix [13] is a conditional adversarial network structure, which is proposed by Berkeley AI Research (BAIR) Laboratory. Compared with classical GAN, it provides a solution of image-to-image translations. In other words, pix2pix accepts image pairs as input. One image pair contains a input image and a target image. Pix2pix will learn the regular pattern of translation from input image to target image, then perform the translation on input image based on the pattern it learned and generate an output image. Considering that image sharpening algorithm only enhances the visual effect of image but not tampers with content, pix2pix is selected to implement similar treatment with USM sharpening algorithm.

2.1 The Network Architecture

The architecture of pix2pix is shown in Fig. 1. The discriminator learns to judged the generated image as unsharpened image and the target image as sharpened image. Meanwhile, the generator learns to deceive the discriminator by adjust the output image it generated. With continuously training of the network, the generated image will be closer and closer to the target image and also has better performance on the resist of detection.

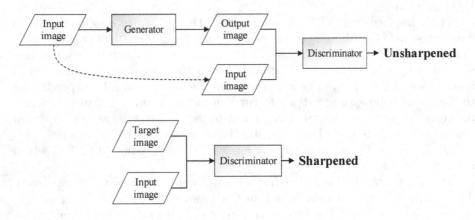

Fig. 1. The architecture of pix2pix

2.2 Generator and Discriminator

The generator in pix2pix is "U-Net" [14], which follows the rule of skip connection. The authors considered that for image translation, the input and the output should share some information from the layers on the bottom of the network. The feature maps in the first half layers from input to output will be added to the symmetrical layers in the second half. As a result, some features on the bottom will be preserved as the reference to output image.

Image generated via $L1$ or $L2$ loss is fuzzy because $L1$ and $L2$ is not effective to restore the high frequency part of image. In order to overcome this draw back, pix2pix provides a discriminator structure called PatchGAN. First, PatchGAN slices image to patches. Then, it tried to classify each patch, respectively. Finally, it averaging the results of all the patches and made its decision. This method can avoid the loss of texture to some extent.

3   Experimental Results

3.1   Datasets

Two image databases were utilized in the experimental. One is named Boss, which was designed for steganoagraphy and steganalysis. Boss contains 10,000 uncompressed grayscale images in "pgm" format. Another image database, which named UCID & NRCS by us, was consisted of 1,000 images from the UCID image database and 1,000 images from NRCS image database. For convenience purposes, all the images from Boss were scaled to the size of 256×256. Since the images of UCID & NRCS are not square, all the images from UCID & NRCS were cropped into the size of 384×384 first and then scaled to the size of 256×256 as well. In addition, all the images were converted to "png" format and grayscale images.

Note that, in Sect. 2, we have introduced two parameters, which were λ and σ. They determine the effect of USM sharpening. In our experiment, we have worked on five combinations of λ and σ, i.e., '$\lambda = 1.5, \sigma = 1.3$', '$\lambda = 1.0, \sigma = 1.5$', '$\lambda = 1.0, \sigma = 1.3$', '$\lambda = 1.0, \sigma = 0.7$', '$\lambda = 1.5, \sigma = 1.0$'. Two image databases that introduced before were sharpened based on these five cases. The original image and its sharpened image, which became a pair of images, were labeled as 0 and 1, respectively. 10,000 Pairs of images generated by Boss were used for training pix2pix model, which can transfer images, and CNN model, which can distinguish images. 2,000 Pairs of images generated by UCID & NRCS were used for testing the performance of generated models.

3.2   Platform and Settings

TensorFlow is one of the most popular deep learning frameworks at present. It has open source feature as well as a large total of convenient APIs. All the pix2pix architecture and CNN architecture were implemented by Tensorflow. The version number of the TensorFlow for this experiment is 1.11.0. The graphics cards employed in the experiment were two NVIDIA GeForce GTX 1080Ti with 10 GB memory. The version number of CUDA is 9.0.

For training pix2pix models, the training batch size was fixed to 1, meaning that for each iteration, 1 images will get into the network. One epoch means all the images in training dataset get into the network once. The number of epochs for training was fixed to 100. Adam optimizer was employed to train the whole network. The initial learning rate of Adam was fixed to 0.0002 and the momentum was fixed to 0.5. The images generated by pix2pix would be classified by the CNN model, which trained though the CNN architecture in [12].

The CNN architecture is shown in Fig. 2. It has four convolutional modules. Each convolutional module has a convolutional layer, a normalization layer, a activation layer and a pooling layer, respectively. The function of activation layers is Relu. Max pooling is adopted in first three convolutional modules. The pooling algorithm in the last convolutional module is average pooling, which concluded the feature maps to 64 single feature elements before getting into classification module. For training CNN models, the batch size is 64 and the number of epochs is 50. The learning rate of Adam is 0.001 and the momentum is 0.9.

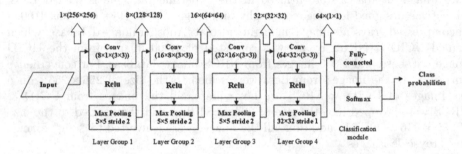

Fig. 2. The architecture of CNN for testing. The configuration of each layer is displayed inside the boxes. The sizes of feature maps are listed on the top, shown as number of feature maps × (height × width). The sizes of convolutional filter groups are shown in the boxes follows number of filters × number of input feature maps × (height × width).

3.3   Results

At first, we used the prepared 10,000 pairs of images, which were generated from Boss, of each five cases to train pix2pix models individually. Second, we used these models to generate images on UCID & NRCS. The samples of the comparison between the generated images, the original images and the sharpened images on the case when $\lambda = 1.5, \sigma = 1.3$ were shown in Fig. 3. Compared with original images, The generated images do have similar sharpening effect with generated images visually.

Then, we still used the image pairs of Boss to training CNN models of each five cases. Finally, 2,000 generated images of each cases were classified by corresponding models. The comparison of the average classification accuracy of generated images and the duration of training pix2pix models for each cases are shown in Table 1. The time consumption indicates the time count on minutes that consumed for the model reach convergence.

Original image   Sharpened image   Generated image

Fig. 3. Two samples of the generated images, the original images and the sharpened images on the case of '$\lambda = 1.5, \sigma = 1.3$'.

Table 1. The average classification accuracy for each cases and the duration of pix2pix training process.

Cases	Accuracy	Time consumption
$\lambda = 1.5, \sigma = 1.3$	87.72%	1259
$\lambda = 1.0, \sigma = 1.5$	83.72%	1267
$\lambda = 1.0, \sigma = 1.3$	78.21%	1260
$\lambda = 1.0, \sigma = 0.7$	73.32%	1255
$\lambda = 1.5, \sigma = 1.0$	85.62%	1260

Considering that the classification accuracy for all the cases are over 98% in [12], the generated images does have anti-forensics property to some extent. Besides, The average value of peak signal to noise ratio (PSNR) for the generated images and the sharpened images of different parameters are computed. The results can be found in Table 2. It is the evidence that the generated images not only possess the sharpening effect, but also higher image quality when compares with the images processed by USM sharpening algorithm.

Table 2. The average PSNR of the generated images and the sharpened images on each cases.

Cases	PSNR(dB)	
	Generated	Sharpened
$\lambda = 1.5, \sigma = 1.3$	30.74	26.00
$\lambda = 1.0, \sigma = 1.5$	33.40	28.02
$\lambda = 1.0, \sigma = 1.3$	33.11	28.94
$\lambda = 1.0, \sigma = 0.7$	35.73	34.64
$\lambda = 1.5, \sigma = 1.0$	31.44	27.94

4   Conclusion

In this paper, an anti-forensics method is proposed. Our method is capable of generating images, which have sharpening effect that aims to deceive the state-of-art sharpening detector. The proposed GAN model consists of a generator and a discriminator. It features generating images with sharpening effect while preserving the image contents. Observed from the experimental results, the generated images can be successfully classified as sharpened images although they have never been sharpened via any traditional sharpening manipulation. In addition, the quality of the generated images are also better with higher PSNR when compare with the real sharpened images. This can be considered as a tremendous success that it shows the potential of GAN models in generating images. In our future work, we will devote ourselves to further explore the potential of GAN.

References

1. Fridrich, J.: Digital image forensics. IEEE Signal Process. Mag. **26**(2), 26–37 (2009)
2. Piva, A.: An overview on image forensics. ISRN Signal Process. **2013**, 22 (2013)
3. Farid, H.: Image forgery detection. IEEE Signal Process. Mag. **26**(2), 16–25 (2009)
4. Cao, G., Zhao, Y., Ni, R.: Detection of image sharpening based on histogram aberration and ringing artifacts. In: Proceedings of the IEEE International Conference on Multimedia and Expo (ICME), pp. 1026–1029 (2009)
5. Cao, G., Zhao, Y., Ni, R., Kot, A.C.: Unsharp masking sharpening detection via overshoot artifacts analysis. IEEE Signal Process. Lett. **18**(10), 603–606 (2011)
6. Ding, F., Zhu, G., Shi, Y.Q.: A novel method for detecting image sharpening based on local binary pattern. In: Shi, Y.Q., Kim, H.-J., Pérez-González, F. (eds.) IWDW 2013. LNCS, vol. 8389, pp. 180–191. Springer, Heidelberg (2014). https://doi.org/10.1007/978-3-662-43886-2_13
7. Ojala, T., Pietikäinen, M., Harwood, D.: A comparative study of texture measures with classfication based on featured distributions. Pattern Recogn. **29**(1), 51–59 (1996)
8. Ojala, T., Pietikainen, M., Maenpaa, T.: Multiresolution gray-scale and rotation invariant texture classfication with local binary patterns. IEEE Trans. Patt. Anal. Mach. Intell. **24**(7), 971–987 (2002)

9. Lu, L., Yang, G., Xia, M.: Anti-forensics for unsharp masking sharpening in digital images. Int. J. Digit. Crime Forensics **5**(3), 53–65 (2013)
10. Ding, F., Zhu, G., Yang, J., Xie, J., Shi, Y.Q.: Edge perpendicular binary coding for USM sharpening detection. IEEE Signal Process. Lett. **22**(3), 327–331 (2015)
11. Ding, F., Zhu, G., Dong, W., Shi, Y.Q.: An efficient weak sharpening detection method for image forensics. J. Vis. Commun. Image Represent. **50**, 93–99 (2018)
12. Ye, J., Shen, Z., Behrani, P., Ding, F., Shi, Y.Q.: Detecting USM image sharpening by using CNN. Signal Process. Image Commun. **68**, 258–264 (2018)
13. Isola, P., Zhu, J.Y., Zhou, T., Efros, A.A.: Image-to-image translation with conditional adversarial networks. In: Proceedings of the IEEE Conference on Computer Vision and Pattern Recognition, pp. 1125–1134 (2017)
14. Ronneberger, O., Fischer, P., Brox, T.: U-Net: convolutional networks for biomedical image segmentation. In: Navab, N., Hornegger, J., Wells, W.M., Frangi, A.F. (eds.) MICCAI 2015. LNCS, vol. 9351, pp. 234–241. Springer, Cham (2015). https://doi.org/10.1007/978-3-319-24574-4_28

Digital Watermarking

A New JPEG Image Watermarking Method Exploiting Spatial JND Model

Liwen Qin[1,2], Xiaolong Li[1,2], and Yao Zhao[1,2(✉)]

[1] Institute of Information Science, Beijing Jiaotong University, Beijing 100044, China
{18120311,lixl,yzhao}@bjtu.edu.cn
[2] Beijing Key Laboratory of Advanced Information Science and Network Technology,
Beijing 100044, China

Abstract. For JPEG images, the current digital watermarking methods mainly embed the watermark by modifying the DCT coefficients, in which the spatial visual performance isn't well taken into account. As a result, significant visual distortion can be observed in smooth and boundary regions of the marked image. Then, to improve the visual quality of the marked image, a new JPEG image watermarking method exploiting the spatial just-noticeable-difference (JND) model is proposed in this paper. In the proposed method, the watermark is embedded into the DCT domain, but the embedding strength is directly determined by a spatial JND model. Moreover, for each DCT block, the variances calculated from the difference blocks along four different directions are controlled to further enhance the imperceptibility. Finally, an optimization problem is summarized and developed to obtain the optimal embedding strength that meets the above requirements. Experimental results show that, with the same PSNR and robustness, the proposed method has better imperceptibility than the prior art.

Keywords: DCT domain digital watermarking · Spatial JND model · Optimization problem

1 Introduction

Digital watermarking provides a way for copyright protection of digital media such as images, videos, and text documents, etc [7]. So far, various image watermarking methods have been proposed, and these methods can be roughly classified into two categories: quantization based and spread spectrum (SS) based. For quantization based methods, the watermark is inserted by using different quantizers to quantize the host image features [3,8,10,14]. For SS based methods, the watermark is embedded into frequency coefficients of the host image as pseudo-random noise, either additively [9,11,15] or multiplicatively [5,6,12].

This work was supported by the National Science Foundation of China (Nos. 61532005 and 61972031), and the Fundamental Research Funds for the Central Universities (No. 2018JBZ001).

H. Wang et al. (Eds.): IWDW 2019, LNCS 12022, pp. 161–170, 2020.
https://doi.org/10.1007/978-3-030-43575-2_13

Nowadays, digital images are commonly stored and transmitted in JPEG format. Hence, most image watermarking methods are designed for JPEG images. For example, in [4], Cheng *et al.* proposed a DCT domain watermarking method. In this work, based on modifying the mean of DCT coefficients in the middle frequencies, the watermark is embedded into a JPEG image. This method can resist JPEG compression and print-and-scan (PS) attack as well. However, significant visual distortion still exists in smooth and boundary areas of the marked image. The main reason is that, when modifying DCT coefficients for watermark embedding, the just-noticeable-difference (JND) model utilized in this work is only defined in DCT domain, while spatial visual distortion isn't well taken into account.

Then, based on the above consideration and to improve the visual quality of the marked image, as an extension of Cheng *et al.*'s work [4], a new JPEG image watermarking method is proposed in this paper. In the proposed method, a spatial JND model, which reveals the visibility thresholds of the human visual system (HVS) for spatial pixels, is directly utilized to determine the embedding strength of middle frequency DCT coefficients. Moreover, in each DCT block of the host image, the variances calculated from the difference blocks along four different directions are controlled to further enhance the imperceptibility. Finally, based on the aforementioned constraints, an optimization problem is summarized and developed to obtain the optimal embedding strength. Experimental results show that, with the same PSNR and robustness, the proposed method has better imperceptibility than the prior art [4].

The rest of this paper is organized as follows. In Sect. 2, Cheng *et al.*'s watermarking method [4] is briefly introduced. Then, the proposed method is described in detail in Sect. 3. The experimental results and the comparison with Cheng *et al.*'s method [4] are shown in Sect. 4. Finally, this work is concluded in Sect. 5.

2   Related Work

In this section, the watermark embedding and extraction procedures of Cheng *et al.*'s method [4] are briefly described as follows.

In the embedding process, first, for the host JPEG image, collect all DCT coefficients $x_{u,v}^k$ in the middle frequency with

$$(u, v, k) \in C \triangleq \{(u, v, k) : 0 \leq u, v \leq 7, \ 3 \leq u + v \leq 6, \ 1 \leq k \leq K\} \quad (1)$$

where (u, v) is the frequency position, k is the block index, and K is the total number of DCT blocks. Then, encode the watermark by a key into a sequence $(w_1, ..., w_M)$ with $w_i \in \{-1, 1\}$. Next, divide the set C into M subsets as

$$C = C_1 \cup ... \cup C_M \quad (2)$$

where the DCT coefficients in each subset C_i have the same frequency. Finally, embed each watermark bit w_i into the host image by shifting the mean value of the elements in C_i, i.e., the marked DCT coefficient is defined as

$$y_{u,v}^k = \begin{cases} x_{u,v}^k + a_{u,v}^k w_i & \text{if } (u,v,k) \in C_i \\ x_{u,v}^k & \text{if } (u,v,k) \notin C \end{cases} \tag{3}$$

where the perceptual mask $a_{u,v}^k$ is defined by, using the HVS model described in [2]

$$a_{u,v}^k = 4\gamma(1 + (\sqrt{2} - 1)\delta_u)(1 + (\sqrt{2} - 1)\delta_v)T_{u,v}\left(\frac{x_{0,0}^k}{\bar{x}_{0,0}}\right)^a \tag{4}$$

where δ is the Kronecker delta function, $\bar{x}_{0,0}$ denotes the mean luminance of the host image, $x_{0,0}^k$ denotes the DC coefficient of the k-th DCT block, the parameter a is set to 0.649, $\gamma \in (0,1)$ is a scaling factor controlling the watermark strength, and $T_{u,v}$ is the visibility threshold for the AC frequency (u,v) defined by (see Ahumada $et\ al.$ [1])

$$\log T_{u,v} = \log \frac{T_{\min}(f_{u,0}^2 + f_{0,v}^2)^2}{(f_{u,0}^2 + f_{0,v}^2)^2 - 4(1-r)f_{u,0}^2 f_{0,v}^2} + F\left(\log \sqrt{f_{u,0}^2 + f_{0,v}^2} - \log f_{\min}\right)^2. \tag{5}$$

Here, in the above equation, $f_{u,0}$ and $f_{0,v}$ are the vertical and horizontal spatial frequency (in cycle/degree), respectively, and the parameters are set as $r = 0.7$, $T_{\min} = 1.1548$, $F = 1.728$ and $f_{\min} = 3.68$ cycles/degree.

In this method, the key issue is that, for each set C_i, the mean value of the DCT coefficients $x_{u,v}^k$ with $(u,v,k) \in C_i$ is approximately 0, i.e.,

$$\sum_{(u,v,k) \in C_i} x_{u,v}^k \approx 0. \tag{6}$$

Then, this mean value is shifted towards left or right according to (3) to embed one watermark bit $w_i \in \{-1,1\}$.

In the extraction process, first, divide the marked image into 8×8 sized blocks and perform DCT on each block. Suppose that the derived DCT coefficients are $z_{u,v}^k$. As the marked image is probably degraded in transmission (such as re-compressing or PS, etc.), we then have, considering (3), for each $(u,v,k) \in C_i$,

$$z_{u,v}^k = y_{u,v}^k + n_{u,v}^k = x_{u,v}^k + a_{u,v}^k w_i + n_{u,v}^k \tag{7}$$

where $n_{u,v}^k$ can be modeled as i.i.d. noise with mean zero. Then, for each $1 \le i \le M$, calculate the detector T_i as

$$T_i = \sum_{(u,v,k) \in C_i} z_{u,v}^k. \tag{8}$$

In this way, based on (6) and (7), we have

$$T_i = \sum_{(u,v,k) \in C_i} (x_{u,v}^k + a_{u,v}^k w_i + n_{u,v}^k) \approx w_i\left(\sum_{(u,v,k) \in C_i} a_{u,v}^k\right). \tag{9}$$

Next, since $a_{u,v}^k$ is always positive, the embedded watermark bit denoted $\widetilde{w}_i$ can be determined by the sign of T_i, i.e.,

$$\widetilde{w}_i = \left\{ \begin{array}{ll} 1 & \text{if } T_i > 0 \\ -1 & \text{if } T_i \leq 0 \end{array} \right. . \tag{10}$$

Finally, the extracted sequence $(\widetilde{w}_1, ..., \widetilde{w}_M)$ is decoded by the same key used in the embedding process to obtain the embedded watermark.

Experimental results show that the scheme can well resist JPEG compression and PS attack. However, regarding (4) and (5), when modifying DCT coefficients for watermark embedding, the JND model utilized in this work is only defined in DCT domain, which may result significant spatial visual distortion in smooth and boundary regions of the marked image.

3   Proposed Method

As an extension of Cheng *et al.*'s work [4], a new JPEG image watermarking method is proposed. In the proposed method, since the spatial JND model can directly reflect the visual thresholds of HVS for host pixels, a spatial JND model is exploited to determine the embedding strength of middle frequency DCT coefficients. Moreover, in each DCT block of the host image, the variances calculated from the difference blocks along horizontal, vertical, diagonal and anti-diagonal directions are controlled to further enhance the imperceptibility. The detailed implementation process is elaborated below.

In the proposed embedding process, the same as Cheng *et al.*'s method [4], we also adopt (3) for data embedding, and the only difference between the proposed method and [4] is the determination of the watermark strength $a_{u,v}^k$. In our work, an optimization problem is established to obtain the optimal $a_{u,v}^k$ based on several constraints.

Suppose that the host and marked spatial pixels are respectively $X_{i,j}^k$ and $Y_{i,j}^k$, where $(X_{i,j}^k)_{0 \leq i,j \leq 7}$ and $(Y_{i,j}^k)_{0 \leq i,j \leq 7}$ are respectively the inverse DCT of $(x_{u,v}^k)_{0 \leq u,v \leq 7}$ and $(y_{u,v}^k)_{0 \leq u,v \leq 7}$. Then, we define

$$D_{i,j}^k = Y_{i,j}^k - X_{i,j}^k \tag{11}$$

as the pixel change due to watermark embedding. Clearly, $(D_{i,j}^k)_{0 \leq i,j \leq 7}$ is the inverse DCT of $(y_{u,v}^k - x_{u,v}^k)_{0 \leq u,v \leq 7}$.

On one hand, we propose to utilize a spatial JND model to control the spatial pixel change, i.e., we impose the following constraint

$$|D_{i,j}^k| \leq S_{i,j}^k \tag{12}$$

where $S_{i,j}^k$ represents the spatial JND threshold. Here, the spatial JND model is obtained based on the work [13].

On the other hand, since the constraint (12) only controls the single pixel change, the correlation between adjacent pixels is not considered. We then propose to control the change of pixel difference. Taking the horizontal direction for example, denote the difference block of the k-th image block as HX^k and HY^k, for the host and marked image, respectively. Specifically, HX^k and HY^k are defined as, for $0 \leq i \leq 6$ and $0 \leq j \leq 7$,

$$HX_{i,j}^k = X_{i,j}^k - X_{i+1,j}^k \quad \text{and} \quad HY_{i,j}^k = Y_{i,j}^k - Y_{i+1,j}^k. \tag{13}$$

Then, based on the variances of HX^k and HY^k, we impose the following constraint to control the change of pixel difference in horizontal direction

$$Var(HY^k) \leq Var(HX^k). \tag{14}$$

Similarly, consider the difference blocks of the k-th image block for the host and marked image along the vertical direction (denoted respectively as VX^k and VY^k), diagonal direction (denoted respectively as DX^k and DY^k) and anti-diagonal direction (denoted respectively as AX^k and AY^k), we also impose the following constraints: $Var(VY^k) \leq Var(VX^k)$, $Var(DY^k) \leq Var(DX^k)$, and $Var(AY^k) \leq Var(AX^k)$.

In summary, based on the above constraints, for the k-th image block, the optimization problem that maximizes the watermark strength, can be expressed as

$$\left\{ \begin{array}{l} \text{minimize} \ -\sum\limits_{(u,v)\in \Lambda} a_{u,v}^k \\ \text{subject to } a_{u,v}^k \geq 0 \\ \qquad |D_{i,j}^k| \leq S_{i,j}^k \\ \qquad Var(HY^k) \leq Var(HX^k) \\ \qquad Var(VY^k) \leq Var(VX^k) \\ \qquad Var(DY^k) \leq Var(DX^k) \\ \qquad Var(AY^k) \leq Var(AX^k) \end{array} \right. \tag{15}$$

where $\Lambda = \{0 \leq u, v \leq 7, \ 3 \leq u + v \leq 6\}$ means the set of middle frequencies. This optimization problem (15) is a standard convex optimization problem, and it can be solved efficiently based on the conventional gradient decent method. Finally, after obtaining the watermark strength $a_{u,v}^k$ for each block, the watermark embedding can be completed by re-defining the marked DCT coefficient as

$$y_{u,v}^k = \begin{cases} x_{u,v}^k + \beta a_{u,v}^k w_i & \text{if } (u,v,k) \in C_i \\ x_{u,v}^k & \text{if } (u,v,k) \notin C \end{cases} \tag{16}$$

where $\beta \in (0,1)$ is a parameter tuning the PSNR of the resulting marked image.

In the proposed extraction process, the same as Cheng *et al.*'s work [4], we also adopt (8) and (10) to extract the watermark bits.

4   Experimental Results

In this section, we use eight standard 512×512 sized gray-scale JPEG images including Lena, Baboon, Airplane, Barbara, Lake, Boat, Peppers, and Elaine to evaluate the fidelity and robustness of the proposed method. In the experiment,

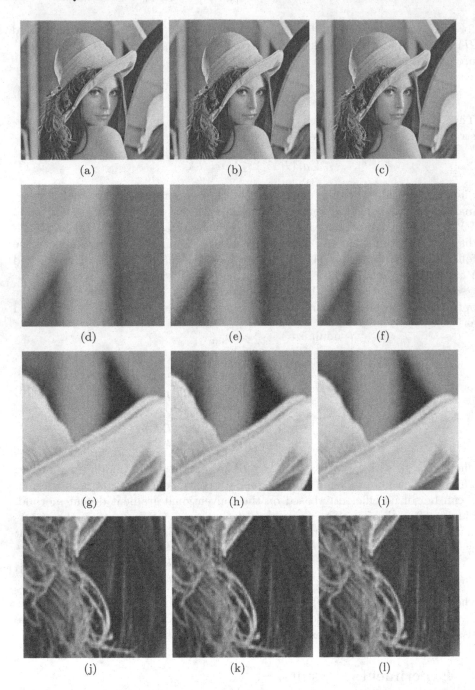

Fig. 1. Visual performance comparison for the image Lena with PSNR=40.35 dB: (a) the host image; (b) the marked image derived from Cheng *et al.*'s method [4]; (c) the marked image derived from the proposed method; (d) (g) (j) 100×100 sized sub-image of (a); (e) (h) (k) 100×100 sized sub-image of (b); (f) (i) (l) 100×100 sized sub-image of (c).

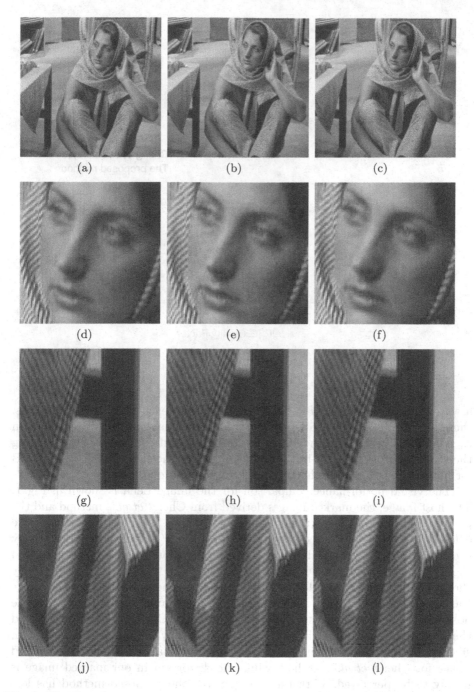

Fig. 2. Visual performance comparison for the image Barbara with PSNR=40.35 dB:
(a) the host image; (b) the marked image derived from Cheng *et al.*'s method [4]; (c)
the marked image derived from the proposed method; (d) (g) (j) 100 × 100 sized sub-
image of (a); (e) (h) (k) 100 × 100 sized sub-image of (b); (f) (i) (l) 100 × 100 sized
sub-image of (c).

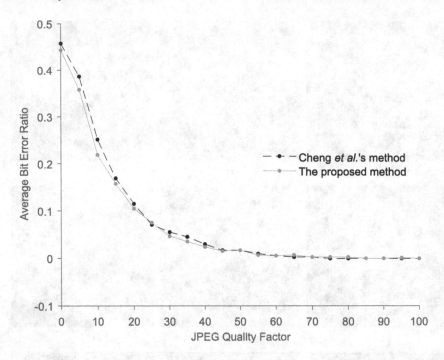

Fig. 3. Average BER for JPEG compression, for eight test images.

a watermark with length $M = 88$ is embedded into each host image, and thus, there are totally $K = 4,096$ DCT blocks for each image and $1,024$ elements in each set C_i. To evaluate the visual performance and robustness, by adjusting the scaling factors γ and β in (4) and (16), we set the same PSNR = 40.35 dB for both Cheng *et al.*'s method [4] and the proposed one.

The visual performance comparison for the image Lena is shown in Fig. 1. The host image, the marked images derived from Cheng *et al.*'s method and the proposed method are respectively shown in Fig. 1(a), (b) and (c). Moreover, we extract three 100×100 sized sub-images from Fig. 1(a), which are respectively shown in Fig. 1(d), (g) and (j). The same operations are also performed on Fig. 1(b) (respectively shown in Figs. 1(e), (h) and (k)) and (c) (respectively shown in Fig. 1(f), (i) and (l)). Similarly, the experimental results for the image Barbara are shown in Fig. 2. As shown in Figs. 1 and 2, compared with the host image, in texture region, the pixel changes in Cheng *et al.*'s method and the proposed one are both hardly to be perceived by human eyes. However, in smooth and boundary regions, there is significant visual distortion in the marked image for Cheng *et al.*'s method, while the distortion in our marked image is hardly to be perceived. With the same PSNR, the proposed method has less obvious visual distortion than Cheng *et al.*'s method. The experimental results for other six images also demonstrate the superiority of the proposed method.

Moreover, to evaluate the robustness, the bit error ratio (BER) for eight host images embedded by Cheng *et al.*'s method and ours, is respectively computed, with different JPEG compression factors. Figure 3 shows the average BER curves. According to this figure, one can see that the robustness of the proposed method is approximately the same as that of Cheng *et al.*'s method, whatever the JPEG quality factor is. Moreover, the proposed method is robust enough for JPEG compression when the JPEG quality factor is above 50.

In conclusion, compared with Cheng *et al.*'s method, with the same PSNR, the watermark in the proposed method is hardly to be perceived by human eyes, and there is almost no degradation for the robustness against to JPEG compression. The spatial JND model is proved to be effective in enhancing the embedding performance of the DCT domain watermarking scheme.

5   Conclusion

In this paper, as an extension of Cheng *et al.*'s work [4], a new JPEG image watermarking method is proposed. In the proposed method, a spatial JND model is exploited to determine the DCT domain watermark embedding strength. Moreover, in each DCT block, the variances calculated from the difference blocks along horizontal, vertical, diagonal and anti-diagonal directions are controlled to further enhance the imperceptibility. By the proposed approach, the embedding strength is in line with the HVS threshold for spatial pixel, and the visual quality of the marked image is guaranteed. Experimental results have demonstrated that the proposed scheme is robust to JPEG compression. And, compared with Cheng *et al.*'s method [4], the proposed scheme has better invisibility with the same PSNR and robustness. For the future work, we will extend the proposed approach to more effective DCT domain image watermarking schemes.

References

1. Ahumada, A.J., Peterso, H.A.: Luminance-model-based DCT quantization for color image compression. In: Human Vision, Visual Processing, Digital Display III. vol. 1666, pp. 365–374 (1992)
2. Briassouli, A., Tsakalides, P., Stouraitis, A.: Hidden messages in heavy-tails: DCT-domain watermark detection using alpha-stable models. IEEE Trans. Multimedia **7**(4), 700–715 (2005)
3. Chen, B., Wornell, G.W.: Quantization index modulation: a class of provably good methods for digital watermarking and information embedding. IEEE Trans. Inf. Theory **47**(4), 1423–1443 (2001)
4. Cheng, D., Li, X., Qi, W., Yang, B.: A statistics-based watermarking scheme robust to print-and-scan. In: 2008 International Symposium on Electronic Commerce and Security, pp. 894–898 (2008)
5. Cheng, Q.: Generalized embedding of multiplicative watermarks. IEEE Trans. Circuits Syst. Video Technol. **19**(7), 978–988 (2009)
6. Cox, I.J., Kilian, J., Leighton, F.T., Shamoon, T.: Secure spread spectrum watermarking for multimedia. IEEE Trans. Image Process. **6**(12), 1673–1687 (1997)

7. Cox, I., Miller, M., Bloom, J., Fridrich, J., Kalker, T.: Digital Watermarking and Steganography, 2nd edn. Morgan Kaufmann Publishers Inc., San Francisco (2007)
8. Li, Q., Cox, I.J.: Using perceptual models to improve fidelity and provide resistance to valumetric scaling for quantization index modulation watermarking. IEEE Trans. Inf. Forensics Secur. **2**(2), 127–139 (2007)
9. Malvar, H.S., Florencio, D.A.F.: Improved spread spectrum: a new modulation technique for robust watermarking. IEEE Trans. Signal Process. **51**(4), 898–905 (2003)
10. Nezhadarya, E., Wang, Z.J., Ward, R.K.: Robust image watermarking based on multiscale gradient direction quantization. IEEE Trans. Inf. Forensics Secur. **6**(4), 1200–1213 (2011)
11. Valizadeh, A., Wang, Z.J.: Correlation-and-bit-aware spread spectrum embedding for data hiding. IEEE Trans. Inf. Forensics Secur. **6**(2), 267–282 (2011)
12. Valizadeh, A., Wang, Z.J.: An improved multiplicative spread spectrum embedding scheme for data hiding. IEEE Trans. Inf. Forensics Secur. **7**(4), 1127–1143 (2012)
13. Wu, J., Lin, W., Shi, G., Wang, X., Li, F.: Pattern masking estimation in image with structural uncertainty. IEEE Trans. Image Process. **22**(12), 4892–4904 (2013)
14. Zareian, M., Tohidypour, H.R.: A novel gain invariant quantization-based watermarking approach. IEEE Trans. Inf. Forensics Secur. **9**(11), 1804–1813 (2014)
15. Zong, T., Xiang, Y., Guo, S., Rong, Y.: Rank-based image watermarking method with high embedding capacity and robustness. IEEE Access **4**, 1689–1699 (2016)

Improved DM-QIM Watermarking Scheme for PDF Document

Minoru Kuribayashi[1(✉)] and KokSheik Wong[2]

[1] Okayama University, Okayama, Japan
kminoru@okayama-u.ac.jp
[2] Monash University Malaysia, Subang Jaya, Selangor, Malaysia
wong.koksheik@monash.edu

Abstract. In any application of watermarking, the selection of feature vectors from a given multimedia content is important from the perspective of robustness and security. In the case of PDF document, the spaces between words and characters are commonly utilized for embedding watermark in the conventional schemes. Instead of modifying the space values directly, researchers proposed to manipulate the frequency components of the space values by using the quantization index modulation (QIM) watermarking method. The QIM method is further combined with dither modulation (DM) to enhance secrecy of watermark. In this paper, we improve the imperceptibility of watermarked PDF document by investigating into the DM operation. The proposed method selects the best secret key among some candidates which minimizes the degradation caused by embedding watermark. Information about the selected key is also embedded as side information so that the embedded watermark can be extracted without referring to the original PDF document. The degree of distortion caused by watermark embedding is quantitatively measured in our experiment. It is verified that the gain in terms of signal-to-noise ratio in the proposed method is increased with the number of secret key candidates.

Keywords: PDF document · Watermark · Dither modulation · Quantization index modulation

1 Introduction

Digital watermarking technique enables us to embed information into multimedia content without causing noticeable perceptual degradation. It is desirable to embed more information with less distortion. Robustness of a watermark, which refers to its ability to withstand common attacks, is also important for actual deployment or application of the watermarking scheme. Such watermarking schemes can be roughly categorized into two classes, namely, (a) spread spectrum [4], and (b) quantization index modulation (QIM) [3]. Due to its high robustness against attacks and low embedding distortion, QIM-based technique has been employed in many watermarking schemes. When adversaries only know

© Springer Nature Switzerland AG 2020
H. Wang et al. (Eds.): IWDW 2019, LNCS 12022, pp. 171–183, 2020.
https://doi.org/10.1007/978-3-030-43575-2_14

the embedding algorithm but not the secret key, they focus on the components (i.e., venues) which may contain watermark signal for attacking the watermark. Hence, such components should be selected according to a secret key, and information leakage by means of direct observation should be prevented from a security point of view. In Chen et al.'s QIM method [3], some extensions are also investigated for enhancing the secrecy of watermark as well as the robustness against additive noise.

Among all multimedia contents, we focus on PDF document in this study. PDF stands for *portable document format* [5], which has been developed by Adobe Systems Society as a page description language. Due to the compatibility requirement in various environments, office documents are commonly stored in the PDF format. With PDF, one can set the permissions to prevent the file from being viewed, copied, printed, and so on. However, the protection against information leakage becomes difficult when such permissions are allowed, even just for one time. In the case of internal leakage by a malicious party (e.g., spy), we need other protection mechanism such as watermark to identify the traitor based on the leaked PDF file.

Since PDF conforms to a standard, we should be mindful not to violate the constraints in PDF document, i.e., format-compliant. Otherwise, a PDF viewer detects irregularities in the format and refuses to open the file. Specifically, in a PDF file, a TJ operator displays strings of text with the specified position and space lengths between characters. In some conventional schemes [1,2,6–10], the space lengths are applied for embedding watermark. For example, Bitar et al. [2] combined QIM with the spread transform dither modulation (STDM) [3] to embed watermark. Due to its spreading operation in STDM, the analysis of watermark becomes difficult. However, the payload is small due to the characteristic of STDM. In [6], an ordinary dither modulation (DM) is used in the QIM method to ensure the secrecy of the watermark. A set of space lengths in each line is regarded as a host vector, and its frequency components are modified for embedding purpose. For the enhancement of secrecy, a random permutation is introduced prior to frequency transformation. The maximum payload of the DM method is significantly larger than the STDM-QIM method, and the payload can be controlled by a rate parameter.

In this paper, we propose a method for suppressing the distortion caused by embedding watermark using the DM-QIM method. A random sequence is used in the DM operation, and it is generated according to a secret key. The proposed method increases the number of the candidates of such random sequence and finds the one that minimizes the distortion. Information of the selected candidate is embedded as side information in order to provide a blind watermarking scheme, which can extract a watermark without referring to the original content. By introducing a spreading operation among every lines, the embedding information is widely spread over all space lengths for not compromising the secrecy of side information as well as watermark. The degree of reduction in distortion and file size are numerically compared with the original DM-QIM method.

2   Preliminaries

In this section, we briefly review the DM-QIM watermarking method and review a conventional watermarking method [6] for PDF document.

2.1   DM-QIM Watermarking

Let d be an element in the feature vector exploited for embedding, and let $w \in \{0,1\}$ be a watermark. In QIM, d is quantized into the nearest even/odd point, which is a multiple of a quantization step size δ. For example, if $\delta = 10$, the resulting quantized value will be a member in the set $\{0, \pm 10, \pm 20, \pm 30, \cdots \}$. If a malicious party knows the embedding algorithm in use, each element of the feature vector can be found by simply observing the values. Therefore, the DM operation is introduced to enhance secrecy.

In the DM operation, a random number k is identically and independently selected from the range $[-\delta/2, \delta/2]$. Then, a watermark w is embedded into d using k as follows:

$$d' = \text{DM-QIM}(d, w, k)$$
$$= \begin{cases} \delta \cdot \left\lfloor \frac{d+k}{\delta} \right\rfloor & \text{if } \left\lfloor \frac{d+k}{\delta} \right\rfloor \bmod 2 = w; \\ \delta \cdot \left(\left\lfloor \frac{d+k}{\delta} \right\rfloor + 1 \right) & \text{otherwise.} \end{cases} \quad (1)$$

The above operation quantizes $d+k$ into the nearest even/odd value according to the watermark bit w. Then, the watermarked element $d^\star$ is calculated as follows:

$$d^\star = d' - k. \quad (2)$$

At the receiver's end, the watermark w is extracted as follows:

$$w = \left\lfloor \frac{d^\star + k + \frac{\delta}{2}}{\delta} \right\rfloor \bmod 2. \quad (3)$$

2.2   PDF File Structure

A PDF file assumes a structured binary file format with four components, namely: header, body, cross-reference table, and trailer. The header is the first line of the PDF file, and it indicates the version of the PDF specification. In the body, there are objects such as text streams, images, other multimedia elements, etc. The body is utilized to hold all the data in the document, which will be rendered by a PDF viewer. The cross-reference table contains the references to all the objects in the document. It allows random access to objects in the file, where each object is represented by one entry in the table. The Trailer is utilized to find the cross-reference table, similar to a dictionary indicating the link to each object.

Within the PDF standard, some operators are defined for representing the text document. Specifically, the Tf operator specifies the text style and font size, and the Td operator specifies the offset of the beginning of the current line. When the current coordinate is (x, y), the Td operator shifts the coordinate to $(x + \Delta x, y + \Delta y)$. The TJ operator shows the text characters and spaces between characters.

For each TJ operator, a collection of space lengths are specified for the text characters. The value of space length indicates the horizontal position of the characters.

2.3   Conventional Method

Without loss of generality, assume that one TJ operator is placed at each line of a PDF document file. The number of space lengths in the t-th line is denoted by ℓ_t, and the collection of space lengths in the t-th line is denoted by a vector $s_t = (s_{t,0}, s_{t,1}, \ldots, s_{t,\ell_t-1})$. When the number of lines is n, the total number of space lengths is $\sum_{t=1}^{n} \ell_t$. The conventional method can embed at most $\ell_t - 1$ watermark bits into the t-th line, and hence, the total amount of embeddable information is $\sum_{t=1}^{n}(\ell_t - 1)$ bits. The embedding operation, which consists of there sub-operations, is executed for each line. The sub-operations, namely, *Feature Extraction*, *Embedding*, and *Inverse Feature Extraction*, are detailed in the following sub-sections.

Feature Extraction. The order of elements in s_t of length ℓ_t is randomly permuted according to a secret key key and the index of line t.

$$\bar{s}_t = \text{Permute}(s_t, key, t, \ell_t), \tag{4}$$

where Permute() is a random permutation function. Then, the permuted vector is transformed by Discrete Cosine Transformation (DCT), i.e.,

$$d_t = \text{DCT}(\bar{s}_t). \tag{5}$$

Embedding. The DC element $d_{t,0}$ is kept unchanged in order to maintain the total space length. Therefore, one can embed at most $(\ell_t - 1)$-bit of watermark information into the t-th line. In order to control the trade-off between distortion and payload, the amount of watermark information is reduced by a factor R where $0 < R \leq 1$. The payload becomes

$$\ell'_t = \lfloor R\ell_t \rfloor - 1. \tag{6}$$

Using a pseudo-random number generator PRNG, the random sequence k_t of length ℓ'_t is generated according to the secret key key:

$$\text{PRNG}(key, t, \ell'_t) = k_t = (k_{t,1}, \ldots, k_{t,\ell'_t}), \tag{7}$$

where the value of $k_{t,j}$ is uniformly distributed over $[-\delta/2, \delta/2]$. The embedding operation is performed as follows:

$$d'_{t,j} = \begin{cases} \text{DM-QIM}(d_{t,j}, w_{t,j}, k_{t,j}) & 1 \leq j \leq \ell'_t; \\ d_{t,j} & \text{otherwise.} \end{cases} \tag{8}$$

Finally, the watermarked DCT coefficients $d^\star_{t,j}$ are calculated as follows for $1 \leq j \leq \ell_t - 1$:

$$d^\star_{t,j} = d'_{t,j} - k_{t,j}. \tag{9}$$

Inverse Feature Extraction. The watermarked DCT coefficients $d^\star_t$ is transformed by IDCT:

$$\bar{s}'_t = \text{IDCT}(d^\star_t). \tag{10}$$

The same permutation function is used to obtain the watermarked vector s'_t:

$$s'_t = \text{Permute}(\bar{s}'_t, key, t, \ell_t). \tag{11}$$

3 Proposed Method

3.1 Expected Degree of Distortion

In the conventional method, a random sequence generated according to a secret key is utilized in dither modulation, where the expected degree of distortion can be theoretically calculated.

During the quantization process, a DCT coefficient $d_{t,j}$ is quantized into its nearest odd/even multiple value with respect to the quantization step δ. Before/after the quantization process, the value $k_{t,j}$ is added/subtracted because of the dither modulation. Due to the randomness of $k_{t,j}$, the difference $d^\star_{t,j} - d_{t,j}$ is uniformly distributed within the range $[-\delta, \delta]$. Hence, the expectation of squared difference can be computed as follows:

$$\mathbb{E}\left[(d^\star_{t,j} - d_{t,j})^2\right] = \frac{1}{\delta} \int_{-\delta}^{\delta} x^2 dx = \frac{\delta^2}{3} \tag{12}$$

If $k_{t,j}$ is selected so that $|d^\star_{t,j} - d_{t,j}| < \delta/2$, the distortion caused by the embedding can be reduced. However, such $k_{t,j}$ must be determined from a given $d_{t,j}$. Thus, the extraction of watermark requires the information about the original $d_{t,j}$, which leads to a non-blind watermarking scheme. Since the advantage of QIM watermarking scheme is its blind property in watermark extraction, the use of the aforementioned strategy for determining $k_{t,j}$ is futile.

3.2 Improved DM-QIM Watermarking

We propose a solution for reducing the distortion by using some potential keys derived from a single master secret key to systematically generate random sequences.

Let α be a positive integer. A random sequence k_α is generated by using a secret key key and α. Specifically,

$$k_\alpha = \text{PRNG2}(key, \alpha, L) = (k_{\alpha,0}, k_{\alpha,1}, k_{\alpha,2}, \ldots, k_{\alpha,L-1}), \tag{13}$$

where PRNG2 is a different pseudo-random number generator from PRNG and

$$L = \sum_{t=1}^{n} \ell_t'. \tag{14}$$

Then, $\tilde{\alpha}$ is determined by the following operation:

$$\tilde{\alpha} = \arg\min_{\alpha}\{D_\alpha\}, \tag{15}$$

where D_α is a parameter for measuring the distortion level. Once $\tilde{\alpha}$ is determined, the watermarked vectors $s_t^\star$ are calculated by embedding watermark. Finally, a watermarked PDF document file is output as the result.

During the extraction of watermark, $\tilde{\alpha}$ as well as the secret key key are required to generate the sequence $k_{\tilde{\alpha}}$. It should be noted that $\tilde{\alpha}$ is dependent on a given PDF file, although key is independent. In order to realize a blind watermarking scheme, $\tilde{\alpha}$ is separately embedded by using DM-QIM technique with key. If the number of candidates for $\tilde{\alpha}$ is N, we need to embed $\log_2 N$ bits to retrieve it, which reduces the payload to $L - \log_2 N$.

From the security point of view, if the $\log_2 N$-bit information about $\tilde{\alpha}$ is embedded in specified positions (e.g., the first line of the document), it is easy for an attacker to make watermarked unextractable by intensively adding noise only to those positions. Even if a secret key key is used in the permutation at each line, such an attack cannot be avoided. To immunize against such an attack, the $\log_2 N$-bit information as well as watermark are randomly spread over all space lengths in the proposed method.

Let $\boldsymbol{\beta}$ be the vector composed of $d_{t,j}$ for $1 \leq j \leq \ell_t'$ and $1 \leq t \leq n$.

$$\begin{aligned}\boldsymbol{\beta} &= (\boldsymbol{d_1}, \boldsymbol{d_2}, \ldots, \boldsymbol{d_n}) \\ &= (d_{1,1}, \ldots, d_{1,\ell_1'}, d_{2,1}, \ldots, d_{2,\ell_1'}, \ldots, d_{n,1}, \ldots, d_{n,\ell_1'})\end{aligned} \tag{16}$$

It is stressed that the DC elements $d_{t,0}$ for $1 \leq t \leq n$ are not involved in the vector $\boldsymbol{\beta}$. Notice that the number of elements in $\boldsymbol{\beta}$ is L. The order of elements in $\boldsymbol{\beta}$ is randomly permuted according to a secret key key with index 0, i.e.,

$$\bar{\boldsymbol{\beta}} = \text{Permute}(\boldsymbol{\beta}, key, 0, L). \tag{17}$$

Then, the permuted vector is transformed by DCT to obtain

$$\boldsymbol{\theta} = \text{DCT}(\bar{\boldsymbol{\beta}}) = (\theta_0, \theta_1, \ldots, \theta_{L-1}). \tag{18}$$

For a given watermark sequence $\boldsymbol{w}$ of length $L - \log_2 N$, the parameter D_α of distortion level is calculated as follows.

$$D_\alpha = \sum_{j=0}^{L-1} \left(\text{DM-QIM}(\theta_j, w_j, k_{\alpha,j}) - \theta_j\right)^2. \tag{19}$$

According to Eq. (15), $\tilde{\alpha}$ is determined by using D_α for $1 \leq \alpha \leq N$.

3.3 Embedding Procedure

The proposed method measures the sum of squared differences using the random sequence k_α for a given α, and finds $\tilde{\alpha}$ which yields the minimum sum. From Eq. (12), the expected value of the sum is $L\delta/12$. As the sum is fluctuated around $L\delta/12$, the sum is decreased as the number of candidates for α increases.

The embedding procedure of the proposed method is summarized as follows.

(1) At each line of a PDF document file, its space vector s_t is permuted by using a secret key key, and it is transformed by DCT.

(2) Except for the DC element $d_{t,0}$, the DCT coefficients $d_{t,j}$ are selected for $1 \le j \le \ell'_t$ and $1 \le t \le n$ to create a single vector β of length L.

(3) The vector β is further permuted by using key and is transformed by DCT.

(4) For $1 \le \alpha \le N$, $\tilde{\alpha}$ is determined from θ by using Eq. (15).

(5) Each watermark bit w_j is embedded into the selected DCT coefficients θ_j using $k_{\tilde{\alpha},j}$. The number of embeddable watermark bits is $L - \log_2 N$.

(6) For the last $\log_2 N$ DCT coefficients θ_j for $L - \log_2 \le j \le L - 1$, a random sequence $k_0 = \text{PRNG}(key, 0, \log_2 N)$ of length $\log_2 N$ is generated using key, and watermarked coefficients θ_j^* are calculated by embedding the binary representation of α using the DM-QIM technique.

(7) By performing inverse operations, the watermarked vectors s_t^* are calculated and a watermarked PDF document file is created.

For the above procedure, steps (1) to (3) are the feature extraction operations, and step (7) is the inverse operation. Steps (4) to (6) are the main embedding operations.

3.4 Extraction Procedure

The watermark is extracted from a suspicious PDF file using the same secret key key following the procedure below.

(1) The same operations detailed in Steps (1) to (3) of the embedding procedure are performed to each line of a suspicious PDF document file.

(2) $\tilde{\alpha}$ is extracted from the last $\log_2 N$ DCT coefficients $\tilde{\theta}_j$ using k_0, which is in turn generated by key.

(3) The random sequence $k_{\tilde{\alpha}}$ is generated, and each watermark bit w_j is extracted from $\tilde{\theta}_j$ for $0 \le j \le L - \log_2 N - 1$ by using Eq. (3).

4 Experimental Results

A PDF document file is generated by Latex using an extended version of dvipdfm-0.13.2c. Specifically, the document is the first 5 chapters of Genesis in the Old Testament of the Bible, which contains 3178 words with 15694 characters and 150 lines. We select lines each having $\ell_t \ge 10$ spaces for embedding purpose, while leaving the rest unchanged. The number of lines for embedding is 147 in this case, and the payload of the PDF file is at most 3810 bits.

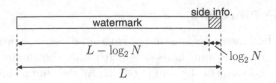

Fig. 1. Embedding data.

Table 1. Payload [bits] in the case of $\log_2 N = 8$.

R	0.1	0.2	0.3	0.4	0.5	0.6	0.7	0.8	0.9	1.0
$L - \log_2 N$	162	581	964	1369	1788	2161	2548	2949	3350	3802

For experiment purpose, 1000 random sequences of zeros and ones are generated and utilized as watermark. Figure 1 illustrates the embedding data which is composed of watermark and side information. The proposed scheme modifies L elements to embed $L - \log_2 N$ watermark. For fair comparison, the payload of the conventional method is reduced to $L - \log_2 N$, where the last $\log_2 N$ DCT coefficients are left unmodified. The payload varied by considering different R values as recorded in Table 1 in the case of $\log_2 N = 8$.

4.1   Distortion

After embedding the watermarks, the average signal-to-noise ratio (SNR) and file size are calculated. We use the following SNR in this experiment:

$$SNR = 10 \log_{10} \left(\frac{\sum \sum (s_{t,j})^2}{\sum \sum (s_{t,j}^\star - s_{t,j})^2} \right) \quad [\text{dB}]. \tag{20}$$

The comparison of SNR between the conventional and proposed methods is shown in Fig. 2. Results suggest that SNR for both the conventional and proposed methods are increased when N increases. However, a higher rate of SNR improvement is observed for the proposed method. The detailed numerical results are recorded in Table 2 for $\log_2 N = 8$. The SNR gain refers to the difference of SNR between the conventional and proposed methods. It is observed that the gain is inversely correlated to the rate R. It means that the sum of squared differences tends to be small when the number of DCT coefficients $d_{t,j}$ is small. A similar trend can be observed from the results in Table 2. From the above results, we can conclude that the proposed method can suppress the distortion caused by embedding watermark into a PDF document.

We use the "PDFtk" toolkit[1] to compress/decompress PDF file. The document of PDF file is compressed when it is created by the dvipdfm tool from Latex. The size of the original PDF file is 24, 767 bytes, while the size becomes

---

[1] https://www.pdflabs.com/tools/pdftk-the-pdf-toolkit/.

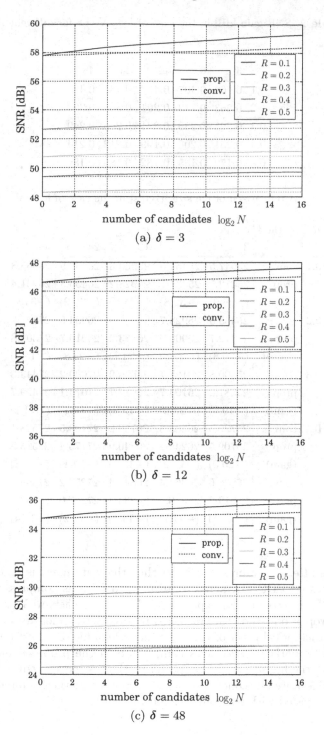

Fig. 2. Comparison of distortions caused by embedding.

Table 2. SNR gain [dB] in the case of $\log_2 N = 8$ for different R.

R	δ				
	3	6	12	24	48
0.1	0.668	0.407	0.453	0.485	0.480
0.2	0.263	0.289	0.291	0.308	0.308
0.3	0.225	0.239	0.231	0.245	0.249
0.4	0.201	0.206	0.199	0.212	0.214
0.5	0.179	0.185	0.182	0.189	0.186

Table 3. Comparison of file size [Bytes] in the case of $\log_2 N = 8$.

R	method	δ				
		3	6	12	24	48
0.1	conv.	25047.5	25464.5	25969.8	26496.5	26965.8
	prop	25012.5	25431.7	25928.2	26456.3	26931.4
	(gain)	(−35.0)	(−32.8)	(−41.6)	(−40.2)	(−34.4)
0.2	conv.	25433.5	25928.7	26457.9	26934.5	27321.2
	prop	25412.7	25900.9	26433.2	26910.7	27302.8
	(gain)	(−20.8)	(−27.8)	(−24.7)	(−23.8)	(−18.4)
0.3	conv.	25600.8	26127.7	26636.9	27090.2	27443.8
	prop	25581.2	26104.7	26617.7	27074.1	27429.7
	(gain)	(−19.6)	(−23.0)	(−19.2)	(−16.1)	(−14.1)
0.4	conv.	25729.5	26263.3	26756.2	27189.5	27528.1
	prop	25709.5	26245.1	26740.9	27175.4	27513.3
	(gain)	(−20.0)	(−18.2)	(−15.3)	(−14.1)	(−14.8)
0.5	conv.	25828.6	26364.4	26847.4	27258.2	27594.9
	prop	25813.2	26346.7	26833.3	27247.0	27583.5
	(gain)	(−15.4)	(−17.7)	(−14.1)	(−11.2)	(−11.4)

$52,445$ bytes after decompression. Note that the watermark is embedded into the decompressed PDF file, and a watermarked PDF is compressed again by using the "PDFtk" tool in our experiment. The file size achieved by the conventional and proposed methods are recorded in Table 3 when $\log_2 N = 8$. From the information theoretical point of view, the increase of file size must be suppressed when the watermarked PDF file is compressed in the proposed method. It is observed that the file size of the proposed method is indeed reduced. From the results in Table 3, we can conclude that the proposed method can reduce the file size when compared with the conventional method.

4.2   Robustness

We evaluate the robustness against additive noise under the following conditions. Neither the vectors $\boldsymbol{\theta}$ nor $\boldsymbol{\beta}$ can be observed without the secret key key, and it is assumed that white Gaussian noise (AWGN) is directly added to the space vectors $\boldsymbol{s}_t$. The watermark-to-noise ratio (WNR) is calculated by using the ratio between the total amount of energy embedded into a PDF and the energy of AWGN:

$$WNR = \frac{\sum_{j=0}^{\ell-1}(s_j^\star - s_j)^2}{\sum_{j=0}^{\ell-1} \epsilon_j^2}. \tag{21}$$

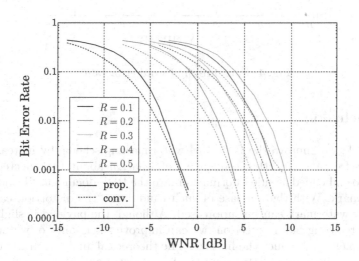

Fig. 3. Comparison of bit error rate.

The bit error rate is calculated as the ratio of *the number of error bits* to *the total bits L*. The results are as summarized as Fig. 3. It is observed that BER of the proposed method is lower than that of the conventional method. It is due to the side information, which is of length $\log_2 N$-bit. If the side information is not correctly extracted, the extraction of payload will fail, and the number of error bits increase significantly in the proposed method. On the other hand, if at least one error appears in the extracted watermark of length L, we regard it as a detection error in the measurement of word error rate. Specifically, in this experiment, we count the average number of detection errors for 10^3 trials, then calculate its ratio as the word error rate. The results are shown in Fig. 4. The results indicate that the probability of error detection is suppressed in the proposed method. It is because the proposed method can suppress the distortion caused by embedding as confirmed in Fig. 2. Nonetheless, error correcting code appears to be a promising approach to further improve robustness, which is left as our future work.

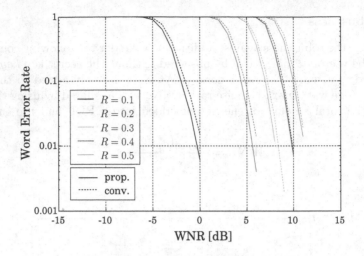

Fig. 4. Comparison of word error rate.

5   Conclusion

In this work, we improve the DM-QIM watermarking scheme by increasing the candidates for random dither sequence. Information about the selected candidate is also embedded as side information into the PDF document file along with the watermark. With the increase of such candidates, the distortion caused by embedding watermark can be suppressed. Although the payload is slightly sacrificed for realizing blind detection, we can improve the quality of watermarked PDF document and reduce the file size. The theoretical analysis on the relationship between the gain and the number of candidates will be pursued as one of our future works.

Acknowledgment. This research has been partially supported by the Kayamori Foundation of Information Science Advancement and JSPS KAKENHI Grant Number 19K22846.

References

1. Bender, W., Gruhl, D., Morimoto, N., Lu, A.: Techniques for data hiding. IBM Syst. J. **35**(3–4), 313–336 (1996)
2. Bitar, A.W., Darazi, R., Couchot, J.F., Couturier, R.: Blind digital watermarking in PDF documents using spread transform dither modulation. Multimedia Tools Appl. **76**(1), 143–161 (2017)
3. Chen, B., Wornell, G.Q.: Quantization index modulation: a class of provably good methods for digital watermarking and information embedding. IEEE Trans. Inf. Theory **47**(4), 1423–1443 (2001)
4. Cox, I.J., Kilian, J., Leighton, F.T., Shamson, T.: Secure spread spectrum watermarking for multimedia. IEEE Trans. Image Process. **6**(12), 1673–1687 (1997)

5. Adobe Systems Incorporated: Document management—portable document format—part 1: PDF 1.7. ISO 32000–1:2008, July 2008
6. Kuribayashi, M., Fukushima, T., Funabiki, N.: Robust and secure data hiding for PDF text document. IEICE Trans. Inf. Syst. **E102-D**(1), 41–47 (2019)
7. Lee, I.S., Tsai, W.H.: A new approach to covert communication via PDF files. Sig. Process. **90**(2), 557–565 (2010)
8. Lin, H.F., Lu, L.W., Gun, C.Y., Chen, C.Y.: A copyright protection scheme based on PDF. Int. J. Innov. Comput. Inf. Control **9**(1), 1–6 (2013)
9. Por, L.Y., Delina, B.: Information hiding: a new approach in text steganography. In: Proceedings of ACACOS 2008, pp. 689–695 (2008)
10. Zhong, S., Cheng, X., Chen, T.: Data hiding in a kind of PDF texts for secret communication. Int. J. Netw. Secur. **4**, 17–26 (2007)

New Paradigm for Self-embedding Image Watermarking with Poisson Equation

Fang Cao[1], Tianwei Wu[2], Chuan Qin[2(✉)], Zhenxing Qian[3], and Xinpeng Zhang[3]

[1] College of Information Engineering, Shanghai Maritime University, Shanghai 200135, China
fangcao@shmtu.edu.cn
[2] School of Optical-Electrical and Computer Engineering, University of Shanghai for Science and Technology, Shanghai 200093, China
705057264@qq.com, qin@usst.edu.cn
[3] School of Computer Science, Fudan University, Shanghai 200433, China
{zxqian,zhangxinpeng}@fudan.edu.cn

Abstract. In this paper, we propose a new self-embedding image watermarking scheme based on reference sharing and Poisson equation. With Laplacian operator, the relationship of each pixel and its neighborhood in original image is established and can be converted to compression bits. Then, after scrambling, compression bits are interleaved through the reference sharing mechanism, which can introduce more redundancy into the reference bits to be embedded for future content recovery. Thus, the relationship between each compression bit and each reference bit is constructed so that the recoverable area for tampered image can be increased effectively. Tampered contents can be recovered with the Laplacian values of tampered blocks and the boundary values around tampered blocks based on tampering localization and Poisson equation solver. Experimental results demonstrate the effectiveness of the proposed scheme.

Keywords: Self-embedding · Reference sharing · Poisson equation · Tampering recovery

1 Introduction

Nowadays, with the rapid development of network technology, the transmission of multimedia data has been increasingly widely. Digital images can also be more easily modified by powerful image processing tools than before. As a result, we cannot ensure whether our received digital images are faked or not [1–3]. Therefore, how to protect the integrity of digital images has been attracted more and more attentions, and many researchers have deeply studied the solutions to image authentication [4–8], which includes tampering detection and content recovery for suspicious images.

Fragile image watermarking is an effective technique for image authentication, which embeds watermark data into original image on the sender side and extracts watermark data from watermarked image on the receiver side for tampering detection and image recovery. If the embedded watermark data is related with the image itself, this technique can also be called as self-embedding watermarking.

© Springer Nature Switzerland AG 2020
H. Wang et al. (Eds.): IWDW 2019, LNCS 12022, pp. 184–191, 2020.
https://doi.org/10.1007/978-3-030-43575-2_15

Chang *et al.* presented a fragile watermarking scheme of ownership detection and tampering detection for digital images [2]. This scheme embedded adaptive least significant bits (LSBs) of the pixels to localize the tampered area accurately. Although the accuracy of tampering detection was high, the function of content recovery for tampered images cannot be achieved. Lin *et al.* proposed a hierarchical self-embedding image watermarking scheme for both tampering detection and content recovery [3]. A 3-level stage detection for tampered blocks based on parity check bits was applied in this scheme, and the average intensity of image block was utilized to recover tampered region. But, this scheme cannot restore images with higher tampering rate very well. Lee and Lin proposed a dual-watermark scheme for image tampering detection and recovery [4]. This scheme provided a second opportunity for content recovery when the first copy of the extracted watermark data was damaged. Even if the watermarked image was destroyed with relatively higher tampering rate, visual quality of recovered image can still be satisfactory. Zhang *et al.* proposed a self-embedding image watermarking scheme in [5], which was capable of recovering the original principal content of damaged region in extensive areas. In this scheme, DCT coefficients were shared to form reference-bits that can be used to recover original principal content when the tampering rate was not greater than 59%, and the PSNR value of recovered image can achieve [26, 29] dB.

In this work, in order to achieve higher visual quality of watermarked images and recovered images, we propose a new paradigm for self-embedding fragile image watermarking based on Poisson equation. In our new paradigm, reference bits for content recovery are derived from two-order Laplacian values of original image after reference sharing. Watermark bits are embedded into 3 LSB planes of original image. On the receiver side, the extractable reference bits from LSB, the intact information from MSB in the undamaged regions and their relationships are employed during the content recovery procedure. Tampered contents can be recovered with the Laplacian values in tampered blocks and the boundary value around tampered blocks through solving Poisson equation. Even if tampering rate is not low, visual quality of recovered image can be satisfactory.

2 Watermark Embedding Procedure

In our scheme, original image is first divided into a series of non-overlapping 8×8 blocks. Each pixel in original image can be transformed into a new value based on the relationship with its neighborhood according to the Laplacian operator. Then, through the reference sharing mechanism, the reference bits for content recovery are produced based on Laplacian values. After that, the authentication bits of each block for tampering detection are also calculated through the hash function. Reference bits after scrambling are embedded into the whole image dispersedly and authentication bits of each block are embedded into the block itself. Thus, the final watermarked image can be obtained. The flowchart of the self-embedding procedure is shown in Fig. 1.

2.1 Laplacian Operator Processing

The 3 LSBs of each pixel are first set to zeros for initialization. In order to establish the connection between each pixel with its neighboring pixels, Laplacian operator processing

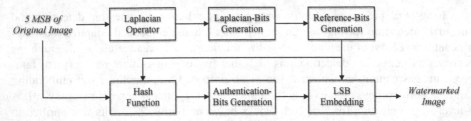

Fig. 1. Flowchart of watermark embedding procedure

is conducted. Four common Laplacian operators are shown in Fig. 2. In order to achieve higher recovery efficiency, Laplacian operator of Type 1 in Fig. 2(a) is applied in our scheme. Original image **A** sized $N_1 \times N_2$ is convolved with the Laplacian operator **L** to construct a new matrix **B**:

$$\mathbf{B} = \mathbf{A} \otimes \mathbf{L}. \tag{1}$$

The value of each pixel in **A** ranges from 0 to 255, which can be represented by 8 bits. In order to make the length of Laplacian bits fixed, the maximum b_{max} and the minimum b_{min} of all the values of pixels in **B** need to be calculated, where b_{min} must be less than or equal to 0. A new matrix of Laplacian value **C** can be obtained by Eq. (2) and the fixed length k of each pixel in **C** can be calculated by Eq. (3), where k is transmitted to the receiver together with other secret keys.

$$\mathbf{C} = \mathbf{B} + |b_{min}|, \tag{2}$$

$$k = \lfloor \log_2(b_{max} - b_{min}) + 1 \rfloor. \tag{3}$$

Then, the matrix **C** is divided into $N/64$ non-overlapping blocks sized 8×8, where $N = N_1 \times N_2$. Thus, each 8×8 block produces $64k$ bits. After all blocks are processed, total $k \cdot N$ Laplacian bits of **C** can be acquired.

2.2 Reference-Bits Generation and Embedding

All the $k \cdot N$ Laplacian bits should be divided into $N/64$ subsets pseudo-randomly according to a secret key, and each subset contains $64k$ Laplacian bits. Denote the i-th subset as $T_i = \{t_{i,1}, t_{i,2}, ..., t_{i,64k}\}$, $i = 1, 2, ..., N/64$. For each 8×8 block of original image

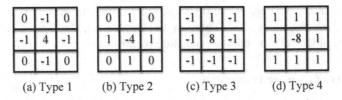

(a) Type 1   (b) Type 2   (c) Type 3   (d) Type 4

Fig. 2. Four common Laplacian operators

A, 160 reference bits for further content recovery are generated from the 64k Laplacian bits:

$$\begin{bmatrix} r_{i,1} \\ r_{i,2} \\ \vdots \\ r_{i,160} \end{bmatrix} = \mathbf{H}_i \cdot \begin{bmatrix} t_{i,1} \\ t_{i,2} \\ \vdots \\ t_{i,64k} \end{bmatrix}, \quad i = 1, 2, \ldots, N/64, \tag{4}$$

where $\mathbf{H}_i$ is a binary matrix sized $160 \times 64k$ and generated according to the secret key. The calculation in Eq. (4) should be module 2.

For each 8×8 block of $\mathbf{A}$, the 32 authentication bits for tampering detection can be gained by feeding its 5 MSB and the corresponding 160 reference bits into a hash function. For each block of $\mathbf{A}$, the 192 watermark bits, including 160 reference bits and 32 authentication bits, are permuted and used to replace 3 LSB of the block itself. After all $N/64$ blocks are processed, the final watermarked image $\mathbf{P}$ can be acquired.

3   Content Recovery Procedure

Suppose that the potential adversary may modify some contents of watermarked image $\mathbf{P}$ without changing image size. Hence, tampering detection and further content recovery should be implemented on the receiver side. The flowchart of content recovery procedure for our scheme is illustrated in Fig. 3.

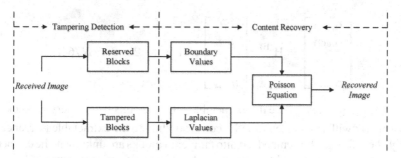

Fig. 3. Flowchart of tampering detection and content recovery

3.1   Tampering Detection

Denote the received, possibly tampered image as $\mathbf{P}'$. First, $\mathbf{P}'$ is divided into 8×8 non-overlapping blocks. For each block, the 192 watermark bits extracted from the 3 LSBs are parsed into two parts, i.e., 160 reference bits and 32 authentication bits, according the same secret key with the sender side. If the extracted 32 authentication bits differ from the hash result of the 320 bits of 5 MSBs and 160 extracted reference bits corresponding to the current block, the block is marked as tampered. Otherwise, the block is marked as intact. In addition, After all blocks in **P'** are conducted with tampering detection, boundary values f of tampered blocks can be obtained, which can be used to recover the tampered blocks f' with the restored Laplacian values in tampered area through solving the Poisson equation, as illustrated in Fig. 4.

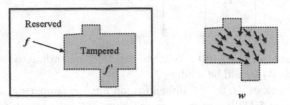

(a) Tampered area and its boundary   (b) Gradient field of tampered area

Fig. 4. Illustration of tampering detection

3.2   Restoration of Laplacian Bits

As mentioned in Sect. 2, the extracted $3N/2$ reference bits are derived from the Laplacian bits scattering in the whole image. When the contents of the blocks containing these reference bits are altered by the adversary, the number of reference bits extractable from intact blocks, u, may be less than 160 in each subset, thus, Eq. (4) can be rewritten as Eq. (5).

$$\begin{bmatrix} r_{i,e(1)} \\ r_{i,e(2)} \\ \vdots \\ r_{i,e(u)} \end{bmatrix} = \mathbf{H}_i^{(E)} \cdot \begin{bmatrix} t_{i,1} \\ t_{i,2} \\ \vdots \\ t_{i,64k} \end{bmatrix}, \quad i = 1, 2, \ldots, N/64, \tag{5}$$

where $r_{i,e(1)}, r_{i,e(2)}, \ldots, r_{i,e(u)}$ are the extractable reference bits from reserved blocks, and $\mathbf{H}_i^{(E)}$ is a matrix with rows taken from $\mathbf{H}_i$ corresponding to the extractable reference bits. Although the reference bits embedded into tampered blocks are unknown, the extractable reference bits can be obtained to recover the Laplacian bits in each subset. $\mathbf{C}_R$ and $\mathbf{C}_T$ are denoted as the two column vectors consisting of Laplacian bits in intact blocks and tampered blocks, respectively. Equation (5) can be re-formulated as:

$$\begin{bmatrix} r_{i,e(1)} \\ r_{i,e(2)} \\ \vdots \\ r_{i,e(u)} \end{bmatrix} - \mathbf{H}_i^{(E,R)} \cdot \mathbf{C}_R = \mathbf{H}_i^{(E,T)} \cdot \mathbf{C}_T, \tag{6}$$

where $\mathbf{H}_i^{(E,T)}$ and $\mathbf{H}_i^{(E,R)}$ are the two matrixes whose columns are those in $\mathbf{H}_i$ corresponding to Laplacian bits in $\mathbf{C}_T$ and $\mathbf{C}_R$, respectively. In Eq. (6), the left side and the matrix $\mathbf{H}_i^{(E,T)}$ are known, only $\mathbf{C}_T$ is unknown and required to be solved. Denote the length of C_T as n_T, so that the binary matrix $\mathbf{H}_i^{(E,T)}$ is sized as $v \times n_T$. As long as Eq. (6) has a unique solution, it can be solved by using the Gaussian elimination algorithm. That is to say, the extractable reference bits and Laplacian bits in intact region can be both utilized to restore the Laplacian bits of tampered blocks in each subset.

3.3 Tampered Content Recovery

After tampering detection and Laplacian-bits restoration are completed, we can recover the tampered contents by solving Poisson equation [9], see Eq. (7).

$$\Delta f' = \nabla \cdot w, \tag{7}$$

where w denotes the gradient field of tampered area and $\nabla \cdot w$ is the Laplacian values in the tampered blocks. The received image can be divided into two parts: reserved blocks and tampered blocks. For the reserved blocks, 5 MSB bits can be kept unchanged without recovery. For the tampered blocks, Laplacian bits solved by Eq. (6) can be rearranged based on the same secret key. As shown in Fig. 4, by solving the Poisson Equation, the pixel values f' of the tampered blocks can be recovered by the pixel values f on the boundary of tampered blocks and the restored Laplacian values within tampered blocks. After all tampered blocks are processed with above described procedures, the recovered image can be acquired.

4 Experimental Results and Comparisons

Experiments were conducted on a large number of images to demonstrate the effectiveness and superiority of our scheme. Two standard images sized 512×512, i.e., *Lena* and *Lake*, are given as examples in this Section. Two corresponding watermarked images are shown in Fig. 5 with PSNR of 37.97 dB and 37.90 dB, respectively. Because of the low volume of embedded watermark bits, the difference between watermarked images and original images cannot be distinguished by human eyes.

(a)   (b)

Fig. 5. Two watermarked images. (a) *Lena* (PSNR $= 37.97$ dB), (b) *Lake* (PSNR $= 37.90$ dB).

The tampered versions of the two watermarked images in Fig. 5 are shown in Figs. 6(a)–(b). The tampering rates for the two images are 8.69% and 9.03%, respectively. The results of tampering detection are shown in Figs. 6(c)–(d), in which the detected, tampered blocks are marked as white. It can be observed that, the tampered blocks can be judged by authentication bits accurately. After tampering detection, the Laplacian bits can be derived to recover tampered contents of received image based on reference sharing and Poisson equation solver, as shown in Fig. 7, and the PSNR of two recovered images are 40.73 dB and 40.68 dB, respectively.

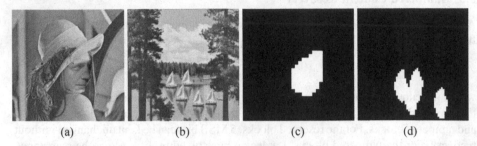

(a)   (b)   (c)   (d)

Fig. 6. Two tampered, watermarked images and tampering detection results. (a) Tampered *Lena*, (b) Tampered *Lake*, (c) Detection result for (a), (d) Detection result for (b).

(a)   (b)

Fig. 7. Recovered images. (a) *Lena* (PSNR = 40.73 dB), (b) *Lake* (PSNR = 40.68 dB).

Table 1. Comparisons of the proposed scheme with the schemes [4–6]

Images	Tampering rate	PSNR of recovered images (dB)			
		[4]	[5]	[6]	Ours
Lena	8.69%	35.82	37.55	35.41	40.73
Lake	9.03%	36.84	37.73	36.15	40.68

Comparisons for the performance of content recovery among the proposed scheme, Lee and Lin's scheme [4], Zhang *et al.*'s scheme [5] and Yang and Shen's scheme [6] were also conducted. PSNR of recovered images for the four schemes are shown in Table 1. Because our scheme can recover original contents of 5 MSB for tampered images correctly, recovered results of our scheme are superior to those of the other three schemes. Possible drawback of our scheme is that the number of Laplacian bits may be great, which may lead to unsuccessful recovery for higher tampering rates.

5 Conclusions

A new self-embedding fragile image watermarking scheme based on Poisson equation is proposed in this paper, which can be utilized for tampering detection and content recovery for images. To obtain the reference bits and the authentication bits, the Laplacian operator, the reference sharing operation and hash function are employed. Because the watermark bits are embedded into 3 LSBs of original image, the visual quality of watermarked image is satisfactory. Higher quality of recovered image can be obtained through deriving Laplacian bits and solving Poisson equation. Compared with some typical reported schemes, the proposed scheme can achieve superior performance of tampering recovery.

Acknowledgments. This work was supported by the National Natural Science Foundation of China (61902239, 61672354). The authors would like to thank the anonymous reviewers for their valuable suggestions.

References

1. Fridrich, J., Goljan, M.: Images with self-correcting capabilities. In: Proceedings of IEEE International Conference on Image Processing, pp. 792–796 (1999)
2. Chang, C.C., Hu, Y.S., Lu, T.C.: A watermarking-based image ownership and tampering authentication scheme. Pattern Recogn. Lett. 27(5), 439–446 (2006)
3. Lin, P.L., Hsieh, C.K., Huang, P.W.: A hierarchical digital watermarking method for image tamper detection and recovery. Pattern Recogn. 38(12), 2519–2529 (2005)
4. Lee, T.Y., Lin, S.D.: Dual watermark for image tamper detection and recovery. Pattern Recogn. 41(11), 3497–3506 (2008)
5. Zhang, X.P., Wang, S.Z., Qian, Z.X., Feng, G.R.: Reference sharing mechanism for watermark self-embedding. IEEE Trans. Image Process. 20(2), 485–495 (2011)
6. Yang, C.W., Shen, J.J.: Recover the tampered image based on VQ indexing. Sig. Process. 90(1), 331–343 (2010)
7. Korus, P., Dziech, A.: Adaptive self-embedding scheme with controlled reconstruction performance. IEEE Trans. Inf. Forensics Secur. 9(2), 169–181 (2014)
8. Qin, C., Ji, P., Chang, C.C., Dong, J., Sun, X.M.: Non-uniform watermark sharing based on optimal iterative BTC for image tampering recovery. IEEE Multimedia 25(3), 36–48 (2018)
9. Perez, P., Gangnet, M., Blake, A.: Poisson image editing. ACM Trans. Graph. 22(3), 313–318 (2003)

Information Hiding

Reversible Data Hiding Based on Partitioning the Prediction Values

Haihang Wu and Fangjun Huang[✉]

Guangdong Provincial Key Laboratory of Information Security Technology, School of Data and Computer Science, Sun Yat-Sen University, Guangzhou 510006, GD, China
huangfj@mail.sysu.edu.cn

Abstract. In this paper, we present a new reversible data hiding (RDH) method. Instead of directly dividing the neighboring pixels into blocks, we sort the pixels according to their prediction values first, and then the sorted sequence is partitioned into non-overlapping blocks. That is, different from that in pixel value ordering (PVO) series only the neighboring pixels can be divided into the same block, in our new scheme the pixels far apart from each other in space may be divided into the same block in case they have the similar pixel values. Thus much redundancy in image can be exploited and a sharper prediction error histogram is easy to be obtained for data embedding. To achieve better performance, a new adaptive embedding strategy is also proposed. The experimental results show that our new method is superior to the traditional PVO based methods.

Keywords: Reversible data hiding · Pixel value ordering · Prediction value

1 Introduction

Traditional data hiding will introduce permanent distortion on the cover medium during the embedding process, which is unacceptable in some sensitive fields, such as military and medical image processing. To solve this deficiency, reversible data hiding (RDH) is proposed, which can not only extract the embedded message bits but also completely restore the cover image.

In general, the classic RDH methods may be classified into three categories: lossless compression (LS) [1, 2], histogram shifting (HS) [3] and difference expansion (DE) [4]. The philosophy behind LS is to losslessly compress a subset of cover image and utilize the saved space to embed message bits. The HS strategy was first proposed by Ni *et al.* [3], and the data hiding is realized by shifting and expanding the histogram bins. The idea of difference expansion (DE) was first presented by Tian [4], in which the difference between pixel pairs is expanded to carry the message bit. Recent studies demonstrated that DE and HS strategies could also be integrated together to form a series of new RDH schemes [5–10].

In [11], a new strategy evolved from DE and HS was proposed by Li *et al.*, called pixel value ordering (PVO). In this new strategy, the image is divided into equal-sized blocks, and in each block the pixels are sorted according to their values. Then, in each

H. Wang et al. (Eds.): IWDW 2019, LNCS 12022, pp. 195–203, 2020.
https://doi.org/10.1007/978-3-030-43575-2_16

sorted block, the second largest pixel and the second smallest pixel are used to predict the largest pixel and the smallest pixel, respectively, and thus a prediction error histogram can be obtained. Finally, data hiding is implemented by shifting and expanding the bins of the prediction error histogram. This new method realizes data embedding in a block-wise manner, and high-fidelity can be easily obtained. Considering that in PVO, only the bins 1 and −1 are expanded to carry message bits, and bin 0 is left untouched, Peng *et al.* [12] improved PVO with considering the relative position of pixels, which was called improved PVO (IPVO). In IPVO, since bin 0 can also be expanded for carrying message bits, both the embedding capacity and visual quality of the marked image can be improved according to various experimental results.

As seen, in PVO series [11, 12], the adjacent pixels are divided into the same block. However, in practice, the values of adjacent pixels may vary considerably. In this paper, we present a new RDH method. Instead of directly dividing the neighboring pixels into the same block, we first sort the pixels according to the prediction values obtained by the rhombus prediction, and then the sorted sequence is partitioned into non-overlapping blocks. As seen, in the partitioning stage, not only the spatial position of the pixels is considered, but also the specific values of the pixels to be grouped are considered. That is, some pixels far apart from each other in space may be divided into the same block in case they have the similar values. To achieve better performance, a new adaptive embedding strategy is also proposed. The experimental results demonstrate that our new method is superior to the traditional PVO based methods.

The structure of this paper is as follows: Sect. 2 review some related works including Li *et al.*'s PVO and Peng *et al.*'s IPVO methods. Our scheme is introduced in Sect. 3. The comparison and analysis of experimental results are discussed in Sect. 4. Finally, a brief summary is given in Sect. 5.

2 Related Works

In this section, the basic principles of PVO and IPVO proposed by Li *et al.* [11] and Peng *et al.* [12] are introduced.

2.1 Li *et al.*'s PVO

In PVO method, the image is divided into pixel blocks with the same size. Suppose that a pixel block P has n pixels $\{p_1, \ldots, p_n\}$. All the pixels $\{p_1, \ldots, p_n\}$ are sorted in ascending order and the sorted sequence is represented with $\{p_{\sigma(1)}, \ldots, p_{\sigma(n)}\}$, where $p_{\sigma(1)} \leq \ldots \leq p_{\sigma(n)}$. After sorting, the second largest pixel is used to predict the largest pixel, and the second smallest pixel is used to predict the smallest pixel. For simplicity, only modification on the largest pixel is exemplified here.

The prediction error is computed as follows.

$$PE_{max} = p_{\sigma(n)} - p_{(n-1)} \tag{1}$$

After computing the prediction error, the message bit can be embedded according to Eq. (2).

$$\overline{PE_{max}} = \begin{cases} PE_{max} & if\ PE_{max} = 0, \\ PE_{max} + b & if\ PE_{max} = 1 \\ PE_{max} + 1 & if\ PE_{max} > 1 \end{cases} \qquad (2)$$

where $b \in \{1, 0\}$ represents the secret message bit to be embedded, and $\overline{PE_{max}}$ represents the prediction error after the message embedding. Correspondingly the largest pixel $p_{\sigma(n)}$ is changed as follows.

$$\overline{p_{\sigma(n)}} = p_{\sigma(n-1)} + \overline{PE_{max}} = \begin{cases} p_{\sigma(n)} & if\ PE_{max} = 0 \\ p_{\sigma(n)} + b & if\ PE_{max} = 1 \\ p_{\sigma(n)+1} & if\ PE_{max} > 1 \end{cases} \qquad (3)$$

where $\overline{p_{\sigma(n)}}$ represents the pixel value in the marked image. Note that modification on the smallest pixel is conducted in the same way. As seen, after data hiding the order of the pixel values remains unchanged, which guarantees the reversibility.

2.2 Peng *et al.*'s IPVO

In [12], Peng *et al.* improved PVO with considering the relative locations of the pixels in each block. As before, suppose that a pixel block P has n pixels $\{p_1, \dots, p_n\}$. All the pixels $\{p_1, \dots, p_n\}$ are sorted in ascending order and the sorted sequence is represented with $\{p_{\sigma(1)}, \dots, p_{\sigma(n)}\}$, where $p_{\sigma(1)} \leq \dots \leq p_{\sigma(n)}$. After sorting, the prediction error is computed according to Eq. (4).

$$d_{max} = p_u - p_v \qquad (4)$$

where

$$\begin{cases} u = min(\sigma(n), \sigma(n-1)) \\ v = max(\sigma(n), \sigma(n-1)) \end{cases} \qquad (5)$$

The prediction error d_{max} is no longer always non-negative, which means that the new defined prediction error lies in the interval $(-\infty, +\infty)$. Therefore both bin 0 and bin 1 can be expanded for carrying message bits as follows.

$$\overline{d_{max}} = \begin{cases} d_{max} - 1 & if\ d_{max} < 0 \\ d_{max} - b & if\ d_{max} = 0 \\ d_{max} + b & if\ d_{max} = 1 \\ d_{max} + 1 & if\ d_{max} > 1 \end{cases} \qquad (6)$$

where $b \in \{0, 1\}$. Then the marked pixel value is obtained as:

$$\overline{p_{\sigma(n)}} = p_{\sigma(n-1)} + |\overline{d_{max}}| = \begin{cases} p_{\sigma(n)} + 1 & if\ d_{max} < 0 \\ p_{\sigma(n)} + b & if\ d_{max} = 0 \\ p_{\sigma(n)} + b & if\ d_{max} = 1 \\ p_{\sigma(n)} + 1 & if\ d_{max} > 1 \end{cases} \qquad (7)$$

As seen, the pixel value order remains unchanged after data embedding, and the decoder can realize data extraction and lossless image restoration. Note that modification on the smallest pixel can be conducted in the same way. For simplicity, only modification on the largest pixel is exemplified here.

3 Proposed Method

In this section, how to partition the prediction values into blocks is introduced first. Then the adaptive embedding strategy is proposed followed by the embedding and extraction steps.

3.1 Partitioning the Prediction Values Based on Rhombus Prediction

The combination of rhombus prediction and RDH was first proposed by Sachnev *et al.* [7]. In [7], all pixels are divided into two sets, *i.e.*, the white set and the black set, which is shown in Fig. 1. The central pixel is predicted by the four surrounding pixels according to Eq. (8),

$$p'_{i,j} = \lfloor (p_{i,j-1} + p_{i-1,j} + p_{i,j+1} + p_{i+1,j})/4 \rfloor \tag{8}$$

where $p'_{i,j}$ is the prediction value of the pixel $p_{i,j}$.

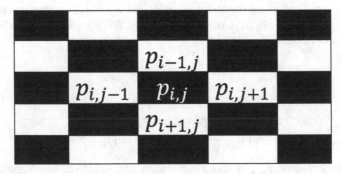

Fig. 1. Dividing pixels into two sets

Note that in [7] the data hiding is processed separately on two types of pixels. In the first round of embedding, the black pixels are used for embedding and the surrounding white pixels are used for computing the prediction values. In the second round, the white pixels are modified for data hiding, and the black pixels are kept unchanged for computing the prediction values.

Here we take the first round of embedding as an example to introduce our new algorithm. After the rhombus prediction, each pixel in the black set has a prediction value. We sort all the pixels in ascending order according to their prediction values, and then divide the sorted pixel sequence into equal-sized groups. As we know, most of the prediction values obtained by the rhombus prediction are close to their real pixel values.

Therefore, after sorting the pixels according to their prediction values, the pixels with similar values may be divided into the same group.

In Table 1, one sorted pixel group of 512×512 Lena image is illustrated. The original pixel values are shown in the first column, their corresponding prediction values are shown in the second column, and their associated coordinates in the original image are shown in the third column. As seen, although those pixels are far away from each other in space, they have the similar pixel values and may be divided into the same group. That is, different from that in PVO and IPVO based algorithms where only the neighboring pixels can be divided into the same block, in our new method the pixels far apart from each other in space may be divided into the same block in case they have the similar pixel values.

Table 1. Example of image block.

Original pixel value	Prediction value	Coordinate
31	30	(200, 265)
31	30	(230, 235)
29	30	(231, 234)
30	30	(309, 186)
30	30	(331, 156)
28	30	(435, 366)
30	30	(439, 366)
29	30	(442, 367)
27	30	(444, 367)

3.2 Adaptive Embedding

In PVO and IPVO based algorithms, only bin 0 and bins ± 1 are expanded for carrying message bits, and the rest of the bins are shifted to make room for data embedding, which is so-called invalid shifting. In general, the prediction value of the pixel will be close to its real value in smooth image blocks (*i.e.*, the pixels belonging to the block are with the similar pixel values). When we sort the pixels in smooth blocks according to their prediction values, the pixels with the similar values (or even the same value) may be divided into the same block. As we predict the largest pixel with the second largest pixel, and predict the smallest pixel with the second smallest pixel in each block, a prediction error histogram having more elements in bin 0 and bins ± 1 can be constructed, which implies that more elements can be expanded for carry message bits and less invalid shifting is needed. On the other hand, the pixels in the rough image block may produce prediction error histogram having less elements in bin 0 and bins ± 1, which means less embedding capacity and more invalid shifting.

Therefore, in our algorithm the pixels in smooth image blocks will take precedence for data hiding. For any pixel p_{ij} to be modified for data hiding, its associated complexity is computed according to Eq. (9).

$$C(p_{ij}) = std(p_{i-1,j}, p_{i,j+1}, p_{i+1,j}, p_{i,j-1})$$ (9)

where $std(X)$ is a function which returns the standard deviation of the vector X.

In the embedding process, the optimized threshold T_Z is exhaustively searched with the step of 0.1. For example, for preselected threshold value T, only those pixels whose associated complexity values are less than T are utilized for data hiding in the embedding process (Note that the preselected threshold should be big enough to ensure that all data can be embedded). That is, only those pixels whose associated complexity values are less than T_Z are grouped together as that in Sect. 3.1, and then PVO or IPVO embedding strategy is applied to compute the resulted distortion. The optimal threshold T_Z is searched according to Eq. (10).

$$\begin{cases} T_Z = argmin\ D(T) \\ subject\ to\ EC(T) \geq Len \end{cases}$$ (10)

where $D(T)$ represents the introduced distortion in the embedding process, $EC(T)$ denotes the embedding capacity with threshold T, and LEN represents the message length to be embedded.

3.3   The Embedding and Extraction Algorithms

In this section, we will introduce the data embedding and extraction procedures in detail. The embedding steps are as follows.

Step 1: Generate the location map.
To avoid the overflow/underflow problem, a location map initialized as empty is constructed first. Then visit the pixels sequentially. If the pixel is with value 254 or 1, append a bit "0" to the location map; if the pixel is with the value of 255 or 0, the pixel is changed to 254 or 1, and append a bit "1" to the location map. In general, there are few pixels with values 0, 1, 254 and 255, and thus it does not need much space to store the location map.

In addition to the location map, the threshold value T_z, the image block size, and the message length also need to be recorded. These auxiliary information can be transmitted to the receiver by replacing the least significant bits (LSBs) of some pseudo-randomly selected pixels (determined by a key). Accordingly, the LSBs of those selected pixels are appended to the message bits to be embedded. Note that all these pseudo-randomly selected pixels are kept unchanged in the next embedding process.

Step 2: Divide the pixels into white and black sets as shown in Fig. 1

Step 3: Embed half of the message bits in the first round.

- Sort the prediction values.
  The white pixels are used to predict the pixels in the black set, and then the black pixels are sorted according to their prediction values.

- Find the optimum block size and threshold value T_z.
  After sorting, the black pixels are divided into $1 \times n (n \geq 3)$ blocks. For a determined block size and the message length to be embedded (note that half of the message bits will be embedded in the first round), the threshold T_z is exhaustively searched with repeatedly applying IPVO embedding strategy on these equal-sized blocks as described in Sect. 3.2. Note that in this step, the block size is another important factor that should be considered. With different block sizes, the obtained marked images may have different visual qualities. In our scheme, the optimal combination of block size and threshold value is exhaustively searched.
- Embed the message bits via the optimized block size and threshold value T_z.
  After finding the combination of optimum block size and threshold value T_z, apply the IPVO embedding strategy on the given image again to get the marked image.

Step 4: Embed the rest half of the message bits in the second round as that in Step 3.

The extraction is the inverse process of embedding, which is as follows.

Step1: Extract the auxiliary information, including the location map, the threshold value T_z, the image block size, and the message length, from those pseudo-randomly selected pixels.
Step2: Extract the half of message bits embedded in the second round. At the same time, partially restore the carrier image.
Step3: Extract the half of the message bits embedded in the first round. At the same time, partially restore the carrier image.
Step3: Replace the LSBs of those pseudo-randomly selected pixels in the embedding process with the extracted information, and restore the original image completely.

4   Experimental Results

In order to demonstrate the efficiency of our new scheme, we compare it with the methods proposed by Li *et al.* [11] and Peng *et al.* [12]. Six standard grayscale images downloaded from the USC-SIPI database are used as the carrier image, including: Lena, Baboon, Barbara, Lake, Airplane (F-16), Boat, which are with the same size of 512×512. The experimental results are shown in Fig. 2. In Fig. 2, the horizontal axis represents the embedded message length and the vertical axis represents the peak signal-to-noise ratio (PSNR), which is computed between the original image and the marked image.

It is observed from Fig. 2 that via using our new embedding strategy, the marked image with higher visual quality (i.e., higher PSNR value) can be easily obtained. It is also observed from Fig. 2 that our new method is particularly efficient for some rough images such as Airplane (F-16) and Baboon. For example, for these two rough images, when the embedding message length is 10000 bits, the PSNR values can be increased by 0.5 db and 0.7 db respectively compared with IPVO algorithm.

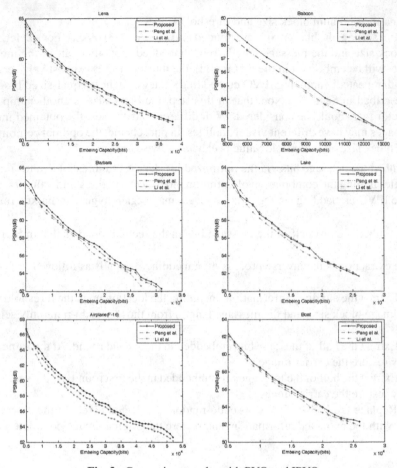

Fig. 2. Comparison results with PVO and IPVO

5   Conclusion

This paper proposes a new RDH method. Instead of directly dividing the neighboring pixels into blocks, in our new method the pixels are sorted first according to their prediction values obtained by the rhombus prediction, and then the sorted sequence is partitioned into non-overlapping blocks. That is, not only the spatial position of the pixels is considered, but also the specific values of the pixels to be grouped are considered in the partitioning stage. Moreover, a new adaptive embedding strategy is proposed based on the characteristics of rhombus prediction. The experimental results demonstrate that our new method is superior to the traditional PVO series.

Acknowledgments. This work is partially supported by the National Natural Science Foundation of China (61772572), the NSFC-NRF Scientific Cooperation Program (61811540409), and the Natural Science Foundation of Guangdong Province of China (2017A030313366).

References

1. Fridrich, J., Goljan, M., Du, R.: Invertible authentication. In: Proceedings SPIE Security Watermarking Multimedia Contents, San Jose, CA, January 2001, pp. 197–208 (2001)
2. Goljan, M., Fridrich, J.J., Du, R.: Distortion-free data embedding for images. In: Moskowitz, I.S. (ed.) IH 2001. LNCS, vol. 2137, pp. 27–41. Springer, Heidelberg (2001). https://doi.org/10.1007/3-540-45496-9_3
3. Ni, Z., Shi, Y., Ansari, N., Su, W.: Reversible data hiding. IEEE Trans. Circuits Syst. Video Technol. **16**(3), 354–362 (2006)
4. Tian, J.: Reversible data embedding using a difference expansion. IEEE Trans. Circuits Syst. Video Technol. **13**(8), 890–896 (2003)
5. Alattar, A.M.: Reversible watermark using the difference expansion of a generalized integer transform. IEEE Trans. Image Process. **13**(8), 1147–1156 (2004)
6. Thodi, D.M., Rodríguez, J.: Expansion embedding techniques for reversible watermarking. IEEE Trans. Image Process. **16**(3), 721–730 (2007)
7. Sachnev, V., Kim, H.J., Nam, J., et al.: Reversible watermarking method using sorting and prediction. IEEE Trans. Circuits Syst. Video Technol. **19**(7), 989–999 (2009)
8. Li, X., Yang, B., Zeng, T.: Efficient reversible watermarking based on adaptive prediction-error expansion and pixel selection. IEEE Trans. Image Process. **20**(12), 3524–3533 (2011)
9. Luo, L., Chen, Z., Chen, M., et al.: Reversible image watermarking using interpolation technique. IEEE Trans. Data Forensics Secur. **5**(1), 187–193 (2010)
10. Yang, W., Chung, K., Liao, M., et al.: Efficient reversible data hiding method based on gradient-based edge direction prediction. J. Syst. Softw. **86**(2), 567–580 (2013)
11. Li, X., Li, J., Li, B., et al.: High-fidelity reversible data hiding scheme based on pixel-value-ordering and prediction-error expansion. Sig. Process. **93**(1), 198–205 (2013)
12. Pen, F., Li, X., Yang, B.: Improved PVO-based reversible data hiding. Digit. Sig. Proc. **25**(2), 255–265 (2014)

A Novel Reversible Data Hiding with Skin Tone Smoothing Effect for Face Images

Yang Yang[✉], Xue Cai, Xingxing Xiao, Jinghan Ye, and Wenyi Shi

School of Electronics and Information Engineering, Anhui University, Hefei, China
sky_yang@ahu.edu.cn

Abstract. In order to improve the visual quality of face images while embedding data reversibly, this paper proposes a novel reversible data hiding (RDH) with skin tone smoothing effect for face images. Firstly, data is embedded into the face images by RDH in color images. Then, the skin tone regions are extracted by an improved skin tone extraction algorithm. Lastly, the skin tone regions are smoothed by the proposed reversible smoothing skin tone algorithm. The experiments show that the visual quality of face images can be effectively improved after embedding the data comparing with other RDH methods and beautification algorithms.

Keywords: Reversible data hiding · Beautification technology · Reversible skin tone smoothing · Face images

1 Introduction

Reversible data hiding (RDH) [1] is a data hiding technique which is the perfect recovery of the cover image and the embedded data. RDH is widely applied to various fields which are not allowed to make any modification in images, such as legal evidence, military imagery and law forensics.

At present, there are already reversible data hiding with contrast enhancement [2] for researching medical and satellite images to improve image quality. However, reversible data hiding for other kinds of images is relatively lacking. Face images have been widely used in social networks and artificial intelligence technology, such as the scene of face recognition. But the quality of face images can not be improved by contrast enhancement. Thus, can we consider embedding data and improving the quality of face images at the same time? Generally, beautification is the main approach to improve the quality of face images. Hence, we consider a novel reversible skin tone smoothing which can beautify face images and embed data.

Supported by the Natural Science Foundation of China under Grant 61502007 and the Natural Science Research Project of Anhui province under Grant 1608085MF125.

H. Wang et al. (Eds.): IWDW 2019, LNCS 12022, pp. 204–212, 2020.
https://doi.org/10.1007/978-3-030-43575-2_17

Skin tone smoothing can improve the quality of face images effectively. Hence, many skin tone smoothing algorithms have been proposed in the past decades. However, almost all of the algorithms can not restore the image losslessly. If the users want to keep the original image, they must save the original image as well as the beautified image, which will cost more storage space and communication bandwidth. So, a reversible skin tone smoothing algorithm is desired. Besides, embedding the user's data into the beautified image by RDH methods can help us to recognize the owner of the image. Therefore, we can consider embedding user's data into the image to achieve skin beautification at the same time.

Hence, a novel reversible data hiding with skin tone smoothing effect for face images is proposed in this paper, which aims at achieving data embedding and skin beautification. The proposed scheme can improve visual quality of face image well comparing with other RDH methods and beautification algorithms.

2   Proposed Method

At present, smoothing algorithms only focus on smoothing the skin regions but hardly ever consider restoring the original image losslessly. Hence, a novel reversible data hiding with skin tone smoothing effect for face images is designed in this paper, which aims at achieving data embedding and skin beautification. This section introduces reversible data hiding and reversible skin tone smoothing respectively.

2.1   Reversible Data Hiding

To protect privacy information of image' user, the proposed method first use Ou's [3] method based on channel-dependent payload partition and adaptive embedding to embed privacy information into the image. Due to the limit of space, we will not give the detailed implementation, which can be found in [3]. The steps of embedding are described briefly as follows.

(1) Calculate prediction-error $e_{i,j}$ of $O_{i,j}$ (Fig. 1) for each channel (R,G,B) by

$$e_{i,j} = O_{i,j} - \lfloor \frac{X_{i-1,j} + X_{i,j-1} + X_{i,j+1} + X_{i+1,j}}{4} \rfloor \qquad (1)$$

Then the prediction-errors sequence $(e_1, ..., e_N)$ is generated according to the scanning order.
(2) Sort the prediction error in each channel according to the integrated complexity Ω_i [3] in an ascending order.
(3) Divide the payload into each channel according to total distortion and embedding capacity.
(4) Select the embedding sub-sequence for single channel.
(5) Obtain the marked prediction-error e_i' in sequence of R, G, B as follows:

$$e_{i,j}' = \begin{cases} 2e_{i,j} + b & \text{if } e_{i,j} \in [-t, t) \\ e_{i,j} + t & \text{if } e_{i,j} \in [t, +\infty) \\ e_{i,j} - t & \text{if } e_{i,j} \in (-\infty, -t) \end{cases} \qquad (2)$$

Where $b \in \{0,1\}$ donates the secret data and t donates the threshold [3]. Finally, the marked pixel $p_{i,j} = O_{i,j} + e'_{i,j}$.

In order to extract data and recover the image losslessly, three location maps of each channel for recording overflow/underflow pixels are embedded into the image as additional data after compressed.

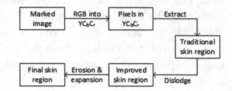

Fig. 1. "x" and "o" pixels.   Fig. 2. Flowchart of the skin region extraction.

2.2   Reversible Skin Tone Smoothing

To improve the quality of face images and realize reversibility, we design reversible skin tone smoothing. This section introduces the proposed reversible skin tone smoothing.

Extraction of Skin-Tone Region. Because smoothing certain parts of faces, such as eyes, mouths and hair leads to visual distortion apparently, the skin region need to be identified accurately. Hsu [4] have proposed a nonlinear transformation of Chroma and the skin model, which showed an advantage of computation comparing with other face detection algorithms and it is suitable for large variations in face images. But the result of Hsu's method [4] contains some interfering pixels which do not belong to the skin region. Hence, we proposed an improved detection of skin-tone regions. Figure 2 is the procedure of the proposed algorithm of skin region extraction. The steps of extraction skin tone are described in this section.

The extraction of skin tone mainly contains the following four steps:

(1) Transform the R, G and B color components into the YC_bC_r color space according to Eqs. (3–5):

$$Y = 0.257 \times R + 0.564 \times G + 0.098 \times B + 16 \tag{3}$$

$$C_b = -0.148 \times R - 0.291 \times G + 0.439 \times B + 128 \tag{4}$$

$$C_r = 0.439 \times R - 0.368 \times G - 0.071 \times B + 128 \tag{5}$$

Where R, G, B donate the pixel in RGB color components, and Y, C_b, C_r donate the transformed pixel in YC_bC_r color space.

(2) Extract the skin-tone according to the skin model.

$$F' = \begin{cases} 0 \text{ if } F \neq 1 or Y < FT \\ 1 \text{ if } F = 1 \end{cases} \tag{6}$$

Where FT is an empirical value. F is the binarization result of skin tone extraction according to the skin model, and donates the pixel is located in the skin regions. F is calculated according to the skin model as follows.

$$F = \frac{(x - ec_x)^2}{a^2} + \frac{(y - ec_y)^2}{b^2} \tag{7}$$

The skin tone model is specified by the centers (donated as $\bar{C}_b(Y)$ and $\bar{C}_r(Y)$) and the spread of the cluster (donated as $W_{C_b}(Y)$ and $W_{C_r}(Y)$). The elliptical model for the skin tones in the transformed $C_b'C_r'$ space is described as Eqs. (8) and (9).

$$\frac{(x - ec_x)^2}{a^2} + \frac{(y - ec_y)^2}{b^2} = 1 \tag{8}$$

$$\begin{bmatrix} x \\ y \end{bmatrix} = \begin{bmatrix} \cos\theta & \sin\theta \\ -\sin\theta & \cos\theta \end{bmatrix} \begin{bmatrix} C_b'(Y) - c_x \\ C_r'(Y) - c_y \end{bmatrix} \tag{9}$$

Where $C_x = 109.38, c_y = 152.02, \theta = 2.53$ (in radian), $ec_x = 1.60, ec_y = 2.41, a = 25.39$ and $b = 14.03$ are computed from skin cluster in the $C_b'C_r'$ space. This is because that the Chroma C_b and C_r are regarded as the function of the luma Y. $C_b'(Y)$ and $C'r(Y)$ are calculated as follows.

$$C_i'(Y) = \begin{cases} (C_i(y) - \bar{C}_i(Y)) \times \frac{W_{C_i}}{W_{C_i}(Y)} + \bar{C}_i(K_h) \text{ if } Y < K_l \\ \qquad\qquad\qquad\qquad\qquad\qquad\text{ or } K_h < Y \\ C_i(Y) \qquad\qquad\qquad\qquad\qquad \text{ if } Y \in [K_l, K_h] \end{cases} \tag{10}$$

Where

$$W_{C_i}(Y) = \begin{cases} WL_{C_i} + \frac{(Y-Y_{min})\times(W_{C_i}-WL_{C_i})}{K_l-Y_{min}} & \text{ if } Y < K_l \\ WH_{C_i} + \frac{(Y_{max}-Y)\times d(W_{C_i}-WH_{C_i})}{Y_{max}-K_h} & \text{ if } K_h < Y \end{cases} \tag{11}$$

$$\bar{C}_b(Y) = \begin{cases} 108 + \frac{(K_l-Y)\times(118-108)}{K_l-Y_{min}} & \text{ if } Y < K_l \\ 108 + \frac{(Y-K_h)\times(118-108)}{Y_{max}-K_h} & \text{ if } K_h < Y \end{cases} \tag{12}$$

$$\bar{C}_r(Y) = \begin{cases} 154 - \frac{(K_l-Y)\times(154-144)}{K_l-Y_{min}} & \text{ if } Y < K_l \\ 154 + \frac{(Y-K_h)\times(154-144)}{Y_{max}-K_h} & \text{ if } K_h < Y \end{cases} \tag{13}$$

Where C_i is either C_b or C_i, $W_{C_b} = 46.97$, $WL_{C_b} = 23$, $WH_{C_b} = 14$, $W_{C_r} = 38.76$, $WL_{C_r} = 20$, $WH_{C_r} = 10$, $K_l = 125$ and $K_h = 188$. All these parameters are estimated from training samples of skin patches from a subset of the HHI images. Y_{min} and Y_{max} in the YC_bC_r are 16 and 235 respectively.

(3) Dislodge the interfering pixels by a $5*5$ template in which the current pixel is the center pixel. If the number of pixels values 1 smaller than 12 in the template, the current pixel values 0, else the current pixel values 1. As Fig. 3 shows, improved value of interfering pixels $u'_{i,j}$ is calculated as follows:

$$u'_{i,j} = \begin{cases} 0 \text{ if } W < 12 \\ 1 \text{ if } W \geq 12 \end{cases} \tag{14}$$

Where W donates the number of pixels valuing 1 among the F' of $u_{i-2,j-2}, u_{i-2,j-1},$
$u_{i-2,j}, \dots, u_{i+2,j+1}, u_{i+2,j+2}.$
(4) Remove the interfering pixels further by erosion and expansion algorithm.

$u_{i-2,j-2}$	$u_{i-2,j-1}$	$u_{i-2,j}$	$u_{i-2,j+1}$	$u_{i-2,j+2}$
$u_{i-1,j-2}$	$u_{i-1,j-1}$	$u_{i-1,j}$	$u_{i-1,j+1}$	$u_{i-1,j+2}$
$u_{i,j-2}$	$u_{i,j-1}$	$u_{i,j}$	$u_{i,j+1}$	$u_{i,j+2}$
$u_{i+1,j-2}$	$u_{i+1,j-1}$	$u_{i+1,j}$	$u_{i+1,j+1}$	$u_{i+1,j+2}$
$u_{i+2,j-2}$	$u_{i+2,j-1}$	$u_{i+2,j}$	$u_{i+2,j+1}$	$u_{i+2,j+2}$

Fig. 3. $5*5$ template.

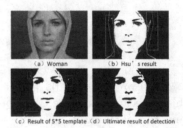

(a) Woman   (b) Hsu's result

(c) Result of 5*5 template   (d) Ultimate result of detection

Fig. 4. Original image and face detection images.

As shown in Fig. 4, the white region donates skin-tone while black donates other region in (b–d). (b) is the extraction of skin-tone by Hsu's method [4]. The red matrixes in (b) contain a lot of interfering pixels, which are not located in the skin regions. (c) is the extracted result after step (3), in which the interfering pixels are obviously decreased in the red matrixes. The ultimate result in (d) almost contains no interfering pixels. Hence, Hsu's method [4] is improved effectively in this paper.

Smoothness of Skin-Tone Region. To restore a portrait image which as same as original image without virtual skin smoothing, a reversible skin smoothing algorithm is proposed in this paper.

Generally, images can be smoothed by mean filtering, but it can not restore the original image losslessly. In order to extract the secret data and restore the original image losslessly, the reversible smoothing skin tone algorithm proposed in this paper first divides pixels into $Dot "O"$ set and $Cross "X"$ set. Note that the two sets (the Cross set and Dot set) are independent of each other. Independence means changes in one set do not affect the other set, and vice versa. Since the two layers' smoothing processes are similar, we only take the layer for illustration. Besides, R, G and B channels are smoothed respectively.

Take Fig. 1 for example, the smoothed value of $O_{i,j}$ is calculated as follows:

$$O'_{i,j} = (X_{i-1,j} + X_{i,j-1} + X_{i,j+1} + O_{i,j}$$
$$+O_{i+1,j-1} + X_{i+1,j} + O_{i+1,j+1}) \times \frac{1}{7} \tag{15}$$

The scanning order of smoothing is from left to right and top to bottom. In order to reverse original image losslessly, the pixel scanning order of our restoration procedure is inverse to that of smoothing.

Figure 5 shows the results of smoothing one time, 3 times, 6 times and 10 times for "Woman". The skin tone is much smoother with the number of smoothing increasing. In order to achieve a significant smoothing effect of the face, the proposed method will use Eq. 14 for L times to smooth the skin-tone region until the realization of visual satisfaction of the smoothing effect.

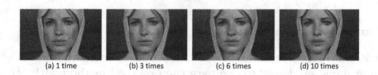

(a) 1 time   (b) 3 times   (c) 6 times   (d) 10 times

Fig. 5. The results of smoothing 1 time, 3 times, 6 times and 10 times.

To achieve reversibility, the number (donated as Num_p) and position of pixels (donated as pos_p, which can be calculated as $pos_p = \lceil log_2 n - 2 \rceil \times Num_p$, where m and n are the size of the image) whose $C_b(Y)$ and $C_r(Y)$ are changed after smoothing are recorded by Least Significant Bit (LSB) of first $8 + pos_p$ in the four sides' h rows and h columns for R, G and B channels. And, L and h are also embedded into the first row of R channel with $O_{embedding flow}$, EC_R, EC_G, EC_B and (t_R^r, t_G^r, t_B^r) by LSB replacement as [2]'s additional data embedding.

2.3 Data Extraction and Image Restoration

For the encoder, it first embeds secret data into the cover image and then smooths the skin tones. Hence, the decoder needs to restore the marked image first and then the secret data and original image can be recovered. The details of data extraction and image restoration are listed as follows.

Step 1. Restore the marked image

Read the LSB of the first row of R channel to obtain L, h, EC_R, EC_G, EC_B and (t_R^r, t_G^r, t_B^r). Then the marked pixels located in the skin region for R, G and B channels are restored for L rounds respectively as

$$O_{i,j} = O'_{i,j} \times 7 - (X_{i-1,j} + X_{i,j-1} + X_{i,j+1}$$
$$+O_{i+1,j-1} + X_{i+1,j} + O_{i+1,j+1}) \tag{16}$$

Step 2. Extract data and restore image

(1) Extract the secret data and recover the G, B, R subsequently. $e'_{i,j}$ is calculated by Eq. (1). $e_{i,j}$ is obtained by

$$e_{i,j} = \begin{cases} \lfloor e'_{i,j}/2 \rfloor & \text{if } e'_{i,j} \in [-2t, 2t) \\ e'_{i,j} - t & \text{if } e'_{i,j} \in [-2t, +\infty) \\ e'_{i,j} + t & \text{if } e'_{i,j} \in (-\infty, -2t) \end{cases} \tag{17}$$

The secret data b is extracted by $b = e'_{i,j} - e_{i,j}$ when $e'_{i,j} \in [-2t, 2t)$. The pixel $O_{i,j}$ is restored by $O_{i,j} = p_{i,j} - e'_{i,j}$.

(2) Replace the four sides' h rows and h columns of R, G and B channel.

3   Experiments

This section presents the performance evaluation of the proposed method in two parts: comparison the proposed method with traditional RDH, comparison the proposed method with other beautification algorithm.

3.1   Comparison with Traditional RDH

To present embedding performance of the proposed method, we choose Fig. 6 (a) as an example randomly to compare the proposed method with other RDH respectively.

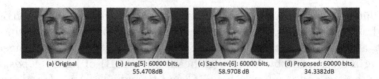

(a) Original   (b) Jung[5]: 60000 bits,   (c) Sachnev[6]: 60000 bits,   (d) Proposed: 60000 bits,
55.4708dB   58.9708 dB   34.3382dB

Fig. 6. Original image and marked images by different methods.

As shown in Fig. 6, the image quality of Jung [5] and Sachnev [6] is only close to the original image and the visual quality of the proposed method is improved well. This is because that [5] and [6] only pursue higher PSNR, but do not consider improving image visual quality. Instead of keeping the smoothed image close to the original image, the proposed method improved the visual quality by smoothing skin tone for face images.

3.2   Compared with Beautification Algorithm

To show the smoothing effect of the proposed method, we choose Fig. 7(a) as an example randomly to compare the proposed method with other beautification algorithm respectively.

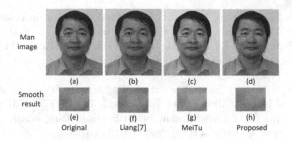

Fig. 7. Original image and smooth results by different algorithms.

Figure 7 is the original images and the smoothing results of Liang [7], MeiTu and the proposed method. For [7], the priori information of facial features is used to produce skin masks, which can better preserve the details of features, but make this part not smoothed. Besides, the skin beautification for faces looks reddish, especially in (f). MeiTu is one of the most popular face beautification softwares in China. We can clear see that skin beautification for faces can not remove all the freckles and wrinkles from (g). (d) is the results obtained after skin smoothness enhancement by the proposed method. The proposed method retains the background of the original image, and only smooths skin-tone region, which is much "closer" to the original image visually. Besides, the beautification operation for skin-tone region is made several rounds to smooth skin-tone effectively. What is more, 60000 bits data are hidden in (d). Hence, the proposed method can reach significant smoothing effect while embedding secret data into the image.

4   Conclusion

This paper proposes a novel reversible data hiding with skin tone smoothing effect for face images, which can improve the image visual quality by reversible smoothing operation after embedding data reversibly. The experiments show that the marked face image visual quality can be effectively improved after embedding data. Besides, the effect of reversible smoothing skin tone is not inferior to the popular beautifying algorithms. In the future, other reversible beautification technologies will be researched.

References

1. Wu, H., Dugelay, J., Shi, Y.: Reversible image data hiding with contrast enhancement. IEEE Sig. Process. Lett. **22**(1), 81–85 (2015)
2. Yang, Y., Zhang, W., Liang, D., Yu, N.: A ROI-based high capacity reversible data hiding scheme with contrast enhancement for medical images. Multimedia Tools Appl. **77**(14), 18043–18065 (2018)
3. Ou, B., Li, X., Zhao, Y., Ni, R.: Efficient color image reversible data hiding based on channel-dependent payload partition and adaptive embedding. Sig. Process. **108**, 642–657 (2015)

4. Hsu, R.-L., Abdel-Mottaleb, M., Jain, A.K.: Face detection in color images. IEEE Trans. Pattern Anal. Mach. Intell. **24**(5), 696–706 (2002)
5. Sachnev, V., Kim, H.J., Nam, J., Suresh, S., Shi, Y.Q.: Reversible watermarking algorithm using sorting and prediction. IEEE Trans. Circ. Syst. Video Technol. **19**(7), 989–999 (2009)
6. Jung, K.: A high-capacity reversible data hiding scheme based on sorting and prediction in digital images. Multimedia Tools Appl. **76**, 13127–13137 (2017)
7. Liang, L., Jin, L., Li, X.: Facial skin beautification using adaptive region-aware masks. IEEE Trans. Cybern. **44**(12), 2600–2612 (2014)

A Novel Lossless Data Hiding Scheme in Homomorphically Encrypted Images

Asad Malik[1], Hongxia Wang[2(✉)], Ahmad Neyaz Khan[3], Yanli Chen[1], and Yi Chen[1]

[1] School of Information Science and Technology, Southwest Jiaotong University, Chengdu 611756, China
[2] College of Cybersecurity, Sichuan University, Chengdu 610065, China
hxwang@scu.edu.cn
[3] School of Computer Science and Engineering, University of Electronic Science and Technology of China, Chengdu 611731, China

Abstract. In this paper, we have presented a novel lossless data hiding scheme in a homomorphically encrypted image. After applying the homomorphic encryption function to the original image by the content owner, the data hider can embed the additional data in a lossless manner, without revealing the original content of the image. Meanwhile, the data hider chooses a threshold value and generates a location map accordingly. This location map is considered as an auxiliary information. The receiver can recover the additional data using the shared auxiliary information in a separable manner. And the original image is recovered losslessly, without any post-processing, by the homomorphic decryption function. In our proposed scheme, no distortion is introduced in the data hiding phase, as a result the directly decrypted image is the same as the original image. The experimental results show that, the scheme has better performance than some of the state-of-the-art methods with high embedding rate and distortionless directly decrypted image.

Keywords: Lossless data hiding · Reversible Data Hiding · Homomorphic cryptography · Cloud computing · High capacity

1 Introduction

Data hiding method enables to embed additional information into digital media, but, in some cases even a slight change in pixel values is inadmissible, like in imagery pertaining to fields of medicine, law, forensics and military. To avoid even the slightest noise, the data is required to be embedded reversibly. Reversible Data Hiding (RDH) [1] is a technique, where after extraction of the embedded information from the digital media, the digital media can be recovered completely. Lossless data hiding is a method where embedding procedure does not effect the original content of digital media and no distortion is introduced.

With the sharp rise in Cloud services usage, users willing to upload the digital data to the Cloud servers have a security concern, due to which they encrypt

© Springer Nature Switzerland AG 2020
H. Wang et al. (Eds.): IWDW 2019, LNCS 12022, pp. 213–220, 2020.
https://doi.org/10.1007/978-3-030-43575-2_18

the cover content prior to upload. In order to deal with the encrypted digital media, the Cloud owner wishes to attach or embed the additional data in it, which could be any origin information or some additional information related to the encrypted content for management purposes. RDH assures that the receiver is able to achieve distortionless cover. Combination of cryptography with RDH results into a new field known as Reversible Data Hiding in Encrypted Images (RDHEI).

Most of the existing RDHEI schemes can be grouped in two categories: (1) RDHEI with symmetric key (2) RDHEI with asymmetric key cryptography. The schemes [4,8,12] are based on symmetric key cryptography, where encryption key and decryption key are the same and need to be shared securely, by the content owner to the receiver. Asymmetric key cryptography (i.e. public key cryptography) also known as homomorphic cryptography has an advantage over the symmetric key cryptography regarding third party key management which is useful in the RDHEI schemes. In asymmetric key cryptography encryption and decryption is done by different keys. Additionally, it provides homomorphic ciphers, which enable security in data processing, without revealing the original content of media. Hence, the homomorphic cryptography is popular with the Cloud computing platform. Some RDHEI schemes [2,5,7,10,13,14] with asymmetric key cryptography having homomorphic property have been proposed in past years. In order to evaluate the performance of RDHEI schemes, two important indicators are the visual quality and embedding rate. The visual quality is normally estimated using the Peak Signal to Noise Ratio (PSNR) and Embedding Rate (ER) is calculated in terms of bit per pixel (bpp).

The rest of this paper is organized as follows: Sect. 2 proposes the general framework of the proposed scheme. Experimental results are shown in Sect. 3. Section 4 gives some concluding remarks.

2   Proposed Scheme

In this section, we have proposed a novel lossless data hiding scheme, in a homomorphically encrypted image. The proposed idea is divided into three primary phases i.e., image encryption, lossless data embedding, data extraction and image recovery. A sketch of the proposed RDHEI scheme can be visualized in Fig. 1. The original image (I) is encrypted by content owner, using Paillier cryptosystem [9], having additive homomorphic and probabilistic properties. Next, after receiving the homomorphically encrypted image (I_e) at the data hiding phase, the data hider embeds the additional data into the encrypted image. Here, embedding is done in a lossless manner, exploiting the additive homomorphic property of Paillier cryptosystem. At the receiver's side, the embedded additional data and recovery of the original image is based on a separable manner. Moreover, the additional data extraction depends on a threshold T value. If T is fixed as minimum, during embedding, in this case all the pixels of I_e will not participate in carrying the additional data. The locations of those pixels, which are unable to carry the additional data, are recorded as auxiliary information. When the value of T is set to maximum, it leads to carry one bit of additional data for each pixel of I_e. In this case, no auxiliary information has to be shared with the receiver. In fact, the original image is recovered losslessly, from the marked encrypted image, only using the secret key.

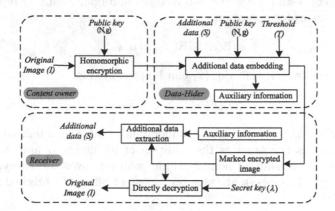

Fig. 1. Illustration of the idea

2.1 Image Encryption

In this phase, the original image of each pixel is encrypted by Paillier cryptosystem [9], with public key (N, g), where $N = p \times q$ is the multiplication of two large prime numbers and $g \in \mathbb{Z}^*_{N^2}$ which follows the condition $gcd(\frac{g^\lambda mod\ N^2 - 1}{N}, N) = 1$. And λ is the secret key, where $\lambda = lcm(p-1, q-1)$. The gcd stands for greatest common divisor and lcm is least common multiple.

Let the original uncompressed gray scale image be (I), having size $L \times B$. Each pixel of the image lies in $[0, 255]$ and is represented by 8 bits. Using the Eq. (1), the content owner of the original image encrypts each pixel of I.

$$c(i,j) = \mathbb{E}[I(i,\ j),\ r] = g^{I(i,\ j)}r^N mod\ N^2 \tag{1}$$

where $c(i,j)$ is the corresponding ciphertext of the original image $I(i,\ j)$, where $1 \leq i \leq L, 1 \leq j \leq B$. $r \in \mathbb{Z}^*_N$ is randomly selected for each pixel, this leads to achieve semantic security and $\mathbb{E}[\cdot]$ denotes the encryption function. Finally, the encrypted image is denoted as I_e, which is sent to the data hider.

2.2 Data Hiding

The data hider, after getting the encrypted image I_e, can successfully embed the additional data, in a lossless manner, into I_e. In fact, without having the knowledge of the original content, the data hider embeds the additional data, by using homomorphic and probabilistic properties of Paillier cryptosystem, in order to achieve a lossless data hiding and the marked encrypted image I_m. The principal of lossless additional data embedding is presented in following subsection.

Lossless Modification in Homomorphic Domain. We have applied the Paillier encryption [9] on the original image and thus the encrypted pixels of the original image have additive homomorphic property inherent in them. The property of additive homomorphism can be explained in the form of following equation, where α and β are the two integers and operation $(\oplus)$ represent the additive homomorphic operation.

$$\mathbb{D}(\mathbb{E}(\alpha) \oplus \mathbb{E}(\beta)) = \alpha + \beta. \tag{2}$$

As a special case when $\beta=0$, Eq. (2) can be presented as:

$$\mathbb{D}(\mathbb{E}(\alpha) \oplus \mathbb{E}(0)) = \alpha. \tag{3}$$

From the Eq. (3), we can easily understand that the value obtained by $\mathbb{D}(\mathbb{E}(\alpha) \oplus \mathbb{E}(0))$ is the same as the addition of plaintexts α and 0. It means, that after applying additive homomorphic property, over the encrypted value $\mathbb{E}(0)$, it changes the ciphertext value but does not affect the original value.

Detailed Embedding Procedure. At the data hiding side, initially the additional data is scrambled using the scrambling key ξ. The scrambled additional data is represented as S. In fact, our embedding scheme shows two types of embedding: first with auxiliary information generation and second without auxiliary information generation. With auxiliary information generation, the data hider can maintain the embedding rate in the range $(0 < \text{ER} < 1)$, by adjusting the threshold T. Initially, the data hider scans the encrypted image I_e in raster scan order. Now, each pixel of I_e is checked for a fixed threshold T, and if either of the two conditions: $(S_k = 0$ and $I_e(i,\ j)$ mod 2=0) or $(S_k = 1$ and $I_e(i,\ j)$ mod 2=1) is met, it means that the data is embedded successfully. On the other side, if the above conditions are not fulfilled for the particular S_k and encrypted pixel of I_e, then upto the particular threshold, the encrypted pixel value is modified using the homomorphic addition property (Eq. (3)). In case, if the encrypted pixel does not meet the condition it is recorded in location map. The location map contains the information about all the pixels, that do not meet the embedding condition which is marked as '1' else '0', after the particular threshold value. The location map is considered as an auxiliary information for the particular threshold. Due to high computational power of Cloud, it is possible to set the threshold value to maximum, so that all the pixels can participate in carrying one bit per pixel of additional data. In this case, there is no need to share the auxiliary information with the receiver, and only with the help of scrambling key ξ, the embedded additional bits are extracted successfully.

2.3   Extraction of Additional Data and Reconstruction of Image

At the receiver's side, the additional data extraction is done with and without the auxiliary information. The data hider can do the embedding in two ways, (1) he/she generates the auxiliary information (with a particular threshold value, not necessarily maximum) and (2) he/she does the embedding without auxiliary information (this is the case when the threshold is set to maximum, until all pixels have been used for embedding). The embedded additional data is extracted using Eq. (4), the shared auxiliary information and the scrambling key ξ.

$$S_k = \begin{cases} 0, & \text{if } I_m(i,\ j) mod\ 2 = 0 \\ 1, & \text{otherwise} \end{cases} \tag{4}$$

In order to recover the original image, the original image is losslessly recovered, by using only the secret key (λ), in both condition i.e. before or after data extraction.

$$R(i,j) = \mathbb{D}[I_m(i,\ j)] = \frac{L(I_m(i,\ j)^\lambda\ mod\ N^2)}{L(g^\lambda\ mod\ N^2)} mod\ N \tag{5}$$

where $R(i,\ j)$ represents the directly decrypted image pixels and $L(x) = (x - 1)/N$. And $\mathbb{D}[\cdot]$ denotes the decryption function. After decryption of all the pixels, the recovered image is R.

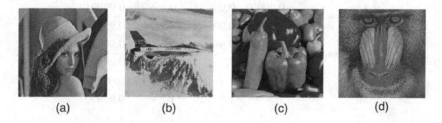

Fig. 2. Test images: (a) Lena, (b) Airplane, (c) Peppers, (d) Baboon

3 Experimental Results

In this section, we evaluate the performance of the proposed method by performing experiments on some standard gray-scale images[1] as shown in Fig. 2. The size of each test image is 512 × 512 pixels.

We investigate our proposed method using standard gray-scale images as shown in the Fig. 2, to show the performance of the purposed scheme with different threshold values. Table 1 shows the maximum embedding rates for different threshold values, where the ER increases with increase in T. Here, we can analyze that Lena, Airplane, Peppers and Baboon images achieve 1 bpp, for T= 17, 17, 18 and 20 respectively.

In order to show the performance of our proposed scheme, we have compared our results with the existing schemes [3,6,11,13]. The comparison shown in Fig. 3, after setting different threshold values, to determine the embedding

[1] http://decsai.ugr.es/cvg/dbimagenes/g512.php.

Table 1. Performance of proposed method with different value of T

Threshold (T)	ER (bpp)			
	Lena	Airplane	Peppers	Baboon
1	0.49997	0.50138	0.50138	0.49969
2	0.74963	0.75019	0.74983	0.74923
3	0.87438	0.87546	0.87433	0.87341
4	0.93713	0.93718	0.93725	0.93717
5	0.96883	0.96833	0.96814	0.96887
6	0.98458	0.98470	0.98510	0.98407
7	0.99225	0.99214	0.99211	0.99246
8	0.99616	0.99599	0.99616	0.99601
9	0.99801	0.99810	0.99807	0.99813
10	0.99902	0.99906	0.99893	0.99901
11	0.99950	0.99957	0.99952	0.99944
12	0.99975	0.99968	0.99977	0.99977
13	0.99989	0.99986	0.99986	0.99989
14	0.99993	0.99991	0.99994	0.99994
15	0.99998	0.99998	0.99998	0.99998
16	0.99998	0.99998	0.99999	0.99999
17	1	1	0.99999	0.99999
18	1	1	1	0.99999
19	1	1	1	0.99999
20	1	1	1	1

rate (bpp) and the quality of directly decrypted image (in terms of PSNR). The comparison is done on the two standard images: Fig. 3(a) Lena and Fig. 3(b) Airplane. After analyzing the results from the Fig. 3, it is notable that our scheme outperforms other compared schemes, in terms of embedding rate and the directly decrypted image quality.

Furthermore, features of our proposed scheme are compared with the related schemes [2, 5, 10, 13]. Table 2 shows that the encryption technique, of the original image, for all the schemes is based on Paillier cryptosystem [9]. The scheme [2] is different from all other schemes, at the receiver's side i.e. non separable in nature, which means the additional data can be extracted but after decryption of the marked encrypted image. The maximum embedding rate and the PSNR of the directly decrypted image, for the schemes [2, 10], are ≤ 0.5 bpp and ≈ 40 dB, which is very low as compared with our scheme. Scheme [2, 5] show extra data expansion whereas our scheme does not show any extra data expansion. Our scheme, like schemes [5, 13], show the perfect recovery of the original image, after applying direct decryption. The maximum embedding capacity of our proposed scheme is 1 bpp, which is similar to [5].

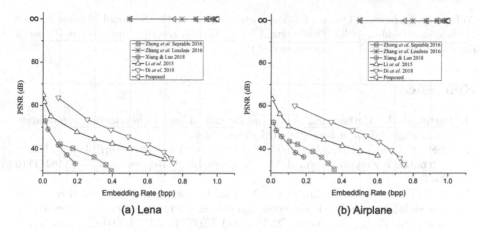

Fig. 3. Performance comparison results with two images: (a) Lena, (b) Airplane

Table 2. Comparative analysis of the proposed scheme with other existing schemes

Schemes	Separable ?	Extra data expansion	ER (bpp)	PSNR (dB)	Encryption method
Chen *et al.* [2]	No	Yes	≤ 0.5	≈ 40	Paillier cryptosystem
Shiu *et al.* [10]	Yes	No	≤ 0.5	≈ 40	Paillier cryptosystem
Zhang *et al.* [13]	Yes	No	≤ 1	$+\infty$	Paillier cryptosystem
Khan *et al.* [5]	Yes	Yes	$= 1$	$+\infty$	Paillier cryptosystem
Proposed	Yes	No	$= 1$	$+\infty$	Paillier cryptosystem

4   Conclusion

In this paper, we have proposed a novel lossless RDHEI scheme in homomorphically encrypted images. The idea is divided into three basic phases: first phase includes encryption of the original image. Lossless embedding of the additional data, in data hiding phase, has been considered in the second phase. The last phase describes the extraction of data and recovery of the original image. However in the first phase, content owner of the original image encrypts the image, by an encryption key using Paillier cryptosystem. In the second phase, without knowing the original content of the original image, the data hider embeds the additional data, in a lossless manner, into the encrypted image by using additive homomorphic and probabilistic property of cryptosystem. Meanwhile, data hider fixes the threshold value and generates the auxiliary information. In the third phase, after the receiver obtains the marked encrypted image that contains the additional data, the receiver extracts the embedded data by using axillary information. The experimental results show that the proposed scheme achieves an embedding rate of 1 bpp, with no auxiliary information when the threshold value is set to maximum. Additionally, it shows separable property in data extraction and the PSNR of the directly decrypted image tends to $+\infty$.

Acknowledgments. This work is supported in part by the National Natural Science Foundation of China (NSFC) under grant No. 61972269, and the Fundamental Research Funds for the Central Universities under the grant No. YJ201881.

References

1. Barton, J.M.: Method and apparatus for embedding authentication information within digital data, 8 July 1997, US Patent 5,646,997
2. Chen, Y.C., Shiu, C.W., Horng, G.: Encrypted signal-based reversible data hiding with public key cryptosystem. J. Vis. Commun. Image Represent. **25**(5), 1164–1170 (2014)
3. Di, F., Duan, J., Zhang, M., Zhang, Y., Liu, J.: Encrypted image-based reversible data hiding with public key cryptography from interpolation-error expansion. In: Barolli, L., Zhang, M., Wang, X.A. (eds.) EIDWT 2017. LNDECT, vol. 6, pp. 138–149. Springer, Cham (2018). https://doi.org/10.1007/978-3-319-59463-7_14
4. Huang, F., Huang, J., Shi, Y.Q.: New framework for reversible data hiding in encrypted domain. IEEE Trans. Inf. Forensics Secur. **11**(12), 2777–2789 (2016)
5. Khan, A.N., Fan, M.Y., Nazeer, M.I., Memon, R.A., Malik, A., Husain, M.A.: An efficient separable reversible data hiding using paillier cryptosystem for preserving privacy in cloud domain. Electronics **8**(6), 682 (2019)
6. Li, M., Xiao, D., Zhang, Y., Nan, H.: Reversible data hiding in encrypted images using cross division and additive homomorphism. Sign. Proces. Image Commun. **39**, 234–248 (2015)
7. Malik, A., et al.: Reversible data hiding in homomorphically encrypted image using interpolation technique. J. Inf. Secur. Appl. **48**, 102374 (2019)
8. Malik, A., Wang, H., Wu, H., Abdullahi, S.M.: Reversible data hiding with multiple data for multiple users in an encrypted image. Int. J. Digit. Crime Forensics (IJDCF) **11**(1), 46–61 (2019)
9. Paillier, P.: Public-key cryptosystems based on composite degree residuosity classes. In: Stern, J. (ed.) EUROCRYPT 1999. LNCS, vol. 1592, pp. 223–238. Springer, Heidelberg (1999). https://doi.org/10.1007/3-540-48910-X_16
10. Shiu, C.W., Chen, Y.C., Hong, W.: Encrypted image-based reversible data hiding with public key cryptography from difference expansion. Sign. Process. Image Commun. **39**, 226–233 (2015)
11. Xiang, S., Luo, X.: Reversible data hiding in homomorphic encrypted domain by mirroring ciphertext group. IEEE Trans. Circuits Syst. Video Technol. **28**(11), 3099–3110 (2017)
12. Zhang, X.: Reversible data hiding in encrypted image. IEEE Sign. Process. Lett. **18**(4), 255–258 (2011)
13. Zhang, X., Long, J., Wang, Z., Cheng, H.: Lossless and reversible data hiding in encrypted images with public-key cryptography. IEEE Trans. Circuits Syst. Video Technol. **26**(9), 1622–1631 (2016)
14. Zheng, S., Wang, Y., Hu, D.: Lossless data hiding based on homomorphic cryptosystem. IEEE Trans. Dependable Secure Comput. 1 (2019). https://doi.org/10.1109/TDSC.2019.2913422

Information Hiding Based on Typing Errors

Linna Zhou[1,2] and Derui Liao[2(✉)]

[1] School of Cyberspace Security,
Beijing University of Posts and Telecommunications, Beijing 100876, China
`zhoulinna@mail.tsinghua.edu.cn`
[2] University of International Relations, Beijing 100091, China
`liaoderui@126.com`

Abstract. Steganography hides secret in carrier. The carrier can be an image, a soundtrack, a video, a text or some other. Text steganography is sometimes more difficulty than others because of the high density of information carried by text. However, we found that most of the online texts is of a kind that tends to contain many typing errors, known as typos, but humans are very good at disambiguation, so these typos often do not frustrate understanding and sometimes it is even difficult to be recognized. This phenomenon can be found both in English and Chinese. In this paper, we propose a text steganography method using carefully injected typos and guarantee the security of the secret and the readability of the texts. With the help of a natural language processing (NLP) model named BERT, we can extract the secret message without the original text. Different from those format-based steganography algorithms, our method can resist format adjustments, OCR re-inputs, etc. Inspired by the text steganography in English text, text steganography in Chinese text with a similar principle is practical. Furthermore, social media platforms always contain many kinds of media, so Cross-Media or even Cross-Social-Network information hiding is practical when combining multi steganography algorithms.

Keywords: Information hiding · Text steganography · Typos

1 Introduction

Steganography has always been an important research direction of information security. It can keep information transmitting in security or protect the copyright. Steganography in image is widely studied and gain a lot of achievements but hiding information in text seems more difficult. Text steganography methods are relatively rare because text contains less information redundancy. However, compared with images, audio, video and other carriers, text has a wider application range and a simpler transmission method which makes text steganography meaningful.

Text steganography mainly includes format-based methods such as adjusting the line spacing, fonts, invisible characters and the format of documents [1], and content-based methods like synonyms or abbreviations substitution [2, 3]. Besides that, text steganography based on text generation [4] using neural network also makes sense. The content-based methods modify the text content to embed secret message in the character

© Springer Nature Switzerland AG 2020
H. Wang et al. (Eds.): IWDW 2019, LNCS 12022, pp. 221–230, 2020.
https://doi.org/10.1007/978-3-030-43575-2_19

streams of the text, which are independent of the additional information such as the format, so they have great advantages in resisting some kinds of attacking methods like format adjustment and OCR re-entry. However, inappropriate modifications may lead to misunderstanding or affect the invisibility of the modification.

In this paper, we propose a text steganography method that can hide secret message with forged typing errors (typos) in plain English text and we can extract the message without using the original text.

2   Online Text and Typing Error

Typing errors exists widely in texts of various languages. Sometimes they do not affect human understanding the text. Rawlinson finds that in English, the skilled reader can still understand the meaning of the text even if the internal alphabetical order of the words is wrong (typoglecymia) [5]. Here is an example:

> *Aoccdrnig to rscheearch at Cmabrigde uinervtisy, it deosn't mttaer waht oredr the ltteers in a wrod are, the olny iprmoetnt tihng is taht the frist and lsat ltteres are at the rghit pclae. The rset can be a tatol mses and you can sitll raed it wouthit a porbelm. Tihs is bcuseae we do not raed ervey lteter by it slef but the wrod as a wlohe.* [6]

A lot of words with inverted characters appear in this text, but it hardly affects understanding. Some people claim that the human brain does not rely on the order of each letter when recognizing words, but from the whole.

Similarly, there is a sentence in Chinese sounds interesting:

> 研表究明,汉字序顺并不定一影阅响读。比如当你看完这句话后,才发这现里的字全是都乱的。

Thus, the phenomenon that some kinds of typos do not affect understanding may be cross-lingual.

Although the examples above are carefully constructed and is unlikely to appear in reality, in fact, unintentional typing errors are common in the text, especially in the online text.

Online texts are texts posted on the Internet. We assume that typing errors in such texts are typos. With the widespread of the Internet, the number of Internet users of various educational levels exploded. Some people are often influenced by their dialects which leads to typos, especially in Chinese. Some online texts on social media are highly informal. For example, when people post text on social media such as Weibo, Twitter or WeChat, expressing their thought is more important than the spelling. Typos often appears in the contents posted by some bloggers, and they even become a characteristic of such bloggers. Some people even use typos to create humor. However, there are also some carefully-constructed harmful typos such as the domain names of some phishing websites.

Commonly, typos in a single word can be one of the following types:

- Duplicated character(s)
- Missing character(s)
- Wrong character(s)
- Reversed characters (reversed character pairs)

And a word with typing error can be either a wrong word or another right word that unsuitable in the context. A wrong word can be conspicuous, but a typo which is another word is stealthy. So, typos can be divided into two parts:

- Non-word typos: they are wrong words that not existed and are conspicuous.
- Right-word typos: they are actually existed words but wrong in the context, and they are stealthy.

However, in an official text, such as official reports, official news, papers, etc., due to their formality and other requirements, they often have multiple rounds of review, and some editing tools provide spelling check, resulting in low input error rate. So creating typo in a text to hide information seems not possible in the texts mentioned above, and is more suitable in an unformal situation such as online texts like texts in Weibo/Twitter and WeChat/messages.

3 Related Work

3.1 BERT and Masked Language Model

Google introduce a powerful language representation model named the BERT [7] (Bidirectional Encoder Representation from Transformers) pre-trained model in 2018. It is pre-trained by two tasks, Masked LM and Next Sentence Prediction. The Masked Language Model (Masked LM, MLM) masks some percentage of the input tokens at random, and then let the model to predict those masked tokens, which enables the model to 'learn' the language in an unsupervised way and build the language model. A pre-trained model can predict a masked token in a context, with some probability to predict the same token as the real one.

3.2 Text Steganography with Typing Errors

Wayner [8] first hide information in the order of shifted characters in English words. But unlimited modifying text may sometimes seriously frustrate human understanding the text and the intensive typo might cause adversary's suspicion. Besides that, swapping characters of a long distance might seems deliberated instead of careless. Liu [9] hide information in English text using matrix coding which has a high embedding rate and guarantee the invisibility by limiting the embedding rate and only swapping the neighboring characters.

However, without understanding the text sometimes it might cause inappropriate modification to the text. Topkara [10] uses Wet-Paper Codes (WPC) to avoid inappropriate modification. They also use computationally asymmetric transformations (CAT) to resist synonym replacement attack and right-word typos to avoid detected by spelling check tools.

4 Steganography Method

4.1 Embedding

BERT can predict the masked token in the context and its probability, so we can let BERT to predict each word in the context one by one and determine whether the prediction is the same as the original word. When BERT predict a same token as the real one, we can recover some missing or wrong token in the context. However, BERT's bidirectional structure makes it difficult recover the original token when modifying more than one tokens each time in each instance that BERT process. So, we select one token at most each time in a single instance to hide information. We transform the selected token into its typo by duplicating a character or swapping a pair of characters. The embedding method steps is as follows:

a. Tokenize the text and divide them into segments by *instance separator* (a character that separate the text into segments which has semantic, for example, comma and period can be used as *instance separators*). Join the segments into instances that no longer than a given length: $len_{instance}$ Then mask and predict one token each time to get each token's prediction and probability in the text.
b. Keep the embeddable tokens that:

   - do not include the octothorpe (#), which means the word should not be *tokenized* to *subtokens*.
   - do not contain numbers, symbols or emoji.
   - *hits*, which means that the token of the highest probability among the predicted candidates is the same as the original token.
   - its probability is greater than P_{embed}
   - is longer than Len_{embed}.

The steps above are designed to find out which word(token) can be modified for embedding.

c. Select an embeddable token to perform typo transformation such as:

   - swapping a pair of neighboring characters
   - duplicating a character
   - deleting a character
   - replacing a character with another different one.

Obviously, four kinds of typo transformations can encode 2 bits. And encoding more bits is practical if more kinds of typo transformations is used. But we perform the transformation by swapping a pair of neighboring characters or duplicating a character here to simplify program. However, in order to make the typo stealthier, it would be better if the typos:

- are right-word typos, which can resist spelling check
- have low ambiguity, typos of high ambiguity are *untouchable words*
- look almost the same as the original word, which means swapping similar characters or replacing a character with a similar one
- try to simulate a real human. For example, we usually only use one keyboard to type, so QWERTY-keyboard typos and 9-key-keyboard typos should not appear in the same context.

4.2 Extracting

A *non-word typo* is likely to be tokenized to subtokens and some of them never appear in the dictionary so they might be converted to the unknown token, the *[UNK]*. The change of the later tokens would affect the prediction of the front tokens because BERT is bidirectional. So tokenized words should be handled before recovering the secret message. But it doesn't matter if the typos were right-word typos. We use non-word typos to enhance the embedding rate, resist synonym replacement and simplify the embedding method, causing complication in extracting, fragility to spelling check and reduction of successful extracting.

We first deal with the tokenized words and then predict each word. Then we find out the typos and identify its type. Finally the secret message can be recovered. Details are as follows:

a. Tokenize the text and convert them into instances.
b. Shrink the tokenized subtokens: Keep the first subtoken of the tokenized word and record its location and its original word.
c. Then mask and predict one token each time to get each token's prediction and probability in the text. Similar in embedding.
d. Compare the original tokens with the predicted tokens, filter out the possible typos and identify their types. Each typo encode one secret bit. Each instance should only have one eligible typo token, otherwise error occurred.
e. Recover the secret message by concatenating the secret bits.

In fact, an extra prediction can be added before shrinking the tokenized subtokens and do not shrink the tokenized subtokens if its predicted probability is greater than a given hyperparameter $P_{tokenized}$. This can reduce the modifications so that the influence to the bidirectional prediction can be minimized.

4.3 Untouchable Words

Untouchable words are words that might seriously frustrate understanding the text after modification such as time, names, and so on. A vanilla method to this problem might be using stop words dictionary to skip these words. Topkara [10] use Wet-Paper Codes [11] to solve this problem. But with the help of MLM, the common untouchable words are hard to predict by the model, so that modifying the untouchable words is of great low probability. So we only filter out the numbers, symbols and emoji.

5 Experiment and Example

5.1 Experiment

We run the PyTorch version BERT model in Python whose parameters are 12-layer, 768-hidden, 12-heads, and 110 M parameters. We use the text copied randomly from an international social media as the carrier. A secret message of 8 bit is embedded in the text as the follows:

> jay chou displays stupendous international popularity, "won't cry " trends # 1 on youtube in various regions including america[1]

> truly iconic. rnb mariah at its finest. every life's happening during its reign is still'vividly emblazoned in my mind'. thanks for the great music to help me remember, queen mc.[2]

> looks like the packaging of apple card will have a nfc tag in there. (unless they **figgure** out how to embed nfc antenna in metal …)[3]

> **tehre** really isn't too many ipad apps with useful external display support 😊hope we'll see some change this year.[4]

> alright now update her sales and upload the hq videos to youtube 😊 📱[5]

> a helicopter crashed in the hudson river after "falling short of the landing pad" on wednesday, nypd and fdny officials say. rescue units are at the incident. according to fdny, the pilot and a heliport worker sustained non-life-**threateninng** injuries due to debris.[6]

> iphone 11 pro lets you capture videos that are beautifully true to life, with greater detail and smoother motion. epic processing power means it can shoot 4 k video with extended dynamic **rannge** and cinematic video stabilization — all at 60 fps. you get more creative control, too, with four times more scene and powerful new editing tools to play with.[7]

---

[1] https://twitter.com/weibo_go/status/1173971748091379713.

[2] https://twitter.com/qtmc1813/status/1173597803987132416.

[3] https://twitter.com/KhaosT/status/1111086092667633666.

[4] https://twitter.com/KhaosT/status/1128176844128129024.

[5] https://twitter.com/slmxny/status/1173807293789589506.

[6] https://twitter.com/Shermanbot/status/1128789210419355648.

[7] https://www.apple.com/iphone-11-pro/.

looks like the internal beta of apple card was turned on for a wider group of audience today ? too bad the enrollment is controlled by apple id whitelist. news team should learn from them 😵[8]

i'll be keeping my 7plus until a phone has teleportation capability or something. it's been repaired once and needs another repair, both of **whichh** are much cheaper than buying new ![9]

there's a jobs age, and then a post-jobs one. apple has lost the creativity and boldness that only jobs could nurture ![10]

innovation has plateaued in the last five **yaers**, there is only so much you can do with it. apple may be making a lot of money but they are doing it behind everyone else.[11]

this ! for daydream's next anniversary, drop the music video already ![12]

such a memorable time, given mariah made it to australia for the **firstt** time. i think this calls for some kodak moments ![13]

jayzhou's new song《# 说好不哭》single digital version of the total sales has broken 10 million yuan, becoming one of the highest digital singles in the **historry** of the platform. # 周杰伦 # zhoujielun # 周杰倫[14]

china's # railway investment maintained stable in the first 8 months of this year, totaling 449. 6 billion yuan (about 63. 6 billion u. s. dollars), according to authorities[15]

now that everybody, in an ever growing global population, wants gadgets and electricity fueled cars, reliable and constant electricity production is needed. most of it produced by coal, gas and oil. crazy environmentalists campaign for scrapping of nuclear power.[16]

from dimly lit restaurants to moonlit beaches, the new night mode uses intelligent software and a13 bionic to deliver low - light shots never before possible on iphone. and it all happens automatically. you can also experiment with manual controls to dial in even more detail and less noise.[17]

it's really lame that beta 2 removed category icons for non-apple issued cards ... i guess this is a sign of a service oriented company, the product no longer put user at the first place ...[18]

---

[8] https://twitter.com/KhaosT/status/1111177188001222656.
[9] https://twitter.com/catchase/status/1174217973298601989.
[10] https://twitter.com/zmanusa54/status/1174268814906798082.
[11] https://twitter.com/VoiceofRaum/status/1174253504543825921.
[12] https://twitter.com/porbidaaaa/status/1173819335007014912.
[13] https://twitter.com/Candour100/status/1173547897226285056.
[14] https://twitter.com/hunantvchina/status/1173836853176201217.
[15] https://twitter.com/PDChina/status/1174302519792668672.
[16] https://twitter.com/CharlesIIIBall/status/1174220891401723907.
[17] https://www.apple.com/iphone-11-pro/.
[18] https://twitter.com/KhaosT/status/1115483276276260864.

can somebody explain what did cai xukun did that he is dissed in comments about jay chou ?[19]

brook lopez started his career exclusively as a post scorer because that's what he was supposed to do. now he runs perimeter to perimeter bombing eight 3's a game. he is finally living his truth and it brings me unbridled joy[20]

iphone 11 and 11 pro review : "we are now living in the golden age of smartphones, where the gadgets' improvements each year are far from seismic," writes @bxchen. "the bottom line ? it's time to reset our upgrade criteria."[21]

today in 1997, @mariahcarey transformed herself & all of us with the release of her sixth album, "butterfly." follow along as we remember some iconic bits from that era, starting with this mimi & the sailors moment from the "honey" music video.[22]

wow !@mariahcarey's 'in the mix' has already climbed to # 1 on the itunes r & b chart in the usa with a 40% lead over its nearest competitor.[23]

it would be nice if we can get a home app redesign this year. the current one just look sad with mar-zipan[24]

bought the cd and didn't stop listening to it the whole week after.[25]

today marks the anniversary of @mariahcarey's signature album, 'butterfly'. regarded as one of the greatest r & b albums in history, this masterpiece was a declaration of personal & musical independence, and it elevated the genre to new heights. timeless. genius. iconic. 🎧[26]

thank u for this unmatched piece of art miss mariah i love u[27]

did we miss a favorite moment of yours from the "butterfly" era ? reply and let us know what your favorite mimi moment is.[28]

And we can extract the secret message without using the original unmodified text. And Fig. 1 is the screenshot of the extraction program result.

5.2   Result

Embedding 8 bits in 4939 characters (including spaces) seems a little bit inefficient compared with Liu [9] and Topkara [10]. But the maximum embedding rate is not only related to the number of characters or the number of words, but also to the semantic of the

---

[19] https://twitter.com/Bunny_Citizen98/status/1173972466059943937.

[20] https://twitter.com/uuords/status/1128855726917640192.

[21] https://www.apple.com/iphone-11-pro/.

[22] https://twitter.com/Sony/status/1173621121331159042.

[23] https://twitter.com/wemissmusic/status/1174254427890507777.

[24] https://twitter.com/KhaosT/status/1125434528699273216.

[25] https://twitter.com/The_Bot/status/1173625354965192706.

[26] https://twitter.com/MariahCareyAU/status/1173538261618135040.

[27] https://twitter.com/patr1ck_w116/status/1173577562230067200.

[28] https://twitter.com/Sony/status/1173621262196891649.

```
... ... ... ,
*** typos are: ***
[type, position, typo, predict]
[1, 88, 'figgure', 'figure']
[0, 99, 'tehre', 'there']
[1, 191, 'threateninng', 'threatening']
[1, 230, 'rannge', 'range']
[1, 332, 'whichh', 'which']
[0, 378, 'yaers', 'years']
[1, 438, 'firstt', 'first']
[1, 485, 'historry', 'history']
msg len = 8
msg is: 0b11011101
```

Fig. 1. Screenshot of the extraction program. 8 bits of secret message extracted.

text. 18 suitable words are found in this experiment and up to 36 bits of secret message can be embedded using 4 kinds of typos and more information could be embedded by using more kinds of typos and by using efficient coding methods. The predicting might change the status of the model and a same order of the sequences should be followed both embedding and extracting. Importantly, the original context should not contain typos, otherwise it might frustrate our embedding and extracting. But we can overcome that by hiding control bits in other typos. Hiding information in typos with NLP methods still have a long way to go.

However, the machine learning and deep learning based natural language processing (NLP) methods are always of great complexity and need huge computing resources, so embedding might take a long time or even doesn't work with lowly equipped machines. But text steganography with the understanding of the text is a cross-lingual idea and it also works in other languages such as Chinese. Although Chinese is extremely different from English, we can also hide information in Chinese text by injecting Chinese typos such as homonym. It also works in other languages, and the only restriction is that an NLP model can learn such a language.

For example, we embed 0b1101 in to a Chinese paragraph using Chinese typos:

如今在一个**网落（网络）**技术快速发展的信息爆炸的时代，网络上每天都有巨量的数据在不断地产生。而网络上的文本往往包含许多拼写错误，这一点在个人用户、自媒体等发布的内容中尤其地明显。并且这种错误往往不影响人类对文本意义的理解，有时甚至难以被发现。这个**限象（现象）**在英文中有出现，在中文中更是如此，所以这一现象似乎是跨语言的。因此，在这样的文本中，人们可以通过明智地输入拼写错误来执行信息隐藏，这并不奇怪。本文**计话（计划）**针对新浪微博或者微信上的文本内容进行中文打字错误的研究，以期望能利用现今的自然语言处理技术研究出基于中文打字错误的信息隐藏算法，该算法能利用精心伪造的打字错误将秘密信息嵌入到中文文本中，并保证文本的可读性与秘密信息的隐蔽性。不同于基于格式的隐写**算发（算法）**，该算法可以抵抗格式调整、OCR重新输入等。并且由于微博、微信包含了多种媒体，该算法可以联合其他算法进行跨媒体甚至跨社交网络的信息隐藏。

6 Conclusion

In this paper we have presented a method that hides secret message in text by creating typing errors with the help of BERT, an NLP model and extracts the message without using the original unmodified text. We proved that NLP method is also applicable to steganography. Our method is suitable for both steganography and digital watermarking in cursory texts of informal situation such as social media, message and chatting.

In the future, we can present a method that hide information in Chinese text with a similar idea. More opportunities might show up with de development of NLP and human's researches of language itself.

Acknowledgment. The work is supported by the National Natural Science Foundation of China (NSFC) under Grant no. U1536207, the National Key Research and Development Program of China under no.2016QY08D1600 and the National Key Research and Development Project of China under no. 2016YFB0801405.

References

1. Por, L.Y., Delina, B.: Information hiding: a new approach in text steganography. In: WSEAS International Conference. Proceedings. Mathematics and Computers in Science and Engineering. No. 7. World Scientific and Engineering Academy and Society (2008)
2. Shirali-Shahreza, M.H., Shirali-Shahreza, M.: Text steganography in chat. In: 2007 3rd IEEE/IFIP International Conference in Central Asia on Internet. IEEE (2007)
3. 甘灿(Can Gan), et al.: "一种改进的基于同义词替换的中文文本信息隐藏方法." (An Improved Chinese Text Steganography Based on Synonym Substitution) 东南大学学报: 自然科学版(Journal of Southeast University: Natural Science Edition) 37.A01, 137–140 (2007)
4. Luo, Y., Huang, Y.: Text steganography with high embedding rate: using recurrent neural networks to generate chinese classic poetry. In: Proceedings of the 5th ACM Workshop on Information Hiding and Multimedia Security. ACM (2017)
5. Rawlinson, Graham: The significance of letter position in word recognition. IEEE Aerosp. Electron. Syst. Mag. **22**(1), 26–27 (2007)
6. Matt Davis. MRC Cognition and Brain Sciences Unit. http://www.mrc-cbu.cam.ac.uk/people/matt.davis/Cmabrigde/. Accessed 30 Oct 2003
7. Devlin, J., Chang, M.W., Lee, K., Toutanova, K.: Bert: pre-training of deep bidirectional transformers for language understanding. arXiv preprint arXiv:1810.04805 (2018)
8. Peter Wayner. Hiding Information in the Order of Letters. http://www.wayner.org/books/discrypt2/wordsteg.html. Accessed 08 Jul 2019
9. Liu, M., Guo, Y., Zhou, L.: Text steganography based on online chat. In: 2009 Fifth International Conference on Intelligent Information Hiding and Multimedia Signal Processing. IEEE (2009)
10. Topkara, M., Topkara, U., Atallah, M.J.: Information hiding through errors: a confusing approach. In: Security, Steganography, and Watermarking of Multimedia Contents IX, vol. 6505. International Society for Optics and Photonics (2007)
11. Fridrich, J., Goljan, M., Soukal, D.: Wet paper codes with improved embedding efficiency. IEEE Trans. Inf. Forensics Secur. **1**(1), 102–110 (2006)

High-Capacity Reversible Data Hiding in Encrypted Images Based on MSB Prediction

Dawen Xu[✉], Bo Guan, Shubing Su, and Xuena Qiu

School of Electronics and Information Engineering,
Ningbo University of Technology, Ningbo 315016, China
dawenxu@126.com

Abstract. Reversible data hiding in encrypted images is an effective technology to embed additional data in the encrypted domain without accessing the content of the original image. During the decoding process, the secret message can be extracted accurately and the original image can be reconstructed perfectly. In this paper, an efficient reversible data hiding scheme for encrypted images based on MSB (most significant bit) prediction is proposed, which has high embedding capacity. Combining with the characteristic of prediction technology, the prediction error is first identified and its location is stored in the location map. The stream cipher is then used to encrypt the original image. According to the location map, the data-hider substitutes up to three MSBs of embeddable pixels in encrypted image with the secret message. At the receiving end, the secret message can be extracted without error, and the original image can be perfectly reconstructed by utilizing MSB prediction technology. Experimental results show that the scheme can achieve higher embedding capacity than most related methods.

Keywords: Reversible data hiding · Image encryption · Image security · MSB prediction · High capacity

1 Introduction

Cloud computing provides the most effective solution for the storage and management of massive image data. However, under the existing cloud computing architecture, users basically lose absolute control over data, which lead to a series of security issues such as confidentiality, privacy and so on. Encryption is an important means to protect the confidentiality and privacy of user data in a cloud computing environment. Users first encrypt sensitive content before uploading it. All the processing and computing in the cloud are performed in the encrypted domain. However, image data loses its original characteristics after encryption, and the effective management, integrity and reliability protection of massive ciphertext image data in the cloud has become an urgent and challenging problem. In recent years, data hiding in encrypted domain has become a research hotspot. It directly embeds some additional messages in the encrypted data, including copyright information, owner identity, or authentication data.

In the past few years, some algorithms for data hiding in encrypted images or videos have been proposed [1–4]. However, within these algorithms, the original carrier is

© Springer Nature Switzerland AG 2020
H. Wang et al. (Eds.): IWDW 2019, LNCS 12022, pp. 231–243, 2020.
https://doi.org/10.1007/978-3-030-43575-2_20

permanently modified during the data embedding process, and cannot be recovered losslessly even after data extraction. This is not feasible in some sensitive areas, such as medical science, law forensics, and military applications [5]. For this reason, reversible Data Hiding in encrypted images (RDH-EI) has become an interesting and challenging research field. At the receiving end, RDH-EI aims to accurately extract secret message and completely restore the original image. Existing RDH-EI methods can be classified into three categories, namely vacating room after encryption (VRAE) [6–11], reserving room before encryption (RRBE) [12–15], and the method based on homomorphic encryption [16–19].

The early VRAE framework is proposed by Zhang [6, 7]. The entire data of an uncompressed image is encrypted directly by a stream cipher. Then the data-hider embeds the additional data by modifying a small portion of encrypted data. Later, Huang et al. [8] designed a new framework for RDH in encrypted domain, which integrates previous difference histogram shifting based RDH approaches via a new encryption strategy. Wu and Sun [9] proposed a separable RDH-EI method, where 1-layer or 2-layer MSBs are emptied for storing the additional bits. The context adaptive interpolation algorithm is adopted to estimate the MSBs. Qian and Zhang [10] proposed a RDH-EI scheme using distributed source coding (DSC). As estimating MSB is much more accurate than estimating LSB planes, the MSB plane can be recovered by DSC decoding with an acceptable decoding error probability. More recently, high capacity reversible data hiding approach with correction of prediction errors and high capacity reversible data hiding approach with embedded prediction errors are presented in [11].

Ma *et al.* [12] first proposed a RRBE method. Specifically, by using traditional RDH method, LSBs of some pixels are embedded into other pixels to empty the room, and then the image is encrypted. So the positions of these LSBs in the encrypted image can be used to embed data. Later, Zhang *et al.* [13] proposed a RDH method in encrypted images based on estimation technique. The additional data is embedded in the encrypted image by modifying the estimating errors. In [14], another RRBE method was proposed by using the interpolation technique to make room for data embedding. Yi *et al.* [15] proposed an RDH-EI method using parametric binary tree labeling scheme. In general, the RDH-EI methods based on RRBE can achieve larger embedding capacity than those based on VRAE. But it is impracticable, because the data hider should know the vacated room created by the content owner before encryption. In addition to VRAE and RRBE, another RDH-EI method suggests to use homomorphic encryption to encrypt the original image [16–19]. However, the most important problem of homomorphic encryption is that it will suffer from pixel expansion.

In this paper, we present an efficient high-capacity reversible data hiding scheme for encrypted images based on MSB prediction. Due to the local correlation, adjacent pixel values in the image are generally close. Therefore, we can use the decrypted previous pixels to predict the current pixel value. During the data hiding phase, three MSBs of each available pixel in the encrypted image are substituted by the secret bits. The rest of the paper is structured as follows. Section 2 describes the details of the proposed scheme including location map generation, image encryption, data embedding, data extraction and original image recovery. Experimental results and comparisons are provided in Sect. 3. Finally, the conclusion is drawn and future work is concluded in Sect. 4.

2   Proposed Scheme

The framework of the proposed RDH-EI method based on MSB prediction is illustrated in Fig. 1. Although there is local correlation in the image, adjacent pixel values can be used to predict the current pixel values. But sometimes there are errors in the prediction. Therefore, the first step is to identify the prediction error and store its position information in the location map. Then, the content owner encrypts the original image using a standard stream cipher. After that, data embedding can be carried out by substituting three MSBs of embeddable pixels in encrypted image with the secret message. At the receiver side, if the receiver only has the data hiding key, he can extract the hidden data. If the receiver only has the encryption key, the original image can be reconstructed. If both the encryption key and the data hiding key are available, the receiver can extract the hidden data without any errors and restore the original image perfectly.

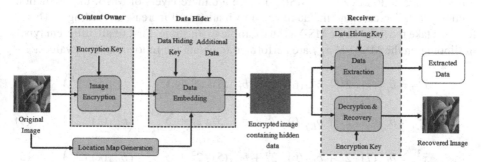

Fig. 1. The framework of proposed RDH-EI scheme

2.1   Generation of Location Map

Without loss of generality, assuming that the size of the original grey image is H × W, and the pixel value is represented by $x_{i,j} \in [0, 255]$, $1 \leq i \leq H$, $1 \leq j \leq W$. According to the prediction mode, all pixels are divided into four categories, that is, $X^I = \{x_{1,1}\}$, $X^{II} = \{x_{1,2}, x_{1,3}, \ldots, x_{1,W}\}$, $X^{III} = \{x_{2,1}, x_{3,1}, \ldots, x_{H,1}\}$, $X^{IV} = \{x_{i,j} | i = 2, 3, \ldots, H, \ j = 2, 3, \ldots, W\}$. The pixel in X^I will be kept unchanged during the whole data embedding phase. On the other hand, the pixels in X^{II}, X^{III}, and X^{IV} will be approximately predicted by those adjacent pixels. Some prediction methods have been proposed to estimate pixel values in spatial domain [20]. In this work, the adjacent pixels are used to predict the target pixel by the following expression.

$$\tilde{x}_{i,j} = \begin{cases} x_{i,j} & x_{i,j} \in X^I \\ x_{i,j-1} & x_{i,j} \in X^{II} \\ x_{i-1,j} & x_{i,j} \in X^{III} \\ \lfloor w_d \cdot x_{i-1,j-1} + w_v \cdot x_{i,j-1} + w_h \cdot x_{i-1,j} \rfloor & x_{i,j} \in X^{IV} \end{cases} \quad (1)$$

where $\lfloor \bullet \rfloor$ is a floor function that maps a real number to the largest previous integer, and $\tilde{x}_{i,j}$ is the predicted pixel value. Weighting coefficients w_h, w_v and w_d are satisfied with

$w_h + w_v + w_d = 1, 0 \le w_h, w_v, w_d \le 1$. For the sake of simplicity, we set $w_h = 0.4$, $w_v = 0.4$ and $w_d = 0.2$.

As the MSB values are substituted by the secret bits during the data embedding phase, it is important to predict them without any errors. To recover the original image perfectly, we need to analyze the image content to detect the possible prediction errors. The difference between the predicted pixel value and the original pixel value can be calculated as $\Delta_{or} = |x_{i,j} - \tilde{x}_{i,j}|$.

Each pixel $x_{i,j}$ with gray value falling into [0, 255] can be represented by 8 bits, $b_{i,j}(0), b_{i,j}(1), \ldots, b_{i,j}(7)$, such that

$$b_{i,j}(k) = \left\lfloor \frac{x_{i,j}}{2^k} \right\rfloor mod\, 2, k = 0, 1, \ldots, 7 \tag{2}$$

where $mod()$ represents the modulo operation. In general, data embedding can be performed using up to three-layer MSB. If there are more layers of MSB, the prediction accuracy will decrease and the auxiliary information will increase accordingly. Therefore, we take the three-layer MSB as an example to illustrate. First of all, different types of flipping on the MSBs of $x_{i,j}$ are performed to obtain the following seven values.

$$\bar{x}_{i,j}^1 = b_{i,j}'(7) \cdot 2^7 + b_{i,j}(6) \cdot 2^6 + b_{i,j}(5) \cdot 2^5 + \sum\nolimits_{k=0}^{4} \left(b_{i,j}(k) \cdot 2^k \right) \tag{3}$$

$$\bar{x}_{i,j}^2 = b_{i,j}(7) \cdot 2^7 + b_{i,j}'(6) \cdot 2^6 + b_{i,j}(5) \cdot 2^5 + \sum\nolimits_{k=0}^{4} \left(b_{i,j}(k) \cdot 2^k \right) \tag{4}$$

$$\bar{x}_{i,j}^3 = b_{i,j}(7) \cdot 2^7 + b_{i,j}(6) \cdot 2^6 + b_{i,j}'(5) \cdot 2^5 + \sum\nolimits_{k=0}^{4} \left(b_{i,j}(k) \cdot 2^k \right) \tag{5}$$

$$\bar{x}_{i,j}^4 = b_{i,j}'(7) \cdot 2^7 + b_{i,j}'(6) \cdot 2^6 + b_{i,j}(5) \cdot 2^5 + \sum\nolimits_{k=0}^{4} \left(b_{i,j}(k) \cdot 2^k \right) \tag{6}$$

$$\bar{x}_{i,j}^5 = b_{i,j}'(7) \cdot 2^7 + b_{i,j}(6) \cdot 2^6 + b_{i,j}'(5) \cdot 2^5 + \sum\nolimits_{k=0}^{4} \left(b_{i,j}(k) \cdot 2^k \right) \tag{7}$$

$$\bar{x}_{i,j}^6 = b_{i,j}(7) \cdot 2^7 + b_{i,j}'(6) \cdot 2^6 + b_{i,j}'(5) \cdot 2^5 + \sum\nolimits_{k=0}^{4} \left(b_{i,j}(k) \cdot 2^k \right) \tag{8}$$

$$\bar{x}_{i,j}^7 = b_{i,j}'(7) \cdot 2^7 + b_{i,j}'(6) \cdot 2^6 + b_{i,j}'(5) \cdot 2^5 + \sum\nolimits_{k=0}^{4} \left(b_{i,j}(k) \cdot 2^k \right) \tag{9}$$

where $b_{(i,j)}'(k)$ is the flipped value of $b_{(i,j)}(k)$, i.e., 0 is converted into 1, and vice versa. The differences between the predicted value and the flipped values are then calculated as $\bar{\Delta}_1 = \left| \bar{x}_{i,j}^1 - \tilde{x}_{i,j} \right|$, $\bar{\Delta}_2 = \left| \bar{x}_{i,j}^2 - \tilde{x}_{i,j} \right|$, $\bar{\Delta}_3 = \left| \bar{x}_{i,j}^3 - \tilde{x}_{i,j}) \right|$, $\bar{\Delta}_4 = \left| \bar{x}_{i,j}^4 - \tilde{x}_{i,j} \right|$, $\bar{\Delta}_5 = \left| \bar{x}_{i,j}^5 - \tilde{x}_{i,j} \right|$, $\bar{\Delta}_6 = \left| \bar{x}_{i,j}^6 - \tilde{x}_{i,j} \right|$, and $\bar{\Delta}_7 = \left| \bar{x}_{i,j}^7 - \tilde{x}_{i,j} \right|$. In addition, the minimum of these differences is defined as follows.

$$\bar{\Delta}_{min} = \left\{ \bar{\Delta}_1, \bar{\Delta}_2, \bar{\Delta}_3, \bar{\Delta}_4, \bar{\Delta}_5, \bar{\Delta}_6, \bar{\Delta}_7 \right\} \tag{10}$$

If $\Delta_{or} \ge \bar{\Delta}_{min}$, it means that there is a prediction error. Otherwise, there is no prediction error because the original pixel value is closer to its predicted pixel value than the flipped values.

In order to ensure that the original image can be completely reconstructed, a binary location map L_1, is introduced to record the positions of the prediction errors. More precisely, if there is a prediction error, the corresponding element is marked as "1" in L_1. Otherwise, the element is marked as "0". The location map is losslessly compressed using arithmetic coding and appended to the front of the payload, along with its size.

2.2 Image Encryption

Decompose pixel $x_{i,j}$ into 8 bits $b_{i,j}(0), b_{i,j}(1), \ldots, b_{i,j}(7)$ using Eq. (2). A pseudo-random binary sequence with $H \times W \times 8$ bits is generated via a standard stream cipher determined by the encryption key K_{en}. Then, the bitwise exclusive-or (XOR) operation is performed between the original bits $b_{i,j}(k)$ and pseudo-random bits $r_{i,j}(k)$ as follow.

$$\hat{B}_{i,j}(k) = b_{i,j}(k) \oplus r_{i,j}(k) \tag{11}$$

where $\oplus$ represents a bitwise XOR operator and $\hat{B}_{i,j}(k)$ denotes the k-th associated encrypted bit. In the next step, the encrypted bits are concatenated orderly as the encrypted pixel value $\hat{x}_{i,j}$.

$$\hat{x}_{i,j} = \sum_{k=0}^{7} \left(\hat{B}_{i,j}(k) \cdot 2^k \right) \tag{12}$$

Thus, an encrypted version of the original image is obtained.

2.3 Data Embedding in Encrypted Image

After receiving the encrypted image, the data hider cannot obtain the plaintext content, because there is no encryption key. However, the data-hider can still embed additional information by MSB substitution technology. Suppose the message to be embedded is a binary sequence. In order to enhance the security, the to-be-embedded message is encrypted by a stream cipher according to the data-hiding key K_{dh}. Thus, the to-be-embedded binary information, i.e., $W = \{w(l)|l = 1, 2, \ldots, K, w(l) \in \{0, 1\}\}$, is an encrypted version. It is difficult for anyone without a data hiding key to recover the message.

During the data hiding phase, the error location map L_1 can be used to detect where it is possible to embed bits of the secret message (i.e. pixels without prediction error). Subsequently, the data hider scans pixels of the encrypted image from left to right, then from top to bottom and substitutes the MSBs of all the available pixels by secret bits.

$$\overline{\overline{X}}_{i,j} = w(l) \cdot 2^7 + w(l+1) \cdot 2^6 + w(l+2) \cdot 2^5 + \sum_{k=0}^{4} \hat{B}_{i,j}(k) \cdot 2^k \tag{13}$$

where $\overline{\overline{X}}_{i,j}$ is the marked encrypted pixels.

2.4 Data Extraction and Original Image Recovery

At the receiving end, the receiver can extract the additional message using the data hiding key and reconstruct the original image using the encryption key. In this section, we will consider the following three scenarios.

(1) Data Extraction with Only Data Hiding Key

After obtaining the marked and encrypted image $\overline{\overline{X}}_{i,j}$, a receiver with the data hiding key K_{dh} and the error location map L_1 can extract the hidden message directly. First of all, the pixels are scanned from left to right, then from top to bottom mentioned above. Then, the MSBs of embeddable pixel are extracted as Eqs. (14)–(16) to retrieve the secret message.

$$\tilde{w}(l) = \left\lfloor \overline{\overline{X}}_{i,j}/2^7 \right\rfloor \tag{14}$$

$$\tilde{w}(l+1) = \left\lfloor mod\left(\overline{\overline{X}}_{i,j}, 2^7\right)/2^6 \right\rfloor \tag{15}$$

$$\tilde{w}(l+2) = \left\lfloor mod\left(\overline{\overline{X}}_{i,j}, 2^6\right)/2^5 \right\rfloor \tag{16}$$

Then, by using the data hiding key K_{dh}, the corresponding plaintext message can be further obtained by decryption. It can be seen that if the receiver only has the data hiding key, he/she can extract the additional message. But without the encryption key, he/she is unable to access the content of the original image.

(2) Image Recovery with Only Encryption Key

In the second scenario, if the receiver only has the encryption key K_{en}, the additional message cannot be extracted. But according to the following steps, he can directly decrypt the marked encrypted image and restore it to the original image.

Step 1. Similar to the image encryption process, the encryption key K_{en} is used to generate pseudo-random sequence with $H \times W \times 8$ bits.
Step 2. The pixels of the marked encrypted image are scanned from left to right, then from top to bottom, and each pixel can be represented by 8 bits, $b'_{i,j}(0), b'_{i,j}(1), \ldots, b'_{i,j}(7)$.

$$b'_{i,j}(k) = \left\lfloor \frac{\overline{\overline{X}}_{i,j}}{2^k} \right\rfloor mod\ 2, k = 0, 1, \ldots, 7 \tag{17}$$

Step 3. Image decryption can then be done as follows.

$$B^{de}_{i,j}(k) = b'_{i,j}(k) \oplus r_{i,j}(k) \tag{18}$$

where $r_{i,j}(k)$ are the key stream bits generated by the encryption key.
Step 4. The decrypted pixel value $x^{de}_{i,j}$ can be calculated as

$$x^{de}_{i,j} = \sum_{k=0}^{7} \left(B^{de}_{i,j}(k) \cdot 2^k\right) \tag{19}$$

Since the MSBs of each pixel (except $\hat{x}_{1,1}$) are substituted with the secret bits during data embedding, these MSBs of $x_{i,j}^{de}$ are different from the MSBs of the original image. For this reason, the prediction of MSBs should be performed.

Since $x_{1,1}$ does not change during the data embedding process, its value can be accurately obtained after decryption. Thus, the estimation of $x_{i,j}$, denoted by $\tilde{x}_{i,j}$, can be obtained using the same prediction technology as Eq. (1). According to the local correlation of the image, the difference between the original pixel and its neighboring pixel is small. On the contrary, the difference between the marked pixel and its neighboring pixel is relatively large. Therefore, in order to recover the MSBs, the following eight values should be first calculated.

$$\overline{\overline{X}}_{i,j}^0 = 0 * 2^7 + 0 * 2^6 + 0 * 2^5 + \sum_{k=0}^{4} \left(B_{i,j}^{de}(k) \cdot 2^k \right)$$

$$\overline{\overline{X}}_{i,j}^1 = 0 * {}^7 + 0 * 2^6 + 1 * 2^5 + \sum_{k=0}^{4} \left(B_{i,j}^{de}(k) \cdot 2^k \right)$$

$$\overline{\overline{X}}_{i,j}^2 = 0 * 2^7 + 1 * 2^6 + 0 * 2^5 + \sum_{k=0}^{4} \left(B_{i,j}^{de}(k) \cdot 2^k \right)$$

$$\overline{\overline{X}}_{i,j}^3 = 0 * 2^7 + 1 * 2^6 + 1 * 2^5 + \sum_{k=0}^{4} \left(B_{i,j}^{de}(k) \cdot 2^k \right)$$

$$\overline{\overline{X}}_{i,j}^4 = 1 * 2^7 + 0 * 2^6 + 0 * 2^5 + \sum_{k=0}^{4} \left(B_{i,j}^{de}(k) \cdot 2^k \right)$$

$$\overline{\overline{X}}_{i,j}^5 = 1 * 2^7 + 0 * 2^6 + 1 * 2^5 + \sum_{k=0}^{4} \left(B_{i,j}^{de}(k) \cdot 2^k \right)$$

$$\overline{\overline{X}}_{i,j}^6 = 1 * 2^7 + 1 * 2^6 + 0 * 2^5 + \sum_{k=0}^{4} \left(B_{i,j}^{de}(k) \cdot 2^k \right)$$

$$\overline{\overline{X}}_{i,j}^7 = 1 * 2^7 + 1 * 2^6 + 1 * 2^5 + \sum_{k=0}^{4} \left(B_{i,j}^{de}(k) \cdot 2^k \right)$$

Then the differences between the predicted value and these eight values are calculated as $\overline{\overline{\Delta}}_0 = \left| \overline{\overline{X}}_{i,j}^0 - \tilde{x}_{i,j} \right|$, $\overline{\overline{\Delta}}_1 = \left| \overline{\overline{X}}_{i,j}^1 - \tilde{x}_{i,j} \right|$, $\overline{\overline{\Delta}}_2 = \left| \overline{\overline{X}}_{i,j}^2 - \tilde{x}_{i,j} \right|$, $\overline{\overline{\Delta}}_3 = \left| \overline{\overline{X}}_{i,j}^3 - \tilde{x}_{i,j} \right|$, $\overline{\overline{\Delta}}_4 = \left| \overline{\overline{X}}_{i,j}^4 - \tilde{x}_{i,j} \right|$, $\overline{\overline{\Delta}}_5 = \left| \overline{\overline{X}}_{i,j}^5 - \tilde{x}_{i,j} \right|$, $\overline{\overline{\Delta}}_6 = \left| \overline{\overline{X}}_{i,j}^6 - \tilde{x}_{i,j} \right|$, and $\overline{\overline{\Delta}}_7 = \left| \overline{\overline{X}}_{i,j}^7 - \tilde{x}_{i,j} \right|$. Similarly, the minimum of these differences is defined as follows.

$$\overline{\overline{\Delta}}_{min} = \left\{ \overline{\overline{\Delta}}_0, \overline{\overline{\Delta}}_1, \overline{\overline{\Delta}}_2, \overline{\overline{\Delta}}_3, \overline{\overline{\Delta}}_4, \overline{\overline{\Delta}}_5, \overline{\overline{\Delta}}_6, \overline{\overline{\Delta}}_7 \right\} \tag{20}$$

Consequently, the original pixel $x_{i,j}$ can be recovered as follows.

$$
x_{i,j} = \begin{cases}
\overline{\overline{X}}_{i,j}^{0} & if\ \overline{\overline{\Delta}}_{min} = \overline{\overline{\Delta}}_{0} \\
\overline{\overline{X}}_{i,j}^{1} & if\ \overline{\overline{\Delta}}_{min} = \overline{\overline{\Delta}}_{1} \\
\overline{\overline{X}}_{i,j}^{2} & if\ \overline{\overline{\Delta}}_{min} = \overline{\overline{\Delta}}_{2} \\
\overline{\overline{X}}_{i,j}^{3} & if\ \overline{\overline{\Delta}}_{min} = \overline{\overline{\Delta}}_{3} \\
\overline{\overline{X}}_{i,j}^{4} & if\ \overline{\overline{\Delta}}_{min} = \overline{\overline{\Delta}}_{4} \\
\overline{\overline{X}}_{i,j}^{5} & if\ \overline{\overline{\Delta}}_{min} = \overline{\overline{\Delta}}_{5} \\
\overline{\overline{X}}_{i,j}^{6} & if\ \overline{\overline{\Delta}}_{min} = \overline{\overline{\Delta}}_{6} \\
\overline{\overline{X}}_{i,j}^{7} & if\ \overline{\overline{\Delta}}_{min} = \overline{\overline{\Delta}}_{7}
\end{cases}
\tag{21}
$$

It can be seen that the method is fully reversible and the original image can be completely reconstructed.

(3) Data Extraction and Image Recovery with Both Keys

If the receiver has both K_{en} and K_{dh}, he can extract the secret message without error and completely restore the original image at the same time. At first, the receiver extracts the secret message from $\overline{\overline{X}}_{i,j}$ by applying the above data extraction procedure. Subsequently, the original image can be further reconstructed by utilizing the above image recovery procedure. Note that data extraction should be carried out before image restoration.

3   Experimental Results and Analysis

In this section, we present the experimental results obtained by applying the proposed method and comparisons with several existing related works. Eight standard gray images shown in Fig. 2 and 80 images selected from the Miscellaneous gray level images database [21] are selected as test images. The size of all images is $512 \times 512 \times 8$. The secret message is a binary sequence created by pseudo random number generator.

3.1   Analysis of Scrambling Effect

In order to show the scrambling effect visually, the original images are demonstrated in Fig. 2, while the corresponding encrypted results are shown in Fig. 3. It can be seen that the data hider cannot obtain any available visual information of the original image from the encrypted image. In addition, PSNR (Peak Signal-to-Noise Ratio) is used as an objective metric to evaluate image visual quality. PSNR values of eight encrypted images are 9.5545 dB, 9.5776 dB, 7.8921 dB, 8.4937 dB, 8.9873 dB, 9.6351 dB, 8.0840 dB, and 7.6121 dB, respectively. We have also applied our proposed method to another 80 images which are selected from the Miscellaneous database [21]. Figure 4 presents the PSNR results of 80 encrypted images. It can be seen that PNSR values of the encrypted images are very low and the visual imperceptibility is guaranteed.

(a) *Lena*   (b) *Baboon*   (c) *Barbara*   (d) *Peppers*

(e) *Boat*   (f) *Truck*   (g) *Airplane*   (h) *Man*

Fig. 2. Eight standard gray images

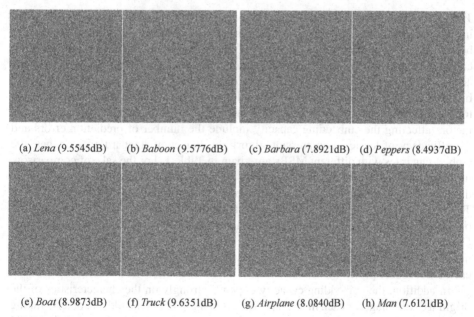

(a) *Lena* (9.5545dB)   (b) *Baboon* (9.5776dB)   (c) *Barbara* (7.8921dB)   (d) *Peppers* (8.4937dB)

(e) *Boat* (8.9873dB)   (f) *Truck* (9.6351dB)   (g) *Airplane* (8.0840dB)   (h) *Man* (7.6121dB)

Fig. 3. The corresponding encrypted images

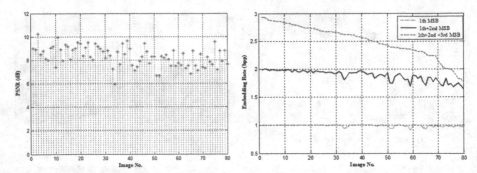

Fig. 4. *PSNR* values of 80 encrypted images   **Fig. 5.** Embedding rates of 80 test images

3.2 Analysis of Reconstructed Image Quality

In the proposed method, with the data hiding key, all embedded bits can be extracted without any error. In addition, with the prediction technology and the location map $L1$, the original image can be perfectly reconstructed after MSB prediction, as indicated by a PSNR which tends to $+\infty$.

3.3 Analysis of Embedding Capacity

The embedding capacity is defined as the maximum number of bits that can be embedded in a given cover image. In general, it is expressed in bit per pixel (bpp) and is expected to be as large as possible in order to hide the maximum amount of information. Embedding capacity is measured by two metrics, namely the total embedding capacity and the actual embedding capacity. The total embedding capacity refers to the total number of bits that can be hidden in the encryption domain. The actual payload should be the total embedding capacity minus the side information. In the proposed approach, the factors affecting the embedding capacity include the number of prediction errors and the efficiency of lossless compression algorithm. For eight standard gray images, the embedding rates with different MSBs are given in Table 1. For the sake of comparison, in addition to providing the test results of the three-layer MSB method proposed in this paper, we also provide the results of the single-layer and two-layer MSB method. The embedding rate of the single-layer MSB method does not exceed 1 bpp, because only one bit of information is embedded in each embeddable pixel by MSB replacement. Compared with the single-layer MSB method, the embedding rate of the two-layer MSB method is improved significantly, because two bits of information can be embedded in each embeddable pixel.

In addition, the embedding capacity depends strongly on the characteristics of the original cover image, as each image has a different number of embeddable pixels. Taking the three-layer MSB method as an example, the maximum embedding capacity is 2.8434 bpp, while the minimum is 1.9918 bpp. The reason is that some pixels cannot be used for information embedding due to prediction errors. In general, for relatively smooth images, the total embedding capacity is large and the encoded auxiliary information is less. In addition, 80 images selected from the Miscellaneous database [21] are also

Table 1. Test results of eight standard images

Standard test images	Total embedding rate (bpp)			Actual embedding rate (bpp)			PSNR
	1-layer MSB	2-layer MSB	3-layer MSB	1-layer MSB	2-layer MSB	3-layer MSB	
Lena	0.9992	1.9782	2.8434	0.9912	1.9159	2.6543	9.5545
Baboon	0.9842	1.7311	1.9918	0.8725	1.2530	1.2205	9.5776
Barbara	0.9652	1.7159	2.2053	0.8339	1.3555	1.7207	7.8921
Peppers	0.9975	1.9656	2.8224	0.9794	1.8722	2.5817	8.4937
Boat	0.9990	1.9419	2.6668	0.9890	1.8076	2.3156	8.9873
Truck	0.9997	1.9696	2.5798	0.9958	1.8594	2.0121	9.6351
Airplane	0.9974	1.9478	2.7731	0.9740	1.8073	2.5036	8.0840
Man	0.9960	1.9260	2.6131	0.9630	1.7531	2.1959	7.6121

tested, and their total embedding rates are shown in Fig. 5. The embedding rates in the best and worst cases are 2.9309 bpp and 1.7534 bpp, respectively, and the average embedding rate is 2.4999 bpp.

3.4 Comparison and Discussion

In terms of embedding rate and reconstructed image quality, several comparisons are made between the proposed method and some existing methods [10, 11, 14]. The comparison of embedding rate is shown in Fig. 6. It can be seen that the embedding capacity of our three-layer MSBs substitution strategy has been greatly improved. In addition, the original image can be reconstructed losslessly (PSNR $\to +\infty$) using only the encryption key. In conclusion, in addition to being error-free during data extraction, the proposed method can provide better performance in terms of embedding capacity and image restoration quality.

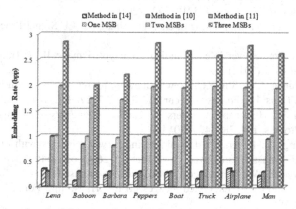

Fig. 6. Comparison of embedding rates between the proposed method and some state-of-the-art methods

4   Conclusions and Future Work

In this paper, we proposed a high-capacity reversible data hiding method in encrypted images based on MSB prediction. To ensure that the original image can be completely reconstructed, information about the position of prediction errors is stored in the binary location map. Then the original image is converted into encrypted form by using encryption key. After that, the data-hider embeds the secret data into the encrypted image by substituting the MSBs of each embeddable pixel with secret bits. Since the data hider cannot access the content of the original image, the confidentiality is guaranteed. In addition, this algorithm can achieve real reversibility, i.e., the original image can be perfectly recovered and the secret message can be extracted without error. Experimental results show that the proposed method can achieve higher embedding capacity compared to most related methods. Future work is aimed at designing more efficient prediction technique to reduce the number of prediction errors. At the same time, an efficient compression technology should be designed for location map to improve the actual embedding capacity.

Acknowledgements. This work is supported by the National Natural Science Foundation of China (61771270), Zhejiang Provincial Natural Science Foundation of China (LY17F020013, LR20F020001), and Ningbo Natural Science Foundation (2018A610054, 2018A610192).

References

1. Subramanyam, A.V., Emmanuel, S., Kankanhalli, M.S.: Robust watermarking of compressed and encrypted JPEG2000 images. IEEE Trans. Multimedia **14**(3), 703–716 (2012)
2. Xu, D.W., Wang, R.D., Shi, Y.Q.: Data hiding in encrypted H.264/AVC video streams by codeword substitution. IEEE Trans. Inf. Forensics Secur. **9**(4), 596–606 (2014)
3. Xu, D.W., Wang, R.D., Shi, Y.Q.: An improved scheme for data hiding in encrypted H.264/AVC videos. J. Vis. Commun. Image Represent. **36**, 229–242 (2016)
4. Xu, D.W., Wang, R.D., Zhu, Y.N.: Tunable data hiding in partially encrypted H.264/AVC videos. J. Vis. Commun. Image Represent. **45**, 34–45 (2017)
5. Shi, Y.Q., Li, X.L., Zhang, X.P., Wu, H.T., Ma, B.: Reversible data hiding: advances in the past two decades. IEEE Access **4**, 3210–3237 (2016)
6. Zhang, X.P.: Reversible data hiding in encrypted image. IEEE Signal Process. Lett. **18**(4), 255–258 (2011)
7. Zhang, X.P.: Separable reversible data hiding in encrypted image. IEEE Trans. Inf. Forensics Secur. **7**(2), 826–832 (2012)
8. Huang, F.J., Huang, J.W., Shi, Y.Q.: New framework for reversible data hiding in encrypted domain. IEEE Trans. Inf. Forensics Secur. **11**(12), 2777–2789 (2016)
9. Wu, X.T., Sun, W.: High-capacity reversible data hiding in encrypted images by prediction error. Signal Process. **104**, 387–400 (2014)
10. Qian, Z., Zhang, X.: Reversible data hiding in encrypted images with distributed source encoding. IEEE Trans. Circuits Syst. Video Technol. **26**(4), 636–646 (2016)
11. Puteaux, P., Puech, W.: An efficient MSB prediction-based method for high-capacity reversible data hiding in encrypted images. IEEE Trans. Inf. Forensics Secur. **13**(7), 1670–1681 (2018)

12. Ma, K.D., Zhang, W.M., Zhao, X.F., et al.: Reversible data hiding in encrypted images by reserving room before encryption. IEEE Trans. Inf. Forensics Secur. **8**(3), 553–562 (2013)
13. Zhang, W.M., Ma, K.D., Yu, N.H.: Reversibility improved data hiding in encrypted images. Sig. Process. **94**, 118–127 (2014)
14. Xu, D.W., Wang, R.D.: Separable and error-free reversible data hiding in encrypted images. Sig. Process. **123**, 9–21 (2016)
15. Yi, S., Zhou, Y.C.: Separable and reversible data hiding in encrypted images using parametric binary tree labeling. IEEE Trans. Multimedia **21**(1), 51–64 (2018)
16. Zhang, X.P., Long, J., Wang, Z.C., Cheng, H.: Lossless and reversible data hiding in encrypted images with public key cryptography. IEEE Trans. Circuits Syst. Video Technol. **26**(9), 1622–1631 (2016)
17. Wu, H.T., Cheung, Y.M., Yang, Z.Y., Tang, S.H.: A high-capacity reversible data hiding method for homomorphic encrypted images. J. Vis. Commun. Image Represent. **62**, 87–96 (2019)
18. Xu, D.W., Chen, K., Wang, R.D., Su, S.B.: Separable reversible data hiding in encrypted images based on two-dimensional histogram modification. Secur. Commun. Netw. **2018**, 1–14 (2018)
19. Xiang, S.J., Luo, X.R.: Reversible data hiding in homomorphic encrypted domain by mirroring ciphertext group. IEEE Trans. Circuits Syst. Video Technol. **28**(11), 3099–3110 (2017)
20. Rad, R.M., Wong, K.S., Guo, J.M.: A unified data embedding and scrambling method. IEEE Trans. Image Process. **23**(4), 1463–1475 (2014)
21. Miscelaneous gray level images. http://decsai.ugr.es/cvg/dbimagenes/g512.php

Steganography and Steganalysis

Image Steganography Using an Eight-Element Neighborhood Gaussian Markov Random Field Model

Yichen Tong[1] , Jiangqun Ni[1,2](✉) , and Wenkang Su[1]

[1] Sun Yat-sen University, Guangzhou, China
tongych@mail2.sysu.edu.cn, issjqni@mail.sysu.edu.cn, swk1004@163.com
[2] Cyberspace Security Research Center, Peng Cheng Laboratory, Shenzhen, China

Abstract. Currently, the design of cost functions which measure the embedding distortion becomes the main task left in steganography with the emergence of Syndrome-Trellis Codes. Whether heuristically designed, e.g., Hill, WOW, or statistical model-based, e.g., HUGO, MiPOD, the embedding distortion is almost a sum of each element's distortion. This paper proposes a new non-additive cost function designed by incorporating an eight-element neighborhood Gaussian Markov Random Field Model (8-GMRF). This proposed scheme, which could be viewed as an extension to MiPOD, derives change probabilities from minimizing the total KL divergence with a given payload and then implements adaptive steganography. Experimental results demonstrate that the proposed 8-GMRF performs superior or comparable to some of the state-of-the-art schemes in resisting steganalysis detectors.

Keywords: Adaptive steganography · Markov Random Field Model · KL divergence

1 Introduction

Spatial image steganography is the art and science of concealing messages into images by modifying pixel values [1]. The most crucial criterion is the ability of resisting the state-of-the-art steganalysis detectors. Since efficient practical coding method which embed near the payload-distortion bound exists, e.g., Syndrome-Trellis Codes (STCs) [2], the main concern in modern steganographic scheme design is the distortion function.

Currently, the design of distortion function is almost in an additive form. The designer starts by assigning costs of changing each element (e.g., pixel or DCT coefficient) and then compute the total distortion as a sum of costs of all modified elements [3]. Assigning pixel cost is often done by empirically quantifying the impact of making an embedding change on outputs of one or more high-pass filters (noise residuals) [3]. For instance, the cost function of HILL (High-pass, Low-pass and Low-pass) [1] is constructed by applying one high-pass filter and two low-pass filters on cover image, sequentially. The cost function of WOW

© Springer Nature Switzerland AG 2020
H. Wang et al. (Eds.): IWDW 2019, LNCS 12022, pp. 247–255, 2020.
https://doi.org/10.1007/978-3-030-43575-2_21

(wavelet obtained weights) [5] which can be adopted in JPEG domain is also designed with the help of a group of directional filters. Only a few distortion functions consider cover model in their design [4]. HUGO [6] is the first attempt, whose distortion is defined as the weighted sum of difference between cover and stego images in SPAM (subtractive pixel adjacency matrix) [7] feature space.

The scheme, which called MG (Multivariate Gaussian) [10], begins to measure statistical detectability in the design of distortion. It employs KL divergence between cover and its stego version, and models the cover pixels as a sequence of independent quantized Gaussians. MG performs comparable to HUGO and subpar with respect to HILL [4]. In [3], the MG is extended by incorporating a Multivariate Generalized Gaussian (MVGG) model with a properly adjusted variance estimator, the MVGG performs superior for the selection-channel aware feature set maxSRMd2 [11] and comparable for SRM, when compared with the state-of-the-art steganographic scheme HILL in spatial images.

MiPOD (Minimizing the Power of Optimal Detector) [4] adopts the same model as [3,10] with better setting of parameters, while minimizes the power of the most powerful detector instead of the KL divergence. Although its security performance is slightly inferior to HILL against SRM, it outperforms HILL against maxSRMd2. However, all models above are additive. In this paper, we propose a non-additive scheme for spatial images by incorporating an eight-element neighborhood Gaussian Markov Random Field Model (8-GMRF). Our steganography task is formulated as an optimization problem to minimize the KL divergence between the cover and stego images. Experimental results demonstrate that the proposed 8-GMRF performs superior or comparable to some of the state-of-the-art methods in resisting steganalysis detectors.

The rest of this paper is organized as follows. In Sect. 2 we introduce notations and review model adopted in MG. Our 8-GMRF are presented in Sect. 3. We demonstrate the effectiveness of our work by comparing to other steganographic scheme experimentally in Sect. 4. Section 5 lies conclusions.

2   Preliminaries and Prior Work

2.1   Notations

Throughout the paper, the symbols $X = (x_i)^n, Y = (y_i)^n$ denote the residual image obtained by using a two-dimensional wiener filter and stego image, respectively. σ_i is the variance of x_i, and ρ_{ij} is the correlation coefficient between x_i and x_j. $i \leftrightarrow j$ represents x_i, x_j is adjacent.

For better readability, $p_{j_1,j_2,...,j_m}^{(i_1,i_2,...,i_m)}$ denotes the joint probability $P\{x_{i_1} = j_1, x_{i_2} = j_2, ..., x_{i_m} = j_m\}$ and $q_{j_1,j_2,...,j_m}^{(i_1,i_2,...,i_m)}$ denotes its stego version. Their superscript or subscript would be elliptical if necessary.

2.2   Model in MG

MG designs the cover model as a sequence of independent but not necessarily identically distributed quantized Gaussians. It's cost function equals the sum of each pixel's KL divergence. By minimizing the total KL divergence by means of Lagrange multipliers, the optimal embedding change probabilities are obtained and used to modify each pixel at most 1 symmetrically and independently.

For an individual pixel x_i with small change rate β_i, the stego pixel distribution and its partial derivative become (1). Then the total KL divergence between the cover and stego objects is well-approximated as (2) by $I_i(0)$, the steganographic Fisher information (FI).

$$q_j(\beta_i) = (1 - 2\beta_i)p_j + \beta_i p_{j-1} + \beta_i p_{j+1}, \frac{\partial q_j}{\partial \beta_i}\big|_{\beta_i=0} = -2p_j + p_{j-1} + p_{j+1}. \quad (1)$$

$$\sum_{i=1}^{n} D_{KL}(p^{(i)}||q^{(i)}(\beta_i)) \approx \sum_{i=1}^{n} \frac{1}{2}\beta_i^2 I_i(0), I_i(0) = \sum_j \frac{1}{p_j^{(i)}}(\frac{\partial q_j^{(i)}(\beta_i)}{\partial \beta_i}\big|_{\beta_i=0})^2 \approx \frac{1}{\sigma_i^2}.$$
$$(2)$$

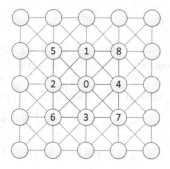

Fig. 1. 8-element neighborhood GMRF Model. Every two pixels are adjacent if connected or independent if disconnected.

3   8-GMRF Model

3.1   Cover Model

In our approach, each cover pixel interacts with its 8 adjacent pixels which are on the upper-left, upper, upper-right, left, right, down-left, downward, and down-right. These 9 pixels $\{0, 1, 2, 3, 4, 5, 6, 7, 8\}$ compose one block shown in Fig. 1, and have 9-variate Gaussian distribution with zero mean, i.e., $p(0 \sim 8) \sim N(0, \Sigma_{9\times9})$. $p(0 \sim 8)$ can be written as (3) by Markovianity (for proof see Appendix A).

$$p(0 \sim 8) = \frac{p(1,0,2,5) \cdot p(3,0,2,6) \cdot p(3,0,4,7) \cdot p(1,0,4,8) \cdot p(0)}{p(0,1) \cdot p(0,2) \cdot p(0,3) \cdot p(0,4)} \quad (3)$$

$$p(v_1, v_2, v_3, v_4) \approx \frac{p(v_1,v_2)p(v_1,v_3)p(v_1,v_4)p(v_2,v_3)p(v_2,v_4)p(v_3,v_4)}{p^2(v_1)p^2(v_2)p^2(v_3)p^2(v_4)} \quad (4)$$

Our cover model is a series of 8-element neighborhood GMRF model blocks, each block's structure is same as Fig. 1. To feasible calculation of the KL divergence of one block, we need to decompose $p(0 \sim 8)$ in terms of 1-variate Gaussian and 2-variate Gaussian, for which we propose an appropriation of 4-variate probability distribution as (4). Thus $p(0 \sim 8)$ and the KL divergence of one block can be approximated in (5)–(6) taking advantage of equation (3)–(4).

$$p(0 \sim 8) \approx \frac{\Pi_{i \leftrightarrow j} p(i,j)}{p^7(0) \cdot \prod_{k=1}^{4} p^4(k) \cdot \prod_{l=5}^{8} p^2(l)}. \tag{5}$$

$$D_{KL}(p^{(0\sim8)}||q^{(0\sim8)}(\beta_0 \sim \beta_8)) \approx \sum_{i \leftrightarrow j} D_{KL}(p^{(i,j)}||q^{(i,j)}(\beta_i,\beta_j))-$$

$$4\sum_{k=1}^{4} D_{KL}(p^{(k)}||q^{(k)}(\beta_k)) - 2\sum_{l=5}^{8} D_{KL}(p^{(l)}||q^{(l)}(\beta_l)) - 7D_{KL}(p^{(0)}||q^{(0)}(\beta_0)). \tag{6}$$

3.2 Stego Image Model

In our work, change probabilities are not mutually independent like MG and MiPOD, but interact between adjacent pixels. For a pair of adjacent pixels x_i, x_j, modified by at most ± 1 with small probabilities $\beta_i = \beta_i^+ = \beta_i^-, \beta_j = \beta_j^+ = \beta_j^-$, their corresponding stego pixels distribution and its partial derivative become:

$$q_{k,l}(\beta_i,\beta_j) = (1-2\beta_i)\beta_j(p_{k,l-1}+p_{k,l+1}) + \beta_i(1-2\beta_j)(p_{k-1,l}+p_{k+1,l})$$

$$+ \beta_i\beta_j(p_{k-1,l-1}+p_{k-1,l+1}+p_{k+1,l-1}+p_{k+1,l+1}) + (1-2\beta_i)(1-2\beta_j)p_{k,l}, \tag{7}$$

$$\frac{\partial q_{k,l}}{\partial \beta_i}|_{\beta_i=0,\beta_j=0} = -2p_{k,l}+p_{k-1,l}+p_{k+1,l}, \quad \frac{\partial q_{k,l}}{\partial \beta_j}|_{\beta_i=0,\beta_j=0} = -2p_{k,l}+p_{k,l-1}+p_{k,l+1}. \tag{8}$$

The total KL divergence is formulated as (9) utilizing (6) and simplifying, where D_{KL}^i denotes the KL divergence of the block centered in the pixel x_i. And $D_{KL}(p^{(i)}||q^{(i)}(\beta_i))$ is given in (2). Two-dimensional KL divergence between the cover and stego object, and its key components, the Fisher Information matrix with size $2*2$ list in (10) (for proof see Appendix B):

$$\sum_{i=1}^{n} D_{KL}^i = 2\sum_{i \leftrightarrow j} D_{KL}(p^{(i,j)}||q^{(i,j)}(\beta_i,\beta_j)) - 31\sum_{i=1}^{n} D_{KL}(p^{(i)}||q^{(i)}(\beta_i)). \tag{9}$$

$$D_{KL}(p^{(i,j)}||q^{(i,j)}(\beta_i,\beta_j)) \approx \frac{1}{2} \begin{bmatrix} \beta_i & \beta_j \end{bmatrix} \begin{bmatrix} I_{ij}^{(11)}(0) & I_{ij}^{(12)}(0) \\ I_{ij}^{(21)}(0) & I_{ij}^{(22)}(0) \end{bmatrix} \begin{bmatrix} \beta_i \\ \beta_j \end{bmatrix},$$

$$I_{ij}^{(11)}(0) \approx \frac{2}{\sigma_i^2(1-\rho_{ij}^2)^2}, I_{ij}^{(22)}(0) \approx \frac{2}{\sigma_j^2(1-\rho_{ij}^2)^2}, I_{ij}^{(12)}(0) = I_{ij}^{(21)}(0) \approx \frac{2\rho_{ij}^2}{\sigma_i\sigma_j(1-\rho_{ij}^2)^2}. \tag{10}$$

3.3   Minimizing the KL Divergence

By means of Lagrange multipliers, we obtain optimal change rates by minimizing the total KL divergence with a given payload constraint. The total payload embed in the image is the sum of entropies as (11). Differentiating the objective function w.r.t. β_i gives (12)–(13). (13) will be solved through several times of iterations such that we embed with the solution and obtain the cost map using $\rho_i = ln(\frac{1}{\beta_i} - 2)$ [3].

$$\alpha n = \sum_{i=1}^{n} h(\beta_i), h(x) = -2x\ln x - (1 - 2x)ln(1 - 2x). \tag{11}$$

$$\frac{\partial}{\partial \beta_i}(\sum_{i=1}^{n} D^i_{KL} - \lambda(\sum_{i=1}^{n} h(\beta_i) - \alpha n)) = 0, \tag{12}$$

$$\sum_{i \leftrightarrow j} (I^{(11)}_{ij}(0) \cdot \beta_i + I^{(12)}_{ij}(0) \cdot \beta_j) - \frac{31}{2} I_i(0) \cdot \beta_i - \lambda ln\frac{1 - 2\beta_i}{\beta_i} = 0. \tag{13}$$

4   Experimental Results and Analysis

In this section, we conduct a series of experiments on BOSSBase ver.1.01 [14], which contains 10,000 gray-scale image with size 512 * 512. The covariance matrices among pixels are estimated by a function named empirical covariance of sklearn package in python. For numerical stability, we adjust the results by: $\rho = min\{0.99, \rho\}, \sigma = max\{0.01, \sigma\}$. Making use of the estimated variance and covariance of pixels above, (13) will be quickly solved for change probabilities. Then we adopt the ternary version of STCs to implement the actual embedding algorithm near its payload-distortion bound.

The security performance is evaluated with two state-of-the-art steganalysis feature sets, i.e., the 34,671-dimensional feature set SRM and its selection-channel-aware version, maxSRMd2 with ensemble classifiers [15]. We adopt the average of the false positive rate and false negative rate by ten times of 5000/5000 randomly database splits as test error, with symbol $\overline{P_E}$. Inspired by MiPOD, we introduce an average filter operation to our cost map with size 9 * 9. This indeed brings promotion if embed with the change rates converted from the filtered cost. Tables 1 and 2 show the average total probability of error $\overline{P_E}$ for payloads $R \in \{0.05, 0.1, 0.2, 0.3, 0.4, 0.5\}$ bpp (bits per pixel) for our 8-GMRF, MG and other prevailing embedding methods.

It is observed that our method outperforms consistently MiPOD and MG for both SRM and maxSRMd2, if the obtained cost values or FIs are not low-pass filtered, as shown in Table 1. Table 2 illustrates the performance comparison of our method (8-GMRF) with HILL and MiPOD when the obtained cost values and FIs are low-pass filtered. Under the circumstance, both our method and MiPOD are superior to HILL against the feature set maxSRMd2, while inferior to HILL against SRM. It is noted that our method outperforms MiPOD consistently for

Table 1. Performance in term of $\overline{P_E}$ versus embedded payload in bits pixels (bpp) for MiPOD without filtered FI, MG and our method without filtered cost using ensemble 1.0 classifier with two feature sets: SRM and maxSRMd2

Feature	Algorithm	Payload (bpp)					
		0.05	0.1	0.2	0.3	0.4	0.5
SRM	MiPOD	0.4511	0.4051	0.3274	0.2723	0.2218	0.1821
	8-GMRF	0.4580	0.4137	0.3348	0.2758	0.2298	0.1909
	MG	0.3689	0.2953	0.2146	0.1658	0.1357	0.1119
maxSRMd2	MiPOD	0.4294	0.3772	0.3037	0.2498	0.2053	0.1683
	8-GMRF	0.4382	0.3856	0.3112	0.2475	0.2039	0.1651
	MG	0.2315	0.1653	0.1161	0.0936	0.0813	0.0715

SRM, while is comparable or slightly inferior to MiPOD for maxSRMd2. These results are expected, because the selection channel aware feature set maxSRMd2 could obtain more statistical information with our method by taking advantages of the GMRF model, thus leading to more accurate steganalysis for our method.

Table 2. Detectability in term of $\overline{P_E}$ versus embedded payload in bits pixels (bpp) for Hill, MiPOD with filtered FI and our method with filtered cost using ensemble 1.0 classifier with two feature sets: SRM and maxSRMd2.

Feature	Algorithm	Payload (bpp)					
		0.05	0.1	0.2	0.3	0.4	0.5
SRM	HiLL	0.4704	0.4330	0.3582	0.2975	0.2450	0.2018
	MiPOD	0.4547	0.4118	0.3419	0.2865	0.2385	0.1986
	8-GMRF	0.4564	0.4170	0.3490	0.2905	0.2409	0.2004
maxSRMd2	HiLL	0.4237	0.3732	0.3094	0.2590	0.2169	0.1789
	MiPOD	0.4426	0.3966	0.3273	0.2700	0.2275	0.1886
	8-GMRF	0.4465	0.4002	0.3320	0.2719	0.2249	0.1852

5   Conclusions

In this paper, we propose a new steganographic scheme (8-GMRF) by incorporating an eight-element neighborhood Gaussian Markov Random Field Model for spatial images. With the GMRF, the task of image steganography is formulated as the optimization problem that minimize the total KL divergence between the cover and stego images for the constraint of given payload. For the 8-element neighborhood GMRF model, we decompose a 4-variate distribution probability in terms of 1-variate and 2-variate form to facilitate the computation of KL divergence. The proposed method could be viewed as an extension to MiPOD.

Experimental results demonstrate that the proposed 8-GMRF outperforms and shows comparable performance to MiPOD for the feature sets SRM and maxS-RMd2, respectively. How to extend the 8-element neighborhood model to GMRF model with neighborhood of arbitrary shape is the topic of our future research work.

Acknowledgments. This work is supported in part by National Natural Science Foundation of China under Grants 61772573 and U1736215, and in part by the Science and Technology Program of Guangzhou under Grants 201707010029 and 201804010265.

Appendix

A. Joint probability of one 8-element neighborhood GMRF block

Recall Fig. 1, which illustrates 9 pixels of one block with index $\{0 \sim 8\}$. Every two pixels are adjacent if connected or independent if disconnected. For those independent (e.g. pixels, i, j), we can easily obtain (14). Accordingly, we proceed with a group of pixels according to Markovianity shown in (15), which will be repeatedly used in this proof.

$$p(i, j) = p(i|j) \cdot p(j) = p(i) \cdot p(j) \tag{14}$$

$$p(i, j_1 ... j_m) = p(i|j_1 ... j_m) \cdot p(j_1 ... j_m) = p(i|j_k, i \leftrightarrow j_k) \cdot p(j_1 ... j_m) \tag{15}$$

Firstly, it is obvious to get (16) using (15) and then take the second term of former formula repeatedly we can get (17). (18) is derived from (17).

$$p(0 \sim 8) = p(5|0 \sim 4, 6 \sim 8) \cdot p(0 \sim 4, 6 \sim 8) = p(5|0, 1, 2) \cdot p(0 \sim 4, 6 \sim 8) \tag{16}$$

$$p(0 \sim 4, 6 \sim 8) = p(6|0, 2, 3) \cdot p(0 \sim 4, 7, 8), p(0 \sim 4, 7, 8) = p(8|0, 1, 4) \cdot p(0 \sim 4, 7)$$

$$p(0 \sim 4, 7) = \frac{p(0, 1, 3, 4)}{p(0, 1, 3)} \cdot p(0, 1, 2, 3), p(0, 1, 2, 3) = \frac{p(0, 1, 2)}{p(0, 2)} \cdot p(0, 2, 3) \tag{17}$$

$$p(0, 1, 3, 4) = \frac{p(0, 3, 4)}{p(0, 4)} \cdot p(0, 1, 4), p(0, 1, 3) = \frac{p(0, 1)}{p(0)} \cdot p(0, 3) \tag{18}$$

Substitute (18) into (17), (17) into (16), $p(0 \sim 8)$ can be formulated as:

$$p(0 \sim 8) = \frac{p(1, 0, 2, 5) \cdot p(3, 0, 2, 6) \cdot p(3, 0, 4, 7) \cdot p(1, 0, 4, 8) \cdot p(0)}{p(0, 1) \cdot p(0, 2) \cdot p(0, 3) \cdot p(0, 4)} \tag{19}$$

B. 2×2 steganographic Fisher Information matrix

Stimulated by one-dimensional steganographic Fisher Information (2) in MG, we construct 2×2 steganographic Fisher Information matrix as following:

$$I_{ij}(0) = \begin{bmatrix} I_{ij}^{(11)}(0) & I_{ij}^{(12)}(0) \\ I_{ij}^{(21)}(0) & I_{ij}^{(22)}(0) \end{bmatrix}, \tag{20}$$

where $I_{ij}^{(12)}(0) = I_{ij}^{(21)}(0) = \sum_{k,l} \frac{1}{p_{k,l}} (\frac{\partial q_{k,l}(\beta_i,\beta_j)}{\partial \beta_i}|_{\beta_i,\beta_j=0}) \cdot (\frac{\partial q_{k,l}(\beta_i,\beta_j)}{\partial \beta_j}|_{\beta_i,\beta_j=0})$,

$$I_{ij}^{(11)}(0) = \sum_{k,l} \frac{1}{p_{k,l}} (\frac{\partial q_{k,l}(\beta_i,\beta_j)}{\partial \beta_i}|_{\beta_i,\beta_j=0})^2, I_{ij}^{(22)}(0) = \sum_{k,l} \frac{1}{p_{k,l}} (\frac{\partial q_{k,l}(\beta_i,\beta_j)}{\partial \beta_j}|_{\beta_i,\beta_j=0})^2.$$

Note that $p_{k,l}$, i.e. $p_{k,l}^{(i,j)}$, equals $P\{x_i = k, x_j = l\}$, which can seemed as a point in the two-dimensional Gaussian distribution $f(x_i,x_j)$ (21). x_i, x_j, k, l are used as continuous for differential and integration in this proof. Given $p_{k,l} = f(k,l), p_{k\pm1,l} = f(k\pm1,l), p_{k,l\pm1} = f(k,l\pm1)$, we have the Taylor approximation at points $(k\pm1,l), (k,l\pm1)$:

$$f(x_i,x_j) = \frac{1}{2\pi\sigma_i\sigma_j\sqrt{1-\rho_{ij}^2}} \exp(-\frac{1}{2(1-\rho_{ij}^2)}(\frac{x_i^2}{\sigma_i^2} - \frac{2\rho_{ij}x_ix_j}{\sigma_i\sigma_j} + \frac{x_j^2}{\sigma_j^2})). \quad (21)$$

$$-2p_{k,l} + p_{k-1,l} + p_{k+1,l} \approx \frac{\partial^2 f(x_i,x_j)}{\partial x_i^2}|_{x_i=k,x_j=1}, \quad (22)$$

$$-2p_{k,l} + p_{k,l-1} + p_{k,l+1} \approx \frac{\partial^2 f(x_i,x_j)}{\partial x_j^2}|_{x_i=k,x_j=1}. \quad (23)$$

After substituting (21)–(23) and (8) into (20), we can finally derive:

$$I_{ij}^{(11)}(0) = \sum_{k,l} \frac{(-2p_{k,l}+p_{k-1,l}+p_{k+1,l})^2}{p_{k,l}} \approx \int_k \int_l (\frac{\partial^2 f(x_i,x_j)}{\partial x_i^2}|_{x_i=k,x_j=l})^2 \frac{dkdl}{f(x_i,x_j)}$$

$$I_{ij}^{(22)}(0) = \sum_{k,l} \frac{(-2p_{k,l}+p_{k,l-1}+p_{k,l+1})^2}{p_{k,l}} \approx \int_k \int_l (\frac{\partial^2 f(x_i,x_j)}{\partial x_j^2}|_{x_i=k,x_j=l})^2 \frac{dkdl}{f(x_i,x_j)}$$

$$I_{ij}^{(12)}(0) = I_{ij}^{(21)}(0) = \sum_{k,l} \frac{(-2p_{k,l}+p_{k-1,l}+p_{k+1,l})(-2p_{k,l}+p_{k,l-1}+p_{k,l+1})}{p_{k,l}}$$

$$\approx \int_k \int_l (\frac{\partial^2 f(x_i,x_j)}{\partial x_i^2}|_{x_i=k,x_j=l})(\frac{\partial^2 f(x_i,x_j)}{\partial x_j^2}|_{x_i=k,x_j=l}) \frac{dkdl}{f(x_i,x_j)}$$

$$I_{ij}^{(11)}(0) \approx \frac{2}{\sigma_i^2(1-\rho_{ij}^2)^2}, I_{ij}^{(22)}(0) \approx \frac{2}{\sigma_j^2(1-\rho_{ij}^2)^2}, I_{ij}^{(12)}(0) = I_{ij}^{(21)}(0) \approx \frac{2\rho_{ij}^2}{\sigma_i\sigma_j(1-\rho_{ij}^2)^2}$$

References

1. Li, B., Wang, M., Huang, J.: A new cost function for spatial image steganography. In: Proceedings IEEE ICIP, Pairs, France, 27–30 October 2014
2. Filler, T., Judas, J., Fridrich, J.: Minimizing additive distortion in steganography using syndrome-trellis codes. IEEE TIFS **6**(3), 920–935 (2011)

3. Sedighi, V., Fridrich, J., Cogranne, R.: Content-adaptive pentary steganography using the multivariate generalized Gaussian cover model. In: Proceedings of the SPIE 9409, Media Watermarking, Security, and Forensics 2015, 9409H, 4 March 2015
4. Sedighi, V., Cogranne, R., Fridrich, J.: Content-adaptive steganography by minimizing statistical detectability. IEEE TIFS **11**(2), 221–234 (2016)
5. Holub, V., Fridrich, J.: Designing steganographic distortion using directional filters. In: Fourth IEEE International Workshop on Information Forensics and Security (2012)
6. Pevný, T., Filler, T., Bas, P.: Using high-dimensional image models to perform highly undetectable steganography. In: Böhme, R., Fong, P.W.L., Safavi-Naini, R. (eds.) IH 2010. LNCS, vol. 6387, pp. 161–177. Springer, Heidelberg (2010). https://doi.org/10.1007/978-3-642-16435-4_13
7. Pevny, T., Bas, P., Fridrich, J.: Steganalysis by subtractive pixel adjacency matrix. IEEE Trans. Inf. Forensics Secur. **5**(2), 215–224 (2010)
8. Fridrich, J., Kodovský, J.: Rich models for steganalysis of digital images. IEEE TIFS **7**, 868–882 (2011)
9. Chen, L., Shi, Y.Q., Sutthiwan, P., Niu, X.: Non-uniform quantization in breaking HUGO. In: Shi, Y.Q., Kim, H.-J., Pérez-González, F. (eds.) IWDW 2013. LNCS, vol. 8389, pp. 48–62. Springer, Heidelberg (2014). https://doi.org/10.1007/978-3-662-43886-2_4
10. Fridrich, J., Kodovský, J.: Multivariate Gaussian model for designing additive distortion for steganography. In: Proceedings of the IEEE ICASSP, 26–31 May 2013
11. Denemark, T., Sedighi, V., Holub, V., Cogranne, R., Fridrich, J.: Selection-channel-aware rich model for steganalysis of digital images. In: Proceedings of the IEEE WIFS, Atlanta, GA, 3–5 December 2014
12. Holub, V., Fridrich, J.: Digital image steganography using universal distortion. In: Proceedings of the First ACM Workshop on Information Hiding and Multimedia Security, pp. 59–68. ACM (2013)
13. Holub, V., Fridrich, J., Denemark, T.: Universal distortion function for steganography in an arbitrary domain. EURASIP J. Inf. Secur. **2014**(1), 1–13 (2014). https://doi.org/10.1186/1687-417X-2014-1
14. Bas, P., Filler, T., Pevný, T.: "Break our steganographic system": the ins and outs of organizing BOSS. In: Filler, T., Pevný, T., Craver, S., Ker, A. (eds.) IH 2011. LNCS, vol. 6958, pp. 59–70. Springer, Heidelberg (2011). https://doi.org/10.1007/978-3-642-24178-9_5
15. Kodovsky, J., Fridrich, J., Holub, V.: Ensemble classifiers for steganalysis of digital media. IEEE Trans. Inf. Forensics Secur. **7**(2), 432–444 (2012)

Broadcasting Steganography in the Blockchain

Mengtian Xu[1], Hanzhou Wu[1]([✉]), Guorui Feng[1], Xinpeng Zhang[1],
and Feng Ding[2]

[1] Shanghai University, Shanghai 200444, China
{mt_xu,grfeng,xzhang}@shu.edu.cn, h.wu.phd@ieee.org
[2] University at Albany, State University of New York, Albany, NY 12222, USA
fding@albany.edu

Abstract. Conventional steganography embeds secret data into an innocent cover object such as image and video. The resulting stego object will be sent to the desired receiver via an insecure channel. Though the channel monitor cannot distinguish between normal objects and objects containing hidden information, he has the ability to intercept and alter the objects so as to break down the covert communication. It inspires us to introduce new steganography in Blockchain in order to overcome the aforementioned problem since an attacker cannot tamper Blockchain data once a block was generated, meaning that, a receiver will always be able to fully retrieve the secret data with the secret key. For the proposed work, the miner serves as the steganographer, who embeds secret data into the transactions within a block during the process of generating the block. To secure the data embedding process within a block, we choose a part of transactions in a block according to a secret key, and embed the secret data by repeatable-address arrangement. Our analysis demonstrates that, it is difficult for an attacker to extract the embedded data. Since the miner collects normal transactions for generating a block and does not generate abnormal transactions, the data embedding process will not arouse suspicion, providing a high level of security.

Keywords: Steganography · Blockchain · Bitcoin · Behavior

1 Introduction

Information hiding [1] is an emerging and interdisciplinary research area covering different applications, among which digital watermarking and steganography [2] are the most common use nowadays. In particular, the ease of use, reproduction, edit and distribution of digital commercial products has led great concern to copyright protection for digital media, leading watermarking to a major activity in media signal processing. Different from digital watermarking, steganography disguises confidential information into unobtrusive general information, thereby achieving the purpose of covert transmission.

© Springer Nature Switzerland AG 2020
H. Wang et al. (Eds.): IWDW 2019, LNCS 12022, pp. 256–267, 2020.
https://doi.org/10.1007/978-3-030-43575-2_22

The principle of steganography can be described as follows. A sender also called steganographer randomly selects a cover such as image from a given database. Then, with a key, he/she embeds a secret message into the cover by slightly modifying the noise-like component of the cover. The resulting stego will not arouse suspicion and be sent to a receiver via an insecure channel. A channel attacker also called steganalyst may intercept the stego and test whether it contains a secret payload or not. If the desired receiver receives the stego, he can extract the embedded data by the pre-shared key. To secure steganographic communication, we expect to reduce the difference between the cover and the stego as much as possible. It inspires us to often design steganographic schemes from two aspects [3], i.e., preserving the cover source model [4], and minimizing the distortion between the cover and the stego [5]. Though both steganography and cryptography provide the access to secret communication, the former even conceals the presence of the present communication while the latter leaves marks on ciphertext for an attacker to trace down.

Recently, with the rise of digital currency, Blockchain has gained more and more attention. As the technology behind Bitcoin [6], Blockchain is a shared and immutable ledger that facilitates the process of recording transactions and tracking assets which can be tangible or intangible in a business network. Blockchain was first mentioned in the year 2008 [6] and thereafter became widely known with the launch of the Bitcoin network[1] in the year 2009. In Bitcoin and its variants, the transfer of digital assets takes place in a distributed system. Bitcoin users can digitally sign and transfer their rights to digital assets to another user and the Bitcoin blockchain records this transfer publicly, allowing all participants of the network to independently verify the validity of the transactions.

Blockchain needs to handle a huge number of transactions, which, actually, can be well exploited for steganography. Compared to conventional media-based steganography, Blockchain-based steganography has two significant advantages:

- Anonymity: In Blockchain, the network nodes are identified by virtual addresses, which are hash values of the public keys that will not reveal the real identities of users. It makes an attacker hard to track the steganographer.
- Non-editability: Blockchain is independently maintained and managed by a distributed group of participants. Along with cryptographic mechanisms, it allows the Blockchain to resist against illegal attempts to alter the ledger later. It is impossible for an attacker to modify blocks and forge transactions to break the steganographic communication, meaning that, the receiver has ability to perfectly retrieve the embedded information.

In addition, as mentioned above, Blockchain records asset-transfer information in a public way. It indicates that, the steganographer only needs to hide the message once in the Blockchain, multiple receivers can easily extract it as long as they have the secret key. Moreover, the steganographer has no need to identify the receivers. This can be considered as a kind of *broadcasting steganography*. Moreover, due to the huge number of users in Blockchain, steganography

---

[1] https://en.wikipedia.org/wiki/Bitcoin_network.

in Blockchain transactions can be easily concealed by the huge number of user normal activities. In particular, a receiver can extract secret information locally without downloading from other communication channels if he/she is a full node. Because in Blockchain, each full node maintains a complete ledger, and once one copy changes, the other copies are updated simultaneously after verification [7].

The first article suggesting Blockchain-based steganography is [8]. In [8], the LSB of an address is used to carry a secret bit. A steganographer sends a payment to the corresponding address, the generated transaction is then verified and packaged into the block, allowing the receiver finally extracts the LSB of the address. Since the steganographer only sends one payment, the embedding capacity for each block is only one bit. Moreover, taking Bitcoin for example, generating a block needs ten minutes, i.e., transmitting one bit takes ten minutes, which is not desirable if we want to convey a large payload.

It is straightforward to extend [8] by sending more payments to carry more data, which, however, may arouse suspicion. The reasons are, the steganographer does not collect transactions for generating a block, and, the miner may not exactly collect all the transactions of the steganographer. It indicates that, the probability of having two *identical* and *specific* addresses in a block is low. Accordingly, once an attacker finds multiple identical addresses in a block, he may infer that steganography is happening. To deal with this problem, we propose to embed secret data into Blockchain transactions during the generation of a block by the miner. The secret data is carried by arranging a list of transactions that are collected by the miner in a block, which allows us to embed a significantly larger secret payload compared to LSB embedding mentioned above. Moreover, we do not require the steganographer to send payments, which will not arouse suspicion, having demonstrated the superiority.

The rest of this paper are organized as follows. We present the basic concepts in Sect. 2. In Sect. 3, we introduce the proposed steganographic scheme exploiting the Blockchain transactions. Thereafter, we provide performance evaluation in Sect. 4. Finally, we conclude this paper in Sect. 5.

2   Preliminaries

Blockchain can be informally defined as [9]: Blockchain is a distributed digital ledger of cryptographically signed transactions that are grouped into blocks. Each block is cryptographically linked to the previous one (making it tamper evident) after validation and undergoing a consensus decision. As new blocks are added, older blocks become more difficult to modify (creating tamper resistance). New blocks are replicated across copies of the ledger within the network, and any conflicts are resolved automatically using established rules.

There are two kinds of Blockchains [10,11]: *permissioned* and *permissionless*. If anyone can release a new block, it is permissionless. If only particular users can publish blocks, it is permissioned. In this paper, we focus on permissionless Blockchain based steganography. However, we would like to point that, our work can be applied to permissioned Blockchain, by appropriate modification.

Blockchain seems to be complex, but it can be simplified by analyzing each component individually. The main components include cryptographic hash functions, transactions, asymmetric-key cryptographic, addresses, ledgers, blocks, and how blocks are chained together [9]. To well present our work, we give brief introduction about transactions, addresses and blocks in the following. For simplicity, we will only introduce those related to our work.

Just similar to what we understand usually, transactions in Blockchain mean the transfer of Bitcoin value [12]. The information about bitcoin transactions can be observed in a specific platform[2] where we can easily find that a normal transaction is composed of the addresses of the payer and recipient and the amount of the transaction. They are broadcast to the network and packed into blocks after verification. The verification here is done by miners. Miners are the nodes which contribute their computing power to mining [13].

Blockchain is the underlying technology of cryptocurrencies, among which Bitcoin and Ethereum are two of the most popular. Throughout this paper, we take Bitcoin as the Blockchain implementation. That is, when we talk about transactions in the Blockchain, one may imagine that we are discussing transactions in Bitcoin network. Let us first review what will happen to the transactions in the Blockchain when they were generated. Firstly, each node verifies the transactions and adds the verified transactions to the transaction pool. The transaction pool, also known as memory pool, is not a network-wide pool, but that each node maintains its own memory pool. Then, each node selects transactions from its memory pool and packs them in its candidate block. Next, each node uses its own computational power to solve a hard mathematical problem to compete the right to create a new block to be chained, which is typically called mining. The winning miner will get rewards and its candidate block will be verified by other nodes in the network and then appended to the end of the Blockchain. Figure 1 shows the sketch of chaining a block, where the nodes represent the miners. The miners are actually competing to solve a mathematical puzzle based on the cryptographic hash algorithm. A miner repeatedly calculates the hash of the block header and continually modifies the nonce until it meets the corresponding requirement. The computational difficulty is dynamically adjusted in real time by Bitcoin network to ensure that a block is usually generated every ten minutes.

The description of Blockchain in [6] is a chain of blocks, each block refers to the hash of the previous block to form a longest chain from the Genesis block to the current block [14]. Blocks in Blockchain are all composed of block header and block body. Block header contains version, nonce, difficulty bits, timestamp, the hash of the previous block and other necessary information. Blocks are connected by the hash of the previous block. If you want to modify something in the one block, you also have to change all the blocks that come after, which makes Blockchain virtually tamper-proof. Block body stores transactions, typically, a block contains at least 500 transactions. A transaction represents a transfer of the cryptocurrency between Blockchain users. Though the data in a transaction can

---

[2] https://www.blockchain.com/explorer?currency=BTC&stat=transactions.

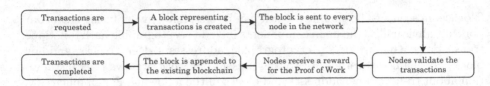

Fig. 1. The sketch for chaining a block.

be different for every Blockchain implementation, the mechanism for transacting is often the same. In Bitcoin network, each transaction records the sender and the receiver information, both of which are identified by an address having a total of 160 bits. We here skip the detailed introduction about the address since it is not the main interest of this work. The only one important thing is that, we will use these addresses to hide secret data. We will not change their values, but rearrange their positions in a block. It should be noted that the address is the unique identifier of the user, and different users have different addresses. A real user may have multiple addresses. He may use different addresses requesting for recording transactions, avoiding exposure and protecting his privacy [15].

3   Proposed Method

In this section, we present a method to realize steganography in the Blockchain. Let us recall the process of generating a block for a miner. Initially, a transaction pool contains a number of transactions. The miner then selects a certain number of transactions from the transaction pool and packs them in his candidate block. The miner uses his own computational power to solve a mathematical problem to compete the right to chain his candidate block. Once he wins the mining game, the block will be appended to the chain. For each transaction to be processed, it usually has one sender address that can be regarded as a stream, which will be used for steganography in this paper. We point that, in a transaction, there actually may be multiple addresses as sender, in this case, we can concatenate the addresses to form a single stream, also called an address stream for the sake of simplicity. For better presentation, we will assume that, in a transaction, we have only one sender address stream below.

The main idea of proposed work is described as follows. First, a steganographer (miner) selects n transactions from his transaction pool. Then, the steganographer packs the selected transactions in an arbitrary order in a new block. Thereafter, according to a key, he selects m transactions out from the block and rearrange them so that the corresponding transaction list matches the secret data to be embedded. Finally, the steganographer produces the new block containing hidden information (also called *stego* block), and tries to chain the stego block with his computational power. Once the stego block is chained, a receiver could extract the hidden information from the stego transactions in the stego block according to the key. We detail the transaction arrangement based data embedding and extraction procedure below. We also provide an example.

3.1 Data Embedding

Let $\mathcal{P} = \{P_1, P_2, ..., P_N\}$ represents the list that contains all the transactions in the transaction pool, where P_i means the i-th transaction in the pool. Each P_i is a data structure consisting of the transaction information including the sender address s_i, receiver address r_i, and so on. Since we only use the sender addresses for steganography, for simplicity, we separate the sender address s_i out from P_i, meaning that, we will use $S = \{s_1, s_2, ..., s_N\}$ to represent the sender address information, namely, s_i means the sender address for the i-th transaction. Notice that, it is possible that $s_i = s_j$ for some $i \neq j$. In addition, N denotes the number of transactions in the pool.

The steganographer first selects $n < N$ transactions out from $\mathcal{P}$. Suppose that the corresponding transaction-index set is $I = \{i_1, i_2, ..., i_n\}$, the selected transactions can be therefore denoted by $\mathcal{B} = \{P_{i_1}, P_{i_2}, ..., P_{i_n}\}$. Without the loss of generality, we assume that $1 \leq i_1 < i_2 < ... < i_n \leq N$. Then, the steganographer uses a secret key to generate $m < n$ different integers in range $[1, n]$, denoted by $T = \{t_1, t_2, ..., t_m\}$, where $1 \leq t_1 < t_2 < ... < t_m \leq n$. Accordingly, the steganographer can determine a sublist of $\mathcal{B}$ as:

$$\mathcal{C} = \{P_{i_{t_1}}, P_{i_{t_2}}, ..., P_{i_{t_m}}\}, \tag{1}$$

which will be used to carry a payload.

The sender address information for $\mathcal{C}$ can be denoted by $S_{\mathcal{C}} = \{s_{i_{t_1}}, s_{i_{t_2}}, ..., s_{i_{t_m}}\}$. It can be seen that, we can sort all the elements in $S_{\mathcal{C}}$ and enumerate all the arrangements according to their values even though they are binary strings. Each arrangement can be associated with an index indicating its order among all arrangements. For example, all arrangements of $\{1, 2, 3\}$ are $\{\{1, 2, 3\}, \{1, 3, 2\}, \{2, 1, 3\}, \{2, 3, 1\}, \{3, 1, 2\}, \{3, 2, 1\}\}$. Thus, we can assign an index "0" to $\{1, 2, 3\}$, "1" to $\{1, 3, 2\}$, ..., and "5" to $\{3, 2, 1\}$. If all elements in $S_{\mathcal{C}}$ are different from each other, then there are a total of $m!$ different arrangements. From a general point, the total number of different arrangements for $S_{\mathcal{C}}$ is

$$L_{\mathcal{C}} = \frac{m!}{\prod_{e \in U_{\mathcal{C}}} f(e)!}, \tag{2}$$

where $U_{\mathcal{C}}$ represents the set containing all the different address values in $S_{\mathcal{C}}$. For example, if $S_{\mathcal{C}} = \{1, 3, 2, 4, 2\}$, then $U_{\mathcal{C}} = \{1, 2, 3, 4\}$. $f(e)$ returns the number of element $e \in U_{\mathcal{C}}$ appearing in $S_{\mathcal{C}}$, e.g., $f(2) = 2$ for the above case. In this way, we can easily determine the total number of different arrangements as $L_{\mathcal{C}}$ for $S_{\mathcal{C}}$ even though there may be identical values in $S_{\mathcal{C}}$. For example, if $S_{\mathcal{C}} = \{1, 1, 2, 3, 1, 4, 5, 2\}$, then $L_{\mathcal{C}} = \frac{8!}{3!2!} = 3360$. Obviously, if we use these arrangements to carry a payload, the embedding capacity is $\log_2 L_{\mathcal{C}}$ bits.

Suppose that, the secret data is a non-negative integer M in range $[0, L_{\mathcal{C}} - 1]$. It is necessary to translate M as an arrangement that can be represented by $S_{\mathcal{C}}$. Without the loss of generality, we assume that, $s_{i_{t_1}} \leq s_{i_{t_2}} \leq ... \leq s_{i_{t_m}}$. We want to find such an arrangement of $\{1, 2, ..., m\}$, denoted by $\{x_1, x_2, ..., x_m\}$, that

$$\{s_{i_{t_{x_1}}}, s_{i_{t_{x_2}}}, ..., s_{i_{t_{x_m}}}\} \tag{3}$$

corresponds to M, i.e., one can always determine M out from this sequence. To solve this problem, we formulate a task as:

Given a sorted sequence $1 \le v_1 \le v_2 \le ... \le v_m \le m$ and an index $M \in [0, D-1]$ where D is the total number of different arrangements of $\{v_1, v_2, ..., v_m\}$, find the M-th lexicographically smallest sequence, e.g., the 8-th lexicographically smallest sequence of $\{1, 2, 3\}$ is $\{2, 3, 1, 1\}$. Here, given two different sequences of the same length $\{a_1, a_2, ..., a_m\}$ and $\{b_1, b_2, ..., b_m\}$, the first one is lexicographically smaller than the second one means there exists an index i that $a_j = b_j$ for all $j < i$ (if any) and $a_j < b_j$ when $j = i$. Two sequences equal each other when each element in one sequence equals the corresponding element in the other one.

It can be easily inferred that the 0-th sequence is $\{v_1, v_2, ..., v_m\}$ and the $(D-1)$-th sequence is $\{v_m, v_{m-1}, ..., v_1\}$. We could determine the M-th sequence from the first element to the last element one by one. For each element position, we collect all possible values, and then identify its value according to the index. Assuming that, there are q different values $U = \{u_1, u_2, ..., u_q\}$ and $u_1 < u_2 < ... < u_q$ in the sequence, it means that, $\forall i \in [1, m], v_i \in U$. Let $Z = \{z_1, z_2, ..., z_m\}$ be the sequence we want to determine out. We first find z_1 as follows. It can be inferred that, if $z_1 = u_i$, M should be in $[x_1, y_1)$, where

$$x_1 = \sum_{j=1}^{i-1} \frac{(m-1)!}{[f(u_j) - 1]! \prod_{e \in U \setminus \{u_j\}} f(e)!} \tag{4}$$

and

$$y_1 = x_1 + \frac{(m-1)!}{[f(u_i) - 1]! \prod_{e \in U \setminus \{u_i\}} f(e)!}. \tag{5}$$

For example, for a sequence $V = \{1, 1, 2, 2, 3\}$, we can find $U = \{1, 2, 3\}$. The number of different arranged sequences that start with 1 is $\frac{4!}{2!} = 12$, meaning that, any $0 \le M < 12$ corresponds to a sequence started with 1. For sequences started with 2, they requires that $12 \le M < 24$. And, $24 \le M < 30$ means a sequence started with 3.

Therefore, given M, we can easily find z_1 out. We continue to determine z_2. This can be done by the similar procedure. Suppose that we have found out that $z_1 = u_i$, then if $z_2 = u_j$, we must have $M - x_1 \in [x_2, y_2)$, where

$$x_2 = \sum_{k=1}^{j-1} \frac{(m-2)!}{\prod_{e \in U} [f(e) - \delta(e, u_i) - \delta(e, u_k)]!} \tag{6}$$

and

$$y_2 = x_2 + \frac{(m-2)!}{\prod_{e \in U} [f(e) - \delta(e, u_i) - \delta(e, u_j)]!}, \tag{7}$$

where $\delta(x, y) = 1$ if $x = y$, and $\delta(x, y) = 0$ for $x \ne y$.

We still take the above example for explanation. If $M = 19$, we have $z_1 = 2$, $x_1 = 12$, $y_1 = 24$. Then, we can find $z_2 = 2$ since $M - x_1 = 19 - 12 = 7 \in [x_2, y_2)$,

---

Algorithm 1. Determine the M-th lexicographically smallest sequence.

Input: Sequence $1 \leq v_1 \leq v_2 \leq ... \leq v_m \leq m$ and M.
Output: M-th lexicographically smallest sequence.
1: Find $D = L_C$ based on Eq. (2)
2: **if** $M \notin [0, D-1]$ **then**
3:    **return** M is out of range
4: **end if**
5: Set R as an empty sequence
6: **for** $i = 1, 2, ..., m$ **do**
7:    **for** $j = 1, 2, ..., q$ **do**
8:       Set $z_i = u_j$
9:       Find x_i and y_i with Eqs. (8, 9)
10:       **if** $M - \sum_{k=1}^{i-1} x_k \in [x_i, y_i)$ **then**
11:          Append u_j to R
12:          Break
13:       **end if**
14:    **end for**
15: **end for**
16: **return** Sequence R

---

where $x_2 = 6$ and $y_2 = 9$ in case $z_1 = z_2 = 2$. It means that, for $M = 19$, the corresponding sequence should start with two 2s.

Generally, given M, if we have determined out the values of $\{z_1, z_2, ..., z_{i-1}\}$, then z_i will be equal to such a *unique* u_j that $M - \sum_{k=1}^{i-1} x_k \in [x_i, y_i)$, where

$$x_i = \sum_{k=1}^{j-1} \frac{(m-i)!}{\prod_{e \in U} [f(e) - \sum_{t=1}^{i-1} \delta(e, u_t) - \delta(e, u_k)]!} \tag{8}$$

and

$$y_i = x_i + \frac{(m-i)!}{\prod_{e \in U} [f(e) - \sum_{t=1}^{i-1} \delta(e, u_t) - \delta(e, u_j)]!}. \tag{9}$$

Therefore, we can correctly construct the required sequence, which allows us to embed M into the corresponding transaction list. Algorithm 1 shows the pseudo-code of determining the M-th lexicographically smallest sequence.

3.2   Data Extraction

Since the blockchain is public to anyone, for a receiver, he will be able to extract all the transactions from the stego block. And, according to the secret key, he can further identify the m transactions containing hidden information, from which the sender addresses can be all parsed. With the address sequence, the receiver can finally reconstruct the embedded integer M, which is equivalent to solving the following problem: *Given* $\{z_1, z_2, ..., z_m\}$, *find its lexicographical order.*

Similarly, let $U = \{u_1, u_2, ..., u_q\}$ and $u_1 < u_2 < ... < u_q$ denote all the different values in the sequence. We can determine M by processing each element in the sequence in order. Let us first consider z_1. Suppose that, $z_1 = u_i$. Then, we count the number of all sequences that start with anyone in $\{u_1, u_2, ..., u_{i-1}\}$, denoted by c_1, which is computed as

$$c_1 = \sum_{j=1}^{i-1} \frac{(m-1)!}{\prod_{e \in U} [f(e) - \delta(e, u_j)]!}. \tag{10}$$

For example, if the given sequence is $\{3, 1, 2, 1\}$, then we have $c_1 = 3! + \frac{3!}{2!} = 9$. It indicates that, the lexicographical order of $\{3, 1, 2, 1\}$ should be no less than 9. Notice that, here, the lexicographical order of a sequence is started from 0. We continue to process the second element. Assuming that, we have $z_1 = u_i, z_2 = u_j$, then the number of all the sequences that the first element is u_i and the second one is anyone in $\{u_1, u_2, ..., u_{j-1}\}$ will be

$$c_2 = \sum_{k=1}^{j-1} \frac{(m-2)!}{\prod_{e \in U} [f(e) - \delta(e, u_i) - \delta(e, u_k)]!}. \tag{11}$$

We still take $\{3, 1, 2, 1\}$ for explanation. Since $z_1 = 3$ and $z_2 = 1$, we have $c_2 = 0$. It means that, the lexicographical order of $\{3, 1, 2, 1\}$ is no less than $c_1 + c_2 = 9$. Generally, given $\{z_1, z_2, ..., z_m\}$, if we have determined out the values of $\{c_1, c_2, ..., c_{i-1}\}$, and suppose that $z_i = u_j$, then c_i will be equal to

$$c_i = \sum_{k=1}^{j-1} \frac{(m-i)!}{\prod_{e \in U} [f(e) - \sum_{t=1}^{i-1} \delta(e, u_t) - \delta(e, u_k)]!}. \tag{12}$$

In this way, M will be determined as:

$$\begin{aligned} M &= \sum_{i=1}^{m} c_i \\ &= \sum_{i=1}^{m} \sum_{j=1}^{q} \sum_{k=1}^{j-1} \frac{\delta(z_i, u_j) \cdot (m-i)!}{\prod_{e \in U} [f(e) - \sum_{t=1}^{i-1} \delta(e, u_t) - \delta(e, u_k)]!}. \end{aligned} \tag{13}$$

3.3   Example

We present an example for better explanation. Suppose that, we have collected a total of 10 transactions to be packed in a block, and intend to use 6 of them to carry a payload. Figure 2 shows the data embedding procedure. In Fig. 2, each A_i $(1 \le i \le 10)$ represents the original sender address in the corresponding transaction. In the Bitcoin network, A_i is a 160-bit stream. One can easily compare two addresses according to their values. From a general perspective, we can use a function denoted by "MAP" for the addresses, which allows us to map a bitstream to an integer. Obviously, there are many ways to define such a function. In this example, we will not discuss its definition since it is a quite simple

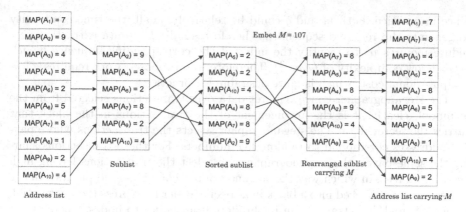

Fig. 2. Example for data embedding.

task, but rather directly assign a value to each address for the sake of simplicity. Notice that, two identical addresses should map to the identical integer.

The steganographer selects 6 addresses from the list according to a key, which constitutes a sublist shown in Fig. 2. According to the sublist, we can construct a sequence according to the mapped values of the addresses, i.e., $\{9, 8, 2, 8, 2, 4\}$. Then, we can sort the sequence as $\{2, 2, 4, 8, 8, 9\}$. The secret integer is $M = 107$. We use the rearrangement of $\{2, 2, 4, 8, 8, 9\}$ to carry M according to Algorithm 1, resulting in a new sequence $\{8, 2, 8, 9, 4, 2\}$ that carries M. The corresponding address list is $\{A_7, A_5, A_4, A_2, A_{10}, A_9\}$. Notice that, since there may be two *identical sender addresses*, the address list that can carry M may be not unique.

The steganographer will insert the "rearranged" sublist into the original address list, and then generate the "stego" block expected to be chained. Once the stego block is chained, a receiver would be able to reconstruct the "rearranged" sublist, and then determine the secret integer according to the proposed data extraction procedure. Accordingly, the steganographic communication is finished.

4   Performance Evaluation

It has been shown that, the embedding capacity for the proposed work is $\log_2 L_C$ bits per block, which is significantly larger than the work introduced in [8]. Though, in theory, there could be many identical addresses in a block, the steganographer may intentionally choose and arrange the transactions to be packed according to a specific rule such that the generated address sublist to be embedded has no two identical addresses (or say, the number of identical addresses is small). It indicates that, the capacity can approach $\log_2 m!$ in practice.

The data embedding procedure requires us to solve a sequence generation problem, which, as shown in Algorithm 1, will need a complexity of $O(m^2 q^2)$.

Since in practice, both m and q could be relatively small, the time complexity to generate the required sequence is therefore small. The data extraction procedure requires us to identify the index of the corresponding sequence, which needs a low complexity of $O(mq^2)$. Therefore, the proposed work requires a low computational cost, which is quite desirable for practice.

The steganographer conveys secret data over transactions selected from the mempool, clearly, it is the arrangement of the transactions in the block that carries the secret data. The steganographer selects the transactions whose payers' addresses correspond to random-like numbers. For those transactions sharing the same payer, the steganographer can select the transactions having high transaction fees, in which way the steganographer can gain good profits. All the transactions are packed into a block in a specific order to express the information to be delivered. The transaction pool differs from nodes to nodes. Therefore, it will not be noticed that the block is abnormal. It is rather hard to distinguish the blocks containing payload from a normal block. Moreover, the steganographer does not generate new transactions, but rather collect normal transactions for data embedding, which will not arouse suspicion.

Besides, even the attacker knows that there is secret information in a certain block, he cannot extract the information without the key. On the contrary, the recipient who shares the key with the transmitter is able to extract the secret information with high reliability. If an attacker wants to retrieve the secret data, he has to identify the address sublist. The probability of reconstructing the required sublist is $1/2^n$, which is quite small for large n, indicating that, the attacker will hardly reconstruct the embedded information, demonstrating the high security. Moreover, in blockchain, each node is identified by an address, which is not associated with its real identity. The attacker will not know about the real identity of the transmitter and recipient.

5   Conclusion

In this paper, we present a new steganographic scheme to blockchain. The secret message is carried by rearranging a part of the sender addresses of transactions within a block. The rearrangement assignment is equivalent to finding the M-th lexicographically smallest sequence for a given sorted sequence where M is the secret integer to be embedded. Since there may be identical elements in the sequence, we present an element-by-element determination algorithm to find the required sequence, which has a very low computational cost. A receiver will be able to effectively retrieve the secret integer from the "stego" sequence by the presented reconstruction algorithm with the secret key. It is analyzed that, the proposed work can provide a high embedding capacity, a low computational cost, and a high security level, which is suitable for practice under condition that the miner has the sufficient ability to chain the stego block.

Acknowledgement. This work was partly supported by the National Natural Science Foundation of China (NSFC) (U1636206, 61525203, and 61902235), the Shanghai Institute for Advanced Communication and Data Science, and the Natural Science Foundation of Shanghai (19ZR1419000).

References

1. Cox, I., Miller, M., Bloom, J., Fridrich, J., Kalker, T.: Digital Watermarking and Steganography. Morgan Kaufmann, Burlington (2008)
2. Mazurczyk, W., Szczypiorski, K.: Trends in steganography. Commun. ACM **57**(3), 86–95 (2014)
3. Wu, H., Wang, W., Dong, J., Wang, H.: New graph-theoretic approach to social steganography. In: Proceedings of the IS&T Electronic Imaging, Media Watermarking, Security and Forensics, pp. 539-1–539-7(7) (2019)
4. Sallee, P.: Model-based steganography. In: Kalker, T., Cox, I., Ro, Y.M. (eds.) IWDW 2003. LNCS, vol. 2939, pp. 154–167. Springer, Heidelberg (2004). https://doi.org/10.1007/978-3-540-24624-4_12
5. Kim, Y., Duric, Z., Richards, D.: Modified matrix encoding technique for minimal distortion steganography. In: Camenisch, J.L., Collberg, C.S., Johnson, N.F., Sallee, P. (eds.) IH 2006. LNCS, vol. 4437, pp. 314–327. Springer, Heidelberg (2007). https://doi.org/10.1007/978-3-540-74124-4_21
6. Nakamoto, S.: Bitcoin: A peer-to-peer electronic cash system (2008). https://bitcoin.org/bitcoin.pdf
7. Iansiti, M., Lakhani, K.R.: The truth about blockchain. Harv. Bus. Rev. **95**(1), 118–127 (2017)
8. Partala, J.: Provably secure covert communication on blockchain. Cryptography **2**(3) (2018). 18 pages
9. Yaga, D., Mell, P., Roby, N., Scarfone, K.: Blockchain technology overview (2018). https://doi.org/10.6028/NIST.IR.8202
10. Belotti, M., Božić, N., Pujolle, G., Secci, S.: A vademecum on blockchain technologies: when, which and how. IEEE Commun. Surv. Tutor. **21**(4), 3796–3838 (2019)
11. Gai, K., Wu, Y., Zhu, L., Xu, L., Zhang, Y.: Permissioned blockchain and edge computing empowered privacy-preserving smart grid networks. IEEE Internet Things J. **6**(5), 7992–8004 (2019)
12. Bakar, N., Rosbi, S., Uzaki, K.: Cryptocurrency framework diagnostics from islamic finance perspective: a new insight of bitcoin system transaction. Int. J. Manage. Sci. Bus. Adm. **4**(1), 19–28 (2017)
13. Jiao, Y., Wang, P., Niyato, D., Suankaewmanee, K.: Auction mechanisms in cloud/fog computing resource allocation for public blockchain networks. IEEE Trans. Parallel Distrib. Syst. **30**(9), 1975–1989 (2019)
14. Christidis, K., Devetsikiotis, M.: Blockchains and smart contracts for the internet of things. IEEE Access **4**, 2292–2303 (2016)
15. Zheng, Z., Xie, S., Dai, H., Chen, X., Wang, H.: Blockchain challenges and opportunities: a survey. Int. J. Web Grid Serv. **14**(4), 352–375 (2018)

Designing Non-additive Distortions for JPEG Steganography Based on Blocking Artifacts Reduction

Yubo Lu, Liming Zhai, and Lina Wang$^{(\boxtimes)}$

Key Laboratory of Aerospace Information Security and Trusted Computing,
Ministry of Education, School of Cyber Science and Engineering, Wuhan University,
Wuhan, China
{lusirer,limingzhai,lnwang}@whu.edu.cn

Abstract. The JPEG image is the most commonly used image format, and the content-adaptive embedding mechanism is widely adopted for JPEG steganography. The embedding distortions for existing adaptive JPEG steganography are mostly additive distortions, while the non-additive distortions in JPEG steganography have not been sufficiently explored. In this paper, we propose a non-additive distortion design method to measure the embedding effects of DCT coefficients on the spatial domain by using blocking artifacts reduction (BAR). The main idea is to reduce the spatial domain blocking artifacts, from which to guide the selection of the polarity of embedding changes for DCT coefficients in the JPEG domain. Because the changes of DCT coefficients will increase the blocking artifacts, the BAR principle can maintain the spatial continuity in both inter-blocks and intra-blocks. The proposed BAR principle can be applied to current additive JPEG steganography. Experimental results show that our method significantly improves the security of additive JPEG steganography, especially for high embedding payloads.

Keywords: JPEG image · Steganography · Blocking artifacts · Non-additive distortion

1 Introduction

Steganography is the art of covert communication, and it conceals the existence of secret messages by slightly modifying the digital carrier without causing suspicions [1]. JPEG image is a commonly used steganographic carrier for its wide application, and the steganography based on JPEG images has become a hot research topic.

The content-adaptive embedding mechanism has been a main trend for image steganography. The adaptive steganography firstly assigns an embedding cost to each element of the cover image to indicate its security level according to the texture complexity of the image, and then embeds the secret message into

© Springer Nature Switzerland AG 2020
H. Wang et al. (Eds.): IWDW 2019, LNCS 12022, pp. 268–280, 2020.
https://doi.org/10.1007/978-3-030-43575-2_23

the image while minimizing the overall distortion with some coding schemes, such as syndrome-trellis codes (STCs) [2]. The representative adaptive JPEG steganographic algorithms include EBS [3], UED [4], UERD [5], JUNIWARD [6] and RBV [7]. The EBS [3] designs the embedding costs based on the entropy of 8×8 DCT coefficient blocks. The authors of UED [4] proposed the idea of uniform embedding, in which the embedding cost are decided by the magnitudes of DCT coefficients, so that the embedding changes are uniformly spread over the DCT coefficients with all possible magnitudes. Similar to UED, UERD [5] also use the uniform embedding strategies to design embedding costs with the statistic model of DCT coefficients. Unlike other steganographic algorithms, JUNIWARD [6] constructs the distortion function in a wavelet domain, and the embedding costs of DCT coefficients are defined as the sum of the relative changes of the directional wavelet coefficients obtained from the decompressed image. RBV [7] evaluates the embedding risk from both spatial domain and JPEG domain, and the embedding costs are based on the filtered residuals of decompressed spatial pixels and the quantization steps of DCT coefficients.

When designing the distortion functions, the above adaptive JPEG steganography all assumes that the modifications between neighboring elements are independent with each other, namely, the embedding distortions are additive. The modification of a DCT coefficient will cause more changes to the corresponding spatial pixels, which are vulnerable to the current successful JPEG steganalytic features [8–10] that are constructed from the spatial domain. Therefore, the adaptive JPEG steganography needs to consider not only the modification magnitudes of spatial pixels but also the interactions among neighboring pixels. However, due to the transformation between DCT coefficients and spatial pixels, the non-additive distortions [11, 12] for spatial domain are difficult to be directly applied to JPEG images. Recently, a principle called block boundary continuity (BBC) [13] is proposed for non-additive distortions in JPEG images. The BBC tries to preserve the spatial continuity at block boundaries in spatial domain, and adjusts the existing additive distortions to non-additive ones by decomposing joint distortion (Dejoin) [14]. However, the BBC only considers the interactions of modifications between neighboring blocks (inter-block), and is not sufficient to measure the interactions among spatial pixels within the same block (intra-block), especially for the spatial modifications caused by high frequency DCT coefficients.

In this paper, we propose a non-additive distortion design method to measure the interactions among neighboring modifications in spatial domain based on blocking artifact reduction (BAR). The blocking artifacts, which mostly result from the block based lossy compression, are typically characterized as the changes of pixel intensities at the block boundaries. For the stego images generated by JPEG steganography, the embedding changes of DCT coefficients also increase the discontinuity of spatial pixels for inter-blocks and intra-blocks, and this embedding effect reflected in spatial domain is similar to the blocking artifacts. This motivates us to use BAR method to preserve the spatial continuity, which can be served as a measurement of interactions among neighboring modi-

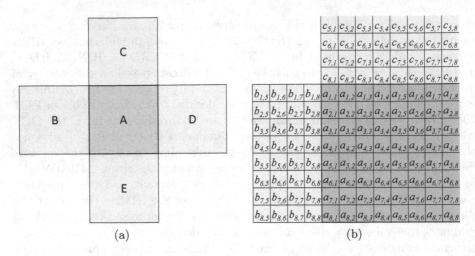

Fig. 1. Neighboring relations of 8 × 8 blocks.

fications. By reducing the blocking artifacts defined on the spatial discontinuity of inter-blocks and intra-blocks, the preferred polarity of embedding changes can be determined and the non-additive embedding can be achieved. Experimental results show that the principle of BAR can be applied to the current adaptive JPEG steganography with additive distortions, and can improve their steganographic security against the advanced JPEG steganalysis, especially at high embedding payloads.

The rest of this paper is organized as follows. In Sect. 2, the blocking artifacts and the quality assessment methods for JPEG images are introduced. Section 3 details the design of non-additive distortion using blocking artifact reduction (BAR). In Sect. 4, extensive experiments are performed to demonstrate the effectiveness of the proposed method. Finally, the paper is concluded in Sect. 5.

2   Preliminaries

Our proposed non-additive distortion design method is based on the reduction of blocking artifacts, so the measurement of blocking artifacts should be firstly introduced. To make this paper more self-contained, this section describes the concept of blocking artifacts, and the quality assessment methods for blocking artifacts in JPEG images.

The blocking artifact is a phenomenon in which the discontinuity of pixel intensities occurs at the edges of spatial blocks due to JPEG lossy compression. The smaller the quality factor (QF) is, the larger the block boundary discontinuity will be. The blocking artifacts can be evaluated by some quality assessment methods. The most widely used one is the no-reference quality assessment method, that is, no information of the original raw image is needed to measure the blocking artifacts. Typical measurements used for no-reference quality assessment methods include the blockiness and flatness measure (BFM) [15] in block boundary, Referenceless quality Measure of Blocking artifacts (RMB) using Tchebichef moments [16], grid strength and regularity (GridSAR) [17] and blockiness and luminance changes (BLC) [18]. In this paper, the quality assessment method with blockiness and flatness measure (BFM) [15] is used for designing non-additive distortions (the selection of quality assessment methods is detailed in Sect. 4.2), so it is introduced as follows.

The BFM [15] measures the local blocking artifacts using the blockiness and flatness across block boundaries in spatial domain. Figure 1 shows the relationships of a spatial 8×8 block and its four neighboring blocks. The blockiness is based on pixel differences, and the horizontal blockiness B_h between block A and B is defined as

$$B_h = \begin{cases} \frac{N_h}{D_h} & \text{if } D_h \neq 0 \\ 0 & \text{otherwise} \end{cases} \tag{1}$$

where N_h and D_h are defined as

$$N_h = \gamma_1 \times \sum_{i=1}^{8} |a_{i,1} - b_{i,8}| \tag{2}$$

and

$$D_h = \gamma_2 \times \sum_{i=1}^{8} \left(\sum_{j=5}^{7} |b_{i,j+1} - b_{i,j}| + \sum_{j=1}^{3} |a_{i,j+1} - a_{i,j}| \right) + \sum_{i=1}^{8} |a_{i,1} - b_{i,8}| \tag{3}$$

In (2) and (3), $a_{i,j}$ and $b_{i,j}$ denote the spatial pixel values, N_h is the inter-block pixel difference by calculating the boundary pixels between block A and B, and D_h is the weighted average of the intra-block pixel difference and inter-block pixel difference. The γ_1 and γ_2 are the weighting coefficients and are set 10 and 1.5, respectively.

The flatness is measured by the proportion of zero-valued pixel difference, and the horizontal flatness between block A and block B is defined as

$$Z_h = \frac{10}{56} \sum_{i=1}^{8} \left(\sum_{j=5}^{7} z(b_{i,j}, b_{i,j+1}) + \sum_{j=1}^{3} z(a_{i,j}, a_{i,j+1}) \right) + \frac{10}{56} \sum_{i=1}^{8} z(a_{i,1}, b_{i,8}) \tag{4}$$

where

$$z(x, y) = \begin{cases} 1 & \text{if } |x - y| = 0 \\ 0 & \text{otherwise} \end{cases} \tag{5}$$

The vertical blockiness B_v and the vertical flatness Z_v between the block A and block C are defined analogically. The BFM [15] only use neighboring blocks B and C for measuring block artifacts; in this paper, the neighboring blocks D and E are also considered. The horizontal blockiness and horizontal flatness

Table 1. Evaluation values of blocking artifacts for different stego images.

Steganography algorithm	BFM [15]	BLC [18]	RMB [16]
Q_Cover	2.1363	2.893	0.52121
Q_EBS	$2.1483 \pm 3.01 \times 10^{-6}$	$3.0517 \pm 1.56 \times 10^{-4}$	$0.51716 \pm 1.80 \times 10^{-5}$
Q_UED	$2.1471 \pm 3.95 \times 10^{-6}$	$3.0099 \pm 3.90 \times 10^{-3}$	$0.51781 \pm 3.65 \times 10^{-6}$
Q_UERD	$2.1388 \pm 1.27 \times 10^{-6}$	$3.0049 \pm 7.82 \times 10^{-5}$	$0.51872 \pm 2.23 \times 10^{-5}$
Q_JUNI	$2.1374 \pm 1.15 \times 10^{-6}$	$2.9931 \pm 1.64 \times 10^{-4}$	$0.52107 \pm 1.88 \times 10^{-6}$

between A and D are denoted by B_h' and Z_h', and the vertical blockiness and vertical flatness between A and E are denoted by B_v' and Z_v'. Finally, the local blocking artifacts Q_{BLK} is defined as

$$Q_{BLK} = \max(B_{BLK}, Z_{BLK}) \tag{6}$$

where

$$B_{BLK} = \frac{B_h + B_v + B_h' + B_v'}{4} \tag{7}$$

and

$$Z_{BLK} = \frac{Z_h + Z_v + Z_h' + Z_v'}{4} \tag{8}$$

The Q_{BLK} is a quality measure for one 8×8 block, and a larger Q_{BLK} value indicates more severe blocking artifacts. The quality of an JPEG image can be measured by averaging the Q_{BLK} values of all 8×8 blocks.

3   Proposed Method

3.1   Motivation

The blocking artifacts are characterized by the discontinuity of pixel values for 8×8 spatial blocks. In addition to the blocking artifacts caused by lossy compression, the ± 1 modifications of DCT coefficients in JPEG images can also result in spatial discontinuity between and within blocks. Intuitively, stego images should lead to little spatial discontinuity to ensure steganographic security. Therefore, if the steganographic embedding can be performed in a blocking artifact reduction manner, the steganographic security can be increased. To verify this conjecture, we conduct an experiment as follows.

First, an uncompressed image named 'Lena.tiff' is compressed into a JPEG image with QF 75, and it is regarded as a cover image. Then, four types of stego images are generated by using the steganographic algorithms J-EBS [3], JC-UED [4], J-UERD [5], J-UNIWARD [6] with payload 0.4 bpnzac (bits per non-zero AC coefficient). Next, three blocking artifact evaluation methods (BFM [15], BLC [18] and RMB [16]) are used to measure the above cover image and all kinds of stego images. Each type of the stego image is repeatedly generated with different random seeds 10 times, and the mean and variance of the evaluation values of the blocking artifacts for stego images are reported in Table 1. Note that for BFM [15] and BLC [18], larger evaluation values mean larger blocking artifacts; while for RMB [16], smaller evaluation values stand for larger blocking artifacts.

It can be seen from Table 1 that all types of stego images have larger blocking artifacts than the cover image, and the securer steganographic algorithm tends to have less blocking artifacts. For example, the J-UNIWARD is the most secure one of all four types of steganographic algorithms, so it has the least blocking artifacts. This demonstrates that the blocking artifacts are related to the steganographic security, and reducing the blocking artifacts of the image is beneficial to improve the security of steganographic algorithms.

3.2   Selection of Modification Directions

The ± 1 modifications on the DCT coefficients lead to the changes of the pixels in the spatial domain, and different modification directions of DCT coefficients have different effects on the blocking artifacts. It is obvious that selecting the proper modification direction which has the least blocking artifacts for each DCT coefficient is more suitable for embedding.

In order to select the best modification direction, the blocking artifacts caused by ± 1 modification on each DCT coefficient should be evaluated, and this can be done by using the quality assessment methods as mentioned in Sect. 2. Let a JPEG cover image be denoted by x, and the JPEG stego images obtained by only $+1$ and -1 on the ij-th DCT coefficient of x be denoted by $y^{+1}_{\sim i,j}$ and $y^{-1}_{\sim i,j}$. For $y^{+1}_{\sim i,j}$ and $y^{-1}_{\sim i,j}$, their corresponding quality scores are denoted by $Q^{+1}_{i,j}$ and $Q^{-1}_{i,j}$, respectively. The quality scores can be obtained by BFM [15], BLC [18] or RMB [16]. If $Q^{+1}_{i,j} < Q^{-1}_{i,j}$, the $+1$ modification produces less blocking artifacts than the -1 modification, and the $+1$ modification is more preferable than the -1 modification. Otherwise, the -1 modification is preferred.

Note that the current quality assessment methods are used to calculate the quality scores for the whole image. For the embedding in the JPEG image, modifying one DCT coefficient will make the 64 pixels in the corresponding 8×8 spatial block to change, and the blocking artifacts caused by embedding only occur at a local area as shown in Fig. 1. Therefore, the $Q^{+1}_{i,j}$ and $Q^{-1}_{i,j}$ are obtained by applying the quality assessment methods on a 24×24 pixel area (see Fig. 1 (a)), and this will reduce computational complexity greatly.

3.3   Embedding with Blocking Artifact Reduction

For the ± 1 modification on a DCT coefficient, the embedding cost corresponding to the preferred modification direction should be decreased, while the embedding cost with opposite modification direction should be increased. Therefore, the embedding costs need to be further adjusted after selecting the modification directions. To capture the mutual embedding impacts in the spatial domain of

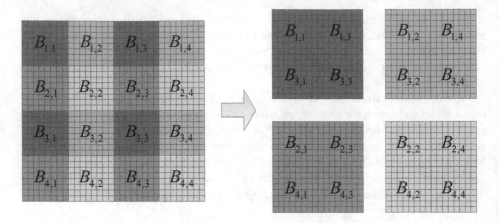

Fig. 2. Division of a JPEG image into sub-images.

the image, the embedding costs are updated in a dynamic way. Inspired by the clustering modified directions (CMD) [11], the decompressed JPEG cover image is first decomposed into several disjoint sub-images, and then the payload is embedded into sub-images sequentially. During the embedding, the embedding costs of the subsequent sub-images are dynamically updated based on the previously modified images. The detailed embedding process is described as follows.

(1) Divide the JPEG cover image x into four disjoint JPEG cover sub-images, and a cover sub-image containing DCT blocks is denoted by

$$x_{u,v} = \{B_{u+2s,v+2t} \mid u = 1,2, v = 1,2, s = 0,...,\frac{S}{2} - 1, t = 0,...,\frac{T}{2} - 1\} \quad (9)$$

where $B_{u+2s,v+2t}$ is a 8×8 DCT block, u,v are the indices of sub-images, and S and T are the number of 8×8 blocks for horizontal and vertical directions. The division of a JPEG image into sub-images is illustrated in Fig. 2.

(2) Segment the embedding payload m into four equal-sized sub-payloads denoted by $m_{u,v}, u = 1,2, v = 1,2$.

(3) Calculate the embedding cost $\rho_{i,j}^{+1} = \rho_{i,j}^{-1} = \rho_{i,j}$ for each DCT coefficient in JPEG cover image x using a specific steganographic algorithm, such as J-UED, J-UERD and J-UNIWARD.

(4) Determine an embedding order for the JPEG cover sub-images, and the horizontal zig-zag order adopted in CMD is used for embedding.

(5) Embed $m_{1,1}$ into the first JPEG cover sub-image $x_{1,1}$ with the initial embedding costs using ternary embedding, and obtain a JPEG stego sub-image denoted by $y_{1,1}$.

(6) Replace the $x_{1,1}$ in x with $y_{1,1}$ to obtain the JPEG stego image y.

(7) Calculate the embedding cost $\rho_{i,j}^{+1} = \rho_{i,j}^{-1} = \rho_{i,j}$ for each DCT coefficient in JPEG stego image y.

(8) For the JPEG sub-image $x_{u,v}, u \neq 1, v \neq 1$, compute the quality scores $Q_{i,j}^{+1}$ and $Q_{i,j}^{-1}$ for each DCT coefficient from the previously obtained stego image, and adjust the embedding cost $\rho_{i,j}^{+1}$ and $\rho_{i,j}^{-1}$ as follows:

$$\rho_{i,j}^{+1} = \begin{cases} \alpha \cdot \rho_{i,j} & \text{if } Q_{i,j}^{+1} < Q_{i,j}^{-1} \\ \rho_{i,j} & \text{otherwise} \end{cases} \tag{10}$$

and

$$\rho_{i,j}^{-1} = \begin{cases} \alpha \cdot \rho_{i,j} & \text{if } Q_{i,j}^{+1} > Q_{i,j}^{-1} \\ \rho_{i,j} & \text{otherwise} \end{cases} \tag{11}$$

where $\alpha \in (0,1)$ is a scaling factor determined by experiments (see Sect. 4.2).

(9) Embed the $m_{u,v}, u \neq 1, v \neq 1$ into the JPEG sub-image $x_{u,v}$ with the adjusted embedding costs using ternary embedding.

(10) Replace the $x_{u,v}$ in y with $y_{u,v}$ to update the JPEG stego image y.

(11) Go back to step (7) until all sub-payloads are embedded into the corresponding JPEG sub-images.

The message extraction is just the reverse process of embedding. First, the stego image is decomposed into four sub-images as did in the embedding. Then the sub-payload is extracted from each sub-image sequentially. Finally, the extracted sub-payloads are merged into a whole message.

4   Experiments

4.1   Experimental Setup

The image database employed for our experiments is the BossBase ver. 1.01 [19], which contains 10,000 gray-scale images of size 512×512 pixels. All the images in the BossBase are JPEG compressed with quality factors (QFs) 75 and 95. The comparative steganographic algorithms include three additive distortion schemes JC-UED [4], J-UERD [5] and J-UNIWARD [6], and their non-additive distortion versions using the principle of BBC [13], namely JC-UED-BBC, J-UERD-BBC, and J-UNI-BBC. All the BBC based steganographic algorithms use the UpDist-DeJoin2 method to update their embedding costs. For simplicity, the optimal embedding simulator [20] instead of STC [2] is used for embedding, and the embedding payload ranges from 0.05 to 0.5 bpnzac (bits per non-zero AC coefficient). The used steganalytic features are DCTR [9] and GFR [10], which are trained with FLD-based ensemble classifier [21]. For each steganographic algorithms, payload and QF, 5,000 cover-stego pairs of images are randomly selected for training, and the remaining 5000 pairs are used for testing. The steganographic security is evaluated by testing error rate, which is the mean value of the false positive rate and the false negative rate. Each experiment is repeated 10 times to obtain the averaged testing error rate.

Table 2. Testing error rates of JC-UED with and without blocking artifact reduction.

Algorithm	QF = 75	QF = 95
JC-UED	0.0450	0.2057
JC-UED-BFM	0.0801	0.2784
JC-UED-BLC	0.0794	0.2717
JC-UED-RMB	0.0581	0.2359

Table 3. Testing error rates of J-UERD with and without blocking artifact reduction.

Algorithm	QF = 75	QF = 95
J-UERD	0.1470	0.3007
J-UERD-BFM	0.1999	0.3305
J-UERD-BLC	0.1998	0.3301
J-UERD-RMB	0.1473	0.3008

Table 4. Testing error rates of J-UNIWARD with and without blocking artifact reduction.

Algorithm	QF = 75	QF = 95
J-UNI	0.1557	0.3336
J-UNI-BFM	0.2470	0.3858
J-UNI-BLC	0.2466	0.3854
J-UNI-RMB	0.1560	0.3346

4.2   Determination of Steganographic Settings

There are two steganographic settings should be determined before implementing embedding: one is the blocking artifact reduction method, and the other is the scaling factor α.

The quality assessment methods described in Sect. 2 are used for artifact reduction methods to design non-additive distortions. Arbitrary blocking artifact reduction methods can be incorporated into the proposed BAR principle, and we select the one that contributes most to steganographic security. Three blocking artifact reduction methods based on BFM [15], BLC [18] and RMB [16] are incorporated into JC-UED with payload 0.4 bpnzac at two QFs, and resulting in three steganographic algorithms named JC-UED-BFM, JC-UED-BLC and JC-UED-RMB. The scaling factor α is 0.7, and the DCTR is used for steganalysis. The testing error rates of JC-UED with and without blocking artifact reduction (BAR) are shown in Table 2. This process is also applied to J-UERD and J-UNIWARD, and the corresponding results are reported in Tables 3 and 4.

We can see from Tables 2, 3 and 4 that all the three blocking artifact reduction methods can improve the security of the original steganographic algorithms, and

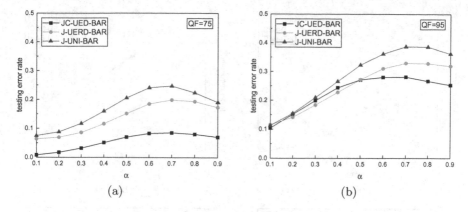

Fig. 3. Effect of different scaling factors on steganographic security.

the non-additive distortion schemes with BFM have the highest testing error. So the BFM [15] is selected for our BAR principle in the following experiments.

For a specific blocking artifact reduction method, Eqs. (10) and (11) use the scaling factor α to adjust the embedding costs of DCT coefficients. To find the best value of α, the blocking artifact reduction method BFM [15] with different α is applied to JC-UED, J-UERD and J-UNIWARD respectively (their non-additive distortion versions are with suffix "BAR" as shown in Fig. 3). The embedding payload 0.4 bpnzac and QF 75 and 95 are used for experiments, and the employed feature set is also DCTR. The testing error rates of BAR based steganographic algorithms are shown in Fig. 3.

The Fig. 3 shows that different scaling factors have different effects on the steganographic security, and the trends of changes of testing error rates for different steganographic algorithms are almost the same. For QF 75, all the steganographic algorithms get the highest testing error rates when the value of α is 0.7, so we set $\alpha = 0.7$ for the JPEG images with QF 75. For QF 95, the scaling factor α is set to be 0.7 for JC-UED-BAR, and 0.8 for JC-UERD-BAR and J-UNI-BAR.

4.3 Comparison to Prior Art

This subsection evaluates the effectiveness of our proposed BAR principle. The JC-UED-BAR, J-UERD-BAR and J-UNI-BAR are compared with the three additive distortion schemes (i.e., JC-UED, J-UERD and J-UNIWARD) and three non-additive distortion schemes (i.e., JC-UED-BBC, J-UERD-BBC and J-UNI-BBC). The feature set GFR is used for steganalysis, and the testing error rates of various steganographic algorithms for two QFs are shown in Fig. 4.

It is observed from Fig. 4 that the BAR based steganographic algorithms significantly outperform their corresponding additive distortion schemes for all payloads and QFs. At QF 75, the BAR principle increases the testing error rates by at most 7%, 6% and 10% for JC-UED, J-UERD and J-UNIWARD,

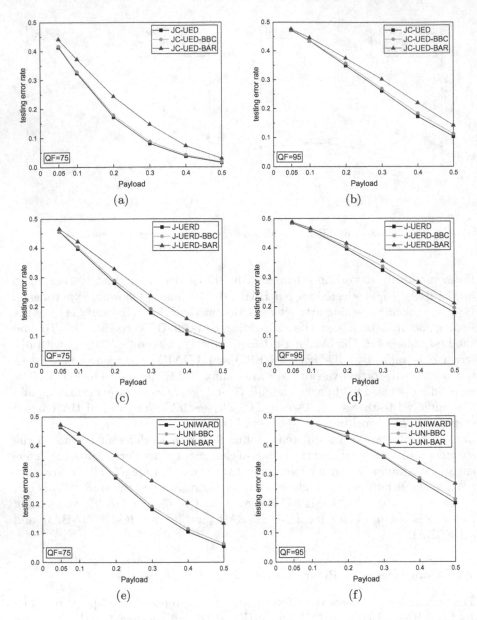

Fig. 4. Testing error rates of various steganographic algorithms for QF 75 and 95.

respectively. Besides, the improvement achieved by BAR is more pronounced for QF 75 than QF 95. This is because the lower QF corresponds to larger quantization steps, and this will lead to greater spatial blocking artifacts, which is conducive to exert the potential of BAR for selecting the polarity of embedding changes.

Compared with the BBC based schemes, the BAR based schemes also have obvious advantages. This is because the BBC uses the DCT coefficient pairs in different blocks to adjust embedding costs, and only preserves the spatial continuity for inter-blocks. While the BAR modulates the embedding costs directly by the reduction of blocking artifacts in the spatial domain, and the evaluation of blocking artifacts also considers the spatial continuity in both inter-blocks and intra-blocks, which fully exploits the interactions of modifications of spatial pixels.

5   Conclusion and Future Work

This paper presents a non-additive distortion design method by using the blocking artifact deduction to adjust the embedding costs. First, the effects of the changes of DCT coefficients on the blocking artifacts are evaluated. Then the DCT coefficients are modified in the direction of reducing blocking artifacts in the spatial domain. Finally, the payload is embedded by decomposing the image into sub-images. The proposed blocking artifact reduction (BAR) method considers the interactions of modifications between and within the blocks in the spatial domain, and the experiments demonstrate that the principle of BAR can significantly increase the undetectability of existing steganographic algorithms.

Acknowledgements. This work was supported by the National Natural Science Foundation of China under U1536204, U1836112, 61876134.

References

1. Fridrich, J.: Steganography in Digital Media: Principles, Algorithms, and Applications. Cambridge University Press, New York (2009)
2. Filler, T., Judas, J., Fridrich, J.: Minimizing additive distortion in steganography using syndrome-trellis codes. IEEE Trans. Inf. Forensics Secur. **6**, 920–935 (2011)
3. Wang, C., Ni, J.: An efficient JPEG steganographic scheme based on the block entropy of DCT coefficients. In: 2012 IEEE International Conference on Acoustics, Speech and Signal Processing (ICASSP), pp. 1785–1788. IEEE, March 2012
4. Guo, L., Ni, J., Shi, Y.Q.: Uniform embedding for efficient JPEG steganography. IEEE Trans. Inf. Forensics Secur. **9**, 814–825 (2014)
5. Guo, L., Ni, J., Su, W., Tang, C., Shi, Y.-Q.: Using statistical image model for JPEG steganography: uniform embedding revisited. IEEE Trans. Inf. Forensics Secur. **10**, 2669–2680 (2015)
6. Holub, V., Fridrich, J., Denemark, T.: Universal distortion function for steganography in an arbitrary domain. EURASIP J. Inf. Secur. **2014**, 1 (2014)
7. Wei, Q., Yin, Z., Wang, Z., Zhang, X.: Distortion function based on residual blocks for JPEG steganography. Multimedia Tools Appl. **77**, 17875–17888 (2018)
8. Holub, V., Fridrich, J.: Phase-aware projection model for steganalysis of JPEG images. In: Media Watermarking, Security, and Forensics 2015, vol. 9409, p. 94090T. International Society for Optics and Photonics, March 2015
9. Holub, V., Fridrich, J.: Low-complexity features for JPEG steganalysis using undecimated DCT. IEEE Trans. Inf. Forensics Secur. **10**, 219–228 (2014)

10. Song, X., Liu, F., Yang, C., Luo, X., Zhang, Y.: Steganalysis of adaptive JPEG steganography using 2D Gabor filters. In: Proceedings of the 3rd ACM Workshop on Information Hiding and Multimedia Security, pp. 15–23. ACM, June 2015

11. Li, B., Wang, M., Li, X., Tan, S., Huang, J.: A strategy of clustering modification directions in spatial image steganography. IEEE Trans. Inf. Forensics Secur. **10**, 1905–1917 (2015)

12. Denemark, T., Fridrich, J.: Improving steganographic security by synchronizing the selection channel. In: Proceedings of the 3rd ACM Workshop on Information Hiding and Multimedia Security, pp. 5–14. ACM, June 2015

13. Li, W., Zhang, W., Chen, K., Zhou, W., Yu, N.: Defining joint distortion for JPEG steganography. In: Proceedings of the 6th ACM Workshop on Information Hiding and Multimedia Security, pp. 5–16. ACM, June 2018

14. Zhang, W., Zhang, Z., Zhang, L., Li, H., Yu, N.: Decomposing joint distortion for adaptive steganography. IEEE Trans. Circuits Syst. Video Technol. **27**, 2274–2280 (2016)

15. Pan, F., et al.: A locally-adaptive algorithm for measuring blocking artifacts in images and videos. In: 2004 IEEE International Symposium on Circuits and Systems (IEEE Cat. No. 04CH37512), vol. 3, pp. III–925. IEEE, May 2004

16. Li, L., Zhu, H., Yang, G., Qian, J.: Referenceless measure of blocking artifacts by Tchebichef kernel analysis. IEEE Signal Process. Lett. **21**, 122–125 (2013)

17. Li, L., Zhou, Y., Wu, J., Lin, W., Li, H.: GridSAR: grid strength and regularity for robust evaluation of blocking artifacts in JPEG images. J. Vis. Commun. Image Represent. **30**, 153–163 (2015)

18. Zhan, Y., Zhang, R.: No-reference JPEG image quality assessment based on blockiness and luminance change. IEEE Signal Process. Lett. **24**, 760–764 (2017)

19. Bas, P., Filler, T., Pevný, T.: "Break our steganographic system": the ins and outs of organizing BOSS. In: Filler, T., Pevný, T., Craver, S., Ker, A. (eds.) IH 2011. LNCS, vol. 6958, pp. 59–70. Springer, Heidelberg (2011). https://doi.org/10.1007/978-3-642-24178-9_5

20. Fridrich, J., Filler, T.: Practical methods for minimizing embedding impact in steganography. In: Security, Steganography, and Watermarking of Multimedia Contents IX, vol. 6505, p. 650502. International Society for Optics and Photonics, February 2007

21. Kodovsky, J., Fridrich, J., Holub, V.: Ensemble classifiers for steganalysis of digital media. IEEE Trans. Inf. Forensics Secur. **7**, 432–444 (2011)

Halftone Image Steganography with Distortion Measurement Based on Structural Similarity

Wanteng Liu, Xiaolin Yin, Wei Lu$^{(\boxtimes)}$ ⓘD, and Junhong Zhang

School of Data and Computer Science, Guangdong Key Laboratory of Information Security Technology, Ministry of Education Key Laboratory of Machine Intelligence and Advanced Computing, Sun Yat-sen University, Guangzhou 510006, China
{liuwt25,yinxl6}@mail2.sysu.edu.cn, luwei3@mail.sysu.edu.cn

Abstract. For halftone image data hiding, it is difficult to achieve good visual quality and statistical security when high embedding capacity is demanded. In this paper, a secure steganographic scheme for halftone image is proposed, which aims to minimize the embedding distortion on structural similarity. Structural distortions are the ones that affect the most the perception of degradation of a halftone image. To evaluate the structural distortions caused by flipping pixels, halftone image structural similarity (HSSIM) is introduced based on a human visual filter, which is trained by Least-Mean-Square (LMS) approach. Utilizing the HSSIM, a distortion measurement is proposed to evaluate the embedding distortions on both vision and statistics. To minimize the embedding distortions, syndrome-trellis code (STC) is employed in the embedding process. The experimental results have demonstrated that the proposed steganographic scheme can achieve high statistical security with good visual quality without degrading the embedding capacity.

Keywords: Halftone image steganography · Distortion measurement · Halftone image structural similarity (HSSIM) · Syndrome-trellis code (STC)

1 Introduction

Steganography aims to transmit secret messages under digital media in public channels, which is a practice of covert communication using hiding messages. With the development of digital multimedia technology, the security of multimedia information has received much attention [4,22–26,31]. As a type of the host media, halftone image is a special kind of binary image, which can be resembled as a grayscale image when viewed from a distance with the low-pass nature of the human visual system (HVS). There are several kinds of digital halftoning methods being developed, including ordered dithering [2], error diffusion [7,17], dot diffusion [19,28] and least squares [12,15,18,33]. In recent years, many data hiding methods have been developed for halftone images [8–11,13,14,20,21,29,30],

© Springer Nature Switzerland AG 2020
H. Wang et al. (Eds.): IWDW 2019, LNCS 12022, pp. 281–292, 2020.
https://doi.org/10.1007/978-3-030-43575-2_24

which can be used for printing security documents such as ID card, currency, as well as confidential documents. In a general way, there are two categories of data hiding schemes on halftone images according to whether the data hiding operation is in the halftoning process or not. The first category is to embed secret messages during the process of halftoning [14,21,29], so the original multi-tone images are required. In this situation, the embedded capacity can be fairly large and the visual distortion of halftone images is negligible. The second category is to embed secret messages directly into the halftone images without the original multi-tone images and the method of halftoning is unknown [8,9,13,20,30]. In most cases, the original multi-tone images are unavailable and we can only embed secret messages into the generated halftone images. Therefore, our work focuses on the second category considering the versatility of steganography.

Many state-of-the-art data hiding schemes on halftone images have been proposed in recent years [8,10,13,16,30]. In the early work, Fu and Au [10] proposed a method named Data Hiding Self Toggling (DHST) which directly toggles the pixel value according to the embedded data. However, the random selections of pixels degrade the quality of stego image. To improve the visual quality, Fu and Au [10] proposed a data-hiding method named Data Hiding Pair Toggling (DHPT) which randomly chooses a pair of pixels to be toggled in order to preserve the local intensity. Furthermore, Fu and Au [8] proposed a modified technique, Data Hiding by Smart Pair Toggling (DHSPT), which achieves the best quality by choosing the minimum connection toggled pixels after data embedding. In [13], Guo further improved the pair toggling method and proposed a method named Pair Toggling with Human Visual System (PTHVS) which can determine the optimum toggled pixel. To improve the embedded capacity, Guo and Zhang [16] proposed a block-based method which employs the Grouping Index Matrix (GIM) to embed secret messages by changing pixels in pairs. The previous halftone image data hiding schemes only focus on improving the visual imperceptibility and embedding capacity.

However, these methods ignore the statistical security against steganalyzers. With the development of the steganalysis techniques, the statistical security is also an important criterion for data hiding schemes. The high undetectability of the secret messages can reduce the suspicion from attackers and thus enhance the security. To this end, Xue et al. [30] proposed a halftone image steganography based on minimizing the distortion of texture structure. They introduced the concept of dispersion degree (DD) which can measure the complexity of the region texture in halftone images. Although the previous DD method can improve the statistical security, the stego halftone images still can be detected easily with the state-of-the-art steganalysis techniques.

In this paper, we proposed a secure halftone image steganographic scheme focusing on both visual quality and the statistical security of anti-steganalysis. As a specific kind of binary image, halftone image has its own unique characteristics. In halftone images, the structural correlation between the local regions is more significant than the value of a single pixel and the textures smoothness and connectivity are less important than ordinary binary images. To this end, we first introduced an objective halftone image quality evaluation named halftone structural similarity (HSSIM) based on a human visual system obtained by Least-Mean-Square (LMS) methods [13,14,29]. Visual distortions caused by embedding messages include structural distortions and non-structural distortions. Structural distortions are the ones that affect the most the perception of degradation of an halftone image, whereas non-structural distortions only slightly affect the perception of degradation. Utilizing the HSSIM, we can distinguish structural distortions from non-structural distortions and assign different distortion scores to different kinds of distortions. In this way, we design a novel distortion measurement based on halftone image structural similarity. To play the advantage of the distortion measurement, syndrome-trellis code (STC) is employed in the embedding process. The experimental results have demonstrated that the proposed steganographic scheme can achieve high statistical security with good visual quality without degrading the embedding capacity.

The rest of this paper is organized as follows. Section 2 introduces the definition of halftone image structural similarity (HSSIM) which is based on a human visual system and develops the construction of distortion map for STC. In Sect. 3, the proposed steganographic scheme is presented. In Sect. 4, experimental results about visual quality and the statistical security are presented. Finally, the conclusion of this paper is given in Sect. 5.

2   The Proposed Method

In this section, halftone structural similarity (HSSIM) is introduced based on a human visual system obtained by Least-Mean-Square (LMS) approach. Utilizing the HSSIM, a distortion measurement is proposed to evaluate the embedding distortions on both vision and statistics. To realize the high embedding capacity and minimize the visual distortion, syndrome-trellis code (STC) is employed in embedding process.

2.1   Halftone Image Structural Similarity

To evaluate the visual quality of halftone images, we define the halftone image structural similarity (HSSIM) in this paper. For a cover halftone image C and a stego halftone image S with size $P \times Q$, the corresponding inverse halftone image X and Y can be obtained by utilizing the human visual filter ω, which are defined as:

$$x_{i,j} = \sum_{m=-M/2}^{M/2} \sum_{n=-N/2}^{N/2} \omega_{m,n} c_{i+m,j+n} \qquad (1)$$

$$y_{i,j} = \sum_{m=-M/2}^{M/2} \sum_{n=-N/2}^{N/2} \omega_{m,n} s_{i+m,j+n} \qquad (2)$$

where the variables $c_{i,j} \in C$ and $s_{i,j} \in S$ denote the values of the cover halftone image and the stego halftone image, the variables $x_{i,j} \in X$ and $y_{i,j} \in Y$ denote the values of the corresponding inverse halftone images and $\omega_{m,n}$ denotes the coefficient of the human visual filter with size $M \times N$.

In this way, HSSIM between the cover halftone image C and the stego halftone image S can be defined as follows:

$$HSSIM(C,S) = SSIM(X,Y) = (l(X,Y))^\alpha (c(X,Y))^\beta (s(X,Y))^\gamma \qquad (3)$$

where $l(X,Y)$, $c(X,Y)$ and $s(X,Y)$ denote the luminance function, contrast function and structure function of inverse halftone image X and Y, respectively, which are defined as follows:

$$l(X,Y) = \frac{2\mu_x\mu_y + C_1}{\mu_x^2 + \mu_y^2 + C_1} \qquad (4)$$

$$c(X,Y) = \frac{2\sigma_x\sigma_y + C_2}{\sigma_x^2 + \sigma_y^2 + C_2} \qquad (5)$$

$$s(X,Y) = \frac{\sigma_{xy} + C_3}{\sigma_x\sigma_y + C_3} \qquad (6)$$

where μ_x and μ_y are the mean intensity of X and Y, σ_x and σ_y are the standard deviation of X and Y, σ_{xy} is the covariance between X and Y, and C_i is included to avoid instability in the measurements.

When the constant C_3 is set as $C_2/2$, as well as $\alpha = \beta = \gamma = 1$, then HSSIM between C and S can be simplified as:

$$HSSIM(C,S) = SSIM(X,Y) = \frac{(2\mu_x\mu_y + C_1)(2\sigma_{xy} + C_2)}{(\mu_x^2 + \mu_y^2 + C_1)(\sigma_x^2 + \sigma_y^2 + C_2)} \qquad (7)$$

The human visual filter ω can be obtained by psychophysical experiments [27]. The other way to derive uses training set of both pairs of gray-level images and good halftone results of them, such as using error diffusion or ordered dithering to produce the set [13,14,29]. In this paper, we employ the Least-Mean-Square (LMS) approach proposed by Guo et al. [13,14,29]. The LMS is described as follows:

$$\hat{g}_{i,j} = \sum_{m=-M/2}^{M/2} \sum_{n=-N/2}^{N/2} \omega_{m,n} h_{i+m,j+n} \qquad (8)$$

$$e_{i,j}^2 = (g_{i,j} - \hat{g}_{i,j})^2 \qquad (9)$$

$$\frac{\partial e_{i,j}^2}{\partial \omega_{m,n}} = -2e_{i,j} h_{i+m,j+n} \qquad (10)$$

$$\omega_{m,n}^{(k+1)} = \omega_{m,n}^k + \begin{cases} \mu e_{i+m,j+n} h_{i+m,j+n}, & \text{if } \frac{\partial e_{i,j}^2}{\partial \omega_{m,n}} < 0 \\ -\mu e_{i+m,j+n} h_{i+m,j+n}, & \text{if } \frac{\partial e_{i,j}^2}{\partial \omega_{m,n}} > 0 \end{cases} \qquad (11)$$

where $g_{i,j}$ and $h_{i,j}$ are the values of the original gray image and the corresponding halftone image, $e_{i,j}$ is the MSE between $g_{i,j}$ and $\hat{g}_{i,j}$, μ is the adjusting parameter used to control the convergent speed of the LMS optimum procedure, which is set to be 10^{-5} in our experiments. In [13,14,29], Guo et al. only used several gray images and the corresponding halftone images in the training process, which are not sufficient to train an accurate human visual filter. In this paper, to train a more suitable LMS-trained filter for human visual system, we utilize the grayscale images in BossBased-1.01 [1] and the corresponding halftone images generated by Floyd error diffusion [7]. For reducing the overall computational complexity, the LMS-trained filter of size 7×7 is employed, which is shown as Fig. 1. With the LMS-trained filter, the structural similarity between the cover halftone image and the stego halftone image can be evaluated by HSSIM which is an objective halftone image quality evaluation method.

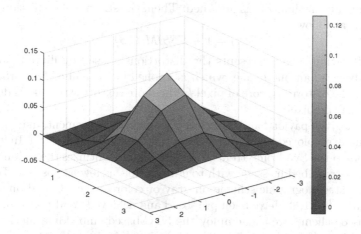

Fig. 1. LMS-trained human visual filter (7×7).

2.2 Distortion Measurement for STC

In this section, based on the HSSIM introduced in Sect. 2.1, we propose a distortion measurement to evaluate the embedding distortions. Different from multitone images, halftone images require only 1 bit per pixel compared with 8 bits per gray pixel or 24 bits per color pixel. Therefore, halftone image data hiding can only embed data by flipping pixels from black to white and vice versa. Compared with the common ±1 embedding operation in grayscale images, flipping pixels arbitrarily in halftone images destroys the texture structure, which leads to significant visual distortions without considering the image content. Thus, distortion measurement is indispensable to evaluate the influence caused by flipping pixels.

In halftone images, the structural correlation between the local regions is more significant than the value of a single pixel. Embedding messages into halftone images will caused different kinds of distortion including structural distortions and non-structural distortions. Structural distortions are the ones that affect the most the perception of degradation of an halftone image, whereas non-structural distortions only slightly affect the perception of degradation.

To minimize the visual distortion and improve the statistical security, the original texture structure should be maintained as much as possible. HSSIM can evaluate the structural similarity between cover halftone image and stego halftone image, based on which, we can minimize the destruction of the association between local regions. Higher structural similarity means less embedding distortion and more the original texture structure can be maintained. It should be noticed that the value of HSSIM is in range of $[0, 1]$. The higher the value of HSSIM, the more similar the structure between two halftone images and when the two images are exactly the same, the value of HSSIM is equal to 1. To this end, given a cover halftone image C, one pixel (denoted as pixel k) is flipped to embed one bit data and a stego halftone image S is obtained. Then, the structural distortion of pixel k is defined as follow:

$$D(k) = 1 - HSSIM(C,S) \tag{12}$$

The distortion score represents the distortions caused by flipping one pixel individually in a halftone image, which is applied in the embedding procedures. The higher the distortion score of pixel k, the more texture structure is destroyed after flipping the pixel.

With the given payload and designed distortion measurement, matrix embedding is usually employed to minimize the total embedding distortion. In [6], Filler et al. proposed the Syndrome-trellis code (STC) which utilizes the redundancy of cover carrier to embed message with toggling pixels as few as possible. Based on STC, many steganographic scheme on gray or color images [6] and on ordinary binary images [4,31,32] have been proposed and achieved good performances. In the proposed scheme, we also employ the STC-based embedding method and a single pixel in halftone image is used as STC's carrier.

3   General Framework of Embedding and Extraction

Based on the proposed distortion measurement and STC-based embedding, the steganographic scheme is constructed in this Section. The embedding and extraction procedures are shown in Figs. 2 and 3, respectively.

3.1   Embedding Procedure

For a given cover halftone image C with size $P \times Q$ and the secret message m, the embedding procedure contains the following steps:

1. Calculate the structural distortion D for each pixel in C by using Eq. (12);
2. Reshape C into an one-dimensional vectors with a random scrambling, donated as V_C;
3. Reshape D into an one-dimensional vectors with a same random scrambling, donated as V_D, which can preserve the mapping relationships between pixels and distortion scores;
4. Employ the STC encoder with V_C, V_D and secret message m, then obtain a one-dimensional stego vector V_S;
5. Descramble and reshape V_S into the size $P \times Q$. In this way, the stego image S is obtained.

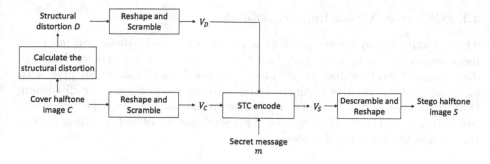

Fig. 2. The framework of embedding procedure.

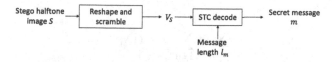

Fig. 3. The framework of extraction procedure.

3.2 Extraction Procedure

In the extraction procedure, the length of the secret message l_m and the random scrambling seed used in the embedding procedure are needed. Given a stego halftone image S of size $P \times Q$, the extraction of secret message m is detailed as follows:

1. Reshape S into an one-dimensional vector with a scrambling via the same seed using in embedding, denoted as V_S.
2. Employ the STC decoder with V_S and l_m. The secret message m is obtained.

4 Experiments and Results

It should be noticed that there is no commonly used halftone image dataset. To construct a suitable halftone image dataset, we convert the grayscale images in BossBase-1.01 [1] to halftone images by Floyd error diffusion method [7]. To demonstrate the high performance and effectiveness of the proposed scheme, some experiments have been conducted, including objective visual imperceptibility comparison and the statistical security comparison. Some classical halftone image data hiding schemes including DHSPT [9], PTHVS [13], GIM [16] and DD [30] are employed for comparison. The DHSPT chooses the minimum connection toggled pixels after data embedding for better visual quality. The PTHVS improves DHSPT by employing a visual distortion measurement to evaluate the candidate slave pixels in a local region. The GIM is a matrix embedding method based on group index matrix to enlarge the embedding capacity. The DD introduces the concept of dispersion degree to measure the complexity of the region texture in halftone images.

4.1   Objective Vision Imperceptibility

The objective vision imperceptibility is evaluated by some distortion measurement approaches proposed in [9] based on the human visual perception. The distortions of halftone images are mainly in the form of salt-and-pepper artifacts due to local clusters of pixels. Large clusters are visually more disturbing than small ones. Thus Fu and Au [9] measure the amount and the size of the salt-and-pepper clusters to evaluate the visual quality of halftone images and they define the following five scores:

$$S_1 = \sum_{i=0}^{4} N_i \tag{13}$$

$$S_2 = \sum_{i=0}^{4} (i+1)N_i \tag{14}$$

$$S_3 = \frac{S_2}{S_1} \tag{15}$$

$$S_4 = \sum_{i=2}^{4} N_i \tag{16}$$

$$S_5 = \sum_{i=0}^{4} iN_i = S_2 - S_1 \tag{17}$$

where the N_i is the total number of the flipping pixels having i neighbors with same pixel values in the 4-neighborhood. The S_1 is the total number of the flipping pixels which are the black pixels in bright region (denoted as class A) and the white pixels in dark region (denoted as class B). The S_2 is the total area covered by the clusters with class A and class B. The S_3 is the average area per cluster. The S_4 is the number of flipping pixels associated with clusters of size 3 or more. The S_5 is a perceptual measure with a linear penalty model, which gives a zero penalty score to isolated black or white pixels which look visually pleasing.

In general, the smaller scores of S_1, S_2, S_3, S_4, S_5 are, the better visual quality the halftone image is. As shown in Table 1, the average scores except S_3 are the smallest among various schemes on the constructed halftone images dataset. The S_3 gives the average area per cluster, which can evaluate the size of salt-and-pepper artifacts because the distortion in halftone image is always exhibited in the form of salt-and-pepper artifacts due to local clusters of pixels. However, pixel clusters also represent texture content in halftone images. Therefore, the experimental result still can demonstrate that the proposed scheme has good performance on objective vision imperceptibility.

Table 1. Average scores (S_1 to S_5) of various schemes on the halftone images dataset with 1024 bits embedded.

	S_1	S_2	S_3	S_4	S_5
Proposed	**126.7**	**420.1**	3.315	**106.16**	**245.9**
DD [30]	385.3	1160.9	**3.013**	269.6	803.2
PTHVS [13]	676.5	2371.5	3.441	533.7	1695.0
DHSPT [9]	786.9	2432.8	3.107	468.2	1645.9
GIM [16]	683.6	2198.5	3.216	398.3	1514.9

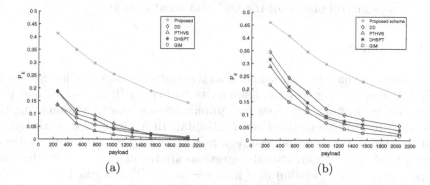

(a)   (b)

Fig. 4. The statistical security comparison of different steganographic schemes. The utilized steganalyzers are (a) PMMTM-320D [5], (b) RLCM-100D [3].

4.2 Statistical Security Comparisons

The undetectability of stego images indicates the statistical security of corresponding steganographic schemes. There have been a number of papers discussing binary image steganalysis [3,5]. Since halftone image is a special kind of binary image, we can employ these binary image steganalysis methods to evaluate the performance of our steganographic scheme. The PMMTM-320D features [5] capture the dependence on texture structures to describe the embedding distortions. The RLCM-100D features [3] employ high-order difference images and extract the run length and co-occurrence matrices as features. The number following each feature name is the dimension of the corresponded feature. These features are sent into soft-margin SVMs with an optimized Gaussian kernel to construct the steganalyzers. The detection performance is measured by the decision error rate P_E defined as follow:

$$P_E = \frac{1}{2}(P_{F_p} + P_{F_n}) \qquad (18)$$

where P_{F_p} is the probabilities of false positive (detecting cover as stego) and P_{F_n} is the probabilities of false negative (detecting stego as cover).

Figure 4 illustrates the statistical security comparisons averaged over 50 random training/testing divisions (half for training and a half for testing) of the constructed halftone image dataset. It can be observed that the statistical security of the proposed scheme is higher than the others, which intuitively demonstrates that the proposed scheme is effective, and the statistical security is significantly improved. The features of PMMTM focus on the correlations between patterns in different shapes and sizes and the features of RLCM focus on the changes of run-length and co-occurrence in local regions. To improve the statistical security, the proposed steganography scheme minimizes the structural distortions and maintains the structural correlations between texture regions. Therefore, the proposed steganographic scheme has the better performance in statistical security. It is worth mentioning that as the embedding payload increases, the proposed scheme still maintains the high statistical security.

5   Conclusions

In this paper, we have introduced an objective halftone image quality evaluation HSSIM to evaluate the structural similarity between halftone images and proposed a secure halftone image steganographic scheme based on minimizing the embedding distortion measured by the HSSIM. In halftone images, the structural correlation between the local regions is more significant than the value of a single pixel. Thus the structural distortions are the ones that affect the most the perception of degradation of a halftone image. HSSIM can help us evaluate the structural similarity between cover halftone image and stego halftone image. Based on HSSIM, we proposed a novel distortion measurement, which can help us minimize the structural distortions after embedding messages. To play the advantage of the distortion measurement, syndrome-trellis code (STC) is employed in the embedding process. The experimental results have demonstrated that the proposed steganographic scheme can achieve high statistical security with good visual quality without degrading the embedding capacity.

In the further research, we will further focus on the visual quality and statistical security in halftone image steganography. Our aim is to reveal the deep relationship between them to design a better steganographic scheme and improve the performance.

Acknowledgements. This work is supported by the National Natural Science Foundation of China (No. U1736118), the Key Areas R&D Program of Guangdong (No. 2019B010136002), the Key Scientific Research Program of Guangzhou (No. 201804020068), the Natural Science Foundation of Guangdong (No. 2016A030313350), the Special Funds for Science and Technology Development of Guangdong (No. 2016KZ010103), Shanghai Minsheng Science and Technology Support Program (17DZ1205500), Shanghai Sailing Program (17YF1420000), the Fundamental Research Funds for the Central Universities (No. 17lgjc45).

References

1. Bas, P., Filler, T., Pevn, Y.T.: Break our steganographic system: the ins and outs of organizing boss. J. Am. Stat. Assoc. **96**(454), 488–499 (2011)

2. Bayers, B.: An optimum method for two level rendition of continuous tone pictures. In: Proceedings of the IEEE International Communication Conference, pp. 2611–2615 (1973)
3. Chiew, K.L., Pieprzyk, J.: Binary image steganographic techniques classification based on multi-class steganalysis. In: Kwak, J., Deng, R.H., Won, Y., Wang, G. (eds.) ISPEC 2010. LNCS, vol. 6047, pp. 341–358. Springer, Heidelberg (2010). https://doi.org/10.1007/978-3-642-12827-1_25
4. Feng, B., Lu, W., Sun, W.: Secure binary image steganography based on minimizing the distortion on the texture. IEEE Trans. Inf. Forensics Secur. 10(2), 243–255 (2014)
5. Feng, B., Lu, W., Sun, W.: Binary image steganalysis based on pixel mesh Markov transition matrix. J. Vis. Commun. Image Represent. 26(C), 284–295 (2015)
6. Filler, T., Judas, J., Fridrich, J.: Minimizing additive distortion in steganography using syndrome-trellis codes. IEEE Trans. Inf. Forensics Secur. 6(3), 920–935 (2011)
7. Floyd, R.W., Steinberg, L.: Adaptive algorithm for spatial greyscale. In: Proceedings of SID, pp. 75–77 (1976)
8. Fu, M.S., Au, O.C.: Data hiding by smart pair toggling for halftone images. In: 2000 IEEE International Conference on Acoustics, Speech, and Signal Processing, Proceedings (Cat. No. 00CH37100), vol. 4, pp. 2318–2321. IEEE (2000)
9. Fu, M.S., Au, O.C.: Halftone image data hiding with intensity selection and connection selection. Signal Process. Image Commun. 16(10), 909–930 (2001)
10. Fu, M.S., Au, O.C.: Data hiding watermarking for halftone images. IEEE Trans. Image Process. 11(4), 477–484 (2002)
11. Fu, M.S., Au, O.C.L.: Data hiding in halftone images with parity coding. In: Security and Watermarking of Multimedia Contents III, vol. 4314, pp. 360–369. International Society for Optics and Photonics (2001)
12. Goyal, P., Gupta, M., Staelin, C., Fischer, M., Shacham, O., Allebach, J.P.: Clustered-dot halftoning with direct binary search. IEEE Trans. Image Process. 22, 473–487 (2013)
13. Guo, J.M.: Improved data hiding in halftone images with cooperating pair toggling human visual system. Int. J. Imaging Syst. Technol. 17(6), 328–332 (2007)
14. Guo, J.M., Liu, Y.F.: Halftone-image security improving using overall minimal-error searching. IEEE Trans. Image Process. 20(10), 2800–2812 (2011)
15. Guo, J.M., Liu, Y.F., Chang, J.Y.: High efficient direct binary search using multiple lookup tables. In: 2012 19th IEEE International Conference on Image Processing, pp. 813–816. IEEE (2012)
16. Guo, M., Zhang, H.: High capacity data hiding for halftone image authentication. In: Shi, Y.Q., Kim, H.-J., Pérez-González, F. (eds.) IWDW 2012. LNCS, vol. 7809, pp. 156–168. Springer, Heidelberg (2013). https://doi.org/10.1007/978-3-642-40099-5_14
17. Jarvis, J.F., Judice, C.N., Ninke, W.H.: A survey of techniques for the display of continuous tone pictures on bilevel displays. Comput. Graph. Image Process. 5(1), 13–40 (1976)
18. Kim, S.H., Allebach, J.P.: Impact of HVS models on model-based halftoning. IEEE Trans. Image Process. 11(3), 258–269 (2002)
19. Knuth, D.E.: Digital halftones by dot diffusion. ACM Trans. Graph. (TOG) 6(4), 245–273 (1987)
20. Lien, B.K., Lan, Z.L.: Improved halftone data hiding scheme using Hilbert curve neighborhood toggling. In: International Conference on Intelligent Information Hiding and Multimedia Signal Processing, pp. 73–76 (2011)

21. Lien, B.K., Pei, W.D.: Reversible data hiding for ordered dithered halftone images. In: IEEE International Conference on Image Processing, pp. 4181–4184 (2009)
22. Lin, C., Lu, W., Huang, X., Liu, K., Sun, W., Lin, H.: Region duplication detection based on hybrid feature and evaluative clustering. Multimedia Tools Appl. **78**(15), 20739–20763 (2019). https://doi.org/10.1007/s11042-019-7342-9
23. Lin, C., et al.: Copy-move forgery detection using combined features and transitive matching. Multimedia Tools Appl. **78**(21), 30081–30096 (2018). https://doi.org/10.1007/s11042-018-6922-4
24. Liu, X., Lu, W., Liu, W., Luo, S., Liang, Y., Li, M.: Image deblocking detection based on a convolutional neural network. IEEE Access **7**, 26432–26439 (2019)
25. Liu, X., Lu, W., Zhang, Q., Huang, J., Shi, Y.Q.: Downscaling factor estimation on pre-JPEG compressed images. IEEE Trans. Circuits Syst. Video Technol. **PP**, 1 (2019)
26. Lu, W., He, L., Yeung, Y., Xue, Y., Liu, H., Feng, B.: Secure binary image steganography based on fused distortion measurement. IEEE Trans. Circuits Syst. Video Technol. **29**, 1608–1618 (2018)
27. Mannos, J., Sakrison, D.: The effects of a visual fidelity criterion of the encoding of images. IEEE Trans. Inf. Theory **20**(4), 525–536 (1974)
28. Mese, M., Vaidyanathan, P.P.: Optimized halftoning using dot diffusion and methods for inverse halftoning. IEEE Trans. Image Process. **9**(4), 691–709 (2000)
29. Pei, S.C., Guo, J.M.: High-capacity data hiding in halftone images using minimal-error bit searching and least-mean square filter. IEEE Trans. Image Process. **15**(6), 1665–1679 (2006)
30. Xue, Y., Liu, W., Lu, W., Yeung, Y., Liu, X., Liu, H.: Efficient halftone image steganography based on dispersion degree optimization. J. Real-Time Image Proc. **16**, 601–609 (2018)
31. Yeung, Y., Lu, W., Xue, Y., Huang, J., Shi, Y.Q.: Secure binary image steganography with distortion measurement based on prediction. IEEE Trans. Circuits Syst. Video Technol. **PP**, 1 (2019)
32. Zhang, J., Lu, W., Yin, X., Liu, W., Yeung, Y.: Binary image steganography based on joint distortion measurement. J. Vis. Commun. Image Represent. **58**, 600–605 (2019)
33. Zhang, X., Allebach, J.P.: Quad-interleaved block level parallel direct binary search algorithm. Electron. Imaging **2016**(20), 1–6 (2016)

A Motion Vector-Based Steganographic Algorithm for HEVC with MTB Mapping Strategy

Mengyuan Guo, Tanfeng Sun[✉], Xinghao Jiang, Yi Dong, and Ke Xu

School of Electronic Information and Electronic Engineering,
Shanghai Jiao Tong University, Shanghai, China
{my.guo,tfsun,xhjiang,aa44,113025816}@sjtu.edu.cn

Abstract. Video is considered an ideal hidden communication cover because of its ample signal space and widespread propagation. In this paper, a novel motion vector-based video steganography algorithm is proposed under the HEVC standard. First, the motion trend of each frame is counted and described by creating a Top-list. According to the motion trend, the Motion Trend Based (MTB) mapping strategy is established between motion vectors and binary bitstream. Finally, the cover is embedded using STC to minimize additional distortion. Experiments are carried out on six original YUV sequences. Performance results demonstrate that our algorithm outperforms previous works in general.

Keywords: Video steganography · Motion vector · HEVC · MTB mapping strategy

1 Introduction

Steganography stems from modern information hiding technology. The video steganography technology has considerable theoretical and practical significance, due to the large signal space of the video cover and common in network transmission.

The existing video steganography methods can be divided into two parts: spatial domain steganography and coding domain steganography. The steganography algorithm in the coding domain can be further divided into prediction mode, motion vector, entropy coding, transformation coefficient, and block mode according to the different types of covers. Due to its high concealment and moderate hiding capacity, motion vector-based hiding has attracted much attention among them. Jing [1] proposed a motion vector concealment algorithm for anti-hiding analysis, which makes the statistical properties of the motion vector population unchanged. Aly [2] proposed to select the motion vector according to the corresponding compression residual size, which can further reduce the distortion. Shanableh et al. [3–7] combined encryption, coding and other technologies to enhance algorithm security. Authors such as Cao [8] used wet paper coding and

© Springer Nature Switzerland AG 2020
H. Wang et al. (Eds.): IWDW 2019, LNCS 12022, pp. 293–306, 2020.
https://doi.org/10.1007/978-3-030-43575-2_25

STC (Syndrome trellis codes) coding for steganography and resisted analysis by maintaining the local optimality of the modified motion vector. Steganography algorithms for H.264/AVC video are now quite mature. However, these methods cannot accommodate the development of High Definition (HD) video.

HEVC (High Efficiency Video Coding) has become a new trend in video covers due to its excellent support for high-definition video in terms of compressed video quality. Although motion vector steganography has many great achievements in the field of H 264, little research has been done in the field of HEVC. Tew [9,10] and Dong et al. [11] studied the intra-pattern steganography algorithm based on HEVC. Chang [12] and Van [13] proposed the DST coefficient concealment algorithm for HEVC standard video earlier. Jiang [14] proposed a CABAC-based video steganography algorithm for HEVC video. Yang [15] and other authors first proposed the information hiding method based on the motion vector for HEVC. These methods extend the scope of video steganography to the HEVC domain. However, some issues are not fully solved in this newly researched region as follows:

(1) Few steganographic algorithms are combined with HEVC, especially using motion vectors as cover.
(2) There are few studies on the steganographic framework in the HEVC field, resulting in insufficient security analysis and performance analysis for steganography.
(3) Both the traditional steganography field and HEVC video steganography have security issues that need to be studied.

In order to solve the issues above, this paper proposes a novel motion vector-based video steganography algorithm for HEVC video, which is mainly used to improve the embedding capacity and video quality. This paper proposes a new MTB mapping strategy, which can maintain the video motion trend constant. The algorithm combines the steganography module with the HEVC coding structure to form an HEVC steganography framework. Besides, the algorithm uses STC for encoding, which guarantees minimum additional distortion and steganography security to some extent. Results of experiments have demonstrated that the proposed algorithm for HEVC video steganography has better performance in embedding capacity and bit rate changing than the method in [15].

2   Proposed Steganographic Strategy

The Steganography algorithm proposed in this paper uses HEVC motion vector as the cover. To ensure the trend of video motion, this paper proposes a new MTB mapping strategy. In this paper, the motion vectors of all PUs in non-merge mode are selected as candidate covers, and the STC method is introduced for minimum distortion, which can further improve the security of the algorithm and reduce the additional distortion.

2.1   Motion Trend Top-List

Video always has a trend of motion between its adjacent frames, and this trend of motion directly represents the change of motion vector in video coding. The motion of video frames is often divided into two types. One is the change of the entire frame, which is usually caused by the relative displacement of the camera and the picture. The other is the change of the small connected area of the frame. Generally, there are many small areas, and the changing trend in each area is also different. The motion trends are shown in Fig. 1.

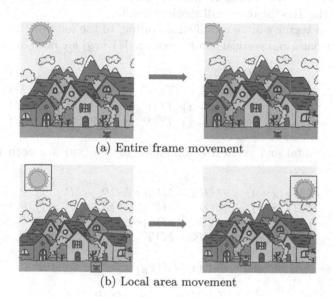

(a) Entire frame movement

(b) Local area movement

Fig. 1. Motion trends of different type

A Top-list of statistical motion vectors is thus constructed to describe the overall distribution trend of the motion vectors. The method for establishing the list is as follows:

step 1: The value and frequency of all horizontal and vertical components of the motion vector in a frame are counted (excluding the component with a value of 0).

step 2: The overall distribution direction of all components is counted as a full-frame trend. Since subsequent embedding only binary embeds the motion vector, the value of this trend $Top_x all$ and $Top_y all$ maybe 1, or -1 for each component to represent the direction of motion. Where x_n and y_n are the horizontal and vertical components of the nth motion vector of a frame.

$$TOP_{xall} = \begin{cases} +1, \cdots\cdots \sum(x_1 + x_2 + ... + x_n) \geqslant 0 \\ -1, \cdots\cdots \sum(x_1 + x_2 + ... + x_n) < 0 \end{cases} \quad (1)$$

$$TOP_{yall} = \begin{cases} +1, \cdots\cdots \sum(y_1 + y_2 + ... + y_n) \geqslant 0 \\ -1, \cdots\cdots \sum(y_1 + y_2 + ... + y_n) < 0 \end{cases} \qquad (2)$$

step 3: Select Top5 of each component as the regional trend and fill in the Top-list.

2.2   MTB Mapping Strategy

For the motion vector in the same frame picture, the mapping strategy and the modification of the candidate motion vector in this frame are determined according to the Top-list of overall motion trend.

The motion vector will be modified according to the following rules:

If the horizontal and vertical components of $MV(xy)$ are both in the Top-list:

$$MV(x',y') = \begin{cases} MV(x+1,y) \ |TOP_x < TOP_y, TOP_x \geqslant MV_x \\ MV(x-1,y) \ |TOP_x < TOP_y, TOP_x < MV_x \\ MV(x,y+1) \ |TOP_x \geqslant TOP_y, TOP_y \geqslant MV_y \\ MV(x,y-1) \ |TOP_x \geqslant TOP_y, TOP_y < MV_y \end{cases} \qquad (3)$$

If the horizontal and vertical components of $MV(xy)$ are both not in the Top-list:

$$MV(x',y') = \begin{cases} MV(x+1,y) \ ||TOP_x - MV_x| \geqslant |TOP_y - MV_y|, TOP_x \geqslant MV_x \\ MV(x-1,y) \ ||TOP_x - MV_x| \geqslant |TOP_y - MV_y|, TOP_x < MV_x \\ MV(x,y+1) \ ||TOP_x - MV_x| < |TOP_y - MV_y|, TOP_y \geqslant MV_y \\ MV(x,y-1) \ ||TOP_x - MV_x| < |TOP_y - MV_y|, TOP_y < MV_y \end{cases} \qquad (4)$$

If only the vertical component of $MV(xy)$ is in the Top-list:

$$MV(x',y') = \begin{cases} MV(x+1,y) \ ||TOP_x \geqslant MV_x \\ MV(x-1,y) \ ||TOP_x < MV_x \end{cases} \qquad (5)$$

If only the horizontal components of $MV(x,y)$ is in the Top-list:

$$MV(x',y') = \begin{cases} MV(x,y+1) \ ||TOP_y \geqslant MV_y \\ MV(x,y-1) \ ||TOP_y < MV_y \end{cases} \qquad (6)$$

Where MVx and MVy are the horizontal and vertical components of the original motion vector, $f(MV_x)$ and $f(MV_y)$ is the position of this component in the Top-list, $MV(x',y')$ is modified alternative embedded motion vector. TOP_x and TOP_y are the value in the Top-list that is closest to the original motion vector.

Figure 2 shows an example of embedding a motion vector. It shows the Top-list of one frame and four motion vector embedding examples that conform to the modification rules. Taking the motion vector $(0,0)$ as an example, both horizontal component 0 and vertical component 0 are not in the Top-list, but the horizontal component 0 is closer to the horizontal component element -1 in the Top-list. Therefore, the value of the horizontal component 0 is shifted

TOP-MVX	TOP-MVY
-1	-31
-56	-15
1	-34
-61	-30
-58	-38

stego data:

(0,0) ->(-1,0)

(1,0) ->(1,-1)

(-52,-20) ->(-53,-20)

(-61,-15) ->(-60,-15)

Fig. 2. An example of embedding motion vector

from -1 to one unit and changed to -1 to obtain the final motion vector $(-1, 0)$. For motion vector $(1, 0)$, because only the horizontal component is in the Top-list, the modified vertical component 0 is closer to the nearest element -15, and the final motion vector $(1, -1)$ is obtained.

Only motion vectors that are not in the merge mode are mapped as alternative motion vectors. It is assumed that the Least Significant Bit (LSB) of cover MV is $X = (x_1, x_2, \cdots, x_n) \in \{0, 1\}^n$, the LSB of corresponding embedded MV is $Y = (y_1, y_2, \cdots, y_n) \in \{0, 1\}^n$. And n represent the length of the cover. If $C = (x_n \oplus y_n) = 1$, it can be judged that the motion vector of the position n is embedded. Then the motion vector $MV(x_n, y_n)$ will use the motion vector $MV(x'_n, y'_n)$ that matches the motion trend change.

2.3 Minimize Distortion Strategy

In the H.264 field, Syndrome-Trellis Codes has become an important way to minimize additive distortion. For defined distortion and a given message length, the STC code minimizes the embedding distortion and allows the receiver to extract the message without synchronizing the distortion information. STC can be expressed as follows:

$$Hx^T = m \tag{7}$$

Where H denotes the parity check matrix generated by the STC algorithm, m is the secret message sequence, and x is the modified cover sequence. Since the MTB mapping strategy in this paper only produces one way of change, this is a binary STC problem. After determining the motion vector that maintains the motion trend, the following equation is used to map them into a binary sequence:

$$c_i = m_i \bmod 2 \tag{8}$$

Where c_i denotes the binary cover and m_i means the original cover.

$$D(X, Y) = \sum_{i=1}^{n} \rho_i |x_i - y_i| \tag{9}$$

Assuming that the embedding operations are independent of each other, the total distortion function is $D(x,y)$. The cost ρ_i is the cost of changing the i th cover element x_i to y_i (i = 1, 2,..., n). As is mentioned above, the main distortion caused for this steganography is D_{SATD}. SATD (Sum of Absolute Transformed Difference) is an image matching algorithm.

$$D_{SATD} = \sum_{xy} |T(P(x,y) - P_{pe}(x,y))| \tag{10}$$

where $T(.)$ represents an orthogonal transform, here a Hadamard transform. $P(.)$ represents the original pixel value, $P_{pe}(.)$ represents the predicted pixel value.

For each motion vector element, the SATD values before and after the change need to be calculated separately. The difference in SATD will be the cost of the motion vector embedding, which will be used in STC coding.

2.4   Security Strategy

At present, the common video motion vector steganalysis algorithms are mainly based on motion vector spatiotemporal correlation statistical property detection and local optimality analysis, etc. The statistical feature detection mainly detects the temporal and spatial correlation of the embedded motion vector and the disturbance caused by the neighborhood correlation. The local optimality analysis uses SAD (Sum Of Absolute Difference) and SATD as distortion metrics to detect local optimal features of the motion vector.

In the proposed algorithm, the MTB mapping strategy can ensure that the temporal and spatial correlation of motion vectors tends to be minimal, thus resisting the detection of spatiotemporal correlation statistics. In addition, since the STC algorithm uses SATD as a parameter to minimize distortion, it is guaranteed that the modification of the embedded sequence minimizes additional SATD distortion. Therefore, the proposed algorithm can resist the steganographic analysis of motion vectors to a certain extent, ensuring the security of steganography.

The motion trend is maintained as much as possible during the mapping and encoding process, and the additional distortion is minimized. Thus the steganography algorithm can minimize the visibility of motion vector variations.

In the STC embedding process and extraction process, the H matrix in Eq. (7) is an essential element, and consistency must be guaranteed in both processes to restore the embedded information. Therefore, the H matrix is equivalent to the key of the encryption process, and the STC process is similar to the symmetric encryption method. This further guarantees the security of steganography.

3   A New Steganography Framework in HEVC

3.1   HEVC Embedding and Coding Integration Framework

Since video is essentially a series of highly correlated frames, inter-frame prediction can effectively utilize temporal correlation to reduce redundancy in video coding, thereby efficiently storing and transmitting video. HEVC eliminates temporal redundancy through ME (Motion Estimation) and MC (Motion Compensation) techniques. The interframe coding structure in HEVC video is shown in the upper part of Fig. 3.

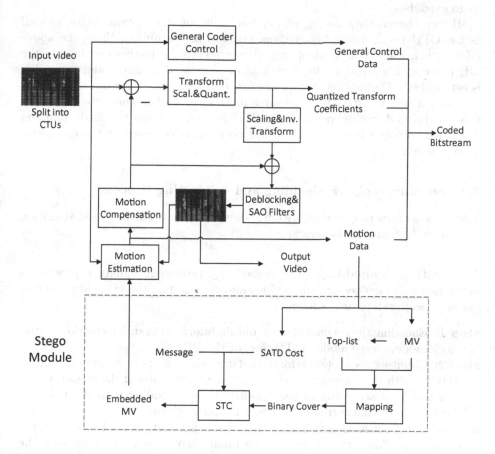

Fig. 3. Integrated steganographic coding framework

The motion vector is a product obtained in the ME phase. ME quickly and efficiently obtains sufficiently accurate motion vectors. Since the proposed steganography algorithm uses motion vector as the cover, we need to fuse the steganography module with the HEVC coding structure and introduce a new integrated steganographic coding framework.

This is an abstract and abbreviated framework of the proposed steganographic algorithm, as shown in Fig. 3. The acquisition of motion vector, SATD Cost, and the replacement of Embedded motion vector occur respectively in different stages of the coding framework. Two motion vector prediction techniques are used in HEVC: merge and AMVP (Advanced Motion Vector Prediction). The merge creates a motion vector candidate list for the current PU, traverses the motion vectors in the list and selects the one with the lowest rate-distortion as the optimal MV. The motion vectors of the merge mode PU will be the same as the motion vector of its neighbor and are not suitable for embedding. Therefore, the proposed method selects the motion vector of the non-merge mode as stego candidate.

Before the entropy coding phase, the value of the motion vector as well as the CTU Data, merge information, etc. are first acquired. Using the above information, the SATD Cost of motion vectors can be further obtained in the ME process. Then the motion vector of one frame is counted, and a Top-list is established. The motion vectors are mapped to a binary stream using MTB mapping strategy. After that, the same method is used to calculate the SATD Cost of changed motion vectors. The STC is used to make the final minimum distortion coding. Finally, the video will be re-encoded based on the embedded motion vector.

3.2   Steganographic Embedding and Extracting Process

The process of the proposed algorithm is shown in Fig. 4. The proposed algorithm can be implemented as follows.

Information Embedding: The embedding process is mainly a process of extracting a motion vector from a video and re-encoding the video after modification. Specific steps are as follows:

step 1: Encoding the original video to obtain information such as motion vector, block mode, merge mode, SATD, etc. of the PU
step 2: Counting the motion information of a frame, and create a motion vector Top-list with the strategy in Sect. 2.1. The modification of the motion vector is determined according to the Top-list. By re-encoding with the modified motion vector, the corresponding SATD cost is obtained.
step 3: Filter out motion vectors in the non-merge mode of one frame. Map the original candidate motion vector to a binary sequence as the cover with the MTB mapping strategy in Sect. 2.2.
step 4: Carry out the STC operation to get the embedded bitstream, and further obtain the embedded motion vector sequence. The distortion function is as the minimize distortion strategy in Sect. 2.3.
step 5: Re-encode the video based on the embedded motion vector sequence. Replace the best motion vector and motion vector candidate list in the ME process with the embedded motion vector.

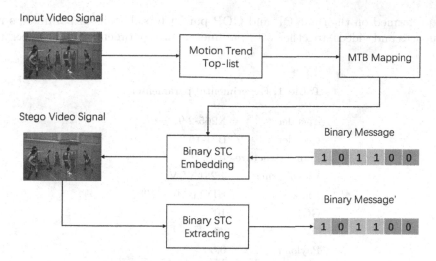

Fig. 4. Process of proposed algorithm

Information Extracting: The extraction process is the opposite of the embedding process, and the ciphertext needs to be extracted from the binary sequence into which the motion vector is mapped. The extracting algorithm can be implemented as follows.

step 1: Decode the steganographic video and obtain the motion vector and block mode, merge mode, etc. according to the same filtering rules as to when it was embedded.
step 2: Map motion vectors in one frame to binary sequences using the LSB of horizontal and vertical components.
step 3: Extract the message from the binary sequence using the STC extraction tool. Make sure that the H matrix used in the STC extraction is consistent with the embedding process.

4 Experiments and Analysis

4.1 Experiment Setting

The experiment of the proposed algorithm is based on the X265 encoder and HEVC reference software decoder. In order to reflect the superior compression characteristics of HEVC on HD video, six YUV sequences with resolution 1920 × 1080 *(BasketballDrive, BQTerrace, Cactus, Kimono1, ParkScene, and Tennis)* used in [15] are selected in this experiment. The shortest video has 240 frames, and the longest video has 600 frames. The video frame encoding sequence structure is IPP..., the GOP is 10, and the QP is 20. Syndrome-Trellis Codes Toolbox is used as the STC embedder. Experiment and comparative experiment are performed on the same QP and GOP parameters. Details of parameters in sequences and videos, together with parameters in experiments could be seen in Table 1.

Table 1. Experimental paramenter

Encoder	X265-2.9
Decoder	HM-16.2
Frame structure	IPP...
Video format	4:2:0 YUV
Video size	HD (1920 × 1080)
GOP	10
QP	20
Payload	0.5

The experiments compare the effects of steganography on video quality and embedding efficiency. This paper tested the performance of multiple payloads and ultimately decided to use the payload of 0.5, which can achieve a better result. Similarly, Yang's method uses the payload of 1, that is, all the motion vector satisfying the conditions in [15] are chosen.

4.2 Embedded Capacity Comparison

This paper calculates the total number of bits of secret messages embedded in each video and compares them with Yang's method [15].

Table 2 presents a comparison of the embedded capacity of six test video sequences. It can be seen that the embedding capacity of the proposed algorithm is directly proportional to the payload. The proposed algorithm has a higher embedding capacity than Yang's for all three payloads. Yang's method has an average video embedding capacity of 193,071 and an average frame embedding capacity of 485. The proposed algorithm has an average video embedding capacity of 667,910, which is 245.94% higher than Yang's method. The average frame embedding capacity is 1,599 bits, which is 229.69% higher than Yang's.

Overall, the proposed algorithm is much higher than Yang's method in the total embedding bits and average frame embedding bits, which proves that the proposed algorithm is effective in improving the embedding capacity.

Table 2. Embedding capacity (bits) of six video sequences

Video sequences	Yang's [15]	AFEC[a]	Proposed	AFEC
Tennis	89530	373.04	216662	902.76
Kimono1	114084	475.35	293594	1223.31
ParkScene	119227	496.78	418884	1745.35
Cactus	251347	502.69	871195	1742.39
BQTerrace	325998	543.33	1300984	2168.31
BasketballDrive	258238	516.48	906144	1812.29
Average	193071	485	667910	1599

[a]AFEC is an abbreviation for Average Frame Embedding Capacity.

4.3 Video Bit Changing Rate Comparison

The video bit changing rate is defined as the ratio of the difference between the number of video bits after steganography and the number of original video bits to the original video size per embedded 100,000 bits.

For a steganography method, which embeds m (100,000) bits, the size of the video before embedding is x, and the size after embedding is y. The bit changing rate $C = (y - x)/mx$. The smaller the result, the smaller the effect of steganography on the size of the video file.

In Table 3, it presents a comparison of the video bit changing rate of six test video sequences with Yang's method.

Table 3. Video bit changing rate (%) of six video sequences

Video sequences	Yang's [15]	Proposed
Tennis	3.10	0.75
Kimono1	2.81	0.75
ParkScene	2.73	0.79
Cactus	0.46	0.17
BQTerrace	0.38	0.11
BasketballDrive	0.0076	0.0019
Average	1.58	0.43

It can be seen that all the six video sequences have lower video bit changing rate than Yang's method. The average video bit changing rate of the proposed algorithm is 0.43%, which is 72.78% lower than Yang's method with the number of 1.58%.

Therefore, it shows that the proposed algorithm can make minor changes to the video file with the same embedding capacity, and it has better performance in reducing the bit changing rate.

4.4 Video Quality Performance

Commonly used video quality assessment criteria can be divided into subjective and objective tests. First, subjective judgments are launched on video sequences. Figure 5 shows a visual comparison of the original and video frames at different embedding payloads of this algorithm for Tennis and Kimono1. It can be seen that none of three embedding payloads adversely affects the subjective visual effects of the frame. Therefore, the proposed algorithm does not have a visual impact on the video quality in subjective judgment.

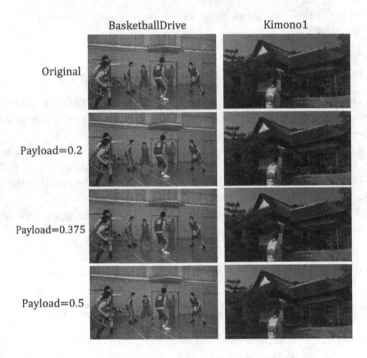

Fig. 5. Visual comparison of the original and hidden frame

Then the PSNR and SSIM metrics of the video are statistically evaluated. Table 4 shows the averages PSNR and SSIM for all frames of the six video sequences. The value of SSIM is approximately close to 1, indicating that the distortion of the frame is smaller. The larger the PSNR value, the smaller the distortion. Moreover, the PSNR higher than 40 dB indicates that the frame quality is excellent, that is, very close to the original frame.

It can be seen that for all video sequences tested experimentally, the PSNR of the proposed algorithm is much higher than 40 dB, although slightly lower than Yang's. The SSIM value exceeds 0.98, which is the same as Yang's method. This indicates that the quality of the video is not significantly affected after embedding using the steganographic algorithm in this paper. The video frame

Table 4. Analysis of video quality

Video sequence	Yang's [15]		Proposed	
	PSNR (dB)	SSIM	PSNR (dB)	SSIM
Tennis	48.71	0.99	47.98	0.99
Kimono1	48.17	0.99	47.67	0.99
ParkScene	46.73	0.99	45.75	0.99
Cactus	45.53	0.98	44.47	0.98
BQTerrace	44.85	0.98	44.39	0.98
BasketballDrive	45.61	0.98	45.21	0.98
Average	46.6	0.985	45.91	0.985

has almost no distortion. Therefore, in terms of video quality, the proposed algorithm performs as well as Yang's method.

5   Conclusion

This paper proposes a steganography method based on motion vector for HEVC video. This paper establishes a Top-list of motion vectors to represent the motion trend and proposes a new motion vector to the binary sequence MTB mapping strategy to reduce the impact of embedding on motion trends. In the embedding phase of the motion vector, STC is used to ensure minimum distortion. The proposed algorithm improves the embedding capacity and bit changing rate on the basis of ensuring that the video quality and video files are not greatly affected.

In future work, there is still room for improvement in the selection and mapping methods of motion vectors, as well as the definition of distortion functions.

Acknowledgment. This work is funded by National Natural Science Foundation of China (Grant No. 61771270, 61572320 & 61572321). It is also supported by National Key Research and Development Projects of China (2018YFC0830700, 2018YFC0831405) and Zhejiang Provincial Natural Science Foundation of China (LR20F020001).

References

1. Jing, H., He, X., Han, Q., Niu, X.: Motion vector based information hiding algorithm for H.264/AVC against motion vector steganalysis. In: Pan, J.-S., Chen, S.-M., Nguyen, N.T. (eds.) ACIIDS 2012. LNCS (LNAI), vol. 7197, pp. 91–98. Springer, Heidelberg (2012). https://doi.org/10.1007/978-3-642-28490-8_10
2. Aly, H.A.: Data hiding in motion vectors of compressed video based on their associated prediction error. IEEE Trans. Inf. Forensics Secur. **6**(1), 14–18 (2011)
3. Shanableh, T.: Matrix encoding for data hiding using multilayer video coding and transcoding solutions. Signal Process. Commun. **27**(9), 1025–1034 (2012)

4. Xu, D., Wang, R., Shi, Y.Q.: Data hiding in encrypted H.264/AVC video streams by codeword substitution. IEEE Trans. Inf. Forensics Secur. **9**(4), 596–606 (2014)
5. Yao, Y., Zhang, W., Yu, N., Zhao, X.: Defining embedding distortion for motion vector-based video steganography. Multimedia Tools Appl. **74**(24), 11163–11186 (2014). https://doi.org/10.1007/s11042-014-2223-8
6. Zhang, Y., Zhang, M., Yang, X., Guo, D., Liu, L.: Novel video steganography algorithm based on secret sharing and error-correcting code for H.264/AVC. Tsinghua ScienceTechnol. **22**(2), 198–209 (2017)
7. Niu, K., Yang, X., Zhang, Y.: A novel video reversible data hiding algorithm using motion vector for H264/AVC. Tsinghua Sci. Technol. **22**(5), 489–498 (2017)
8. Zhang, H., Cao, Y., Zhao, X.: Motion vector-based video steganography with preserved local optimality. Multimedia Tools Appl. **75**(21), 13503–13519 (2015). https://doi.org/10.1007/s11042-015-2743-x
9. Tew, Y., Wong, K.S.: Information hiding in HEVC standard using adaptive coding block size decision. In: 2014 IEEE International Conference on Image Processing (ICIP), France, Paris, pp. 5502–5506 (2014)
10. Tew, Y., Wong, K.S., Phan, C.W.: HEVC video authentication using data embedding technique. In: IEEE International Conference on Image Processing, Quebec City, Canada, pp. 1265–1269 (2015)
11. Dong, Y., Jiang, X., Sun, T., Xu, D.: Coding efficiency preserving steganography based on HEVC steganographic channel model. In: Kraetzer, C., Shi, Y.-Q., Dittmann, J., Kim, H.J. (eds.) IWDW 2017. LNCS, vol. 10431, pp. 149–162. Springer, Cham (2017). https://doi.org/10.1007/978-3-319-64185-0_12
12. Chang, P.C., Chung, K.L., Chen, J.J., Lin, C.H., Lin, T.J.: An error propagation free data hiding algorithm in HEVC intra-coded frames. In: Signal and Information Processing Association Summit and Conference, Kaohsiung, Taiwan, pp. 1–9 (2013)
13. Van, L.P., De Praeter, J., Van Wallendael, G., Cock, J.D., Walle, R.V.D.: Out-of-the-loop information hiding for HEVC video. In: IEEE International Conference on Image Processing, Quebec City, Canada, pp. 3610–3614 (2015)
14. Jiang, B., Yang, G., Chen, W.: A CABAC based HEVC video steganography algorithm without bitrate increase. J. Comput. Inf. Syst. **11**(6), 2121–2130 (2015)
15. Yang, J., Li, S.: An efficient information hiding method based on motion vector space encoding for HEVC. Multimedia Tools Appl. **77**(10), 11979–12001 (2017). https://doi.org/10.1007/s11042-017-4844-1

New Steganalytic Approach for AMR Steganography Based on Block-Wise of Pulse Position Distribution and Neighboring Joint Density

Chen Gong[1,2] and Xianfeng Zhao[1,2]([✉])

[1] State Key Laboratory of Information Security, Institute of Information
Engineering, Chinese Academy of Sciences, Beijing 100093, China
{gongchen,zhaoxianfeng}@iie.ac.cn
[2] School of Cyber Security, University of Chinese Academy of Sciences,
Beijing 100049, China

Abstract. Adaptive multi-rate (AMR) is a popular audio compression
standard, various AMR FCB (Fixed Codebook) steganographic algorithms have been developed and more readily available for the popularity of AMR in mobile communication and mobile Internet, an effective
steganalysis techniques are called for cyber security. In this paper, we
propose a well-designed steganalytic scheme to effectively detect FCB
steganography. For this purpose, we first elaborately to model the pulse
position 2-D arrays formed on the pulses positions. Neighboring joint
density features are constructed based on the intra-block and inter-block
from multi scales and multi directions extracted. Experimental results
show that, our method prominently outperforms the existing FCB based
steganalysis, especially in detecting the STC-based steganographic systems at low embedding rate.

1 Introduction

Steganography is the technology to conceal the very existence of hidden messages
into digital covers such as image, video, audio, speech and document. Steganalysis is the countermeasure technology of steganography used to detect presence
of hidden data in a cover object.

AMR is an ideal carrier that has recently gained increasing attention in the
information hiding community. Due to its extensive usage in mobile communication and considerable coding redundancy. AMR audio codec is a worldwide
speech compression standard for wireless communication transmission, including
3G and 4G. Besides that, such codec is also an audio file format standard with
extension AMR for storing spoken audio recordings, which is the used by various mobile phones as the default audio storage. In addition, most popular social

---

This work was supported by NSFC under 61972390, U1736214 and 61902391, and
National Key Technology R&D Program under 2019QY0700 and 2016QY15Z2500.

H. Wang et al. (Eds.): IWDW 2019, LNCS 12022, pp. 307–321, 2020.
https://doi.org/10.1007/978-3-030-43575-2_26

softwares also adopt AMR as the speech compression format, such as WeChat and QQ. Especially, the frequent interchange of digital speech nowadays makes AMR steganography very promising.

So far research in the field of FCB steganography has become a research hotspot. Many steganographic techniques operating on FCB have been published. In general, AMR is based on algebraic code excited line prediction (ACELP) coding, so there are three feasible embedding domains in AMR codec, including FCB [6,13,17], Liner Prediction Coefficient (LPC) [11,12,19] and Adaptive CodeBook (ACB) [7,9,15]. FCB gained more attention recently for the maximum hidden capacity and good imperceptibility compared with other embedding domains. First, AMR performed on each frame of 20 ms and produces 244 bits code stream at 12.2 kb/s mode, while FCB takes up 140 bits which is a significant proportion ($140/244 = 57.38\%$) of the total bits. Furthermore, FCB is the residual of the speech signal after long-term prediction and short-term, and the search procedure of FCB is the depth-first tree, it means modification of the FCB parameters will introduce slightly degradation of the perceptible. Based on this, several steganographic methods on FCB have emerged.

The existing effective hand-crafted features are extracted from paired pulses [14,16]. These steganalytic features are constructed by the paired pulses in the same track. Miao *et al.* [14] designed a set of features, including Markov transition probabilities, joint entropy and conditional entropy. Ren *et al.* [16] extracted the correlation characteristics based on the probability of the pulse position being the same in the same track (SPP).

Recently, deep learning attracted attentions of the steganalysis research community [8,10,18]. The first deep learning based FCB steganalytic algorithm using RNN combined with CNN (SRCNet) was proposed in [8]. However, the study of deep-learned features still have much room for improvement. First, the performance of in detecting STC-based [5] adaptive FCB steganography [17] (AFA) at low embedding rate is not perfect [8], it indicated that the steganalytic feature cannot be effectively learned by deep networks. Since SRCNet is a fully connected recurrent neural network, the training and testing process of the model will be slowed down with the time length increased. The size of model is dependent on the length of input speech, so that it would directly influences the model's practicability. Moreover, deep learning tools are essentially a black box method since it is not easy to mathematically formulate the features that are learned within its different layers of representation. At the same time, hand-crafted features [14,16] does not consider specific time sequence existing in pulse position, which has been proven in work [8]. Obviously, the advantage of pulse position may not be fully exploited. Therefore, it is still necessary to study and improve hand-crafted steganalytic features. Please remind that, the most successful collaborations is to learn from the each other.

To study this issue, a new set of steganalytic features that not only consider steganography specific FCB artifacts in characteristics of the codewords but also in the property of time serials. We first to model the PP 2-D arrays to formulate features for steganalysis. FCB 2-D arrays which utilize intrablock and interblock correlation among pulses positions are then used to generally enhance changes caused by FCB steganography. Neighboring joint distribution is applied to model all these FCB 2-D arrays for steganalysis. The experimental works are presented to demonstrate that the proposed scheme has outperformed the state-of-the-arts in attacking AFA, Geiser and Miao. The proposed 2-D pulse position model has the characteristic of clear mathematic description, easily calculation and convenient to analysis, which may be useful for further relevant studies. The 2-D mode array may be extended to other embedding domain, such as LPC and ACB.

The rest of paper is organized as follows. In Sect. 2, we briefly introduces the basic knowledge, including the AMR codec, FCB steganography, FCB steganalysis and the analysis of the neighboring joint statistical model on the pulses position distribution caused by information-hiding. The feature construction procedure is presented in Sect. 3. The results of experiments are presented in Sect. 4. Finally, the conclusions and future work are given in Sect. 5.

2   Preliminaries

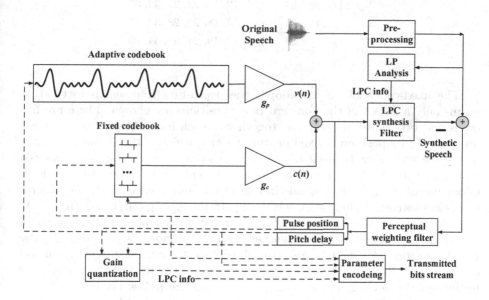

Fig. 1. Block diagram of the AMR encoding.

2.1   AMR Codec

The AMR coder [1] is based on the Algebraic Code Excited Linear Prediction (ACELP). The encoding diagram of ACELP is presented in Fig. 1. The speech codec operates on each speech frames of 20 ms corresponding to 160 samples at a sampling rate of 8000 samples per second. The input speech are represented using 16 bit linear Pulse Code Modulation (PCM). For every 20 ms frame, the input speech is analyzed to extract the parameters of the ACELP, including linear prediction coefficient, adaptive codebook, fixed codebook, gain quantization and so on. In order to determine the optimal synthesized speech signal, a linear prediction synthesis filter is used to synthesize the output signal by filtering the output of the sum of the two excitation vectors from adaptive and fixed codebook. The optimum excitation sequence in a codebook is chosen by minimizing the weighted error which between the original speech and the synthesized speech using a so-called analysis-by-synthesis (ABS) search approach. Finally, the encoded parameters are obtained and transmitted through a public channel.

Table 1. The structure of FCB for AMR at mode 12.2 kbps. i_t and i_{t+5} represent the two pulses in the same track $t(0 \leq t \leq 4)$ respectively.

Track	Pulse	Sign	Position
0	i_0, i_5	±1	0, 5, 10, 15, 20, 25, 30, 35
1	i_1, i_6	±1	1, 6, 11, 16, 21, 26, 31, 36
2	i_2, i_7	±1	2, 7, 12, 17, 22, 27, 32, 37
3	i_3, i_8	±1	3, 8, 13, 18, 23, 28, 33, 38
4	i_4, i_9	±1	4, 9, 14, 19, 24, 29, 34, 39

The fixed-codebook search adopts the depth-first tree search method, it means only a subset of the non-zero pulse positions are chosen. There are five levels and two pulses are searched together in each level. At level 1, i_0 do not need search, its position is fixed on the position which is the global maximum of the reference signals in all tracks. The position of i_1 can then be followed by the four iterations. In each iterations, i_1 is tentatively assigned to the local maximum of the reference signals in one of the four tracks. Next, the other 8 pulses are searched in four levels within a pair: $(i_2, i_3), (i_4, i_5), (i_6, i_7), (i_8, i_9)$. At level 2, pulse i_2 and i_3 are searched in their respective tracks. Pulse i_2 with all 8 candidate positions is tested together with all 8 candidate positions of pulse i_3. The position of i_2 and i_3 are determined once the current target signal was the maximum in all $8 \times 8 = 64$ test combinations. The next of the three levels is the same as level 2. After having determined the pulses positions, FCB is constructed on the interleaved single pulse permutation (ISPP) design. 2 pulses are placed in one track, each pulse has 8 different positions, so there are 10 pulse positions are encoded in a sub-frame. The goal of FCB search is to search 10 pulses' optimal position in 40 candidate position, all 40 positions are divided into 5 tracks of interleaved positions, as shown in Table 1.

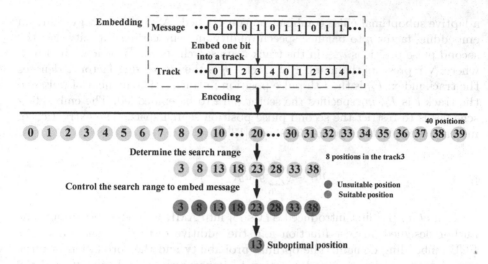

Fig. 2. The embedding process of FCB to embed a binary bit into a track. Here, we embed binary 1 into track 3. The embedding process has 2 mainly steps. First, determine the positions of the last position i_8 in track3 from 40 positions. Second, control the search range to find the suboptimal position from 8 positions.

2.2 FCB Steganography

The principle of the existing schemes of AMR FCB steganography [6,13,17] is to limit the search scope of the last pulse position in each track. As illustrated by the Fig. 2.

Geiser *et al.* [6] designed a steganographic FCB rule for AMR-NB 12.2 kbit/s mode. Assuming that i_t and i_{t+5} respectively represent the first pulse position and the second pulse position in the same track t ($0 \leq t \leq 4$). $(m)_{2k,2k+1}$, ($k \in [0,4]$) is a binary 2 bit message to be embedded into the track t. The two candidates positions for i_{t+5} are calculated by Eq. 1, where $gray$ and $gray^{-1}$ respectively represent the gray encoding and the gray decoding, $\oplus$ is the bitwise exclusive operation of two binary strings, $\lfloor x \rfloor = max\{n \in \mathbb{Z} \mid n \leq x\}$ rounds down x, $\lfloor \frac{i_t}{5} \rfloor$ calculates the 3 bit pulse position index in the track t.

$$i_t = \begin{cases} gray^{-1}(gray(\lfloor \frac{i_{t+5}}{5} \rfloor) \oplus (m)_{0,1}) \cdot 5 + t \\ gray^{-1}(gray(\lfloor \frac{i_{t+5}}{5} \rfloor) \oplus (m)_{0,1} + 4) \cdot 5 + t \end{cases} \tag{1}$$

The embedded 2 bit hidden message $(m)_{2k,2k+1}$, ($k \in [0,4]$) is extracted by Eq. 2.

$$(m)_{2k,2k+1} = (gray(\lfloor \frac{i_t}{5} \rfloor) \oplus gray(\lfloor \frac{i_{t+5}}{5} \rfloor))\%4 \tag{2}$$

Miao *et al.* [13] extended Geiser's FCB steganographic scheme for AMR-WB speech codec. The author implemented message embedding during the FCB search by controlling the pulse positions. Different from [6], Miao introduced an adaptive suboptimal pulse combination constrained (ASOPP) strategy using an embedding factor η to balance speech quality and embedding capacity. For the second pulse positions i_{t+5} in the track t, its search space is restricted by Eq. 3, where N represents the number of tracks. η is the embedding factor. t denotes the track index. P_{t_i} is the i-th pulse position in track t. The number of pulses in the track t is P_t. m_t specifies the secret data to be embedded. The embedding schemes is to restrict the second pulse position search space. The extraction of message are calculated by Eq. 3 as well [13].

$$m_t = (\sum_{i=0}^{P_t} gray(\lfloor \frac{P_{t_i}}{N} \rfloor)) \oplus \eta \qquad (3)$$

Ren *et al.* [17] first introduced STCs [5] into AMR FCB steganography. The author designed an cost function and the additive distortion function in the FCB embedding domain. The optimal probability and the correlation of pulse were introduced into the cost function to improve the speech quality and the statistical security.

3   Feature Construction

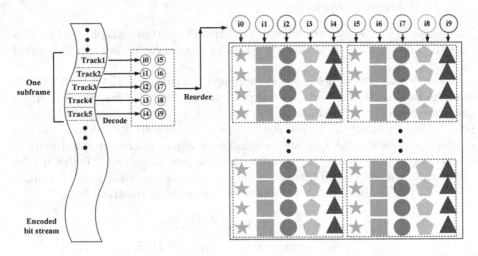

Fig. 3. A sketch of pulses positions 2-D array. A mode (4×5) pulses positions 2-D array in a block, which is denoted with the dotted box. One row for each sub-frame. One sub-frame has 5 tracks, and each frame are divided into 4 sub-frames.

Feature construction is a key step in the steganalysis. As mentioned above, conventional steganorgraphic methods deeply affect distributions of the pulses positions, while the adaptive algorithm AFA have made great efforts to keep the changes on the distributions of the pulses positions caused by information hiding as less as possible. So that, current steganalytic method [3,4,14,16] are not effective in detecting AFA especially at low embedding rate.

In this section, we first define the block-based pulses positions 2-D array, followed by introducing the pulses positions. We then propose to model the pulses positions 2-D array using neighbor joint matrix. Our proposed features are derived from the neighbor joint matrix.

3.1 Pulses Positions 2-D Array

In this part, we first study the property of pulses positions. For a given speech, consider the 2-D array consisting of all the pulses positions. That is, this 2-D array is filled up with the first five pulses in a track, so do the last five pulses, resulting in a 2-D array as shown in Fig. 3. We name this 2-D array as pulses positions 2-D array in this paper. The features proposed in this scheme are formed from the pulses positions 2-D array.

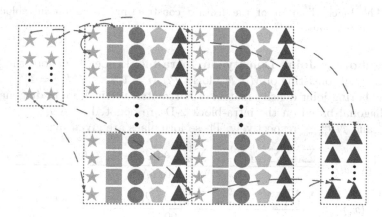

Fig. 4. The generation of intrablock and interblock pulses position 2-D arrays.

3.2 Neighboring Joint Density and Block-Based FCB Feature

We have shown that speech signals have long-term and short-term correlations. To fully exploit this time series correlation, here we construct multi scales and multi directions pulses positions based on neighboring joint density of pulses positions between intrablock and interblock (NJPB). These pulse positions 2-D arrays are shown in Fig. 4. We propose to use both the intrablock and the interblock correlations for steganalysis. The feature extraction procedure can be summarized in Fig. 5.

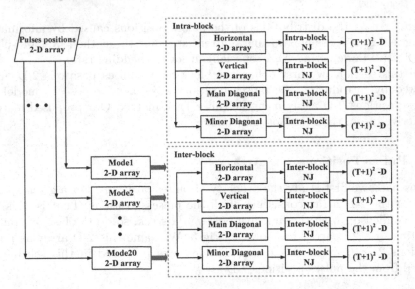

Fig. 5. The block diagram of the feature constructing based on intrablock and interblock correlations.

A. Neighboring Joint Density on Intra-block. Let P denote the pulses positions array consisting of $M \times N$ blocks $P_{ij}, (i = 1, 2, \ldots, M; j = 1, 2, \ldots, N)$. The neighboring joint density matrix of horizontal, vertical, main diagonal, and minor diagonal based on the intra-block 2-D are denoted as NJ_{intra}^h, NJ_{intra}^v, NJ_{intra}^m, and NJ_{intra}^d respectively. These formulaes are given by:

$$NJ_{intra}^h(x,y) = \frac{\sum_{i=1}^{M} \sum_{j=1}^{N} \sum_{m=1}^{9} \sum_{n=1}^{10} \delta \left(Q_{ijmn} = x, Q_{ij(m+1)n} = y \right)}{90MN} \quad (4)$$

$$NJ_{intra}^v(x,y) = \frac{\sum_{i=1}^{M} \sum_{j=1}^{N} \sum_{m=1}^{9} \sum_{n=1}^{10} \delta \left(Q_{ijmn} = x, Q_{ijm(n+1)} = y \right)}{90MN} \quad (5)$$

$$NJ_{intra}^m(x,y) = \frac{\sum_{i=1}^{M} \sum_{j=1}^{N} \sum_{m=1}^{9} \sum_{n=1}^{9} \delta \left(Q_{ijmn} = x, Q_{ij(m+1)(n+1)} = y \right)}{90MN}$$
$$\quad (6)$$

$$NJ_{intra}^d(x,y) = \frac{\sum_{i=1}^{M} \sum_{j=1}^{N} \sum_{m=1}^{9} \sum_{n=1}^{9} \delta \left(Q_{ij(m+1)n} = x, Q_{ijm(n+1)} = y \right)}{90MN}$$
$$\quad (7)$$

where Q_{ijmn} is the pulse position located at the m_{th} row and the n_{th} column in the block P_{ij}; $\delta = 1$ if its arguments are satisfied, otherwise $\delta = 0$; x and y are integers. In our prior detection, the values of x and y are in the range $[0, 7]$, and each NJ_{intra} consists of 64 features. For computational efficiency, we define $NJ_{intra}(x,y)$ as the neighboring joint density features on intra-block, calculated as follows:

$$NJ_{intra}(x,y) = \{NJ_{intra}^h(x,y) + NJ_{intra}^v(x,y) + NJ_{intra}^m(x,y) + NJ_{intra}^d(x,y)\}/4$$
$$\quad (8)$$

B. Neighboring Joint Density on Inter-block. Similarly, the inter-block neighboring joint density matrix on horizontal direction NJ_{inter}^h, the matrix on vertical direction NJ_{inter}^v, the matrix on main diagonal NJ_{inter}^m, and the matrix on minor diagonal NJ_{inter}^d are constructed as follows:

$$NJ_{inter}^h(x,y) = \frac{\sum_{m=1}^{4}\sum_{n=1}^{5}\sum_{i=1}^{M}\sum_{j=1}^{N-1}\delta\left(Q_{ijmn} = x, Q_{(i+1)jmn} = y\right)}{25M(N-1)} \quad (9)$$

$$NJ_{inter}^v(x,y) = \frac{\sum_{m=1}^{4}\sum_{n=1}^{5}\sum_{i=1}^{M-1}\sum_{j=1}^{N}\delta\left(Q_{ijmn} = x, Q_{i(j+1)mn} = y\right)}{25(M-1)N} \quad (10)$$

$$NJ_{inter}^m(x,y) = \frac{\sum_{m=1}^{4}\sum_{n=1}^{4}\sum_{i=1}^{M-1}\sum_{j=1}^{N}\delta\left(Q_{ijmn} = x, Q_{(i+1)(j+1)mn} = y\right)}{16(M-1)(N-1)} \quad (11)$$

$$NJ_{inter}^d(x,y) = \frac{\sum_{m=1}^{4}\sum_{n=1}^{4}\sum_{i=1}^{M-1}\sum_{j=1}^{N}\delta\left(Q_{(i+1)jmn} = x, Q_{i(j+1)mn} = y\right)}{16(M-1)(N-1)} \quad (12)$$

Similarly, the values of x and y are in $[0, 7]$ and each NJ_{inter} has 64 features. We define $NJ_{inter}(x,y)$ as the neighboring joint density features on inter-block, calculated as follows:

$$NJ_{inter}(x,y) = \{NJ_{inter}^h(x,y) + NJ_{inter}^v(x,y) + NJ_{inter}^m(x,y) + NJ_{inter}^d(x,y)\}/4 \quad (13)$$

4 Experiments and Results

To evaluate the detection performance of the proposed NJPB steganalysis method, several experiments are conducted, the results are compared with some state of the art FCB steganalysis method to verify the validity of the proposed model. This section starts with an introduction of the data-set used in this work, followed by the structure and the training details of the model. Then, we evaluate the importance of four kinds of FCB correlations. Finally, we compare the performance of the proposed model and other state of the art FCB steganalysis models under different conditions, including different embedding rates, different durations and so on.

4.1 Setup

The proposed NJPB was primarily evaluated and contrasted on the speech data-set published by Lin *et al.* [10]. This data-set contains 41 h of Chinese speech, 72 h of English speech and different gender. The speech data-set includes different male and female speakers. The origin speech samples have been cut into 100 ms segments. The same length segments are successive and non-overlapped. All the segments are converted from their origin WAV format to PCM format with mono, 8 kHz, 16 bits quantization by FFmpeg. Those segments are used to generate the

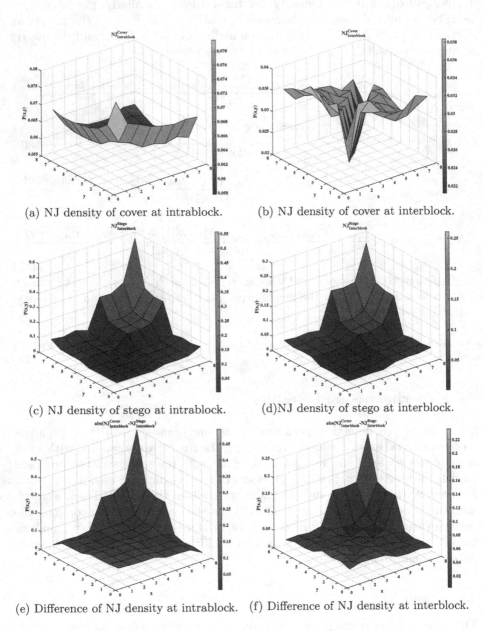

(a) NJ density of cover at intrablock.

(b) NJ density of cover at interblock.

(c) NJ density of stego at intrablock.

(d)NJ density of stego at interblock.

(e) Difference of NJ density at intrablock.

(f) Difference of NJ density at interblock.

Fig. 6. Neighboring joint densities of the pulses positions 2-D arrays and the absolute differences arrays between intrablock and interblock respectively. The samples in this experiment are generated by Geiser method using 300,000 sub-frames, at 12.2 kbit/s mode and 100% embedding rate from 300,000 sub-frames.

cover segment data-set and stego segment data-set respectively. There are three methods involved in the steganographic experiments, Geiser [6], Miao [13] at the modes of η =1, 2 and 3 respectively, one adaptive steganography AFA [17] (with constraint height h = 7 in the STCs). In the experiments, we use the RBR (Relative embedding rate) to denote the embedding ratio, which represents the ratio of length of message m to the length of cover audio n. 20%, 40%, ..., 100% RBR are used to generate the corresponding stego.

The classification accuracy P_A is used to measure the detection performance, which is defined as the proportion of the tested AMR audio correctly classified for each of the categories. The calculation of P_A is shown in (14)

$$P_A = \frac{P_{TP} + P_{TN}}{2} \tag{14}$$

where P_{TP} is the probability of the true positives correctly distinguished, that is the stego samples correctly distinguished, P_{TN} is the probability of the true negatives correctly distinguished, that is the cover samples correctly distinguished. P_A shows the accuracy rate of the steganalysis scheme which is used to detect the tested steganography schemes. Larger values of P_A correspond to better steganalysis and thus more effective detectability but lower security.

For each experiment, randomly chosen 2000 of the samples for training, the remaining 2000 of the samples were used for testing, and we applied those parameters to all later experiments. The number of cover samples and the number of stego are in pair, that is the ratio of cover and stego in all experiments is half and half. Besides that, each experiment picked up the cover and stego samples respectively according to the required language, embedding rate and sample length. In order to compare with other methods, we also conducted the comparison tasks on the two state of the art FCB steganalysis methods: Fast-SPP [16] and MTJCE [14]. We used the soft-margin support vector machines (C-SVM) [2] with Gaussian kernel and default parameters as the classifiers.

4.2 Embedding Effect on Pulses Positions Distributions

In this part, we explored the statistical property of pulses positions and found that, most FCB steganographic systems modify the pulses positions and hence change the correlation of neighboring pulses positions. Specifically, embedding of the message modify the neighboring joint distribution, so that, Markov transition probabilities are affected. Our study also shows that, that Markov approach does not completely represent the neighboring joint relation, that is, it falls short of fully exploring the modification caused by information-hiding. The steganalysis method described in this paper exploits the independence of the stego noise as well. An example of the modification of the joint density is illustrated by Fig. 6. Figure 6(a) and (b) show the cover between intrablock and interblock of the neighboring joint density probability, respectively. (c) and (d) show the stego respectively. Figure 6(e) and (f) are the difference of the intrablock and interblock neighboring joint features respectively. Although Fig. 6(c) and (d) look

Table 2. Detection accuracy (%) of 100 ms samples under different embedding rate for English language at 12.2 kb/s mode. The number in the parentheses indicates a corresponding dimension of the steganalytic feature.

Steganalysis scheme	Steganography scheme	Embedding rate (RBR)				
		0.2	0.4	0.6	0.8	1.0
Fast-SPP (7-D) [16]	AFA [17]	52.90	56.10	60.48	65.19	71.09
	Geiser [6]	77.82	89.82	95.91	98.40	99.62
	Miao ($\eta=1$) [13]	60.58	67.44	71.66	76.78	81.92
	Miao ($\eta=2$) [13]	58.55	65.62	71.77	77.48	81.60
	Miao ($\eta=3$) [13]	58.78	65.24	72.24	76.71	80.74
MTJCE (66-D) [14]	AFA	52.74	56.08	60.97	70.05	78.19
	Geiser	87.82	97.94	99.84	100.00	100.00
	Miao ($\eta=1$)	60.95	72.35	81.94	89.24	94.43
	Miao ($\eta=2$)	58.58	66.40	73.73	80.79	86.00
	Miao ($\eta=3$)	58.55	66.32	73.66	80.08	85.25
NJPB (128-D)	AFA	**52.75**	**57.41**	**63.20**	**74.12**	**84.27**
	Geiser	**96.34**	**99.84**	**99.99**	**100.00**	**100.00**
	Miao ($\eta=1$)	**64.47**	**78.74**	**88.85**	**95.03**	**98.03**
	Miao ($\eta=2$)	**58.73**	**68.27**	**76.00**	**83.41**	**89.02**
	Miao ($\eta=3$)	**59.05**	**67.79**	**76.54**	**83.43**	**89.17**

identical, the neighboring joint densities are different. The differences are given in Fig. 6(c) and (f), indicating that information hiding modifies the neighboring joint density. Figures 6(a) and (c) also demonstrate that the intrablock-based feature is a effective feature to detect FCB steganography.

4.3   Results and Discussion

We use two most related steganalytic feature sets for comparison, Fast-SPP [16] with 7-D features and MTJCE [14] with 66-D features. As the Table 2 shows, the proposed NJBP scheme always achieves the best detection accuracy than Fast-SPP and MTJCE. These experiments results is in accordance with the theoretical analysis. Beside the paired pulse, the intricate correlation which exist among pulse and its neighbouring pulse at different direction is useful.

Since deep learning is different machine learning method such as SVM, we would like to investigate the method utilization and efficiency. On one hand, we compare the detection accuracy of NJBP to deep learning method, SRCNet [8]. On the other hand, we compare the model efficiency. Table 3 shows the performance of each model for different FCB steganography. We can observe that when the payload rate is low, SRCNet is better than NJBP. When the payload rate is high, the advantage in SRCNet is not prominent for AFA, Geiser, and Miao.

Table 3. Detection accuracy (%) of NJPB vs. SRCNet [8] with 100 ms samples under different embedding rate for English language at 12.2 kb/s mode.

Steganalysis scheme	Steganography scheme	RBR				
		0.2	0.4	0.6	0.8	1.0
SRCNet [8]	AFA	52.85	56.95	62.58	74.18	82.13
	Geiser	99.92	100.00	100.00	100.00	100.00
	Miao ($\eta = 1$)	80.80	89.55	93.89	97.06	98.25
	Miao ($\eta = 2$)	68.80	76.08	82.41	85.83	88.29
	Miao ($\eta = 3$)	71.08	75.38	83.16	85.29	89.48
NJPB	AFA	**52.75**	**57.41**	**63.20**	**74.12**	**84.27**
	Geiser	**96.34**	**99.84**	**99.99**	**100.00**	**100.00**
	Miao ($\eta = 1$)	**64.47**	**78.74**	**88.85**	**95.03**	**98.03**
	Miao ($\eta = 2$)	**58.73**	**68.27**	**76.00**	**83.41**	**89.02**
	Miao ($\eta = 3$)	**59.05**	**67.79**	**76.54**	**83.43**	**89.17**

It is interesting to observe NJPB performs slightly better SRCNet for AFA. The features learned by SRCNet is the speech content itself not the feature caused by information hiding. It also indicate that no matter how powerful a learning tool, the primary issue in steganalytic schemes is to design a efficient features.

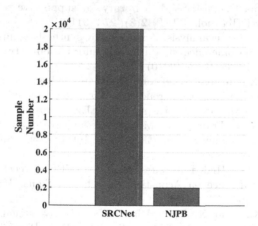

Fig. 7. Training samples comparison.

We also tested the detection efficiency of these two models. The results are shown in Fig. 7. Significant different order of magnitude between the two schemes. The training samples in SRCNet is far more than in the NJPB. However, the collection of training samples is both time consuming and quite costly.

The quantity and quality of enough training samples are important for SRCNet to obtain an accurate classification. For training a deep network, a appropriate training data set has become more important than that of SVM. Detection accuracy is important, but efficiency is equally important. So NJPB is more practical.

5   Conclusion

In this paper, we propose a novel block-based steganalysis method for the FCB steganography. We conducted extensive experimental results to compare the performance of NJPB as well that of two state-of-the-art steganalysis methods known as the Markov method and the Fast-SPP method. Three two steganographic methods under consideration were Geiser, Miao and AFA. The training samples is only one-tenth of SRCNet. These results demonstrate that the proposed NJPB method offers a effective and practical performance for both steganographic methods. In particular, NJPB achieves the significant improvements for detecting the STC-based adaptive AMR steganography at low embedding rate.

References

1. Bessette, B., et al.: The adaptive multirate wideband speech codec (AMR-WB). IEEE Trans. Speech Audio Process. **10**(8), 620–636 (2002)
2. Chang, C.C., Lin, C.J.: LIBSVM: a library for support vector machines. ACM Trans. Intell. Syst. Technol. (TIST) **2**(3), 27 (2011)
3. Ding, Q., Ping, X.: Steganalysis of analysis-by-synthesis compressed speech. In: 2010 International Conference on Multimedia Information Networking and Security (MINES), pp. 681–685. IEEE (2010)
4. Ding, Q., Ping, X.: Steganalysis of compressed speech based on histogram features. In: 2010 6th International Conference on Wireless Communications Networking and Mobile Computing (WiCOM), pp. 1–4. IEEE (2010)
5. Filler, T., Judas, J., Fridrich, J.: Minimizing additive distortion in steganography using syndrome-trellis codes. IEEE Trans. Inf. Forensics Secur. **6**(3), 920–935 (2011)
6. Geiser, B., Vary, P.: High rate data hiding in ACELP speech codecs. In: IEEE International Conference on Acoustics, Speech and Signal Processing, ICASSP 2008, pp. 4005–4008. IEEE (2008)
7. Gong, C., Yi, X., Zhao, X.: Pitch delay based adaptive steganography for AMR speech stream. In: Yoo, C.D., Shi, Y.-Q., Kim, H.J., Piva, A., Kim, G. (eds.) IWDW 2018. LNCS, vol. 11378, pp. 275–289. Springer, Cham (2019). https://doi.org/10.1007/978-3-030-11389-6_21
8. Gong, C., Yi, X., Zhao, X., Ma, Y.: Recurrent convolutional neural networks for AMR steganalysis based on pulse position. In: Proceedings of the ACM Workshop on Information Hiding and Multimedia Security, pp. 2–13. ACM (2019)
9. Huang, Y., Liu, C., Tang, S., Bai, S.: Steganography integration into a low-bit rate speech codec. IEEE Trans. Inf. Forensics Secur. **7**(6), 1865–1875 (2012)

10. Lin, Z., Huang, Y., Wang, J.: RNN-SM: fast steganalysis of VoIP streams using recurrent neural network. IEEE Trans. Inf. Forensics Secur. **13**(7), 1854–1868 (2018)
11. Liu, P., Li, S., Wang, H.: Steganography in vector quantization process of linear predictive coding for low-bit-rate speech codec. Multimedia Syst. **23**(4), 485–497 (2017)
12. Liu, P., Li, S., Wang, H.: Steganography integrated into linear predictive coding for low bit-rate speech codec. Multimedia Tools Appl. **76**(2), 2837–2859 (2017)
13. Miao, H., Huang, L., Chen, Z., Yang, W., Al-Hawbani, A.: A new scheme for covert communication via 3G encoded speech. Comput. Electr. Eng. **38**(6), 1490–1501 (2012)
14. Miao, H., Huang, L., Shen, Y., Lu, X., Chen, Z.: Steganalysis of compressed speech based on Markov and entropy. In: Shi, Y.Q., Kim, H.-J., Pérez-González, F. (eds.) IWDW 2013. LNCS, vol. 8389, pp. 63–76. Springer, Heidelberg (2014). https://doi.org/10.1007/978-3-662-43886-2_5
15. Nishimura, A.: Data hiding in pitch delay data of the adaptive multi-rate narrowband speech codec. In: Fifth International Conference on Intelligent Information Hiding and Multimedia Signal Processing, IIH-MSP 2009, pp. 483–486. IEEE (2009)
16. Ren, Y., Cai, T., Tang, M., Wang, L.: AMR steganalysis based on the probability of same pulse position. IEEE Trans. Inf. Forensics Secur. **10**(9), 1801–1811 (2015)
17. Ren, Y., Wu, H., Wang, L.: An AMR adaptive steganography algorithm based on minimizing distortion. Multimedia Tools Appl. **77**(10), 12095–12110 (2018)
18. Wang, Y., Yang, K., Yi, X., Zhao, X., Xu, Z.: CNN-based steganalysis of MP3 steganography in the entropy code domain. In: Proceedings of the 6th ACM Workshop on Information Hiding and Multimedia Security, pp. 55–65. ACM (2018)
19. Xiao, B., Huang, Y., Tang, S.: An approach to information hiding in low bit-rate speech stream. In: Global Telecommunications Conference, IEEE GLOBECOM 2008, pp. 1–5. IEEE (2008)

A Novel Feature Selection Model for JPEG Image Steganalysis

Liran Yang[1], Jing Zhong[1], Ping Zhong[2(✉)], Yiming Xue[1], and Juan Wen[1]

[1] College of Information and Electrical Engineering,
China Agricultural University, Beijing 100083, China
[2] College of Science, China Agricultural University, Beijing 100083, China
zping@cau.edu.cn

Abstract. Image steganalysis is a very important research topic in the field of information security. The existing feature based image steganalysis methods have achieved the appealing performance. The performance of them greatly depends on the quality of the hand-crafted steganalysis feature vectors, such as Cartesian Calibration PEV (CC-PEV), DCT Residuals (DCTR), and so on. However, these feature vectors may contain some redundant elements that will reduce the discrimination power and increase the computation cost. In this paper, a novel feature selection model is proposed for JPEG image steganalysis. Specifically, the proposed model imposes an $l_{2,1}$-structural constraint on the projection matrix for feature selection. Further, to make the model insensitive to noises and outliers, a capped l_2-norm based loss function is adopted. Moreover, a graph-based manifold regularization term which exploits the intrinsic local geometric structure of the data is added into the objective function to select the effective feature elements. Finally, an alternately iterative optimization algorithm with proven convergence is given to solve the proposed model. The extensive experiments on three state-of-the-art JPEG steganographic algorithms with 0.1 and 0.2 embedding rates and two JPEG quality factors show that the proposed model can effectively remove some irrelevant and redundant elements meanwhile retaining high detection accuracy.

Keywords: Steganalysis · Feature selection · JPEG image · Dimensionality reduction · Sparsity

1 Introduction

Steganography is the science of hiding secret messages within the innocent cover media, such as text, image, audio, video, and so on. Among these embedding covers, image is considered to be one of the most appropriate ones due to its wide-use for information storage and transmission in modern society. Thus, image steganography has attracted great attention over the past few decades [1,2].

As the counter-measure of steganography, steganalysis is the technology of detecting the presence of hidden data. In recent years, numerous image steganalysis methods based on the hand-crafted features have been proposed.

H. Wang et al. (Eds.): IWDW 2019, LNCS 12022, pp. 322–336, 2020.
https://doi.org/10.1007/978-3-030-43575-2_27

The detection performance usually depends on these features. Thus, many studies are devoted to design good feature extractors, such as CC-PEV [3], Cartesian-Calibrated JPEG Rich Model (CC-JRM) [4], DCTR [5], Gabor Filter Residuals (GFR) [6] and GFR-Gabor Symmetric Merging (GFR-GSM) [7]. However, the extracted steganalysis features might contain some redundant elements due to the small difference between the cover and stego images. The performance and computational efficiency are disturbed by the redundant features. To tackle this problem, feature selection technique is introduced to image steganalysis tasks, and it shows the promising effects. For example, Mohammadi and Abadeh [8] presented a novel feature-based blind JPEG image steganalysis method by employing an artificial bee colony based feature selection strategy. Based on the particle swarm optimization (PSO) algorithm, Chhikara et al. [9] proposed a feature selection method by combining the filter algorithm and a novel wrapper algorithm. Adeli and Broumandnia [10] developed an adaptive PSO based feature selection method, in which the inertia weight of PSO is adaptively adjusted. Pathak et al. [11] introduced a novel levy flight-based grey wolf optimization method to select the prominent features from a set of original features. Ma et al. [12] put forward a universal steganalysis feature selection approach based on the decision rough set α-positive region reduction to measure the importance of feature components and select the ones with high attribute separability.

It is noteworthy that feature selection technique is also extensively used in other fields, such as machine learning. With the arrival of the era of big data, the amount of the data increases rapidly. This brings some problems: over-fitting, dimension curse, high complexity and low efficiency. Therefore, dimensionality reduction is important and necessary. Recently, more and more scholars concentrate on feature selection which is an effective dimension reduction way. For example, Du et al. [13] proposed a feature learning model through the matrix factorization. Lan et al. [14] proposed a new feature selection approach by combining the capped l_2-norm loss and $l_{2,p}$-norm regularizer. Chang et al. [15] proposed an unsupervised feature selection method to select the discriminative features by using dual self-representation and manifold regularization. Zheng et al. [16] proposed a feature selection learning method from the view of sparse subspace learning. Nie et al. [17] developed an adaptive-weighting feature learning method by introducing a discriminative regression-based structure.

Inspired by these feature selection methods in machine learning, a novel feature selection model for image steganalysis is proposed in this paper. Specifically, on the one hand, the structurally sparse projection matrix W constrained by the $l_{2,1}$-norm is adopted to achieve the purpose of feature selection. On the other hand, the capped l_2-norm based loss function is introduced to make the model insensitive to outliers and noises. In addition, a graph-based manifold regularization term is incorporated into the objective function to make full use of the geometric structure information of the data. In this way, the possibly redundant feature elements can be removed, and the most prominent ones can be selected from the original feature vector. Subsequently, these selected feature elements are fed into a classifier for classification. The extensive comparison experiments demonstrate the effectiveness of the proposed model for JPEG image steganalysis.

In sum, the paper makes the following contributions:

- A new feature selection model is proposed for image steganalysis, by which the discriminative power of the data can be maintained or enhanced. Thus, it can promote the detection performance of image steganalysis.
- By adopting a capped l_2-norm based loss function, the proposed feature selection model can both remove the outliers and alleviate the negative impact of noises.
- By imposing a structurally sparse constraint on the projection matrix, the rows corresponding to the inessential features can be enforced to become zeros or close to zeros.
- By introducing a manifold regularization term based on the geometric graph to the objective function, the proposed method can preserve the local structure of the data.
- The effectiveness of the proposed method is demonstrated through extensive comparison experiments on three commonly used steganographic algorithms with two different embedding rates.

In the rest of this paper, we first describe the different phases of image steganalysis method: feature selection and classification. In the feature selection step, we formulate the optimization problem and its corresponding solution of the proposed model. And then, extensive experiments are conducted in Sect. 3. At last, Sect. 4 is the conclusion.

2   Proposed Method

Let $X = [\boldsymbol{x}_1, \boldsymbol{x}_2, \ldots, \boldsymbol{x}_n] \in \mathbb{R}^{d \times n}$ be the training data, where d is the number of features and n is the number of samples, respectively. The corresponding labels are represented by $Y = [\boldsymbol{y}_1, \cdots, \boldsymbol{y}_n] \in \mathbb{R}^{c \times n}$ with one-hot encoding, where $\boldsymbol{y}_i = [y_i^1, \cdots, y_i^c]^T \in \mathbb{R}^c$ is the label vector related to the i-th sample $\boldsymbol{x}_i$, and c is the number of the classes. Let $W = [\boldsymbol{w}^1; \boldsymbol{w}^2; \ldots; \boldsymbol{w}^d] \in \mathbb{R}^{d \times c}$ be the projection matrix with $\boldsymbol{w}^i \in \mathbb{R}^{1 \times c}$ being the projection vector corresponding to the i-th feature.

2.1   Feature Selection Step

In practice, least square regression is one of the most commonly used losses in virtue of its smoothness. However, it is sensitive to noises and outliers. Inspired by [14], we utilize the capped l_2-norm based loss:

$$\min_W \sum_{i=1}^n \min(\|W^T \boldsymbol{x}_i - \boldsymbol{y}_i\|_2, \epsilon) \tag{1}$$

where ϵ is the thresholding parameter. According to Eq. (1), when the i-th sample $\boldsymbol{x}_i$ is an outlier, the value of $\|W^T \boldsymbol{x}_i - \boldsymbol{y}_i\|_2$ will be larger than ϵ accordingly, and thus, the loss of $\boldsymbol{x}_i$ will be capped as ϵ. This reduces the impact of outliers.

Besides, the residual $\|W^T x_i - y_i\|_2$ is not squared and thus noises have less importance than the squared one. Thus, the capped l_2-norm loss is insensitive to noises.

For better solving Eq. (1), we usually cap the residual of outliers as zero. Thus, Eq. (1) can be further rewritten as

$$\min_{W} \sum_{i=1}^{n} u_i \|W^T x_i - y_i\|_2 \tag{2}$$

where u_i is defined as

$$u_i = \begin{cases} 1, & \text{if } \|W^T x_i - y_i\|_2 \le \epsilon \\ 0, & \text{otherwise} \end{cases} \tag{3}$$

To preserve the intrinsic geometrical structure of the data, the graph-based manifold regularizer is introduced. Conventionally, the manifold regularization is usually applied to the unsupervised or semi-supervised settings so as to make use of abundant unlabeled samples. While we apply it to the supervised feature selection with all labels available, and consider that if the true labels of x_i and x_j are the same, their corresponding predicted labels $\hat{y}_i$ and $\hat{y}_j$ should also be identical. So the geometry structure of the data in the feature space can be preserved by minimizing the following function

$$R(\hat{Y}) = \frac{1}{2} \sum_{i,j=1}^{n} \|\hat{y}_i - \hat{y}_j\|_2^2 S_{ij} = tr(\hat{Y} L \hat{Y}^T) = tr[(W^T X) L (W^T X)^T] \tag{4}$$

where S_{ij} is denoted as the pair-wise similarity between two data points x_i and x_j, and it is measured as

$$S_{ij} = \begin{cases} 1, & \text{if } y_i = y_j \\ 0, & \text{otherwise} \end{cases} \tag{5}$$

L is the graph Laplacian matrix:

$$L = \hat{S} - S \tag{6}$$

where $\hat{S}$ is a diagonal matrix with diagonal elements $\hat{S}_{ii} = \sum_{j=1}^{n} S_{ij}$, and $S = [S_{ij}]_{n \times n}$ is the graph adjacency matrix.

In order to fulfill feature selection, we insert an $l_{2,1}$-norm regularization given by $\|W\|_{2,1} = \sum_{j=1}^{d} \|w^j\|_2$ into the objective function. The $l_{2,1}$-norm regularizer has the effects of enforcing row sparseness of the projection matrix W, thus is particularly suitable for feature selection. As a result, the proposed objective function is

$$\min_{W} \sum_{i=1}^{n} u_i \|W^T x_i - y_i\|_2 + \lambda_1 tr[(W^T X) L (W^T X)^T] + \lambda_2 \|W\|_{2,1} \tag{7}$$

where $\lambda_1 > 0$ and $\lambda_2 > 0$ are two regularization parameters to balance the importance of each quantity.

Optimization Algorithm. In this part, an efficiently iterative algorithm is proposed to solve the problem (7). Firstly, define a diagonal matrix $M \in \mathbb{R}^{n \times n}$ with the i-th diagonal element

$$M_{ii} = u_i \|W^T \boldsymbol{x}_i - \boldsymbol{y}_i\|_2^{-1} \tag{8}$$

Then the objective function (7) can be converted into

$$\min_{W,M} \sum_{i=1}^{n} M_{ii} \|W^T \boldsymbol{x}_i - \boldsymbol{y}_i\|_2^2 + \lambda_1 tr[(W^T X)L(W^T X)^T] + \lambda_2 \|W\|_{2,1} \tag{9}$$

Since

$$\sum_{i=1}^{n} M_{ii} \|W^T \boldsymbol{x}_i - \boldsymbol{y}_i\|_2^2$$

$$= \sum_{i=1}^{n} M_{ii}(W^T \boldsymbol{x}_i - \boldsymbol{y}_i)^T (W^T \boldsymbol{x}_i - \boldsymbol{y}_i)$$

$$= tr[(W^T X - Y)M(W^T X - Y)^T] \tag{10}$$

and

$$\|W\|_{2,1} = tr(W^T D W) \tag{11}$$

where $D \in \mathbb{R}^{d \times d}$ is a diagonal matrix

$$D = \begin{bmatrix} \frac{1}{2\|\boldsymbol{w}^1\|_2} & & \\ & \ddots & \\ & & \frac{1}{2\|\boldsymbol{w}^d\|_2} \end{bmatrix} \tag{12}$$

with $\boldsymbol{w}^i$ being the i-th row of W, Eq. (9) can be transformed into the following matrix form:

$$\min_{W,D,M} tr[(W^T X - Y)M(W^T X - Y)^T] + \lambda_1 tr[(W^T X)L(W^T X)^T]$$

$$+ \lambda_2 tr(W^T D W) \tag{13}$$

By setting derivative of (13) with respect to W to zero, we have

$$W = (XMX^T + \lambda_1 XLX^T + \lambda_2 D)^{-1} XMY^T \tag{14}$$

The proposed algorithm is shown in Algorithm 1, where $Obj(t)$ is denoted as the value of the objective function (7) at the t-th iteration

$$Obj(t) = \sum_{i=1}^{n} u_i \|W_{(t)}^T \boldsymbol{x}_i - \boldsymbol{y}_i\|_2 + \lambda_1 tr[(W_{(t)}^T X)L(W_{(t)}^T X)^T] + \lambda_2 \|W_{(t)}\|_{2,1} \tag{15}$$

Algorithm 1. Solving problem (7)

Input: Data matrix X, label matrix Y, regularizer parameters λ_1 and λ_2, thresholding parameter ϵ
Initialization: Set $t = 0$, $D_0 = [1]_{d \times d}$, $M_0 = [1]_{d \times d}$
Compute the graph Laplacian matrix L by Eq. (6)
While not converged **do**
1. Update $W_{(t+1)}$ by Eq. (14)
2. Update $M_{(t+1)}$ by Eq. (8)
3. Update $D_{(t+1)}$ by Eq. (12)
4. Compute $er = |Obj(t+1) - Obj(t)|$
5. $t = t + 1$
End while
Output: Projection matrix W

Convergence Analysis. Before analyzing the convergence of the proposed optimization algorithm, a lemma provided in [18] is given firstly.

Lemma 1. *For any two positive values a and b, the following inequality holds*

$$\sqrt{a} - \frac{a}{2\sqrt{b}} \leq \sqrt{b} - \frac{b}{2\sqrt{b}} \tag{16}$$

By referring to [19, 20], the following theorem guarantees the convergence property of the proposed optimization algorithm.

Theorem 1. *In Algorithm 1, the objective values monotonically decrease until convergence.*

Proof. Please refer to the Appendix for the detailed proof of Theorem 1.

2.2 Classification Step

Through the above feature selection step, we obtain the projection matrix W calculated by Algorithm 1. According to the learned W, we can select the most discriminant feature elements. After selecting, we perform the last step of the proposed method. That is, constructing a steganography detector based on the selected prominent feature elements to distinguish stego images from cover images. Steganalysis detection is usually cast as a supervised classification problem implemented using machine learning, and it is required to train a classification model. As we all know, the ensemble classifier is a favorable and fast tool for classification. Thus, we employ the Fisher Linear Discriminant (FLD) ensemble classifier [21] which is built by fusing decisions of weak and unstable base learners implemented as the FLD.

3   Experiments

3.1   Experimental Data and Setup

In the experiments, 10,000 gray-scale images with size of 512×512 coming from the Bossbase 1.01 database are converted into JPEG images with quality factors (QFs) 75 and 95 as experimental cover images. The stego images are generated by hiding messages using three popular embedding algorithms nsF5 [22], UED [23] and J-UNIWARD [24] with payloads of 0.1 and 0.2 bits per nonzero AC DCT coefficient (bpnzac). The experiments are tested on data sets generated by extracting two sets of features: CC-PEV [3] and DCTR [5] from these cover and stego images, where the lengths of the two feature vectors are 548 and 8,000, respectively.

To evaluate the effectiveness of the proposed method, the original features (548-D or 8,000-D) without feature selection (denoted by Allfea) is taken as the baseline and two state-of-the-art feature selection methods proposed in [14] and [17] are selected as the compared algorithms. We arrange all the features in a descending sort based on the values of $\|w^i\|_2$, $i = 1, 2, \ldots, d$, where w^i is the i-th row of W. And then we respectively select the top-K features as the inputs of subsequent classifier. Here, $K = \lfloor ratio \times d \rfloor$, where $ratio$ varies from 10% to 90%. In the experiments, the classification error is quantified using the minimal total error under equal priors $P_E = \min_{P_{FA}} \frac{1}{2}(P_{FA} + P_{MD})$, where P_{FA} and P_{MD} represent the false alarm and missed-detection probabilities, respectively. We consider the median value of P_E over 5 random tests (denoted by $\overline{P}_E$) as the performance evaluation metric. For fair comparison, all algorithms are evaluated using the FLD ensemble classifier [21].

3.2   Experimental Results and Analysis

The experimental results are shown in Tables 1, 2, 3, 4, 5, 6, 7 and 8, where the results with best performance are presented in bold.

Table 1. Detection results ($\overline{P}_E$) with payload of 0.1 bpnzac for QF 75 when steganalyzed with CC-PEV feature vector.

Selected ratio	nsF5			UED			J-UNIWARD		
	[14]	[17]	Proposed	[14]	[17]	Proposed	[14]	[17]	Proposed
10%	0.3124	0.3058	0.2906	0.4622	0.4382	0.4220	0.4942	0.4858	0.4776
30%	0.3008	0.2886	0.2778	0.4508	0.4272	0.4202	0.4862	0.4720	0.4718
50%	0.2926	0.2842	0.2852	0.4534	0.4252	0.4186	0.4830	0.4798	**0.4704**
70%	**0.2832**	0.2874	0.2870	0.4272	0.4274	**0.4118**	0.4796	0.4752	0.4716
90%	0.2916	0.2922	0.2874	0.4332	0.4284	0.4188	0.4780	0.4784	0.4708
Allfea	0.2908			0.4300			0.4850		

Table 2. Detection results $(\overline{P}_E)$ with payload of 0.1 bpnzac for QF 95 when steganalyzed with CC-PEV feature vector.

Selected ratio	nsF5			UED			J-UNIWARD		
	[14]	[17]	Proposed	[14]	[17]	Proposed	[14]	[17]	Proposed
10%	0.2642	0.2542	0.2456	0.4864	0.4828	0.4816	0.4932	0.4904	0.4800
30%	0.2330	0.2262	0.2214	0.4930	0.4936	0.4796	0.4890	0.4888	0.4846
50%	0.2228	0.2190	**0.2150**	0.4862	0.4856	**0.4792**	0.4856	0.4872	0.4812
70%	0.2230	0.2240	0.2182	0.4868	0.4876	0.4810	0.4878	0.4866	**0.4770**
90%	0.2230	0.2288	0.2226	0.4908	0.4902	0.4834	0.4850	0.4812	0.4776
Allfea	0.2336			0.4872			0.4838		

Table 3. Detection results $(\overline{P}_E)$ with payload of 0.2 bpnzac for QF 75 when steganalyzed with CC-PEV feature vector.

Selected ratio	nsF5			UED			J-UNIWARD		
	[14]	[17]	Proposed	[14]	[17]	Proposed	[14]	[17]	Proposed
10%	0.1054	0.1058	0.0798	0.3978	0.3586	0.3538	0.4596	0.4316	**0.4160**
30%	0.0860	0.0668	**0.0592**	0.3756	0.3426	**0.3322**	0.4478	0.4300	0.4170
50%	0.0774	0.0662	0.0602	0.3576	0.3460	0.3328	0.4288	0.4258	0.4172
70%	0.0670	0.0656	0.0614	0.3568	0.3488	0.3338	0.4304	0.4306	0.4272
90%	0.0672	0.0628	0.0636	0.3516	0.3442	0.3396	0.4324	0.4310	0.4334
Allfea	0.0684			0.3516			0.4380		

Table 4. Detection results $(\overline{P}_E)$ with payload of 0.2 bpnzac for QF 95 when steganalyzed with CC-PEV feature vector.

Selected ratio	nsF5			UED			J-UNIWARD		
	[14]	[17]	Proposed	[14]	[17]	Proposed	[14]	[17]	Proposed
10%	0.0444	0.0386	0.0282	0.4750	0.4724	0.4572	0.4738	0.4722	0.4604
30%	0.0204	0.0146	0.0168	0.4652	0.4588	0.4546	0.4668	0.4724	0.4610
50%	0.0204	0.0148	0.0146	0.4628	0.4608	**0.4446**	0.4664	0.4674	**0.4534**
70%	0.0150	0.0124	**0.0118**	0.4586	0.4656	0.4554	0.4662	0.4714	0.4588
90%	0.0140	0.0124	**0.0118**	0.4628	0.4554	0.4558	0.4704	0.4692	0.4642
Allfea	0.0128			0.4610			0.4746		

Table 5. Detection results $(\overline{P}_E)$ with payload of 0.1 bpnzac for QF 75 when steganalyzed with DCTR feature vector.

Selected ratio	nsF5			UED			J-UNIWARD		
	[14]	[17]	Proposed	[14]	[17]	Proposed	[14]	[17]	Proposed
10%	0.2198	0.2390	0.2168	0.3442	0.3354	0.3368	0.4680	0.4600	0.4520
30%	**0.2122**	0.2218	0.2150	0.3294	0.3304	0.3288	0.4494	0.4454	0.4466
50%	0.2194	0.2246	0.2124	0.3272	0.3292	0.3220	0.4462	0.4436	0.4450
70%	0.2212	0.2250	0.2174	0.3222	0.3276	**0.3212**	0.4482	**0.4424**	0.4440
90%	0.2276	0.2274	0.2222	0.3306	0.3278	0.3278	0.4486	0.4442	0.4436
Allfea	0.2328			0.3370			0.4500		

Table 6. Detection results $(\overline{P}_E)$ with payload of 0.1 bpnzac for QF 95 when steganalyzed with DCTR feature vector.

Selected ratio	nsF5			UED			J-UNIWARD		
	[14]	[17]	Proposed	[14]	[17]	Proposed	[14]	[17]	Proposed
10%	0.2160	0.2296	0.1784	0.4748	0.4762	0.4644	0.4956	0.4828	0.4874
30%	0.1750	0.1818	0.1612	0.4674	0.4704	0.4636	0.4852	0.4868	0.4824
50%	0.1710	0.1684	0.1560	0.4660	0.4644	0.4628	0.4852	0.4868	0.4830
70%	0.1612	0.1612	0.1546	0.4664	0.4656	**0.4626**	0.4898	0.4842	**0.4804**
90%	0.1560	0.1570	**0.1496**	0.4706	0.4710	0.4638	0.4882	0.4868	0.4810
Allfea	0.1584			0.4772			0.4940		

Table 7. Detection results $(\overline{P}_E)$ with payload of 0.2 bpnzac for QF 75 when steganalyzed with DCTR feature vector.

Selected ratio	nsF5			UED			J-UNIWARD		
	[14]	[17]	Proposed	[14]	[17]	Proposed	[14]	[17]	Proposed
10%	0.0476	0.0572	0.0457	0.1892	0.1946	0.1852	0.3960	0.3854	0.3828
30%	0.0456	0.0476	**0.0430**	0.1712	0.1744	0.1660	0.3800	0.3736	0.3748
50%	0.0496	0.0520	0.0478	0.1650	0.1680	**0.1602**	0.3746	0.3648	0.3652
70%	0.0516	0.0570	0.0494	0.1694	0.1702	0.1658	0.3698	0.3650	0.3654
90%	0.0578	0.0568	0.0540	0.1660	0.1720	0.1668	0.3660	0.3690	**0.3646**
Allfea	0.0600			0.1708			0.3728		

Table 8. Detection results ($\overline{P}_E$) with payload of 0.2 bpnzac for QF 95 when steganalyzed with DCTR feature vector.

Selected ratio	nsF5			UED			J-UNIWARD		
	[14]	[17]	Proposed	[14]	[17]	Proposed	[14]	[17]	Proposed
10%	0.0356	0.0216	0.0124	0.4204	0.4240	0.4204	0.4672	0.4588	0.4546
30%	0.0154	0.0140	0.0096	0.4142	0.4138	0.4054	0.4672	0.4542	**0.4510**
50%	0.0102	0.0102	0.0074	0.4062	0.4070	**0.3964**	0.4608	0.4606	0.4546
70%	0.0106	0.0114	0.0080	0.4026	0.4046	0.3968	0.4612	0.4580	0.4538
90%	0.0108	0.0096	**0.0072**	0.3994	0.4036	0.3968	0.4626	0.4570	0.4534
Allfea	0.0090			0.4066			0.4636		

From these experimental results, the following findings can be given.

(1) The performance of the different number of the selected feature elements (10%, 30%, 50%, 70%, 90%) is generally better than that of the Allfea, which shows that there are redundant elements in the original steganalysis feature vectors.

(2) The detection errors are not always decreased with the increase of the number of the selected features, which indicates that the detection performance is not always improved by selecting more features.

(3) The proposed method achieves the lowest detection errors on most cases by only selecting not more than 70% of features. Specifically, the proposed method obtains the best detection performance on 21 out of 24 steganalysis tasks.

To sum up, the proposed feature selection model is superior to the other feature selection ones on steganalysis applications, which implies that it is a powerful algorithm for the dimension reduction on JPEG image steganalysis tasks.

3.3   Parameter Sensitivity Analysis

In this part, we discuss the influence of the different parameters involved in the proposed feature selection model. The model includes a thresholding parameter ϵ as well as two regularization parameters λ_1 and λ_2. Taking UED and J-UNIWARD steganographic algorithms for examples, the detection performance of the proposed model with respect of ϵ as well as λ_1 and λ_2 under different values is shown in Figs. 1 and 2, where ϵ is tuned within $\{0, 0.2, 0.4, 0.6, 0.8, 1\}$ as well as λ_1 and λ_2 are tuned within $\{0.001, 0.01, 0.1, 1, 10, 100, 1000\}$. From Fig. 1, it can be seen that the detection performance is almost invariable when the values of ϵ is controlled in $[0.2, 1]$, which means that the performance of the proposed algorithm is insensitive to the parameter ϵ provided that its value in a reasonable range. From Fig. 2, it can be observed that the proposed model can obtain roughly consistent detection performance. In other words, the proposed model is insensitive to the regularization parameters λ_1 and λ_2.

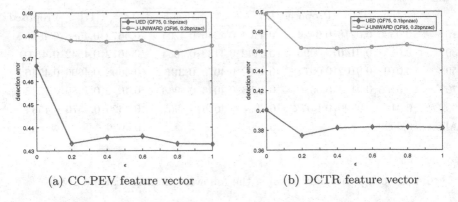

(a) CC-PEV feature vector   (b) DCTR feature vector

Fig. 1. The sensitivity of the proposed model with respect to the choice of ϵ.

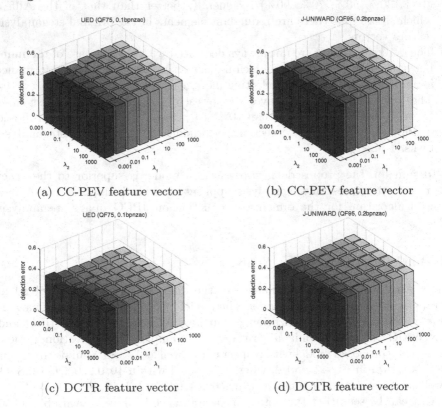

(a) CC-PEV feature vector   (b) CC-PEV feature vector

(c) DCTR feature vector   (d) DCTR feature vector

Fig. 2. The sensitivity of the proposed model with respect to the choice of λ_1 and λ_2.

4 Conclusion

In many image steganalysis tasks, there are some correlations and redundan-
cies in the hand-crafted feature vector due to the small distribution difference
between the cover and stego images. This will result in low detection performance and large computational costs. To this end, this paper proposes a novel
feature selection model for JPEG image steganalysis. Specifically, a structurally
sparse projection matrix imposed by an $l_{2,1}$-norm is adopted to exploit the correlation information among features. It is able to select the most significant and
influential feature elements. Meanwhile, a capped l_2-norm based loss function is
introduced to remove the outliers and reduce the impact of noises. A graph-based
manifold regularization term is inserted into the objective function to preserve
the geometric structure information of the data. It is helpful to select the significant and influential feature elements. In this way, the most discriminant ones
are selected, and so, the performance of steganalysis is improved. Finally, an
iterative algorithm is proposed to optimize the problem, whose computational
complexity and convergence are discussed. A series of experiments are conducted
on two kinds of typical feature vectors (548-D CC-PEV and 8,000-D DCTR).
The experimental results show that the performance of our method is superior to the baseline and state-of-the-art methods, which verifies the validity of
the proposed method. In the future, the experiments will be further extended,
and higher dimensional steganalysis features, such as CC-JRM [4], GFR [6] and
GFR-GSM [7], will be explored to examine the effectiveness of the model.

Acknowledgements. The work is supported by the National Natural Science Foundation of China (Grant No. 61872368). The authors gratefully acknowledge the helpful
comments and suggestions of the reviewers, which have improved the presentation.

Appendix

Proof of Theorem 1. According to the step 1 of Algorithm 1 in the t-th
iteration and Eq. (11), we have

$$
\begin{aligned}
W_{(t+1)} &= \arg\min_{W} \sum_{i=1}^{n} u_i \| W^T \boldsymbol{x}_i - \boldsymbol{y}_i \|_2 + \lambda_1 tr[(W^T X)L(W^T X)^T] + \lambda_2 \| W \|_{2,1} \\
&= \arg\min_{W} \sum_{i=1}^{n} u_i \| W^T \boldsymbol{x}_i - \boldsymbol{y}_i \|_2 + \lambda_1 tr[(W^T X)L(W^T X)^T] \\
&\quad + \lambda_2 tr(W^T D_{(t)} W)
\end{aligned}
\tag{17}
$$

which indicates that

$$\sum_{i=1}^{n} u_i \|W_{(t+1)}^T \boldsymbol{x}_i - \boldsymbol{y}_i\|_2 + \lambda_1 tr[(W_{(t+1)}^T X)L(W_{(t+1)}^T X)^T]$$

$$+ \lambda_2 tr(W_{(t+1)}^T D_{(t)} W_{(t+1)})$$

$$\leq \sum_{i=1}^{n} u_i \|W_{(t)}^T \boldsymbol{x}_i - \boldsymbol{y}_i\|_2 + \lambda_1 tr[(W_{(t)}^T X)L(W_{(t)}^T X)^T]$$

$$+ \lambda_2 tr(W_{(t)}^T D_{(t)} W_{(t)}) \tag{18}$$

According to Eq. (12), the following equations hold:

$$tr(W_{(t+1)}^T D_{(t)} W_{(t+1)}) = \sum_{i=1}^{d} \frac{\|\boldsymbol{w}_{(t+1)}^i\|_2^2}{2\|\boldsymbol{w}_{(t)}^i\|_2} \tag{19}$$

$$tr(W_{(t)}^T D_{(t)} W_{(t)}) = \sum_{i=1}^{d} \frac{\|\boldsymbol{w}_{(t)}^i\|_2^2}{2\|\boldsymbol{w}_{(t)}^i\|_2} \tag{20}$$

Thus, Eq. (18) can be transformed into the following form:

$$\sum_{i=1}^{n} u_i \|W_{(t+1)}^T \boldsymbol{x}_i - \boldsymbol{y}_i\|_2 + \lambda_1 tr[(W_{(t+1)}^T X)L(W_{(t+1)}^T X)^T] + \lambda_2 \sum_{i=1}^{d} \frac{\|\boldsymbol{w}_{(t+1)}^i\|_2^2}{2\|\boldsymbol{w}_{(t)}^i\|_2}$$

$$\leq \sum_{i=1}^{n} u_i \|W_{(t)}^T \boldsymbol{x}_i - \boldsymbol{y}_i\|_2 + \lambda_1 tr[(W_{(t)}^T X)L(W_{(t)}^T X)^T] + \lambda_2 \sum_{i=1}^{d} \frac{\|\boldsymbol{w}_{(t)}^i\|_2^2}{2\|\boldsymbol{w}_{(t)}^i\|_2} \tag{21}$$

Further, the above inequality can be rewritten as

$$\sum_{i=1}^{n} u_i \|W_{(t+1)}^T \boldsymbol{x}_i - \boldsymbol{y}_i\|_2 + \lambda_1 tr[(W_{(t+1)}^T X)L(W_{(t+1)}^T X)^T]$$

$$+ \lambda_2 \sum_{i=1}^{d} \left(\frac{\|\boldsymbol{w}_{(t+1)}^i\|_2^2}{2\|\boldsymbol{w}_{(t)}^i\|_2} + \|\boldsymbol{w}_{(t+1)}^i\|_2 - \|\boldsymbol{w}_{(t+1)}^i\|_2 \right)$$

$$\leq \sum_{i=1}^{n} u_i \|W_{(t)}^T \boldsymbol{x}_i - \boldsymbol{y}_i\|_2 + \lambda_1 tr[(W_{(t)}^T X)L(W_{(t)}^T X)^T]$$

$$+ \lambda_2 \sum_{i=1}^{d} \left(\frac{\|\boldsymbol{w}_{(t)}^i\|_2^2}{2\|\boldsymbol{w}_{(t)}^i\|_2} + \|\boldsymbol{w}_{(t)}^i\|_2 - \|\boldsymbol{w}_{(t)}^i\|_2 \right) \tag{22}$$

By replacing a and b in Lemma 1 with $\|\boldsymbol{w}_{(t+1)}^i\|_2^2$ and $\|\boldsymbol{w}_{(t)}^i\|_2^2$, we get

$$\|\boldsymbol{w}_{(t+1)}^i\|_2 - \frac{\|\boldsymbol{w}_{(t+1)}^i\|_2^2}{2\|\boldsymbol{w}_{(t)}^i\|_2} \leq \|\boldsymbol{w}_{(t)}^i\|_2 - \frac{\|\boldsymbol{w}_{(t)}^i\|_2^2}{2\|\boldsymbol{w}_{(t)}^i\|_2} \tag{23}$$

By adding Eqs. (22) and (23) on both sides (note that Eq. (23) is repeated for $1 \leq i \leq d$), we have

$$\sum_{i=1}^{n} u_i \|W_{(t+1)}^T x_i - y_i\|_2 + \lambda_1 tr[(W_{(t+1)}^T X)L(W_{(t+1)}^T X)^T] + \lambda_2 \sum_{i=1}^{d} \|w_{(t+1)}^i\|_2$$

$$\leq \sum_{i=1}^{n} u_i \|W_{(t)}^T x_i - y_i\|_2 + \lambda_1 tr[(W_{(t)}^T X)L(W_{(t)}^T X)^T] + \lambda_2 \sum_{i=1}^{d} \|w_{(t)}^i\|_2 \qquad (24)$$

That is to say,

$$Obj(t+1) \leq Obj(t) \qquad (25)$$

Since the values of objective function (7) decrease monotonously and are greater than zeros, so Algorithm 1 is convergent. Theorem 1 is proven.

References

1. Pevný, T., Filler, T., Bas, P.: Using high-dimensional image models to perform highly undetectable steganography. In: Böhme, R., Fong, P.W.L., Safavi-Naini, R. (eds.) IH 2010. LNCS, vol. 6387, pp. 161–177. Springer, Heidelberg (2010). https://doi.org/10.1007/978-3-642-16435-4_13

2. Denemark, T., Fridrich, J.: Steganography with multiple JPEG images of the same scene. IEEE Trans. Inf. Forensics Secur. **12**(10), 2308–2319 (2017)

3. Kodovský, J., Fridrich, J.: Calibration revisited. In: 11th Multimedia and Security Workshop (MMSec), New Jersey, USA, pp. 63–74. ACM (2009)

4. Kodovský, J., Fridrich, J.: Steganalysis of JPEG images using rich models. In: SPIE 8303, Media Watermarking, Security, and Forensics, p. 83030A. SPIE (2012)

5. Holub, V., Fridrich, J.: Low complexity features for JPEG steganalysis using undecimated DCT. IEEE Trans. Inf. Forensics Secur. **10**(2), 219–228 (2015)

6. Song, X., Liu, F., Yang, C., Luo, X., Zhang, Y.: Steganalysis of adaptive JPEG steganography using 2D Gabor filters. In: 3rd ACM Workshop on Information Hiding and Multimedia Security (IH&MMSec), Portland, Oregon, USA, pp. 15–23. ACM (2015)

7. Xia, C., Guan, Q., Zhao, X., Xu, Z., Ma, Y.: Improving GFR steganalysis features by using Gabor symmetry and weighted histograms. In: 5th ACM Workshop on Information Hiding and Multimedia Security (IH&MMSec), Philadelphia, Pennsylvania, USA, pp. 55–66. ACM (2017)

8. Mohammadi, F.G., Abadeh, M.S.: Image steganalysis using a bee colony based feature selection algorithm. Eng. Appl. Artif. Intell. **31**, 35–43 (2014)

9. Chhikara, R.R., Sharma, P., Singh, L.: A hybrid feature selection approach based on improved PSO and filter approaches for image steganalysis. Int. J. Mach. Learn. Cybern. **7**(6), 1195–1206 (2016). https://doi.org/10.1007/s13042-015-0448-0

10. Adeli, A., Broumandnia, A.: Image steganalysis using improved particle swarm optimization based feature selection. Appl. Intell. **48**, 1609–1622 (2018). https://doi.org/10.1007/s10489-017-0989-x

11. Pathak, Y., Arya, K.V., Shailendra, T.: Feature selection for image steganalysis using levy flight-based grey wolf optimization. Multimedia Tools Appl. **78**, 1473–1494 (2019). https://doi.org/10.1007/s11042-018-6155-6

12. Ma, Y., Luo, X., Li, X., Bao, Z., Zhang, Y.: Selection of rich model steganalysis features based on decision rough set α-positive region reduction. IEEE Trans. Circuits Syst. Video Technol. **29**(2), 336–350 (2018)
13. Du, A., Ma, Y., Li, S., Ma, Y.: Robust unsupervised feature selection via matrix factorization. Neurocomputing **241**, 115–127 (2017)
14. Lan, G., Hou, C., Nie, F., Luo, T., Yi, D.: Robust feature selection via simultaneous capped norm and sparse regularizer minimization. Neurocomputing **283**, 228–240 (2018)
15. Tang, C., Liu, X., Li, M.: Robust unsupervised feature selection via dual self-representation and manifold regularization. Knowl. Based Syst. **145**, 109–120 (2018)
16. Zheng, W., Yan, H., Yang, J., Yang, J.: Robust unsupervised feature selection by nonnegative sparse subspace learning. Neurocomputing **334**, 156–171 (2019)
17. Yang, M., Cheng, D., Nie, F.: Adaptive-weighting discriminative regression for multi-view classification. Pattern Recogn. **88**, 236–245 (2019)
18. Nie, F., Huang, H., Cai, X., Ding, C.: Efficient and robust feature selection via joint $L_{2,1}$-norms minimization. In: 23rd International Conference on Neural Information Processing Systems (NIPS), Vancouver, BC, Canada, pp. 1813–1821. Curran Associates Inc. (2010)
19. Zhu, X., Li, X., Zhang, S.: Block-row sparse multiview multilabel learning for image classification. IEEE Trans. Cybern. **46**(2), 450–461 (2016)
20. Huang, S., Zhao, K., Xu, Z.: Self-weighted multi-view clustering with soft capped norm. Knowl. Based Syst. **158**, 1–8 (2018)
21. Kodovský, J., Fridrich, J., Holub, V.: Ensemble classifiers for steganalysis of digital media. IEEE Trans. Inf. Forensics Secur. **7**(2), 432–444 (2012)
22. Fridrich, J., Pevný, T., Kodovsky, J.: Statistically undetectable JPEG steganography: dead ends challenges, and opportunities. In: 9th Multimedia and Security Workshop (MMSec), Dallas, Texas, USA, pp. 3–14. ACM (2007)
23. Guo, L., Ni, J., Shi, Y.Q.: Uniform embedding for efficient JPEG steganography. IEEE Trans. Inf. Forensics Secur. **9**(5), 814–825 (2014)
24. Holub, V., Fridrich, J., Denemark, T.: Universal distortion function for steganography in an arbitrary domain. EURASIP J. Inf. Secur. **2014**, 1–13 (2014)

New Steganalytic Features for Spatial Image Steganography Based on Non-negative Matrix Factorization

Hui Ge, Donghui Hu$^{(\boxtimes)}$, Haiyan Xu, Meng Li, and Shuli Zheng

College of Computer Science and Information Engineering,
Hefei University of Techonology, Hefei 230009, Anhui, China
15555387016gehui@gmail.com, {hudh,mengli}@hfut.edu.cn,
xu_haiyan0314@sina.com, zsl251@163.com

Abstract. The traditional steganalysis feature extraction method can be mainly divided into two steps. First, the residual image is calculated by convolution filtering, and then the co-occurrence matrix of residual image is calculated to obtain the final feature. Previous work calculates the residual image usually through a set of fixed high-pass filter or a manually designed residual sub-model, and does not utilize the consistency between pixels in the local area of the natural image. In this paper, we propose the Non-negative Matrix Factorization (NMF) based steganalysis feature extraction method for spatial image. Considering the number of pixels used by NMF for prediction and its positional relationship with the predicted pixels, a plurality of sets of residual sub-models for acquiring residual images are designed; and then, a new residual combination method is proposed, combining Local Binary Pattern (LBP), co-occurrence matrix and other statistical information, and the parameters in feature extraction is optimized. Finally, we compare the performance of the designed features with existing steganalysis features and analyze the validity of the designed features. In addition, we combine the existing artificially designed spatial steganalysis features with the designed features and analyze the validity and complementarity of each type of features, such as Spatial Rich Model (SRM) and Threshold LBP (TLBP).

Keywords: Steganalysis · Non-negative Matrix Factorization · Pixel-wise mutual prediction · Information hiding

1 Introduction

Steganography refers to concealing secret information in multimedia data without causing suspicion during steganalysis [8,13]. As the opposite art of steganography, steganalysis analyses the statistical properties of an image, detecting whether the image contains secret information.

This work was supported by the National Natural Science Foundation of China (NSFC) under the grant No. U1836102.

© Springer Nature Switzerland AG 2020
H. Wang et al. (Eds.): IWDW 2019, LNCS 12022, pp. 337–351, 2020.
https://doi.org/10.1007/978-3-030-43575-2_28

The traditional steganalysis is to extract the high-dimensional features of an image, and then use machine-learning classifiers [2,5] to detect whether the image contains secret information. The features can be designed in an ad hoc or empirical manner relying on the designer's ability, or as the recently new trend of being automatically learned via convolutional neural networks (CNNs). The most popular hand-crafted features are extracted from the rich models, in which the Spatial Rich Model (SRM) [4] is a standard approach for evaluating the security of spatial image steganography. In the SRM feature extraction framework, the features are extracted from an image by a set of high-pass filters to obtain residual images. Then, steganalytic features are generated by computing and merging the fourth order co-occurrence matrices of quantized residuals. The different shapes and orientations of linear and non-linear high-pass filters, together with several residual quantization steps, contribute the diversity of the model. The steganalytic features modeled the intricate high-order relationships between pixels and have the powerful ability of detecting (adaptive) steganography. And the feature of maxSRM [3], which consider selection-channel side information, further improve the detection ability. Li et al. [7] presented a set of derivative filters to obtain residual images, the residual images were then fed to an extended version of Local Binary Pattern (LBP) [11] to generate the steganalytic features with a non-linear mapping.

Though the recently rapidly development deep learning attracted attentions of the steganalysis research community [14,16–19], traditional hand-crafted steganalytic features still have significance in the research community. For example, though some operations such as forming histogram can be simulated by specially designed network layers, recent studies also suggest that some important operations from the SRM framework, such as truncation and quantization, cannot be effectively learned by deep networks.

In this paper, we propose a new set of steganalytic features based on Non-negative Matrix Factorization (NMF) [6]. As shown in Fig. 1, with parallel comparison to SRM and the Threshold LBP (TLBP) proposed in [7], the new feature extraction method contains three phases. First, in order to capture intricate relationships among pixels, NMF with different decomposition ranks and sizes is designed to generate residual images. This stage resembles the high-pass filtering and derivative filters used in SRM and method proposed in [7], respectively. Second, we use TLBP to capture the deviation caused by steganography in residual images. Third, we calculate the features from second-order co-occurrence matrix of the TLBP images, and then aggregate second-order features and utilize non-linearly mapping to improve feature effectiveness.

The contributions of this work are summarized as follows.

1. Compared with a large number of unsystematically designed high-pass filters and mathematical derivative filter, the proposed method utilize NMF to design a set of nonlinear features, which can use the complex relationships between neighboring pixels to evaluate target pixels.
2. Under different conditions, the proposed NMF features achieve good steganalysis performance. When analyzing the effectiveness of features with different

experiments, the proposed features achieve the comparable detection ability, especially in the cover source mismatch cases.

3. When combining with SRM and TLBP features, more powerful detection ability can be achieved, and even in some cases exceed the maxSRM feature based on the selected channel, which proves the three features come from different feature extraction methods are mutually supplementary.

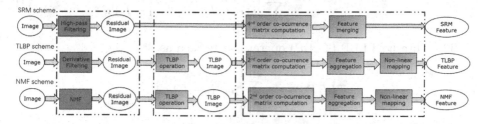

Fig. 1. The feature extraction flows for SRM, TLBP, and the proposed NMF scheme.

The rest of this paper is organized as follows. Section 2 describes the $TLBP_{P,R,T}^{riu^2}$ for obtaining TLBP images. Section 3 describes the NMF for obtaining residual images, and Sect. 4 explains the detailed feature extraction steps. Experimental results are demonstrated in Sect. 5. Finally, we conclude the paper in Sect. 6.

2 Fundamentals of Threshold Local Binary Pattern

In this section we review the $LBP_{8,1}^{riu2}$ of R_i proposed in [7].

2.1 Definition of TLBP

LBP [11] is proposed to model the statistics of a texture unit defined within its neighboring pixels in given distance. Each of neighboring pixels I_p ($p \in \{0, \ldots, P-1\}$) in given distance R ($R > 0$) is thresholded by the gray value of its central pixel I_c to form an P-bit binary pattern. And the P pixels in the neighborhood can be selected in a clockwise manner. The LBP operator is defined as

$$LBP_{P,R} = \sum_{p=0}^{P-1} s(I_p - I_c) \cdot 2^p, \tag{1}$$

where $s(\cdot)$ is the binarization function defined as

$$s(x) = \begin{cases} 1, & x \geqslant 0, \\ 0, & x < 0. \end{cases} \tag{2}$$

A popular extension is called rotation invariant uniform LBP ($LBP_{P,R}^{riu2}$) [12].

$$LBP_{P,R}^{riu2} = \begin{cases} \sum_{p=0}^{P-1} s(I_p - I_c), & \text{if } U(LBP_{P,R} \leqslant 2), \\ P+1, & \text{otherwise.} \end{cases} \tag{3}$$

$$U(LBP_{P,R}) = |s(I_{p-1} - I_c) - s(I_0 - I_c)| \\ + \sum_{p=1}^{P-1} |s(I_p - I_c) - s(I_{p-1} - I_c)|. \tag{4}$$

The Threshold LBP (TLBP) operator is defined as

$$TLBP_{P,R,T} = \sum_{p=0}^{P-1} s_T(I_p - I_c) \cdot 2^p, \tag{5}$$

where $s_T(\cdot)$ is the binarization function defined as

$$s_T(x) = \begin{cases} 1, & |x| \geqslant T \\ 0, & |x| < T. \end{cases} \tag{6}$$

2.2 TLBP Features for Steganalysis

In order to model pixel relationship in different scales, several values of radius R are used in the operator defined in Eq. (5). The checkerboard distance ($D8$ distance) is used to define the spatial distance R between I_p and I_c. When R is set to 1, 2, and 3, respectively, P equals to 8, 16, and 24. To reduce the number of LBP codes, neighboring pixels of I_c with a distance of R are divided into R subsets. Therefore, six neighboring pixel sets are formed, each one with $P = 8$, and six resultant TLBP images are generated for each residual image. The details of the process please see [7].

In our scheme, the $LBP_{8,1}^{riu2}$ of R_i operator is used to obtain TLBP images. Therefore, the value of TLBP image elements ranges from 0 to 9.

3 Obtaining Residual Images with Non-negative Matrix Factorization

3.1 Definition of Non-negative Matrix Factorization

NMF is developed as a matrix factorization technique, which decomposes non-negative matrices into physically meaningful data in two dimensional signal analysis, and has been used for image representation, document analysis and clustering for its parts-based representation property. In spatial image steganalysis, an image is represented by a two-dimensional matrix whose elements are non-negative. Thus, NMF can be applied to images. We predict the value of a central pixel based on its neighboring pixels via NMF and then calculate the residuals between the original and predicted values. In this paper, because the residuals between the original and predicted values satisfy a normal distribution, we use the Euclidean distance and iterative addition operations to obtain the NMF solution. Based on the Euclidean distance, we can express the objective function for NMF as follows:

$$e_{ij}^2 = \sum_{i=1}^{m}\sum_{j=1}^{n}(R_{ij} - \sum_{k=1}^{K}(P_{ik} \cdot Q_{kj}))^2 + \frac{\beta}{2}(||P_{ik}||^2 + ||Q_{kj}||^2), \qquad (7)$$

where β is a regularization coefficient that is introduced to avoid over-fitting, R_{ij} represent the pixel value of original image at location (i, j), P_{ik} and Q_{kj} represent the corresponding pixel value in the sub-matrix. By using this objective function, we can find the partial derivatives of P_{ik} and Q_{kj}:

$$\frac{\partial e_{ij}^2}{\partial P_{ik}} = \sum_{i=1}^{m}\sum_{j=1}^{n}[2(R_{ij} - \sum_{k=1}^{K}(P_{ik} \cdot Q_{kj})) \cdot (-Q_{kj})] + \beta \cdot P_{ik}$$
$$= -2[(RQ^T)_{ik} - (PQQ^T)_{ik}] + \beta \cdot P_{ik}, \qquad (8)$$

$$\frac{\partial e_{ij}^2}{\partial Q_{kj}} = \sum_{i=1}^{m}\sum_{j=1}^{n}[2(R_{ij} - \sum_{k=1}^{K}(P_{ik} \cdot Q_{kj})) \cdot (-P_{ik})] + \beta \cdot Q_{kj}$$
$$= -2[(P^T R)_{kj} - (P^T PQ)_{kj}] + \beta \cdot Q_{kj}. \qquad (9)$$

Then, we can iteratively use the gradient descent method to obtain the solutions for P_{ik} and Q_{kj}:

$$P_{ik} = P_{ik} + \alpha \cdot [(RQ^T)_{ik} - (PQQ^T)_{ik} - \frac{\beta}{2} \cdot P_{ik}], \qquad (10)$$

$$Q_{kj} = Q_{kj} + \alpha \cdot [(P^T R)_{kj} - (P^T PQ)_{kj} - \frac{\beta}{2} \cdot Q_{kj}], \qquad (11)$$

where α denotes the learning step. The larger α and the smaller β, the faster the speed of convergence. However, if the speed of convergence is too fast, it may suddenly exceed the extreme point, resulting in over-fitting. And if the speed of convergence is too slow, it may require very high time costs to iterate. Therefore, it is important to choose suitable α and β. In this paper, we choose 0.001 and 0.02 for α and β by multiple experiments, respectively. The prediction errors under different αs and βs are show in Fig. 2.

3.2   Application of NMF in Obtaining Residuals

This paper uses NMF and correlation between pixels to predict central pixel values and design steganalysis features. According to redundant information in the natural image, the central pixel value usually maintains a strong correlation with its neighboring pixels. By using the consistency relationship between neighboring pixels in the image, the central pixel can be obtained based on NMF with

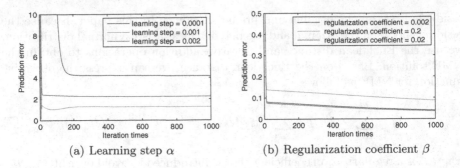

(a) Learning step α (b) Regularization coefficient β

Fig. 2. The prediction errors under different αs and βs.

multiple neighboring pixels. And then we can calculate the difference between the predicted pixel and the original pixel to obtain the residuals. Figure 3 illustrates the process of using NMF to predict the target pixel. For an image block of 3×3, we select the central (target) pixel r_{22} as the target pixel to be predicted, the directly neighboring 8 pixels (with the value of the central pixel set to 0) form the matrix $R_{3 \times 3}$ to be decomposed. Through the NMF solution, we can obtain the central pixel prediction value $\hat{r}_{22}$ and its residual $d = r_{22} - \hat{r}_{22}$.

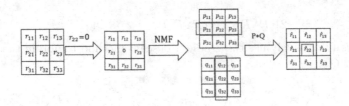

Fig. 3. The illustration of using NMF to predict the target pixel.

In order to obtain more versatile steganalysis features, Non-negative Matrix Factorization Features (NMFF) will be composed of multiple residual sub-models, which corresponding to different orders of magnitude and different positional relationships, or matrix decomposition of different degrees, etc. The specific residual sub-models are shown in Figs. 4 and 5. The dots in the figure represent the pixels to be predicted (we call target pixel in this paper), and the squares represent the pixels to be decomposed. We use the pixel values and NMF to calculate the predicted values of the target pixels. For example, the sub-model 1a) predict the target pixel located (1,1) by the other three pixels located (1,2), (2,1) and (2,2). For different sub-models, the naming rule is {"size", "nmff", "the position of target pixel"}. There are five sizes as 2×2, 2×3, 3×2, 3×3 and 5×5. Since the different sizes and shapes of sub-matrix contain different pixels to be decomposed, this enhance the diversity of final prediction results (and finally enhance the diversity of predicted residuals and effectiveness of the generated features).

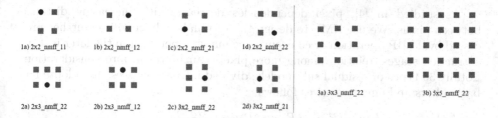

1a) 2x2_nmff_11   1b) 2x2_nmff_12   1c) 2x2_nmff_21   1d) 2x2_nmff_22

2a) 2x3_nmff_22   2b) 2x3_nmff_12   2c) 3x2_nmff_22   2d) 3x2_nmff_21   3a) 3x3_nmff_22   3b) 5x5_nmff_22

Fig. 4. The different matrix size in NMF.

In addition, considering that the selection of the decomposition rank in the matrix decomposition process will also affect the final decomposition result, we subdivide the decomposition of four cases as $K = 2, K = 3, K = 4$ and $K = 5$.

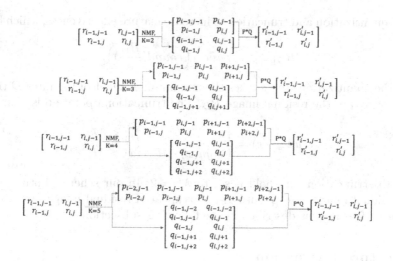

Fig. 5. The different decomposition rank of NMF with matrix size 2×2.

3.3 Non-linear Filtering

We introduce non-linearity by "max" and "min" operators. The "max" (or "min") operator computes the maximum (or minimum) values among the residuals obtained aforementioned NMF based process with different decomposition ranks. The output residual is designated as $R_{D^{max}}$ (or $R_{D^{min}}$). For example,

$$R_{D_{2 \times 2}^{max}} = \max\left\{R_{D_{2 \times 2}^{k=2}}, R_{D_{2 \times 2}^{k=3}}, R_{D_{2 \times 2}^{k=4}}, R_{D_{2 \times 2}^{k=5}}\right\}, \tag{12}$$

$$R_{D_{2 \times 2}^{min}} = \min\left\{R_{D_{2 \times 2}^{k=2}}, R_{D_{2 \times 2}^{k=3}}, R_{D_{2 \times 2}^{k=4}}, R_{D_{2 \times 2}^{k=5}}\right\}. \tag{13}$$

As studied in [4], pixel dependencies decrease with increasing distance between pixels. We use NMF to design the residuals, which will be further processed by TLBP operation or co-occurrence matrix operation in the later feature extraction stages, relation among more pixels can be taken into consideration. Totally 30 types of residual sub-models, divided into five classes, are adopted as basic filters and enumerated as follows:

- $C\#1 : R_{D_{2\times2}^{k=2}}, R_{D_{2\times2}^{k=3}}, R_{D_{2\times2}^{k=4}}, R_{D_{2\times2}^{k=5}}, R_{D_{2\times2}^{max}}, R_{D_{2\times2}^{min}}.$
- $C\#2 : R_{D_{2\times3}^{k=2}}, R_{D_{2\times3}^{k=3}}, R_{D_{2\times3}^{k=4}}, R_{D_{2\times3}^{k=5}}, R_{D_{2\times3}^{max}}, R_{D_{2\times3}^{min}}.$
- $C\#3 : R_{D_{3\times2}^{k=2}}, R_{D_{3\times2}^{k=3}}, R_{D_{3\times2}^{k=4}}, R_{D_{3\times2}^{k=5}}, R_{D_{3\times2}^{max}}, R_{D_{3\times2}^{min}}.$
- $C\#4 : R_{D_{3\times3}^{k=2}}, R_{D_{3\times3}^{k=3}}, R_{D_{3\times3}^{k=4}}, R_{D_{3\times3}^{k=5}}, R_{D_{3\times3}^{max}}, R_{D_{3\times3}^{min}}.$
- $C\#5 : R_{D_{5\times5}^{k=2}}, R_{D_{5\times5}^{k=3}}, R_{D_{5\times5}^{k=4}}, R_{D_{5\times5}^{k=5}}, R_{D_{5\times5}^{max}}, R_{D_{5\times5}^{min}}.$

3.4   Residual Quantization and Truncation

We use quantization and truncation to increase feature effectiveness, which forms as

$$[R_D]_{q,M} = trunc_M\left(round(\frac{R_D}{q})\right), \tag{14}$$

where the quantization step q takes the maximum element of the filter D that is used to generate the residual image R_D. The truncation operation is defined as

$$trunc_M(x) = \begin{cases} x, & |x| \leqslant M; \\ sign(x) \cdot M, & |x| > M, \end{cases} \tag{15}$$

where the truncation threshold is set to $M = 2$. In our scheme, both unquantized residual images and quantized-and-truncated residual images are used for generating features, as described in the following subsections.

4   Feature Extraction

4.1   Co-occurrence Matrix Formation

For the residuals calculated in Sect. 3, we compute the $LBP_{8,1}^{riu2}$ of R_i proposed in [7]. Let $B(i,j)$ $(0 \leqslant i \leqslant U - 1, 0 \leqslant j \leqslant V - 1)$ be a pixel of a TLBP image at location (i,j). Standard second-order co-occurrence matrices are formed along horizontal, vertical, diagonal, and anti-diagonal directions as:

$$C^{0°}(k,l) = \frac{\sum_{i=0}^{U-1}\sum_{j=0}^{V-2} \delta(B(i,j) - k, B(i,j+1) - l)}{U \cdot (V - 1)}, \tag{16}$$

$$C^{90°}(k,l) = \frac{\sum_{i=0}^{U-2}\sum_{j=0}^{V-1} \delta(B(i,j) - k, B(i+1,j) - l)}{(U - 1) \cdot V}, \tag{17}$$

$$C^{45°}(k,l) = \frac{\sum_{i=0}^{U-2}\sum_{j=0}^{V-2} \delta(B(i,j) - k, B(i+1,j+1) - l)}{(U-1)\cdot(V-1)}, \tag{18}$$

$$C^{135°}(k,l) = \frac{\sum_{i=1}^{U-2}\sum_{j=0}^{V-1} \delta(B(i+1,j) - k, B(i,j+1) - l)}{(U-1)\cdot(V-1)}, \tag{19}$$

where $k, l \in \{0, 1, \cdots, 9\}$, and

$$\delta(m,n) = \begin{cases} 1, & m = n = 0, \\ 0, & \text{otherwise}. \end{cases} \tag{20}$$

4.2 Feature Aggregation

In order to minimize the dimensions of statistical features, we need to add and compress the co-occurrence matrices in different directions. In SRM [4], it is found that the closer the distance among pixels, the stronger the correlation among them. Therefore, the correlation between a pixel and its horizontal (or vertical) neighboring pixels is stronger than the correlation between the pixel and its diagonal (or anti-diagonal) neighboring pixels. Therefore, for the second-order co-occurrence matrices of 0°, 90°, 45° and 135° generated by the same image, they are merged as follows:

$$C^{+}(k,l) = \frac{1}{2}\left(C^{0°}(k,l) + C^{90°}(k,l)\right), \tag{21}$$

$$C^{\times}(k,l) = \frac{1}{2}\left(C^{45°}(k,l) + C^{135°}(k,l)\right). \tag{22}$$

In steganalysis, when counting the pixel values of the co-occurrence matrix, the order between the pixel values has little effect on the final statistical results. Therefore, we can perform some fold operations when calculating the co-occurrence matrix. The operation embodied in the co-occurrence matrix is to fold the diagonal line between the upper left and the lower right of the co-occurrence matrix. The corresponding position values are directly added, the values at the diagonal position remain unchanged, and finally the folded co-occurrence matrix is converted into one dimension vector, the calculation process is as follows:

$$c^{+}\left(9k - \frac{k(k-1)}{2} + l\right) = \begin{cases} C^{+}(k,l), & k = l, \\ C^{+}(k,l) + C^{+}(l,k), & k < l. \end{cases} \tag{23}$$

$$c^{\times}\left(9k - \frac{k(k-1)}{2} + l\right) = \begin{cases} C^{\times}(k,l), & k = l, \\ C^{\times}(k,l) + C^{\times}(l,k), & k < l. \end{cases} \tag{24}$$

$$c = c^{+} \cup c^{\times}. \tag{25}$$

4.3 Non-linear Mapping

The dynamic range of non-zero elements of the aggregated features is large. For instance, the range is from 10^{-6} (i.e., $\frac{1}{(U-1) \times V}$ when $U = V = 512$) to 10^{-1}. This is due to the nature of co-occurrence matrix in which the diagonal elements are often large, while off-diagonal elements are often small. Large feature values might dominate the classification performance. In order to increase the efficiency of small features, we take the logarithm of features as:

$$f' = \log_{10}(f + \triangle), \tag{26}$$

where f represents the original co-occurrence matrix, and f' represents new co-occurrence matrix obtained by nonlinear mapping. In order to prevent mathematical calculation errors when value of f is 0, we add a constant $\triangle$ ($\triangle = 1/[(U-1) \times V])$ to f.

5   Performance Analysis

5.1 Experimental Settings

This section presents and analyses the experimental results of the proposed NMFF steganalysis features. All experiments in this paper were performed in the BOSSbase ver.1.01 [1], which contains 10,000 grayscale images of 512×512 size. The detected steganographic algorithms are HILL [9], MiPOD [15] and CMD_HILL [10], and the average error rate of random ten experiments is used as the evaluation metric of steganalysis. Among them, each experiment randomly selected 5000 images from the BOSSBase1.01 as the training set, and another 5000 images as the test set. For the steganalysis performance comparison experiment, this section selects the 29040-dimensional TLBP [7] steganalysis features, the 34671-dimensional SRM [4] steganalysis features, and the 34671-dimensional maxSRM [3] steganalysis features based on the selection channel. Fisher linear discriminant (FLD) based ensemble classifier [5] was applied for classification.

5.2 Performance of Each Feature Subset

In this subsection, we evaluate the performance of the NMF residual sub-models designed in Sect. 3. NMF based features with different types of residual sub-models and post process are compared with the experimental results shown in Table 1. From the table we can see, in the residual sub-model category, when the size of the sub-matrix is 3×3 ($C\#4$), the final feature performance is the best; when the size of the sub-matrix is 2×2 ($C\#1$) and 5×5 ($C\#5$), the performance is good; while the performance of other categories of residual sub-models are relative poor. We can also find that, when only use the linear features, their performance is better than that of only use nonlinear features. For the quantization truncation operation, we can see that the performance of features processed by quantization truncation operation are significantly better than that do not use quantization truncation operation. Finally, we combine linear and nonlinear features, quantized truncation and non-quantized truncation features to obtain all features based on NMF, and the detection effect is optimal compared to the single model or single operation sub-features.

Table 1. Detection performance under different sets of features.

Grouping criterion	Feature subset	Feature dimension	HILL	MiPOD	CMD-HILL
Filter class	C#1	7920-D	.3547 ± .0039	.3663 ± .0018	.4174 ± .0018
	C#2	7920-D	.4371 ± .0030	.4342 ± .0034	.4533 ± .0048
	C#3	7920-D	.4470 ± .0018	.4327 ± .0057	.4584 ± .0022
	C#4	7920-D	**.3159 ± .0029**	**.3130 ± .0048**	**.3626 ± .0021**
	C#5	7920-D	.3912 ± .0050	.3956 ± .0048	.4140 ± .0044
Residual type	Linear	26400-D	**.3125 ± .0026**	**.3107 ± .0061**	**.3600 ± .0019**
	Nonlinear	13200-D	.3206 ± .0048	.3145 ± .0024	.3649 ± .0021
Quantization operation	Quantized-and-Truncated	19800-D	**.3104 ± .0028**	**.3052 ± .0028**	**.3594 ± .0027**
	Unquantized	19800-D	.3326 ± .0024	.3249 ± .0034	.3804 ± .0019
All feature		39600-D	**.3052 ± .0034**	**.2984 ± .0061**	**.3554 ± .0046**

5.3 Comparison with Prior Arts

In order to verify the validity of the proposed steganalysis feature NMFF, we compare NMFF with the existing steganalysis features SRM and TLBP when detecting HILL [9], MiPOD [15] and CMD_HILL [10] at embedding rates of 0.1 bpp to 0.5 bpp. The detailed experimental results are shown in Table 2. We can see from the table that the proposed feature has certain effectiveness in detecting the above three steganographic algorithms, but it does not achieve better detection performance than the existing steganalysis features such as SRM.

5.4 Performance of Cover Source Mismatch

To further analyze the effectiveness of the proposed NMFF, we also compare the performance of NMFF with SRM and TLBP in the cover source mismatch (CSM) scenarios, where the source (*i.e.*, camera brand) of the test image are different from that of the training images. HILL with an embedding rate of 0.4 bpp is used as the example. We use BOSSbase ver.1.01 database [1] from a full-resolution color images in RAW format (CR2 or DNG). We first converted this images to grayscale, and eventually cropped to 512 × 512 pixels. Crossover experiments of 1000 images as the training set and 500 images as the test in CSM cases were conducted. The experimental results are shown in Table 3.

Table 2. Average detection error PE for three embedding algorithms with three steganalysis feature.

Algorithms	Features	0.1 bpp	0.2 bpp	0.3 bpp	0.4 bpp	0.5 bpp
HILL	TLBP	.4102 ± .0020	.3402 ± .0044	.2808 ± .0042	.2295 ± .0032	.1888 ± .0021
	SRM	.4360 ± .0033	.3632 ± .0024	.2996 ± .0020	.2482 ± .0032	.2038 ± .0021
	NMFF	.4450 ± .0014	.3795 ± .0028	.3052 ± .0034	.2653 ± .0038	.2219 ± .0055
MiPOD	TLBP	.4075 ± .0043	.3361 ± .0025	.2768 ± .0034	.2271 ± .0044	.1872 ± .0024
	SRM	.4150 ± .0047	.3442 ± .0032	.2893 ± .0055	.2398 ± .0023	.1969 ± .0032
	NMFF	.4297 ± .0027	.3539 ± .0029	.2984 ± .0061	.2527 ± .0037	.2107 ± .0025
CMD-HILL	TLBP	.4408 ± .0029	.3838 ± .0024	.3350 ± .0043	.2881 ± .0030	.2489 ± .0027
	SRM	.4529 ± .0036	.3945 ± .0033	.3424 ± .0029	.2987 ± .0036	.2542 ± .0018
	NMFF	.4642 ± .0057	.4069 ± .0053	.3554 ± .0046	.3123 ± .0032	.2674 ± .0025

Table 3. The comparison experiment with single training set under the case of cover-source mismatch

Training sets	Features	Test sets from different cover sources					
		Canon Eos 7D	Canon Eos 400D	Nikon D70	Pentax K20D	Canon Eos Digital Rebel XSi	Laica M9
Canon Eos 7D	SRM		.3219 ± .0055	.4156 ± .0040	.2978 ± .0071	.4166 ± .0057	.2718 ± .0129
	TLBP		.2817 ± .0080	.3310 ± .0076	.2828 ± .0098	.3730 ± .0065	.3090 ± .0144
	NMFF		.2890 ± .0086	.3930 ± .0050	.2747 ± .0045	.3750 ± .0010	.2540 ± .0056
Canon Eos 400D	SRM	.4057 ± .0046		.3120 ± .0053	.2187 ± .0042	.3436 ± .0058	.2219 ± .0038
	TLBP	.3552 ± .0153		.3208 ± .0064	.2158 ± .0048	.3154 ± .0081	.2452 ± .0114
	NMFF	.3900 ± .0020		.3393 ± .0059	.2433 ± .0110	.3267 ± .0068	.2543 ± .0040
Nikon D70	SRM	.4405 ± .0076	.3117 ± .0044		.3113 ± .0066	.3715 ± .0062	.2615 ± .0078
	TLBP	.3590 ± .0104	.2476 ± .0117		.2522 ± .0138	.3410 ± .0127	.2466 ± .0191
	NMFF	.4220 ± .0054	.2837 ± .0015		.2693 ± .0040	.3807 ± .0103	.2737 ± .0042
Pentax K20D	SRM	.4085 ± .0069	.2446 ± .0033	.3324 ± .0078		.3535 ± .0071	.2045 ± .0051
	TLBP	.3764 ± .0056	.2194 ± .0038	.3246 ± .0049		.3296 ± .0062	.2090 ± .0037
	NMFF	.3833 ± .0038	.2513 ± .0086	.3317 ± .0046		.3507 ± .0086	.2313 ± .0031
Canon Eos Digital Rebel XSi	SRM	.4102 ± .0059	.2561 ± .0077	.3059 ± .0042	.2401 ± .0070		.2249 ± .0104
	TLBP	.3936 ± .0056	.2228 ± .0060	.2878 ± .0066	.2180 ± .0045		.2464 ± .0204
	NMFF	.4040 ± .0010	.2483 ± .0051	.3110 ± .0010	.2430 ± .0046		.2497 ± .0031
Laica M9	SRM	.4074 ± .0079	.2501 ± .0036	.3227 ± .0042	.2348 ± .0044	.3625 ± .0051	
	TLBP	.3732 ± .0060	.2328 ± .0043	.3544 ± .0058	.2202 ± .0050	.3304 ± .0047	
	NMFF	.3730 ± .0096	.2513 ± .0042	.3700 ± .0066	.2543 ± .0050	.3613 ± .0067	

From Table 3 we can see that the NMFF features designed in this paper do not achieve the same effects as the existing SRM and TLBP features in CSM cases. The sensitivity of different steganalysis features to different camera images is not the same. The TLBP feature is better than the SRM features in many CSM cases and the NMFF feature is better than the SRM and TLBP features in some CSM cases. Compared with TLBP and SRM features, the CSM has less influence on the NMFF features, this may because that the residuals of NMFF are calculated with dynamic filters that derived from the image itself, whereas the filters of SRM and TLBP used are relative constant.

5.5   Performance of Combined Feature Set

The steganalysis features NMFF designed in this paper are basically different from the existing SRM and TLBP features in calculating the residual image. Therefore, the above three features are supplementary. We conducted experiments to test the effectiveness of combining the three features together.

As shown in Fig. 6, we directly combine NMFF with SRM and TLBP to form high-dimensional features. The experimental results show that the combined feature sets are improved to some extent compared to each of the single feature set NMFF, SRM or TLBP, and even in some cases, exceed the maxSRM feature based on the selected channel.

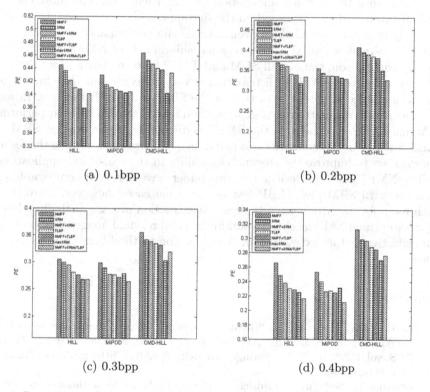

(a) 0.1bpp   (b) 0.2bpp

(c) 0.3bpp   (d) 0.4bpp

Fig. 6. Detection performance of TLBP, SRM, NMFF, the combination of NMFF and SRM, and the combination of TLBP and NMFF. (a)–(d) are steganographic algorithm embedding rates of 0.1 bpp, 0.2 bpp, 0.3 bpp, and 0.4 bpp, respectively.

6   Conclusion

This paper has designed a set of linear and nonlinear residual sub-models based on NMF to calculate the image residuals, and combined the local binary model and the co-occurrence matrix to extract the residual image to obtain the final feature NMFF for steganalysis. Based on the theoretical analysis of NMF, we choose the appropriate matrix decomposition size and decomposition rank in designing the sub-model. We choose the sub-model according to the results of experiments and the nature of NMF, and finally obtain 20 linear and 10 nonlinear sub-models used to calculate the residual image; through the residual sub-model of NMF design, the sub-models of different matrix decomposition ranks and different sizes of decomposed sub-matrixes, resulting in the variety of the residuals. Finally, the coded map of the residual image and the co-occurrence matrix in different directions are obtained to generate the final steganalysis feature NMFF. Compared with the existing steganalysis features, the NMFF feature proposed in this paper completely depends on the mutual relationship between image pixels to calculate the residual and obtain the final features. The most effective residual sub-model (3×3) based on the decomposition matrix design has good steganalysis performance, which even exceeds the performance of SRM feature optimal sub-models, but the other residual sub-models of NMFF are less effective. By comparison, the overall SRM and TLBP feature distributions are more uniform, whereas the NMFF distribution is very concentrated. The final detection performance is weaker than that of the SRM and TLBP features. In some the cover source mismatch cases, experimental results show NMFF outperformed SRM and TLBP. And because the NMFF is distinct from the existing SRM and TLBP features in designing the residual image, we also can combine the feature sets together to improve the steganalysis ability in the real-world applications.

The NMFF features designed in this paper have achieved comparable performance with SRM and TLBP features in some cases, however, there is still much room for improvement in the feature extraction process, including designing more optimal NMF method to obtain the valid residual images, and designing more effective feature extraction and combination method based on the residual images.

References

1. Bas, P., Filler, T., Pevný, T.: "Break our steganographic system": the ins and outs of organizing BOSS. In: Filler, T., Pevný, T., Craver, S., Ker, A. (eds.) IH 2011. LNCS, vol. 6958, pp. 59–70. Springer, Heidelberg (2011). https://doi.org/10.1007/978-3-642-24178-9_5
2. Cogranne, R., Sedighi, V., Fridrich, J., Pevny, T.: Is ensemble classifier needed for steganalysis in high-dimensional feature spaces? In: IEEE International Workshop on Information Forensics and Security, pp. 1–6 (2016)
3. Denemark, T., Sedighi, V., Holub, V., Cogranne, R., Fridrich, J.: Selection-channel-aware rich model for steganalysis of digital images. In: IEEE International Workshop on Information Forensics and Security, pp. 48–53 (2014)
4. Fridrich, J., Kodovsky, J.: Rich models for steganalysis of digital images. IEEE Trans. Inf. Forensics Secur. **7**(3), 868–882 (2012)
5. Kodovsky, J., Fridrich, J., Holub, V.: Ensemble classifiers for steganalysis of digital media. IEEE Trans. Inf. Forensics Secur. **7**(2), 432–444 (2012)
6. Lee, D.D., Seung, H.S.: Learning the parts of objects by non-negative matrix factorization. Nature **401**(6755), 788–791 (1999)

7. Li, B., Li, Z., Zhou, S., Tan, S., Zhang, X.: New steganalytic features for spatial image steganography based on derivative filters and threshold LBP operator. IEEE Trans. Inf. Forensics Secur. **13**(5), 1242–1257 (2018)

8. Li, B., He, J., Huang, J., Shi, Y.Q.: A survey on image steganography and steganalysis. J. Inf. Hiding Multimedia Signal Process. **2**(3), 288–289 (2011)

9. Li, B., Wang, M., Huang, J., Li, X.: A new cost function for spatial image steganography. In: 2014 IEEE International Conference on Image Processing (ICIP), pp. 4206–4210. IEEE (2014)

10. Li, B., Wang, M., Li, X., Tan, S., Huang, J.: A strategy of clustering modification directions in spatial image steganography. IEEE Trans. Inf. Forensics Secur. **10**(9), 1905–1917 (2015)

11. Ojala, T., Harwood, I.: A comparative study of texture measures with classification based on feature distributions. Pattern Recogn. **29**(1), 51–59 (1996)

12. Ojala, T., Pietikäinen, M., Mäenpää, T.: Multiresolution gray-scale and rotation invariant texture classification with local binary patterns. IEEE Trans. Pattern Anal. Mach. Intell. **7**, 971–987 (2002)

13. Pevný, T., Fridrich, J.: Benchmarking for steganography. In: Solanki, K., Sullivan, K., Madhow, U. (eds.) IH 2008. LNCS, vol. 5284, pp. 251–267. Springer, Heidelberg (2008). https://doi.org/10.1007/978-3-540-88961-8_18

14. Qian, Y., Dong, J., Wang, W., Tan, T.: Deep learning for steganalysis via convolutional neural networks. In: Proceedings of SPIE - The International Society for Optical Engineering, vol. 9409, pp. 94090J-1–94090J-10 (2015)

15. Sedighi, V., Cogranne, R., Fridrich, J.: Content-adaptive steganography by minimizing statistical detectability. IEEE Trans. Inf. Forensics Secur. **11**(2), 221–234 (2015)

16. Tan, S., Li, B.: Stacked convolutional auto-encoders for steganalysis of digital images. In: Signal and Information Processing Association Summit and Conference, pp. 1–4 (2014)

17. Xu, G., Wu, H.Z., Shi, Y.Q.: Ensemble of CNNs for steganalysis: an empirical study. In: ACM Workshop on Information Hiding and Multimedia Security, pp. 103–107 (2016)

18. Xu, G., Wu, H.Z., Shi, Y.Q.: Structural design of convolutional neural networks for steganalysis. IEEE Signal Process. Lett. **23**(5), 708–712 (2016)

19. Zeng, J., Tan, S., Li, B., Huang, J.: Large-scale JPEG image steganalysis using hybrid deep-learning framework. IEEE Trans. Inf. Forensics Secur. **13**(5), 1200–1214 (2018)

IStego100K: Large-Scale Image Steganalysis Dataset

Zhongliang Yang[1]([✉]), Ke Wang[1], Sai Ma[2], Yongfeng Huang[1], Xiangui Kang[3], and Xianfeng Zhao[2]

[1] Beijing National Research Center for Information Science and Technology, Tsinghua University, Beijing 100084, China
{yangzl15,k-w17}@mails.tsinghua.edu.cn, yfhuang@tsinghua.edu.cn
[2] State Key Laboratory of Information Security, Institute of Information Engineering, Chinese Academy of Sciences, Beijing 100093, China
{masai,zhaoxianfeng}@iie.ac.cn
[3] Guangdong Key Lab of Information Security, Sun Yat-sen University, Guangzhou, China
isskxg@mail.sysu.edu.cn

Abstract. In order to promote the rapid development of image steganalysis technology, in this paper, we construct and release a multivariable large-scale image steganalysis dataset called IStego100K. It contains 208,104 images with the same size of 1024*1024. Among them, 200,000 images (100,000 cover-stego image pairs) are divided as the training set and the remaining 8,104 as testing set. In addition, we hope that IStego100K can help researchers further explore the development of universal image steganalysis algorithms, so we try to reduce limits on the images in IStego100K. For each image in IStego100K, the quality factors is randomly set in the range of 75–95, the steganographic algorithm is randomly selected from three well-known steganographic algorithms, which are J-uniward, nsF5 and UERD, and the embedding rate is also randomly set to be a value of 0.1–0.4. In addition, considering the possible mismatch between training samples and test samples in real environment, we add a test set (DS-Test) whose source of samples are different from the training set. We hope that this test set can help to evaluate the robustness of steganalysis algorithms. We tested the performance of some latest steganalysis algorithms on IStego100K, with specific results and analysis details in the experimental part. We hope that the IStego100K dataset will further promote the development of universal image steganalysis technology (The description of IStego100K and instructions for use can be found here: https://github.com/YangzlTHU/IStego100K).

Keywords: IStego100K · Image steganalysis · Dataset

1 Introduction

Concealment system, together with encryption system and privacy system, is classified into three basic information security systems by Shannon [1].

© Springer Nature Switzerland AG 2020
H. Wang et al. (Eds.): IWDW 2019, LNCS 12022, pp. 352–364, 2020.
https://doi.org/10.1007/978-3-030-43575-2_29

Among them, the latter two security systems mainly guarantee the security of information content, but they may expose the existence and importance of information while protecting it. But for concealment system, it mainly protects the information from the perspective of behavioral security, hiding the existence of information and communication behavior, thus ensuring the security of important information. Due to its powerful information hiding ability, concealment system plays an important role in protecting the privacy and security in cyberspace.

There are various media forms of carrier that can be used for information hiding, including image [2,3], audio [4,5], text [6–8] and so on [9]. Among them, image has the characteristics of large information capacity, which has become a widely studied and used steganographic carrier in recent years. However, while protecting the security of information, these concealment systems may also be used by criminals and transmit some malicious information, thus bringing potential risks to cyberspace security [10]. Therefore, studying and developing effective steganalysis techniques becomes an increasingly promising and challenging task.

For a concealment system, we can usually model it as follows. Suppose there is a carrier space $\mathcal{C}$, a key space $\mathcal{K}$, and a secret information space $\mathcal{M}$. Alice chooses a secret information m from the secret space $\mathcal{M}$, under the guidance of the secret key $k \in \mathcal{K}$, uses the steganographic algorithm $f()$ to embed m into a carrier $c \in \mathcal{C}$ and form the steganographic carrier s, that is:

$$Emb : \mathcal{C} \times \mathcal{K} \times \mathcal{M} \to \mathcal{S}, f(c, k, m) = s. \qquad (1)$$

Generally speaking, once we insert additional information into the carrier, it will inevitably lead to changes in the distribution of some features of the carriers. In order to ensure the security of the steganographic system, the steganographic algorithm $f()$ chosen by Alice should minimize the statistical differences between the carriers before and after steganography, that is:

$$d_f(P_\mathcal{C}, P_\mathcal{S}) \le \varepsilon. \qquad (2)$$

Steganalysis technology is the countermeasure technology of steganography. Its main purpose is to detect whether covert information is contained in the information carrier being transmitted in cyberspace. It can help identify potential network attacks in cyberspace and maintain cyberspace security. Any steganalysis can be described by a map $F : \mathbb{R}^d \to \{0, 1\}$, where $F = 0$ means that x is detected as cover, while $F = 1$ means that x is detected as stego. Therefore, steganalysis researchers usually construct a variety of corresponding statistical features, and based on these features to find the differences in the statistical distribution between cover and stego carriers [11–13, 13–18].

This paper is motivated in three aspects. Firstly, in order to achieve higher performance steganalysis technology, researchers usually need to analyze the statistical distribution differences between a large number of normal samples and steganographic samples [11–13]. Especially with the development of deep learning technology, some image steganalysis methods based on deep neural network have a growing demand for data [13–15]. However, existing steganalysis datasets, such as the widely used BOSS dataset [19], are small in scale (10,000 images for training and 1,000 for testing), it may cause the model to ignore potential subtle differences in statistical feature distributions. Secondly, at present, many image steganalysis methods have strong pertinence. They are usually aimed at one specific steganalysis algorithm. This may lead to some steganalysis algorithms giving very good results in detecting a particular steganalysis algorithm, but might fail in detecting other steganography techniques. In order to help realize the universal steganalysis algorithm and make it more practical, we need a more diverse and universal steganalysis dataset. Thirdly, current steganalysis models are usually trained and tested on images from the same source. But in reality, it is difficult to have such perfect condition. We want to know whether the existing steganalysis models can still maintain good performance when training samples and test samples come from different image sources.

In order to promote the development of image steganalysis technology, especially the progress of universal image steganalysis technology, in this paper, we construct and release a large-scale image steganalysis dataset called IStego100K. For the first motivation, we collected 100,000 cover-stego image pairs with the same size of 1024*1024 to construct the training set. For the second motivation, each steganographic image in IStego100K is randomly embedded with three widely used image steganography (J-uniward [20], nsF5 [21] and UERD [22]) with a random embedding rate (bit per non-zero AC-DCT coefficient (bpnzac): 0.1–0.4). For the third motivation, we constructed two test sets. The first test set (SS-Test) contains 8,104 images from the same source as the training set. The second test set (DS-Test) contains 11,809 images from different sources of the training set. We also choose some of the latest and widely used image steganalysis models to train and test their performance on IStego100K. The experimental results are shown in details in the experimental section. We hope that IStego100K will further advance the development of image steganalysis.

In the remainder of this paper, Sect. 2 introduces related image steganalysis datasets. Section 3 introduces the detailed information of the IStego100K dataset, including data collection and preprocessing, information embedding algorithms. The Following part, Sect. 4, describes the steganalysis benchmarks we use and their performance on IStego100K dataset. Finally, conclusions are drawn in Sect. 5.

2   Related Dataset

BOSS dataset [19] is currently the most widely used image steganalysis dataset. It contains two databases of images, which are BOSSBase for training and BOSS-Rank for testing. BOSS dataset has greatly promoted the development of image steganalysis in previous years. However, with the advancement of technology, this dataset currently shows increasingly limitations.

Firstly, on the scale of the dataset, BOSSBase contains 10,000 grayscale images with the same size of 512*512, and BOSSRank database contains 1,000 512*512 grayscale images. However, IStego100K contains 200,000 images for

Table 1. The main characteristics of BOSS and IStego100K.

Dataset	BOSS		IStego100K		
	BOSSBase	BOSSRank	Train	SS-Test	DS-Test
Number	10,000	1,000	200,000	8,104	11,809
Size	512*512		1024*1024		
Image style	grayscale		color		
bpnzac	0.4		0.1–0.4		
Steganography	HUGO		J-uniward, nsF5, UERD		

training (100,000 cover-stego image pairs), each of which is a 1024*1024 color image. The core of the stegaalysis is to find the statistical distribution difference between normal carriers and steganographic carriers through the analysis model. In general, the more samples, the more helpful for the model to discover the statistical distribution differences between the carrier features.

Secondly, steganographic images in BOSS datasets are embedded using a single steganographic algorithm HUGO [19], which hides messages into least significant bits of grayscale images represented in the spatial domain. However, a single steganographic algorithm can only bring differences in the statistical distribution of samples in a limited way. In complex real-world environments, the steganography algorithms used by Alice may be varied. It is often difficult for the detector to know which steganographic algorithm is used for a sample that may contain covert information. We hope to further promote the development of universal image steganalysis technology, so that the steganalysis model can have certain detection capabilities for a variety of steganographic methods. Therefore, we set up a variety of randomness settings for the steganographic samples in IStego100K. For example, image quality factor, image steganography algorithm and embedding rate are all set in a certain dynamic range for steganographic images in IStego100K.

Thirdly, in the real environment, the source-mismatch of training samples and test samples is a very important problem. In reality, it is a very realistic and challenging problem to train and detect sample source inconsistencies. Because in reality, it's hard for Eve to know the source of the steganographic samples Alice and Bob are transmitting, and it's equally difficult to get a large number of training samples from the same source. In fact, this requires that image steganalysis algorithms have strong robustness and can still have high steganalysis ability for different source image samples. We believe that in order to achieve more practical and general steganalysis algorithm, the problem of sample source mismatch is worth considering. Therefore, different from the BOSS dataset, we present two test sets from different sources, one from the same source as the training sample (SS-Test) and the other from different sources (DS-Test).

In order to compare the IStego100K and BOSS more intuitively, we present the main characteristics of the two datasets in Table 1.

3   The Construction of IStego100K

In this section, we will introduce in details of the construction process of IStego100K, including source image collection, image preprocessing and information hiding. Finally, we give the overall distribution characteristics of IStego100K.

3.1   Source Image Collection

All of the training images in IStego100K were crawled from Unsplash[1], a copyright-free photography website[2]. We first used the API provided by Unsplash website to randomly crawl a large number of high quality photographic images. From these original images, we then selected pictures whose shortest edge is greater than 1024 and whose quality factor is higher than 95. At the same time, we also filter some images with similar content and single scene artificially. Finally, we obtained 108,104 original images. In addition, in order to explore the problem of image source mismatch, we have built another test set. We collected daily photos taken by more than 30 people using their mobile phones (without private information and they all agreed to make them public for research). After manually deleting some images that did not meet the requirements, we collected a total of 11,809 images.

3.2   Image Preprocessing

For image steganalysis, there are many factors that can affect the final detection results, such as steganographic algorithm, image size, image quality factor (QF), steganography embedding rate, etc. To construct a universal dataset for image steganalysis, in IStego100K, we only unified the image size to be 1024*1024, and the other three factors are randomly set within a certain range. For image size, we firstly cut images into square according to the length of the short edge. Secondly, we resized the clipped images into 1024*1024. For image quality factor, we randomly adjusted the quality factor (QF) for the images obtained from Unsplash to be $\{75, 80, 85, 90, 95\}$. And we maintain the QF distribution of images obtained from the phone unchanged.

3.3   Information Embedding

In order to construct a general and practical dataset for image steganalysis, we choose a variety of widely used steganographic algorithms, which are J-uniward [20], nsF5 [21] and UERD [22], to embed covert information into samples of IStego100K. We first randomly selected 100,000 images from the original images in IStego100K as the training set, and the remaining 8,104 images as the test set. In the information embedding process, we randomly selected one

---

[1] https://unsplash.com/.

[2] https://unsplash.com/license.

of the three steganographic algorithms and used them to embed the random
bits stream into all the images in the training set and the random half of the
test set (both SS-Test set and DS-Test set). For each steganographic image, the
embedding rate was randomly set to be 0.1, 0.2, 0.3, and 0.4.

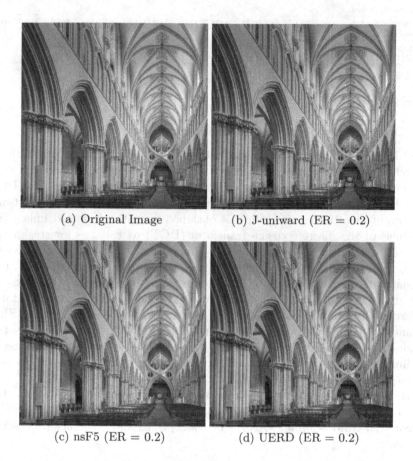

(a) Original Image   (b) J-uniward (ER = 0.2)

(c) nsF5 (ER = 0.2)   (d) UERD (ER = 0.2)

Fig. 1. Pictures that are embedded random bitstream by different steganographic algorithms at the same payload (bpnzac = 0.2).

3.4 Overall Details of IStego100K

After these above operations, the overall characteristics of IStego100K are shown
in Table 2. Figure 1 shows the case when the same image is embedded by different
steganographic algorithms at the same payload (bpnzac = 0.2). From the
examples in Fig. 1, we find that it is very difficult to distinguish the normal
image from the steganographic images visually.

Table 2. The overall characteristics of IStego100K.

IStego100K	Training set	SS-Test set	DS-Test set
Image Number(Cover:Stego)	100,000:100,000	4,052:4,052	5,904:5,905
Number for different steganography (Uerd:nsf5:j-uniward)	33,416:33,404:33,180	1,347:1,325:1,380	1,969:1,981:1,955
Number for different payloads (0.1:0.2:0.3:0.4)	25,077:24,878:25,251:24,794	1,047:984:1,045:976	1,484:1,500:1,451:1,470
Steganographic images of different QF (75:80:85:90:95)	10,058:9,925:9,979:10,032:10,006	803:806:820:798:825	95.369±1.664

4 Experimental

4.1 Benchmark Methods and Evaluation Metrics

To evaluate the difficulty of IStego100K and provide benchmark results for researchers who subsequently use this dataset, we tested four latest and widely used image steganalysis methods on this proposed dataset, which are DCTR [11], GFR [12], XuNet [23] and SRNet [13]. DCTR [11] extracts the first-order statistics of quantized noise residuals obtained from the inputted image using 64 kernels of the discrete cosine transform (DCT) as features for steganalysis. GFR [12] extracts features based on 2-dimensional (2D) Gabor filters, which have certain optimal joint localization properties in the spatial domain and in the spatial frequency domain and can describe the image texture features from different scales and orientations, therefore it can detect the changes of statistical feature distribution before and after steganography. XuNet [23] and SRNet [13] and based on convolutional neural networks (CNN), for which, XuNet [23] contains a 20-layer CNN and SRNet [13] designed a deep residual architecture to minimize the use of heuristics and extract features, finally these features are sent to classifiers for steganlysis.

We use several evaluation indicators commonly used in classification tasks to evaluate the performance of our model, which are precision (P), recall (R), F1-score (F1) and accuracy (Acc). The conceptions and formulas are described as follows:

- Accuracy measures the proportion of true results (both true positives and true negatives) among the total number of cases examined

$$Accuracy = \frac{TP + TN}{TP + FN + FP + TN}. \tag{3}$$

- Precision measures the proportion of positive samples in the classified samples.

$$Precision = \frac{TP}{TP + FP}. \tag{4}$$

- Recall measures the proportion of positives that are correctly identified as such.

$$Recall = \frac{TP}{TP + FN}. \tag{5}$$

– F1-score is a measure of a test's accuracy. It considers both the precision and the recall of the test. The F1 score is the harmonic average of the precision and recall, where an F1 score reaches its best value at 1 and worst at 0.

$$F1 - score = \frac{2 \times Precision \times Recall}{Precision + Recall}. \tag{6}$$

TP (True Positive) represents the number of positive samples that are predicted to be positive by the model, FP (False Positive) indicates the number of negative samples predicted to be positive, FN (False Negative) illustrates the number of positive samples predicted to be negative and TN (True Negative) represents the number of negative samples predicted to be negative. All these indicators are the higher the better.

4.2   Detection Results of Benchmark Methods

We first used the training set in IStego100K to train various steganalysis models and then used both SS-Test set and DS-Test set for testing. Table 3 records the test performance of each steganalysis model on both test set. In the process of model training, we are surprised to find that the two steganalysis methods based on neural network, which are XuNet [23] and SRNet [13], are hardly to converge on IStego100K. This may be caused by various reasons. To run these two models, we downloaded their training codes from https://github.com/GuanshuoXu/ caffe_deep_learning_for_steganalysis and http://dde.binghamton.edu/download/ respectively. We adopted the default training parameters, and then trained them in the environment of GTX1080TI and CUDA8.0. The small GPU memory (about 11G) may limited the performance of the model. Another main reason we thought is the diversity of samples in IStego100K, including multi-steganography, multi-quality factors, multi-embedding rates. These results at least indicate that although neural network technology and neural network-based image steganalysis models [13,23] have developed rapidly in recent years, they still face enormous challenges in the face of more complex real-world environments. Although the neural network-based image steganalysis model can achieve better results than the manual feature-based steganalysis model [11,12] in some specific scenarios, there is still much room for improvement in the practicality and generality of the model.

In addition, Table 3 also compares the detection performance of DCTR [11] and GFR [11] on the two test sets. Firstly, we noticed that the detection results of both DCTR and GFR on SS-Test is better than that on DS-Test. This result is in line with our expectations, since after all, the samples in DS-Test do not come from the same source as those in the training set. But we are also glad to see that these two steganalysis algorithms still have certain detection ability even in the case of source mis-match. This results reflect the robustness of these two steganalysis algorithms to some extent.

360   Z. Yang et al.

Table 3. The overall performance of each benchmark methods.

Dataset	Methods	Acc(%)	P(%)	R(%)	F1(%)
SS-Test	DCTR [11]	71.34	79.72	57.23	66.63
	GFR [12]	66.26	69.58	57.97	63.25
	XuNet [23]	Not Convergent			
	SRNet [13]	Not Convergent			
DS-Test	DCTR [11]	56.95	55.50	70.11	61.95
	GFR [12]	59.12	61.61	48.42	54.22
	XuNet [23]	Not Convergent			
	SRNet [13]	Not Convergent			

Table 4. The detection performance of each benchmark methods for different steganography algorithms in IStego100K.

Test Set	Steganalysis	Steganography	Acc(%)	P(%)	R(%)	F1(%)
SS-Test	DCTR [11]	UERD [22]	71.77	79.75	58.36	67.40
		nsF5 [21]	84.44	85.10	83.51	84.30
		J-uniward [20]	57.73	67.58	29.71	41.27
	GFR [12]	UERD [22]	68.47	71.34	61.75	66.20
		nsF5 [21]	71.61	72.72	69.18	70.91
		J-uniward [20]	58.81	62.91	42.92	51.02
DS-Test	DCTR [11]	UERD [22]	53.96	53.35	63.06	57.80
		nsF5 [21]	62.28	60.56	87.59	71.61
		J-uniward [20]	51.67	51.43	59.83	55.31
	GFR [12]	UERD [22]	56.05	58.40	42.09	48.92
		nsF5 [21]	67.24	68.21	64.58	66.35
		J-uniward [20]	54.59	56.62	39.26	46.37

On the basis of Table 3, we have made a more detailed analysis of the detection results on test sets. We analyzed the impact of different steganographic algorithms on the detection results. We calculated the test results of different steganalysis methods on the test set for each steganographic algorithm. The results are shown in Table 4.

From the results in Table 4, we can find that, firstly, when these three steganographic algorithms are mixed together, whether using DCTR or GFR for steganalysis, J-uniward [20] seems to be the most difficult to detect, and nsF5 [21] is relatively easier to detect. To some extent, it proves that the concealment of the three steganography algorithms from strong to weak seems to be J-uniward [20], UERD [22] and nsF5 [21]. Secondly, when we compare the detection accuracy of two steganalysis algorithms on the two test sets, we find a very interesting phenomenon: the detection accuracy of DCTR on SS-Test seems to be better than that of GFR, but on DS-Test, GFR's detection accuracy seems to be better than DCTR's. This seems to indicate that the robustness of the GFR model is better than the robustness of the DCTR.

Table 5. The detection performance of each benchmark methods for different embedding rates in IStego100K.

Test Set		SS-Test				DS-Test			
Steganalysis	Payload	Acc(%)	P(%)	R(%)	F1(%)	Acc(%)	P(%)	R(%)	F1(%)
DCTR [11]	0.1	58.55	67.84	32.51	43.96	52.86	52.42	61.90	56.77
	0.2	71.43	80.19	56.90	66.57	56.21	54.99	68.40	60.97
	0.3	76.30	82.22	67.11	73.90	58.56	56.53	74.11	64.13
	0.4	79.55	83.74	73.35	78.20	60.17	57.72	76.05	65.63
GFR [12]	0.1	55.87	59.40	37.10	45.67	52.29	53.42	35.79	42.86
	0.2	63.51	67.98	51.08	58.33	56.66	58.87	44.19	50.49
	0.3	70.83	72.04	67.89	69.95	62.15	64.65	53.65	58.63
	0.4	75.71	74.89	76.75	72.05	65.40	67.18	60.22	63.51

We further analyzed the impact of different embedding rates on the test results. We calculate the detection performance of each steganalysis method for images with different embedding rates in the test set. The results are shown in Table 5. From the results in Table 5, we can easily find a very obvious change rule, that is, as the embedding rate increases, the detection performance of each detection model is gradually improved. For example, for the DCTR algorithm [11], when the embedding rate is 0.1, the detection accuracy is only 58.55%. When the embedding rate is increased to 0.4, the detection is also improved to 79.55%. This trend can be explained by Formula (2). Embedding additional information in the original image carrier is equivalent to introducing noise into the original signal, which will inevitably change the statistical distribution characteristics of the original signal carrier. The higher the embedding rate, the more extra information is embedded, which will cause this statistical distribution to become larger and therefore easier to be detected. In Table 5, we found the same phenomenon as in Table 4. That is to say, from the detection accuracy, the detection accuracy of DCTR on SS-Test is higher than that of GFR, but it turns to the opposite on DS-Test.

Further more, we also want to know how the image quality factors affect steganalysis performance. Therefore, we also calculated the detection accuracy of different detection algorithms for different quality factor images in the test sets. The results are shown in Table 6. From the results in Table 6, we can see that as the image quality factor increases, the detection accuracy of various detection algorithms gradually decreases. This seems to indicate that the higher the image quality factor within a certain range, the harder it is to detect a steganographic image. Finally, Fig. 2 shows the ROC curves of these two steganography algorithms on IStego100K in different situations.

Table 6. The detection performance of each benchmark methods for different quality factors in IStego100K.

Test Set		SS-Test			
Steganalysis	QF	Acc(%)	P(%)	R(%)	F1(%)
DCTR [11]	75	75.23	85.63	60.64	71.00
	80	71.50	86.48	61.56	71.82
	85	74.09	84.34	59.18	69.55
	90	69.04	76.09	55.54	64.21
	95	62.12	66.41	49.05	56.43
GFR [12]	75	70.08	75.06	60.15	66.78
	80	69.91	74.98	59.75	66.50
	85	68.42	71.54	61.17	65.95
	90	64.67	67.02	57.75	62.04
	95	58.30	59.76	50.82	54.93

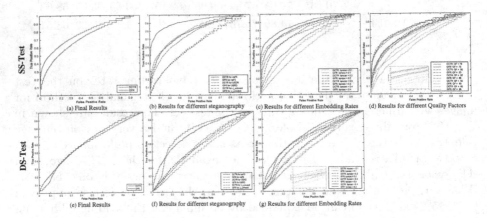

(a) Final Results (b) Results for different steganography (c) Results for different Embedding Rates (d) Results for different Quailty Factors

(e) Final Results (f) Results for different steganography (g) Results for different Embedding Rates

Fig. 2. The ROC curves of these two steganography algorithms on IStego100K in different situations.

5 Conclusion

In this paper, we construct and release a large-scale image steganalysis dataset called IStego100K. It contains 208,104 images with the same size of 1024*1024, of which 200,000 images (100,000 cover-stego image pairs) construct the training set and the remaining 8,104 are as testing sets. Each steganographic image is randomly steganized with three widely used image steganography (J-uniward [20], NSF5 [21] and UERD [22]) with a random embedding rate (0.1-0.4). At the same time, we also choose some latest steganalysis algorithms to test IStego100K dataset. These results show some interesting phenomena. Firstly, although image analysis techniques based on convolutional neural networks have been greatly developed in recent years, and there have also appeared more and more image steganalysis techniques based on CNN. However, our detection results show that when facing with more general detection scenarios, these methods seem to still have great limitations. Secondly, the results of Tables 3, 4 and 5 show that the detection performance of existing steganalysis methods will be greatly affected when facing different source detection samples from training samples. This further encourages researchers to explore more general steganalysis models for more realistic scenarios. Thirdly, the results of Tables 5 and 6 show that the image quality factor and embedding rate can significantly affect the detection performance. Generally speaking, increasing the embedding rate and reducing the quality factor in a certain range will be more helpful for steganalysis. We hope that this paper will serve as a reference guide for researchers to facilitate the design and implementation of better image steganalysis method.

Acknowledgment. This work was supported in part by the National Key Research and Development Program of China under Grant 2018YFB0804103 and the National Natural Science Foundation of China (No.U1536207, No.U1705261 and No.U1636113).

References

1. Shannon, C.E.: Communication theory of secrecy systems. Bell Labs Tech. J. **28**(4), 656–715 (1949)
2. Fridrich, J.: Steganography in Digital Media: Principles, Algorithms, and Applications. Cambridge University Press, Cambridge (2009)
3. Chen, K., Zhou, H., Zhou, W., Zhang, W., Yu, N.: Defining cost functions for adaptive JPEG steganography at the microscale. IEEE Trans. Inf. Forensics Secur. **14**(4), 1052–1066 (2019)
4. Yang, Z., Peng, X., Huang, Y.: A sudoku matrix-based method of pitch period steganography in low-rate speech coding. In: Lin, X., Ghorbani, A., Ren, K., Zhu, S., Zhang, A. (eds.) SecureComm 2017. LNICST, vol. 238, pp. 752–762. Springer, Cham (2018). https://doi.org/10.1007/978-3-319-78813-5_40
5. Yang, Z., Du, X., Tan, Y., Huang, Y., Zhang, Y.-J.: AAG-Stega: automatic audio generation-based steganography. arXiv preprint arXiv:1809.03463 (2018)
6. Yang, Z.-L., Guo, X.-Q., Chen, Z.-M., Huang, Y.-F., Zhang, Y.-J.: RNN-Stega: linguistic steganography based on recurrent neural networks. IEEE Trans. Inf. Forensics Secur. **14**(5), 1280–1295 (2019)
7. Yang, Z., Zhang, P., Jiang, M., Huang, Y., Zhang, Y.-J.: RITS: real-time interactive text steganography based on automatic dialogue model. In: Sun, X., Pan, Z., Bertino, E. (eds.) ICCCS 2018. LNCS, vol. 11065, pp. 253–264. Springer, Cham (2018). https://doi.org/10.1007/978-3-030-00012-7_24
8. Yang, Z., Jin, S., Huang, Y., Zhang, Y., Li, H.: Automatically generate steganographic text based on Markov model and Huffman coding. arXiv preprint arXiv:1811.04720 (2018)
9. Johnson, N.F., Sallee, P.A.: Detection of Hidden Information, Covert Channels and Information Flows. Wiley Handbook of Science and Technology for Homeland Security (2008)
10. Theohary, C.A.: Terrorist Use of the Internet: Information Operations in Cyberspace. DIANE Publishing (2011)

11. Holub, V., Fridrich, J.: Low-complexity features for JPEG steganalysis using undecimated DCT. IEEE Trans. Inf. Forensics Secur. **10**(2), 219–228 (2014)
12. Song, X., Liu, F., Yang, C., Luo, X., Zhang, Y.: Steganalysis of adaptive JPEG steganography using 2D Gabor filters. In: Proceedings of the 3rd ACM Workshop on Information Hiding and Multimedia Security, pp. 15–23. ACM (2015)
13. Boroumand, M., Chen, M., Fridrich, J.: Deep residual network for steganalysis of digital images. IEEE Trans. Inf. Forensics Secur. **14**(5), 1181–1193 (2019)
14. Xu, G., Wu, H.-Z., Shi, Y.-Q.: Structural design of convolutional neural networks for steganalysis. IEEE Signal Process. Lett. **23**(5), 708–712 (2016)
15. Wu, S., Zhong, S., Liu, Y.: Deep residual learning for image steganalysis. Multimedia Tools Appl. **77**(9), 437–453 (2018)
16. Yang, Z., Wang, K., Li, J., Huang, Y., Zhang, Y.: TS-RNN: text steganalysis based on recurrent neural networks. IEEE Signal Process. Lett., 1 (2019)
17. Yang, Z., Huang, Y., Zhang, Y.-J.: A fast and efficient text steganalysis method. IEEE Signal Process. Lett. **26**(4), 627–631 (2019)
18. Yang, Z., Yang, H., Hu, Y., Huang, Y., Zhang, Y.-J.: Real-time steganalysis for stream media based on multi-channel convolutional sliding windows. arXiv preprint arXiv:1902.01286 (2019)
19. Bas, P., Filler, T., Pevný, T.: Break our steganographic system: the ins and outs of organizing BOSS. In: Filler, T., Pevný, T., Craver, S., Ker, A. (eds.) IH 2011. LNCS, vol. 6958, pp. 59–70. Springer, Heidelberg (2011). https://doi.org/10.1007/978-3-642-24178-9_5
20. Holub, V., Fridrich, J., Denemark, T.: Universal distortion function for steganography in an arbitrary domain. EURASIP J. Inf. Secur. **2014**(1), 1 (2014)
21. Fridrich, J., Pevný, T., Kodovský, J.: Statistically undetectable jpeg steganography: dead ends challenges, and opportunities. In: Proceedings of the 9th Workshop on Multimedia & Security, pp. 3–14. ACM (2007)
22. Guo, L., Ni, J., Su, W., Tang, C., Shi, Y.-Q.: Using statistical image model for JPEG steganography: uniform embedding revisited. IEEE Trans. Inf. Forensics Secur. **10**(12), 2669–2680 (2015)
23. Xu, G.: Deep convolutional neural network to detect J-UNIWARD. In: Proceedings of the 5th ACM Workshop on Information Hiding and Multimedia Security, pp. 67–73. ACM (2017)

BNS-CNN: A Blind Network Steganalysis Model Based on Convolutional Neural Network in IPv6 Network

Danyang Zhao and Kaixi Wang[✉] (iD)

College of Computer Science and Technology, Qingdao University, Qingdao,
Shandong Province, China
kxwang@qdu.edu.cn

Abstract. There still exists the difficulties in the feature extraction and
few approaches can detect multiple network steganographic algorithms
currently in the IPv6 network. A unified network steganalysis model
based on convolutional neural network, abbreviated as BNS-CNN, is
proposed to detect multiple network storage steganographic algorithms.
After preprocessing the network traffic, the model divides them by field
to preserve the integrality of traffic feature to the maximum extent to
build a matrix. Multiple convolution kernels and the K-max pooling are
effectively combined to perform the feature extraction to speed up the
model convergence; the full connection layer is designed to improve the
ability of feature integration and boosts up the robustness of the model.
Compared with the traditional network steganalysis method, the model
can automatically extract data features and identify multiple storage
covert channels at the same time. The experimental results show that
the detection accuracy of BNS-CNN model is as high as 99.98% with
low time complexity and favorable generalization performance.

Keywords: Network steganalysis · Network steganography ·
Convolutional neural network · Deep learning

1 Introduction

Compared with other carriers, network steganography either uses redundant
fields and loopholes in protocol rules or leverages the protocol timing to transmit
a secret message. Both of them have the same distinct feature that the carriers,
i.e., the network traffic, are dynamic, this makes it more covert than the static
covers, such as an image. But the existing IPv6 security mechanism has no
measures in resisting network steganography.

This paper analyzes the IPv6 network protocols and the existing network
steganography and steganalysis. A blind network steganalysis model based on
convolutional neural Network, i.e. BNS-CNN is proposed to detect the storage
channels in the IPv6 headers.

This work was supported in part by the NSFC-General Technical Research Foundation
Joint Fund of China under Grant U1536113, and in part by the CERNET Innovation
Project under Grant NGII20180405.

© Springer Nature Switzerland AG 2020
H. Wang et al. (Eds.): IWDW 2019, LNCS 12022, pp. 365–373, 2020.
https://doi.org/10.1007/978-3-030-43575-2_30

2   Related Work

2.1   Network Steganography

The network steganography refers to all information hiding methods used in communication networks for secret information exchange, mainly by constructing covert channels. Usually, it is mainly divided into storage covert channels and timing covert channels.

The covert storage channel modifies the network protocol header [10] and the payload for steganography, which is currently the main way to construct covert channels on network. Graf [5] implemented embedding secret information into IPv6 destination options. Miller et al. [6] encoded the source address field of the IPv6 packet header by means of MAC address and forged packet, and used 64-bit interface identifier to implement secret information transmission. Lucena et al. [3] demonstrated the embedding of information in the IPv6 hop limit field.

The covert timing channel encodes secret information in the timing of protocol messages for steganography, such as changing the order of the packets, adding delay. Li [2] described a timing channel where a covert sender affects the performance of a switch to change the throughput of a packet flow from a third party to a covert receiver. Zander et al. [14] encoded the covert information only in the least significant part of the interpacket gaps of existing traffic.

2.2   Network Steganalysis

Network steganalysis is the inverse of network steganography. The existing network steganalysis techniques are mainly divided into two categories: statistical steganalysis and machine learning steganalysis.

Statistical steganalysis mainly uses mathematical and statistical techniques to establish statistical models to describe the probability distribution of steganographic systems or vectors. Pack et al. [8] presented a system to detect HTTP covert channels. Berk et al. [1] studied the channel capacity of Internet-based timing channels and proposed a methodology for detecting covert timing channels based on the proximity of the signal source and the capacity of channel.

Although the statistical steganalysis methods have higher accuracy, their analysis is time-consuming, which makes the steganalysis analysis less efficient. But machine learning technology has great advantages in data analysis and feature selection. The machine learning steganalysis method can automatically select features from the steganographic carrier, and use the machine learning method to train the classifier to implement steganalysis [13].

Sohn et al. [11] demonstrated that high-precision detection is performed using the support vector machine in the IP ID field the TCP ISN field. The authors evaluated the set of different features to achieve a classification accuracy rate higher than 99%. Similarly for the IP ID field and the TCP ISN field, Apurva et al. [4] proposed method is based on Naive Bayes classifier for network steganalysis, which achieved good detection results and greatly reduced computational complexity. Qian et al. [9] used deep learning techniques to replace the traditional statistical analysis methods for steganalysis, and proposed a five-layer CNN model. The model test works well and shows the great potential of neural networks in the field of steganalysis. Oplatkova et al. [7] discussed a neural network model that detects the secret information embedded in normal packets by the program OutGuess. Tumoian et al. [12] evaluated the accuracy of using the neural network to detect Rutkowska's TCP ISN covert channel. The study found that the correct rate for continuous ISNs monitoring can reach 99%, and the accuracy of steganalysis is high.

3 The Unified Network Steganalysis Model Based on Convolutional Neural Network (BNS-CNN)

This paper mainly detect the steganography using headers of IP, TCP and UDP protocols. We construct a model BNS-CNN that includes input layer, convolutional layer, two fully connected layers, and a softmax layer to detect the covert channel in these protocols' headers. The network structure of the BNS-CNN model is shown in Fig. 1.

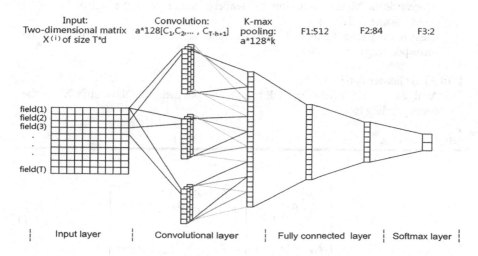

Fig. 1. BNS-CNN network structure (a denotes the type of different size filters)

3.1 Constructing Input Matrix

In order to preserve the data characteristics to the greatest extent and ensure the filters' feature extraction effective, the input layer extracts the IP, TCP and UDP headers of the IPv6 packet into a two-dimensional matrix, whose size is $T*d$. The total number of fields is T and the length of the longest field is d. The fields that the package does not contain or the fields whose length is shorter than the longest field are padded with 0. Thus, all packets can be converted to a unified fixed size vector.

According to RFC2460, RFC793 and RFC768, we comprehensively consider the nature and size of each field, combine the IP, TCP, and UDP protocol headers in the IPv6 network with the BNS-CNN unified input unit of 54 fields. They are arranged in the order of the packets, with the TCP header placed after the UDP header. Algorithm 1 describes the method in detail, and the matrix x$^{(i)}$ is figured out and illustrated in Eq. (1).

Algorithm 1: Packet Preprocessing

Input: Packet S$^{(i)}$
Output: Matrix X$^{(i)}$ of size T*d
Traverse packet S$^{(i)}$ and get the longest field length d;
Create a matrix X$^{(i)}$ of size T*d and initialize its element by zero;
Get all the fix fields in the IPv6 header format and put them into the matrix in order;
headercounter = 0;
While (the next header is the extension header) {
    headercounter++;
    Get the fields according to its extended header format and put them into the corresponding position of the matrix X$^{(i)}$;
}
Move forwards the MaxHeaderCounter − headercounter rows in the Matrix.
If (the next header is TCP) {
    Analyze the packet fields in TCP format and put them into the matrix X$^{(i)}$ at the corresponding rows;
}
If (the next header is UDP) {
    Analyze the packet fields in UDP format and put them into the matrix X$^{(i)}$ at the corresponding rows;
}
return matrix X$^{(i)}$

$$X^{(i)} = \begin{bmatrix} field^{(1)} \\ field^{(2)} \\ \vdots \\ field^{(T)} \end{bmatrix} = \begin{bmatrix} x^{(1,1)} & x^{(1,2)} & \cdots & x^{(1,d)} \\ x^{(2,1)} & x^{(2,2)} & \cdots & x^{(2,d)} \\ \vdots & \vdots & & \vdots \\ x^{(T,1)} & x^{(T,2)} & \cdots & x^{(T,d)} \end{bmatrix} \tag{1}$$

3.2 Convolutional Layer

The BNS-CNN model uses different sizes of filters for feature extraction. Its filters' size can be $n^{(j)} * d$, where $j \in \{1, 2, ..., s\}$, $n^{(j)} \in T$, $s < T + 2$. The filter width d is the same as the column width of the matrix, this can ensure that the feature is recognized by a field unit. For the filter height $h \in n^{(j)}$, a filter w can produce a new feature c_p on a window of size $h*d$ starting from p line.

$$c_p = f\left(W * X^{(i)}_{p:p+h-1} + b\right) \tag{2}$$

where b is a bias term and f is a non-linear function. Our model chooses the ReLU function as f, that is, $f(x) = \max(0, x)$. The filter slides up and down on the matrix $X^{(i)}$. A series of extracted feature values form a feature map C.

$$C = [c_1, c_2, ..., c_{T-h+1}] \tag{3}$$

Each filter in the model repeats the same operation to form different feature map. The specific process of the convolution operation is shown in Fig. 2.

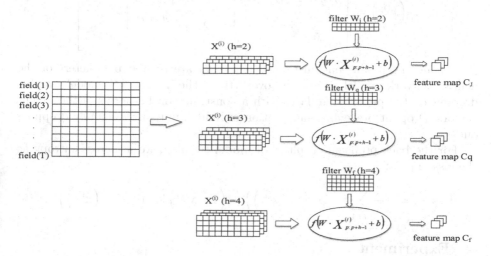

Fig. 2. Specific example of BNS-CNN convolution operation

The network steganography algorithm makes the steganographic embedding rate generally low in order to ensure concealment, the steganographic noise is usually small. The traditional max pooling and average pooling are prone to oversampling, which is not conducive to model convergence. Therefore, the BNS-CNN model uses K-max pooling to aggregate statistics on features.

In addition, the model uses the K-max pooling to reduce data size, increase computational speed and improve feature robustness. The output of the convolution is pooled, taking the largest K values of all feature values, and retaining the original order of these feature values. K-max pooling can reflect the strength of certain types of features and retain some location information. K-max pooling can achieve the connection between fields that are further away in the matrix, and provide more feature information for feature integration of the full-connection layer and improve the effect of model classification.

3.3   Softmax Function and Loss Function

The output by the convolution layer are put into the fully connected layer, which can enhance the ability to integrate model features. Finally, the softmax function is used to determine the possible final classification. We assume that the training set is $\{(\mathrm{x}^{(1)}, \mathrm{y}^{(1)}), \ldots, (\mathrm{x}^{(m)}, \mathrm{y}^{(m)})\}$, where m represents the number of samples; label $y^{(i)} \in \{1, 2, \ldots, k\}$, $i \in m$. For input x, We use the softmax prediction function to estimate the probability value $p(y = j|x)$ for each category $j \in \{1, 2, \ldots, k\}$, and adjusting the model output between $[0, 1]$. The prediction function $h_\theta\left(x^{(i)}\right)$ is as follows:

$$
h_\theta\left(x^{(i)}\right) =
\begin{bmatrix}
p\left(y^{(i)} = 1|x^{(i)}; \theta\right) \\
p\left(y^{(i)} = 2|x^{(i)}; \theta\right) \\
\vdots \\
p\left(y^{(i)} = k|x^{(i)}; \theta\right)
\end{bmatrix}
= \frac{1}{\sum_{j=1}^{k} e^{\theta_j^T x(i)}}
\begin{bmatrix}
e^{\theta_1^T x(i)} \\
e^{\theta_2^T x(i)} \\
\vdots \\
e^{\theta_k^T x(i)}
\end{bmatrix}
\tag{4}
$$

Among the prediction function, $\theta_1, \theta_2, \ldots, \theta_k$ are related parameters of the neural network model. To avoid overfitting, the BNS-CNN model employ dropout on the penultimate layer with a constraint on L2-norms of the weight vectors. Dropout prevents co-adaptation of hidden units by randomly dropping out.

For the back propagation phase of model training, we use cross entropy as the loss function.

$$
\mathrm{loss}\,(\theta) = -\frac{1}{m} \sum_{i=1}^{m} \mathrm{y}^{(i)} \log\left(h_\theta\left(\mathrm{x}^{(i)}\right)\right) + \left(1 - \mathrm{y}^{(i)}\right) \log\left(1 - h_\theta\left(\mathrm{x}^{(i)}\right)\right)
\tag{5}
$$

4   Experiment

4.1   Data Set and Experimental Setup

A network steganographic dataset is built with a total of 24,000 packets. The network steganographic packet is generated by embedding covert data in the carrier's IPv6 source address field [6], hop limit field [3], and TCP ISN [10]. The specific division of the data set is shown in Table 1.

The batch size is set to 100. A epoch, i.e. 180 iterations, is performed. Experiments show that the detection accuracy is no longer improved when the model is trained for 10 epochs. We choose a filter with 2, 3, 4 height respectively, and 128 filters for each size, and a k value of 3 is set in the K-max pooling layer to generate 1152 values into the fully connected layer. The first full connection layer contains 512 neurons, and the second full connection layer contains 84 neurons, all of which apply the ReLU non-linear function.

Table 1. Number of samples in the training set and test set.

	Training set	Test set
Steganographic packet	6000	2000
Non-steganographic packet	12000	4000

Loss Optimizer. The experiment compares two optimization methods commonly used in machine learning algorithms: stochastic gradient descent and Adam optimizer. We evaluate the degree of convergence of the loss value and the accuracy of the model in the model training process. As can be seen from Fig. 3, the Adam optimizer performs better in both loss and accuracy.

Reduce the Convolutional Layer. Experiments show that, since the BNS-CNN model considers the characteristics of the packet header, the field is the minimum unit of feature extraction to retain the data feature. The convolutional method with filter size $n*n$ will destroy the field features. And the steganographic information accounts for a small proportion of all data. Too many convolutional layers can also lead to loss of steganographic information, and the accuracy of model detection decreases, shown in Fig. 4. Therefore, the BNS-CNN model reduces the number of convolutional layers, uses the filters of size $n*d$ and increases the number of filters to improve feature extraction.

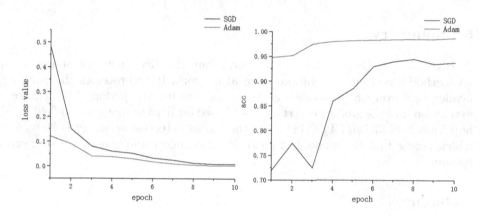

Fig. 3. Effect of SGD and Adam optimizer on loss value and detection accuracy

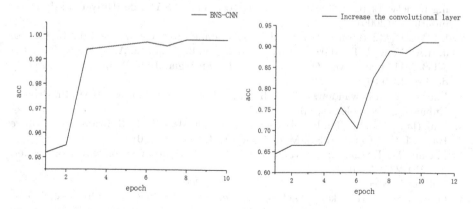

Fig. 4. Model accuracy changes after increasing the convolutional layer

4.2 Experimental Results and Analysis

The BNS-CNN model is compared with other common shallow convolutional neural network models in three dimensions, i.e. the false alarm (FPR), the missing alarm (FNR) and the accuracy (ACC). As show in Table 2, its detection rate can reach 99.98% and its execution time is low. This shows that this model works well for detecting multiple network steganography algorithms, the model detection efficiency is high and it has strong generalization ability.

Table 2. Comparing the performance of each model.

Model	FPR/%	FNR/%	ACC/%	Testing time/m
LeNet	17.25	15.13	83.33	43.31
AlexNet	2.58	3.17	97.34	338.23
BNS-CNN	0.037	0.021	99.98	52.50

5 Summary

A BNS-CNN model is proposed to carry out the IPv6 network steganalysis method based on convolutional neural network. It preprocesses the packet header, and every field is taken as the minimum unit to perform the feature extraction. For the storage covert channel based on IPv6 source address field [6], hop limit field [3], and TCP ISN [10], the model detection accuracy is 99.98%, which proves that the model has good detection effect and generalization performance.

References

1. Berk, V., Giani, A., Cybenko, G., Hanover, N.: Detection of covert channel encoding in network packet delays. Rapport technique TR536, de lUniversité de Dartmouth, 19 (2005)
2. Li, W., He, G.: Towards a protocol for autonomic covert communication. In: Calero, J.M.A., Yang, L.T., Mármol, F.G., García Villalba, L.J., Li, A.X., Wang, Y. (eds.) ATC 2011. LNCS, vol. 6906, pp. 106–117. Springer, Heidelberg (2011). https://doi.org/10.1007/978-3-642-23496-5_8
3. Lucena, N.B., Lewandowski, G., Chapin, S.J.: Covert channels in IPv6. In: Privacy Enhancing Technologies, pp. 147–166 (2006)
4. Mahajan, A.N., Shaikh, I.R.: Detect covert channels in TCP/IP header using Naive Bayes. Int. J. Comput. Sci. Mob. Comput. 4, 881–883 (2015)
5. Mavani, M., Ragha, L.: Covert channel in IPv6 destination option extension header, pp. 219–224, April 2014
6. Miller, B.: Steganography in IPv6, December 2008
7. Oplatkova, Z., Holoska, J., Zelinka, I., Senkerik, R.: Steganography detection by means of neural networks. In: 2008 19th International Workshop on Database and Expert Systems Applications, pp. 571–575. IEEE (2008)

8. Pack, D.J., Streilein, W., Webster, S., Cunningham, R.: Detecting http tunneling activities. Technical report, Massachusetts Inst of Tech Lexington Lincoln Lab. (2002)

9. Qian, Y., Dong, J., Wang, W., Tan, T.: Deep learning for steganalysis via convolutional neural networks. In: Media Watermarking, Security, and Forensics, vol. 9409, p. 94090J (2015)

10. Rowland, C.H.: Covert channels in the TCP/IP protocol suite. First Monday **2**(2), 32–48 (1997)

11. Sohn, T., Seo, J.T., Moon, J.: A study on the covert channel detection of TCP/IP header using support vector machine. In: International Conference on Information and Communications Security, pp. 313–324 (2003)

12. Tumoian, E., Anikeev, M.: Network based detection of passive covert channels in TCP/IP. In: The IEEE Conference on Local Computer Networks 30th Anniversary (LCN 2005) l, pp. 802–809. IEEE (2005)

13. Xu, G., Wu, H.Z., Shi, Y.Q.: Structural design of convolutional neural networks for steganalysis. IEEE Sig. Process. Lett. **23**(5), 708–712 (2016)

14. Zander, S., Armitage, G., Branch, P.: Stealthier inter-packet timing covert channels. In: Domingo-Pascual, J., Manzoni, P., Palazzo, S., Pont, A., Scoglio, C. (eds.) NETWORKING 2011. LNCS, vol. 6640, pp. 458–470. Springer, Heidelberg (2011). https://doi.org/10.1007/978-3-642-20757-0_36

Authentication and Security

Behavioral Security in Covert Communication Systems

Zhongliang Yang[1,2]([⊠]), Yuting Hu[1,2], Yongfeng Huang[1,2], and Yujin Zhang[1,2]

[1] The Department of Electronic Engineering, Tsinghua University,
Beijing 100084, China
{yangzl15,huyt16}@mails.tsinghua.edu.cn,
{yfhuang,zhang-yj}@tsinghua.edu.cn
[2] Beijing National Research Center for Information Science and Technology,
Beijing 100084, China

Abstract. The purpose of the covert communication system is to implement the communication process without causing third party perception. In order to achieve complete covert communication, two aspects of security issues need to be considered. The first one is to cover up the existence of information, that is, to ensure the content security of information; the second one is to cover up the behavior of transmitting information, that is, to ensure the behavioral security of communication. However, most of the existing information hiding models are based on the "Prisoners' Model", which only considers the content security of carriers, while ignoring the behavioral security of the sender and receiver. We think that this is incomplete for the security of covert communication. In this paper, we propose a new covert communication framework, which considers both content security and behavioral security in the process of information transmission. In the experimental part, we analyzed a large amount of collected real Twitter data to illustrate the security risks that may be brought to covert communication if we only consider content security and neglect behavioral security. Finally, we designed a toy experiment, pointing out that in addition to most of the existing content steganography, under the proposed new framework of covert communication, we can also use user's behavior to implement behavioral steganography. We hope this new proposed framework will help researchers to design better covert communication systems.

Keywords: Covert communication · Content security · Behavioral security · Behavioral steganography

1 Introduction

Covert communication system, encryption system and privacy system are three basic information security systems which have been summarized by Shannon [1]. These three types of information security systems protect people's information security and privacy in cyberspace from different aspects. Among them,

© Springer Nature Switzerland AG 2020
H. Wang et al. (Eds.): IWDW 2019, LNCS 12022, pp. 377–392, 2020.
https://doi.org/10.1007/978-3-030-43575-2_31

the encryption system mainly encrypts important information, makes the unauthorized people cannot decode and read normally, so as to ensure information security [2]. The privacy system mainly controls the access to important information and thus ensures the security of information [3]. These two systems can only guarantee the security of information content, but can not cover up the behavior of transmitting secret information. The most important characteristic of a covert communication system is that it can conceal the fact of transmitting secret information, that is, to complete the communication process without causing suspicion from third parties.

In order to achieve truly effective covert communication and avoid being perceived by third parties, there are two aspects of security issues that need to be considered: the concealment of information content and the concealment of information transmission behavior, which correspond to content security and behavioral security, respectively. For a covert communication process, these two issues are indispensable, and they together ensure the concealment and security of the communication process.

Currently, most covert communication systems are under the framework of "Prisoners' Model" [4], which is described in detail as follows. Alice and Bob are two prisoners locked in different cells in the prison. They are planning a jailbreak. They are allowed to communicate with each other, but all communicate information must be reviewed by guard Eve. Once Eve finds that they are transmitting secret information, they will be handed over to a cell with the highest security level where they will never be able to escape from. Therefore, they intend to use covert communication methods to embed secret information into common carriers, such as images [5], voices [6], texts [7], and then communicating with each other. Such information hiding technology is called steganography. Eve's task is to determine as accurately as possible whether the information they are transmitting contains secret information. The technology she uses is called steganalysis.

In the past few decades, with the development of technology, the steganography and steganalysis methods under the framework of the "Prisoners' Model" have achieved rapid development and progress on various carriers [5–13]. However, with the development of these steganography and steganalysis techniques, we have noticed the limitations of "Prisoners' Model" which only focus on content security.

A typical communication system consists of three important components: an information sender, a communication channel and an information receiver [1]. The task of the sender is to generate and send information, which can be in the form of images, voices, texts and so on. The communication channel is to pass the signal generated by the sender to the receiver. The receiver is to receive the information carrier transmitted from the channel and obtain the information therein. Simmons' "Prisoners' Model" only emphasizes content security in the process of information transmission, but ignores the behavioral security of the sender and the receiver. In the scenario it assumes, it even has a very strong assumption that Alice and Bob are allowed to communicate point-to-point.

However, in reality, it might be that Alice and Bob's behavior of establishing such point-to-point communication alone is enough to arouse suspicion from others, thus failing to achieve truly covert communication. Therefore, if we want to realize the truly concealment of transmitting secret information, in addition to ensuring the content security in the communication channel, we should also conside the behavioral security of both sender and receiver of the communication system.

In this paper, we propose a new security framework of covert communication system, which considers both content security and behavioral security in the process of information transmission. We collected and analyzed the behavioral of a large number of active Twitter users, trying to illustrate the security risks that may be brought to covert communication if we only consider content security and neglect behavioral security. Finally, we designed a toy experiment, pointing out that in addition to most of the existing content steganography, under the proposed new framework of covert communication, we can even only rely on user behavior to achieve behavioral steganography, which may bring new ideas and methods to the future covert communication.

In the remainder of this paper, Sect. 2 introduces several related works. Section 3 describes the proposed framework in detail. In Sect. 4, we analyzed the behavioral of a large number of active Twitter users and conducted a series of analytical experiments. Finally, conclusions are drawn in Sect. 5.

2   Related Works

2.1   Steganography and Steganalysis Under the "Prisoners' Model"

Previous information hiding methods which under the framework of the "Prisoners' Model" [4] mainly focus on content security, they try to find the best way to hide secret information into common carriers. These steganographic methods can be divided into different types according to different kinds of carrier, like image steganography [5], text steganography [7], audio steganography [6] and so on. In addition, according to different steganography means, they can also be classified to modification-based steganography [5] and generation-based steganography [6,7].

Figure 1 shows the overall framework of the "Prisoners' Model" and we can model it in the following mathematical form. Assuming that there are three spaces: carrier space $\mathcal{C}$, key space $\mathcal{K}$, and secret message space $\mathcal{M}$. The process of information hiding can be represented by the function $f()$. If Alice adopts a steganographic method based on the modification mode, she selects a common carrier c from the carrier space $\mathcal{C}$, which can be an image, voice or text. Then, under the control of the secret key k_A from the key space $\mathcal{K}$, Alice embeds the secret information m into the carrier c by modifying it, that is:

$$Emb : \mathcal{C} \times \mathcal{K} \times \mathcal{M} \rightarrow \mathcal{S}, f_{mod}(c, k_A, m) = s. \tag{1}$$

Correspondingly, if Alice adopts the steganographic method based on the carrier automatic generation, she does not need to be given a carrier in advance.

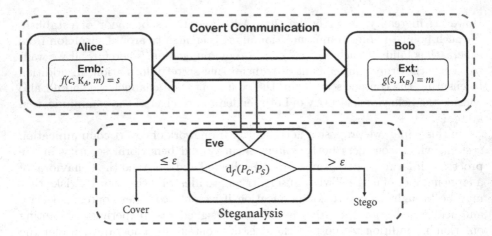

Fig. 1. Steganography and steganalysis within the framework of "Prisoners' Model".

She can automatically generate a steganographic carrier s according to the secret information m that needs to be transmitted, that is:

$$Emb : \mathcal{K} \times \mathcal{M} \rightarrow \mathcal{S}, f_{gen}(k_A, m) = s. \qquad (2)$$

When Bob receives the carrier s containing secret information from Alice, under the control of the decoding key k_B, he can extract the embedded secret message m from the steganographic carrier s by using the corresponding extraction function $g()$, that is:

$$Ext : \mathcal{S} \times \mathcal{K} \rightarrow \mathcal{M}, g(s, k_B) = m. \qquad (3)$$

In order not to arouse suspicion of Eve and ensure the security of secret information, according to Cachin's analysis of steganographic security [14], Alice and Bob should try their best to reduce the statistical distribution differences between normal carriers and steganographic carriers, that is:

$$d_f(P_C, P_S) \leq \varepsilon_f. \qquad (4)$$

Among them, P_C and P_S represent the statistical distribution of normal carriers and steganographic carriers respectively. ε_f is a number greater than 0, which can be used to measure the concealment of steganographic algorithm $f()$. For Eve, her job is to analyze and judge whether the information carrier being transmitted has deviated from the statistical distribution of the normal carriers, and then determine whether the carrier contains secret information.

The limitation of "Prisoners' Model" is that it only considers the content security in the communication process and ignores the behavioral security of the communication ends, which we think is incomplete for achieving truly effective covert communication.

2.2   Behavioral Concealment and Behavioral Analysis

At present, most covert communication models mainly focus on the content security of the information transmitted in the intermediate channel, but in fact, both ends of the communication system can also participate in the entire covert communication process. For example, during World War II, some people used several specific behaviors agreed in advance to convey covert information [15]. In recent years, some researchers have begun to study how to use specific online behaviors to convey covert information. For example, Pantic *et al.* [16] proposed a steganographic method that represents different secret information by controlling the length of Twitter published. Zhang [17] suggested that different secret messages could be conveyed by giving "love" marks to the information on social media. Li *et al.* [15] defined a "bits to activities" mapping algorithm and tried to use different online behaviors to convey secret message.

These covert communication methods can be implemented smoothly because they utilize the blind area of current steganalysis methods under the "Prisoners' Model" framework, that is, the lack of modeling and analysis of user's behavior. However, it is noteworthy that in recent years, with the development of technology, more and more methods for detecting abnormal behaviors on the Internet have emerged [18–21]. In this case, if we still only consider the content security in the covert communication process, without considering the behavior security, it will bring a great security risk to the entire covert communication system no matter how concealment the secret information is embedded.

3   The Proposed Framework

In order to describe the proposed framework more conveniently, we first describe a virtual scene. We assume that Alice and Bob are two intelligence personnel disguised as ordinary people. Their job is to gather intelligence. They have sneaked into two different target hostile areas and each of them have collected some intelligence information. Now they need to communicate with each other, exchange the information they have acquired and verify them with each other in order to make the best decisions. However, due to previous actions, these two areas have been suspected by the enemy, which can be collectively refered as Eve. Eve suspects that Alice and Bob have infiltrated these two areas, but she is not sure who they are. She was authorized to review all the communications between these two regions in the hope of finding Alice and Bob. According to Kerckhoffs's principle [1], we can expand Eve's capabilities as much as possible. We assume that Eve can get the content of each communication between any two people in these two regions, so she can perform steganalysis by analyzing the statistical distribution characteristics of the communication content. In addition, she can also know the communication behavior between any two people in these two regions, so she can also perform steganalysis by analyzing the communication behavior. We should also assume that Eve is familiar with all kinds of steganographic algorithms that Alice and Bob may adopt, and only does not know the specific steganography parameters (i.e. the secret key) that Alice and Bob adopt.

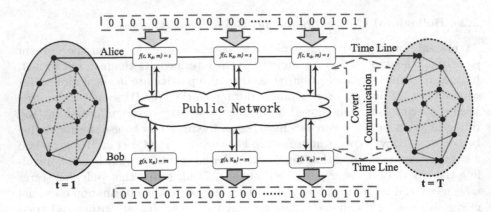

Fig. 2. Covert communication in public cyberspace.

For Alice and Bob, in order to successfully accomplish the task and ensure their own safety, they need to consider two aspects of security. Firstly, they need to ensure that the information they transmit is well concealed and not easily to be detected; secondly, they should behave as normal as possible and thus not expose themselves. They first ruled out the use of encryption methods to transmit information, because the transmission of encrypted information in the public channel will likely arouse suspicions. They eventually choose to use steganographic methods for covert communication. But only assurance the content concealment of each point-to-point communication as required by the "Prisoners' Model" is obviously not enough. They need to disguise themselves as normal people in a public communication network, cover up their behavior of exchanging secret information, and ensure the content security of each communication at the same time, thus they can achieve real covert communication.

The framework of the whole scenario is shown in Fig. 2 and the mathematical descriptions for this scenario and task are as follows. We define the entire public communication network as a graph series $\mathbf{G} = \{G_t\}_{t=1}^T$, where G_t denotes the graph at the t-th moment. Graph G_t of time step t is composed of vertices set V_t and edges set E_t, that is:

$$\mathbf{G} = \{G_t\}_{t=1}^T. \quad s.t. \quad \forall t \in [1, T], G_t = \{V_t, E_t \subseteq (V_t \times V_t)\}. \tag{5}$$

The vertices in G_t represent the users in the social network and edges represent the connections between users:

$$\forall i, j \in [1, N], \forall t \in [1, T],$$
$$V_t = \cup_{n=1}^N \{v_t^i\}, \quad E_t = \cup \{e_t^{i,j}\}|_{i,j \in [1,N]}, \quad e_t^{i,j} : v_t^i \to v_t^j. \tag{6}$$

We can represent Alice and Bob in this public network as v^A and v^B. Without affecting the nature of this problem, for the convenience of the following discussion, we assume that all the secret information is sent by Alice and extracted by Bob. According to the previous description, in order to achieve real covert communication, we need to consider both content security and behavioral security in the communication process. At the same time, we notice from Fig. 2 that the content and behavior of each user in the network have instantaneous and temporal characteristics. Next we will discuss and model them separately.

- **Instantaneous Content Security**

  In order to ensure instantaneous content security, Alice and Bob only need to ensure that at each time, the difference in the statistical distribution characteristics of the carrier they are transmitting and the normal carriers is small enough. This is very similar to formula (1)–(4). We assume that at time step t, Alice needs to pass a covert message m_t to Bob. Alice selects a carrier c_t from the carrier space $\mathcal{C}$, uses a steganographic function $f_t()$ to embed the secret information m_t into common carrier c_t under the guidance of the secret key $k_t^A \in \mathcal{K}$, and gets the steganographic carrier s_t. To minimize the impact on the statistical features distributions of carriers, so as to avoid arousing suspicion of other people about the transmission content, the steganographic function $f_t()$ needs to satisfy the following constraints:

  $$\forall t \in [1, T], \quad \begin{cases} f_t(c_t, k_t^A, m_t) = s_t, \\ g_t(s_t, k_t^B) = m_t, \\ d_1(P_\mathcal{C}, P_\mathcal{S}) \leq \varepsilon_1. \end{cases} \tag{7}$$

  Where $g_t()$ and k_t^B are the extraction function and the extraction key corresponding to $f_t()$ and k_t^A, respectively. $P_\mathcal{C}$ and $P_\mathcal{S}$ represent the statistical distribution characteristics of the normal carriers and the steganographic carriers, respectively, and $d_1()$ is a measurement function for measuring the statistical distribution difference between the normal carriers and the steganographic carriers. ε_1 is a value greater than 0 and it measures the security of the steganographic function $f_t()$. The smaller the value of ε_1, the stronger the concealment of $f_t()$.

- **Temporal Content Security**

  However, it is not enough to only guarantee the content security of a single communication. For users in social networks, according to their own interests and characteristics, usually the contents they publish or pay attention to have a certain relevance. Therefore, for Alice and Bob, the content they upload and download should also have a certain temporal correlation. For example, if a person is a big fan of basketball and his social media content in the past short term is sports-related, then we have reason to guess that the next content may also be sports-related. Or if a person always publishes negative content on social media for a long time, we can also estimate that the emotions contained in the following content may be negative. Conversely, if a social account publishes multiple messages in a short period of time (e.g. within an hour) and the topic changes frequently, or emotional switching frequently, we can at least suspect that the account is unusually. We use $c_{t_1:t_2}^i$ to represent the sequence of information published or downloaded by user v^i during the period from t_1 to t_2. Suppose $H()$ is a function which can measure the temporal relevance of sequence information. Therefore, in order to achieve temporal content security, Alice and Bob should ensure:

$$\forall t_1, t_2 \in [1, T], t_1 < t_2, \quad \begin{cases} d_2(H(s_{t_1:t_2}^A), \overline{H(c_{t_1:t_2})}) \leq \varepsilon_2. \\ d_2(H(s_{t_1:t_2}^B), \overline{H(c_{t_1:t_2})}) \leq \varepsilon_2. \end{cases} \tag{8}$$

where $\overline{H(c_{t_1:t_2})}$ represents the average score of a large number of sequence social information published by normal users. $d_2()$ reflects the difference between temporal relevance score of sequence social information published by Alice and normal users. ε_2 is a value greater than 0, the smaller it is, the stronger the concealment.

– **Instantaneous Behavioral Security**

For each moment $t \in [1, T]$, the behavioral security of each user v_t^i in cyberspace can be divided into two aspects: one is the behavioral security of himself, the other is the contacts with the people around him, that is, the behavioral security of a single vertex and the edges around it. Extreme examples such like Bob only downloads information published by Alice, or Alice publishs an unusually large amount of content in a very short time (for example, 100 images in one minute), may bring risks of suspicion. Here, we define two behavior scoring functions $I()$ and $J()$ to analyze the behavior of vertexes and edges in the public network, respectively. Then to achieve instantaneous behavioral security, Alice and Bob's behavior at each moment needs to meet the following constraints:

$$\begin{cases} \forall t \in [1, T], \\ d_3(I(v_t^A), \overline{I(v_t)}) \leq \varepsilon_3, \quad d_3(I(v_t^B), \overline{I(v_t)}) \leq \varepsilon_3, \\ d_4(J(E_t^A), \overline{J(E_t)}) \leq \varepsilon_4, \quad d_4(J(E_t^B), \overline{J(E_t)}) \leq \varepsilon_4. \end{cases} \tag{9}$$

Where E_t^A and E_t^B represents all the edge sets associated with Alice and Bob at t-th time step, and $\overline{I(v_t)}$ and $\overline{J(E_t)}$ represent the average behavior score of the normal users and their connections, respectively. For instantaneous behavioral security, the statistical distribution difference between Alice's and Bob's online behavior and that of normal users' behavior should be less than a threshold ε_3 and ε_4.

– **Temporal Behavioral Security**

Costa et al. [18] and Daniel et al. [19] have found that for many ordinary users, when logging in and using these social media, their behavioral records have a significant time distribution. This shows that users may have their own habits of using these social media and these behavior on social media is likely to have a temporal correlation. For example, some people are accustomed to watching a video on social media before going to bed, or browsing their friends' information and commenting on social media after getting up every day. From the perspective of behavioral security, it would be much less likely for Alice and Bob to expose themselves if they found a large number of normal users' usage habits and statistical characteristics and then imitated their usage habits. The temporal characteristics of users' online behavior can

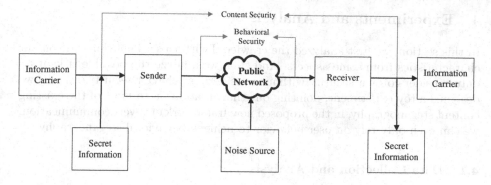

Fig. 3. The overall framework for covert communication in public networks.

also be divided into two aspects: vertex behavior and edge behavior, then the constraints should be:

$$
\begin{cases}
\forall t_1, t_2 \in [1, T], t_1 < t_2, \\
d_5(H(v^A_{t_1:t_2}), \overline{H(v_{t_1:t_2})}) \le \varepsilon_5, \quad d_5(H(v^B_{t_1:t_2}), \overline{H(v_{t_1:t_2})}) \le \varepsilon_5. \\
d_6(H(E^A_{t_1:t_2}), \overline{H(E_{t_1:t_2})}) \le \varepsilon_6, \quad d_6(H(E^B_{t_1:t_2}), \overline{H(E_{t_1:t_2})}) \le \varepsilon_6.
\end{cases}
\tag{10}
$$

Where $H(v^A_{t_1:t_2})$, $H(v^B_{t_1:t_2})$ and $H(E^A_{t_1:t_2})$, $H(E^B_{t_1:t_2})$ represent the temporal relevance of their sequential behavior of Alice and Bob themselves and their interaction with the people around them, respectively. $\overline{H(v_{t_1:t_2})}$ and $\overline{H(E_{t_1:t_2})}$ represent the corresponding distribution characteristics of ordinary users. To ensure temporal behavioral security, the difference of their distribution should be less than the threshold ε_5 and ε_6.

Based on the above analysis, the overall framework for covert communication in public networks has been summarised in Fig. 3, and in order to achieve real covert communication, the security constraints that Alice and Bob need to meet are shown in Table 1.

Table 1. Steganographic security constraints for covert communication systems.

Steganographic Security	Single Communication	Continuous Communication
Content Security	$\forall t \in [1, T], \begin{cases} f_t(c_t, k^A_t, m_t) = s_t \\ g_t(s_t, k^B_t) = m_t \\ d_1(P_C, P_S) \le \varepsilon_1 \end{cases}$	$\begin{cases} \forall t_1, t_2 \in [1, T], t_1 < t_2 \\ d_2\left(H(s^A_{t_1:t_2}), \overline{H(c_{t_1:t_2})}\right) \le \varepsilon_2 \\ d_2\left(H(s^B_{t_1:t_2}), \overline{H(c_{t_1:t_2})}\right) \le \varepsilon_2 \end{cases}$
Behavioral Security	$\begin{cases} \forall t \in [1, T] \\ d_3(I(v^A_t), \overline{I(v_t)}) \le \varepsilon_3, d_3(I(v^B_t), \overline{I(v_t)}) \le \varepsilon_3 \\ d_4(J(E^A_t), \overline{J(E_t)}) \le \varepsilon_4, d_4(J(E^B_t), \overline{J(E_t)}) \le \varepsilon_4 \end{cases}$	$\begin{cases} \forall t_1, t_2 \in [1, T], t_1 < t_2 \\ d_5\left(H(v^A_{t_1:t_2}), \overline{H(v_{t_1:t_2})}\right) \le \varepsilon_5, d_5\left(H(v^B_{t_1:t_2}), \overline{H(v_{t_1:t_2})}\right) \le \varepsilon_5 \\ d_6\left(H(E^A_{t_1:t_2}), \overline{H(E_{t_1:t_2})}\right) \le \varepsilon_6, d_6\left(H(E^B_{t_1:t_2}), \overline{H(E_{t_1:t_2})}\right) \le \varepsilon_6 \end{cases}$

4   Experiments and Analysis

In this section, we first analyzed the crawled Twitter user behavior and content characteristics from some aspects. And then we analyze the possible risks if we only consider content security without considering behavior security. Finally, we designed a toy experiment, pointing out that in addition to most of the existing content steganography, in the proposed new framework of covert communication, we can even only rely on user behavior to achieve behavioral steganography.

4.1   Data Collection and Analysis

According to the previous section, in order to achieve truly effective covert communication, Alice and Bob need to cover up themselves from both content and behavior aspects. To achieve this goal, we first need to analyze the content and behavioral characteristics of a large number of normal users on public networks. In this work, we crawled 317,375 tweets from 1,147 active Twitter users (defined as publish Twitter messages more than 90 in a month) for the period from 2019-06-15 00:00:00 to 2019-07-15 23:59:59. Some detail information about these users and tweets can be found in Table 2.

Table 2. Some detail information about the crawled twitter users and tweets

User number	Tweet number	Rate of retweet	Average forwarding
1,147	317,375	34.55%	151.0
Average comments	Average follower	Average following	
1871.7	23,036	8761.2	

We made some statistical analyses of these crawled Tweets, and the results are shown in Fig. 4. From these results, we can at least see that when these unrelated users publish content on social networks, their behavior will show a regular distribution on the whole, rather than disorder. For example, Fig. 4(b) reflects the relationship between the total number of Twitters and the rate of original Twitters published by these active users in a month. It forms a very regular fan-shaped distribution. If Alice ignores these statistical rules, Twitter publishing falls outside the sector. Even if the content she publishes is normal, it may be recognized as abnormal behavior and expose herself. Figure 4(d) shows the statistical distribution of the average number of Twitters posted by users within 24 h a day. They also form a very regular distribution. If the time when Alice publishes information does not coincide with that of most people, such as always publishing information at the lowest point of normal people's probability of republishingleasing information, it may also be considered abnormal.

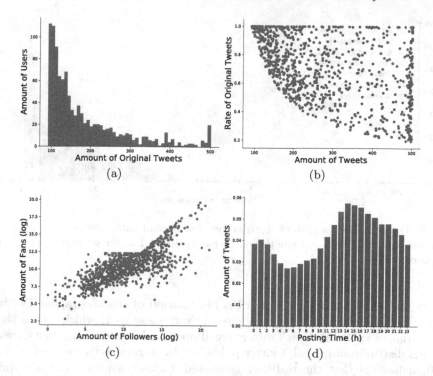

Fig. 4. Some statistical distribution characteristics of online behaviors of active twitter users.

In addition, from the perspective of content security, we analyzed in Sect. 3 that social information published by users (especially active users) is likely to have temporal content relevance. We use the VADER model proposed in [22] to analyze the sentiment of crawling Twitters. The sentiment score of each Twitter is distributed between $[-1, 1]$. The closer the value is to 1, the more positive it is, and the closer it is to -1, the more negative it is. Then, we use permutation entropy [23] to calculate the random degree of Twitter sentiment values of these active users within a month. As a measure, permutation entropy (PE) is widely used in the analysis, prediction and detection tasks of time series. The value of PE (in a range of $[0, 1]$) represents the degree of randomness or predictability of the time series, the closer to 0, the more regular the sequence is.

In contrast, we have also constructed 100 virtual users and used recently appeared steganographic text generation algorithm [7] to generate 100 steganographic twitters for each virtual user. Then we use the same method to calculate the sentiment value of each steganographic Twitter and then use permutation entropy to calculate its random degree. We use different embedding rates (bits per word) to generate multiple sets of Twitters, and the final test results are shown in Fig. 5.

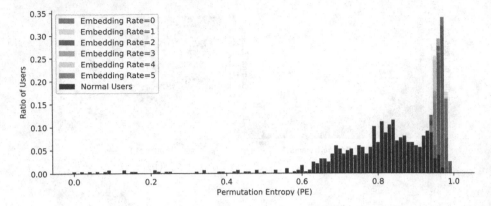

Fig. 5. The permutation entropy distribution of sentiment values of Twitter published by normal users within one month and steganographic Twitter generated by model proposed in [7].

As can be seen from Fig. 5, the PE distribution of steganographic Twitter (regardless of embedding rate) generated is very close to 1, which means that the sentiment values of these Twitters are almost random sequences. In contrast, the PE distribution of real Twitter published by normal active users is closer to 0, indicating that the real user generated Twitter sequence has a certain predictability of sentiment state. This further validates our previous analysis that no matter how concealment the steganographic samples generated by Alice each time, once the temporal correlation is ignored, it is very likely to expose itself.

These analyses show that a large number of normal users' online content and behavior have certain statistical characteristics, and neglecting any aspect of them will bring security risks, so that effective covert communication cannot be realized. Therefore, in order to achieve real covert communication, whether single communication or continuous communication, we need to consider both content security and behavioral security to ensure the concealment of communication.

4.2 Behavioral Steganography Based on Posting Time

In fact, by effectively expanding the "Prisoners' Model", on the one hand, it brings greater challenges to Alice and Bob, but on the other hand, it also brings them new ideas of steganography. They may even not need to modify the content of the original carrier, only use the online behavior to transmit secret information, which can be called behavioral steganography. In this section, we will present a very simple but effective method, to illustrate how can we conduct behavioral steganography.

The steganography models based on the "Prisoners' Model" usually need to analyze the statistical distribution characteristics of the normal carrier, and then modify the insensitive features of it and thus to embed secret information.

This kind of methods can be called content steganography. Similarly, in order to implement behavioral steganography, we first need to analyze the statistical distribution characteristics of a large number of normal users' behaviors.

Figure 4(d) shows the statistical distribution of the posting time within 24 h a day. Therefore, we can consider using the behavior of posting time to transmit secret information. For example, if Alice divides each day into hours, she can get 24 time periods for sending information and also the probability of sending information in each time hour according to Fig. 4(d), that is:

$$\begin{cases} \{h_1, h_2, ..., h_{24}\}, \\ \{P(h_1), P(h_2), ..., P(h_{24})\}. \end{cases} \tag{11}$$

Then Alice can construct a Huffman tree and encode each time period according to the corresponding probability. Each leaf node represents a period of time, and the encoding rule can be 0 on the left and 1 on the right. The Huffman coding for each time period can be find in Table 3.

Table 3. Huffman code table for each posting time during one day.

O'clock	Code	O'clock	Code	O'clock	Code	O'clock	Code	O'clock	Code	O'clock	Code
0–1	11001	1–2	11011	2–3	11000	3–4	10110	4–5	10011	5–6	01010
6–7	01011	7–8	10010	8–9	10100	9–10	10101	10–11	10111	11–12	11100
12–13	11111	13–14	0100	14–15	1000	15–16	0111	16–17	0110	17–18	0011
18–19	0010	19–20	0000	20–21	0001	21–22	11110	22–23	11101	23–24	11010

Then each time according to the secret bit stream, Alice searches from the root node of Huffman tree until the corresponding leaf node is found, indicating that the steganographic information should be sent out in the corresponding time. We simulated Alice to transmit secret information at a specified time using the above method and embed random bit streams into the sending time. We simulated Alice sending 5,000 messages, and then we counted the distribution of these sending times, results have been shown in Fig. 6. From Fig. 6, we can see that for this steganographic method, while transmitting hidden information, Alice can still obey the statistical characteristics of normal users' behavior, so it can achieve a certain degree of behavioral security. At the same time, it is worth noting that Alice has not made any changes to the carrier content, so the content security can also be guaranteed.

Although this is just a simple example of using network behavior to carry covert information. But it proves that we can jump out of the scope of content security, and only use the behavior to achieve covert communication. We think that this may inspire more new types of covert communication technologies and methods in the future.

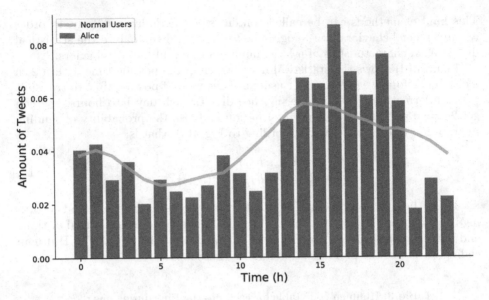

Fig. 6. The statistical distribution difference between the steganographic behavior and the real behavior after carrying the covert information with the transmission time.

5   Conclusion

In this paper, we propose a new covert communication framework, which considers both content security and behavioral security in the process of information transmission. We give a complete security constraint under the proposed new framework of covert communication. In the experimental part, we use a large amount of collected real Twitter data to illustrate the security risks that may be brought to covert communication if we only consider content security and neglect behavioral security. Finally, we designed a toy experiment, pointing out that in addition to most of the existing content steganography, in the proposed new framework of covert communication, we can even only rely on user behavior to achieve behavioral steganography. We think this new proposed framework is an important development to the current covert communication system. We hope that this paper will serve as a reference guide for researchers to facilitate the design and implementation of better covert communication systems.

Acknowledgment. The authors thank Dr. Shujun Li for constructive communications. This work was supported in part by the National Key Research and Development Program of China under Grant 2018YFB0804103 and the National Natural Science Foundation of China (No. U1536207, No. U1705261 and No. U1636113).

References

1. Shannon, C.E.: Communication theory of secrecy systems. Bell Labs Tech. J. **28**(4), 656–715 (1949)

2. Rivest, R.L., Shamir, A., Adleman, L.: A method for obtaining digital signatures and public-key cryptosystems. Commun. ACM **21**(2), 120–126 (1978)
3. Beller, M.J., Chang, L.-F., Yacobi, Y.: Privacy and authentication on a portable communications system. IEEE J. Sel. Areas Commun. **11**(6), 821–829 (1993)
4. Simmons, G.J.: The prisoners' problem and the subliminal channel. In: Chaum, D. (ed.) Advances in Cryptology, pp. 51–67. Springer, Boston (1984)
5. Fridrich, J.: Steganography in Digital Media: Principles, Algorithms, and Applications. Cambridge University Press, New York (2009)
6. Yang, Z., Du, X., Tan, Y., Huang, Y., Zhang, Y.-J.: AAG-stega: automatic audio generation-based steganography. arXiv preprint arXiv:1809.03463 (2018)
7. Yang, Z.-L., Guo, X.-Q., Chen, Z.-M., Huang, Y.-F., Zhang, Y.-J.: RNN-stega: linguistic steganography based on recurrent neural networks. IEEE Trans. Inf. Forensics Secur. **14**(5), 1280–1295 (2019)
8. Yang, Z., Peng, X., Huang, Y.: A sudoku matrix-based method of pitch period steganography in low-rate speech coding. In: Lin, X., Ghorbani, A., Ren, K., Zhu, S., Zhang, A. (eds.) SecureComm 2017. LNICST, vol. 238, pp. 752–762. Springer, Cham (2018). https://doi.org/10.1007/978-3-319-78813-5_40
9. Yang, Z., Wei, N., Sheng, J., Huang, Y., Zhang, Y.-J.: TS-CNN: text steganalysis from semantic space based on convolutional neural network. arXiv preprint arXiv:1810.08136 (2018)
10. Yang, Z., Jin, S., Huang, Y., Zhang, Y., Li, H.: Automatically generate steganographic text based on Markov model and Huffman coding. arXiv preprint arXiv:1811.04720 (2018)
11. Yang, Z., Yang, H., Hu, Y., Huang, Y., Zhang, Y.-J.: Real-time steganalysis for stream media based on multi-channel convolutional sliding windows. arXiv preprint arXiv:1902.01286 (2019)
12. Yang, Z., Wang, K., Li, J., Huang, Y., Zhang, Y.: TS-RNN: text steganalysis based on recurrent neural networks. IEEE Sig. Process. Lett. **26**, 1743–1747 (2019)
13. Yang, Z., Zhang, P., Jiang, M., Huang, Y., Zhang, Y.-J.: RITS: real-time interactive text steganography based on automatic dialogue model. In: Sun, X., Pan, Z., Bertino, E. (eds.) ICCCS 2018. LNCS, vol. 11065, pp. 253–264. Springer, Cham (2018). https://doi.org/10.1007/978-3-030-00012-7_24
14. Cachin, C.: An information-theoretic model for steganography. Inf. Comput. **192**(1), 41–56 (2004)
15. Li, S., Ho, A.T., Wang, Z., Zhang, X.: Lost in the digital wild: hiding information in digital activities. In: Proceedings of the 2nd International Workshop on Multimedia Privacy and Security, pp. 27–37. ACM (2018)
16. Pantic, N., Husain, M.I.: Covert botnet command and control using twitter. In: Proceedings of the 31st Annual Computer Security Applications Conference, pp. 171–180. ACM (2015)
17. Zhang, X.: Behavior steganography in social network. In: Pan, J.S., Tsai, P.W., Huang, H.C. (eds.) Advances in Intelligent Information Hiding and Multimedia Signal Processing. SIST, vol. 63, pp. 21–23. Springer, Cham (2017). https://doi.org/10.1007/978-3-319-50209-0_3
18. Costa, A.F., Yamaguchi, Y., Traina, A.J.M., Faloutsos, C., et al.: Modeling temporal activity to detect anomalous behavior in social media. ACM Trans. Knowl. Discov. Data (TKDD) **11**(4), 49 (2017)
19. Chino, D.Y., Costa, A.F., Traina, A.J., Faloutsos, C.: VolTime: unsupervised anomaly detection on users' online activity volume. In: Proceedings of the 2017 SIAM International Conference on Data Mining, pp. 108–116. SIAM (2017)

20. Ranshous, S., Shen, S., Koutra, D., Harenberg, S., Faloutsos, C., Samatova, N.F.: Anomaly detection in dynamic networks: a survey. Wiley Interdisc. Rev. Comput. Stat. **7**(3), 223–247 (2015)
21. Anand, K., Kumar, J., Anand, K.: Anomaly detection in online social network: a survey. In: 2017 International Conference on Inventive Communication and Computational Technologies (ICICCT), pp. 456–459. IEEE (2017)
22. Hutto, C.J., Gilbert, E.: VADER: a parsimonious rule-based model for sentiment analysis of social media text. In: Eighth International AAAI Conference on Weblogs and Social Media (2014)
23. Bandt, C., Pompe, B.: Permutation entropy: a natural complexity measure for time series. Phys. Rev. Lett. **88**(17), 174102 (2002)

Image Visually Meaningful Cryptography Based on Julia Set Generating and Information Hiding

Longfu Zhou[1], Sen Bai[1(✉)], Yuqiang Cao[2], and YingLong Wang[1]

[1] College of Software and Artificial Intelligence, Chongqing Institute of Engineering,
Chongqing 400056, China
baisencq@126.com
[2] College of Computer, Chongqing Institute of Engineering, Chongqing 400056, China

Abstract. Secret and private image security storage and fast transmission are a relatively concerned issue in the field of information security. In existed image encryption schemes, plain image is transformed to meaningless random noise signal which is vulnerable to attack with suspicion. Image visually meaningful cryptography (IVMC) based on information hiding is difficult to hide large size images because of limited hiding capacity. To solve this problem,a new IVMC based on Julia set images (JSI) generating and information hiding was proposed.In this solution, firstly, JSI are generated by utilizing Julia set generating parameters (JSGP) and specific pixel coloring scheme (SPCS), as keys, escape-time algorithm (ETA). Then the secret image or the encrypted secret image is embedded into JSI's detail-rich small areas to form a beautiful stego-JSI, so as to achieve the purpose of IVMC. The receiver can use the same JSGP and SPCS keys to generate the same cover-JSI, which greatly facilitates the extraction and decryption of the encrypted image. Theoretical analysis and experimental results show that the proposed method has good artistic beauty, high hiding capacity, good imperceptibility, strong anti-compression performance and good anti-steganalysis ability, as well as large key space and good key sensitivity.

Keywords: Image encryption · Image visually meaningful cryptography (IVMC) · Information hiding · Julia set

1 Introduction

1.1 The Difference Between VC and IVMC

Traditional visual cryptography (VC) method is based on image sharing. It is a powerful technique in which a secret image can be divided into two or more shares and the decryption can be done using human visual system [1]. As the name suggests, visual cryptography has relationship with the human visual system. The decoding is carried out by the human eyes, if k shares are stacked together. This qualifies everyone to use the system, regardless of their information about cryptography and any computations. These methods have the disadvantages of reducing contrast and increasing image size.

H. Wang et al. (Eds.): IWDW 2019, LNCS 12022, pp. 393–406, 2020.
https://doi.org/10.1007/978-3-030-43575-2_32

In this paper, we propose an image visually meaningful cryptography (IVMC), which is different from visual cryptography (VC). It encrypts plain images into visually meaningful images, i.e. Julia set images (JSI), so as to reduce the suspicion of the enemy and reduce the possibility of being attacked.

1.2 Related Work

In steganography, different fractal images of Julia set are generated in [2] by embedding the secret data in the fractal creation process. The secret data are regarded as the parameters which are necessary for the generation of fractal images. This method does not hide image data directly, but hides bit information 0 and 1, resulting in low hiding capacity and imperceptibility. In addition, the beauty, complexity and controllability of the Julia sets images (JSI) are poor because of the randomness of generation. In 2018, Mohammed pointed out the weakness and limitations of using fractal images in [3], especially Julia sets images (JSI), as a cover in steganography system that may contribute in detect the hidden information within these images. Therefore, from the point of view of information hiding, using JSI as a cover and using information hiding only for IVMC is easy to be steganlyzed. Although the key space of using JSI as a key of image encryption is very large [4], the result of encryption is similar to random noise, which exposes the importance of image and is easily attacked by the adversary. Therefore, we try to combine information hiding and JSI generating to construct IVMC to overcome the low hiding capacity, poor imperceptibility and controllability.

The rest of this paper is organized as follows. After introducing the framework of JSI generating method in Sect. 2, we show how to generate JSI by controlling various parameters. In Sect. 3, the proposed IVMC encryption scheme and decryption scheme are presented. In Sect. 4, We demonstrate the experimental results and analyze the performance of the proposed algorithm. We draw conclusions in Sect. 5.

2 Julia Sets Image Generating Based on Improved Newton-Raphson Method

2.1 Improved Newton-Raphson Method

Julia set is a type of algebraic fractal image which yield chaotic or unpredictable image. Each Julia set creates a unique image, which is called the Julia set image (JSI). Julia set is the maximal set of points that gets mapped onto itself under the function $f(z) = z^m + c(m \in \mathbf{C}, c \in \mathbf{C})$, and is usually created with the escape-time algorithm.

For simplicity, in this study, we adopted quadratic polynomials of Julia set to create fractal images. The quadratic polynomials can be expressed as $F(Z) = z^2 + c$, where $z = x + yi$, $c = p + qi$, and $i = \sqrt{-1}$. The c value controls on the shape of JSI. To produce an image, the process of all points must repeat. Julia set use the parameters z and c, as a key, to generate images. Image color and shape change as input parameter c. The value of c is constant in creation of each image.

Su et al. proposed an improved Newton-Raphson method for JSI generation [5]. Zhang et al. also used this escape-time algorithm (ETA) to generate JSI [2], which is described as follows.

Algorithm 1. *Escape-time algorithm* **(ETA)**

Step 1. Assume that the size of fractal image is $a \times b$. Given $c = p + qi$ (initial parameter, saved as the embedded key), the escape radius threshold R, and the escape time threshold T. Set $x_{\min} = -\alpha$, $y_{\min} = -\beta$, $x_{\max} = \alpha$, $y_{\max} = \beta$.

Let

$$\Delta x = (x_{\max} - x_{\min})/(a - 1) \tag{1}$$

$$\Delta y = (y_{\max} - y_{\min})/(b - 1) \tag{2}$$

Complete Step 2–4 for all points (n_x, n_y), where $n_x = 0, 1, 2, \cdots, a - 1$, and $n_y = 0, 1, 2, \cdots, b - 1$.

Step 2. Given starting values $Z_0 = x_0 + y_0 i$, where $x_0 = x_{\min} + n_x \times \Delta x$, and $y_0 = y_{\min} + n_y \times \Delta y$. Set $t = 0$.

Step 3. Set $x_{t+1} = x_t^2 - y_t^2 + p$, $y_{t+1} = 2x_t y_t + q$, and $t = t + 1$

Step 4. Set $r = x_t^2 + y_t^2$.

If $r > R$, draw points (n_x, n_y) with coloring mode $K = (C_r, C_g, C_b)$ and compute the next point. Then go to Step 3. If $t = T$, draw points (n_x, n_y) with fixed color 0 (black) and compute the next point. Then go to Step 3. If $r \leq R$ and $t < T$, turn to Step 3 and continue the iteration.

In this algorithm, we add the definition of *coloring mode*, which is defined as $K = (C_r, C_g, C_b)$, in which C_r, C_g and C_b are arbitrary natural numbers. This corresponds to the RGB color of drawing (n_x, n_y) points, and its calculation method is as follows: $R_t = \mod(t \times C_r, 256)$, $G_t = \mod(t \times C_g, 256)$, $B_t = \mod(t \times C_b, 256)$.

2.2 Julia Set Images Generating

Next, we will examine the influence of each parameter in Algorithm 1 on JSI, and give some results. The values of p and q have great influence on the shape and aesthetic feeling of JSI. The smaller the α and β are, the more details of JSI are displayed, as shown in Figs. 1 and 2. In Figs. 1 and 2, the coloring mode $K = (13, 21, 17)$.

The modification of parameters a and b can change the size of JSI, which are not discussed here. Now we discuss the impact of the modification of the coloring mode on JSI. Through theoretical analysis of Algorithm 1, the modification of the coloring mode

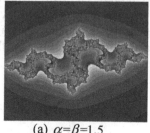
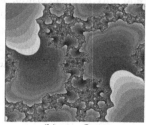

(a) $\alpha = \beta = 1.5$ (b) $\alpha = \beta = 0.5$

Fig. 1. Julia set images with $a = 1200$, $b = 1000$, $p = -0.835$, $q = -0.2321$

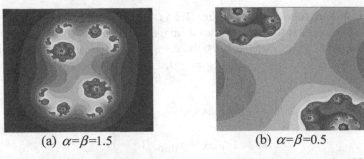

(a) $\alpha=\beta=1.5$ (b) $\alpha=\beta=0.5$

Fig. 2. Julia set images with $a = 1200$, $b = 1000$, $p = 0.45$, $q = -0.1428$

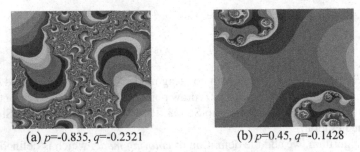

(a) $p=-0.835$, $q=-0.2321$ (b) $p=0.45$, $q=-0.1428$

Fig. 3. The influence of coloring mode on JSI (with $a = 1200$, $b = 1000$, $\alpha = \beta = 0.5$)

don't change the shape of JSI, but can only change the color of each region of JSI, as shown in Fig. 3, where the coloring mode is $K = (113, 211, 117)$. The coloring mode will be used in the IVMC algorithm proposed in next section.

3   Image Visually Meaningful Cryptosystem Based on JSI and Information Hiding

3.1   Diagram of the Cryptosystem

There are some areas which include very rich details showed in the JSI of Figs. 1 and 3(a), and the color of these areas is very close to the encrypted image after pixel position scrambling and gray value diffusion. Therefore, we propose an IVMC algorithm based on information hiding and JSI. The basic idea is to replace the details of the JSI with the encrypted secret image, so as to obtain an image which is similar to the original JSI, and form the image which hides the secret image and is visually meaningful, thus it can reduce the possibility of being suspected and attacked.

The diagram of the algorithm is shown in Fig. 4.

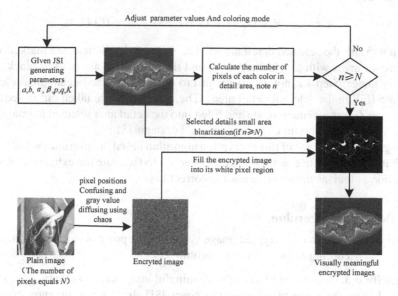

Adjust parameter values And coloring mode

GIven JSI generating parameters $a,b, \alpha, \beta, p, q, K$

Calculate the number of pixels of each color in detail area, note n

$n \geq N$

No

Yes

Selected details small area binarization(if $n \geq N$)

Fill the encrypted image into its white pixel region

pixel positions Confusing and gray value diffusing using chaos

Plain image (The number of pixels equals N)

Encryted image

Visually meaningful encrypted images

Fig. 4. The diagram of the image visually meaningful cryptography based on IH and JSI

3.2 Encryption and Decryption Algorithm Steps

3.2.1 Encryption Algorithm

Suppose that the plain image to be encrypted is $\mathbf{S} = [a_{ij}]_{h \times w}$, then according to the diagram of visually meaningful image cryptosystem in Fig. 4, the encryption steps are as follows.

Algorithm 2. *Visually meaningful image cryptosystem*

Step 1 (Pre-encrypt plain image): a plain image $\mathbf{S}$ is encrypted by a common methods of pixel position confusion and gray scale diffusion, then an encrypted image $\mathbf{S}'$ is obtained. Initialize parameters $a, b, \alpha, \beta, p, q$ and coloring mode $K = (C_r, C_g, C_b)$, *counter* $= 0$.

Step 2 (Generate JSI). update a, b, α, β according to $a = a - 5 \times counter, b = b - 5 \times counter, \alpha = \alpha - 0.1 \times counter, \beta = \beta - 0.1 \times counter$, and modify the coloring mode K to generate RGB JSI according to Sect. 2 Algorithm 1. Note that the generated JSI is $\mathbf{J}$. Here the parameters $a, b, \alpha, \beta, p, q$ and $K = (C_r, C_g, C_b)$ can be used as keys. *counter* $= counter + 1$.

Step 3 (Select the small color areas to be replaced). Using the following formula (3) to transform generated RGB image $\mathbf{J}$ into the gray image $\mathbf{J}'$. For $l = 0, 1, 2, \cdots, 255$, calculate the number of pixels C_l in $\mathbf{J}'$. Let $\mathbf{V} = \{ l | C_l/(a \times b) \leq \gamma \}$, if $\sum_{l \in \mathbf{V}} C_l \geq N = h \times w$, then go to Step 4. Here γ is the proportion of small area pixels to the whole image **J'** pixels, usually less than 0.02, which can also be used as a key. Otherwise, go back to the Step 2.

$$Gray = R \times 0.299 + G \times 0.587 + B \times 0.144 \tag{3}$$

Step 4 (Mark the selected detail areas). The selected detail areas are marked white (those are the areas with gray value $l \in V$) and the other areas are marked black to get the binary image. Step 4 is not necessary, just to show the selected detail areas clearly.

Step 5 (Fill in the selected detail area). The pixels in **S'** are taken out in sequence according to Zigzag scanning mode and filled into the detail area selected in image **J'** to obtain a visually meaningful encrypted image, i.e. stego-JSI.

The greatest advantage of this encryption algorithm based on information hiding and JSI is that it can generate exactly the same cover-JSI to facilitate the extraction of secret information as long as the receiver has the correct key.

3.2.2 Decryption Algorithm

The decryption process of encrypted image is the inverse process of encryption, which is carried out according to the steps of algorithm 3 below.

Algorithm 3. Decryption of visually meaningful image cryptosystem

Step 1 (Get the key and generate the cover-JSI). In order to decrypt, cover-JSI generation keys $a, b, \alpha, \beta, p, q, C_r, C_g, C_b$ and γ need to be obtained. Then, use these keys to generate cover-JSI, note that the generated JSI is **J**. Using the formula (3), transform generated RGB image **J** into the gray image **J'**. Here **J** and **J'** are exactly the same as **J** and **J'** generated in encryption Algorithm 2, which is the greatest advantage of this algorithm and the guarantee of correctly decrypting the encrypted secret image.

Step 2 (Select small color areas that have been replaced). This step is similar to the Step 3 in encryption Algorithm 2.

Step 3 (Extract encrypted secret image from selected areas). In Stego-JSI, we find the regions corresponding to the small areas selected in step 2, extract the pixel values from them by Zigzag scanning, and combine them into size $h \times w$ image to get encrypted secret image **S'**.

Step 4 (Decrypt encrypted image to get plain image). The original plain image **S** is obtained by de-confusion and de-diffusion with the encryption method in Step 1 of Algorithm 2.

4   Experiment Results and Safety Analysis

4.1   Experiment Results of the Algorithm

In this study, secrete image were embedded with the Algorithm 2 described previously. Set $a = 1000, b = 600, \alpha = \beta = 0.5, p = -0.835, q = -0.2321$ and $K = (13, 21, 17)$, and use Algorithm 1 to get the cover-JSI as shown in Fig. 5(a). Using Step 3 of Algorithm 2, the selected detail area (white) is shown in Fig. 5(b), where $\gamma = 0.0167$. The original 256×256 plain image Lena and its chaotic encrypted image are shown in Fig. 5(c) and (d), respectively. In the absence of the original JSI, it is difficult to see the encrypted image hidden in Fig. 5(e). Therefore, the proposed algorithm has good imperceptibility from the perspective of information hiding, and achieves image encryption with visual significance from the perspective of encryption.

(a) Cover-JSI   (b) Selected details small areas (white)

(c)Original Lena   (d) Encrypted Lena   (e) Stego-JSI after (d) is embedded in JSI

Fig. 5. The effect of Lena image encryption using the proposed algorithm

When decrypting, the same JSI can be generated by using the same key parameters, and the location and size of the small areas embedded in secret information can also be determined. Then J' can be extracted from it. Then, the inverse process of chaotic encryption is used to de-confuse the position of the pixels and de-diffuse the gray value. The decrypted image consistent with the Lena of Fig. 5(c) can be obtained.

4.2   Algorithm Performance Analysis

The IVMC algorithm proposed in this paper is based on information hiding and JSI generation. Therefore, its performance includes two aspects: the performance in the field of information hiding and the performance in the field of encryption. However, IVMC as a new encryption and hiding paradigm, we think that it is not suitable to copy the performance of these two fields completely, and there should be new performance indicators to measure the performance of IVMC. From the point of view of encryption, the key space size, key sensitivity and the correlation of the encrypted image pixels are very important performance indicators. Considering from the angle of information hiding, its imperceptibility, hiding capacity and anti-steganalysis ability are very important performance indicators. In view of the particularity of JSI image and the new encryption and hiding paradigm, we choose the artistic aesthetics and hiding capacity of JSI, the imperceptibility, anti-compression and anti-steganalysis performance of Stego-JSI, the size of key space and key sensitivity to discuss the performance of the proposed algorithm. The presentation and discussion of other performance indicators will be our future research work.

4.2.1   JSI Art Aesthetics and Hidden Capacity Analysis

The IVMC proposed in this paper requires that cover-JSI not only have a sense of aesthetics, but also have high hiding capacity. From Figs. 1, 2 and 3, we can see that the aesthetics of cover-JSI is related not only to the values of p and q, but also to the coloring mode K. The hiding capacity of cover-JSI is related to the number of its detail areas. Generally, the smaller the values of α and β, the more detail areas it displays, and the larger the hiding capacity. This can be seen in Figs. 1(a) and (b).

Through a lot of experiments, we find that when $a = 1000$, $b = 600$, $K = (13, 21, 17)$, p and q satisfy formula (4). Cover-JSI generated by ETA can have a better sense of aesthetics and higher hiding capacity at the same time, as shown in Fig. 6. As can be seen from Fig. 6, only from the aesthetic point of view, Fig. 6 (c) and (d) show that image's artistry is better because they are similar to marbling art works [6, 7]. In fact, JSI images satisfying good aesthetics and high hiding capacity are far more than those limited by formula (4) as long as appropriate α, β and K are selected.

$$\begin{cases} -0.9 \leq p \leq -0.7 \\ -0.5 \leq q \leq -0.3 \\ |p+q| < 1.2 \end{cases} \quad or \quad \begin{cases} 0 \leq p \leq 0.4 \\ -0.5 \leq q \leq 0.8 \\ |p| + |q| < 1.2 \end{cases} \tag{4}$$

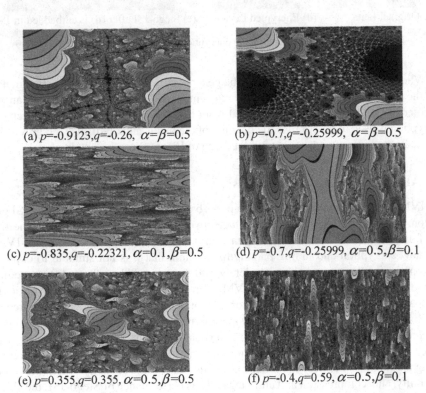

(a) p=-0.9123,q=-0.26, α=β=0.5   (b) p=-0.7,q=-0.25999, α=β=0.5

(c) p=-0.835,q=-0.22321, α=0.1,β=0.5   (d) p=-0.7,q=-0.25999, α=0.5,β=0.1

(e) p=0.355,q=0.355, α=0.5,β=0.5   (f) p=-0.4,q=0.59, α=0.5,β=0.1

Fig. 6. The cover-JSI generated given different parameters

When the cover-JSI is generated, the main factor affecting the hiding capacity and imperceptibility is γ, which is the proportion of pixels in each detail small area to the whole image pixels. The relationship between the generating parameters p, q and the hidden capacity (the total number of pixels in all small detail areas) is shown in Table 1. As can be seen from Table 1, except for $p = -0.7$ and $q = -0.455$, the hidden capacity is larger than that in reference [2, 9, 10], and increases with the increase of γ, which is consistent with the theoretical analysis. However, with the increase of hiding capacity, the aesthetics of stego-JSI is also damaged to a certain extent. The underlined Bold Italic numbers in Table 1 represent the corresponding images, and some of the steganographic images are shown in Fig. 7. Comparing the cover-JSI of Fig. 6(c) with the stego-JSIs of Fig. 7, we can find that there is a certain loss of artistic aesthetics.

Table 1. The relation between hidden capacity and JSI generation parameters p and q

q capacity	p capacity							
	p	−0.9123	−0.9	−0.835	−0.7456	−0.7234	−0.7	−0.7
	q	−0.26	−0.25	−0.2321	−0.2345	−0.2345	−0.455	−0.2599
Hidden pixel number	$\gamma = 0.005$	76899	62878	25896	42136	85430	14489	***165045***
	$\gamma = 0.010$	121302	80075	57311	78122	***221560***	24248	***209823***
	$\gamma = 0.017$	216517	153449	85164	107331	***388478***	71979	***267086***
Bit/pixel	0.5 in [2] <0.1 in [9] 1 in [10]	>3.0759	>2.5152	>1.0358	>1.6854	>3.4172	>0.5795	>6.6018

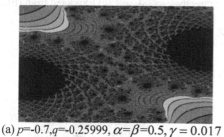 

(a) p=-0.7,q=-0.25999, α=β=0.5, $\gamma = 0.017$ (b) p=-0.7,q=-0.25999, α=β=0.5, $\gamma = 0.005$

Fig. 7. The stego-JSI with artistic aesthetic loss

4.2.2 Imperceptibility Analysis

Because the JSI generated by ETA has very detail-rich small areas (DSA), the color of these DSA has very high similarity with the color of color image after chaotic encryption visually, and the Algorithm 2 proposed by us is to hide the encrypted image in these DSA, so it has very good imperceptibility. This can be seen from Fig. 5(a) and (e). Even in less beautiful Fig. 7(a) and (b), without the original cover-image, it is difficult to distinguish whether their color differences are due to different *coloring mode* or other reasons.

On the other hand, it should be noted that although we borrow the concept of information hiding here, encryption is the main purpose. Moreover, even the imperceptibility of information hiding cannot be measured by peak signal-to-noise ratio (PSNR) in each case. Therefore, we do not use PSNR to measure imperceptibility here.

4.2.3 Anti-compression Analysis

When stego-JSI (for example, Fig. 5(e)) is lossless compressed, the secret image J' hidden in stego-JSI can be extracted correctly. But when Fig. 5(e) is compressed by lossy JPEG, the original plain image can't be decrypted at all, as shown in Fig. 8(a). This is because stego-JSI is compressed to change its gray value, and a gray value change based on position scrambling and gray value diffusion will lead to incorrect decryption. However, if the plain image Lena is embedded directly into JSI according to the Step 2 to Step 5 of Algorithm 2, it can be also decrypted and extracted after compression as shown in Fig. 8(b) and (c), except that the color of the image is different from original image, so our algorithm has a certain compression resistance.

 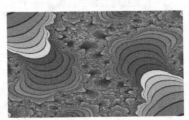 

(a)Compressed stego-JSI extracting and decrypted   (b) Lena is embedded directly into JSI   (c) Extracted from (b)

(d) Calculate details areas (white) from (b)   (e) Extracted without cover-JSI

Fig. 8. The encrypted image is compressed with JPGE and decrypted image

Further theoretical and experimental analysis shows that the advantage of compression resistance is brought by the new information hiding paradigm proposed in this paper. If the key parameters are not used to generate the cover-JSI, the small information hiding area determined from Stego-JSI is wrong as shown in Fig. 8(d), this leads to extraction and decryption errors as shown in Fig. 8(e).

4.2.4 Key Space

The key space is a vital index to evaluate the performance of the encryption system. Only a large key space can defend against exhaustive attack. In our proposed IVMC algorithm, the size of the key space is mainly affected by two parts: (1) Chaotic pre-encrypted key space for plain image, which has been discussed in other literature, and we will not discuss it; (2) The parameters of JSI generation, which is the focus of our discussion.

According to Sect. 3.2.1, the key of the encryption algorithm proposed in this paper includes $a, b, \alpha, \beta, p, q, C_r, C_g, C_b$ and γ. Since the size of JSI a, b is exposed in stego-JSI, they are not be considered as keys. γ as a control parameter of hidden capacity, we do not use them as keys for the time being. Here, we will only discuss the number of keys using $\alpha, \beta, p, q, C_r, C_g$ and C_b as keys. Considering the beauty and detail richness of JSI images, set the range of values of α and β is $[-3, 3]$. Assuming that the precision of α and β is 10^{-8}, there are 7×10^8 values of α and β, respectively. From formula (4), we can get 3×10^4 values of p and q, respectively. C_r, C_g and C_b determine the total number of color patterns, there are $256 \times 256 \times 256$. Note that the absolute values of $x_{min}, x_{max}, y_{min}$ and y_{max} in formula (1) and (2) can be different, so the key space is

$$7 \times 10^8 \times 7 \times 10^8 \times 7 \times 10^8 \times 7 \times 10^8 \times 3 \times 10^4 \times 3 \times 10^4 \times 256^3 > 2^{171} \quad (5)$$

Formula (5) shows that although the key space is smaller than that in reference [8], there is no statistical key space for plain image pre-encrypted.

4.2.5 Key Sensitivity Analysis

A secure encryption system should have a strong key sensitivity. Because the IVMC proposed in this paper is different from the encryption method which encrypts the image into random noise, it cannot be measured by the usual NPCR (Number of Pixel Changing Rate) and UACI (Unified Average Changing Intensity) [4]. Here we use the extremely small change of the key to examine the effect of extracting and decrypting the hidden image, thus demonstrating the sensitivity of the key of the proposed algorithm in this paper.

Let $a = 1000, b = 600, \alpha = \beta = 0.5, p = -0.7234$ and $q = -0.2345$, and the cover-JSI generated by Algorithm 1 is shown in Fig. 9(a). In order to display conveniently, the plain image Peppers (Fig. 9(b)) of 256×256 is directly hidden into cover-JSI, and a visually meaningful stego-JSI is obtained, as shown in Fig. 9(c). When all keys are correct, Peppers can be correctly retrieved from Fig. 9(c), as shown in Fig. 9(d). If only 0.0001 is added to the key p, Peppers cannot be extracted correctly, as shown in Fig. 9(e) and (f). Keeping $a = 1000, b = 600, p = -0.7234$ and $q = -0.2345$ unchanged, only adding 0.0001 to α or subtracting 0.0001 from β, the JSI generated by Algorithm 1 has no visual difference (Fig. 9(g) (h)), but the Peppers images cannot be extracted correctly, as shown in Fig. 9(i) and (j). These results show that our proposed encryption scheme has good key sensitivity.

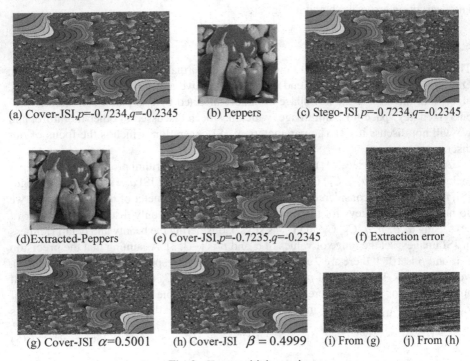

(a) Cover-JSI,p=-0.7234,q=-0.2345   (b) Peppers   (c) Stego-JSI p=-0.7234,q=-0.2345

(d)Extracted-Peppers   (e) Cover-JSI,p=-0.7235,q=-0.2345   (f) Extraction error

(g) Cover-JSI α=0.5001   (h) Cover-JSI $\beta = 0.4999$ (i) From (g)   (j) From (h)

Fig. 9. Key sensitivity testing

4.2.6   Analysis of Anti-steganalysis Ability

The IVMC algorithm proposed in this paper is based on information hiding. As an important performance of information hiding, it has the ability of anti-covert analysis.

Reference [3] focuses on the weak points and limitations of using fractal images, especially Julia sets images, as a cover in steganography system that may contribute in detect the hidden information within these images. These weak points and limitations mainly include: (I) The effect of the reflective or rotational symmetry in Julia set images; (II) JSIs have the properties of self-similarity; (III) The effect of changing the parameters values. (IV) Embedding in the JSI after decomposed into R, G, B colors. (V) Background of JSI: There are a large number of points from JSI containing only the information of background which are the non-chaotic points; there is a big similarity between pixel values. (VI) Amount of data can be hidden in JSI.

In fact, as long as the values of x_{min}, x_{max}, y_{min} and y_{max} in formula (1) and (2) are as different as possible, the shortcomings mentioned above (I) and (II) can be avoided. Similarly, it is difficult to guess the value of parameters p and q by adjusting these parameters to a relatively small range and displaying only the local and beautiful details of JSI images. Therefore, the weak point of (III) pointed out in reference [3] can be overcome. Our steganography does not decompose the cover-JSI color into R, G, B, so there is no weakness mentioned above (IV). In addition, our steganography is to hide the secret image directly in the detail-rich area of JSI without any change in the large background area, which will not provide a good detection opportunity for attackers. That is to say, disadvantage (V) does not exist in our method. As for the deficiency of (VI), it is a challenging problem to increase the hiding capacity and reduce the possibility of being breached by steganalysit, which needs to be further studied and solved. The plain image should be pre-encrypted first in the algorithm 2 proposed in this paper. So its security is guaranteed. The steganography of this paper is to add another layer of protection to the secret image.

5 Conclusion

In this paper, we proposed an image encryption scheme based on the Julia set Images and steganography. We embedded the secret image into JSI's detail-rich small areas to form a beautiful JSI image with high hiding capacity and good imperceptibility, and can overcome many shortcomings of existing JSI-based information hiding schemes. Simulation results show that our encryption scheme has more excellent performance and is a new paradigm in the field of visual cryptography and secret image sharing. Therefore, our IVMC scheme is safe, and the Julia set is an excellent set for visual cryptography.

Acknowledgement. The work was supported by the Science and Technology Research Program of Chongqing Municipal Education Commission (Grant No. KJZD-K201801901).

References

1. Thomas, S.A., Gharge, S.: Review on various visual cryptography schemes. In: International Conference on Current Trends in Computer, Electrical, Electronics and Communication (ICCTCEEC 2017), pp. 1164–1167 (2017)
2. Zhang, H.X., Hu, J., Wang, G., et al.: A steganography scheme based on fractal images. In: Second International Conference on Networking and Distributed Computing, Beijing, China, pp. 28–31, September 2011
3. Mohammed, N.Q., Hussein, Q.M., Ahmed, M.S.: Suitability of using Julia set images as a cover for hiding information. In: Al-Mansour International Conference on New Trends in Computing, Communication, and Information Technology, NTCCIT 2018, pp. 71–74 (2018)
4. Gao, W.J., Sun, J., Qiao, W., et al.: Digital image encryption scheme based on generalized Mandelbrot-Julia set. Opt. Int. J. Light. Electron Opt. **185**, 917–929 (2019)
5. Su, X.H., Li, D., Hu, M.Z.: The resulting of the symmetric fractal art images with improved Newton-Raphson method. Chin. J. Comput. **22**(11), 1147–1152 (1999)
6. Acar, R., Boulanger, P.: Digital marbling: a multiscale fluid model. IEEE Trans. Vis. Comput. Graph. **12**(4), 600–614 (2006)
7. Lu, S.F., Mok, P.Y., Jin, X.G.: From design methodology to evolutionary design: an interactive creation of marble-like textile patterns. Eng. Appl. Artif. Intell. **32**, 124–135 (2014)

8. Zhou, N., Yan, X., Liang, H., et al.: Multi-image encryption scheme based on quantum 3D Arnold transform and scaled Zhongtang chaotic system. Quantum Inf. Process. **17**, 338 (2018)
9. Agaian, S.S., Susmilch, J.M.: Fractal steganography using artificially generated images. In: Proceedings of SPIE - The International Society for Optical Engineering, vol. 6982, pp. 312–317 (2008)
10. Patel, H.N., Khant, D.R., Prajapati, D.: Design of a color palette based image steganography algorithm for fractal images. In: 2017 International Conference on Wireless Communications, Signal Processing and Networking (IEEE WiSPNET 2017), pp. 2584–2589 (2017)

Multi-attack Reference Hashing Generation for Image Authentication

Ling Du[1]([✉]), Yijing Wang[1], and Anthony T. S. Ho[2,3,4]

[1] School of Computer Science and Technology,
Tianjin Polytechnic University, Tianjin 300387, China
`duling@tjpu.edu.cn`, `1831125506@stu.tjpu.edu.cn`
[2] Department of Computer Science, University of Surrey,
Guildford, Surrey GU2 7XH, UK
`a.ho@surrey.ac.uk`
[3] Tianjin University of Science and Technology, Tianjin 300457, China
[4] Wuhan University of Technology, Wuhan 430070, China

Abstract. Perceptual hashing for image authentication has been intensively investigated owing to the speed and memory efficiency. How to determine the reference hashing code, which is used for similarity measures between the distorted hashes and reference hashes, is important but less considered for image hashing design. In this paper, we present a Multi-Attack Reference Hashing (MRH) method based on hashing cluster for image authentication, which is expected to use prior information, i.e. the supervised content-preserving images and multiple attacks for feature generation and final reference hashing code generation. Extensive experiments on benchmark datasets have validated the effectiveness of our proposed method.

Keywords: Reference hashing · Multi-attack · Image authentication

1 Introduction

With the rapid development of internet and multimedia, image content authentication [1] becomes the research hotspots of multimedia information security. Different from digital watermarking [2] and digital signature [3], perceptual hashing [4] is used for multimedia content identification and authentication through perception digests based on the understanding of multimedia content. It provides a more convenient way for solving the management problems associated with multimedia authentication.

Currently the majority of image perceptual hashing algorithms can roughly be divided into five categories: statistic based schemes, relation based schemes, coarse representation based schemes, low level feature based schemes and learning based schemes [5,6]. Statistic based schemes generate reference hashing by calculating image statistics in the spatial domain, such as mean, variance, and histograms of image blocks [7–10]. Relation based schemes take the advantage

© Springer Nature Switzerland AG 2020
H. Wang et al. (Eds.): IWDW 2019, LNCS 12022, pp. 407–420, 2020.
https://doi.org/10.1007/978-3-030-43575-2_33

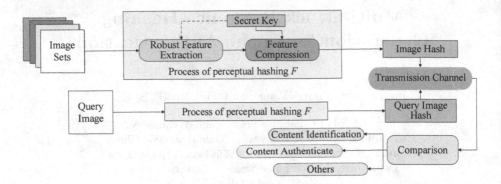

Fig. 1. A generic framework of perceptual image hashing.

of some invariant relations of discrete cosine transform (DCT) coefficients or wavelet transform (DWT) coefficients to generate reference hashes [11–13]. In coarse representation based category of methods, the reference hashes are generated by utilizing the coarse information of the original image. For example, the spatial distribution of significant wavelet coefficients, the low-frequency coefficients of Fourier transform, etc [14–17]. Local feature points based hashes are generated by extracting the striking image feature points [18–21]. These methods typically perform the DCT or SIFT transform on the original image, and then generate reference hashes using different algorithms [22–24]. In category of learning based schemes, efficient learning can be incorporated into the image hash generation process by taking advantages of the training data at the owner side. The hashing codes were obtained based on the existing learned parameters [25–27].

The well-established paradigm of perceptual hashing consists of three major steps, i.e., extract robust features, feature compression, and hash comparison as shown in Fig. 1. The first stage is to extract robust features from the image sets and conduct compression, quantification, coding and other operations on the perceptual features. This procedure is known as perceptual hash process F. These original reference hashes are generated and transmitted through a secure channel. In the second stage, the same perceptual hash process F will apply to the queried image to be authenticated, so as to obtain the hashing codes of the query image. In the third stage, the reference hashes will be compared with image hashes in the test database for content authentication.

For the total framework of perceptual hashing based image authentication, only few studies have been devoted to the reference hashing generation. Lv et al. [29] proposed obtaining an optimal estimate of the hash centroid using kernel density estimation (KDE). In this method, the centroid was obtained as the value which yields the maximum estimated distribution. Its major drawbacks are that the binary codes are obtained by using a data independent method. Moreover, in the current literature of image hashing, prior information, i.e. the distorted copies by image processing attacks of original images are generally less explored

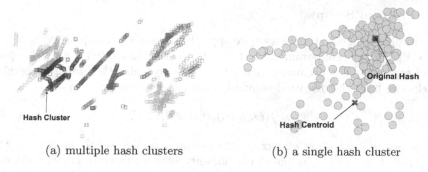

(a) multiple hash clusters   (b) a single hash cluster

Fig. 2. The examples of hash clusters

in image hashing generation. Therefore, how to put on efforts of exploring prior information and efficiently learn reference hashing code for solving multimedia security problems is an important topic for current research.

In this paper, we propose a Multi-Attack Reference Hashing (MRH) method based on cluster for image authentication. According to the requirement of authentication application, we propose to build the prior information set based on the help of multiple virtual prior attacks, which is produced by applying virtual prior distortions and attacks on the original images. An extensive set of experiments on two image datasets for four current baseline hashing algorithms demonstrate the advantages of the proposed method.

2   Proposed Method

2.1   Prior Information Set

Perceptual hashing for image content authentication is expected to be able to survive on acceptable content-preserving manipulations. For given original images and its various distorted copies, image hashing for image authentication is actually an infinite clustering problem. However, the image hashes arising from the original image may not the hash centroid of the distorted copies. As shown in Fig. 2(a), where we apply 15 classes of attacks on 5 original images and represent their hashes in 2-dimensional space for both the original images and their distorted copies. From Fig. 2(a), we can observe 5 clusters in the hashing space. From Fig. 2(b) by zooming into one hash cluster, we note a observation that the hashes of the original image actually may not be the centroid of its cluster.

How to determine the hashing centroid (Reference Hashing), which is used for similarity measures between the distorted hashes and reference hashes, is important for image hashing design. In this paper, the original images and their distorted copies compose the so-called prior information set. We take the reference hashing generation as a multi-attack based cluster problem in the prior information set. The goal of our algorithm is to infer the cluster centroid and the corresponding central image.

2.2 Problem Setup

For l original images in the dataset, we apply V types of content preserving attack with different types of parameter settings to generate simulated distorted copies. Let Θ represents the original image set, $f_v(\cdot)$ represent v-th content-preserving attacks, we have the distorted copy set after virtual attacks:

$$\Psi_v = f(\Theta, f_v(\cdot)), v = 1, 2, ..., V. \tag{1}$$

Let us denote the feature matrix of attacked instances in set Ψ_v as $\mathbf{X}^v \in \mathbb{R}^{m \times t}$. Here, $v = 1, 2, ..., V$, m is the dimensionality of data feature, t is the number of instances for attack v. Finally, we get the feature matrices for the total n instance as $\mathbf{X} = \{\mathbf{X}^1, ..., \mathbf{X}^V\}$, and here $n = tV$. Note that, the feature matrices are normalized to zero-centered.

For certain original image set and its various distorted copies, image hashing for image authentication is actually an infinite clustering problem. Therefore, we take the prior image set as training data. We aim to infer the clustering centroids for reference hashing generation, which is used for similarity measure.

2.3 Multi-attack Reference Hashing

We now elaborate the formulation of our proposed multi-attack based hashing method, which jointly exploits the information from various content preserving multi-attack data.

By considering the total reconstruction errors of all the training objects, we have the following minimization problem in a matrix form:

$$J_1(\tilde{\mathbf{U}}, \tilde{\mathbf{X}}) = \alpha(||\tilde{\mathbf{X}} - \tilde{\mathbf{U}}\mathbf{X}||_F^2 + \beta||\tilde{\mathbf{U}}||_F^2), \tag{2}$$

where $\tilde{\mathbf{X}}$ is shared latent multi-attack feature representations. The matrix $\tilde{\mathbf{U}}$ can be viewed as the basis matrix, which mapping the input multi-attack features into the corresponding latent features. Parameter α, β is a nonnegative weighting vector to balance the significance.

From the information-theoretic point of view, the variance over all data is measured, and taken as a regularization term:

$$J_2(\tilde{\mathbf{U}}) = \gamma||\tilde{\mathbf{U}}\mathbf{X}||_F^2, \tag{3}$$

where γ is a nonnegative constant parameter.

As shown in Fig. 2, image hashing for image authentication is actually an infinite clustering problem. The reference hashing code is generated based on the cluster centroid image. Therefore, we also consider keeping the cluster structures. We formulate this objective function as:

$$J_3(\mathbf{C}, \mathbf{G}) = \lambda||\tilde{\mathbf{X}} - \mathbf{C}\mathbf{G}||_F^2, \tag{4}$$

where $\mathbf{C} \in \mathbb{R}^{k \times l}$ and $\mathbf{G} \in \{0, 1\}^{l \times n}$ are the clustering centroid and indicator.

Finally, the formulation of our proposed MRH algorithm can be written as:

$$\min_{\tilde{U},\tilde{X},C,G} \alpha||\tilde{X} - \tilde{U}X||_F^2 + \beta||\tilde{U}||_F^2 - \gamma||\tilde{U}X||_F^2 + \lambda||\tilde{X} - CG||_F^2. \tag{5}$$

Our objective function simultaneously learns the feature representations $\tilde{X}$ and finds the mapping matrix $\tilde{U}$, the cluster centroid C and indicator G. The iterative optimization algorithm is as follows.

Fixing all variables but **optimize** $\tilde{U}$: The optimization problem Eq. (5) reduces to:

$$\min J(\tilde{U}^v) = \alpha||\tilde{X} - \tilde{U}X||_F^2 + \beta||\tilde{U}||_F^2 - \gamma \mathrm{tr}(\tilde{U}XX^T\tilde{U}^T), \tag{6}$$

By setting the derivation $\frac{\partial J(\tilde{U})}{\partial \tilde{U}} = 0$, we have:

$$\tilde{U} = \tilde{X}X^T((\alpha - \gamma)XX^T + \beta I)^{-1} \tag{7}$$

Fixing all variables but **optimize** $\tilde{X}$: Similarly, we solve the following optimization problem:

$$\min F(\tilde{X}) = \alpha||\tilde{X} - \tilde{U}X||_F^2 + \lambda||\tilde{X} - CG||_F^2, \tag{8}$$

which has a closed-form optimal solution:

$$\tilde{X} = \alpha\tilde{U}X + \lambda CG. \tag{9}$$

Fixing all variables but C and G: For the cluster centroid C and indicator G, we obtain the following problem:

$$\min_{C,G} ||\tilde{X} - CG||_F^2. \tag{10}$$

Inspired by the optimization algorithm ADPLM (Adaptive Discrete Proximal Linear Method) [30], we initialize $C = \tilde{X}G^T$ and update C as follows:

$$C^{p+1} = C^p - \frac{1}{\mu} \nabla \Gamma(C^p), \tag{11}$$

where $\Gamma(C^p) = ||B - CG||_F^2 + \rho||C^T 1||$, $\rho = 0.001$, $p = 1, 2, ...5$ denote the p-th iteration.

The indicator matrix G at indices (i, j) is obtained by:

$$g_{i,j}^{p+1} = \begin{cases} 1 & j = \arg\min_s H(b_i, c_s^{p+1}) \\ 0 & otherwise \end{cases}, \tag{12}$$

where $H(b_i, c_s)$ is the distance between the i-th feature codes x_i and the s-th cluster centroid c_s.

After we infer the cluster centroid C and the multi-attack feature representations $\tilde{X}$, the corresponding l reference hashing code is generated. The basic idea is to compare the hashing distance among the nearest content preserving attacked neighbors of each original image and corresponding cluster centroid. The complete algorithm is shown in Algorithm 1.

Algorithm 1. Optimization Algorithm for MRH

1: **Input**: Multi-attack matrices: $\mathbf{X} = \{\mathbf{X}^1, ..., \mathbf{X}^V\}$, parameter α, β, γ, λ, and the dimension k of latent multi-attack feature representations $\tilde{\mathbf{X}}$.

2: **Initialize**: $\alpha = 1.000$, $\beta = 0.003$, $\gamma = 0.001$, $\lambda = 0.00001$; Initialize $\tilde{\mathbf{U}}$ and $\tilde{\mathbf{X}}$ with random values.

3: **while** *not converged* **do**

4:     Update the variables $\tilde{\mathbf{U}}$ and $\tilde{\mathbf{X}}$ according to Eq. (7) and

5:     Eq. (9).

6:     Update parameter $\mathbf{C}$ and $\mathbf{G}$ according to Eq. (11) and Eq. (12).

7:     Check the convergence for Eq. (5).

8: **end**

9: **Output**: $\tilde{\mathbf{U}}$, $\tilde{\mathbf{X}}$, $\mathbf{C}$ and $\mathbf{G}$

---

3 Experiments

3.1 Experiment Setting

We compare our multi-attack reference hashing approach with a number of baselines. In particular, we compare with:

Wavelet-based image hashing [31]: It is an invariant feature transform based method, which develop an image hash from the various sub-bands in a wavelet decomposition of the image and makes it convenient to transform from the space-time domain to the frequency.

SVD-based image hashing [16]: It belongs to dimension reduction based hashing and it use spectral matrix invariants as embodied by singular value decomposition. The invariant features based on matrix decomposition show good robustness against noise addition, blurring and compressing attacks.

RPIVD-based image hashing [32]: It incorporates ring partition and invariant vector distance to image hashing by calculating the images statistics. The statistic information of the images includes: mean, variance, standard deviation and kurtosis, etc.

Quaternion-based image hashing [33]: This method considers the multiple features, and constructs quaternion image to implement quaternion Fourier transform for hashing generation.

In this paper, the involved experiments are carried out on two real-world datasets. The first comes from the **CASIA** [34], which contains 918 image pairs, including 384×256 real images and corresponding distorted images with different texture characteristics. The other one is **RTD** [35,36], which contains 220 real images and corresponding distorted images with resolution 1920×1080. For performance evaluation, we report F1 and Precision, Recall and Area Under Receiver Operating Curve (AUC) as the metrics for hash performance.

3.2 Perceptual Robustness

To validate our perceptual robustness, we apply the content preserving operations. Twelve types of content-preserving attacks are tested: (a) Gaussian noise

Table 1. Hashing distances under different content-preserving manipulations.

Method	Manipulation	ORH			MRH		
		Max	Min	Mean	Max	Min	Mean
Wavelet	Gaussian noise	0.02828	0.00015	0.00197	0.02847	0.00014	0.00196
	Salt & Pepper	0.01918	0.00021	0.00252	0.01918	0.00024	0.00251
	Gaussian blurring	0.00038	0.00005	0.00017	0.00067	0.00006	0.00019
	Circular blurring	0.00048	0.00006	0.00022	0.00069	0.00006	0.00021
	Motion blurring	0.00034	0.00006	0.00015	0.00065	0.00005	0.00016
	Average filtering	0.00071	0.00007	0.00033	0.00071	0.00009	0.00030
	Median filtering	0.00704	0.00006	0.00099	0.00753	0.00007	0.00099
	Wiener filtering	0.00101	0.00008	0.00028	0.00087	0.00008	0.00028
	Image sharpening	0.00906	0.00009	0.00115	0.00906	0.00010	0.00114
	Image scaling	0.00039	0.00005	0.00013	0.00064	0.00006	0.00018
	Illumination correction	0.08458	0.00447	0.02759	0.08458	0.00443	0.02757
	JPEG compression	0.00143	0.00009	0.00026	0.00275	0.00013	0.00051
SVD	Gaussian noise	0.00616	0.00007	0.00031	0.00616	0.00007	0.00030
	Salt & Pepper	0.00339	0.00008	0.00034	0.00338	0.00007	0.00033
	Gaussian blurring	0.00017	0.00007	0.00010	0.00113	0.00007	0.00011
	Circular blurring	0.00018	0.00006	0.00010	0.00114	0.00006	0.00011
	Motion blurring	0.00017	0.00007	0.00010	0.00113	0.00006	0.00011
	Average filtering	0.00025	0.00007	0.00011	0.00111	0.00006	0.00012
	Median filtering	0.00166	0.00007	0.00015	0.00190	0.00007	0.00016
	Wiener filtering	0.00035	0.00005	0.00011	0.00113	0.00007	0.00012
	Image sharpening	0.00104	0.00007	0.00018	0.00099	0.00007	0.00018
	Image scaling	0.00016	0.00007	0.00010	0.00114	0.00007	0.00011
	Illumination correction	0.00662	0.00014	0.00149	0.00674	0.00014	0.00150
	JPEG compression	0.00031	0.00007	0.00010	0.00053	0.00008	0.00012
RPIVD	Gaussian noise	0.25827	0.00864	0.03086	0.29081	0.01115	0.03234
	Salt & Pepper	0.22855	0.01131	0.02993	0.25789	0.01191	0.03033
	Gaussian blurring	0.03560	0.00411	0.01471	0.14023	0.00545	0.01786
	Circular blurring	0.06126	0.00447	0.01713	0.13469	0.00565	0.01924
	Motion blurring	0.03570	0.00362	0.01432	0.18510	0.00473	0.01825
	Average filtering	0.07037	0.00543	0.02109	0.20190	0.00591	0.02237
	Median filtering	0.06126	0.00512	0.02234	0.18360	0.00625	0.02465
	Wiener filtering	0.07156	0.00421	0.01803	0.20421	0.00581	0.02041
	Image sharpening	0.06324	0.00609	0.02442	0.18283	0.00706	0.02765
	Image scaling	0.03311	0.00275	0.01154	0.18233	0.00381	0.01761
	Illumination correction	0.11616	0.00769	0.02864	0.20944	0.01047	0.02920
	JPEG compression	0.07037	0.00543	0.02109	0.06180	0.00707	0.02155
QFT	Gaussian noise	6.97151	0.13508	0.73563	6.30302	0.11636	0.60460
	Salt & Pepper	7.63719	0.16998	0.66200	7.50644	0.15073	0.63441
	Gaussian blurring	0.26237	0.00513	0.02519	0.10820	0.00318	0.01449
	Circular blurring	0.26529	0.00712	0.03163	0.17937	0.00460	0.02075
	Motion blurring	0.26408	0.00465	0.02286	0.10729	0.00300	0.01318
	Average filtering	0.30154	0.00976	0.04403	0.30719	0.00760	0.03263
	Median filtering	0.95120	0.03084	0.19822	0.87149	0.02706	0.19345
	Wiener filtering	0.64373	0.01746	0.08046	0.68851	0.01551	0.07616
	Image sharpening	6.55606	0.05188	1.52398	6.55596	0.05189	1.52398
	Image scaling	0.51083	0.04031	0.10067	0.52404	0.02800	0.09827
	Illumination correction	4.37001	0.27357	0.84280	4.36692	0.27348	0.84170
	JPEG compression	7.55523	0.13752	1.29158	13.1816	0.13585	1.46682

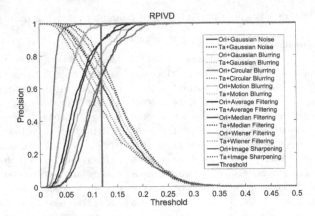

Fig. 3. Image authentication performances with varying thresholds.

addition with the variance of 0.005; (b) Salt & Pepper noise addition with density as 0.005; (c) Gaussian blurring with the standard deviation of the filter as 10; (d) Circular blurring with radius of 2; (e) Motion blurring with the amount of the linear motion as 3 and the angle of the motion blurring filter as 45; (f) Average filtering with filter size as 5; (g) Median filtering with filter size as 5; (h) Wiener filtering with filter size as 5; (i) Image sharpening with the parameter alpha as 0.49; (j) Image scaling with the percentage as 1.2; (k) Illumination correction with parameter gamma as 1.18; (l) JPEG compression with quality factor as 20.

We extract the reference hashing code based on original image (ORH) and our proposed multi-attack reference hashing (MRH). For the content-preserving distorted images, we calculate the corresponding distance between reference hashing codes and content-preserving images's hashing codes. The statistical results under different attacks are presented in Table 1. Just as shown, the hashing distance for the four baseline methods are small enough. For threshold determination, the precision distribution of the authentication results with varying threshold are shown in Fig. 3. The results shown by the solid line and dashed line indicate the performance of similar images and tampered images under different content preserving manipulations on CASIA dataset for RPIVD method. It can be easily seen that the results are approximately intersected at threshold $\tau = 0.12$. Therefore, in our experiments, we set to $\tau = 0.12$ distinguish the similar images and forgery images on CASIA dataset for PRIVD method. Similarly, for the other three methods, we set the threshold as 1.2, 0.0012 and 0.008 correspondingly.

3.3   Discriminative Capability

Discriminative capability of image hashing means that visually distinct images should have significantly different hashes [37]. In other words, two images that visually distinct should have a very low probability of generating similar hashes.

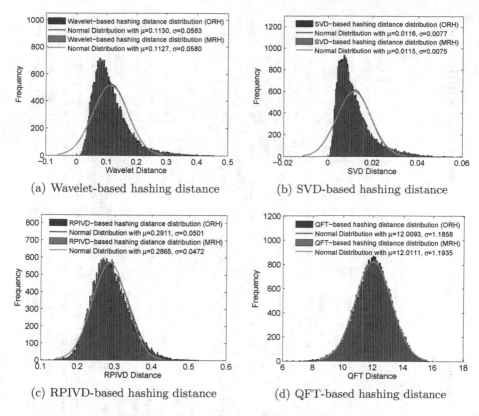

(a) Wavelet-based hashing distance

(b) SVD-based hashing distance

(c) RPIVD-based hashing distance

(d) QFT-based hashing distance

Fig. 4. Distribution of hashing distances between hashing pairs with varying thresholds.

Here, RTD Dataset consisting of 220 different uncompressed color images is adopted to validate discriminative capability of our proposed multi-attack reference hashing algorithm. We first extracted reference hashing codes for all 220 images in RTD and then calculated the hashing distance for each image with the other 219 images. Thus, we can finally obtain $220 \times (220-1)/2 = 24090$ hashing distances. Figure 4 shows the distribution of these 24090 hashing distances between hashing pairs with varying thresholds, where the abscissa is the hashing distance and the ordinate represents the frequency of hashing distance. It can be seen clearly from the histogram that the methods proposed by us has good discriminative capability. For instance, we set to $\tau = 0.12$ as threshold on CASIA dataset when extract the reference hashing by RPIVD method. The minimum value for hashing distance is 0.1389 which above the threshold. The results show that the multi-attack reference hashing can replace the original image based reference hashing with good discrimination.

Table 2. Comparisons between original image based reference hashing and the proposed multi-attack reference hashing (RTD dataset).

Manipulation	Wavelet				SVD				RPIVD				QFT			
	Precision	Recall	F1	AUC	Precision	Recall	F1	AUC	Precision	Recall	F1	AUC	Precision	Recall	F1	AUC
Original image based reference hashing																
Gaussian noise	0.6257	0.9500	0.7545	0.8442	0.8537	0.4773	0.6122	0.8501	0.8326	0.8211	0.8268	0.8991	0.8978	0.7591	0.8227	0.9241
Salt & Pepper	0.5485	0.9773	0.7026	0.8043	0.8537	0.4773	0.6122	0.8507	0.8806	0.8119	0.7449	0.9088	0.8851	0.7727	0.8252	0.9184
Gaussian blurring	1.0000	0.8727	0.9320	0.9866	1.0000	0.4409	0.6120	0.9874	1.0000	0.7465	0.8549	0.9557	1.0000	0.7227	0.8391	0.9948
Circular blurring	1.0000	0.8733	0.9346	0.9787	1.0000	0.4364	0.6076	0.9852	0.9821	0.7604	0.8571	0.9447	1.0000	0.7227	0.8391	0.9948
Motion blurring	1.0000	0.8727	0.9346	0.9787	1.0000	0.4273	0.5987	0.9868	1.0000	0.7477	0.8556	0.9572	1.0000	0.7227	0.8391	0.9949
Average filtering	1.0000	0.8864	0.9398	0.9665	1.0000	0.4318	0.6032	0.9790	0.9598	0.7661	0.8520	0.9351	1.0000	0.7227	0.8391	0.9948
Median filtering	0.6967	0.9500	0.8038	0.9012	0.9898	0.4409	0.6101	0.9544	0.9399	0.7890	0.8579	0.9212	1.0000	0.7409	0.8512	0.9721
Wiener filtering	0.9847	0.8773	0.9279	0.9713	1.0000	0.4318	0.6032	0.9822	0.9880	0.7569	0.8571	0.9427	1.0000	0.7227	0.8391	0.9950
Image sharpening	0.7178	0.9364	0.8126	0.8872	0.9709	0.4545	0.6192	0.9368	0.8980	0.8073	0.8502	0.9155	0.8851	0.8537	0.8537	0.8537
Image scaling	1.0000	0.8773	0.9346	0.9892	1.0000	0.4318	0.6032	0.9873	1.0000	0.7385	0.8496	0.9677	0.8851	0.7727	0.8252	0.9184
Illumination correction	0.5000	1.0000	0.6667	0.5593	0.5479	0.8318	0.6606	0.6754	0.9021	0.8028	0.8495	0.9073	0.6429	0.9000	0.7500	0.8498
JPEG compression	1.0000	0.4909	0.6585	0.9271	1.0000	0.4318	0.6032	0.9846	1.0000	0.3073	0.4702	0.9408	0.9273	0.6955	0.7948	0.9015
Multi-attack reference hashing																
Gaussian noise	0.8345	0.5273	0.6462	0.8465	0.8462	0.3000	0.4430	0.8846	0.9600	0.3303	0.4915	0.8948	0.9279	0.8773	0.9019	0.9588
Salt & Pepper	0.7619	0.5818	0.6598	0.8046	0.9507	0.6136	0.7459	0.9263	0.9706	0.3028	0.4615	0.9057	0.9500	0.6909	0.8000	0.9355
Gaussian blurring	1.0000	0.6000	0.7500	0.9955	1.0000	0.6045	0.7535	0.9904	0.9927	0.6415	0.7794	0.9880	1.0000	0.6818	0.8108	0.9952
Circular blurring	1.0000	0.4955	0.6626	0.9811	1.0000	0.6045	0.7535	0.9904	0.9926	0.6368	0.7759	0.9870	1.0000	0.6818	0.8108	0.9953
Motion blurring	1.0000	0.4909	0.6585	0.9849	1.0000	0.6000	0.7500	0.9955	0.9855	0.6415	0.7771	0.9857	1.0000	0.6818	0.8108	0.9952
Average filtering	1.0000	0.4955	0.6626	0.9709	1.0000	0.6091	0.7571	0.9955	0.9714	0.3119	0.4722	0.9270	1.0000	0.6818	0.8108	0.9952
Median filtering	0.9590	0.5318	0.6842	0.9013	0.9926	0.6091	0.7549	0.9803	1.0000	0.3211	0.4861	0.9258	1.0000	0.6818	0.8108	0.9809
Wiener filtering	1.0000	0.4909	0.6585	0.9703	1.0000	0.6045	0.7535	0.9901	0.9854	0.6368	0.7736	0.9858	1.0000	0.6864	0.8140	0.9950
Image sharpening	0.8986	0.5636	0.6927	0.8884	1.0000	0.2864	0.4452	0.9313	0.9722	0.3211	0.4828	0.9071	0.9167	0.7000	0.7938	0.9011
Image scaling	1.0000	0.4955	0.6626	0.9828	1.0000	0.6000	0.7500	0.9955	0.9855	0.6415	0.6415	0.9868	0.9494	0.6818	0.7937	0.9607
Illumination correction	0.5046	1.0000	0.6707	0.7791	0.6376	0.8318	0.7219	0.7848	0.9714	0.3119	0.4722	0.9062	0.7500	0.7909	0.7699	0.8405
JPEG compression	1.0000	0.4909	0.6585	0.9256	1.0000	0.6045	0.7535	0.9900	1.0000	0.3073	0.4702	0.9264	0.9403	0.8591	0.8979	0.9598

Table 3. Comparisons between original image based reference hashing and the proposed multi-attack reference hashing (CASIA dataset).

Manipulation	Wavelet				SVD				RPIVD				QFT			
	Precision	Recall	F1	AUC	Precision	Recall	F1	AUC	Precision	Recall	F1	AUC	Precision	Recall	F1	AUC
Original image based reference hashing																
Gaussian noise	0.7451	0.6623	0.8010	0.7909	0.8385	0.7015	0.7639	0.8825	0.9782	0.6830	0.8044	0.9021	0.8802	0.8965	0.8883	0.9520
Salt & Pepper	0.8128	0.6481	0.7212	0.8307	0.8978	0.6983	0.7855	0.9164	0.9699	0.6329	0.7660	0.9282	0.8837	0.8856	0.8847	0.9572
Gaussian blurring	0.9694	0.5861	0.7305	0.9434	0.9937	0.6852	0.8811	0.9512	0.9502	0.6452	0.7685	0.8981	1.0000	0.8638	0.9269	0.9989
Circular blurring	0.9399	0.5959	0.7293	0.9526	0.9696	0.6939	0.8089	0.8274	0.8124	0.6856	0.7436	0.8467	1.0000	0.8638	0.9269	0.9989
Motion blurring	0.9745	0.5817	0.7285	0.9526	0.9952	0.6797	0.8078	0.9642	0.9827	0.6201	0.7604	0.9161	1.0000	0.8638	0.9269	0.9989
Average filtering	0.8786	0.6231	0.7291	0.8917	0.8728	0.7179	0.7878	0.8835	0.6562	0.7738	0.7101	0.7739	1.0000	0.8638	0.9269	0.9989
Median filtering	0.8838	0.6503	0.7307	0.8457	0.9269	0.7048	0.8007	0.9047	0.7296	0.7216	0.7256	0.8080	1.0000	0.8649	0.9276	0.9939
Wiener filtering	0.8997	0.6155	0.7309	0.9055	0.9485	0.7015	0.8065	0.9212	0.8227	0.6921	0.7539	0.8506	1.0000	0.8638	0.9269	0.9980
Image sharpening	0.7194	0.7197	0.7186	0.7878	0.8089	0.7702	0.7891	0.8656	0.6526	0.8268	0.7295	0.8014	0.6565	0.9390	0.7727	0.8653
Image scaling	0.9868	0.5719	0.7241	0.9640	0.9952	0.6808	0.8085	0.9672	0.9581	0.6234	0.7553	0.9180	1.0000	0.8627	0.9263	0.9986
Illumination correction	0.5008	0.9978	0.6669	0.6063	0.6256	0.8573	0.7233	0.7541	0.9941	0.5579	0.7147	0.9810	0.8854	0.9085	0.8968	0.9616
JPEG compression	1.0000	0.4909	0.6585	0.9271	0.9676	0.6830	0.8008	0.9580	0.9565	0.6495	0.7736	0.9076	0.7148	0.9281	0.8076	0.8861
Multi-attack reference hashing																
Gaussian noise	0.7604	0.6569	0.7049	0.7993	0.8647	0.6961	0.7713	0.8902	0.9429	0.8638	0.9016	0.9578	0.9130	0.8922	0.9025	0.9646
Salt & Pepper	0.8415	0.6362	0.7246	0.8407	0.9261	0.6961	0.7948	0.9202	0.9738	0.8497	0.9075	0.9693	0.8906	0.8954	0.8930	0.9614
Gaussian blurring	1.0000	0.5664	0.7232	0.9797	1.0000	0.6634	0.7976	0.9807	0.9584	0.8046	0.8748	0.9481	1.0000	0.8758	0.9338	0.9989
Circular blurring	0.9943	0.5708	0.7253	0.9624	0.9951	0.6645	0.7969	0.9644	0.8596	0.8155	0.8370	0.9081	1.0000	0.8758	0.9338	0.9989
Motion blurring	1.0000	0.5654	0.7223	0.9800	1.0000	0.6656	0.7992	0.9857	0.9867	0.8079	0.8884	0.9618	1.0000	0.8758	0.9338	0.9989
Average filtering	0.9451	0.6002	0.7342	0.9201	0.9574	0.6852	0.7987	0.9203	0.6915	0.8328	0.7556	0.8349	1.0000	0.8758	0.9338	0.9989
Median filtering	0.7954	0.6438	0.7116	0.8366	0.9077	0.6961	0.7879	0.9038	0.7795	0.8297	0.8038	0.8851	1.0000	0.8769	0.9344	0.9958
Wiener filtering	0.9818	0.5871	0.7348	0.9369	0.9842	0.6776	0.8026	0.9542	0.8659	0.8177	0.8411	0.9195	1.0000	0.8769	0.9344	0.9984
Image sharpening	0.7271	0.7081	0.7174	0.7958	0.7901	0.7789	0.7844	0.8581	0.6722	0.9292	0.7801	0.8982	0.6579	0.9434	0.7749	0.8685
Image scaling	0.9923	0.5599	0.7159	0.9521	0.9952	0.6754	0.8047	0.9657	0.9716	0.8210	0.8899	0.9640	1.0000	0.8780	0.9350	0.9988
Illumination correction	0.5008	0.9978	0.6669	0.6043	0.6003	0.8638	0.7084	0.7389	0.9973	0.8111	0.8946	0.9915	0.8843	0.9161	0.8999	0.9649
JPEG compression	0.9925	0.5763	0.7292	0.9420	0.9779	0.6754	0.7990	0.9537	0.9720	0.8368	0.8994	0.9627	0.7145	0.9270	0.8070	0.8859

3.4   Authentication Results

In this subsection, we compare the performance of the reference hashing based on original image (ORH) and our proposed multi-attack reference hashing (MRH) on four state-of-the-art image hashing methods, i.e., Wavelet-based image hashing, SVD-based image hashing, RPIVD-based image hashing and QFT-based image hashing, with twelve content-preserving operations.

The results are shown in Tables 2 and 3. Note that, higher values indicate better performance for all metrics. It is observed that, the proposed MRH algorithm outperform the ORH algorithm by a clear margin, irrespective of the content preserving operation and image datasets (RTD and CASIA). This is particularly evident for illumination correction. For instance, in contrast to original image based reference hashing, the multi-attack reference hashing increase the AUC of illumination correction by 21.98% on the RTD image dataset when get the reference hashing by wavelet as shown in Table 2. For the QFT approach, the multi-attack reference hashing we proposed are more stable and outstanding than other corresponding reference hashings. Since the QFT robust image hashing technique is used to process the three channels of the color image, the chrominance information of the color image can be prevented from being lost and image features are more obvious. Therefore, the robustness of generated multi-attack reference hashing is more prominent in resisting geometric attack and content preserving operations. For instance, the multi-attack reference hashing increase the precision of gaussian noise by 3.28% on the RTD image.

3.5   Conclusions

In this paper, we have proposed a Multi-Attack Reference Hashing (MRH) method based on cluster for image authentication. We effectively exploited simultaneously the supervised content-preserving images and multiple attacks for feature generation and the hashing learning. We performed extensive experiments on two image datasets and compared with the reference hashing based on original image (ORH) on state-of-the-art hashing baselines. Experimental results demonstrated that the proposed method yields superior performance. The current work can be extended with the design of co-regularized hashing for multiple features, which is expected to show even better performance.

Acknowledgments. This work was supported by National Natural Science Foundation of China (Grant No. 61602344, 61602341, 61902280), Science & Technology Development Fund of Tianjin Education Commission for Higher Education, China (Grant No. 2017KJ091) and Natural Science Foundation of Tianjin (Grant No. 17JCQNJC00600, 19JCYBJC15600).

References

1. Kobayashi, H., Kiya, H.: Robust image authentication using hash function. In: IEEE Region 10 Annual International Conference, pp. 435–438 (2004)

2. Schneider, M., Chang, S.F.: A robust content based digital signature for image authentication. In: IEEE International Conference on Image Processing, pp. 227–230 (1996)
3. Fridrich, J., Goljan, M.: Robust hash function for digital watermarking. In: Proceedings of International Conference on Information Technology: Coding and Computing, pp. 173–178 (2000)
4. Kalker, T., Haitsma, J., Oostveen, J.C.: Issues with digital watermarking and perceptual hashing. In: Proceedings of SPIE, vol. 4518, pp. 189–197 (2001)
5. Hadmi, A., Ouahman, A.A., Said, B.A.E., Puech, W.: Perceptual image hashing. INTECH Open Access Publisher (2012)
6. Zhu, G., Huang, J., Kwong, S.: Fragility analysis of adaptive quantization-based image hashing. IEEE Trans. Inf. Forensics Secur. **5**(1), 133–147 (2010)
7. Khelifi, F., Jiang, J.: Perceptual image hashing based on virtual watermark detection. IEEE Trans. Image Process. **19**, 981–994 (2010)
8. Schneider, M., Chang, S.F.: A robust content based digital signature for image authentication. In: Proceedings of the IEEE International Conference on Image Processing, pp. 227–230 (1996)
9. Tang, Z., Zhang, X., Li, X.: Robust image hashing with ring partition and invariant vector distance. IEEE Trans. Inf. Forensics Secur. **11**(1), 200–214 (2015)
10. Huang, Z., Liu, S.: Robustness and discrimination oriented hashing combining texture and invariant vector distance. In: Proceedings of the 26th ACM International Conference on Multimedia, pp. 1389–1397 (2018)
11. Huang, Z., Liu, S.: Robustness and discrimination oriented hashing combining texture and invariant vector distance. In: Proceedings of the 2018 ACM Multimedia Conference on Multimedia Conference, pp. 1389–1397 (2018)
12. Lin, C., Chang, Y.: A robust image authentication method distinguishing JPEG compression from malicious manipulation. IEEE Trans. Circuits Syst. Video Technol. **11**(2), 153–168 (2001)
13. Lu, C., Liao, S.: Structural digital signature for image authentication: an incidental distortion resistant scheme. IEEE Trans. Multimedia **5**(2), 161–173 (2003)
14. Venkatesan, R., Koon, S.M., Jakubowski, M.H.: Robust image hashing. In: Proceedings of the IEEE International Conference on Image Processing (ICIP), pp. 664–666 (2000)
15. Fridrich, J., Goljan, M.: Robust hash functions for digital watermarking. In: Proceedings of the International Conference on Information Technology: Coding and Computing (ITCC), pp. 178–183 (2000)
16. Kozat, S., Venkatesan, R.: Robust perceptual image hashing via matrix invariants. In: Proceedings of the IEEE International Conference on Image Processing (ICIP), pp. 3443–3446 (2004)
17. Swaminathan, A., Mao, Y., Wu, M.: Robust and secure image hashing. IEEE Trans. Inf. Forensics Secur. **1**(2), 215–230 (2006)
18. Yan, C., Pun, C., Yuan, X.: Multi-scale image hashing using adaptive local feature extraction for robust tampering detection. Signal Process. **121**, 1–16 (2016)
19. Pun, C.-M., Yan, C.-P., Yuan, X.-C.: Robust image hashing using progressive feature selection for tampering detection. Multimedia Tools Appl. **77**(10), 11609–11633 (2017). https://doi.org/10.1007/s11042-017-4809-4
20. Kang, I.S., Seo, Y.H., Kim, D.W.: Blind digital watermarking methods for omnidirectional panorama images using feature points. Korean Inst. Broadcast Media Eng. **22**(6), 785–799 (2017)
21. Qi, S., Zhao, Y.: Perceptual hashing for color image based on color opponent component and quadtree structure. Signal Process. **166**, 107244 (2020)

22. Cui, C., Wang, S.: Depth information estimation-based DIBR 3D image hashing using SIFT feature points. In: Pan, J.-S., Li, J., Tsai, P.-W., Jain, L.C. (eds.) Advances in Intelligent Information Hiding and Multimedia Signal Processing. SIST, vol. 157, pp. 371–379. Springer, Singapore (2020). https://doi.org/10.1007/978-981-13-9710-3_39

23. Bhattacharjee, S., Kutter, M.: Compression tolerant image authentication. In: Proceedings of the IEEE International Conference on Image Processing (ICIP), pp. 435–439 (1998)

24. Monga, V., Evans, B.L.: Perceptual image hashing via feature points: performance evaluation and tradeoffs. IEEE Trans. Image Process. 15(11), 3452–3465 (2006)

25. Abdoun, N., El Assad, S.: Secure hash algorithm based on efficient chaotic neural network. In: 2016 International Conference on Communications (COMM), pp. 405–410 (2016)

26. Abdoun, N., El Assad, S., Deforges, O., Assaf, R., Khalil, M.: Design and security analysis of two robust keyed hash functions based on chaotic neural networks. J. Ambient Intell. Hum. Comput. 1–25 (2019). https://doi.org/10.1007/s12652-019-01244-y

27. Liu, Z., Qin, J., Li, A., Wang, Y.: Adversarial binary coding for efficient person re-identification. In: 2019 IEEE International Conference on Multimedia and Expo (ICME), pp. 700–705 (2019)

28. Han, S., Chu, C.H.: Content-based image authentication: current status, issues, and challenges. Int. J. Inf. Secur. 9(1), 19–32 (2010)

29. Lv, X., Wang, A.: Compressed binary image hashes based on semisupervised spectral embedding. IEEE Trans. Inf. Forensics Secur. 8(11), 1838–1849 (2013)

30. Zheng, Z., Li, L.: Binary multi-view clustering. IEEE Trans. Pattern Anal. Mach. Intell. 41(7), 1774–1782 (2019)

31. Venkatesan, R., Koon, S.M., Jakubowski, M.H., Moulin, P.: Robust image hashing. In: Proceedings of IEEE International Conference on Image Processing, pp. 664–666 (2001)

32. Tang, Z., Zhang, X., Li, X., Zhang, S.: Robust image hashing with ring partition and invariant vector distance. IEEE Trans. Inf. Forensics Secur. 11(1), 200–214 (2016)

33. Yan, C., Pun, C., Yuan, X.: Quaternion-based image hashing for adaptive tampering localization. IEEE Trans. Inf. Forensics Secur. 11(12), 2664–2677 (2016)

34. Dong, J., Wang, W.: CASIA image tampering detection evaluation database. In: 2013 IEEE China Summit and International Conference on Signal and Information Processing, pp. 422–426 (2013)

35. Korus, P., Huang, J.: Evaluation of random field models in multi-modal unsupervised tampering localization. In: 2016 IEEE International Workshop on Information Forensics and Security, pp. 1–6 (2016)

36. Korus, P., Huang, J.: Multi-scale analysis strategies in PRNU-based tampering localization. IEEE Trans. Inf. Forensics Secur. 12(4), 809–824 (2017)

37. Qin, C., Sun, M., Chang, C.: Perceptual hashing for color images based on hybrid extraction of structural features. Signal Process. 142, 194–205 (2018)

Cheating Detection in (k, n) Secret Image Sharing Scheme

Jianfeng Ma, Liping Yin, and Peng Li[✉]

Department of Mathematics and Physics, North China Electric Power University,
Baoding 071003, Hebei, China
lphit@163.com

Abstract. Secret image sharing will inevitably be threatened by various types of attacks in practical applications, of which cheating behavior is the most prone. In this paper, in order to prevent deceivers from threatening the security of secret image transmission process, a polynomial based cheating detection scheme is proposed. The (k, n) secret image sharing scheme must ensure that any k or more participants can restore the secret image, and less than k participants cannot get any information of the secret image. In our scheme, only one honest shareholder can detect the collusion from other $k - 1$ deceivers. Furthermore, our scheme reduces the size of shadow images thus saving storage space and transmission time. Theory and experiments show that our scheme is effective and feasible in cheating detection.

Keywords: Secret image sharing · Cheating detection · Shadow image · Secret sharing

1 Introduction

Shamir [1] and Blakley [2] introduced the idea of secret sharing in 1979. In a (k, n) threshold secret sharing scheme, the dealer encrypts the secret into n shares and assigns them to n participants. Only k or more participants can recover the secret, less than k shares cannot get any information of the secret. Therefore, the system is secure even when a small number of participants $(<k)$ have their shares filched.

Secret sharing will inevitably be threatened by cheating in practical applications. Therefore, many scholars have carried out extensive research on anti-cheating secret sharing scheme. Tompa and Woll [3] proposed the problem of cheating in the secret sharing scheme firstly. One of the cases is that the deceiver seizes the true secret alone by submitting the bogus share to recover the false secret. There's another case, external deceivers impersonate authorized participants to participate in secret reconstruction to filch secret. Schemes for preventing cheating are mainly divided into two categories: cheating detection [4–6] and deceiver identification [7–9]. The former can only detect the existence of cheating, while the latter can identify who the deceiver is.

Pieprzyk and Zhang [6] considered the cheating detection in linear secret sharing, their model extended the Tompa-Woll attack. Liu [4] proposed a linear (k, n) secret

© Springer Nature Switzerland AG 2020
H. Wang et al. (Eds.): IWDW 2019, LNCS 12022, pp. 421–428, 2020.
https://doi.org/10.1007/978-3-030-43575-2_34

sharing scheme against cheating which is based on Shamir's scheme and the size of share almost reaches its theoretic lower bound in (k, n) secret sharing scheme with cheating detection. In Liu et al.'s work [7], two cheating identification algorithms based on bivariate polynomial was proposed. The scheme given by Carpentieri [8] is similar to the scheme of Rabin and Ben-Or [11], both of which are prefect and unconditionally secure secret sharing scheme that the honest participants can identify the deceivers. The advantage of the former scheme is the information distributed to each participant is smaller. Pasailă et al. [9] analyzed the cheating detection and deceiver identification problems for schemes [14, 15] which based on Chinese remainder theorem and proved that the majority of the solutions for Shamir's scheme can be translated to these schemes.

Thien-Lin's scheme [10] is derived from the (k, n) threshold scheme, the secret image is divided into several blocks. k pixels of each block are taken as coefficients of a polynomial of degree $k - 1$ to calculate sub-shadows, thereby reducing the size of the shadow image. On this basis, Liu's scheme [5] considered the cheating detection problem. In this paper, further discussion is made to make the proposed scheme not only have the performance of cheating detection, but also reduce the size of shadows.

The rest of this paper is organized as follows. Predecessor's schemes are formulated in Sect. 2. We describe the proposed scheme in Sect. 3. Section 4 illustrates the experiments and comparisons with previous schemes. We conclude in Sect. 5.

2 Preliminary

2.1 Thien-Lin's Secret Image Sharing Scheme

Thien and Lin proposed a (k, n) secret image sharing scheme based on Shamir's scheme such that every k pixels in the image are grouped together and taken as the coefficients of $k - 1$th degree polynomial, rather than randomly selected like the Shamir's scheme. The size of shadow is smaller than secret image.

Share Generation Phase: Input secret image I, output n shadow images.

Step 1 The dealer decomposes the secret image I into t non-overlapping blocks $B_1, B_2, \ldots, B_t$, and each block contains k pixels.

Step 2 For block B_j, the dealer takes k pixels $a_{j,0}, a_{j,1}, \ldots, a_{j,k-1} \in GF(251)$ as coefficients and generates a polynomial $f_j(x) \in GF(251)[X]$ of degree $k - 1$.

Step 3 Dealer computes n shares $v_{j,1} = f_j(1), v_{j,2} = f_j(2), \ldots, v_{j,n} = f_j(n), j \in [1, t]$.

Step 4 Output n shadow images $V_i = v_{1,i} || v_{2,i} || \cdots || v_{t,i}, i = 1, 2, \ldots, n$.

Secret image Reconstruction Phase: Input k shadows. Output the secret image I.

Step 1 Extract the sub-share $v_{1,j}, v_{2,j}, \ldots, v_{k,j}$ of block B_j from $V_1, V_2, \ldots, V_k$.

Step 2 Reconstruct the polynomial of degree $k - 1$ according to Lagrange interpolation formula. Then block B_j is recovered such that $B_j = a_{j,0} || a_{j,1} || \cdots || a_{j,k-1}$.

Step 3 Output the secret image $I = B_1 || B_2 || \cdots || B_t$.

2.2 Liu-Sun-Yang's Scheme

On the basis of Thien-Lin's scheme, Liu-Sun-Yang's scheme considers the problem of cheating detection in polynomial-based (k, n) secret image sharing scheme.

Shadow Generation Phase: Input the secret image I, output n shadow images.

Step 1 The dealer divides image I into t non-overlapping blocks $B_1, B_2, \ldots, B_t$.

Step 2 There are $2k - 2$ pixels $a_{i,0}, \ldots, a_{i,k-1}, b_{i,2}, \ldots, b_{i,k-1} \in GF(251)$ in B_i. Take the first k pixels as coefficients to generate a polynomial of degree $k - 1$ $f_i(x)$.

Step 3 A value $r_i \in GF(251)$ is selected randomly by the dealer and $b_{i,0}, b_{i,1}$ are computed via $r_i a_{i,0} + b_{i,0} = 0$, $r_i a_{i,1} + b_{i,1} = 0$. Then another polynomial $g_i(x) = b_{i,0} + b_{i,1}x + \cdots + b_{i,k-1}x^{k-1}$ is constructed.

Step 4 For B_i, the shadow for each participant P_j is $V_j = v_{1,j}||v_{2,j}||, \cdots, ||v_{t,j}$. where $v_{i,j} = \{m_{i,j}, d_{i,j}\}$, $m_{i,j} = f_i(j)$, $d_{i,j} = g_i(j)$, $j = 1, 2, \ldots, n$.

Image Reconstruction Phase: Input k shadows. Let k shadows are $V_1, V_2, \ldots, V_k$.

Step 1 Extract $v_{i,j} = \{m_{i,j}, d_{i,j}\}$, $i = 1, 2, \ldots, t$, $j = 1, 2, \ldots, k$ from $V_1, V_2, \ldots, V_k$.

Step 2 Lagrange interpolation is used to reconstruct $f_i(x)$ and $g_i(x)$ respectively.

Step 3 If there is a common constant $r_i \in GF(251)$ that satisfies verification information, reconstruct B_i, then get the secret image $I = B_1||B_2||, \cdots, ||B_t$. Otherwise, cheating behavior is detected with the output $\perp$.

3   The Proposed Scheme

In order to prevent deceivers from threatening the security of secret transmission process, we propose a (k, n) secret image sharing scheme with the performance of cheating detection in this part. Our proposed scheme to detect cheating is based on Thien-Lin's scheme and Liu-Sun-Yang's scheme and reduces the size of shadow images. Just one honest shareholder can detect the collusion of $k - 1$ deceivers. The specific algorithm is as follows:

Shadow Generation Phase: Input the secret image I, output n shadows $V_1, V_2, \ldots, V_n$ of I.

Step 1 Scramble secret image with Arnold transformation.

Step 2 Decompose the scrambled image I' into t non-overlapping blocks $B_1, B_2, \ldots, B_t$ each block contains $2k - 1$ pixels.

Step 3 For each block B_i, $i \in [1, t]$, there are $2k - 1$ secret pixels, denoted by $a_{i,0}, a_{i,1}, \ldots, a_{i,k-1}, b_{i,1}, b_{i,2}, \ldots, b_{i,k-1} \in GF(251)$. The dealer generates a $k - 1$ order polynomial $f_i(x) = a_{i,0} + a_{i,1}x + \cdots + a_{i,k-1}x^{k-1} \in GF(251)[X]$ using the first k pixel values as the coefficients.

Step 4 The dealer chooses a value $r_i \in GF(251)$ randomly and gets $b_{i,0}$ via $r_i a_{i,0} + b_{i,0} = 0$. Where r_i is public information. Then another polynomial which takes $b_{i,0}$ as the constant terms and remaining $k-1$ pixels as coefficients is constructed $g_i(x) = b_{i,0} + b_{i,1}x + \cdots + b_{i,k-1}x^{k-1}$.

Step 5 The dealer calculates sub-shadows $v_{i,j} = \{m_{i,j}, d_{i,j}\}$, $m_{i,j} = f_i(j)$, $d_{i,j} = g_i(j)$, $j = 1, 2, \ldots, n$ of each block B_i, $i \in [1, t]$ for each participant P_j. The shadow that participant P_j gets is $V_j = v_{1,j} || v_{2,j} ||, \cdots, || v_{t,j}$.

Image Reconstruction Phase: Input k shadows. Without loss of generality, the k shadows are $V_1, V_2, \ldots, V_k$. Output the secret image I or cheating signal $\perp$.

Step 1 Extract $v_{i,j} = \{m_{i,j}, d_{i,j}\}$, $i = 1, 2, \ldots, t$, $j = 1, 2, \ldots, k$ from $V_1, V_2, \ldots, V_k$.

Step 2 For k points $(1, v_{i,1}), (2, v_{i,2}), \ldots, (k, v_{i,k})$, $i \in [1, t]$, Lagrange interpolation is used to reconstruct $f_i(x)$ and $g_i(x)$ respectively.

Step 3 Let $a_{i,0}$ and $b_{i,0}$ be constant terms of $f_i(x)$ and $g_i(x)$ respectively.

- If there is a constant $r_i' = r_i \in GF(251)$ that satisfies $r_i a_{i,0} + b_{i,0} = 0$, reconstruct $B_i = \{a_{i,0}, a_{i,1}, \cdots, a_{i,k-1}, b_{i,1}, b_{i,2}, \cdots, b_{i,k-1}\}$, then get the scrambled image $I' = B_1 || B_2 ||, \cdots, || B_t$. Finally, recover the secret image I with the Arnold inverse transformation.
- Else, there are bogus shadows in the process of image reconstruction. Cheating behavior is detected with the output $\perp$.

Theorem 1. The proposed scheme is a perfect (k, n) secret image sharing scheme, that is to say, any k or more than k shareholders can recover the secret image taking advantage of their shadows. Nevertheless, less than k shareholders can't get any information about the secret.

Proof. Firstly, we prove that k or more than k shareholders can recover the secret. Next, prove that $k-1$ shareholders can't get any information about the secret. Since each block is processed the same way, we only need to analyze one block.

(1) For B_i, we hide $2k-1$ pixels as the coefficients of two polynomials $f_i(x)$, $g_i(x)$ and generate shares according to Shamir's scheme which satisfies the property of (k, n) threshold. Apparently, in our scheme, k or more than k shareholders can reconstruct $f_i(x)$ and $g_i(x)$, then we can get B_i, scrambled image I', secret image I in turn.

(2) For B_i, suppose the first $k-1$ shareholders want to get secret privately, they only have $k-1$ correct shares. Therefore, a value needs to be randomly selected on $GF(251)$ as the share of the kth shareholder. Assuming that the selected value is m_k^*, a polynomial $f_i'(x)$ of order $k-1$ can be obtained by using the correct share $(1, m_1), (2, m_2), \ldots, (k-1, m_{k-1})$ and (k, m_k^*). Let a_0' be the constant term of $f_i'(x)$. Deceivers can take the coefficients $b_0', b_1', \ldots, b_{k-1}'$ as unknowns of k linear equations: $g'(1) = d_1, g'(2) = d_2, \ldots, g'(k-1) = d_{k-1}, r_i a_0' + b_0' = 0$, k unknowns can be solved, then $g_i'(x)$ can be obtained. Although r_i is known, the share of the kth shareholder is selected randomly, the calculated polynomial $f_i'(x)$ is not necessarily

correct, i.e. $a'_0, b'_0, b'_1, \ldots, b'_{k-1}$ is not necessarily the real values given by dealer, which means that regardless of which value of the $GF(251)$ the deceivers choose as the share of the kth shareholder, they will get the corresponding $b'_0, b'_1, \ldots, b'_{k-1}$, that is they will think that each value is valid. In general, deceivers don't get any secret information. □

In order to explain the proof process more clearly, we give an example.

Example 1. When $k = 5$, $a_0 = 1$, $a_1 = 5$, $a_2 = 2$, $a_3 = 2$, $a_4 = 1$, $b_1 = 6$, $b_2 = 1$, $b_3 = 3$, $b_4 = 2$ over $GF(7)$ is known, so $f(x) = 1 + 5x + 2x^2 + 2x^3 + x^4$. Assuming r chosen by dealer is 5, $b_0 = 2$ is calculated from $ra_0 + b_0 = 0$, then $g(x) = 2 + 6x + x^2 + 3x^3 + 2x^4$. Let P_1, P_2, P_3, P_4, P_5 be the five shareholders, and shares for them are $P_1: (m_1 = 4, d_1 = 0)$, $P_2: (m_2 = 2, d_2 = 4)$, $P_3: (m_3 = 1, d_3 = 6)$, $P_4: (m_4 = 3, d_4 = 4)$, $P_5: (m_5 = 6, d_5 = 2)$. Suppose P_1, P_2, P_3, P_4 are deceivers. As described in the previous proof, they can randomly choose $m_5^* = 0$ as the share of P_5 and obtain $f'(x) = 2 + 2x^2 + x^3 + 6x^4$ according to Lagrange interpolation. Then they set up the following equations: $ra'_0 + b'_0 = 0$, $b'_0 + b'_1 + b'_2 + b'_3 + b'_4 = 0$, $b'_0 + 2b'_1 + 4b'_2 + b'_3 + 2b'_4 = 4$, $b'_0 + 3b'_1 + 2b'_2 + 6b'_3 + 4b'_4 = 6$, $b'_0 + 4b'_1 + 2b'_2 + b'_3 + 4b'_4 = 4$, Get $g'(x) = 4 + 3x + x^2 + x^3 + 5x^4$ by solving the above equations, which satisfies $5a'_0 + b'_0 = 0$. They were misled into thinking that the result is correct. Actually, the secret they have been got is wrong.

Next, we discuss the performance of our scheme for detecting cheating.

Theorem 2. Our scheme has the capability that only one honest shareholder can detect the cheating behavior from $k - 1$ deceivers.

Proof. For each block B_i, suppose k shareholders $P_1, P_2, \ldots, P_k$ participate in the secret reconstruction and $P_1, P_2, \ldots, P_{k-1}$ are deceivers. Let $v_i^* = (m_i^*, d_i^*)$, $i = 1, 2, \ldots, k - 1$ denotes the $k - 1$ bogus shares and (m_k, d_k) be the share of the kth shareholders. Two polynomials obtained by interpolation according to $v_i^* = (m_i^*, d_i^*)$, $i = 1, 2, \ldots, k - 1$ and (m_k, d_k) are $f^*(x)$ and $g^*(x)$. There must exist a number r^* which satisfy $r^* a_0^* + b_0^* = 0$. Distinctly, the cheating is successful only when r^* is equal to r_i that determined by the dealer. Since all the pixels are in $GF(251)$, according to the proof analysis of theorem 1, the probability of successful cheating is $\varepsilon = \frac{1}{251}$, which means that our proposed scheme is effective in detecting cheating. □

4 Experiments and Comparisons

4.1 An Example for Cheating Detection

In this part, we use an example to simulate the process of cheating detection. A $(5, 7)$ threshold secret sharing scheme is adopt in the example. Suppose $2k - 1 = 9$ pixels are 37, 249, 154, 78, 59, 182, 94, 68, 167 in B_i and r selected by dealer is 7, then generate two $k - 1 = 4$th degree polynomials $f(x) = 37 + 249x + 154x^2 + 78x^3 + 59x^4$ and $g(x) = 243 + 182x + 94x^2 + 68x^3 + 167x^4$ which satisfy $7 * 37 + 243 = 0 \pmod{251}$. The

$n = 7$ shares for 7 shareholders of B_i are $v_1 = (75, 1)$, $v_2 = (209, 183)$, $v_3 = (19, 181)$, $v_4 = (250, 132)$, $v_5 = (51, 165)$, $v_6 = (238, 150)$, $v_7 = (31, 200)$, Without loss of generality, 5 shareholders P_1, P_2, P_3, P_4, P_5 participate in the secret reconstruction and P_1, P_2, P_3, P_4 are deceivers. Assuming that the 4 bogus shares provided by deceivers are $v_1^* = (92, 40)$, $v_2^* = (136, 112)$, $v_3^* = (35, 75)$, $v_4^* = (128, 20)$, and the correct share of P_5 is $v_5 = (51, 165)$. They get two polynomials $f^*(x) = 116 + 235x + 17x^2 + 203x^3 + 23x^4$ and $g^*(x) = 146 + 75x + 92x^2 + 25x^3 + 204x^4$ using Lagrange interpolation. Obviously, $55 * 116 + 146 = 0 \pmod{251}$, $r^* = 55 \neq r = 7$, so P_5 detects cheating from $k - 1$ deceivers.

4.2 Share and Recover a Secret Image Utilize the Proposed Scheme

In this section, we apply the famous image "Lena" as the secret image I to our scheme. Let $(k, n) = (5, 7)$, then each block contains $2k - 1 = 9$ pixels. In order to avoid the occurrence of overflow, we use an image with the size of 510×510. For the sake of improving the security of the scheme and prevent secret image information from appearing in shadow image, Arnold transform is firstly used to scramble the original image. The scrambled image I' will be divided into 28900 blocks and we can get 7 shadow images whose size are 2/9 of I. The experimental results are depicted in Fig. 1. Obviously, the recovered image is distortion free.

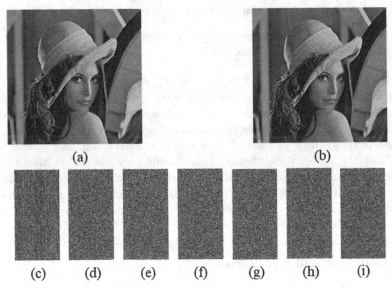

Fig. 1. Experimental results: (a) a 510×510 secret image; (b) the image recovered from 5 shadow images; (c)–(i): the shadow images whose size are 340×170.

4.3 Comparison

There are k pixels in each block in Thien-Lin's scheme, each shadow only receives one value as the sub-share, the size of shadow is $1/k$ of the secret image. In Liu-Sun-Yang's scheme, the share $v_{ij} = (m_{ij}, d_{ij})$ is generated from each $2k - 2$ pixels, so the size of image shadow is $1/(k - 1)$ of the original image. Similarly, the size of image shadow in our scheme is $2/(2k - 1)$ of the secret image which is smaller than Liu-Sun-Yang's scheme. The small size of shadow image is a great feature in practice especially in saving storage space and transmission time. Table 1 depicts the comparisons between cheating detection schemes, where P is for the number of pixels in the secret image, $|S|$ represents the size of the secret image.

Table 1. Comparisons between cheating detection schemes.

Scheme	Probability of cheating success	Cheating detection	Size of shadow
Scheme [10]	$(1/251)^{P/k}$	No	$1/k|S|$
Scheme [5]	$(1/251)^{P/k}$	Yes	$1/(k - 1)|S|$
Scheme [12]	$(1/251)^{P/k}$	Yes	$1/k|S|$
Scheme [13]	$(1/251)^{P/k}$	No	$1/k|S|$
Scheme [14]	$(1/256)^{P/k}$	No	$1/k|S|$
Scheme [15]	$(1/128)^{P/k}$	No	$|S|$
Scheme [16]	$(1/256)^{P/k}$	Yes	$(\lceil k/4 \rceil + 1)/k|S|$
Our scheme	$(1/251)^{P/k}$	Yes	$2/(2k - 1)|S|$

5 Conclusion

In this paper, we propose a cheating detection algorithm based on Thien-Lin's scheme and Liu-Sun-Yang's scheme. Our scheme can detect the cheating of the collusion of $k - 1$ cheaters by only one honest shareholder who participates in secret image reconstruction. Furthermore, the shadow image size of our scheme is smaller than Liu-Sun-Yang's scheme that reduce storage space and transmission time for shares. The cheating detection in our scheme only involves the interpolation of linear polynomials, and does not contain any redundant information in the shares. Therefore, the proposed scheme is feasible and effective in detecting cheating and can be adopted in other polynomial based secret image sharing schemes.

Acknowledgements. This work was supported in part by the National Natural Science Foundation of China (No. 61602173), Natural Science Foundation of Hebei Province of China (No. F2019502173) and the Fundamental Research Funds for Central Universities (No. 2019MS116).

428   J. Ma et al.

References

1. Shamir, A.: How to share a secret. Commun. ACM **22**(11), 612–613 (1979)
2. Blakley, G.R.: Safeguarding cryptographic keys. In: Proceedings of the AFIPS, pp. 313–317 (1979)
3. Tompa, M., Woll, H.: How to share a secret with cheaters. J. Cryptol. **1**(3), 133–138 (1989)
4. Liu, Y.: Linear (k, n) secret sharing scheme with cheating detection. Secur. Commun. Netw. **9**(13), 2115–2121 (2016)
5. Liu, Y.-X., Sun, Q.-D., Yang, C.-N.: (k,n) secret image sharing scheme capable of cheating detection. EURASIP J. Wirel. Commun. Netw. **2018**(1), 1–6 (2018). https://doi.org/10.1186/s13638-018-1084-7
6. Pieprzyk, J., Zhang, X.-M.: Cheating prevention in linear secret sharing. In: Batten, L., Seberry, J. (eds.) ACISP 2002. LNCS, vol. 2384, pp. 121–135. Springer, Heidelberg (2002). https://doi.org/10.1007/3-540-45450-0_9
7. Liu, Y., Yang, C., Wang, Y., et al.: Cheating identifiable secret sharing scheme using symmetric bivariate polynomial. Inf. Sci. **453**, 21–29 (2018)
8. Carpentieri, M.: A perfect threshold secret sharing scheme to identify cheaters. Des. Codes Crypt. **5**(3), 183–187 (1995)
9. Pasailă, D., Alexa, V., Iftene, S.: Cheating detection and cheater identification in CRT-based secret sharing schemes. Int. Sci. J. Comput. **9**(2), 107–117 (2010)
10. Thien, C., Lin, J.: Secret image sharing. Comput. Graph. **26**(5), 765–770 (2002)
11. Rabin, T., Ben-Or, M.: Verifiable secret sharing and multiparty protocols with honest majority. In: Proceeding of the Symposium on theory of Computing, pp. 73–85 (1989)
12. Zhao, R., Zhao, J., Dai, F., et al.: A new image secret sharing scheme to identify cheaters. Comput. Stand. Interfaces **31**(1), 252–257 (2009)
13. Lin, Y., Wang, R.: Scalable secret image sharing with smaller shadow images. IEEE Signal Process. Lett. **17**(3), 316–319 (2010)
14. Wu, K.-S.: A secret image sharing scheme for light images. EURASIP J. Adv. Signal Process. **2013**(1), 1–5 (2013). https://doi.org/10.1186/1687-6180-2013-49
15. Chen, C., Fu, W.: A geometry-based secret image sharing approach. J. Inf. Sci. Eng. **24**(5), 1567–1577 (2008)
16. Nag, A., Biswas, S., Sarkar, D., et al.: A new (k, n) verifiable secret image sharing scheme (VSISS). Egypt. Inform. J. **15**(3), 201–209 (2014)

Author Index

Printed in the United States
By Bookmasters